Introduction to Wavelet Transforms

Introduction to Wavelet Transforms

by

Nirdosh Bhatnagar

CRC Press

Taylor & Francis Group

Boca Raton London New York

CRC Press is an imprint of the
Taylor & Francis Group, an **informa** business

A CHAPMAN & HALL BOOK

CRC Press
Taylor & Francis Group
6000 Broken Sound Parkway NW, Suite 300
Boca Raton, FL 33487-2742

First issued in paperback 2021

© 2020 by Taylor & Francis Group, LLC
CRC Press is an imprint of Taylor & Francis Group, an Informa business

No claim to original U.S. Government works

ISBN-13: 978-0-367-43879-1 (hbk)
ISBN-13: 978-1-03-217483-9 (pbk)
DOI: 10.1201/9781003006626

**Visit the Taylor & Francis Web site at
http://www.taylorandfrancis.com**

**and the CRC Press Web site at
http://www.crcpress.com**

For Rishi

Contents

Part III. Signal Processing

Preface

The purpose of this book on wavelet transforms is to provide the reader with the basics of this fascinating subject in a self-contained manner. Applications of wavelet transform theory permeate our daily lives. Therefore, it is imperative to have a strong foundation for this subject.

Contents of the Book

It is the author's belief that learning becomes relatively simpler by proper segmentation of main ideas. The textbook is therefore divided into four main parts. These are:

1. Basics of wavelet transforms
2. Intermediate topics
3. Signal processing concepts
4. Mathematical concepts

The first part, on the basics of wavelet transforms, consists of chapters on the introduction to wavelets, continuous and discrete wavelet transforms, and Daubechies wavelets. It also contains a chapter on some elementary examples of wavelets. The basics of certain well-known applications are also provided.

The chapters in the second part are essentially vignettes from certain intermediate topics on wavelet transforms. These are periodic and biorthogonal wavelet transforms, coiflets, lifting technique, wavelet packets, and lapped orthogonal transforms.

The above-mentioned topics rely upon important concepts from the world of signal processing. Therefore, the third part has chapters on discrete Fourier transform, the z-transform and discrete-time Fourier transform, and elements of continuous- and discrete-time signal processing.

The fourth part, not surprisingly, is on the mathematical concepts. A chapter on set-theoretic concepts and number theory is provided. This is followed by a chapter on matrices and determinants. Subsequently, chapters on applied analysis and Fourier theory are provided. These later topics are essentially the foundations of wavelet transform theory. In addition, a chapter on probability theory and stochastic processes is also provided.

A list of Greek and commonly used symbols is also provided. This is followed by a bibliography and an index.

Why Read This Book?

The main features of this book are listed below.

(a) *Self-contained*: A primary goal of this book is to present this subject in a *self-contained* manner. That is, sufficient mathematical background is provided to complete the discussion of different topics. No prior knowledge of the subject is assumed. Notation is generally introduced in the definitions. Relatively easy consequences of the definitions are listed as observations, and important results are stated as theorems. Examples are provided for clarity and to enhance the reader's understanding of the subject.

(b) *Student-friendly format via segmentation of main ideas*: Different topics have been properly segmented for easy learning. This makes the textbook student-friendly, pedagogical, and unique.

(c) *List of observations*: Several significant results are listed precisely as observations. Proofs of some of these observations are outlined in the Problems section at the end of each chapter.

(d) *Examples and figures*: Each chapter is interspersed with examples. These examples serve to clarify, enhance, and sometimes motivate different results. It is the author's belief that examples play a crucial role in getting a firm grasp of the fundamentals of a subject. If and where necessary, figures are provided to improve the clarity of the presentation.

(e) *Problems*: Each chapter is provided with a problem section. Besides enhancing the material presented in the main chapter, each problem states a significant result. A majority of the problems are provided with sufficient hints. In order to keep the continuity and not clutter with too many details, proofs of important observations made in the chapter are relegated to the problem section. It is strongly suggested that the reader peruse the problem section.

(f) *Bibliography*: A bibliography is provided at the end of the textbook.

(g) *User-friendly index*: A comprehensive and user-friendly Index of topics is provided at the end of the textbook.

Target Audience of the Book

This book has essentially been crafted for an enthusiastic student who is learning wavelet transforms for the first time, and who wants a proper foundation. The book can be used either in an upper-level undergraduate or first-year graduate class in electrical engineering or computer science or applied mathematics. It should also serve as a useful reference for professionals and practitioners of the art of signal processing.

Commissions and Omissions

It is quite possible that the author has not provided complete credit to the different contributors of the subject. To them, the author offers a sincere apology for any such inadvertent omission. Receiving information about errors will be greatly appreciated.

Acknowledgements

A very special thanks is extended to the creators of the wavelet transform techniques. These researchers are responsible for making it an important theoretical and practical tool. An initial draft of this work was prepared using the Scientific Work-Place software. This is a product of MacKichan Software, Inc. The author owes an immense debt of gratitude to this product.

This is my second time around working with Randi Cohen, publisher at the Taylor and Francis Group. As usual, she has been most professional in all of my interactions with her. Initial coordination of the publication process was facilitated by Talitha Duncan-Todd. The production editor, Paul Boyd was most cooperative. Expert editing of the manuscript was provided by Rebecca Condit; I am immensely grateful for her help. Shashi Kumar provided the final formatting of the manuscript.

Comments and encouragement provided by Vikram M. Gadre are certainly appreciated. This work would not have been possible without the inspiration of my students and esteemed teachers. A very special thanks is extended to family, friends, and colleagues for their steadfast support.

NB
San Jose, California
Email address: nbhatnagar@alumni.stanford.edu

List of Symbols

Different types of commonly used symbols are categorized as:

1. Logical operators
2. Set operators
3. Sets of numbers
4. Basic arithmetic operators
5. More arithmetic operators
6. Arithmetical relationships
7. Analysis
8. Complex numbers
9. Vectors
10. Matrices
11. Mappings
12. Combinatorial functions
13. Probability theory
14. Mathematical constants

Logical Operators

$\leftarrow$	assignment operator
$\rightarrow$, $\Rightarrow$	logical implication
$\Leftrightarrow$, iff	if and only if

Set Operators

$\in$	belongs to
$\notin$	does not belong to, negation of $\in$
$\ni$	such that
$\forall$	universal quantifier, for all
$\exists$	existential quantifier, there exists
$\nexists$	there does not exist
$\cap$	set intersection operator
$\cup$	set union operator
$\setminus$	set difference operator
$\subset$	proper subset containment operator
$\subseteq$	subset operator
$\varnothing$	empty set
$\oplus$	set addition operator
$\square$	end of: proof, definition, example, or observation
$\{\cdot, \cdots, \cdot\}$	set list
$\sim$	equivalence between sets
$\perp$	set orthogonality operator
$\not\perp$	set nonorthogonality operator
$A^c, \overline{A}$	complement of the set A
$\lvert A \rvert$	cardinality of the set A
$A^\perp$	set orthogonal to the set A
$A \times B$	Cartesian product of sets A and B
$A^{(n)}, A^n$	Cartesian product of the set A with itself, n times over
$\{x \mid R(x)\}, \{x : R(x)\}$	set of all x for which the relationship $R(x)$ is true

Sets of Numbers

$\mathbb{C}$	set of complex numbers
$\mathbb{P}$	set of positive numbers $\{1, 2, 3, \ldots\}$
$\mathbb{N}$	set of natural numbers $\{0, 1, 2, 3, \ldots\}$
$\mathbb{Q}$	set of rational numbers
$\mathbb{R}$	set of real numbers
$\mathbb{R}_0^+$	set of nonnegative real numbers $\mathbb{R}^+ \cup \{0\}$
$\mathbb{R}^+$	set of positive real numbers
$\mathbb{R}^n$	n-dimensional real vector space, where $n \in \mathbb{P}$
$\mathbb{Z}$	set of integers $\{\ldots, -2, -1, 0, 1, 2, \ldots\}$
$\mathbb{Z}_n$	set of integers modulo n, the set $\{0, 1, 2, \ldots, n-1\}$

Basic Arithmetic Operators

$+$	addition operator
$-$	subtraction operator
$\times, \cdot$	multiplication operator
$\div, /$	division operator
$\pm$	plus or minus operator
$\sqrt{\cdot}$	square root operator
$\lceil \cdot \rceil$	ceiling operator; for $x \in \mathbb{R}$, $\lceil x \rceil = $ least integer greater than or equal to x
$\lfloor \cdot \rfloor$	floor operator; for $x \in \mathbb{R}$, $\lfloor x \rfloor = $ greatest integer less than or equal to x
$[\cdot]$	round-off operator; for $x \in \mathbb{R}$, $[x] = $ integer closest to x
$\cdot \mid \cdot$	divisibility operator; $a \mid m$ means nonzero integer a can divide integer m
$\cdot \nmid \cdot$	nondivisibility operator; $a \nmid m$ means nonzero integer a cannot divide integer m

More Arithmetic Operators

$\lvert a \rvert$	absolute value (magnitude) of $a \in \mathbb{R}$
$\langle n \rangle_p$	modulus operator $n \pmod{p}$, $p \in \mathbb{P}$
$\sum$	discrete summation operator
$\prod$	product operator
$*$	convolution operator
$\gcd(a, b)$	greatest common divisor of a and b; $a, b \in \mathbb{P}$
$\max\{\ldots\}, \max(\ldots)$	maximum operator
$\min\{\ldots\}, \min(\ldots)$	minimum operator
$\max(a, b)$	maximum of a and b; $a, b \in \mathbb{R}$
$\min(a, b)$	minimum of a and b; $a, b \in \mathbb{R}$
mod	modulo operator
a^+, a_+	$\max(0, a)$, $a \in \mathbb{R}$
a^-, a_-	$\max(0, -a)$, $a \in \mathbb{R}$
$\exp(\cdot)$	exponential function with base e
$\ln(\cdot)$	natural logarithm
$\log_a(\cdot)$	logarithm to the base a, where $a \in \mathbb{R}^+$
$sgn(\cdot)$	signum function

Arithmetical Relationships

$=$	equality operator
$\neq$	not equal to
$\sim$	asymptotically equal
$\simeq$	approximate relationship between functions
$\approx$	approximate relationship between numbers within a constant
$\geq$	greater than or equal to
$\leq$	less than or equal to
$\gg$	much greater than
$\ll$	much less than
$\rightarrow$	approaches, tends towards
$\propto$	proportional to
$\equiv$	congruent to
$\not\equiv$	not congruent to

Analysis

∞	infinity
$\lim$	limit
$\frac{d}{dt}$	differentiation operator
$f'(t), \dot{f}(t)$	$\frac{d}{dt}f(t),\ t \in \mathbb{R}$
$\frac{\partial}{\partial t}$	partial differentiation operator
$\int$	integration operator
$\|\cdot\|$	norm of a vector
l^2	square summable sequences
$L^2(\mathbb{R})$	set of square-integrable functions
$\leftrightarrow$	Fourier transform pair
$\arg\max_x f(x)$	$\{x \mid f(y) \leq f(x)\ \forall\, y\}$
$\arg\min_x f(x)$	$\{x \mid f(y) \geq f(x)\ \forall\, y\}$
$\delta_{ij};\ i,j \in \mathbb{Z}$	Kronecker's delta function.
$f \circ g(\cdot)$	$f(g(\cdot))$ function composition
$\circ,\ \langle\cdot,\cdot\rangle,\ \langle\cdot\mid\cdot\rangle$	inner (dot) product operators
$\times$	cross product operator

Complex Numbers

i	$\sqrt{-1}$
$\bar{z}$	complex conjugate of $z \in \mathbb{C}$
$\|z\|$	magnitude of $z \in \mathbb{C}$
$\mathrm{Re}\,(z)$	real part of $z \in \mathbb{C}$
$\mathrm{Im}\,(z)$	imaginary part of $z \in \mathbb{C}$
$\arg(z)$	argument of $z \in \mathbb{C}$

Vectors

$\boxplus$	vector addition
$\otimes$	vector multiplication
$u^{\perp}$	a vector orthogonal to vector u
$x \perp y$	vectors x and y are orthogonal

Matrices

A^T	transpose of matrix A
$A^\dagger$	Hermitian transpose of matrix A
A^{-1}	inverse of square matrix A
I	identity matrix
$[a_{ij}]$	matrix with entries a_{ij}
$tr\,(A)$	trace of the square matrix A
$\det A, |A|$	determinant of the square matrix A

Mappings

$f : A \to B$	f is a mapping from the set A to the set B
$f(x)$	image of $x \in A$ under the mapping f
$f(X)$	$\{f(x) \mid x \in X\}$ for $f : A \to B$ and $X \subset A$
$\triangleq$	definition, or alternate notation

Combinatorial Functions

$n!$	$n \in \mathbb{N}$, factorial of n
$\binom{n}{k}$	$k, n \in \mathbb{N}, 0 \le k \le n$, binomial coefficient

Probability Theory

$\stackrel{d}{=}$	equality in distribution
$\stackrel{d}{\to}$	convergence in distribution
$P(\cdot)$	probability function
$\sim$	distribution of a random variable
$\mathcal{E}(X), \mathcal{E}[X]$	expectation of random variable X
$Var\,(X)$	variance of random variable X
$Cov\,(X, Y)$	covariance between random variables X and Y

Mathematical Constants

π	$3.141592653\ldots$
e	$2.718281828\ldots$, Euler's number

Greek Symbols

A list of lower- and upper-case Greek letters and their spelling in English.

Lower-case	Upper-case	Name
α	A	alpha
β	B	beta
γ	Γ	gamma
δ	Δ	delta
ϵ, ε	E	epsilon
ζ	Z	zeta
η	H	eta
θ, ϑ	Θ	theta
ι	I	iota
κ	K	kappa
λ	Λ	lambda
μ	M	mu

Lower-case	Upper-case	Name
ν	N	nu
ξ	Ξ	xi
o	O	omicron
π	Π	pi
ρ	P	rho
σ, ς	Σ	sigma
τ	T	tau
υ	Υ	upsilon
ϕ, φ	Φ	phi
χ	X	chi
ψ	Ψ	psi
ω	Ω	omega

PART I

Basics of Wavelet Transforms

CHAPTER 1

Introduction to Wavelets

1.1 Introduction

Wavelets are the latest tool in constructing function spaces. The spaces which can be constructed are more localized than that can be built with Fourier theory. These have recently found several applications in signal processing.

The purpose of signal processing, is to collect data, analyze it, and transmit it efficiently to a destination. The received signal is subsequently reconstructed at the destination. Alternately, the processed (transformed) signal can also be stored. The ultimate aim of such processes is to implement the transmission or storage of information via efficient utilization of resources.

The goal of Fourier and wavelet analysis is to represent functions in terms of "simpler" functions. These simple functions can be considered to be the building blocks of a set of functions. Given a function $f(t) \in \mathbb{R}$, where $t \in \mathbb{R}$, the aim is to expand this function in terms of a set of orthonormal basis functions $\{\varphi_n(t) \in \mathbb{R} \mid t \in \mathbb{R}, n \in \mathbb{Z}\}$. The set of basis functions can be considered to be a set of building blocks in order to construct a signal. Orthonormality of basis functions implies

$$\int_{-\infty}^{\infty} \varphi_m(t)\,\varphi_n(t)\, dt = \begin{cases} 1, & m = n \\ 0, & m \neq n \end{cases} \qquad m, n \in \mathbb{Z}$$

Then

$$f(t) = \sum_{n \in \mathbb{Z}} \alpha_n \varphi_n(t), \qquad t \in \mathbb{R}$$

$$\alpha_n = \int_{-\infty}^{\infty} f(t)\varphi_n(t)\, dt, \qquad n \in \mathbb{Z}$$

The coefficient α_n is a measure of the function $f(\cdot)$ along the basis $\varphi_n(\cdot)$, for all values of n. Therefore, instead of transmitting (or storing) the function $f(\cdot)$, it might be efficient to transmit (or store) the coefficients α_n, $n \in \mathbb{Z}$. Then the recipient of the coefficients at the receiver can reconstruct the function $f(\cdot)$ using the above relationships. However, if some of these coefficients are close to zero in magnitude, then their values need not be transmitted (or stored). Therefore, only a finite subset of values of α_n's need be transmitted (or stored). This implies efficient utilization of resources.

The set of basis functions has to be chosen such that only a few coefficients α_n's are required to represent the function $f(\cdot)$. Given a signal, the challenge is to find an optimum set of basis functions.

Well-known techniques in representation of functions are initially explored in this chapter. This is followed by an introduction to Fourier analysis. Its advantages and disadvantages are specified. Subsequently basics of wavelet analysis are discussed. Motivation for the use wavelets, and a brief history is also provided. Finally some popular applications of wavelets are listed.

1.2 Representation of Functions

A useful technique to represent a function consists of specifying it as a linear combination of some simple functions. Let the set of useful functions be $\{g_\omega \mid \omega \in \Omega\}$, where the set Ω is countable. A possible representation of a function f is

$$f = \sum_{\omega \in \Omega} c_\omega g_\omega$$

In the above representation, the function f is represented by $r = \{c_\omega \mid \omega \in \Omega\}$. The function f can be reconstructed from the representation r. It is hoped that $|r|$ is a small number. Some of the possible representations of a function are:

- Basis representation
- Representation via frames
- Riesz basis representation
- Representation via multiresolution
- Representation via dictionaries

1.2.1 Basis Representation

A possible technique to represent a function f in space $\mathcal{F}$ is via its basis set. Let a basis set of the space $\mathcal{F}$ be $B = \{g_n \in \mathcal{F} \mid n \in \mathbb{Z}\}$. The elements of the set B are linearly independent. A representation of $f \in \mathcal{F}$ is a sequence $\{\alpha_n \mid n \in \mathbb{Z}\}$ such that

$$f = \sum_{n \in \mathbb{Z}} \alpha_n g_n$$

As the above representation might possibly have an infinite number of terms, we should have

$$\lim_{m\to\infty} \left\| f - \sum_{n=-m}^{m} \alpha_n g_n \right\| \to 0$$

where $\|\cdot\|$ is a norm in space $\mathcal{F}$.

In order to guarantee uniqueness of the representation of the function f, we let the space $\mathcal{F}$ be a Hilbert space. Recall that in a Hilbert space H, basis is a complete orthonormal set $S = \{\varphi_n \mid n \in \mathbb{Z}\}$. That is, it satisfies:

- Orthogonality: $\langle \varphi_n, \varphi_m \rangle = 0$, if $n, m \in \mathbb{Z}, n \neq m$, where $\langle \cdot, \cdot \rangle$ is the inner product operator.

- Normalization: $\langle \varphi_n, \varphi_n \rangle = 1$, for all values of $n \in \mathbb{Z}$.

- Completeness: Given $x \in H$ and $\langle x, \varphi_n \rangle = 0$, $\forall n \in \mathbb{Z}$, then $x = 0$.
  For every $f \in H$ the following expansions are valid.

$$f = \sum_{n\in\mathbb{Z}} \alpha_n \varphi_n,$$

$$\text{where } \alpha_n = \langle f, \varphi_n \rangle, \ n \in \mathbb{Z}$$

$$\|f\|^2 = \sum_{n\in\mathbb{Z}} |\alpha_n|^2$$

Complete orthonormal sets like S are also called the orthonormal basis of Hilbert spaces. The result $\|f\|^2 = \sum_{n\in\mathbb{Z}} |\alpha_n|^2$, is called Parseval's relationship.

1.2.2 Representation via Frames

Representation of functions in terms of orthonormal basis might be too restrictive. Nevertheless, it is possible to have representation of a function by relaxing the condition of orthonormality, and linear independence on the set of functions $S = \{\varphi_n \mid n \in \mathbb{Z}\}$. Recall that orthogonality implies linear independence.

The set $S = \{\varphi_n \mid n \in \mathbb{Z}\}$ of functions which belong to the Hilbert space H is a frame if there exist two constants $A > 0$ and $B < \infty$ such that for every $f \in H$ we have:

$$A\|f\|^2 \leq \sum_{n\in\mathbb{Z}} |\langle f, \varphi_n \rangle|^2 \leq B\|f\|^2$$

A and B are called the frame bounds. The frame is said to be tight if $A = B$. In this case, for $f \in H$:

$$f = A^{-1} \sum_{n\in\mathbb{Z}} \alpha_n \varphi_n,$$

$$\text{where } \alpha_n = \langle f, \varphi_n \rangle, \ n \in \mathbb{Z}$$

As noted earlier, the set of functions $\{\varphi_n \mid n \in \mathbb{Z}\}$ can be linearly dependent. Hence the above expansion need not be unique. Note that the frames are also complete, but do not necessarily satisfy Parseval's relationship in general. Further, $A = B = 1$ results in Parseval's relationship.

1.2.3 Riesz Basis Representation

If the set of functions $\{e_n \mid n \in \mathbb{Z}\}$ belonging to the Hilbert space H is a frame, and is also linearly independent, then it is a Riesz basis. Since frames are complete, so is the Riesz basis. If $\{e_n \mid n \in \mathbb{Z}\}$ is a Riesz basis for Hilbert space H, and for any $f \in H$ we have

$$A \|f\|^2 \leq \sum_{n \in \mathbb{Z}} |\langle f, e_n \rangle|^2 \leq B \|f\|^2$$

For each $f \in L^2(\mathbb{R})$ its representation is

$$\sum_{n \in \mathbb{Z}} \langle f, e_n \rangle e_n$$

Any Riesz basis can be made into a Hilbert basis by the Gram–Schmidt orthogonalization process.

1.2.4 Multiscale Representation

Human beings recognize an object via a multiscale scheme. We initially perceive an object at a coarse scale, and subsequently at finer scales. It is also possible to describe functions in this manner. That is, functions can be described at different scales. A function $f \in L^2(\mathbb{R})$ can be approximated by projecting it onto a space V_j as $P_j[f]$, where P_j is the projection operator and $j \in \mathbb{Z}$. Thus a sequence of approximating functions $\{P_j[f] \mid j \in \mathbb{Z}\}$ is obtained, so that

$$\lim_{j \to \infty} P_j[f] = f$$

Next consider the difference between two consecutive approximations. This is

$$Q_j[f] = P_{j+1}[f] - P_j[f]$$

Note that $Q_j[f]$ can be considered as the projection of the function f onto the detail space W_j. The detail space W_j is restricted so that $V_j \cap W_j = \{0\}, V_{j+1} = V_j \oplus W_j,$ $V_j \perp W_j, \forall j \in \mathbb{Z}$. Thus

$$f = \sum_{j \in \mathbb{Z}} Q_j[f]$$

The basis of the spaces W_j's are indeed the wavelets. This scheme is formally described as multiresolution analysis in a subsequent chapter.

1.2.5 Representation via Dictionaries

The idea of representation of a function via the use of a dictionary of functions is analogous to the idea of representing human thoughts via the proper use of vocabulary. The richer the vocabulary, the more precise is the representation of an idea.

A dictionary within the context of function representation is a family of vectors. In the function space $\mathcal{F}$, let $\mathcal{D} = \{g_\gamma \in \mathcal{F} \mid \gamma \in \Gamma\}$, where the set Γ is not necessarily countable. A possible representation of a function f is

$$f = \sum_{\gamma \in \Gamma} \alpha_\gamma g_\gamma$$

In the above representation, the function f is represented by $r = \{\alpha_\gamma \mid \gamma \in \Gamma\} \in l^2$. The goal of this representation is to specify a function using smallest number of words (vectors) from the dictionary. This scheme is very flexible if the size of the dictionary $\mathcal{D}$ is very large. However, this comes at the cost of determining different sets of vectors to represent different functions. A possible scheme to obtain a representation of the function f is described below.

Let the function f be represented by its approximation f_M. Further, let I_M be the index set of the vectors that are used in specifying the function f_M. Let

$$f_M = \sum_{m \in I_M} \langle f, g_m \rangle \, g_m$$

The set I_M is selected so that the error

$$\epsilon_M = \|f - f_M\|^2 = \sum_{m \notin I_M} |\langle f, g_m \rangle|^2$$

is minimized.

1.2.6 Redundancy in Representation

Redundancy, in contrast to uniqueness, in representation of a function is possible.

For example, if a function is built using frames which are not linearly independent vectors, then there might be redundancy in its representation. That is, correlation might exist between elements of the representation sequence.

In some cases redundancy might also be useful. Redundancy offers a certain level of robustness in the representation and reconstruction of functions.

1.3 Fourier Analysis

Fourier analysis involves the study of expansion of arbitrary functions in terms of trigonometric functions (sines and cosines). Fourier methods transform the original signal into a function in the transform domain. Note that a signal is simply a function. The domain of this transformation can either be time or space. The transformed domain is often referred to as the frequency or spectral domain.

1.3.1 Fourier Series

Fourier series was developed by Jean-Baptiste-Joseph Fourier (1768–1830) of France in the year 1807. He was a contemporary of Napoleon-Bonaparte. He expanded a real-valued periodic function $f(t)$ defined on $[-\pi, \pi]$ as a weighted sum of trigonometric functions.

$$f(t) = a_0 + \sum_{n=1}^{\infty} (a_n \cos(nt) + b_n \sin(nt))$$

$$a_0 = \frac{1}{2\pi} \int_{-\pi}^{\pi} f(t)\, dt$$

$$a_n = \frac{1}{\pi} \int_{-\pi}^{\pi} f(t) \cos(nt)\, dt, \quad b_n = \frac{1}{\pi} \int_{-\pi}^{\pi} f(t) \sin(nt)\, dt, \quad n = 1, 2, \ldots$$

Notice that the Fourier basis functions are of infinite duration. A snapshot of a typical trigonometric basis function which is defined for all values of $t \in \mathbb{R}$ is shown in Figure 1.1.

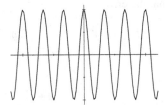

Figure 1.1. A typical trigonometric basis function.

1.3.2 Fourier Transform and Spectral Analysis

If a function $f(t)$, $t \in \mathbb{R}$ is not periodic, then the frequency content of a signal can be studied via Fourier transform. The Fourier transform of this function is defined as $F(\omega)$, where

$$F(\omega) = \int_{-\infty}^{\infty} f(t) e^{-i\omega t}\, dt$$

and

$$f(t) = \frac{1}{2\pi} \int_{-\infty}^{\infty} F(\omega) e^{i\omega t}\, d\omega$$

Note that, in order to evaluate $F(\omega)$, the entire time axis is utilized. Therefore, what is obtained with the Fourier transform is a composite view of the frequency content of the signal. This spectral analysis is global in time. It does not provide a local picture of signal variations. Consequently, this transform is not suitable if the signal is localized and nonstationary. A function is stationary, if its statistical properties do not change over time.

In order to overcome this disadvantage, Dennis Gabor (1900–1979) introduced short-time Fourier transform. In this scheme, a window-function extracts data over an interval, and then computes the Fourier transform. Note that the window-function is a weighting function which acts upon the data. This is a suitable scheme for functions which are locally stationary, but globally nonstationary. This can also capture transient effects in the signal. This scheme is called time-dependent spectral analysis, because the window slides along the time axis to compute Fourier transform of different segments of the signal.

Let the window function be $g(t-\tau)$, and $\|g\|_2$ is the $L^2(\mathbb{R})$ norm of the window function $g(t)$. Then the short-time Fourier transform is given by $F(\omega,\tau)$.

$$F(\omega,\tau) = \int_{-\infty}^{\infty} f(t)g(t-\tau)e^{-i\omega t}dt$$

$$f(t) = \frac{1}{2\pi\|g\|_2^2} \int_{-\infty}^{\infty}\int_{-\infty}^{\infty} F(\omega,\tau)\overline{g(t-\tau)}e^{i\omega t}d\omega d\tau$$

A disadvantage of the short-time Fourier transform is that, a window of fixed size provides an upper bound on the frequency resolution. This is a consequence of the so-called Heisenberg's uncertainty principle. In other words, if the window width is narrower, the signal is better localized in the time domain, but it is poorly localized in the spectral domain. The short-time Fourier transform is also called the Gabor transform.

1.4 Wavelet Analysis

Wavelet analysis is based upon the concept of *scale*, rather than frequency. Wavelets are wave-like functions, and are simply "small waves." That is, these are localized in time. See Figure 1.2.

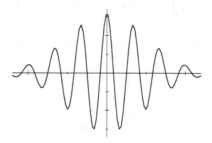

Figure 1.2. A wavelet.

Further, these functions generally have a compact support. From a single wavelet, several wavelets can be constructed by scaling and translating the original wavelet. This is in contrast to the short-time Fourier transform, where a window of constant shape and size is translated.

The original wavelet $\psi(t)$, $t \in \mathbb{R}$ is called the *mother wavelet*. The family of functions thus generated from the mother wavelet, can be used to represent a function mathematically. The basis functions are

$$\psi_{a,b}(t) = \frac{1}{\sqrt{|a|}} \psi\left(\frac{t-b}{a}\right), \qquad a, b \in \mathbb{R}, a \neq 0, \text{ and } t \in \mathbb{R}$$

Observe that these basis functions can either be of short-duration or long-duration. If these are of short-duration, then they can represent high-frequencies. However, if these are of long-duration, then they can represent low-frequencies. The continuous wavelet transform is given by

$$W_f(\psi, a, b) = \int_{-\infty}^{\infty} f(t) \overline{\psi_{a,b}(t)} dt$$

$$f(t) = \frac{1}{C_\psi} \int_{-\infty}^{\infty} \int_{-\infty}^{\infty} W_f(\psi, a, b) \, \psi_{a,b}(t) \, \frac{dadb}{a^2}$$

$$C_\psi = \int_{-\infty}^{\infty} \frac{|\Psi(\omega)|^2}{|\omega|} d\omega < \infty$$

where $\Psi(\omega)$ is the Fourier transform of $\psi(t)$, and C_ψ is well defined if $\Psi(0) = 0$, which implies $\int_{-\infty}^{\infty} \psi(t) \, dt = 0$. This is called the admissibility condition. A discrete version of wavelet transform is defined as follows. The function $f(t)$ is expanded as

$$f(t) = \sum_{m,n \in \mathbb{Z}} d(m,n) \, \psi_{mn}(t)$$

$$\psi_{mn}(t) = 2^{\frac{m}{2}} \psi(2^m t - n), \quad t \in \mathbb{R}, \qquad m, n \in \mathbb{Z}$$

$$d(m,n) = \int_{-\infty}^{\infty} f(t) \overline{\psi_{mn}(t)} dt, \qquad m, n \in \mathbb{Z}$$

The wavelets $\{\psi_{mn}(t) \mid m, n \in \mathbb{Z}\}$ form an orthonormal basis.

$$\int_{-\infty}^{\infty} \psi_{mn}(t) \overline{\psi_{m'n'}(t)} dt = \delta_{mm'} \delta_{nn'}, \qquad m, n \in \mathbb{Z}$$

$$\delta_{jk} = \begin{cases} 1, & j = k \\ 0, & j \neq k \end{cases} \qquad j, k \in \mathbb{Z}$$

δ_{jk} is called Kronecker's delta function.

Example 1.1. The mathematician Haar constructed a wavelet, which is a piece-wise constant function. The Haar wavelet is

$$\psi(t) = \begin{cases} 1, & 0 \le t < 1/2 \\ -1, & 1/2 \le t < 1 \\ 0, & \text{elsewhere} \end{cases}$$

The translations and dilations of this wavelet function form an orthonormal basis for space $L^2(\mathbb{R})$.   □

1.5 Why Use Wavelets?

Wavelets provide an excellent mathematical representation of a function due to:

- Orthogonality: The basis functions of a wavelet series are orthogonal to one another. This feature is identical to the Fourier series expansion of a function.

- Compact support: The wavelet series can provide compact support. This is very much unlike its Fourier cousin, where the trigonometric basis functions are defined over the entire real line.

  A consequence of the compact support is that wavelets can approximate sharp transitions (discontinuities) in a signal much more efficiently than the Fourier techniques.

  Also because of this property, the wavelet transforms can be used for extracting the localized time-frequency information of a signal much more efficiently than Fourier transform. In short, wavelets provide a better local description of a signal than their Fourier counterpart.

- Hierarchical representation: Wavelet analytic techniques are hierarchical representations of functions. These techniques are also called multiresolution methods.

  The concept of hierarchical representation of a function is simple. A function is divided into two parts by the wavelet transform. These parts are the *detailed* component, and the *residual* component. In the language of digital filter theory, the detailed part is the *low-pass*, and the residual part is the *high-pass*. This decomposition is again applied to the detailed or the low-pass component. This process is repeated until a desired level of resolution is achieved.

- Complexity of computation: If the length of the data vector is N, then the computational complexity of wavelet transform is typically $O(N)$. This is in contrast to the computational complexity of the fast Fourier transform algorithm, which is $O(N \log N)$.

1.6 Story of Wavelets

Story of wavelets goes as far back as the work of the mathematician Karl Weierstrass (1815–1897). In the year 1873, he constructed functions from scaled copies of a given specific function. He essentially described fractal functions. These were everywhere continuous but nowhere differentiable functions.

In the year 1909, Alfred Haar constructed a set of compactly supported, orthonormal system of functions in his doctoral dissertation. The functions that he constructed, are now called Haar wavelets in his honor.

Dennis Gabor developed a noncompact (Gaussians) and nonorthogonal basis set of functions in the year 1946.

Physicists Claude Galand and Daniel Esteban discover subband coding in 1976. It was a technique used for digital transmission over telephone communication lines.

Jean Morlet, a geophysicist used wavelets for analyzing seismic data in the early 1980's. Alex Grossman and Jean Morlet studied these seismic wavelets mathematically in more detail. They discovered that seismic signals can be modeled by simple translations and dilations of an oscillatory function of finite duration. Morlet and Grossman introduced the term *wavelet* in one of their papers, in the year 1984.

Yves Meyer recognized the deep connection between the signal-analytic studies of Grossman and Morlet and the study of singular integral operators. He discovers the first smooth orthogonal wavelet.

It was Stephane Mallat, who showed that discrete wavelet transform of a function can be computed fast via a cascade-like algorithm in the year 1986. He showed that the Haar basis, the idea of subband filtering are all interrelated via the wavelet-based algorithms. Yves Meyer and Stephane Mallat are generally credited with developing the notion of multiresolution analysis during the years 1986 through 1988.

In her epoch-making work, Ingrid Daubechies developed a family of compactly supported orthogonal wavelets in the year 1987. This work made wavelet theory a practical tool for scientists and engineers.

David Donho, and Iain Johnstone use wavelets to "denoise" images in 1990. This resulted in sharper images. In the year 1992, FBI uses wavelet technology to compress its large database of fingerprints.

In 1994, W. Sweldens developed the "lifting technique." All finite wavelet filters can be derived by using this technique.

Besides the luminaries mentioned above, several other people made significant contributions to this field. Actually wavelet theory in the present form is due to the synthesis of different ideas from many different fields like geophysics, image processing, mathematics, signal processing, and so on.

1.7 Applications

Wavelets have found applications in astronomy, econometrics, geophysics, mathematics, medicine, numerical analysis, signal processing, statistics, and many other diverse fields. More specifically, some of these applications are:

- Signal compression. This is necessary for efficient transmission of information over links, where bandwidth is a premium. The goal of compression is a parsimonious representation of data. This is the celebrated Ockham's razor principle. Signal compression also results in efficient storage of the signal.

- Signal denoising. Denoising means removal of noise from signals. Noise is the unwanted component of a signal. Audio signals and images benefit from denoising.

- Storing of fingerprint files. Wavelet transforms can be used to compress the large amount of data stored in the fingerprint files.

- Speech recognition technology uses wavelet techniques to differentiate consonants and vowels.

- Wavelets can be used for image enhancement, image recognition, and object detection.

- Detection of transients in signals.

- Biomedical engineers can use wavelets in analyzing signals from electrocardiogram and electroencephalogram. Biological signals are sometimes more amenable to wavelet techniques, because they are occasionally organized into different scales.

- Analyzing self-similar signals. Wavelets have found application in analyzing the traffic on the Internet.

- Wavelets can be used to find numerical solutions of boundary value problems.

- Used in finance industry for tracking quick variation of values.

- Metallurgical industry uses it for describing rough surfaces.

- Biologists use it for characterizing cell membranes.

- For automatic target recognition in defense industry.

- Machine learning, and artificial intelligence in general.

Problems

1. Increase the size of the list of applications of wavelet transforms given in the chapter.

CHAPTER 2

Continuous Wavelet Transform

2.1 Introduction

Wavelet transform is a technique for local analysis of signals. This transform is an alternative but not a replacement of the Fourier transform. The building blocks in wavelet analysis are derived by translation and dilation of a mother function. It uses wavelets (short waves) instead of long waves. These wavelets are localized functions. Instead of oscillating forever, as in the case of the basis functions used in Fourier analysis (trigonometric functions), wavelets eventually drop to zero. Wavelet transforms can be either continuous or discrete.

Continuous wavelet transforms are studied in this chapter. We initially study basics of continuous wavelet transforms. This is followed by a description of properties of continuous wavelet transforms. Certain examples of wavelets and elementary examples of continuous wavelet transforms are also given. A brief description of regularity of a wavelet is also provided. Regularity of a wavelet is a degree of its smoothness.

2.2 Basics of Continuous Wavelet Transform

The wavelet transform is a mapping of a function defined in time domain, into a function which has a *time-scale* representation. That is, the wavelet transformation is a two-dimensional representation of a one-dimensional function. In the following definition of wavelet transform, $L^2(\mathbb{R})$ is the space of square-integrable functions. Let $f(t)$, $t \in \mathbb{R}$ be the signal that has to be transformed, where $f(\cdot) \in L^2(\mathbb{R})$. That is, $\int_{-\infty}^{\infty} |f(t)|^2 \, dt < \infty$. The wavelet transform of the function $f(\cdot)$ is defined below. It is computed by shifting and scaling of the mother wavelet function $\psi(t)$, $t \in \mathbb{R}$, where $\psi(\cdot) \in L^2(\mathbb{R})$.

Definition 2.1. *Continuous wavelet transform.*

(a) *The signal to be transformed is:* $f(t) \in \mathbb{R}$, $t \in \mathbb{R}$, *and* $f(\cdot) \in L^2(\mathbb{R})$.

(b) *The function* $\psi : \mathbb{R} \to \mathbb{C}$, *where* $\psi(\cdot) \in L^2(\mathbb{R})$, *is called the mother wavelet or the prototype function.*

(i) $\Psi(\cdot)$ *is the Fourier transform of* $\psi(\cdot)$. *That is,* $\psi(t) \leftrightarrow \Psi(\omega)$.

(ii) *The function* $\Psi(\cdot)$ *should also satisfy the following condition*

$$C_\psi = \int_{-\infty}^{\infty} \frac{|\Psi(\omega)|^2}{|\omega|} d\omega < \infty \tag{2.1a}$$

This relationship is also called the admissibility condition. It is required for recovering $f(t)$ *from the wavelet transform.*

(c) *Let* $a, b \in \mathbb{R}$, *and* $a \neq 0$. *Let*

$$\psi_{a,b}(t) = \frac{1}{\sqrt{|a|}} \psi\left(\frac{t-b}{a}\right), \quad t \in \mathbb{R} \tag{2.1b}$$

(d) *The continuous wavelet transform of the function* $f(\cdot)$ *is*

$$W_f(\psi, a, b) = \int_{-\infty}^{\infty} f(t) \overline{\psi_{a,b}(t)} dt \tag{2.1c}$$

$\square$

Observe that

$$\left\|\psi_{a,b}\right\|^2 = \int_{-\infty}^{\infty} \left|\psi_{a,b}(t)\right|^2 dt = \int_{-\infty}^{\infty} |\psi(t)|^2 dt = \|\psi\|^2 \tag{2.2}$$

Further, the admissibility condition implies that $\Psi(0) = 0$. That is, $\int_{-\infty}^{\infty} \psi(t) dt = 0$. This is required for recovering $f(\cdot)$ from its wavelet transform $W_f(\cdot, \cdot, \cdot)$. The variables a and b, are the *scale* and *translation* parameters respectively. Generally a is positive. For $|a| > 1$, the function $\psi_{a,b}(\cdot)$ becomes a stretched version (long-time duration) of $\psi(\cdot)$. In this case, $\psi_{a,b}(\cdot)$ is a low-frequency function. However, for $|a| < 1$, the function $\psi_{a,b}(\cdot)$ becomes a contracted version (short-time duration) of $\psi(\cdot)$. In this case, $\psi_{a,b}(\cdot)$ is a high-frequency function. The parameter b simply shifts the mother wavelet. In order to preserve smoothness, the mother wavelet is also required to have zero values for the first few moments. This requirement is termed the *regularity condition*.

The existence of continuous wavelet transform of $f(\cdot) \in L^2(\mathbb{R})$ is guaranteed by applying the Bunyakovsky–Cauchy–Schwartz inequality to the relationship $W_f(\psi, a, b) = \int_{-\infty}^{\infty} f(t) \overline{\psi_{a,b}(t)} dt$. However, if the mother wavelet is bounded, then the transform will exist provided $f(\cdot) \in L^1(\mathbb{R})$.

Observation 2.1. The inversion formula of the wavelet transform is

$$f(t) = \frac{1}{C_\psi} \int_{-\infty}^{\infty} \int_{-\infty}^{\infty} W_f(\psi, a, b) \psi_{a,b}(t) \frac{da\,db}{a^2} \tag{2.3}$$

$\square$

See the problem section for a proof of the validity of this inversion formula.

A Property of the Mother Wavelet Function

Let the mother wavelet $\psi(t)$ be centered at t_0, $\Psi(\omega)$ be centered at ω_0. Define the spread of these functions by σ_t and σ_ω respectively.

$$\sigma_t^2 = \int_{-\infty}^{\infty} (t - t_0)^2 \, |\psi(t)|^2 \, dt$$

$$\sigma_\omega^2 = \int_{-\infty}^{\infty} (\omega - \omega_0)^2 \, |\Psi(\omega)|^2 \, d\omega$$

Let $\psi_{a,b}(t) \leftrightarrow \Psi_{ab}(\omega) = \sqrt{|a|}\Psi(a\omega) e^{-ib\omega}$. Then $\psi_{a,b}(t)$ is centered at $t = at_0 + b$, and $\Psi_{ab}(\omega)$ is centered at ω_0/a. Let the spread of the functions $\psi_{a,b}(t)$ and $\Psi_{ab}(\omega)$ be $\sigma_{a,b,t}$ and $\sigma_{a,b,\omega}$ respectively. Then

$$\sigma_{a,b,t}^2 = \int_{-\infty}^{\infty} (t - at_0 - b)^2 \, |\psi_{ab}(t)|^2 \, dt = a^2 \sigma_t^2$$

$$\sigma_{a,b,\omega}^2 = \int_{-\infty}^{\infty} \left(\omega - \frac{\omega_0}{a}\right)^2 |\Psi_{ab}(\omega)|^2 \, d\omega = \frac{\sigma_\omega^2}{a^2}$$

It follows that

$$\sigma_t \sigma_\omega = \sigma_{a,b,t} \sigma_{a,b,\omega}$$

The above equation implies that in the wavelet transform, there is a trade-off between time and frequency resolutions.

2.3 Properties of Continuous Wavelet Transform

Certain important properties of continuous wavelet transforms are listed.

1. Linear superposition

$$g(t) = f_1(t) + f_2(t)$$
$$W_g(\psi, a, b) = W_{f_1}(\psi, a, b) + W_{f_2}(\psi, a, b)$$

2. Translation

$$g(t) = f(t - t_0)$$
$$W_g(\psi, a, b) = W_f(\psi, a, b - t_0)$$

3. Scaling

$$g(t) = \sqrt{\alpha}f(\alpha t), \quad \alpha \in \mathbb{R}^+$$
$$W_g\left(\psi, a, b\right) = W_f\left(\psi, \alpha a, \alpha b\right)$$

4. Fourier representation of the continuous wavelet transform. A Fourier representation of the continuous wavelet transform can be obtained by using Parseval's relationship. Let $f(t) \leftrightarrow F(\omega)$. Then

$$W_f\left(\psi, a, b\right) = \int_{-\infty}^{\infty} f\left(t\right)\overline{\psi_{a,b}\left(t\right)}dt$$
$$= \frac{1}{2\pi}\int_{-\infty}^{\infty} F(\omega)\overline{\Psi_{ab}\left(\omega\right)}d\omega$$

Consequently

$$W_f\left(\psi, a, b\right) = \frac{\sqrt{|a|}}{2\pi}\int_{-\infty}^{\infty} F(\omega)\overline{\Psi\left(a\omega\right)}e^{ib\omega}d\omega$$

5. Parseval type of relationship for continuous wavelet transform. Let $f(t), g(t) \in L^2\left(\mathbb{R}\right)$. Then

$$\int_{-\infty}^{\infty}\int_{-\infty}^{\infty} W_f\left(\psi, a, b\right)\overline{W_g\left(\psi, a, b\right)}\frac{dadb}{a^2} = C_\psi\int_{-\infty}^{\infty} f\left(t\right)\overline{g\left(t\right)}dt$$

and

$$\int_{-\infty}^{\infty}\int_{-\infty}^{\infty} |W_f\left(\psi, a, b\right)|^2\frac{dadb}{a^2} = C_\psi\int_{-\infty}^{\infty} |f\left(t\right)|^2 dt$$

6. Regularity of wavelets. Regularity of wavelets represents the degree of its smoothness. In addition to the admissibility conditions on the wavelet function, it is required that the wavelet function has additional properties. This is required so that the wavelet transform coefficients decrease quickly with decreasing values $|a|$. This important feature is discussed later in the chapter.

7. Wavelet transform of an analytic function. A function $f\left(t\right) \in \mathbb{C}$, for $t \in \mathbb{R}$ is analytic, if its Fourier transform $F\left(\omega\right)$ is equal to zero for negative values of ω. Let $f\left(t\right) = \left(f_r\left(t\right) + if_i\left(t\right)\right)$, where $f_r\left(t\right)$ and $f_i\left(t\right)$ are real and imaginary parts of $f\left(t\right)$ respectively. Also, $f_r\left(t\right) \leftrightarrow F_r\left(\omega\right)$. Then $F\left(\omega\right) = 2u\left(\omega\right)F_r\left(\omega\right)$, where $u\left(\cdot\right)$ is the unit step function. Let $W_f\left(\psi, a, b\right)$ and $W_{f_r}\left(\psi, a, b\right)$ be the wavelet transforms of $f\left(t\right)$ and $f_r\left(t\right)$ respectively. Then

$$W_f\left(\psi, a, b\right) = 2W_{f_r}\left(\psi, a, b\right)$$

This equation implies that the wavelet transform of an analytic function is completely determined by the wavelet transform of its real part.   □

2.4 Examples

Certain well-known examples of wavelets are specified. Elementary examples of continuous time wavelet transforms are also discussed.

2.4.1 Wavelets

Some commonly used wavelets are discussed below. In these examples $t \in \mathbb{R}$.

Haar wavelet: The Haar wavelet, named after Alfred Haar (1885–1933) is defined as

$$\psi(t) = \begin{cases} 1, & 0 \le t < 1/2 \\ -1, & 1/2 \le t < 1 \\ 0, & \text{elsewhere} \end{cases}$$

See Figure 2.1.

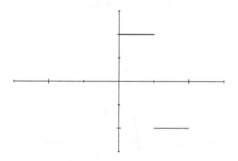

Figure 2.1. Haar wavelet $\psi(\cdot)$.

Note that this wavelet satisfies the admissibility condition $\int_{-\infty}^{\infty} \psi(t)\,dt = 0$. Observe that this wavelet is only piecewise-continuous. Its Fourier transform is given by

$$\Psi(\omega) = 2ie^{-i\omega/2}\frac{\left(1 - \cos\frac{\omega}{2}\right)}{\omega}$$

Morlet wavelet: Morlet wavelet is a complex exponential with a Gaussian window. This function is not a wavelet as per the definition.

$$\psi(t) = \frac{1}{\sqrt{2\pi}}e^{-i\omega_0 t}e^{-t^2/2}$$

Its Fourier transform is given by

$$\Psi(\omega) = e^{-(\omega+\omega_0)^2/2}$$

The function $\psi(\cdot)$ does not satisfy the admissibility condition $\int_{-\infty}^{\infty} \psi(t)\,dt = 0$. However, ω_0 can be chosen such that $\Psi(0)$ is very close to zero. Consider the real part of $\psi(t)$, which is $\mathrm{Re}\,(\psi(t)) = \psi_c(t)$. It is given by

$$\psi_c(t) = \frac{e^{-t^2/2}}{\sqrt{2\pi}}\cos\omega_0 t$$

If $\psi_c(t) \leftrightarrow \Psi_c(\omega)$, then

$$\Psi_c(\omega) = \left[e^{-(\omega+\omega_0)^2/2} + e^{-(\omega-\omega_0)^2/2} \right] / 2$$

Note that $\Psi_c(0) = e^{-\omega_0^2/2} \neq 0$. However the value of ω_0 can be chosen large enough such that $\Psi_c(0) \simeq 0$. In this case the $\psi(\cdot)$ is said to be "approximately analytic." Morlets are named after the French geophysicist Jean Morlet (1931–2007). Morlet and his colleague Alexander Grossman (1930–) did pioneering work in wavelet transform theory.

Mexican-hat wavelet: The Mexican-hat wavelet is defined as

$$\psi(t) = \left(1 - t^2\right) e^{-t^2/2}$$

See Figure 2.2.

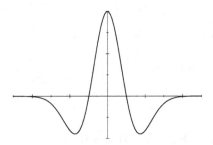

Figure 2.2. Mexican-hat wavelet $\psi(\cdot)$.

This function is related to the second derivative of the Gaussian function $g(t) = e^{-t^2/2}$. That is,

$$\psi(t) = -\frac{d^2}{dt^2} g(t)$$

Also

$$\Psi(\omega) = \sqrt{2\pi}\,\omega^2 e^{-\omega^2/2}$$

This wavelet satisfies the admissibility condition $\Psi(0) = 0$. All the derivatives of $\psi(t)$ and $\Psi(\omega)$ exist. Furthermore, this function has superb localization in both time and frequency domains. It is widely used in image processing. The Mexican-hat wavelet was originally introduced by the physicist Dennis Gabor.

2.4.2 Continuous Wavelet Transforms

Some elementary examples of continuous time wavelet transforms are:

1. $f(t) = k \in \mathbb{R}$. It turns out that $W_f (\psi, a, b) = 0$. This follows by using the admissibility condition $\int_{-\infty}^{\infty} \psi (t) \, dt = 0$.

2. $f(t) = \delta (t - t_0)$. Then $W_f (\psi, a, b) = \overline{\psi_{a,b} (t_0)}$.

3. $f(t) = e^{i\omega_0 t}$. Then $W_f (\psi, a, b) = \overline{\Psi_{a,b} (\omega_0)}$.

4. $f(t) = t$. Then $W_f (\psi, a, b) = -i \frac{d}{d\omega} \overline{\Psi_{a,b} (\omega)} \big|_{\omega=0}$.   □

2.5 Regularity of Wavelets

Regularity of a wavelet is a measure of its smoothness. Continuity of $\psi (\cdot)$ and sufficient number of its derivatives help in overcoming the artifacts in the analysis of a signal via the wavelet itself. Thus, in addition to the admissibility conditions, it is required that the wavelet function has additional properties. This is required so that the value of the wavelet transform decreases quickly with decreasing values of $|a|$. Let

$$\mathcal{N}_j = \int_{-\infty}^{\infty} t^j \psi (t) \, dt = 0, \qquad j = 0, 1, 2, \ldots n$$

$$\Psi^{(j)} (\omega) \triangleq \frac{d^j}{d\omega^j} \Psi(\omega), \quad j \in \mathbb{P}$$

We show that $W_f (\psi, a, b)$ decays as fast as $|a|^{n+1.5}$ for a smooth function $f(t)$. A wavelet which satisfies this condition is called a wavelet of order n. The Fourier transform of the wavelet of order n satisfies $\Psi^{(j)} (0) = 0$ for $j = 0, 1, 2, \ldots n$.

Expand the function $f(t)$ in its Taylor series.

$$f(t) = \sum_{j=0}^{n} f^{(j)} (0) \frac{t^j}{j!} + R(t)$$

$$R(t) = \int_{0}^{t} \frac{(t - t')^n}{n!} f^{(n+1)} (t') \, dt'$$

where

$$f^{(j)} (t) \triangleq \frac{d^j}{dt^j} f(t), \quad j = 0, 1, 2, \ldots (n + 1)$$

$$f^{(j)} (0) \triangleq \frac{d^j}{dt^j} f (t) \Big|_{t=0}, \quad j = 0, 1, 2, \ldots n$$

Let $b = 0$, then

$$W_f(\psi, a, 0) = \frac{1}{\sqrt{|a|}} \left[|a| \sum_{j=0}^{n} f^{(j)}(0) \overline{\mathcal{N}_j} \frac{a^j}{j!} + O(|a|^{n+2}) \right]$$

Therefore, the wavelet transform coefficient decays as fast as $O(|a|^{n+1.5})$. This observation follows from the fact that $\mathcal{N}_j = \Psi^{(j)}(0) = 0$ for $j = 0, 1, 2, \ldots n$. Also note that $\mathcal{N}_0 = 0$ is indeed the admissibility condition for the existence of the continuous wavelet transform. Further, the wavelet transform decays to zero for smaller values of $|a|$. The value of the wavelet transform is largely determined by the first nonzero moment of the wavelet. Thus the regularity of a wavelet forces its low-order moments to zero. In brief, the wavelets should satisfy certain regularity conditions so that the wavelet coefficients decrease sufficiently fast with decreases in the value of magnitude of the scale.

Problems

1. Establish the inversion formula of the continuous wavelet transform.
   Hint: Let $f(t) \leftrightarrow F(\omega)$, $\psi(t) \leftrightarrow \Psi(\omega)$, and $\psi_{a,b}(t) \leftrightarrow \Psi_{a,b}(\omega)$. Then

   $$\Psi_{a,b}(\omega) = \sqrt{|a|}\Psi(a\omega)e^{-ib\omega}, \quad \text{and} \quad \psi_{a,b}(t) = \frac{\sqrt{|a|}}{2\pi} \int_{-\infty}^{\infty} \Psi(a\upsilon)e^{i\upsilon(t-b)}d\upsilon$$

   Also using a generalized Parseval's type of relationship yields

   $$W_f(\psi, a, b) = \frac{\sqrt{|a|}}{2\pi} \int_{-\infty}^{\infty} F(\omega)\overline{\Psi(a\omega)}e^{ib\omega}d\omega$$

   Thus

   $$\frac{1}{C_\psi} \int_{-\infty}^{\infty} \int_{-\infty}^{\infty} W_f(\psi, a, b)\psi_{a,b}(t) \frac{dadb}{a^2}$$

   $$= \frac{1}{4\pi^2 C_\psi} \int_{-\infty}^{\infty} \int_{-\infty}^{\infty} \int_{-\infty}^{\infty} \int_{-\infty}^{\infty} F(\omega)\overline{\Psi(a\omega)}\Psi(a\upsilon)e^{i\upsilon t}e^{ib(\omega-\upsilon)}d\omega d\upsilon \frac{dadb}{|a|}$$

   $$= \frac{1}{2\pi C_\psi} \int_{-\infty}^{\infty} \int_{-\infty}^{\infty} \int_{-\infty}^{\infty} F(\omega)\overline{\Psi(a\omega)}\Psi(a\upsilon)e^{i\upsilon t}\delta(\omega-\upsilon)d\omega d\upsilon \frac{da}{|a|}$$

   $$= \frac{1}{2\pi C_\psi} \int_{-\infty}^{\infty} \int_{-\infty}^{\infty} F(\upsilon)|\Psi(a\upsilon)|^2 e^{i\upsilon t}d\upsilon \frac{da}{|a|}$$

   $$= \frac{1}{2\pi C_\psi} \int_{-\infty}^{\infty} \frac{|\Psi(x)|^2}{|x|}dx \int_{-\infty}^{\infty} F(\upsilon)e^{i\upsilon t}d\upsilon = f(t)$$

2. A Parseval type of relationship for continuous wavelet transform is established. Let $f(t), g(t) \in L^2(\mathbb{R})$. Then

$$\int_{-\infty}^{\infty} \int_{-\infty}^{\infty} W_f\left(\psi, a, b\right) \overline{W_g\left(\psi, a, b\right)} \frac{dadb}{a^2} = C_\psi \int_{-\infty}^{\infty} f\left(t\right) \overline{g\left(t\right)} dt$$

Hint: The proof uses Parseval's relationship of the Fourier transforms

$$W_f\left(\psi, a, b\right) = \int_{-\infty}^{\infty} f\left(t\right) \overline{\psi_{a,b}\left(t\right)} dt = \frac{\sqrt{|a|}}{2\pi} \int_{-\infty}^{\infty} F(\omega) \overline{\Psi\left(a\omega\right)} e^{ib\omega} d\omega$$

$$\overline{W_g\left(\psi, a, b\right)} = \int_{-\infty}^{\infty} \overline{g\left(t\right)} \psi_{a,b}\left(t\right) dt = \frac{\sqrt{|a|}}{2\pi} \int_{-\infty}^{\infty} \overline{G(\upsilon)} \Psi\left(a\upsilon\right) e^{-ib\upsilon} d\upsilon$$

$$\int_{-\infty}^{\infty} \int_{-\infty}^{\infty} W_f\left(\psi, a, b\right) \overline{W_g\left(\psi, a, b\right)} \frac{dadb}{a^2}$$

$$= \int_{-\infty}^{\infty} \int_{-\infty}^{\infty} \int_{-\infty}^{\infty} \frac{1}{4\pi^2 |a|} F(\omega) \overline{G(\upsilon)} \Psi\left(a\omega\right) \Psi\left(a\upsilon\right) \int_{-\infty}^{\infty} e^{ib(\omega - \upsilon)} db d\omega d\upsilon da$$

$$= \int_{-\infty}^{\infty} \int_{-\infty}^{\infty} \int_{-\infty}^{\infty} \frac{1}{2\pi |a|} F(\omega) \overline{G(\upsilon)} \Psi\left(a\omega\right) \Psi\left(a\upsilon\right) \delta\left(\omega - \upsilon\right) d\omega d\upsilon da$$

$$= \int_{-\infty}^{\infty} \int_{-\infty}^{\infty} \frac{1}{2\pi |a|} F(\upsilon) \overline{G(\upsilon)} \left|\Psi\left(a\upsilon\right)\right|^2 d\upsilon da$$

$$= \int_{-\infty}^{\infty} \frac{\left|\Psi\left(x\right)\right|^2}{|x|} dx \frac{1}{2\pi} \int_{-\infty}^{\infty} F(\upsilon) \overline{G(\upsilon)} d\upsilon$$

$$= C_\psi \int_{-\infty}^{\infty} f(t) \overline{g(t)} dt$$

3. A function $f(t) \in \mathbb{C}$, for $t \in \mathbb{R}$ is analytic, if its Fourier transform $F(\omega)$ is equal to zero for negative values of ω. Let $f(t) = (f_r(t) + if_i(t))$, where $f_r(t)$ and $f_i(t)$ are real and imaginary parts of $f(t)$ respectively. Also, $f_r(t) \leftrightarrow F_r(\omega)$. Prove that $F(\omega) = 2u(\omega) F_r(\omega)$, where $u(\cdot)$ is the unit step function. Hint: This result is established in three steps.

Step 1: It is known that

$$u(t) \leftrightarrow \pi\delta\left(\omega\right) + \frac{1}{i\omega}, \quad \text{and} \quad \frac{\delta\left(t\right)}{2} + \frac{i}{2\pi t} \leftrightarrow u\left(\omega\right)$$

$$sgn\left(t\right) \leftrightarrow \frac{2}{i\omega}, \quad \text{and} \quad \frac{i}{\pi t} \leftrightarrow sgn\left(\omega\right)$$

Step 2: As $f(\cdot)$ is an analytic function, we have $F(\omega) = u(\omega) F(\omega)$. This implies

$$f(t) = \left\{ \frac{\delta\left(t\right)}{2} + \frac{i}{2\pi t} \right\} * f(t)$$

That is,

$$f(t) = \frac{i}{\pi t} * f(t)$$

Thus

$$f_r(t) + if_i(t) = \frac{i}{\pi t} * (f_r(t) + if_i(t))$$

This leads to

$$f_r(t) = -\frac{1}{\pi t} * f_i(t), \quad \text{and} \quad f_i(t) = \frac{1}{\pi t} * f_r(t)$$

Therefore,

$$f(t) = f_r(t) + if_i(t) = f_r(t) + \frac{i}{\pi t} * f_r(t)$$

Step 3: The above result implies

$$F(\omega) = (1 + sgn(\omega)) F_r(\omega) = 2u(\omega) F_r(\omega)$$

CHAPTER 3

Discrete Wavelet Transform

3.1 Introduction

A discrete version of the continuous wavelet transform is discussed in this chapter. Initially, basics of discrete wavelet transform are outlined. This is followed by an exposition of a multiresolution-analysis scheme to study discrete wavelets. This leads to the study of scaling function and the characterization of the W_j-spaces (detail spaces), where $j \in \mathbb{Z}$. As we shall see, these spaces are orthogonal to each other. Theory is also developed to expand a function $f \in L^2(\mathbb{R})$ in terms of the scaling function and mother wavelet. An explanation of this expansion is also provided in the language of digital filters. Subsequently, a scheme is outlined for the computation of scaling function. Finally, an alternate and more powerful multiresolution analysis scheme is provided. In this chapter t is real-valued. That is, $t \in \mathbb{R}$.

3.2 Basics of Discrete Wavelet Transform

Recall that the continuous wavelet transform of a real-valued function $f(t)$ is given by

$$W_f(\psi, a, b) = \int_{-\infty}^{\infty} f(t)\,\overline{\psi_{a,b}(t)}\,dt$$

where for $t, a, b \in \mathbb{R}$, and $a \neq 0$

$$\psi_{a,b}(t) = \frac{1}{\sqrt{|a|}}\psi\left(\frac{t-b}{a}\right)$$

Further, $\psi(\cdot)$ satisfies the admissibility conditions. Discrete wavelet transform is the evaluation of the continuous wavelet transform at a discrete set of values of a and b, specified by

$$a = a_0^{-m}, \quad b = nb_0 a_0^{-m}, \quad a_0, b_0 \in \mathbb{R}, \quad a_0 \neq 0, \quad m, n \in \mathbb{Z}$$

In the discrete world, discrete wavelets are defined as

$$\psi_{mn}(t) = |a_0|^{\frac{m}{2}} \psi(a_0^m t - nb_0), \quad t \in \mathbb{R} \qquad m, n \in \mathbb{Z}$$

The discrete wavelet transform is also useful in analyzing time series.

Definition 3.1. *Let $f((t)$, $t \in \mathbb{R}$ where $f \in L^2(\mathbb{R})$. Also let $a_0 \in \mathbb{R}^+$, and $b_0 \in \mathbb{R}$.*

(a) *Discrete wavelet transform of the function $f(\cdot)$, is*

$$d(m,n) = \int_{-\infty}^{\infty} f(t) \overline{\psi_{mn}(t)} dt, \quad \forall\, m, n \in \mathbb{Z} \tag{3.1a}$$

$$\psi_{mn}(t) = a_0^{\frac{m}{2}} \psi(a_0^m t - nb_0), \quad \forall\, m, n \in \mathbb{Z} \tag{3.1b}$$

where $\psi(\cdot)$ is the mother wavelet. The values $d(m,n)$ are called the wavelet coefficients, and the $\psi_{mn}(\cdot)$'s are called the wavelets.

(b) *If the wavelets form an orthonormal basis of $L^2(\mathbb{R})$, then*

$$f(t) = \sum_{m,n \in \mathbb{Z}} d(m,n)\,\psi_{mn}(t) \tag{3.1c}$$

Note that the wavelets $\{\psi_{mn}(t) \mid m, n \in \mathbb{Z}\}$ form an orthonormal basis if

$$\int_{-\infty}^{\infty} \psi_{mn}(t) \overline{\psi_{m'n'}(t)} dt = \delta_{mm'}\delta_{nn'}, \quad \forall\, m, n \in \mathbb{Z} \tag{3.1d}$$

$$\delta_{jk} = \begin{cases} 1, & j = k \\ 0, & j \ne k \end{cases}, \quad \forall\, j, k \in \mathbb{Z} \tag{3.1e}$$

δ_{jk} is called the Kronecker's delta function. □

Observe that the discrete wavelet transform is the transform of a continuous time function, but the scale and translation parameters are discretized. Also note that some authors have elected to define $\psi_{mn}(t)$ as $a_0^{-\frac{m}{2}} \psi(a_0^{-m} t - nb_0)$, for all $m, n \in \mathbb{Z}$.

The necessary and sufficient conditions for a set of wavelets to form a frame or an orthonormal basis can be found in the superb monograph by Daubechies (1992).

3.3 Multiresolution Analysis

A special family of wavelets can be constructed in $L^2(\mathbb{R})$ by using the principle of multiresolution analysis. Multiresolution analysis is basically a hierarchy of approximation spaces. This is a sequence of closed subspaces, where each subspace represents a resolution level. The set difference of successive subspaces represents the detail required to reach the next finer resolution subspace. This concept of multiresolution analysis was formulated by Stéphane Mallat and Yves Meyer. The axioms of multiresolution analysis (MRA) are listed.

Notation: $\overline{A}$ is the closure of the set A.   □

Axioms: The multiresolution analysis of $L^2(\mathbb{R})$ is a sequence of closed subspaces $\{V_j \mid V_j \subseteq L^2(\mathbb{R}), j \in \mathbb{Z}\}$, and a function $\phi(\cdot)$ called the *scaling function*, so that the following assumptions are satisfied.

1. *Nesting property*: $V_j \subset V_{j+1}$, for all values of $j \in \mathbb{Z}$. This is the so called nesting property of the subspaces. This hierarchy of approximation spaces is often represented as

$$\ldots \subset V_{-2} \subset V_{-1} \subset V_0 \subset V_1 \subset V_2 \subset \ldots$$

2. *Upward completeness*: $\overline{\cup_{j\in\mathbb{Z}}V_j} = L^2(\mathbb{R})$. This is the closure property.

3. *Downward completeness*: $\cap_{j\in\mathbb{Z}}V_j = \{0\}$. Coarser approximations are obtained as $j \to -\infty$. Consequently $\lim_{j\to-\infty} V_j = \{0\}$.

4. *Scaling property*: $f(\cdot) \in V_j \Leftrightarrow f(2\cdot) \in V_{j+1}$, for all values of $j \in \mathbb{Z}$.

5. *Existence of scaling function*: A scaling function $\phi(\cdot) \in V_0$, where $\phi : \mathbb{R} \to \mathbb{C}$ exists such that $\{\phi(\cdot - n) \mid n \in \mathbb{Z}\}$ forms an orthonormal basis of V_0. The function $\phi(\cdot)$ is also called a *refinable function* or *father wavelet* or an *orthonormal MRA generator.*
   This formulation is called an *orthogonal MRA*.   □

Axiom 4 states the important property of MRA. That is, each V_j contains functions, which are in V_0, but compressed by a factor 2^j. Axioms 4 and 5 help in determining an orthonormal basis set for the space V_j.

The scaling function should have some additional properties. The scaling function $\phi(\cdot)$ should decay to zero, as $|t| \to \infty$. This implies localization of the scaling function in time. In addition, it is assumed that $\int_{-\infty}^{\infty} \phi(t)\,dt = 1$.

It turns out that, scaling functions are relatively easy to specify. However, the discovery of orthogonal multiresolution approximations is harder. A more general MRA formulation is given later in the chapter. A later chapter studies biorthogonal MRA. A few observations about the V_j and W_j spaces are next summarized.

Observations 3.1. These observations follow from the MRA axioms.

1. $V_{-\infty} = \{0\}$, and $V_\infty = L^2(\mathbb{R})$.

2. $f(t) \in V_0 \Leftrightarrow f(t-n) \in V_0, \forall t \in \mathbb{R}$ and $\forall n \in \mathbb{Z}$.

3. $f(\cdot) \in V_0 \Leftrightarrow f(2^j\cdot) \in V_j$, for all values of $j \in \mathbb{Z}$. The space V_j is a scaled version of the space V_0.

4. Also

$$\langle \phi(\cdot - m), \phi(\cdot - n) \rangle = \int_{-\infty}^{\infty} \phi(t-m)\,\overline{\phi(t-n)}dt = \delta_{mn}, \qquad m, n \in \mathbb{Z}$$

5. For all $j \in \mathbb{Z}$, the set V_j is spanned by the orthonormal basis $\{\phi_{jk}(\cdot) \mid k \in \mathbb{Z}\}$, where

$$\phi_{jk}(t) = 2^{j/2}\phi(2^j t - k), \qquad \forall k \in \mathbb{Z}, \forall t \in \mathbb{R}$$

$$\langle \phi_{jk}, \phi_{jl} \rangle = \int_{-\infty}^{\infty} \phi_{jk}(t)\,\overline{\phi_{jl}(t)}dt = \delta_{kl}, \qquad \forall k, l \in \mathbb{Z}$$

If $j > 0$, $\phi_{jk}(\cdot)$ is narrower, and the spanned space is larger. This implies finer information.

If $j < 0$, $\phi_{jk}(\cdot)$ is wider, and the spanned space is smaller. This implies coarser information.

Note that $\phi(\cdot) = \phi_{00}(\cdot)$, Also let $\phi_{j0}(\cdot) \triangleq \phi_j(\cdot)$.

6. We have

$$\langle \phi_{jk}, \phi_{jk} \rangle = \int_{-\infty}^{\infty} |\phi_{jk}(t)|^2\, dt = \int_{-\infty}^{\infty} |\phi(t)|^2\, dt, \qquad \forall j, k \in \mathbb{Z}$$

7. Let W_0 be the space so that

$$V_0 \cap W_0 = \{0\}, \quad V_1 = V_0 \oplus W_0, \quad V_0 \perp W_0$$

where $\oplus$ is the direct sum operator of vector spaces. Then W_j is a space so that

$$V_j \cap W_j = \{0\}, \quad V_{j+1} = V_j \oplus W_j, \quad V_j \perp W_j, \forall j \in \mathbb{Z}$$

The space W_j, is called the detail space. The spaces V_j and W_j are said to be orthogonal complement of each other in space V_{j+1}.

8. Note that
$$V_j \cap V_k = V_k, \qquad k \leq j, \ \forall j, k \in \mathbb{Z}$$

9. Observe that $V_j \subset V_{j+1}$; however $W_j \cap W_k = \{0\}$, where $j \neq k$ and $\forall j, k \in \mathbb{Z}$.

10. The spaces W_j, $j \in \mathbb{Z}$, also obey the scaling property. $f(\cdot) \in W_0 \Leftrightarrow f(2\cdot) \in W_1$.
   Similarly $f(\cdot) \in W_0 \Leftrightarrow f(2^j \cdot) \in W_j$ for all values of $j \in \mathbb{Z}$.

11. Space W_j is orthogonal to space W_k. And $W_j \cap W_k = \{0\}$, where $j \neq k$, $\forall j, k \in \mathbb{Z}$. It can be concluded that, while the elements of the set $\{V_j \mid j \in \mathbb{Z}\}$ are nested by hypothesis, the elements of the set $\{W_j \mid j \in \mathbb{Z}\}$ are mutually orthogonal.

12. Note that
$$V_j \cap W_k = \{0\}, \qquad j \leq k, \ j, k \in \mathbb{Z}$$

13. Also

$$V_{j+1} = \bigoplus_{n=-\infty}^{j} W_n, \quad j \in \mathbb{Z}$$

14. $L^2(\mathbb{R}) = \ldots W_{-2} \oplus W_{-1} \oplus W_0 \oplus W_1 \oplus W_2 \oplus \ldots = \bigoplus_{n \in \mathbb{Z}} W_n.$

15. Let $j_0 \in \mathbb{Z}$, then $L^2(\mathbb{R}) = V_{j_0} \oplus W_{j_0} \oplus W_{j_0+1} \oplus W_{j_0+2} \oplus \ldots.$ $\qquad\square$

3.4 Scaling Function

Note from the last section that V_1 is spanned by the orthonormal basis

$$\{\phi_{1k}(\cdot) \mid k \in \mathbb{Z}\}$$

Also $\phi(\cdot) \in V_0$ and $V_0 \subset V_1 \Rightarrow \phi(\cdot) \in V_1$. Therefore,

$$\phi(t) = \sum_{n \in \mathbb{Z}} h(n) \sqrt{2}\phi(2t - n), \quad t \in \mathbb{R}$$

where $h(n) = \langle \phi(\cdot), \sqrt{2}\phi(2 \cdot -n) \rangle$, $n \in \mathbb{Z}$. Also $\{h(n) \mid n \in \mathbb{Z}\} \in l^2(\mathbb{Z})$. The above equation is also called the *refinement equation*. We make this result formal in the next definition.

Definition 3.2. *Refinement equation, and scaling function coefficients. Let*

$$\phi(t) = \sum_{n \in \mathbb{Z}} h(n) \sqrt{2}\phi(2t - n), \quad t \in \mathbb{R} \tag{3.2}$$

where $h(n) \in l^2(\mathbb{Z})$, $\forall n \in \mathbb{Z}$. The above equation is also called the refinement equation, or two-scale relation, or dilation equation, or MRA equation. The $h(n)$'s are called scaling function coefficients. $\qquad\square$

Observations about the scaling function $\phi(t)$, $t \in \mathbb{R}$.

Observations 3.2. Let $\omega \in \mathbb{R}$. Define $\Phi(\omega)$ and $H(\omega)$ as

$$\Phi(\omega) = \int_{-\infty}^{\infty} \phi(t) e^{-i\omega t} dt$$

$$H(\omega) = \sum_{n \in \mathbb{Z}} h(n) e^{-i\omega n}$$

where $\Phi(\omega)$ is the Fourier transform of $\phi(t)$. That is, $\phi(t) \leftrightarrow \Phi(\omega)$.

1. The relationship $\int_{-\infty}^{\infty} \phi(t) dt = 1$ implies $\Phi(0) = 1$.

2.
$$\langle \phi\left(\cdot\right), \phi\left(2 \cdot - k\right)\rangle = \int_{-\infty}^{\infty} \phi\left(t\right)\overline{\phi\left(2t - k\right)}dt = \frac{h\left(k\right)}{\sqrt{2}}, \qquad k \in \mathbb{Z}$$

3.
$$\sum_{n \in \mathbb{Z}} |\Phi\left(\omega + 2\pi n\right)|^2 = 1, \qquad \forall\, \omega \in \mathbb{R}$$

The result follows directly from the observation that $\{\phi\left(t - n\right) \mid n \in \mathbb{Z}\}$ form an orthonormal sequence.

4.
$$\Phi\left(\omega\right) = \frac{1}{\sqrt{2}}H\left(\frac{\omega}{2}\right)\Phi\left(\frac{\omega}{2}\right)$$

Consequently

$$\Phi\left(\omega\right) = \prod_{k \in \mathbb{P}}\left\{\frac{1}{\sqrt{2}}H\left(\frac{\omega}{2^k}\right)\right\}\Phi\left(0\right)$$

$$H\left(0\right) = \sum_{n \in \mathbb{Z}} h\left(n\right) = \sqrt{2}$$

where it is assumed that $\Phi\left(0\right)$ is well defined. As per our assumption $\Phi\left(0\right) = 1$. Result is immediate from the refinement equation.

5.
$$\sum_{n \in \mathbb{Z}} h\left(n\right)\overline{h\left(n - 2m\right)} = \delta_{m0}, \qquad m \in \mathbb{Z}$$

$$\sum_{n \in \mathbb{Z}} |h\left(n\right)|^2 = 1$$

6.
$$|H\left(\omega\right)|^2 + |H\left(\omega + \pi\right)|^2 = 2, \qquad \forall\, \omega \in \mathbb{R}$$

7. $H\left(\pi\right) = 0$. This result is obtained by substituting $\omega = 0$, in the last observation.

8.
$$\sum_{n \in \mathbb{Z}} h\left(2n\right) = \sum_{n \in \mathbb{Z}} h\left(2n + 1\right) = \frac{1}{\sqrt{2}}$$

9.
$$\Phi\left(2\pi n\right) = \delta_{n0}, \qquad n \in \mathbb{Z}$$

10.
$$\sum_{n \in \mathbb{Z}} \phi\left(t - n\right) = 1, \quad \forall\, t \in \mathbb{R}$$

This equation is said to represent partition of unity.

11.
$$\sum_{n \in \mathbb{Z}} \phi\left(\frac{n}{2^m}\right) = 2^m, \qquad m \in \mathbb{N}$$

12.

$$t^j = \sum_{n \in \mathbb{Z}} M_n \phi(t - n), \quad j \in \mathbb{P}, \ \forall t \in \mathbb{R}$$

$$M_n = \int_{-\infty}^{\infty} t^j \overline{\phi(t - n)} dt, \quad n \in \mathbb{Z}$$

The result is true, as the sequence $\{\phi\,(\cdot - n) \mid n \in \mathbb{Z}\}$ is orthonormal.

13.

$$\sum_{n \in \mathbb{Z}} \phi_{j0}\,(t + n) = 2^{-j/2}, \quad j \leq 0, \ \forall t \in \mathbb{R}$$

This result is useful in studying periodic wavelets. $\square$

3.5 Characterization of the W_j Spaces

It has been noted earlier that the spaces W_j's are orthogonal to each other, and their direct sum over all values of $j \in \mathbb{Z}$ is equal to $L^2\,(\mathbb{R})$. Let the sequence of orthonormal functions $\{\xi_{jk}\,(\cdot) \mid k \in \mathbb{Z}\}$ span the set $W_j, j \in \mathbb{Z}$. Also, let $\xi_{0,k}\,(\cdot) \triangleq \xi\,(\cdot - k)$, $k \in \mathbb{Z}$. It trivially follows from the definition that $\{\xi\,(\cdot - n) \mid n \in \mathbb{Z}\}$ forms an orthonormal basis of W_0.

Observe that $\xi\,(\cdot) \in W_0$ and $W_0 \subset V_1 \Rightarrow \xi\,(\cdot) \in V_1$. Therefore,

$$\xi\,(t) = \sum_{n \in \mathbb{Z}} g\,(n)\,\sqrt{2}\phi(2t - n), \quad \forall t \in \mathbb{R}$$

where $g\,(n) = \langle \xi\,(\cdot), \sqrt{2}\phi\,(2 \cdot -n) \rangle$, and $g\,(n) \in l^2\,(\mathbb{Z}), \forall n \in \mathbb{Z}$. A relationship between $g\,(n)$ and $h\,(n) \ \forall n \in \mathbb{Z}$ is developed subsequently. The $g\,(n)$'s are called *wavelet function coefficients*. Also since W_j is orthogonal to V_j and $W_j \subset V_{j+1}$, define $\xi_{jk}\,(\cdot)$ as

$$\xi_{jk}\,(t) = 2^{j/2}\xi(2^j t - k), \quad k \in \mathbb{Z}, \ \forall t \in \mathbb{R}$$

$\xi_{jk}\,(\cdot)$ thus defined, indeed belongs to the set $W_j, j \in \mathbb{Z}$.

Finally, since $L^2\,(\mathbb{R}) = \bigoplus_{n \in \mathbb{Z}} W_n$, the function $f \in L^2\,(\mathbb{R})$ can be represented as

$$f(t) = \sum_{m,n \in \mathbb{Z}} F\,(m, n)\,\xi_{mn}(t), \quad \forall t \in \mathbb{R}$$

$$F\,(m, n) = \langle f, \xi_{mn} \rangle = \int_{-\infty}^{\infty} f\,(t)\,\overline{\xi_{mn}\,(t)} dt, \quad m, n \in \mathbb{Z}$$

This equation is similar to the discrete wavelet series equation developed earlier in the chapter. Therefore, $\xi_{mn}(t)$ can be replaced by $\psi_{mn}(t)$, $\forall\, t \in \mathbb{R}$; and $F(m,n)$ by $d(m,n)$, $\forall\, m, n \in \mathbb{Z}$, to describe the spaces W_j, $j \in \mathbb{Z}$. The function $\psi_{mn}(\cdot)$ is generated by the wavelet function $\psi(\cdot)$. Therefore, $\psi(\cdot)$ is sometimes called the *mother wavelet function*. The above discussion is summarized in the following observation.

Observation 3.3. The basis set for space W_j, $j \in \mathbb{Z}$ is an orthonormal set $\{\psi_{jk}(\cdot) \mid k \in \mathbb{Z}\}$. Further

$$\psi(\cdot) \in W_0$$

$$\psi_{jk}(\cdot) \in W_j, \qquad j, k \in \mathbb{Z}$$

$$\psi_{jk}(\cdot) = 2^{j/2}\psi(2^j \cdot - k), \qquad j, k \in \mathbb{Z}$$

$$\langle \psi_{jk}, \psi_{jl}\rangle = \int_{-\infty}^{\infty} \psi_{jk}(t)\,\overline{\psi_{jl}(t)}dt = \delta_{kl}, \quad j, k, l \in \mathbb{Z}$$

$$\langle \psi_{jk}, \psi_{ml}\rangle = \int_{-\infty}^{\infty} \psi_{jk}(t)\,\overline{\psi_{ml}(t)}dt = 0, \quad j \neq m \;\; j, k, l, m \in \mathbb{Z}$$

$$\langle \phi_{jk}, \psi_{ml}\rangle = \int_{-\infty}^{\infty} \phi_{jk}(t)\,\overline{\psi_{ml}(t)}dt = 0, \quad j \leq m \;\; j, k, l, m \in \mathbb{Z}$$

$$\psi(t) = \sum_{n \in \mathbb{Z}} g(n)\,\sqrt{2}\phi(2t - n), \;\; \forall\, t \in \mathbb{R}$$

$$g(n) = \left\langle \psi(\cdot), \sqrt{2}\phi(2 \cdot - n)\right\rangle, \;\; and \;\; g(n) \in l^2(\mathbb{Z}), \forall\, n \in \mathbb{Z}$$

$$\int_{-\infty}^{\infty} \psi(t)\,dt = 0, \quad \text{admissibility condition}$$

$$\langle \psi, \psi\rangle = \int_{-\infty}^{\infty} |\psi(t)|^2\,dt = 1, \quad \text{required for orthonormality.}$$

$\square$

Observations 3.4. Let $\omega \in \mathbb{R}$. Define $\Psi(\omega)$ and $G(\omega)$ as

$$\Psi(\omega) = \int_{-\infty}^{\infty} \psi(t)\,e^{-i\omega t}dt$$

$$G(\omega) = \sum_{n \in \mathbb{Z}} g(n)\,e^{-i\omega n}$$

where $\Psi(\omega)$ is the Fourier transform of $\psi(t)$. That is, $\psi(t) \leftrightarrow \Psi(\omega)$.

1.

$$\langle \phi(\cdot - k), \psi(\cdot - l)\rangle = \int_{-\infty}^{\infty} \phi(t - k)\,\overline{\psi(t - l)}dt = 0, \qquad k, l \in \mathbb{Z}$$

The result follows by letting $j = m = 0$ in the following equation:

$$\langle \phi_{jk}, \psi_{ml} \rangle = \int_{-\infty}^{\infty} \phi_{jk}(t) \overline{\psi_{ml}(t)} dt = 0, \qquad j \leq m \quad \text{and} \quad j, k, l, m \in \mathbb{Z}$$

2. The result $\psi(\cdot) = \sum_{n \in \mathbb{Z}} g(n) \sqrt{2} \phi(2 \cdot -n)$ in Fourier domain is

$$\Psi(\omega) = \frac{1}{\sqrt{2}} G\left(\frac{\omega}{2}\right) \Phi\left(\frac{\omega}{2}\right)$$

Consequently,

$$\Psi(\omega) = \left\{ \frac{1}{\sqrt{2}} G\left(\frac{\omega}{2}\right) \right\} \prod_{k \in \mathbb{P}} \left\{ \frac{1}{\sqrt{2}} H\left(\frac{\omega}{2^{k+1}}\right) \right\} \Phi(0)$$

$$G(0) = \sum_{n \in \mathbb{Z}} g(n)$$

where it is assumed that $\Phi(0)$ is well defined. As per our assumption $\Phi(0) = 1$.

3. $\Psi(4\pi n) = 0, n \in \mathbb{Z}$.

4.
$$\langle \psi, \phi(2 \cdot -k) \rangle = \int_{-\infty}^{\infty} \psi(t) \overline{\phi(2t - k)} dt = \frac{g(k)}{\sqrt{2}}, \qquad k \in \mathbb{Z}$$

5.
$$\sum_{n \in \mathbb{Z}} g(n) \overline{h(n - 2m)} = 0, \qquad m \in \mathbb{Z}$$

$$\sum_{n \in \mathbb{Z}} h(n) \overline{g(n - 2m)} = 0, \qquad m \in \mathbb{Z}$$

$$\sum_{n \in \mathbb{Z}} g(n) \overline{h(n)} = 0$$

6.
$$\sum_{n \in \mathbb{Z}} \overline{\Phi(\omega + 2\pi n)} \Psi(\omega + 2\pi n) = 0, \qquad \forall \, \omega \in \mathbb{R}$$

7. Also $\forall \, \omega \in \mathbb{R}$

$$\overline{H(\omega)} G(\omega) + \overline{H(\omega + \pi)} G(\omega + \pi) = 0$$
$$H(\omega) \overline{G(\omega)} + H(\omega + \pi) \overline{G(\omega + \pi)} = 0$$

8. $G(0) = \sum_{n \in \mathbb{Z}} g(n) = 0$.

9.
$$\sum_{n \in \mathbb{Z}} g(n) \overline{g(n - 2m)} = \delta_{m0}, \qquad m \in \mathbb{Z}$$

$$\sum_{n \in \mathbb{Z}} |g(n)|^2 = 1$$

10.
$$\sum_{n \in \mathbb{Z}} |\Psi(\omega + 2\pi n)|^2 = 1, \qquad \forall \, \omega \in \mathbb{R}$$

The result follows directly from the observation that $\{\psi(\cdot - n) \mid n \in \mathbb{Z}\}$ form an orthonormal sequence.

11.
$$|G(\omega)|^2 + |G(\omega + \pi)|^2 = 2, \qquad \forall \, \omega \in \mathbb{R}$$

This equation is similar to an earlier result.

12. $G(\pi) = \sqrt{2}$. Substitute $\omega = 0$ in the equation $|G(\omega)|^2 + |G(\omega + \pi)|^2 = 2$. This leads to
$$|G(0)|^2 + |G(\pi)|^2 = 2$$

As $G(0) = 0$, the result follows.

13.
$$\sum_{n \in \mathbb{Z}} g(2n) = \frac{1}{\sqrt{2}}, \quad \text{and} \quad \sum_{n \in \mathbb{Z}} g(2n+1) = -\frac{1}{\sqrt{2}}$$

14. For $\forall \, \omega \in \mathbb{R}$
$$|G(\omega)| = |H(\omega + \pi)|$$
$$|G(\omega + \pi)| = |H(\omega)|$$

15.
$$g(n) = \pm(-1)^n \, \overline{h(2m+1-n)}, \qquad m \in \mathbb{Z}$$
$$G(\omega) = \mp e^{-i(2m+1)\omega} \overline{H(\omega + \pi)}, \qquad m \in \mathbb{Z}$$

16. Also $\forall \, \omega \in \mathbb{R}$
$$\begin{bmatrix} H(\omega) & H(\omega + \pi) \\ G(\omega) & G(\omega + \pi) \end{bmatrix} \begin{bmatrix} \overline{H(\omega)} & \overline{G(\omega)} \\ \overline{H(\omega + \pi)} & \overline{G(\omega + \pi)} \end{bmatrix} = 2 \begin{bmatrix} 1 & 0 \\ 0 & 1 \end{bmatrix}$$

This equation is often expressed in the following notation. Let I be a 2×2 identity matrix, and
$$M(\omega) = \begin{bmatrix} H(\omega) & H(\omega + \pi) \\ G(\omega) & G(\omega + \pi) \end{bmatrix}$$

Then
$$M(\omega)\overline{M(\omega)}^T = 2I$$

The matrix $M(\omega)$ is often called the modulation matrix.

17.
$$\sum_{n \in \mathbb{Z}} \psi_{j0}(t+n) = 0, \qquad j \le -1, \ \forall \, t \in \mathbb{R}$$

$\square$

3.6 Expansions and Transformations

Functions can be expressed in terms of the scaling and the mother wavelet functions. Relationships between wavelet coefficients at different scales is also determined in this section. A so-called pyramid algorithm (fast wavelet algorithm) is also described for representing a function.

Assume that $f \in L^2(\mathbb{R})$. Also let P_j be the orthogonal projection operator into subspace V_j. That is,

$$f_j \triangleq P_j f = \sum_{k \in \mathbb{Z}} \langle f, \phi_{jk} \rangle \, \phi_{jk}$$

Thus f_j is an approximation of the function f at scale 2^{-j}. Similarly, let Q_j be the orthogonal projection operator into subspace W_j. That is,

$$g_j \triangleq Q_j f = \sum_{k \in \mathbb{Z}} \langle f, \psi_{jk} \rangle \, \psi_{jk}$$

The observations $V_j \cap W_j = \{0\}$, and $V_{j+1} = V_j \oplus W_j$ imply

$$f_{j+1} = f_j + g_j$$

The following observations readily follow from the above discussion.

Observations 3.5. Basic projection-related results.

1. The observation $L^2(\mathbb{R}) = \bigoplus_{n \in \mathbb{Z}} W_n$ implies $f = \sum_{j \in \mathbb{Z}} g_j$.

2. Let $j_0 \in \mathbb{Z}$, and $L^2(\mathbb{R}) = V_{j_0} \oplus W_{j_0} \oplus W_{j_0+1} \oplus W_{j_0+2} \oplus \dots$. Therefore,

$$f = f_{j_0} + \sum_{j=j_0}^{\infty} g_j$$

3. As $V_{j_0} = \bigoplus_{j \leq (j_0-1)} W_j$

$$f_{j_0} = \sum_{j \leq (j_0-1)} g_j$$

$\square$

Wavelet Series Expansions

Two wavelet series expansions of a function $f \in L^2(\mathbb{R})$ are presented explicitly.

Expansion 1: Let $j_0 \in \mathbb{Z}$, and $L^2(\mathbb{R}) = V_{j_0} \oplus W_{j_0} \oplus W_{j_0+1} \oplus W_{j_0+2} \oplus \dots$. For any $f \in L^2(\mathbb{R})$

$$f(t) = \sum_{k \in \mathbb{Z}} c(j_0, k)\, \phi_{j_0 k}(t) + \sum_{j=j_0}^{\infty} \sum_{k \in \mathbb{Z}} d(j, k)\, \psi_{jk}(t), \quad \forall\, t \in \mathbb{R}$$

$$c(j_0, k) = \langle f, \phi_{j_0 k} \rangle = \int_{-\infty}^{\infty} f(t)\overline{\phi_{j_0 k}(t)}\, dt, \qquad k \in \mathbb{Z}$$

$$d(j, k) = \langle f, \psi_{jk} \rangle = \int_{-\infty}^{\infty} f(t)\overline{\psi_{jk}(t)}\, dt, \qquad j \ge j_0,\ k \in \mathbb{Z}$$

As the scaling and wavelet functions form an orthonormal basis, Parseval's relationship holds.

$$\int_{-\infty}^{\infty} |f(t)|^2\, dt = \sum_{k \in \mathbb{Z}} |c(j_0, k)|^2 + \sum_{j=j_0}^{\infty} \sum_{k \in \mathbb{Z}} |d(j, k)|^2$$

Expansion 2: Let $j_0 \to -\infty$, then $L^2(\mathbb{R}) = \bigoplus_{n \in \mathbb{Z}} W_n$, and for any $f \in L^2(\mathbb{R})$

$$f(t) = \sum_{m,n \in \mathbb{Z}} d(m, n)\, \psi_{mn}(t), \quad \forall\, t \in \mathbb{R}$$

$$d(m, n) = \langle f, \psi_{mn} \rangle = \int_{-\infty}^{\infty} f(t)\overline{\psi_{mn}(t)}\, dt, \qquad m, n \in \mathbb{Z}$$

The corresponding Parseval's relationship is

$$\int_{-\infty}^{\infty} |f(t)|^2\, dt = \sum_{m,n \in \mathbb{Z}} |d(m, n)|^2$$

3.6.1 Coefficient Relationships between Different Scales

The wavelet coefficient relationships between different scales are noted.

Lemma 3.1. *Let $t \in \mathbb{R}$*

$$\phi_{jk}(t) = \sum_{m \in \mathbb{Z}} h(m - 2k)\, \phi_{j+1,m}(t), \qquad j, k \in \mathbb{Z} \tag{3.3a}$$

$$\psi_{jk}(t) = \sum_{m \in \mathbb{Z}} g(m - 2k)\, \phi_{j+1,m}(t), \qquad j, k \in \mathbb{Z} \tag{3.3b}$$

Proof. Recall that $\forall\, t \in \mathbb{R}$

$$\phi(t) = \sum_{n \in \mathbb{Z}} h(n)\, \sqrt{2}\phi(2t - n)$$

$$\phi_{jk}(t) = 2^{j/2}\phi(2^j t - k)$$

Then

$$\phi_{jk}(t) = 2^{j/2} \sum_{n \in \mathbb{Z}} \sqrt{2} h(n) \phi\left(2^{j+1} t - 2k - n\right)$$

A change of variable yields the first result. The second result is proved similarly. □

Lemma 3.2. *Let* $f(\cdot) \in V_{j+1}, j \in \mathbb{Z}$.

$$f(t) = \sum_{k \in \mathbb{Z}} c(j+1,k)\,\phi_{j+1,k}(t), \quad \forall\, t \in \mathbb{R} \tag{3.4a}$$

$$c(j+1,k) = \langle f, \phi_{j+1,k} \rangle = \int_{-\infty}^{\infty} f(t)\overline{\phi_{j+1,k}(t)}dt, \quad k \in \mathbb{Z} \tag{3.4b}$$

$$f(t) = \sum_{k \in \mathbb{Z}} c(j,k)\,\phi_{jk}(t) + \sum_{k \in \mathbb{Z}} d(j,k)\,\psi_{jk}(t) \tag{3.4c}$$

$$c(j,k) = \langle f, \phi_{jk} \rangle = \int_{-\infty}^{\infty} f(t)\overline{\phi_{jk}(t)}dt, \quad k \in \mathbb{Z} \tag{3.4d}$$

$$d(j,k) = \langle f, \psi_{jk} \rangle = \int_{-\infty}^{\infty} f(t)\overline{\psi_{jk}(t)}dt, \quad k \in \mathbb{Z} \tag{3.4e}$$

Then

$$c(j,k) = \sum_{m \in \mathbb{Z}} \overline{h(m-2k)}c(j+1,m), \quad j,k \in \mathbb{Z} \tag{3.4f}$$

$$d(j,k) = \sum_{m \in \mathbb{Z}} \overline{g(m-2k)}c(j+1,m), \quad j,k \in \mathbb{Z} \tag{3.4g}$$

$$c(j+1,k) = \sum_{m \in \mathbb{Z}} c(j,m)\,h(k-2m) + \sum_{m \in \mathbb{Z}} d(j,m)\,g(k-2m), \quad j,k \in \mathbb{Z} \tag{3.4h}$$

Proof. For $j,k \in \mathbb{Z}$

$$c(j,k) = \int_{-\infty}^{\infty} f(t)\overline{\phi_{jk}(t)}dt$$

$$= \int_{-\infty}^{\infty} f(t) \sum_{m \in \mathbb{Z}} \overline{h(m-2k)}\; \overline{\phi_{j+1,m}(t)}dt$$

$$= \sum_{m \in \mathbb{Z}} \overline{h(m-2k)}c(j+1,m)$$

Expression for $d(j,k)$ is similarly evaluated. It remains to evaluate $c(j+1,k)$. For $\forall\, t \in \mathbb{R}$

$$f(t) = \sum_{k \in \mathbb{Z}} c(j,k)\,\phi_{jk}(t) + \sum_{k \in \mathbb{Z}} d(j,k)\,\psi_{jk}(t)$$

$$= \sum_{k \in \mathbb{Z}} c(j,k) \sum_{m \in \mathbb{Z}} h(m-2k)\,\phi_{j+1,m}(t)$$

$$+ \sum_{k \in \mathbb{Z}} d(j,k) \sum_{m \in \mathbb{Z}} g(m-2k)\,\phi_{j+1,m}(t)$$

Then for $r \in \mathbb{Z}$

$$c(j+1, r) = \int_{-\infty}^{\infty} f(t)\overline{\phi_{j+1,r}(t)}dt$$
$$= \sum_{k \in \mathbb{Z}} c(j, k) h(r - 2k) + \sum_{k \in \mathbb{Z}} d(j, k) g(r - 2k)$$

The result follows by simply swapping the variables. $\square$

3.6.2 Pyramid Algorithm

A fast wavelet algorithm for representing a function $f(\cdot) \in V_J$, $J \in \mathbb{Z}$ due to Mallat is described. It is also called the pyramid algorithm. The scaling function expansion of $f(\cdot)$ is

$$f(t) = \sum_{k \in \mathbb{Z}} c(J, k) \phi_{Jk}(t), \quad \forall\, t \in \mathbb{R}$$

$$c(J, k) = \langle f, \phi_{Jk} \rangle = \int_{-\infty}^{\infty} f(t)\overline{\phi_{Jk}(t)}dt, \qquad \forall\, k \in \mathbb{Z}$$

The wavelet function expansion of $f(\cdot)$ is given in the following lemma. A recursive procedure to compute the coefficients of the expansion is also outlined. Note that for signals encountered in practice, there exists an upper scale $j = J$, beyond which $|d(j, k)| \simeq 0$, where $(J + 1) \leq j \in \mathbb{Z}$, and $k \in \mathbb{Z}$. The pyramid algorithm uses the following observation.

Observation 3.6. For a sufficiently smooth function $f(\cdot)$, $c(J, k)$ can be approximated as $2^{-J/2} f(2^{-J}k)$. $\square$

See the problem section for a justification of the above observation.

Lemma 3.3. *Pyramid algorithm. Let* $f(\cdot) \in V_J$, *and* $j_0 < J$, *then the wavelet expansion is*

$$f(t) = \sum_{k \in \mathbb{Z}} c(j_0, k) \phi_{j_0 k}(t) + \sum_{j=j_0}^{J-1} \sum_{k \in \mathbb{Z}} d(j, k) \psi_{jk}(t), \quad \forall\, t \in \mathbb{R} \quad (3.5a)$$

$$c(j_0, k) = \langle f, \phi_{j_0 k} \rangle = \int_{-\infty}^{\infty} f(t)\overline{\phi_{j_0 k}(t)}dt, \qquad k \in \mathbb{Z} \quad (3.5b)$$

$$d(j, k) = \langle f, \psi_{jk} \rangle = \int_{-\infty}^{\infty} f(t)\overline{\psi_{jk}(t)}dt, \qquad j, k \in \mathbb{Z} \quad (3.5c)$$

Parseval's relationship is

$$\int_{-\infty}^{\infty} |f(t)|^2 \, dt = \sum_{k \in \mathbb{Z}} |c(j_0, k)|^2 + \sum_{j=j_0}^{J-1} \sum_{k \in \mathbb{Z}} |d(j, k)|^2 \quad (3.5d)$$

Initially compute the sequence $\{c\,(J,k)\mid k\in\mathbb{Z}\}$. If the function $f(\cdot)$ is sufficiently smooth then

$$c\,(J,k)\simeq 2^{-J/2}f(2^{-J}k) \tag{3.5e}$$

Using $\{c\,(j,k)\mid k\in\mathbb{Z}\}$; compute $\{c\,(j-1,k)\mid k\in\mathbb{Z}\}$ and $\{d\,(j-1,k)\mid k\in\mathbb{Z}\}$ for $j=J,J-1,\ldots,(j_0+1)$, via the recursion

$$c\,(j-1,k)=\sum_{m\in\mathbb{Z}}\overline{h\,(m-2k)}c(j,m),\qquad k\in\mathbb{Z} \tag{3.5f}$$

$$d\,(j-1,k)=\sum_{m\in\mathbb{Z}}\overline{g\,(m-2k)}c(j,m),\qquad k\in\mathbb{Z} \tag{3.5g}$$

The inverse fast wavelet transform is obtained recursively form

$$c\,(j,k)=\sum_{m\in\mathbb{Z}}c\,(j-1,m)\,h\,(k-2m)+\sum_{m\in\mathbb{Z}}d\,(j-1,m)\,g(k-2m),\quad k\in\mathbb{Z} \tag{3.5h}$$

for $j=(j_0+1),(j_0+2),\ldots,J$. $\qquad\qquad\qquad\qquad\qquad\qquad\qquad\qquad$ $\square$

3.7 Digital Filter Interpretation

Let $\{f\,(n)\mid n\in\mathbb{Z}\}$ be a function with a finite support, which has to be transformed. Let its z-transform be denoted by $\mathcal{F}(z)$. The wavelet transformation of this signal is performed in multiple stages. This signal (function) is passed through the $\{h\,(n)\mid n\in\mathbb{Z}\}$ (low-pass) and $\{g\,(n)\mid n\in\mathbb{Z}\}$ (high-pass) filters. The output of the low-pass filter resembles the original signal, but at a lower resolution, while the output of the high-pass filter contains the detail information. Observe that the outputs of these low-pass and high-pass filters, each contain half as many samples as the original input signal.

The low-frequency output of a particular stage during the forward wavelet transformation is then successively passed though the same set of two (the low-pass and high-pass) filters. The low-frequency output of the very last iteration, and the high-frequency output of all the iterations (or stages) is preserved. This actually constitutes the wavelet transform.

The reconstruction of the original signal simply proceeds in the opposite direction. Inverse filtering is done as follows. In each stage, the low-pass and high-pass components are made to pass through the $\{h\,(n)\mid n\in\mathbb{Z}\}$ and $\{g\,(n)\mid n\in\mathbb{Z}\}$ filters respectively, and the result is then merged together. In the language of digital filtering theory, this scheme of decomposing and reconstructing a function is called subband filtering.

Define the z-transforms of $\{h\,(n)\mid n\in\mathbb{Z}\}$ and $\{g\,(n)\mid n\in\mathbb{Z}\}$, as $\mathcal{H}(z)$ and $\mathcal{G}(z)$ respectively. For $j=j_0,(j_0+1),(j_0+2),\ldots,J$ define the z-transforms of the sequences $\{c(j,k) \mid k \in \mathbb{Z}\}$ and $\{d(j,k) \mid k \in \mathbb{Z}\}$ to be $\mathcal{C}(j,z)$ and $\mathcal{D}(j,z)$ respectively.

Lemma 3.4. For $j = J, J-1, \ldots, (j_0 + 1)$

$$\mathcal{C}\left(j-1, z^2\right) = \frac{1}{2}\left[\overline{\mathcal{H}(z)}\mathcal{C}(j, z) + \overline{\mathcal{H}(-z)}\mathcal{C}(j, -z)\right]$$

$$\mathcal{D}\left(j-1, z^2\right) = \frac{1}{2}\left[\overline{\mathcal{G}(z)}\mathcal{C}(j, z) + \overline{\mathcal{G}(-z)}\mathcal{C}(j, -z)\right]$$

and for $j = (j_0 + 1), (j_0 + 2), \ldots, J$

$$\mathcal{C}(j, z) = \left[\mathcal{H}(z)\mathcal{C}\left(j-1, z^2\right) + \mathcal{G}(z)\mathcal{D}\left(j-1, z^2\right)\right]$$

These equations correspond to decomposition and reconstruction of a function respectively.

Proof. See the problem section.   □

3.8 Computation of the Scaling Function

An iterative procedure is outlined for the computation of the scaling function $\phi(\cdot)$. Recall that for $t \in \mathbb{R}$

$$\phi(t) = \sum_{n \in \mathbb{Z}} h(n)\sqrt{2}\phi(2t - n)$$

Initialize the scaling function by $\phi_0(\cdot)$, and then iterate as follows

$$\phi_{k+1}(t) = \sum_{n \in \mathbb{Z}} h(n)\sqrt{2}\phi_k(2t - n), \qquad k \in \mathbb{N}$$

where $\phi_k(\cdot)$ is scaling function computed in the k-th iteration.

Note that $\int_{-\infty}^{\infty} \phi_k(t)\,dt$ is constant. This can be observed as follows. Let $\phi_k(t) \leftrightarrow \Phi_k(\omega)$. Then

$$\Phi_{k+1}(\omega) = \frac{1}{\sqrt{2}}H\left(\frac{\omega}{2}\right)\Phi_k\left(\frac{\omega}{2}\right)$$

Therefore,

$$\Phi_{k+1}(0) = \frac{1}{\sqrt{2}}H(0)\Phi_k(0)$$

The observation $H(0) = \sum_{n \in \mathbb{Z}} h(n) = \sqrt{2}$ leads to $\Phi_{k+1}(0) = \Phi_k(0)$. This in turn implies that $\int_{-\infty}^{\infty} \phi_k(t)\,dt$ is constant. This procedure, for obvious reasons is sometimes called the *cascade algorithm*. The algorithm will converge for suitable initializing function $\phi_0(\cdot)$.

Once the scaling function is determined, the wavelet function can be computed from the following equation

$$\psi(t) = \sum_{n \in \mathbb{Z}} g(n) \sqrt{2} \phi(2t - n) \quad \forall t \in \mathbb{R}$$

3.9 An Alternate Multiresolution Analysis

An alternate and more powerful scheme for multiresolution analysis is specified. It uses the concept of frames.

Axioms: The multiresolution analysis of $L^2(\mathbb{R})$ is a sequence of closed subspaces $\{V_j \mid V_j \subseteq L^2(\mathbb{R}),\ j \in \mathbb{Z}\}$, and a function $\phi(\cdot)$ called the scaling function, such that:

1. *Nesting property:* $V_j \subset V_{j+1}$, for all values of $j \in \mathbb{Z}$. This is the so called nesting property of the subspaces. This hierarchy of approximation spaces is often represented as

$$\ldots \subset V_{-2} \subset V_{-1} \subset V_0 \subset V_1 \subset V_2 \subset \ldots$$

2. *Upward completeness:* $\overline{\cup_{j \in \mathbb{Z}} V_j} = L^2(\mathbb{R})$.

3. *Downward completeness:* $\cap_{j \in \mathbb{Z}} V_j = \{0\}$.

4. *Scaling property:* $f(\cdot) \in V_j \Leftrightarrow f(2\cdot) \in V_{j+1}$, for all values of $j \in \mathbb{Z}$.

5. *Invariance under integral translations:* $f(t) \in V_0 \Leftrightarrow f(t+1) \in V_0, \forall t \in \mathbb{R}$.

6. *Existence of scaling function:* A scaling function $\phi(\cdot) \in V_0$, where $\phi : \mathbb{R} \to \mathbb{C}$ exists such that $\{\phi(\cdot - n) \mid n \in \mathbb{Z}\}$ forms a so-called *stable basis* of V_0. The function $\phi(\cdot)$ is also called the *refinable function* or *MRA generator.*   □

Multiresolution analysis allows us to approximate a function f by a function $f_j \in V_j$. The function f_j is called the *approximation of f at resolution j*. Axiom 2 guarantees that $f = \lim_{j \to \infty} f_j$.

The stable basis is also called an *unconditional basis*, or *Riesz basis* of V_0. Axiom number 6, implies that any $f \in V_0$ can be expressed uniquely as

$$f(t) = \sum_{n \in \mathbb{Z}} c_n \phi(t - n), \quad t \in \mathbb{R}$$

with convergence in the space $L^2(\mathbb{R})$. Further, there also exist constants A and B, independent of f which satisfy

$$A \sum_{n \in \mathbb{Z}} |c_n|^2 \leq \|f\|^2 \leq B \sum_{n \in \mathbb{Z}} |c_n|^2$$

The constants A and B are called the *lower-* and *upper-Riesz bounds*, respectively. Note that $0 < A \le B < \infty$. The above result is called the *stable condition*. A function which satisfies it is called a *stable function*.

The stability of $\{\phi(\cdot - n) \mid n \in \mathbb{Z}\}$ does not guarantee orthogonality. Nevertheless, it is possible to orthonormalize a stable scaling function.

Observation 3.7. Let $\{\phi(\cdot - n) \mid n \in \mathbb{Z}\}$ be an unconditional basis of V_0. Also let $\phi(t) \leftrightarrow \Phi(\omega)$. Define $\xi(\cdot) \in V_0$, where $\xi(t) \leftrightarrow \Xi(\omega)$ and

$$\Xi(\omega) = \frac{\Phi(\omega)}{\left\{ \sum_{n \in \mathbb{Z}} |\Phi(\omega + 2\pi n)|^2 \right\}^{1/2}}, \quad \forall \omega \in \mathbb{R}$$

Then $\{\xi(\cdot - n) \mid n \in \mathbb{Z}\}$ is an orthonormal basis of V_0.   □

The above observation is true, because $\sum_{n \in \mathbb{Z}} |\Xi(\omega + 2\pi n)|^2 = 1$. See the chapter on Fourier analysis for further justification.

Problems

1. Prove that

$$\int_{-\infty}^{\infty} \phi(t)\,\overline{\phi(2t - k)}\,dt = \frac{h(k)}{\sqrt{2}}, \qquad k \in \mathbb{Z}$$

Hint: Use of the refinement equation leads to, for any $k \in \mathbb{Z}$

$$\int_{-\infty}^{\infty} \phi(t)\,\overline{\phi(2t - k)}\,dt = \sum_{n \in \mathbb{Z}} \sqrt{2}h(n) \int_{-\infty}^{\infty} \phi(2t - n)\,\overline{\phi(2t - k)}\,dt$$

$$= \frac{1}{\sqrt{2}} \sum_{n \in \mathbb{Z}} h(n)\,\delta_{nk} = \frac{h(k)}{\sqrt{2}}$$

2. Prove that

$$\sum_{n \in \mathbb{Z}} |\Phi(\omega + 2\pi n)|^2 = 1, \quad \forall \omega \in \mathbb{R}$$

Hint: Let

$$F(\omega) = \sum_{n \in \mathbb{Z}} |\Phi(\omega + 2\pi n)|^2, \quad \omega \in \mathbb{R}$$

Observe that $F(\omega)$ is a periodic function with period 2π. Its Fourier series expansion is

$$F\left(\omega\right) = \sum_{n\in\mathbb{Z}} c_k e^{ik\omega}, \text{ where } c_k = \frac{1}{2\pi}\int_0^{2\pi} F\left(\omega\right)e^{-ik\omega}d\omega, \quad \forall\, k\in\mathbb{Z}$$

Therefore,

$$
\begin{aligned}
c_k &= \frac{1}{2\pi}\int_0^{2\pi} \sum_{n\in\mathbb{Z}} \left|\Phi\left(\omega+2\pi n\right)\right|^2 e^{-ik\omega}d\omega \\
&= \frac{1}{2\pi}\int_{-\infty}^{\infty} \left|\Phi\left(\omega\right)\right|^2 e^{-ik\omega}d\omega = \frac{1}{2\pi}\int_{-\infty}^{\infty} \Phi\left(\omega\right)\overline{\Phi\left(\omega\right)}e^{ik\omega}d\omega \\
&= \int_{-\infty}^{\infty} \phi\left(t\right)\overline{\phi\left(t+k\right)}dt = \delta_{0,-k}
\end{aligned}
$$

where $\delta_{0,-k}$ is equal to unity if $k=0$, and equal to zero otherwise. Thus $F\left(\omega\right)$ is simply equal to 1 for $\forall\,\omega\in\mathbb{R}$.

3. Prove that

$$\sum_{n\in\mathbb{Z}} h\left(n\right)\overline{h\left(n-2m\right)} = \delta_{m0}, \qquad m\in\mathbb{Z}$$

$$\sum_{n\in\mathbb{Z}} \left|h\left(n\right)\right|^2 = 1$$

Hint: Use the refinement equation and the following equation

$$\phi\left(t-m\right) = \sum_{k\in\mathbb{Z}} \sqrt{2}\phi\left(2t-2m-k\right)h(k), \qquad m\in\mathbb{Z}$$

For any $m\in\mathbb{Z}$

$$
\begin{aligned}
\delta_{m0} &= \int_{-\infty}^{\infty} \phi\left(t\right)\overline{\phi\left(t-m\right)}dt \\
&= 2\sum_{n,k\in\mathbb{Z}} h\left(n\right)\overline{h\left(k\right)}\int_{-\infty}^{\infty} \phi\left(2t-n\right)\overline{\phi\left(2t-2m-k\right)}dt \\
&= \sum_{n,k\in\mathbb{Z}} h\left(n\right)\overline{h\left(k\right)}\delta_{n-2m,k} = \sum_{n\in\mathbb{Z}} h\left(n\right)\overline{h\left(n-2m\right)}
\end{aligned}
$$

The last result follows by substituting $m=0$ in the above equation.

4. Prove that
$$\left|H\left(\omega\right)\right|^2 + \left|H\left(\omega+\pi\right)\right|^2 = 2, \qquad \forall\,\omega\in\mathbb{R}$$

Hint: Use the results from earlier observations.

$$\Phi\left(\omega\right) = \frac{1}{\sqrt{2}}H\left(\frac{\omega}{2}\right)\Phi\left(\frac{\omega}{2}\right)$$

Substitute $(2\omega+2\pi n)$ for ω in the above equation. This results in

$$\Phi\left(2\omega + 2\pi n\right) = \frac{1}{\sqrt{2}} H\left(\omega + \pi n\right) \Phi(\omega + \pi n), \quad n \in \mathbb{Z}$$

$$1 = \sum_{n \in \mathbb{Z}} |\Phi\left(2\omega + 2\pi n\right)|^2 = \frac{1}{2} \sum_{n \in \mathbb{Z}} |H\left(\omega + \pi n\right)|^2 |\Phi\left(\omega + \pi n\right)|^2$$

Split the right-hand summation into two parts, one taken over the even values of n and the other over odd values of n. Thus

$$2 = \sum_{n \in \mathbb{Z}} |H\left(\omega + 2\pi n\right)|^2 |\Phi\left(\omega + 2\pi n\right)|^2 +$$

$$\sum_{n \in \mathbb{Z}} |H\left(\omega + \pi + 2\pi n\right)|^2 |\Phi\left(\omega + \pi + 2\pi n\right)|^2$$

$$= |H\left(\omega\right)|^2 \sum_{n \in \mathbb{Z}} |\Phi\left(\omega + 2\pi n\right)|^2 + |H\left(\omega + \pi\right)|^2 \sum_{n \in \mathbb{Z}} |\Phi\left(\omega + \pi + 2\pi n\right)|^2$$

The result follows.

5. Prove that

$$\sum_{n \in \mathbb{Z}} h\left(2n\right) = \sum_{n \in \mathbb{Z}} h\left(2n + 1\right) = \frac{1}{\sqrt{2}}$$

Hint: The result is a consequence of the following observations.

$$0 = H\left(\pi\right) = \sum_{n \in \mathbb{Z}} h\left(n\right) e^{-in\pi}, \quad \text{and} \quad \sum_{n \in \mathbb{Z}} h\left(n\right) = \sqrt{2}$$

6. Prove that

$$\Phi\left(2\pi n\right) = \delta_{n0}, \quad n \in \mathbb{Z}$$

Hint: From an earlier observation, it is known that $\Phi\left(0\right) = 1$. Next consider the following equation

$$\Phi\left(\omega\right) = \frac{1}{\sqrt{2}} H\left(\frac{\omega}{2}\right) \Phi\left(\frac{\omega}{2}\right)$$

Substitute $\omega = 2\pi$ in the above equation. Thus $\Phi\left(2\pi\right) = 0$, as $H\left(\pi\right) = 0$. Substitute again $\omega = 4\pi$ in the above equation. This leads to $\Phi\left(4\pi\right) = 0$, since $\Phi\left(2\pi\right) = 0$. Similarly, by using induction it can be shown that $\Phi\left(2\pi n\right) = 0$ for $n \in \mathbb{P}$. As $H\left(\omega\right)$ is a periodic function, with period 2π, these values can be extended to negative values of n.

7. Prove that

$$\sum_{n \in \mathbb{Z}} \phi\left(t - n\right) = 1, \quad \forall\, t \in \mathbb{R}$$

Hint: It is known that

$$\Phi\left(2\pi n\right) = \delta_{n0}, \quad n \in \mathbb{Z}$$

Use of the Poisson summation formula yields

$$\sum_{n\in\mathbb{Z}} \phi(t-n) = \sum_{n\in\mathbb{Z}} \Phi(2\pi n)\, e^{2\pi i n t} = \sum_{n\in\mathbb{Z}} \delta_{n0} e^{2\pi i n t} = 1$$

This equation is said to represent partition of unity.

8. Prove that

$$\sum_{n\in\mathbb{Z}} \phi\left(\frac{n}{2^m}\right) = 2^m, \qquad m\in\mathbb{N}$$

Hint: It is known that $\sum_{n\in\mathbb{Z}} \phi(t-n) = 1$. Therefore, $\sum_{n\in\mathbb{Z}} \phi(n) = 1$. The refinement equation gives

$$\phi\left(\frac{n}{2}\right) = \sum_{k\in\mathbb{Z}} \sqrt{2}\,\phi(n-k)\,h(k), \qquad n\in\mathbb{N}$$

Sum both sides of the above equation over all values of n.

$$\sum_{n\in\mathbb{Z}} \phi\left(\frac{n}{2}\right) = \sqrt{2} \sum_{n\in\mathbb{Z}} \sum_{k\in\mathbb{Z}} \phi(n-k)\,h(k)$$

$$= \sqrt{2} \sum_{k\in\mathbb{Z}} h(k) \sum_{n\in\mathbb{Z}} \phi(n-k) = \sqrt{2} \sum_{k\in\mathbb{Z}} h(k) \sum_{n\in\mathbb{Z}} \phi(n)$$

$$= \sqrt{2} \sum_{k\in\mathbb{Z}} h(k) = 2$$

Therefore, $\sum_{n\in\mathbb{Z}} \phi\left(\frac{n}{2}\right) = 2$. To get further insight $\sum_{n\in\mathbb{Z}} \phi\left(\frac{n}{2^2}\right)$ is evaluated.

$$\sum_{n\in\mathbb{Z}} \phi\left(\frac{n}{2^2}\right) = \sqrt{2} \sum_{n\in\mathbb{Z}} \sum_{k\in\mathbb{Z}} \phi\left(\frac{n}{2}-k\right) h(k)$$

$$= \sqrt{2} \sum_{k\in\mathbb{Z}} h(k) \sum_{n\in\mathbb{Z}} \phi\left(\frac{n-2k}{2}\right) = \sqrt{2} \sum_{k\in\mathbb{Z}} h(k) \sum_{n\in\mathbb{Z}} \phi\left(\frac{n}{2}\right)$$

$$= 2\sqrt{2} \sum_{k\in\mathbb{Z}} h(k) = 2^2$$

The final result can be proved inductively, using similar technique.

9. Prove that

$$\sum_{n\in\mathbb{Z}} \phi_{j0}(t+n) = 2^{-j/2}, \qquad j \le 0$$

Hint: The following results and Poisson's summation formula yield the stated result.

$$\phi_{j0}(t) \leftrightarrow 2^{-j/2} \Phi\left(\frac{\omega}{2^j}\right), \qquad j\in\mathbb{Z}$$

$$\Phi(2\pi n) = \delta_{n0}, \qquad n\in\mathbb{Z}$$

From Poisson's summation result

$$\sum_{n \in \mathbb{Z}} \phi_{j0}(t+n) = 2^{-j/2} \sum_{n \in \mathbb{Z}} e^{i2\pi nt} \Phi\left(\frac{2\pi n}{2^j}\right)$$

$$= 2^{-j/2} \sum_{n \in \mathbb{Z}} e^{i2\pi nt} \delta_{n/2^j,0} = 2^{-j/2}$$

The last step of the equation is true if $n/2^j$ is an integer, which is true if $j \leq 0$. This result is useful in studying periodic wavelets.

10. Prove that

$$\Psi(4\pi n) = 0, \quad n \in \mathbb{Z}$$

Hint: Consider the following equation

$$\Psi(\omega) = \frac{1}{\sqrt{2}} G\left(\frac{\omega}{2}\right) \Phi\left(\frac{\omega}{2}\right)$$

It is know that $\Phi(2\pi n) = \delta_{n0}$, $n \in \mathbb{Z}$, substituting $\omega = 4\pi n$ in the above equation results in

$$\Psi(4\pi n) = \frac{1}{\sqrt{2}} G(2\pi n) \delta_{n0}, \quad n \in \mathbb{Z}$$

As $\Psi(0) = 0$, from the admissibility condition, the result follows.

11. Prove that

$$\int_{-\infty}^{\infty} \psi(t) \overline{\phi(2t-k)} dt = \frac{g(k)}{\sqrt{2}}, \quad k \in \mathbb{Z}$$

Hint: Consider the result $\psi(t) = \sum_{n \in \mathbb{Z}} g(n) \sqrt{2} \phi(2t-n)$. For any $k \in \mathbb{Z}$

$$\int_{-\infty}^{\infty} \psi(t) \overline{\phi(2t-k)} dt = \sum_{n \in \mathbb{Z}} \sqrt{2} g(n) \int_{-\infty}^{\infty} \phi(2t-n) \overline{\phi(2t-k)} dt$$

$$= \frac{1}{\sqrt{2}} \sum_{n \in \mathbb{Z}} g(n) \delta_{nk} = \frac{g(k)}{\sqrt{2}}$$

12. Prove that

$$\sum_{n \in \mathbb{Z}} g(n) \overline{h(n-2m)} = 0, \quad m \in \mathbb{Z}$$

$$\sum_{n \in \mathbb{Z}} h(n) \overline{g(n-2m)} = 0, \quad m \in \mathbb{Z}$$

$$\sum_{n \in \mathbb{Z}} g(n) \overline{h(n)} = 0$$

Hint: The following equations

$$\psi(t) = \sum_{n \in \mathbb{Z}} g(n) \sqrt{2} \phi(2t-n)$$

$$\phi(t-m) = \sum_{k \in \mathbb{Z}} h(k) \sqrt{2} \phi(2t-2m-k) \quad m \in \mathbb{Z}$$

lead to

$$0 = \int_{-\infty}^{\infty} \psi(t) \overline{\phi(t-m)} dt$$

$$= 2 \sum_{n,k \in \mathbb{Z}} g(n) \overline{h(k)} \int_{-\infty}^{\infty} \phi(2t-n) \overline{\phi(2t-2m-k)} dt$$

$$= \sum_{n,k \in \mathbb{Z}} g(n) \overline{h(k)} \delta_{n,2m+k} = \sum_{n \in \mathbb{Z}} g(n) \overline{h(n-2m)}$$

The second result follows similarly. The last result follows by substituting $m = 0$ in the above equation.

13. Prove that

$$\sum_{n \in \mathbb{Z}} \overline{\Phi(\omega + 2\pi n)} \Psi(\omega + 2\pi n) = 0, \qquad \forall \, \omega \in \mathbb{R}$$

Hint: We proceed as in an earlier problem. Let

$$F(\omega) = \sum_{n \in \mathbb{Z}} \overline{\Phi(\omega + 2\pi n)} \Psi(\omega + 2\pi n), \quad \omega \in \mathbb{R}$$

Observe that $F(\omega)$ is a periodic function with period 2π. Its Fourier series expansion is

$$F(\omega) = \sum_{k \in \mathbb{Z}} c_k e^{ik\omega}, \quad \text{where} \quad c_k = \frac{1}{2\pi} \int_0^{2\pi} F(\omega) e^{-ik\omega} d\omega, \quad \forall \, k \in \mathbb{Z}$$

Therefore,

$$c_k = \frac{1}{2\pi} \int_0^{2\pi} \sum_{n \in \mathbb{Z}} \overline{\Phi(\omega + 2\pi n)} \Psi(\omega + 2\pi n) e^{-ik\omega} d\omega$$

$$= \frac{1}{2\pi} \int_{-\infty}^{\infty} \overline{\Phi(\omega)} \Psi(\omega) e^{-ik\omega} d\omega = \frac{1}{2\pi} \int_{-\infty}^{\infty} \Psi(\omega) \overline{\Phi(\omega) e^{ik\omega}} d\omega$$

$$= \int_{-\infty}^{\infty} \psi(t) \overline{\phi(t+k)} dt = 0$$

Therefore, $F(\omega) = \sum_{k \in \mathbb{Z}} c_k e^{ik\omega} = 0, \, \forall \, \omega \in \mathbb{R}$.

14. Prove that $\forall \, \omega \in \mathbb{R}$

$$\overline{H(\omega)} G(\omega) + \overline{H(\omega + \pi)} G(\omega + \pi) = 0$$
$$H(\omega) \overline{G(\omega)} + H(\omega + \pi) \overline{G(\omega + \pi)} = 0$$

Hint: The results from earlier observations are used.

$$\Phi(\omega) = \frac{1}{\sqrt{2}} H\left(\frac{\omega}{2}\right) \Phi\left(\frac{\omega}{2}\right)$$

$$\Psi(\omega) = \frac{1}{\sqrt{2}} G\left(\frac{\omega}{2}\right) \Phi\left(\frac{\omega}{2}\right)$$

Substitute $(2\omega + 2\pi n)$ for ω in the above equations. Thus

$$\Phi\left(2\omega + 2\pi n\right) = \frac{1}{\sqrt{2}}H\left(\omega + \pi n\right)\Phi(\omega + \pi n), \quad n \in \mathbb{Z}$$

$$\Psi\left(2\omega + 2\pi n\right) = \frac{1}{\sqrt{2}}G\left(\omega + \pi n\right)\Phi(\omega + \pi n), \quad n \in \mathbb{Z}$$

From the last problem, we have

$$\sum_{n\in\mathbb{Z}} \overline{\Phi\left(\omega + 2\pi n\right)}\Psi\left(\omega + 2\pi n\right) = 0, \quad \forall\,\omega \in \mathbb{R}$$

Therefore,

$$0 = \sum_{n\in\mathbb{Z}} \overline{\Phi\left(2\omega + 2\pi n\right)}\Psi\left(2\omega + 2\pi n\right)$$

$$= \frac{1}{2}\sum_{n\in\mathbb{Z}} \overline{H\left(\omega + \pi n\right)}G\left(\omega + \pi n\right)\left|\Phi\left(\omega + \pi n\right)\right|^{2}$$

Split the above summation into two parts, one taken over the even values of n and the other over odd values of n. This results in

$$0 = \sum_{n\in\mathbb{Z}} \overline{H\left(\omega + 2\pi n\right)}G\left(\omega + 2\pi n\right)\left|\Phi\left(\omega + 2\pi n\right)\right|^{2} +$$

$$\sum_{n\in\mathbb{Z}} \overline{H\left(\omega + \pi + 2\pi n\right)}G\left(\omega + \pi + 2\pi n\right)\left|\Phi\left(\omega + \pi + 2\pi n\right)\right|^{2}$$

$$= \overline{H\left(\omega\right)}G\left(\omega\right)\sum_{n\in\mathbb{Z}}\left|\Phi\left(\omega + 2\pi n\right)\right|^{2} +$$

$$\overline{H\left(\omega + \pi\right)}G\left(\omega + \pi\right)\sum_{n\in\mathbb{Z}}\left|\Phi\left(\omega + \pi + 2\pi n\right)\right|^{2}$$

The first result follows. The second result is the complex-conjugate of the first result.

15. Prove that $G\left(0\right) = \sum_{n\in\mathbb{Z}} g\left(n\right) = 0$.

Hint: Substitute $\omega = 0$ in the equation $\overline{H\left(\omega\right)}G\left(\omega\right) + \overline{H\left(\omega + \pi\right)}G\left(\omega + \pi\right) = 0$. This implies

$$\overline{H\left(0\right)}G\left(0\right) + \overline{H\left(\pi\right)}G\left(\pi\right) = 0$$

As $H\left(0\right) = \sqrt{2}$, and $H\left(\pi\right) = 0$ the result follows.

16. Prove that

$$\sum_{n\in\mathbb{Z}} g\left(n\right)\overline{g\left(n - 2m\right)} = \delta_{m0}, \quad m \in \mathbb{Z}$$

$$\sum_{n\in\mathbb{Z}}\left|g\left(n\right)\right|^{2} = 1$$

Hint: Consider the following equations, for $t \in \mathbb{R}$

$$\psi(t) = \sum_{n \in \mathbb{Z}} g(n) \sqrt{2} \phi(2t - n)$$

$$\psi(t - m) = \sum_{k \in \mathbb{Z}} g(k) \sqrt{2} \phi(2t - 2m - k), \qquad m \in \mathbb{Z}$$

Thus

$$\delta_{m0} = \int_{-\infty}^{\infty} \psi(t) \overline{\psi(t - m)} dt$$

$$= 2 \sum_{n,k \in \mathbb{Z}} g(n) \overline{g(k)} \int_{-\infty}^{\infty} \phi(2t - n) \overline{\phi(2t - 2m - k)} dt$$

$$= \sum_{n,k \in \mathbb{Z}} g(n) \overline{g(k)} \delta_{n,2m+k} = \sum_{n \in \mathbb{Z}} g(n) \overline{g(n - 2m)}$$

The last result follows by substituting $m = 0$ in the above equation.

17. Prove that

$$\sum_{n \in \mathbb{Z}} g(2n) = \frac{1}{\sqrt{2}}, \quad \text{and} \quad \sum_{n \in \mathbb{Z}} g(2n + 1) = -\frac{1}{\sqrt{2}}$$

Hint: The result is a consequence of the following observations.

$$\sqrt{2} = G(\pi) = \sum_{n \in \mathbb{Z}} g(n) e^{-in\pi}$$

and

$$G(0) = \sum_{n \in \mathbb{Z}} g(n) = 0$$

18. Verify that $\int_{-\infty}^{\infty} \psi(t) \, dt = 0$. This result proves that the admissibility condition follows from the axioms of MRA.

Hint: Integrate both sides of the following equation

$$\psi(t) = \sum_{n \in \mathbb{Z}} g(n) \sqrt{2} \phi(2t - n)$$

Then

$$\int_{-\infty}^{\infty} \psi(t) \, dt = \int_{-\infty}^{\infty} \sum_{n \in \mathbb{Z}} \sqrt{2} \phi(2t - n) g(n) \, dt$$

$$= \frac{1}{\sqrt{2}} \sum_{n \in \mathbb{Z}} g(n) \int_{-\infty}^{\infty} \phi(t) \, dt = 0$$

19. Prove that $\forall \, \omega \in \mathbb{R}$

$$|G(\omega)| = |H(\omega + \pi)|$$
$$|G(\omega + \pi)| = |H(\omega)|$$

Hint: We eliminate $H(\omega)$ and $G(\omega + \pi)$ from the following equations to obtain the first result.

$$|H(\omega)|^2 + |H(\omega + \pi)|^2 = 2 \qquad\qquad \text{(A)}$$
$$|G(\omega)|^2 + |G(\omega + \pi)|^2 = 2 \qquad\qquad \text{(B)}$$
$$\overline{H(\omega)}G(\omega) + \overline{H(\omega + \pi)}G(\omega + \pi) = 0 \qquad\qquad \text{(C)}$$

Equation (C) leads to

$$|H(\omega)|^2 \, |G(\omega)|^2 = |H(\omega + \pi)|^2 \, |G(\omega + \pi)|^2 \qquad\qquad \text{(D)}$$

Equation (A) yields

$$|H(\omega)|^2 = \left\{ 2 - |H(\omega + \pi)|^2 \right\}$$

Equation (B) yields

$$|G(\omega + \pi)|^2 = \left\{ 2 - |G(\omega)|^2 \right\}$$

Substitute these results in equation (D). This leads to

$$\left\{ 2 - |H(\omega + \pi)|^2 \right\} |G(\omega)|^2 = |H(\omega + \pi)|^2 \left\{ 2 - |G(\omega)|^2 \right\}$$

Simplification results in

$$|G(\omega)|^2 = |H(\omega + \pi)|^2$$

That is, $|G(\omega)| = |H(\omega + \pi)|$. Substitute $(\omega + \pi)$ for ω in the first result, then the second result follows.

20. Prove that

$$g(n) = \pm(-1)^n \, \overline{h(2m+1-n)}, \qquad m \in \mathbb{Z}$$
$$G(\omega) = \mp e^{-i(2m+1)\omega} \overline{H(\omega + \pi)}, \qquad m \in \mathbb{Z}$$

Hint:

$$\overline{H(\omega)}G(\omega) + \overline{H(\omega + \pi)}G(\omega + \pi) = 0$$

Therefore,

$$G(\omega) = -A(\omega)\overline{H(\omega + \pi)}$$
$$A(\omega) = \frac{G(\omega + \pi)}{H(\omega)}$$

Also

$$A(\omega) = -\frac{G(\omega)}{H(\omega + \pi)} = -A(\omega + \pi)$$

$$A(\omega) + A(\omega + \pi) = 0$$

It has also been established that $|G(\omega + \pi)| = |H(\omega)|$. Thus $|A(\omega)| = 1$, which further implies that

$$A(\omega) = \pm e^{-i(2m+1)\omega}, \qquad m \in \mathbb{Z}$$

Substituting this value results in

$$G(\omega) = \sum_{n \in \mathbb{Z}} g(n) e^{-i\omega n} = \pm (-1) e^{-i(2m+1)\omega} \sum_{n \in \mathbb{Z}} \overline{h(n)} e^{i(\omega + \pi)n}, \qquad m \in \mathbb{Z}$$

$$= \sum_{n \in \mathbb{Z}} \pm (-1)^n \overline{h(2m+1-n)} e^{-i\omega n}, \qquad m \in \mathbb{Z}$$

The result follows.

21. Prove that $\forall \, \omega \in \mathbb{R}$

$$\begin{bmatrix} H(\omega) & H(\omega + \pi) \\ G(\omega) & G(\omega + \pi) \end{bmatrix} \begin{bmatrix} \overline{H(\omega)} & \overline{G(\omega)} \\ \overline{H(\omega + \pi)} & \overline{G(\omega + \pi)} \end{bmatrix} = 2 \begin{bmatrix} 1 & 0 \\ 0 & 1 \end{bmatrix}$$

This equation is often expressed in the following notation. Let I be a 2×2 identity matrix, and

$$M(\omega) = \begin{bmatrix} H(\omega) & H(\omega + \pi) \\ G(\omega) & G(\omega + \pi) \end{bmatrix}$$

Then

$$M(\omega) \overline{M(\omega)}^T = 2I$$

Hint: The above equation is a matrix representation of the following results derived earlier.

$$|H(\omega)|^2 + |H(\omega + \pi)|^2 = 2$$
$$|G(\omega)|^2 + |G(\omega + \pi)|^2 = 2$$
$$\overline{H(\omega)} G(\omega) + \overline{H(\omega + \pi)} G(\omega + \pi) = 0$$
$$H(\omega) \overline{G(\omega)} + H(\omega + \pi) \overline{G(\omega + \pi)} = 0$$

22. Prove that

$$\sum_{n \in \mathbb{Z}} \psi_{j0}(t + n) = 0, \qquad j \leq -1, \forall \, t \in \mathbb{R}$$

Hint: The following results and Poisson's summation formula yields the stated result.

$$\psi_{j0}(t) \leftrightarrow 2^{-j/2}\Psi\left(\frac{\omega}{2^j}\right), \qquad j \in \mathbb{Z}$$

$$\Psi(4\pi n) = 0, \qquad n \in \mathbb{Z}$$

From Poisson's summation result

$$\sum_{n \in \mathbb{Z}} \psi_{j0}(t+n) = 2^{-j/2}\sum_{n \in \mathbb{Z}} e^{i2\pi nt}\Psi\left(\frac{2\pi n}{2^j}\right) = 0$$

The last line of the equation is true if $j \leq -1$. This result is used in studying periodic wavelets.

23. Prove that for a sufficiently smooth function $f(\cdot)$, $c(J,k)$ can be approximated as $2^{-J/2}f(2^{-J}k)$.

   Hint: We have

$$c(J,k) = \langle f, \phi_{Jk}\rangle = \int_{-\infty}^{\infty} f(t)\overline{\phi_{Jk}(t)}dt = \int_{-\infty}^{\infty} f(t)\overline{2^{J/2}\phi(2^J t - k)}dt$$

$$= 2^{-J/2}\int_{-\infty}^{\infty} f(2^{-J}(t+k))\overline{\phi(t)}dt \simeq 2^{-J/2}f(2^{-J}k)$$

24. Let

$$a \triangleq \{a(n) \mid n \in \mathbb{Z}\}$$

$$a_e \triangleq \{a(2n) \mid n \in \mathbb{Z}\}$$

$$a_o \triangleq \{a(2n+1) \mid n \in \mathbb{Z}\}$$

That is, a_e and a_o are respectively the even and odd subsequences of the sequence a. Thus $a = a_e \cup a_o$. Let the z-transforms of the sequences a, a_e, and a_o be $\mathcal{A}(z)$, $\mathcal{A}_e(z)$, and $\mathcal{A}_o(z)$ respectively. Prove that

$$\mathcal{A}_e(z^2) = \frac{1}{2}\{\mathcal{A}(z) + \mathcal{A}(-z)\}$$

$$\mathcal{A}_o(z^2) = \frac{1}{2z^{-1}}\{\mathcal{A}(z) - \mathcal{A}(-z)\}$$

Hint: Observe that

$$\mathcal{A}(z) = \mathcal{A}_e(z^2) + z^{-1}\mathcal{A}_o(z^2)$$

$$\mathcal{A}(-z) = \mathcal{A}_e(z^2) - z^{-1}\mathcal{A}_o(z^2)$$

The result follows.

25. Let the z-transforms of $\{h(n) \mid n \in \mathbb{Z}\}$ and $\{g(n) \mid n \in \mathbb{Z}\}$ be $\mathcal{H}(z)$ and $\mathcal{G}(z)$ respectively. For $j = j_0, (j_0+1), (j_0+2), \ldots, J$; let the z-transforms of the sequences $\{c(j,k) \mid k \in \mathbb{Z}\}$, and $\{d(j,k) \mid k \in \mathbb{Z}\}$ be $\mathcal{C}(j,z)$ and $\mathcal{D}(j,z)$ respectively.

(a) For $j = J, J - 1, \ldots, (j_0 + 1)$ prove

$$C\left(j - 1, z^2\right) = \frac{1}{2}\left[\overline{\mathcal{H}\left(z\right)}C(j, z) + \overline{\mathcal{H}\left(-z\right)}C(j, -z)\right]$$

$$\mathcal{D}\left(j - 1, z^2\right) = \frac{1}{2}\left[\overline{\mathcal{G}\left(z\right)}C(j, z) + \overline{\mathcal{G}\left(-z\right)}C(j, -z)\right]$$

(b) For $j = (j_0 + 1), (j_0 + 2), \ldots, J$ prove

$$C(j, z) = \left[\mathcal{H}\left(z\right)C\left(j - 1, z^2\right) + \mathcal{G}\left(z\right)\mathcal{D}\left(j - 1, z^2\right)\right]$$

Hint:

(a) For $j = J, J - 1, \ldots, (j_0 + 1)$; we have

$$c\left(j - 1, k\right) = \sum_{m \in \mathbb{Z}} \overline{h\left(m - 2k\right)} c\left(j, m\right), \qquad k \in \mathbb{Z}$$

$$d\left(j - 1, k\right) = \sum_{m \in \mathbb{Z}} \overline{g\left(m - 2k\right)} c\left(j, m\right), \qquad k \in \mathbb{Z}$$

Let

$$a\left(j, k\right) = \sum_{m \in \mathbb{Z}} \overline{h\left(m - k\right)} c\left(j, m\right), \qquad k \in \mathbb{Z}$$

Also let the z-transform of the above sequence $\{a\left(j, k\right) \mid k \in \mathbb{Z}\}$ be $\mathcal{A}(j, z)$. Therefore,

$$\mathcal{A}(j, z) = \overline{\mathcal{H}\left(z\right)}C(j, z)$$

Use of the result of the last problem yields

$$C\left(j - 1, z^2\right) = \frac{1}{2}\left\{\mathcal{A}\left(j, z\right) + \mathcal{A}\left(j, -z\right)\right\}$$

$$= \frac{1}{2}\left\{\overline{\mathcal{H}\left(z\right)}C(j, z) + \overline{\mathcal{H}\left(-z\right)}C(j, -z)\right\}$$

It can similarly be proved that

$$\mathcal{D}\left(j - 1, z^2\right) = \frac{1}{2}\left[\overline{\mathcal{G}\left(z\right)}C(j, z) + \overline{\mathcal{G}\left(-z\right)}C(j, -z)\right]$$

(b) For $j = (j_0 + 1), (j_0 + 2), \ldots, J$, we have

$$c\left(j, k\right)$$
$$= \sum_{m \in \mathbb{Z}} c\left(j - 1, m\right) h\left(k - 2m\right) + \sum_{m \in \mathbb{Z}} d\left(j - 1, m\right) g\left(k - 2m\right), \quad k \in \mathbb{Z}$$

The z-transform of the sequence $\left\{\sum_{m \in \mathbb{Z}} c\left(j - 1, m\right) h\left(k - 2m\right) \mid k \in \mathbb{Z}\right\}$ is

$$\sum_{k \in \mathbb{Z}} \sum_{m \in \mathbb{Z}} c\left(j-1, m\right) h\left(k-2m\right) z^{-k}$$

$$= \sum_{k \in \mathbb{Z}} \sum_{m \in \mathbb{Z}} c\left(j-1, m\right) z^{-2m} h\left(k-2m\right) z^{-(k-2m)}$$

$$= \mathcal{H}\left(z\right) \mathcal{C}\left(j-1, z^2\right)$$

Similarly, the z-transform of the sequence

$$\left\{ \sum_{m \in \mathbb{Z}} d\left(j-1, m\right) g\left(k-2m\right) \mid k \in \mathbb{Z} \right\}$$

is

$$\mathcal{G}\left(z\right) \mathcal{D}\left(j-1, z^2\right)$$

The result follows.

CHAPTER 4

Daubechies Wavelets

4.1 Introduction

Daubechies wavelets are discussed in this chapter. Daubechies compact and orthonormal wavelets were discovered by none other than Ingrid Daubechies in the year 1988. This is an important milestone in the development of wavelet transform theory. She discovered a hierarchy of wavelets, of which the Haar wavelet is the simplest. All of the Daubechies wavelets are continuous except the Haar wavelet.

Before the construction of Daubechies wavelets is described, a quantitative definition of smoothness or regularity is given. Regularity of a function is related to its moments. As we shall see, Daubechies wavelets satisfy certain regularity conditions. Daubechies wavelets have a compact support. Therefore, the compactness of a function and its consequences, as it relates to scaling and mother wavelet functions is initially explored. Using Bezout's theorem, Daubechies developed expressions for scaling coefficients. Using these coefficients, wavelet coefficients are determined. Finally, a scheme for computing scaling and mother wavelet functions is indicated.

Notation: The jth derivative of a real-valued function $f\left(\cdot\right)$ evaluated at a point $a \in \mathbb{R}$ is denoted as

$$f^{(j)}\left(a\right) \triangleq \left.\frac{d^j}{dx^j} f\left(x\right)\right|_{x=a}, \quad j = 0, 1, 2, \ldots,$$

Observe that $f^{(0)}\left(a\right)$ is simply equal to $f\left(a\right)$. □

4.2 Regularity and Moments

It is possible to build wavelets with different levels of smoothness. Smoothness of a function is related to its rate of decay. As wavelets have a compact support, smoothness is certainly one of its desired features. This feature is also often referred to as its regularity. This characteristic of wavelets also helps in its localization in both time and frequency domains. Regularity of the wavelet function implies its localization in the frequency domain. Thus smoothness and the moments of a function are closely related.

4.2.1 Regularity

Regularity of a function is a measure of its smoothness. Note that if $f(t) \leftrightarrow F(\omega)$, then

$$\frac{d^n}{dt^n} f(t) \leftrightarrow (i\omega)^n F(\omega), \quad n \in \mathbb{P}$$

provided the derivatives exist. This implies that the decay of the Fourier spectrum of a function is related to the existence of its derivatives. Thus the decay of $F(\cdot)$ determines the regularity (smoothness) of $f(\cdot)$.

The regularity of a function $f(\cdot)$ is the maximum value of r in the inequality

$$|F(\omega)| \leq \frac{c}{(1+|\omega|)^{r+1}}, \quad \text{for some } c > 0, \text{ and } \forall \, \omega \in \mathbb{R}$$

That is, $|F(\omega)|$ decays as $O\left(|\omega|^{-r-1}\right)$ for large values of $|\omega|$. Further, $f(\cdot)$ has $(r-1)$ continuous derivatives, and the rth derivative exists, but might possibly be discontinuous.

It is also possible to define smoothness in terms of the *Hölder regularity index*. A function $f(\cdot)$ is called *Lipschitz of order* β, where $0 < \beta \leq 1$; if for all $t, t' \in \mathcal{S} \subseteq \mathbb{R}$, we have

$$|f(t) - f(t')| < c |t - t'|^{\beta}$$

for some $c > 0$. The constant β is called *Lipschitz constant* of the function $f(\cdot)$. The function $f(\cdot)$ becomes "smoother" as β increases from 0 to 1. The function $f(\cdot)$ is also called *Hölder continuous* in region $\mathcal{S}$.

Next assume that the function $f(\cdot)$ is n times differentiable in some region $\mathcal{S}$, and its nth derivative $f^{(n)}(\cdot)$ is Hölder continuous with Lipschitz constant β. Let $\alpha = (n + \beta)$, then $f(\cdot)$ belongs to the class C^{α}. The coefficient α is termed the Hölder regularity index of $f(\cdot)$. For instance $C^{4.7}$ denotes the class of functions which are four times differentiable and the fourth derivatives are Hölder continuous with Lipschitz constant equal to 0.7.

Under this interpretation of regularity, if

$$|F(\omega)| \leq \frac{c}{(1+|\omega|)^{1+\alpha+\varepsilon}}, \quad \text{for some } c, \varepsilon > 0, \text{ and } \forall \, \omega \in \mathbb{R}$$

then $F(\omega)(1+|\omega|)^{\alpha}$ is bounded by the integrable function $c/(1+|\omega|)^{1+\varepsilon}$. It can then be shown that $f(\cdot) \in C^{\alpha}$. This discussion is applicable to both scaling and wavelet functions.

4.2.2 Moments

Moments of the scaling and mother wavelet functions are related to the moments of the $h(\cdot)$ and $g(\cdot)$ sequences. Recall that $\phi(\cdot)$ is the scaling function, $\psi(\cdot)$ is the wavelet function, $h(n)$'s are the scaling function coefficients, and $g(n)$'s are the wavelet coefficients. Also, $\phi(t) \leftrightarrow \Phi(\omega)$, $\psi(t) \leftrightarrow \Psi(\omega)$, $H(\omega) = \sum_{n \in \mathbb{Z}} h(n) e^{-i\omega n}$, and $G(\omega) = \sum_{n \in \mathbb{Z}} g(n) e^{-i\omega n}$.

Definitions 4.1. *Derivatives of $\Phi(\omega)$, $\Psi(\omega)$, $H(\omega)$, and $G(\omega)$ with respect to ω. Moments of: scaling and wavelet functions, and scaling function and wavelet function coefficients.*

1. *The jth derivative of $\Phi(\omega)$, $\Psi(\omega)$, $H(\omega)$, and $G(\omega)$, with respect to ω are denoted by $\Phi^{(j)}(\omega)$, $\Psi^{(j)}(\omega)$, $H^{(j)}(\omega)$, and $G^{(j)}(\omega)$ respectively, where $j \in \mathbb{N}$. Also, $\Phi^{(0)}(\omega) = \Phi(\omega)$, $\Psi^{(0)}(\omega) = \Psi(\omega)$, $H^{(0)}(\omega) = H(\omega)$, and $G^{(0)}(\omega) = G(\omega)$.*

2. *The moments of the scaling and wavelet functions are*

$$\mathcal{M}_j = \int_{-\infty}^{\infty} t^j \phi(t)\, dt, \qquad j \in \mathbb{N} \tag{4.1a}$$

$$\mathcal{N}_j = \int_{-\infty}^{\infty} t^j \psi(t)\, dt, \qquad j \in \mathbb{N} \tag{4.1b}$$

3. *The discrete moments of the $h(n)$'s and $g(n)$'s sequences are*

$$\zeta(j) = \sum_{n \in \mathbb{Z}} n^j h(n), \qquad j \in \mathbb{N} \tag{4.2a}$$

$$\eta(j) = \sum_{n \in \mathbb{Z}} n^j g(n), \qquad j \in \mathbb{N} \tag{4.2b}$$

□

Observation 4.1. We have for $j \in \mathbb{N}$

$$\Phi^{(j)}(0) = (-i)^j \mathcal{M}_j, \quad \Psi^{(j)}(0) = (-i)^j \mathcal{N}_j$$
$$H^{(j)}(0) = (-i)^j \zeta(j), \quad G^{(j)}(0) = (-i)^j \eta(j)$$

In particular, $\mathcal{M}_0 = \Phi(0) = 1$, $\mathcal{N}_0 = \Psi(0) = 0$, $\zeta(0) = \sqrt{2}$, and $\eta(0) = 0$.   □

Recursive relationship between the moments of the scaling and mother wavelet functions is stated in the following observation.

Observation 4.2. Recursive relationship between the moments of the scaling function $\phi(\cdot)$, and the $h(n)$-sequence; and also recursive relationship between the moments of the wavelet function $\psi(\cdot)$, and the $g(n)$-sequence.

$$\mathcal{M}_j = \frac{1}{\sqrt{2}(2^j - 1)} \sum_{k=1}^{j} \binom{j}{k} \mathcal{M}_{j-k} \zeta(k), \qquad j \in \mathbb{P}$$

$$\mathcal{N}_j = \frac{1}{2^{j+1/2}} \sum_{k=1}^{j} \binom{j}{k} \mathcal{M}_{j-k} \eta(k), \qquad j \in \mathbb{P}$$

□

The above observation is established in the problem section.

Wavelet Vanishing Moment

It is known that $\int_{-\infty}^{\infty} \psi(t)\, dt = 0$, that is, $\Psi(0) = 0$. In order to extend the degree of smoothness of the wavelet function $\psi(\cdot)$, it is further required that

$$\mathcal{N}_j = 0, \qquad j = 0, 1, 2, \ldots, N$$

The consequences of this requirement are summarized in the following observations.

Observations 4.3. Some results related to moments of the wavelets.

1. Let the first through the Nth moments of the wavelet function $\psi(\cdot)$ vanish. That is, $\mathcal{N}_j = 0$, $j = 1, 2, \ldots, N$. Then

   (a)
   $$\Psi^{(j)}(0) = 0, \quad j = 1, 2, \ldots, N$$

   Note that $\mathcal{N}_0 = \Psi^{(0)}(0) = 0$ is the admissibility condition. Thus this result implies that $\Psi(\omega)$ has a root of multiplicity $(N+1)$ at $\omega = 0$.

   (b)
   $$G^{(j)}(0) = 0, \quad j = 0, 1, 2, \ldots, N$$

   This result implies that $G(\omega)$ has a root of multiplicity $(N+1)$ at $\omega = 0$.

   $$H^{(j)}(\pi) = 0, \quad j = 0, 1, 2, \ldots, N$$

   This result implies that $H(\omega)$ has a root of multiplicity $(N+1)$ at $\omega = \pi$.

   (c)
   $$\sum_{n \in \mathbb{Z}} n^j g(n) = 0, \quad j = 0, 1, 2, \ldots, N$$

   $$\sum_{n \in \mathbb{Z}} (-1)^n\, n^j h(n) = 0, \quad j = 0, 1, 2, \ldots, N$$

2. If the first through the Nth moments of the wavelet function vanish, then

   (a)
   $$\Phi^{(j)}(2\pi n) = \delta_{n0}\,(-i)^j \mathcal{M}_j, \quad n \in \mathbb{Z},\ j = 0, 1, 2, \ldots, N$$

   where $\delta_{n0} = 1$, if $n = 0$, and equal to 0 otherwise. This result is sometimes called the Strang–Fix condition.

   (b)
   $$\sum_{n \in \mathbb{Z}} (t - n)^j\, \phi(t - n) = \mathcal{M}_j, \quad j = 0, 1, 2, \ldots, N$$

3. Let

$$t^j = \sum_{k \in \mathbb{Z}} M_k \phi(t - k), \qquad j = 0, 1, 2, \ldots, N$$

$$\text{then } M_n = \int_{-\infty}^{\infty} t^j \overline{\phi(t - n)} dt, \qquad n \in \mathbb{Z}$$

The above result implies

$$\int_{-\infty}^{\infty} t^j \psi(t)\, dt = 0, \qquad j = 0, 1, 2, \ldots, N$$

This result implies that the scaling function can be represented as a polynomial up to degree N exactly, when the first N moments of the wavelet function vanish.   □

Notation: For $m \in \mathbb{N}$, the elements of the space $C^{(m)}([a, b])$ are a set of functions defined on the interval $[a, b] \subseteq \mathbb{R}$ which have continuous derivatives up to the mth order in this interval.   □

The following result relates the degree of smoothness of the wavelet function, and its moments.

Observation 4.4. Let $\psi(\cdot)$ be a wavelet function so that $\{\psi_{jk}(\cdot) \mid j, k \in \mathbb{Z}\}$ is an orthonormal set of functions in the space $L^2(\mathbb{R})$. If $\psi(\cdot) \in C^m$, where the kth derivative $\psi^{(k)}(\cdot)$ is bounded for $k \le m$, and if

$$|\psi(t)| \le \frac{c}{(1 + |t|)^{m+1+\varepsilon}}$$

where c is a real-valued positive constant, and $\varepsilon > 0$; then $\psi(\cdot)$ has the moments $\mathcal{N}_j = \int_{-\infty}^{\infty} t^j \psi(t)\, dt = 0$ for $j = 0, 1, 2, \ldots, m$. This result was established by Daubechies in her 1992 opus (Corollary 5.5.2, p. 154).   □

4.3 Compactness

Before compactly supported wavelets are studied, a compact interval, and compact support of a function are defined.

Definitions 4.2. *Compact interval, and compact support of a function defined on a set $\mathbb{S}$. The set $\mathbb{S}$ can be either $\mathbb{R}$ or $\mathbb{Z}$.*

1. *Let $s_1, s_2 \in \mathbb{S}$, and $A_I \subset \mathbb{S}$ is an interval which contains both its end points s_1, s_2, then A_I is a compact interval. Note that $A_I = [s_1, s_2]$.*

2. *A real or complex-valued function $f(s), s \in \mathbb{S}$ has a compact support on a compact interval A_I, if $f(s_1) \neq 0$, $f(s_2) \neq 0$, and $f(s) = 0$, $\forall\, s \in \mathbb{S} \backslash A_I$, then*

$$supp\, f(s) = A_I \qquad (4.3a)$$

The length of the support interval is also called the diameter of the support of the function.

(a) *Let $\mathbb{S} = \mathbb{R}$. The length of the support interval is equal to $(s_2 - s_1)$. It is denoted as*

$$diam\, supp\, f(s) = (s_2 - s_1) \qquad (4.3b)$$

(b) *Let $\mathbb{S} = \mathbb{Z}$. The length of the support interval is equal to $(s_2 - s_1 + 1)$. It is denoted as*

$$diam\, supp\, f(s) = (s_2 - s_1 + 1) \qquad (4.3c)$$

$\square$

Next assume that the scaling coefficients $h(n)$'s have a compact support. A consequence of this fact is that the scaling function $\phi(\cdot)$, the coefficients $g(n)$'s, and the wavelet function $\psi(\cdot)$ all have a compact support. In establishing this result, the following equations are used.

$$\phi(t) = \sum_{n \in \mathbb{Z}} h(n) \sqrt{2}\phi(2t - n), \quad t \in \mathbb{R}$$

$$h(n) = \sqrt{2} \int_{-\infty}^{\infty} \phi(t)\, \overline{\phi(2t - n)}\, dt, \quad n \in \mathbb{Z}$$

$$\psi(t) = \sum_{n \in \mathbb{Z}} g(n) \sqrt{2}\phi(2t - n), \quad t \in \mathbb{R}$$

$$g(n) = \sqrt{2} \int_{-\infty}^{\infty} \psi(t)\, \overline{\phi(2t - n)}\, dt, \quad n \in \mathbb{Z}$$

It is also known that

$$g(n) = \pm(-1)^n\, \overline{h(2m + 1 - n)}, \qquad m \in \mathbb{Z}$$

$$\psi(t) = \sum_{n \in \mathbb{Z}} g(n) \sqrt{2}\phi(2t - n)$$

$$= \sum_{n \in \mathbb{Z}} \pm\sqrt{2}\,(-1)^n\, \overline{h(2m + 1 - n)}\phi(2t - n), \qquad m \in \mathbb{Z}$$

The above results were derived in a different chapter. Compactness-related results are summarized in the following observation.

Observations 4.5. Suppose that the support of the scaling coefficients $h(n)$'s is finite. Let $supp\, h(n) = [0, N_s]$, where N_s is a positive integer.

1. $supp\, \phi(t) = [0, N_s]$.

2. Assume
$$g(n) = \pm(-1)^n \overline{h(2m+1-n)}, \qquad m, n \in \mathbb{Z}$$

If $(2m+1) = N_s$, then

$$supp\ g(n) = [0, N_s], \quad \text{and} \quad supp\ \psi(t) = [0, N_s]$$

$\square$

See the problem section for proofs of these observations. Some immediately useful results in frequency domain, which were derived in the chapter on discrete wavelet transform are summarized. These are useful in the next section.

$$\Phi(\omega) = \int_{-\infty}^{\infty} \phi(t) e^{-i\omega t} dt, \quad H(\omega) = \sum_{n \in \mathbb{Z}} h(n) e^{-i\omega n}$$

$$\Psi(\omega) = \int_{-\infty}^{\infty} \psi(t) e^{-i\omega t} dt, \quad G(\omega) = \sum_{n \in \mathbb{Z}} g(n) e^{-i\omega n}$$

Also

$$|H(\omega)|^2 + |H(\omega + \pi)|^2 = 2$$

$$G(\omega) = \mp e^{-i(2m+1)\omega} \overline{H(\omega + \pi)}, \qquad m \in \mathbb{Z}$$

$$\Psi(\omega) = \frac{1}{\sqrt{2}} G\left(\frac{\omega}{2}\right) \Phi\left(\frac{\omega}{2}\right)$$

$$= \mp \frac{1}{\sqrt{2}} e^{-i(m+1/2)\omega} \overline{H\left(\frac{\omega}{2} + \pi\right)} \Phi\left(\frac{\omega}{2}\right), \qquad m \in \mathbb{Z}$$

4.4 Construction of Daubechies Scaling Coefficients

It has been assumed while stating the axioms of multiresolution analysis, that $\int_{-\infty}^{\infty} \phi(t)\, dt = 1$. Thus $\Phi(0) \neq 0$. Further assume that the scaling function is compactly supported, then it has been observed that $h(n)$'s, $g(n)$'s and $\psi(t)$ are all finitely supported. Let $\psi(t) \leftrightarrow \Psi(\omega)$ be the Fourier transform pair.

Also assume that the mother wavelet function $\psi(t)$ is such that $\int_{-\infty}^{\infty} t^k \psi(t) dt = 0$, for $k = 0, 1, 2, \ldots, (N-1)$, which implies

$$\Psi^{(k)}(0) = 0, \text{ for } k = 0, 1, 2, \ldots, (N-1)$$

Then $\Psi(\omega)$ has a zero of order N at $\omega = 0$. As

$$\Psi(\omega) = \mp \frac{1}{\sqrt{2}} e^{-i(m+1/2)\omega} \overline{H\left(\frac{\omega}{2} + \pi\right)} \Phi\left(\frac{\omega}{2}\right), \qquad m \in \mathbb{Z}$$

$\Psi(\omega)$ has a zero of order N at $\omega = 0$, then $H(\omega)$ has a zero of order N at $\omega = \pi$. This assertion was established in an earlier section. Next define

$$H(\omega) = R(\omega) Q(\omega)$$

where $R(\omega)$ has N zeros at $\omega = \pi$, and $R(0) = 1$. Consequently

$$R(\omega) = \left(\frac{1 + e^{-i\omega}}{2} \right)^N$$

and

$$|H(\omega)|^2 = \left| \cos^2 \frac{\omega}{2} \right|^N |Q(\omega)|^2$$

As $|H(\omega)|^2$ and $|Q(\omega)|^2$ are even functions of ω, these can be written as polynomials in $\cos \omega$. Also, as $\cos \omega = (1 - 2\sin^2 \omega/2)$, let $|Q(\omega)|^2 = B(\sin^2 \omega/2)$. Thus

$$|H(\omega)|^2 = \left| \cos^2 \frac{\omega}{2} \right|^N B\left(\sin^2 \frac{\omega}{2} \right)$$

Using the equation

$$|H(\omega)|^2 + |H(\omega + \pi)|^2 = 2$$

and letting $y = \sin^2 \omega/2$, and defining $P(y) = B(y)/2$, results in

$$(1 - y)^N P(y) + y^N P(1 - y) = 1, \qquad y \in [0, 1]$$

Daubechies finds the solution of the above equation by using Bézout's theorem. Bézout's theorem is named after the mathematician Etienne Bézout (1730–1783).

Theorem 4.1. *Bézout. Let $p_1(\cdot)$, and $p_2(\cdot)$ be two polynomials of degree n_1 and n_2 respectively. These two polynomials have no common zeros. Then there exist unique polynomials $q_1(\cdot)$ and $q_2(\cdot)$ of degrees at most $(n_2 - 1)$ and $(n_1 - 1)$ respectively, so that*

$$p_1(y) q_1(y) + p_2(y) q_2(y) = 1 \tag{4.4}$$

Proof. See the problem section.   □

Use of Bézout's theorem provides unique polynomials $q_1(\cdot)$ and $q_2(\cdot)$ of degrees at most $(n_2 - 1)$ and $(n_1 - 1)$ respectively. It is quite possible that polynomials of higher degrees might exist, and yet satisfy the stated conditions.

A unique solution of the equation, $(1 - y)^N P(y) + y^N P(1 - y) = 1, y \in [0, 1]$ is possible, if the degree of polynomial $P(\cdot)$ is constrained to be at most $(N - 1)$. This is

$$P(y) = \sum_{k=0}^{N-1} \binom{N+k-1}{k} y^k, \qquad y \in [0, 1]$$

A justification of this result is provided in the problem section. Observe that the polynomial $P(y)$ is an even function of ω. Also as $y = \sin^2 \omega/2$, and $\cos \omega = 1 - 2\sin^2 \omega/2$, $P(y)$ can be written as

$$P(y) = \sum_{k=0}^{N-1} d_k \cos^k \omega, \quad d_k \in \mathbb{R}$$

Let $z = e^{i\omega}$, then $\cos \omega = \left(z + z^{-1}\right)/2$, and $(2 - 4y) = \left(z + z^{-1}\right)$. Therefore, there exists a polynomial $A(z)$, such that $P(y) = |A(z)|^2$, where

$$A(z) = \sum_{k=0}^{N-1} a_k z^{-k}, \quad a_k \in \mathbb{R}, \ 0 \le k \le (N-1), \text{ and } a_{N-1} \ne 0$$

As a_k's are real numbers, $|A(z)|^2 = A(z)A(z^{-1})$, and the zeros of polynomial $A(z)$ are either real, or if they are complex, they occur in complex conjugate pairs.

Therefore, in general the zeros of the polynomial $|A(z)|^2$ occur in groups of four $\left\{z_n, \overline{z_n}, z_n^{-1}, \overline{z_n}^{-1}\right\}$, $z_n \in \mathbb{C}$, $z_n \ne 0$. If z_n is either real, or lies on the unit circle, then the zeros occur in groups of twos $\left\{z_n, z_n^{-1}\right\}$, $z_n \in \mathbb{C}$. Note that if a root occurs inside the unit circle, then its reciprocal root occurs outside of it. As $P(0) = 1$, $A(z)$ is normalized so that $A(1) = 1$. That is,

$$\sum_{k=0}^{N-1} a_k = 1$$

The coefficients of the polynomial $A(z)$ are evaluated as follows. Compute $(N-1)$ zeros of the polynomial $P(y)$. The roots of this polynomial $P(y)$ can be either real, or if they are complex, they occur in complex conjugate pairs. Let these roots be $y_n, 1 \le n \le (N-1)$. The zeros of the polynomial $|A(z)|^2$ are obtained from the relationship $(2 - 4y_n) = \left(z_n + z_n^{-1}\right), 1 \le n \le (N-1)$.

Of the $2(N-1)$ zeros, select the $(N-1)$ number of z_n's which are inside the unit circle to form the polynomial $A(z)$. It is quite possible to select other roots as well. Roots inside the unit circle are chosen, so that $A(z)$ is the transfer function of a minimum-phase-lag filter. This filter has its energy concentrated at smaller values of $k, 0 \le k \le (N-1)$. Thus

$$|H(\omega)|^2 = \left|\cos^2 \frac{\omega}{2}\right|^N B\left(\sin^2 \frac{\omega}{2}\right)$$

$$= 2\left|\cos^2 \frac{\omega}{2}\right|^N P(y)$$

$$= 2\left|\cos^2 \frac{\omega}{2}\right|^N |A(z)|^2$$

$$A(z) = \prod_{k=1}^{N-1} \frac{\left(1 - z_k z^{-1}\right)}{\left(1 - z_k\right)}, \quad 2 \le N$$

Note that $A(1) = 1$. Thus

$$H(\omega) = \sqrt{2} \left(\frac{1 + z^{-1}}{2} \right)^N A(z)$$

$H(\omega)$ is a polynomial in z^{-1} of degree $(2N - 1)$. That is,

$$H(\omega) = \sum_{n=0}^{2N-1} h(n)e^{-in\omega} = \sum_{n=0}^{2N-1} h(n)z^{-n}$$

The coefficients $h(n)$'s, can be computed, once the polynomial $A(z)$ is evaluated. Daubechies construction is summarized in the following observation.

Observation 4.6. Daubechies technique for determining compactly supported scaling coefficients. Let the mother wavelet function $\psi(t)$ be such that

$$\int_{-\infty}^{\infty} t^k \psi(t)dt = 0, \quad k = 0, 1, 2, \ldots, (N - 1)$$

which implies that

$$\Psi^{(k)}(0) = 0, \quad k = 0, 1, 2, \ldots, (N - 1)$$

and $\Psi(\omega)$ has a zero of order N at $\omega = 0$. Then $supp\, h(n) = [0, 2N - 1]$. The $h(n)$'s are constructed as follows.

Step 1: Find the roots of the polynomial

$$P(y) = \sum_{k=0}^{N-1} \binom{N + k - 1}{k} y^k, \quad 0 \le y \le 1$$

Let these roots be $\{y_n \mid y_n \in \mathbb{C}, 1 \le n \le (N - 1)\}$.

Step 2: For each value of $n \in [1, N - 1]$, find the roots of the equation $(2 - 4y_n) = (z + z^{-1})$. Of the $2(N - 1)$ roots, select $(N - 1)$ roots inside the unit circle. Construct a polynomial $A(z)$ with these $(N - 1)$ roots. This polynomial is normalized so that $A(1) = 1$.

Step 3: The sequence of $h(n)$'s is obtained from the following equation

$$H(\omega) = \sum_{n=0}^{2N-1} h(n)z^{-n}$$

$$= \sqrt{2} \left(\frac{1 + z^{-1}}{2} \right)^N A(z)$$

$\square$

Observation 4.7. An alternate expression for the polynomial $P(y)$ which satisfies

$$(1-y)^N P(y) + y^N P(1-y) = 1, \quad y \in [0,1]$$

is

$$P(y) = \sum_{k=0}^{N-1} \binom{2N-1}{k} y^k (1-y)^{N-1-k}, \quad y \in [0,1]$$

□

Summary of Results for Compactly Supported Wavelets

A summary of results for wavelets with compact support is given for ready reference. The mother wavelet function $\psi(t)$ is such that $\int_{-\infty}^{\infty} t^k \psi(t)dt = 0$, for $k = 0, 1, 2, \ldots, (N-1)$. Therefore, $\Psi(\omega)$ has a zero of order N at $\omega = 0$. The support relationships are:

$$supp\ \phi(t) = [0, 2N-1]$$
$$supp\ h(n) = [0, 2N-1]$$
$$supp\ g(n) = [0, 2N-1]$$
$$supp\ \psi(t) = [0, 2N-1]$$

The refinement equation and wavelet function are given by

$$\phi(t) = \sum_{n=0}^{2N-1} \sqrt{2}h(n)\phi(2t-n)$$

$$g(n) = (-1)^n \overline{h(2N-1-n)}, \quad n \in [0, 2N-1]$$

$$\psi(t) = \sum_{n=0}^{2N-1} \sqrt{2}g(n)\phi(2t-n)$$

The *max* and *min* functions are defined as follows. Let $a, b \in \mathbb{R}$.

$$\max\ [a,b] = \begin{cases} a, & \text{if } a \geq b \\ b, & \text{if } a < b \end{cases}$$

$$\min\ [a,b] = \begin{cases} b, & \text{if } a \geq b \\ a, & \text{if } a < b \end{cases}$$

Results with $h(n)$'s

$$\sum_{n=0}^{2N-1} h(n) = \sqrt{2}$$

$$\sum_{n=0}^{N-1} h(2n) = \sum_{n=0}^{N-1} h(2n+1) = \frac{1}{\sqrt{2}}$$

$$\sum_{n=0}^{2N-1} |h(n)|^2 = 1$$

$$\sum_{n=\max [0,2m]}^{\min [2N-1,2N-1+2m]} h(n)\,\overline{h}\,(n-2m) = \delta_{m0}, \quad m \in [-(N-1),(N-1)] \subset \mathbb{Z}$$

Also

$$\sum_{n=0}^{2N-1} g(n) = 0$$

$$\sum_{n=0}^{N-1} g(2n) = -\sum_{n=0}^{N-1} g(2n+1) = \frac{1}{\sqrt{2}}$$

$$\sum_{n=0}^{2N-1} |g(n)|^2 = 1$$

$$\sum_{n=\max [0,2m]}^{\min [2N-1,2N-1+2m]} g(n)\,\overline{g}\,(n-2m) = \delta_{m0}, \quad m \in [-(N-1),(N-1)] \subset \mathbb{Z}$$

Equations involving both $h(n)$'s and $g(n)$'s

$$\sum_{n=\max [0,2m]}^{\min [2N-1,2N-1+2m]} g(n)\,\overline{h}\,(n-2m) = 0, \quad m \in [-(N-1),(N-1)] \subset \mathbb{Z}$$

The result with the regularity condition is

$$\sum_{n=0}^{2N-1} (-1)^n\, n^j h(n) = 0, \quad j = 0,1,2,\dots,(N-1)$$

Example 4.1. $\Psi(\omega)$ has a zero of order $N = 1$ at $\omega = 0$. Then $supp\ h(n) = [0,1]$, $supp\ g(n) = [0,1]$, $supp\ \phi(t) = [0,1]$, and $supp\ \psi(t) = [0,1]$. $P(y) = 1$, therefore $A(z) = 1$, and $H(\omega) = (1+z^{-1})/\sqrt{2}$. The relationship $H(\omega) = \sum_{n=0}^{1} h(n)z^{-n}$ implies

$$h(0) = h(1) = \frac{1}{\sqrt{2}}$$

and

$$g(0) = \frac{1}{\sqrt{2}}, \quad g(1) = -\frac{1}{\sqrt{2}}$$

These values correspond to the Haar wavelet. The following equations are verified

$$h(0) + h(1) = \sqrt{2}$$
$$|h(0)|^2 + |h(1)|^2 = 1$$

$$g(0) + g(1) = 0$$
$$|g(0)|^2 + |g(1)|^2 = 1$$
$$g(0)h(0) + g(1)h(1) = 0$$
$$h(0) - h(1) = 0$$

The scaling and the mother wavelet functions are

$$\phi(t) = \begin{cases} 1, & 0 \le t < 1 \\ 0, & \text{otherwise} \end{cases}$$

$$\psi(t) = \begin{cases} 1, & 0 \le t < 1/2 \\ -1, & 1/2 \le t < 1 \\ 0, & \text{otherwise} \end{cases}$$

Observe that the mother wavelet $\psi(\cdot)$ satisfies

$$\int_{-\infty}^{\infty} \psi(t)\, dt = 1$$

The Hungarian mathematician Alfréd Haar (1885–1933) showed that the translates and dilations of this scaling function form an orthonormal basis for $L^2(\mathbb{R})$. The Haar function is discontinuous in time, and consequently poorly localized in the frequency domain. □

Example 4.2. $\Psi(\omega)$ has a zero of order $N = 2$ at $\omega = 0$. Then $supp\ h(n) = [0,3]$, $supp\ g(n) = [0,3]$, $supp\ \phi(t) = [0,3]$, and $supp\ \psi(t) = [0,3]$. $P(y) = (2y+1)$. Therefore, $y_1 = -1/2$ is a root of the polynomial $P(y)$. The zeros of the polynomial $A(z)$ can be determined from the equation $2 - 4y_1 = z_1 + z_1^{-1}$. The roots are $2 \pm \sqrt{3}$. Select the root inside the unit circle, which is $2 - \sqrt{3}$, and normalize polynomial $A(z)$ such that $A(1) = 1$. Then

$$A(z) = \frac{\left(1 - \left(2 - \sqrt{3}\right) z^{-1}\right)}{\left(1 - 2 + \sqrt{3}\right)}$$

$$= \frac{\left(1 - \sqrt{3}\right)}{2} \left(z^{-1} - 2 - \sqrt{3}\right)$$

Therefore, $a_1 = \left(1 - \sqrt{3}\right)/2$ and $a_0 = \left(1 + \sqrt{3}\right)/2$. These coefficients could have also been evaluated as follows.

$$P(y) = 2 - \frac{1}{2}\left(z + z^{-1}\right)$$
$$A(z) = \left(a_1 z^{-1} + a_0\right), \quad A(1) = 1$$
$$P(y) = |A(z)|^2 = \left(a_1 z + a_0\right)\left(a_1 z^{-1} + a_0\right)$$

Comparing coefficients

$$a_0 + a_1 = 1$$

$$a_0^2 + a_1^2 = 2$$

$$a_0 a_1 = -\frac{1}{2}$$

a_1 and a_0 are the roots of the equation $\left(x^2 - x - 0.5\right) = 0$. This quadratic equation will once again yield $a_1 = \left(1 - \sqrt{3}\right)/2$ and $a_0 = \left(1 + \sqrt{3}\right)/2$. The coefficients $h(0)$ and $h(1)$ are evaluated as follows.

$$H(\omega) = \sqrt{2} \left(\frac{1 + z^{-1}}{2}\right)^2 A(z)$$

where $z = e^{i\omega}$. As $H(\omega) = \sum_{n=0}^{3} h(n) z^{-n}$, simplification yields

$$h(0) = \frac{\left(1 + \sqrt{3}\right)}{4\sqrt{2}} \approx 0.482962913$$

$$h(1) = \frac{\left(3 + \sqrt{3}\right)}{4\sqrt{2}} \approx 0.836516304$$

$$h(2) = \frac{\left(3 - \sqrt{3}\right)}{4\sqrt{2}} \approx 0.224143868$$

$$h(3) = \frac{\left(1 - \sqrt{3}\right)}{4\sqrt{2}} \approx -0.129409523$$

The assumption $g(n) = (-1)^n \, \overline{h(3-n)}$, $n \in [0,3]$ implies $g(0) = \overline{h(3)}$, $g(1) = -\overline{h(2)}$, $g(2) = \overline{h(1)}$, and $g(3) = -\overline{h(0)}$. Also $g(n) = 0$ for values of $n \notin [0,3]$. The following equations are then readily verified.

$$h(0) + h(1) + h(2) + h(3) = \sqrt{2}$$

$$(h(0) + h(2)) = (h(1) + h(3)) = \frac{1}{\sqrt{2}}$$

$$h(0)\overline{h(2)} + h(1)\overline{h(3)} = 0$$

$$|h(0)|^2 + |h(1)|^2 + |h(2)|^2 + |h(3)|^2 = 1$$

$$h(2)\overline{h(0)} + h(3)\overline{h(1)} = 0$$

$$g(0) + g(1) + g(2) + g(3) = 0$$

$$(g(0) + g(2)) = -(g(1) + g(3)) = \frac{1}{\sqrt{2}}$$

$$g(0)\overline{g(2)} + g(1)\overline{g(3)} = 0$$

$$|g(0)|^2 + |g(1)|^2 + |g(2)|^2 + |g(3)|^2 = 1$$

$$g(2)\overline{g(0)} + g(3)\overline{g(1)} = 0$$

$$g(0)\overline{h(2)} + g(1)\overline{h(3)} = 0$$
$$g(0)\overline{h(0)} + g(1)\overline{h(1)} + g(2)\overline{h(2)} + g(3)\overline{h(3)} = 0$$
$$g(2)\overline{h(0)} + g(3)\overline{h(1)} = 0$$

The regularity conditions give

$$h(0) - h(1) + h(2) - h(3) = 0$$
$$0h(0) - 1h(1) + 2h(2) - 3h(3) = 0$$

The scaling function $\phi(t)$ can be computed by an iterative technique, and the wavelet function can then be constructed.   □

Example 4.3. $\Psi(\omega)$ has a zero of order $N = 3$ at $\omega = 0$. Then *supp* $h(n) = [0, 5]$, *supp* $g(n) = [0, 5]$, *supp* $\phi(t) = [0, 5]$, and *supp* $\psi(t) = [0, 5]$. $P(y) = (6y^2 + 3y + 1)$. Substituting $y = (2 - (z + z^{-1}))/4$

$$P(y) = \frac{3}{8}\left(z^2 + z^{-2}\right) - \frac{9}{4}\left(z + z^{-1}\right) + \frac{19}{4}$$

The relationship $A(z) = (a_2 z^{-2} + a_1 z^{-1} + a_0)$, $a_2, a_1, a_0 \in \mathbb{R}$ implies

$$P(y) = A(z)A(z^{-1})$$
$$= \left(a_0 + a_1 z + a_2 z^2\right)\left(a_0 + a_1 z^{-1} + a_2 z^{-2}\right)$$

Comparing coefficients of like powers

$$a_0 a_2 = \frac{3}{8}$$
$$a_0 a_1 + a_1 a_2 = -\frac{9}{4}$$
$$a_0^2 + a_1^2 + a_2^2 = \frac{19}{4}$$

The condition $A(1) = 1$ gives

$$a_0 + a_1 + a_2 = 1$$

These equations give

$$a_1^2 - a_1 - \frac{9}{4} = 0$$
$$a_1 = \frac{\left(1 \pm \sqrt{10}\right)}{2}$$

and

$$a_0 + a_2 = \frac{\left(1 \mp \sqrt{10}\right)}{2}$$

Therefore, a_2 and a_0 are solutions of equation

$$x^2 - x \left(\frac{1 \mp \sqrt{10}}{2} \right) + \frac{3}{8} = 0$$

The upper sign in the above equations gives complex values of a_2 and a_0. Therefore, use of the lower sign leads to

$$x = \frac{1}{4} \left[\left(1 + \sqrt{10} \right) \pm \sqrt{5 + 2\sqrt{10}} \right]$$

In summary

$$a_0 = \frac{1}{4} \left[\left(1 + \sqrt{10} \right) + \sqrt{5 + 2\sqrt{10}} \right]$$

$$a_1 = \frac{\left(1 - \sqrt{10} \right)}{2}$$

$$a_2 = \frac{1}{4} \left[\left(1 + \sqrt{10} \right) - \sqrt{5 + 2\sqrt{10}} \right]$$

As

$$H(\omega) = \sqrt{2} \left(\frac{1 + z^{-1}}{2} \right)^3 \left(a_0 + a_1 z^{-1} + a_2 z^{-2} \right) = \sum_{n=0}^{5} h(n) z^{-5}$$

Thus

$$h(0) = \frac{\sqrt{2}}{8} a_0 = \frac{\sqrt{2}}{32} \left[\left(1 + \sqrt{10} \right) + \sqrt{5 + 2\sqrt{10}} \right]$$

$$h(1) = \frac{\sqrt{2}}{8} (3a_0 + a_1) = \frac{\sqrt{2}}{32} \left[\left(5 + \sqrt{10} \right) + 3\sqrt{5 + 2\sqrt{10}} \right]$$

$$h(2) = \frac{\sqrt{2}}{8} (3 - 2a_2) = \frac{\sqrt{2}}{32} \left[\left(10 - 2\sqrt{10} \right) + 2\sqrt{5 + 2\sqrt{10}} \right]$$

$$h(3) = \frac{\sqrt{2}}{8} (3 - 2a_0) = \frac{\sqrt{2}}{32} \left[\left(10 - 2\sqrt{10} \right) - 2\sqrt{5 + 2\sqrt{10}} \right]$$

$$h(4) = \frac{\sqrt{2}}{8} (a_1 + 3a_2) = \frac{\sqrt{2}}{32} \left[\left(5 + \sqrt{10} \right) - 3\sqrt{5 + 2\sqrt{10}} \right]$$

$$h(5) = \frac{\sqrt{2}}{8} a_2 = \frac{\sqrt{2}}{32} \left[\left(1 + \sqrt{10} \right) - \sqrt{5 + 2\sqrt{10}} \right]$$

The numerical values are

$$h(0) \approx 0.332670553$$
$$h(1) \approx 0.806891509$$
$$h(2) \approx 0.459877502$$
$$h(3) \approx -0.135011020$$

$$h(4) \approx -0.085441274$$
$$h(5) \approx 0.035226292$$

The relationship

$$g(n) = (-1)^n \, \overline{h\,(5-n)}, \; n \in [0,5]$$

leads to $g(0) = \overline{h(5)}$, $g(1) = -\overline{h(4)}$, $g(2) = \overline{h(3)}$, $g(3) = -\overline{h(2)}$, $g(4) = \overline{h(1)}$, and $g(5) = -\overline{h(0)}$. Also $g(n) = 0$ for values of $n \notin [0,5]$. It is easy to check the following equations.

$$\sum_{n=0}^{5} h(n) = \sqrt{2}$$

$$\sum_{n=0}^{2} h(2n) = \sum_{n=0}^{2} h(2n+1) = \frac{1}{\sqrt{2}}$$

$$\sum_{n=0}^{5} |h(n)|^2 = 1$$

$$\sum_{n=\max\,[0,2m]}^{\min\,[5,5+2m]} h\,(n)\,\overline{h\,(n-2m)} = \delta_{m0}, \qquad m \in [-2,2] \subset \mathbb{Z}$$

$$\sum_{n=0}^{5} g(n) = 0$$

$$\sum_{n=0}^{2} g(2n) = -\sum_{n=0}^{2} g(2n+1) = \frac{1}{\sqrt{2}}$$

$$\sum_{n=0}^{5} |g(n)|^2 = 1$$

$$\sum_{n=\max\,[0,2m]}^{\min\,[5,5+2m]} g\,(n)\,\overline{g\,(n-2m)} = \delta_{m0}, \qquad m \in [-2,2] \subset \mathbb{Z}$$

$$\sum_{n=\max\,[0,2m]}^{\min\,[5,5+2m]} g\,(n)\,\overline{h\,(n-2m)} = 0, \qquad m \in [-2,2] \subset \mathbb{Z}$$

The regularity condition gives

$$\sum_{n=0}^{5} (-1)^n \, n^j h\,(n) = 0, \; j = 0,1,2$$

□

4.5 Computation of Scaling and Mother Wavelet Functions

In the last section, we learned about the determination of the $h(n)$ and $g(n)$ coefficients of the Daubechies compact wavelet scheme. These are the scaling and wavelet coefficients respectively. Expression for these coefficients were derived earlier in the chapter.

An iterative procedure (cascade algorithm) was described in the chapter on discrete wavelet transform to determine the scaling function $\phi(\cdot)$. It uses the dilation equation $\phi(t) = \sum_{n \in \mathbb{Z}} h(n) \sqrt{2} \phi(2t - n)$, $t \in \mathbb{R}$.

Having determined the scaling function $\phi(\cdot)$, the mother wavelet $\psi(\cdot)$ can be determined from the wavelet equation $\psi(t) = \sum_{n \in \mathbb{Z}} g(n) \sqrt{2} \phi(2t - n)$, $\forall\, t \in \mathbb{R}$.

Problems

1. Establish the recursive relationship between the moments of the scaling function $\phi(\cdot)$, and the $h(n)$-sequence; and also the recursive relationship between the moments of the wavelet function $\psi(\cdot)$, and the $g(n)$-sequence.

$$M_j = \frac{1}{\sqrt{2}\,(2^j - 1)} \sum_{k=1}^{j} \binom{j}{k} M_{j-k}\zeta(k), \qquad j \in \mathbb{P}$$

$$N_j = \frac{1}{2^{j+1/2}} \sum_{k=1}^{j} \binom{j}{k} M_{j-k}\eta(k), \qquad j \in \mathbb{P}$$

Hint: Recall that the refinement equation is

$$\phi(t) = \sum_{n \in \mathbb{Z}} h(n) \sqrt{2} \phi(2t - n)$$

Then

$$M_j = \int_{-\infty}^{\infty} t^j \sum_{n \in \mathbb{Z}} h(n) \sqrt{2} \phi(2t - n)\, dt$$

$$= \sqrt{2} \sum_{n \in \mathbb{Z}} h(n) \int_{-\infty}^{\infty} t^j \phi(2t - n)\, dt$$

Substitution of $y = (2t - n)$, in the above equation, and use of the binomial expansion leads to

$$M_j = \frac{1}{2^j \sqrt{2}} \sum_{k=0}^{j} \binom{j}{k} M_{j-k} \zeta(k)$$

The first result follows immediately. The second result is proved similarly.

2. Let the first through the Nth moments of the wavelet function $\psi(\cdot)$ vanish. That is,

$$\mathcal{N}_j = \int_{-\infty}^{\infty} t^j \psi(t)\, dt = 0, \qquad j = 1, 2, \ldots, N$$

Then prove:

(a)

$$\Psi^{(j)}(0) = 0, \quad j = 0, 1, 2, \ldots, N$$

This result implies that $\Psi(\omega)$ has a root of multiplicity $(N+1)$ at $\omega = 0$.

(b)

$$G^{(j)}(0) = 0, \quad j = 0, 1, 2, \ldots, N$$

This result implies that $G(\omega)$ has a root of multiplicity $(N+1)$ at $\omega = 0$.

$$H^{(j)}(\pi) = 0, \quad j = 0, 1, 2, \ldots, N$$

This result implies that $H(\omega)$ has a root of multiplicity $(N+1)$ at $\omega = \pi$.

(c)

$$\sum_{n \in \mathbb{Z}} n^j g(n) = 0, \quad j = 0, 1, 2, \ldots, N$$

$$\sum_{n \in \mathbb{Z}} (-1)^n n^j h(n) = 0, \quad j = 0, 1, 2, \ldots, N$$

Hint:

(a) The relationship $\psi(t) \leftrightarrow \Psi(\omega)$ implies

$$\Psi^{(j)}(\omega) = (-i)^j \int_{-\infty}^{\infty} t^j \psi(t) e^{-i\omega t}\, dt, \quad j = 0, 1, 2, \ldots, N$$

The result follows.

(b) The following results are used.

$$\Psi(\omega) = \frac{1}{\sqrt{2}} G\left(\frac{\omega}{2}\right) \Phi\left(\frac{\omega}{2}\right)$$

$$G(\omega) = \mp e^{-i(2m+1)\omega} \overline{H(\omega + \pi)}, \qquad m \in \mathbb{Z}$$

$$\overline{H(\omega + \pi)} = \sum_{n \in \mathbb{Z}} \overline{h(n)} e^{i(\omega + \pi)n}$$

$$\Phi(0) = 1, \quad \text{and} \quad H(\pi) = 0$$

Therefore, $G(0) = 0$. Further

$$\frac{d}{d\omega}\Psi(\omega) = \frac{1}{\sqrt{2}}\left\{\frac{d}{d\omega}G\left(\frac{\omega}{2}\right)\right\}\Phi\left(\frac{\omega}{2}\right) + \frac{1}{\sqrt{2}}G\left(\frac{\omega}{2}\right)\left\{\frac{d}{d\omega}\Phi\left(\frac{\omega}{2}\right)\right\}$$

Substitute $\omega = 0$ in the above equation, and use result from part (a) of the problem. This yields

$$\left.\frac{d}{d\omega}G(\omega)\right|_{\omega=0} = 0$$

Also

$$\frac{d}{d\omega}G(\omega) = \mp e^{-i(2m+1)\omega}\left\{(-i(2m+1))\overline{H(\omega+\pi)} + \frac{d}{d\omega}\overline{H(\omega+\pi)}\right\}$$

Substitute $\omega = 0$ in the above equation. This yields

$$\left.\frac{d}{d\omega}H(\omega)\right|_{\omega=\pi} = 0$$

Subsequent results can be proved similarly by using induction on j, where $j = 0, 1, 2, \ldots, N$.

(c) These relationships follow by using the definition of $H(\cdot)$ and $G(\cdot)$, and results from part (b).

3. If the first through the Nth moments of the wavelet function vanish, then prove:

(a)
$$\Phi^{(j)}(2\pi n) = \delta_{n0}(-i)^j \mathcal{M}_j, \quad n \in \mathbb{Z}, \ j = 0, 1, 2, \ldots, N$$

where $\delta_{n0} = 1$, if $n = 0$, and equal to 0 otherwise. This result is sometimes called the Strang-Fix condition.

(b)
$$\sum_{n\in\mathbb{Z}} (t-n)^j \phi(t-n) = \mathcal{M}_j, \quad j = 0, 1, 2, \ldots, N$$

Hint:

(a) This result was proved in a different chapter when $j = 0$. That is, $\Phi(2\pi n) = \delta_{n0}, n \in \mathbb{Z}$. From the Fourier transform theory, it follows that

$$\Phi^{(j)}(0) = (-i)^j \mathcal{M}_j, \quad j = 0, 1, 2, \ldots, N$$

An earlier problem implies that if $\mathcal{N}_j = 0, j = 0, 1, 2, \ldots, N$, then $H(\omega)$ has a root of multiplicity $(N+1)$ at $\omega = \pi$. Therefore, it follows from the following equation

$$\Phi(\omega) = \frac{1}{\sqrt{2}}H\left(\frac{\omega}{2}\right)\Phi\left(\frac{\omega}{2}\right)$$

that $\Phi(\omega)$ has a root of multiplicity $(N+1)$ at $\omega = 2\pi$. Therefore,

$$\Phi^{(j)}(2\pi) = 0, \quad j = 0, 1, 2, \ldots, N$$

Applying this reasoning successively, it can be concluded inductively that

$$\Phi^{(j)}(2\pi n) = 0, \quad n \in \mathbb{P}, \; j = 0, 1, 2, \dots, N$$

As $H(\omega)$ is a periodic function,

$$\Phi^{(j)}(2\pi n) = 0, \quad n \in \mathbb{Z}\backslash\{0\}, \; j = 0, 1, 2, \dots, N$$

(b) Use of part (a) of the problem results in

$$i^j \Phi^{(j)}(2\pi n) = \delta_{n0} \mathcal{M}_j, \quad n \in \mathbb{Z}, \; j = 0, 1, 2, \dots, N$$

Also

$$t^j \phi(t) \leftrightarrow i^j \Phi^{(j)}(\omega), \quad j \in \mathbb{P}$$

Use of Poisson's summation formula leads to

$$\sum_{n \in \mathbb{Z}} (t-n)^j \phi(t-n) = \sum_{k \in \mathbb{Z}} i^j \Phi^{(j)}(2\pi k) e^{i2\pi kt}$$

Next use part (a) result. Thus

$$\sum_{n \in \mathbb{Z}} (t-n)^j \phi(t-n) = i^j \Phi^{(j)}(0) = i^j (-i)^j \mathcal{M}_j = \mathcal{M}_j$$

4. Let

$$t^j = \sum_{k \in \mathbb{Z}} M_k \phi(t-k), \quad j = 0, 1, 2, \dots, N$$

$$\text{then } M_n = \int_{-\infty}^{\infty} t^j \overline{\phi(t-n)} dt, \quad n \in \mathbb{Z}$$

Prove that

$$\int_{-\infty}^{\infty} t^j \psi(t) \, dt = 0, \quad j = 0, 1, 2, \dots, N$$

Hint:

$$\int_{-\infty}^{\infty} t^j \overline{\psi(t)} dt = \sum_{n \in \mathbb{Z}} M_n \int_{-\infty}^{\infty} \phi(t-n) \overline{\psi(t)} dt = 0$$

Also

$$\int_{-\infty}^{\infty} t^j \overline{\psi(t)} dt = 0 \text{ implies } \int_{-\infty}^{\infty} t^j \psi(t) \, dt = 0$$

5. Suppose that the support of the scaling coefficients $h(n)$'s is finite. Let *supp* $h(n) = [0, N_s]$, where N_s is a positive integer.
   (a) *supp* $\phi(t) = [0, N_s]$.

(b) Assume

$$g(n) = \pm(-1)^n \, \overline{h(2m + 1 - n)}, \qquad m, n \in \mathbb{Z}$$

If $(2m + 1) = N_s$, then

$$supp \, g(n) = [0, N_s], \quad \text{and} \quad supp \, \psi(t) = [0, N_s]$$

Hint:

(a) Assume that $supp \, \phi(t) = [a, b]$. Consider the equation

$$\phi(t) = \sum_{n=0}^{N_s} \sqrt{2} h(n) \phi(2t - n)$$

It follows from the hypothesis that

$$supp \, \phi(2t - n) = \left[\frac{a+n}{2}, \frac{b+n}{2} \right], \qquad n \in \mathbb{Z}$$

The support of $\phi(t)$ is $[a, b]$ as per the assumption, and the support of the right-hand side expression is

$$\left[\frac{a}{2}, \frac{b + N_s}{2} \right]$$

Therefore,

$$a = \frac{a}{2}, \quad \text{and} \quad b = \frac{b + N_s}{2}$$

This implies $a = 0$, and $b = N_s$. Therefore, $supp \, \phi(t) = [0, N_s]$.

(b) The support of $g(n)$ is next determined. Let

$$g(n) = \pm(-1)^n \, \overline{h(N_s - n)}, \qquad n \in \mathbb{Z}$$

The relationship $(N_s - n) \in [0, N_s]$ implies $n \in [0, N_s]$. Therefore, $supp$ $g(n) = [0, N_s]$.

Support of $\psi(t)$ is determined from the following equation

$$\psi(t) = \sum_{n=0}^{N_s} \sqrt{2} g(n) \phi(2t - n)$$

The relationships

$$supp \, \phi(2t) = \left[0, \frac{N_s}{2} \right]$$

$$supp \, \phi(2t - N_s) = \left[\frac{N_s}{2}, N_s \right]$$

imply

$$supp \, \psi(t) = [0, N_s]$$

6. Prove Bézout's theorem.

    Hint: See Daubechies (1992). There is an analogous Bézout's theorem for integers. A constructive proof of this later theorem is based upon the Euclidean algorithm for determining the greatest common divisor of two integers, and the extended Euclidean algorithm. Daubechies' proof is similar to its number-theoretic analog.

7. Determine the solution of the equation

$$(1 - y)^N P(y) + y^N P(1 - y) = 1, \qquad y \in [0, 1]$$

    so that the degree of the polynomial $P(y)$ is at most $(N - 1)$.

    Hint: The result is established in several steps.

    Step 1: Apply Bézout's theorem to the polynomials $(1 - y)^N$ and y^N. As per this theorem, there exist unique polynomials $Q_1(y)$ and $Q_2(y)$ of degrees less than N, so that

$$(1 - y)^N Q_1(y) + y^N Q_2(y) = 1$$

    Replace y by $(1 - y)$ in the above equation. This results in

$$y^N Q_1(1 - y) + (1 - y)^N Q_2(1 - y) = 1$$

    Uniqueness of the polynomials $Q_1(y)$ and $Q_2(y)$ imply

$$Q_1(y) = Q_2(1 - y)$$

    Thus

$$Q_1(y) = (1 - y)^{-N} \left\{ 1 - y^N Q_1(1 - y) \right\}$$

    Step 2: The Taylor expansion for $(1 - y)^{-N}$ is

$$(1 - y)^{-N} = \sum_{k \in \mathbb{N}} \binom{N + k - 1}{k} y^k$$

$$= \sum_{k=0}^{N-1} \binom{N + k - 1}{k} y^k + O(y^N)$$

    Step 3: Use of results in Steps 1 and 2 lead to

$$Q_1(y) = (1 - y)^{-N} \left\{ 1 - y^N Q_1(1 - y) \right\}$$

$$= (1 - y)^{-N} - \frac{y^N}{(1 - y)^N} Q_1(1 - y)$$

$$= \sum_{k=0}^{N-1} \binom{N + k - 1}{k} y^k + O(y^N) - \frac{y^N}{(1 - y)^N} Q_1(1 - y)$$

$$= \sum_{k=0}^{N-1} \binom{N + k - 1}{k} y^k + O(y^N)$$

Step 4: As per Bézout's theorem, the degree of the polynomial $Q_1(y)$ is at most $(N-1)$. Therefore, let

$$Q_1(y) = \sum_{k=0}^{N-1} \binom{N+k-1}{k} y^k$$

The above expression for $Q_1(y)$ is an explicit and unique solution of least degree of the stated equation. Denote it by $P_N(y)$. Let $P(y)$ be another solution of higher degree. Thus

$$(1-y)^N \{P(y) - P_N(y)\} + y^N \{P(1-y) - P_N(1-y)\} = 0, \quad y \in [0,1]$$

The above result implies that $\{P(y) - P_N(y)\}$ is divisible by y^N, as $(1-y)^N$ is not divisible by y^N. Therefore, let

$$P(y) - P_N(y) = y^N R(y)$$

Consequently

$$(1-y)^N y^N R(y) + y^N (1-y)^N R(1-y) = 0$$

That is,

$$R(y) + R(1-y) = 0$$
$$R(y) = -R(1-y)$$

This in turn implies

$$R\left(\frac{1}{2} - y\right) = -R\left(\frac{1}{2} + y\right)$$

Thus, $R(y)$ has an odd symmetry about $y = 1/2$. This result implies that $R(\cdot)$ is antisymmetric with respect to $1/2$. In summary,

$$P(y) = \sum_{k=0}^{N-1} \binom{N+k-1}{k} y^k + y^N R\left(\frac{1}{2} - y\right)$$

where $R(y)$ is a polynomial of odd degree, with odd symmetry about $y = 1/2$. If it is assumed that the polynomial $R(y) \neq 0$, then a new family of Daubechies wavelets can be achieved. Actually it is assumed that $R(y) \neq 0$ in the construction of coiflets. Coiflets are discussed in a different chapter.

8. For each $n \in \mathbb{P}$, prove that

$$\binom{2n}{n} = 2\binom{2n-1}{n-1}$$

9. For each $N \in \mathbb{P}$, establish the following trigonometric identity.

$$A_N \triangleq c^{2N} \sum_{k=0}^{N-1} \binom{N-1+k}{k} s^{2k} + s^{2N} \sum_{k=0}^{N-1} \binom{N-1+k}{k} c^{2k} = 1$$

where $c = \cos \alpha$, and $s = \sin \alpha$. This result can be used to verify that

$$P(y) = \sum_{k=0}^{N-1} \binom{N+k-1}{k} y^k$$

is indeed a solution of the equation $(1-y)^N P(y) + y^N P(1-y) = 1$, $y \in [0,1]$.

Hint: See van Fleet (2008). Observe that $A_1 = 1$. It is next demonstrated that for $N \geq 2$, $(A_N - A_{N-1}) = 0$. Begin with

$$(A_N - A_{N-1})$$
$$= c^{2N-2} \left\{ c^2 \sum_{k=0}^{N-1} \binom{N-1+k}{k} s^{2k} - \sum_{k=0}^{N-2} \binom{N-2+k}{k} s^{2k} \right\}$$
$$+ s^{2N-2} \left\{ s^2 \sum_{k=0}^{N-1} \binom{N-1+k}{k} c^{2k} - \sum_{k=0}^{N-2} \binom{N-2+k}{k} c^{2k} \right\}$$

The above equation is expressed as

$$(A_N - A_{N-1}) = c^{2N-2} P_N + s^{2N-2} Q_N$$

where

$$P_N = c^2 \sum_{k=0}^{N-1} \binom{N-1+k}{k} s^{2k} - \sum_{k=0}^{N-2} \binom{N-2+k}{k} s^{2k}$$

$$Q_N = s^2 \sum_{k=0}^{N-1} \binom{N-1+k}{k} c^{2k} - \sum_{k=0}^{N-2} \binom{N-2+k}{k} c^{2k}$$

The expression for P_N is simplified as follows.

$$P_N$$
$$= \sum_{k=0}^{N-1} \binom{N-1+k}{k} s^{2k} - \sum_{k=0}^{N-1} \binom{N-1+k}{k} s^{2k+2}$$
$$- \sum_{k=0}^{N-2} \binom{N-2+k}{k} s^{2k}$$

On the right-hand side of the above equation, there are three summations. These are expressed as follows. The first summation is

$$\sum_{k=0}^{N-1}\binom{N-1+k}{k}s^{2k} = 1 + \sum_{k=1}^{N-2}\binom{N-1+k}{k}s^{2k} + \binom{2N-2}{N-1}s^{2N-2}$$

The second summation is

$$\sum_{k=0}^{N-1}\binom{N-1+k}{k}s^{2k+2} = \sum_{k=1}^{N}\binom{N-2+k}{k-1}s^{2k}$$

$$= \sum_{k=1}^{N-2}\binom{N-2+k}{k-1}s^{2k} + \binom{2N-3}{N-2}s^{2N-2} + \binom{2N-2}{N-1}s^{2N}$$

The third summation is

$$\sum_{k=0}^{N-2}\binom{N-2+k}{k}s^{2k} = 1 + \sum_{k=1}^{N-2}\binom{N-2+k}{k}s^{2k}$$

Collection of the expressions for the three summations leads to

$$P_N = \sum_{k=1}^{N-2}\left\{\binom{N-1+k}{k} - \binom{N-2+k}{k-1} - \binom{N-2+k}{k}\right\}s^{2k}$$

$$+ \left\{\binom{2N-2}{N-1} - \binom{2N-3}{N-2}\right\}s^{2N-2} - \binom{2N-2}{N-1}s^{2N}$$

Observe that

$$\binom{N-1+k}{k} - \binom{N-2+k}{k-1} - \binom{N-2+k}{k} = 0$$

and use of the result of the last problem yields

$$\binom{2N-2}{N-1} - \binom{2N-3}{N-2} = \frac{1}{2}\binom{2N-2}{N-1}$$

Therefore, the expression for P_N simplifies to

$$P_N = \frac{1}{2}\binom{2N-2}{N-1}s^{2N-2} - \binom{2N-2}{N-1}s^{2N}$$

$$= \binom{2N-2}{N-1}s^{2N-2}\left(\frac{1}{2} - s^2\right)$$

It can similarly be shown that

$$Q_N = \binom{2N-2}{N-1}c^{2N-2}\left(\frac{1}{2} - c^2\right)$$

Thus

$$(A_N - A_{N-1}) = c^{2N-2}P_N + s^{2N-2}Q_N$$

$$= \binom{2N-2}{N-1}(cs)^{2N-2}\left(1 - c^2 - s^2\right)$$

$$= 0$$

10. An alternate expression for the polynomial $P(y)$ which satisfies

$$(1 - y)^N P(y) + y^N P(1 - y) = 1, \quad y \in [0, 1]$$

is

$$P(y) = \sum_{k=0}^{N-1} \binom{2N-1}{k} y^k (1 - y)^{N-1-k}, \quad y \in [0, 1]$$

Establish this assertion.

Hint: Let $c = \cos \alpha$, $s = \sin \alpha$, $y = s^2$, and $(1 - y) = c^2$. Use of the binomial theorem leads to

$$1 = (y + (1 - y))^{2N-1}$$

$$= \sum_{k=0}^{2N-1} \binom{2N-1}{k} y^k (1 - y)^{2N-1-k}$$

$$= A + B$$

where

$$A = \sum_{k=0}^{N-1} \binom{2N-1}{k} y^k (1 - y)^{2N-1-k}$$

$$B = \sum_{k=N}^{2N-1} \binom{2N-1}{k} y^k (1 - y)^{2N-1-k}$$

Thus

$$A = (1 - y)^N \sum_{k=0}^{N-1} \binom{2N-1}{k} y^k (1 - y)^{N-1-k}$$

$$= (1 - y)^N P(y)$$

and

$$B = \sum_{k=N}^{2N-1} \binom{2N-1}{k} y^k (1 - y)^{2N-1-k}$$

$$= y^N \sum_{k=N}^{2N-1} \binom{2N-1}{2N-1-k} y^{k-N} (1 - y)^{2N-1-k}$$

Substitute $(2N - 1 - k) = j$ in the above summation. Thus

$$B = y^N \sum_{j=0}^{N-1} \binom{2N-1}{j} (1 - y)^j y^{N-1-j}$$

$$= y^N P(1 - y)$$

The stated result is verified.

CHAPTER 5

Some Examples of Wavelets

5.1 Introduction

Some illustrative examples of wavelets are discussed in this chapter. The Haar wavelet, Morlet wavelet, and Mexican-hat wavelet have been discussed in the chapter on continuous wavelet transforms. Daubechies wavelets are described in a different chapter. In this chapter, the Shannon wavelet, Meyer wavelet, and spline-based wavelets are discussed.

5.2 Shannon Wavelets

Shannon wavelets are also called sinc wavelets. Shannon wavelets are named in honor of C. E. Shannon (1916-2001). Recall that as per Shannon's sampling theorem a band-limited function can be expanded in terms of sinc functions. Shannon wavelets use sinc functions as scaling functions. Unlike Haar wavelets, sinc wavelets are spread out in time, but are discontinuous in the frequency domain.

Definitions 5.1. *Sinc and rectangular functions.*

1. *Sinc function $sinc(\cdot)$:*

$$sinc(t) = \frac{\sin t}{t}, \quad t \in \mathbb{R} \tag{5.1}$$

2. *Rectangular or gate function for $\omega_c > 0$, is $g_{\omega_c}(\omega)$, $\omega \in \mathbb{R}$, where*

$$g_{\omega_c}(\omega) = \begin{cases} 1, & \omega \in [-\omega_c, \omega_c] \\ 0, & \omega \notin [-\omega_c, \omega_c] \end{cases} \tag{5.2}$$

3. *Unit step function $u(\cdot)$ is:*

$$u(t) = \begin{cases} 1, & t > 0 \\ 0, & t < 0 \end{cases} \tag{5.3}$$

□

Observations 5.1. Some observations about sinc functions.

1. Fourier transform relationships.

$$\frac{\omega_c}{\pi} sinc\, \omega_c t \leftrightarrow g_{\omega_c}(\omega)$$

$$sinc\,(\omega_c t - n\pi) \leftrightarrow \frac{\pi}{\omega_c} g_{\omega_c}(\omega)\, e^{-i\pi n\omega/\omega_c}, \qquad n \in \mathbb{Z}$$

2. Orthogonality related results.

$$\int_{-\infty}^{\infty} sinc\,(\omega_c t - m\pi)\; sinc\,(\omega_c t - n\pi)\, dt = \frac{\pi}{\omega_c}\delta_{mn}, \qquad m, n \in \mathbb{Z}$$

Substitute $\omega_c = \pi$ in the last equation. This yields

$$\int_{-\infty}^{\infty} sinc\,\pi\,(t - m)\; sinc\,\pi\,(t - n)\, dt = \delta_{m,n}, \qquad m, n \in \mathbb{Z}$$

In the above equations, δ_{mn} is the Kronecker's delta function, where $\delta_{mn} = 1$ if $m = n$, and equal to 0 otherwise. Therefore, $\{sinc\,\pi\,(t - n) \mid n \in \mathbb{Z}\}$ form an orthonormal set.   □

The scaling function of a Shannon wavelet is $\phi(t) = sinc\,(\pi t)$, $t \in \mathbb{R}$. See Figure 5.1a.

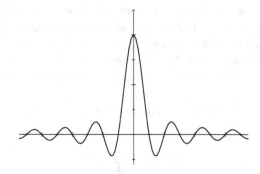

Figure 5.1a. Scaling function of Shannon's wavelet.

Observations 5.2. The scaling function of Shannon's wavelet is $\phi(t) = sinc\,\pi t$, $t \in \mathbb{R}$; and the mother wavelet function is $\psi(t)$, $t \in \mathbb{R}$. The corresponding Fourier transform pairs are: $\phi(t) \leftrightarrow \Phi(\omega)$, and $\psi(t) \leftrightarrow \Psi(\omega)$.

1. $\{\phi(t - n) \mid n \in \mathbb{Z}\}$ form an orthonormal set.

2. $\Phi(\omega) = g_\pi(\omega)$, $\omega \in \mathbb{R}$.

3. The scaling coefficients are:

$$h\left(n\right) = \frac{1}{\sqrt{2}} sinc\,\frac{n\pi}{2}, \qquad n \in \mathbb{Z}$$

Therefore,

$$h\left(0\right) = \frac{1}{\sqrt{2}}$$

$$h\left(2n\right) = 0, \qquad n \in \mathbb{Z} \setminus \{0\}$$

$$h\left(2n+1\right) = \frac{\left(-1\right)^{n}\sqrt{2}}{\pi\left(2n+1\right)}, \qquad n \in \mathbb{Z}$$

4. The mother wavelet and its Fourier transform are

$$\psi\left(t\right) = -2\phi\left(2t-1\right) + \phi\left(t - \frac{1}{2}\right), \qquad t \in \mathbb{R}$$

$$= \frac{\left(\sin 2\pi t - \cos \pi t\right)}{\pi\left(t - 1/2\right)}$$

$$\Psi\left(\omega\right) = e^{-i\omega/2} g_{\pi}\left(\omega\right) - g_{\pi}\left(\left(\omega/2\right)\right), \qquad \omega \in \mathbb{R}$$

Figure 5.1b shows Shannon's mother wavelet.

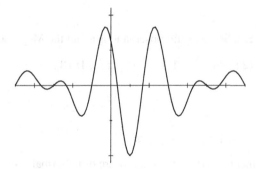

Figure 5.1b. Shannon's mother wavelet.

□

The above set of observations are established in the problem section.

5.3 Meyer Wavelets

The Shannon scaling function and wavelets have sharp discontinuities in the frequency domain. Therefore, these functions have poor localization properties in the time domain. The Meyer scaling function addresses this problem by smoothing out

$\Phi(\omega)$, $\omega \in \mathbb{R}$. This is done by using a smoothening function. Smoothening implies continuous differentiability of a smooth function. The Meyer wavelets are named after Yves Meyer, a pioneer in the study of wavelet transforms. The Meyer wavelet is defined in terms of the function $\zeta(x)$, $x \in \mathbb{R}$. Let

$$\zeta(x) = 0, \qquad x \leq 0$$
$$\zeta(x) = 1, \qquad x \geq 1$$
$$\zeta(x) + \zeta(1 - x) = 1$$

An example of the function $\zeta(\cdot)$ is $\zeta(x) = x$, for $x \in [0, 1]$. Families of different functions have been described in the literature. Meyer defined the Fourier transform $\Phi(\omega)$ as

$$\Phi(\omega) = \begin{cases} 1, & 0 \leq |\omega| \leq 2\pi/3 \\ \cos\left[\dfrac{\pi}{2}\zeta\left(\dfrac{3}{2\pi}|\omega| - 1\right)\right], & 2\pi/3 \leq |\omega| \leq 4\pi/3 \\ 0, & \text{elsewhere} \end{cases}$$

Observe that the function $\Phi(\omega)$ has a compact support, $supp\,\Phi(\omega) = [-4\pi/3, 4\pi/3]$. Also $0 \leq \Phi(\omega) \leq 1$. Further $\Phi(\omega)$ is a real and even function of $\omega \in \mathbb{R}$. Consequently $\phi(t)$, $t \in \mathbb{R}$ is a real function. More properties of this function are noted below.

Observations 5.3. Some useful observations about the Meyer wavelet.

1. $|\Phi(\omega)|^2 + |\Phi(2\pi - \omega)|^2 = 1, \forall |\omega| \in [2\pi/3, 4\pi/3]$.
2.
$$\int_{-\infty}^{\infty} |\Phi(\omega)|^2\,d\omega = 2\pi$$

3. $\sum_{n \in \mathbb{Z}} |\Phi(\omega + 2\pi n)|^2 = 1, \forall \omega \in \mathbb{R}$.
4. The set of elements $\{\phi(t - n) \mid n \in \mathbb{Z}\}$ are orthonormal.
5. $H(\omega) = \sqrt{2}\sum_{n \in \mathbb{Z}} \Phi(2\omega + 4\pi n), \forall \omega \in \mathbb{R}$.
6. The Fourier transform of the mother wavelet is

$$\Psi(\omega) = -e^{-i\omega/2}\Phi\left(\frac{\omega}{2}\right)[\Phi(\omega - 2\pi) + \Phi(\omega + 2\pi)], \qquad \forall \omega \in \mathbb{R}$$

$$\Psi(\omega) = \begin{cases} -e^{-i\omega/2}\sin\left[\dfrac{\pi}{2}\zeta\left(\dfrac{3}{2\pi}|\omega| - 1\right)\right], & |\omega| \in [2\pi/3, 4\pi/3] \\ -e^{-i\omega/2}\cos\left[\dfrac{\pi}{2}\zeta\left(\dfrac{3}{4\pi}|\omega| - 1\right)\right], & |\omega| \in [4\pi/3, 8\pi/3] \\ 0, & \text{elsewhere} \end{cases}$$

7. $\psi(t) = \psi(1-t)$, $t \in \mathbb{R}$. $\square$

Let $\zeta(x) = x$ in the definition of $\Phi(\omega)$, for $\frac{2\pi}{3} \leq |\omega| \leq \frac{4\pi}{3}$. Thus

$$\Phi(\omega) = \cos\left[\frac{\pi}{2}\zeta\left(\frac{3}{2\pi}|\omega| - 1\right)\right]$$

$$= \cos\left[\frac{3}{4}|\omega| - \frac{\pi}{2}\right] = \sin\left[\frac{3}{4}|\omega|\right]$$

Observations 5.4. Consider a special case of the Meyer wavelet. Let

$$\Phi(\omega) = \begin{cases} 1, & 0 \leq |\omega| \leq 2\pi/3 \\ \sin\left[\frac{3}{4}|\omega|\right], & 2\pi/3 \leq |\omega| \leq 4\pi/3 \\ 0, & \text{elsewhere} \end{cases}$$

1. For $t \in \mathbb{R}$

$$\phi(t) = \frac{2}{3}sinc\left(\frac{2\pi t}{3}\right) + \frac{4}{\pi(9 - 16t^2)}\left[3\cos\left(\frac{4\pi t}{3}\right) + 4t\sin\left(\frac{2\pi t}{3}\right)\right]$$

2.

$$h(n) = \frac{\sqrt{2}}{2}\phi\left(\frac{n}{2}\right), \quad n \in \mathbb{Z}$$

$$= \frac{\sqrt{2}}{3}sinc\left(\frac{\pi n}{3}\right) + \frac{2\sqrt{2}}{\pi(9 - 4n^2)}\left[3\cos\left(\frac{2\pi n}{3}\right) + 2n\sin\left(\frac{\pi n}{3}\right)\right]$$

$\square$

5.4 Splines

Splines are piecewise polynomials, with smooth conjunctions between the pieces. Specifically, splines are polynomials of degree n over intervals of fixed lengths, and have continuous derivatives up to order $(n - 1)$ at the junctions of the intervals. Splines occur in numerical analysis, where one of its uses is interpolation.

Splines have been used by G. Battle and P. G. Lemarié to construct wavelets. As will be evident, these wavelets are sometimes called semiorthogonal wavelets. A procedure to create wavelets via an example is first illustrated.

Example 5.1. Consider a piecewise linear spline,

$$b(t) = \begin{cases} 1 - |t|, & 0 \leq |t| \leq 1 \\ 0, & \text{otherwise} \end{cases}$$

The function $b(\cdot)$ has a compact support, $[-1, 1]$. See Figure 5.2.

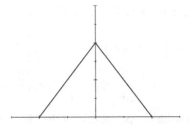

Figure 5.2. A piecewise linear spline.

Further

$$b\left(t\right) \leftrightarrow B\left(\omega\right) = \left(sinc\left(\frac{\omega}{2}\right)\right)^2$$

It can also be checked that

$$b(t) = \frac{1}{2}b(2t+1) + b(2t) + \frac{1}{2}b(2t-1)$$

Observe that the function $b\left(\cdot\right)$ follows a two-scale relation. This is analogous to the two-scale relation of the dilation function $\phi\left(\cdot\right)$. In analogy with the latter's two-scale relationship, a function

$$P(\omega) = \sum_{n\in\mathbb{Z}} p\left(n\right) e^{-i\omega n}$$

is obtained so that

$$B\left(\omega\right) = \frac{1}{\sqrt{2}}P(\frac{\omega}{2})B(\frac{\omega}{2})$$

$$b(t) = \sum_{n\in\mathbb{Z}} \sqrt{2}p\left(n\right) b(2t-n)$$

The sequence $\{b\left(t-n\right) \mid n \in \mathbb{Z}, t \in \mathbb{R}\}$ is a basis but not an orthogonal set. This basis set is orthogonalized as follows. For $\omega \in \mathbb{R}$ let

$$\mathcal{L}\left(\omega\right) = \sum_{n\in\mathbb{Z}} \left|B\left(\omega + 2\pi n\right)\right|^2$$

$$\Phi\left(\omega\right) = \frac{B\left(\omega\right)}{\sqrt{\mathcal{L}\left(\omega\right)}}$$

where $\phi\left(t\right) \leftrightarrow \Phi\left(\omega\right)$. Then $\{\phi\left(t-n\right) \mid n \in \mathbb{Z}, t \in \mathbb{R}\}$ forms an orthonormal basis set, because $\sum_{n\in\mathbb{Z}} \left|\Phi\left(\omega + 2\pi n\right)\right|^2 = 1$. It is proved later in the chapter that $\mathcal{L}\left(\omega\right) = \left(2 + \cos\omega\right)/3$, for $\omega \in \mathbb{R}\backslash 2\pi\mathbb{Z}$. Therefore, for $\omega \in \mathbb{R}\backslash 2\pi\mathbb{Z}$ we have

$$\Phi\left(\omega\right) = \frac{\sqrt{3}\left(sinc\left(\omega/2\right)\right)^2}{\sqrt{\left(2 + \cos\omega\right)}}$$

From the two-scale relationship $\Phi(\omega) = H(\omega/2)\,\Phi(\omega/2)/\sqrt{2}$ it can be concluded that

$$H(\omega) = \sqrt{2}\cos^2\left(\frac{\omega}{2}\right)\sqrt{\frac{(2+\cos\omega)}{(2+\cos 2\omega)}}$$

$\Psi(\omega)$ can be computed via relationships

$$\Psi(\omega) = \frac{1}{\sqrt{2}}G\left(\frac{\omega}{2}\right)\Phi\left(\frac{\omega}{2}\right)$$

$$G(\omega) = -e^{-i\omega}\overline{H(\omega+\pi)}$$

The wavelets thus generated are often called Battle–Lemarié wavelets.   □

Properties of certain splines called B-splines (basis-splines), and general theory and technique to generate orthogonal scaling and wavelet functions are next described.

Definitions 5.2. *B-splines.*

1. *First-order B-spline* $b_1(t),\ t \in \mathbb{R}$ *is*

$$b_1(t) = \begin{cases} 1, & t \in [0,1) \\ 0, & t \notin [0,1) \end{cases} \tag{5.4a}$$

2. *The m-th-order B-spline* $b_m(t), t \in \mathbb{R}, m \in \mathbb{P}\backslash\{1\}$ *is*

$$b_m(t) = b_{m-1}(t) * b_1(t) \tag{5.4b}$$

where $*$ is the convolution operator. Note that $b_m(t) = b_1(t)*b_1(t)*\ldots*b_1(t)$, where the convolution operator $*$ occurs $(m-1)$ times.

3. *The Fourier transform of $b_m(\cdot)$ is $B_m(\omega),\ \omega \in \mathbb{R}$.*   □

5.4.1 Properties of B-Splines

In the following properties of B-splines; $t,\omega \in \mathbb{R}$, and $m \in \mathbb{P}$ unless specified otherwise.

1. $b_m(t) = \int_0^1 b_{m-1}(t-x)\,dx$, $m = 2,3,4,\ldots$..
2. $B_1(\omega) = (1 - e^{-i\omega})/(i\omega) = e^{-i\omega/2}\,sinc\,(\omega/2)$.
3. $B_m(\omega) = \{B_1(\omega)\}^m$
4. $\int_0^m b_m(t)\,dt = 1$
5. $b_m(t) > 0$, for $t \in (0,m)$; $b_m(0) = \delta_{m1}$, and $b_m(m) = 0$. Note that δ_{m1} is equal to 1 if $m = 1$, and equal to 0 for $m > 1$.

6. *supp* $b_m(t) = [0, m]$. That is, splines have compact support.

7. Partition of unity. $\sum_{n \in \mathbb{Z}} b_m(t - n) = 1, \forall t \in \mathbb{R}$.

8. $b_m(t)$ is symmetric with respect to $t = m/2$.

$$b_m \left(\frac{m}{2} + t \right) = b_m \left(\frac{m}{2} - t \right), \quad t \in \mathbb{R}$$

If $b_m(t)$ is computed at integer values of t, then this symmetry property can be exploited.

9. The two-scale equation for $b_m(t)$:

$$b_m(t) = \sum_{n=0}^{m} p_m(n) \, b_m(2t - n)$$

where

$$p_m(n) = 2^{-m+1} \binom{m}{n}, \quad 0 \le n \le m$$

10. Define $x_+ = max(x, 0), x \in \mathbb{R}$. Then

$$b_m(t) = \sum_{n=0}^{m} (-1)^n \binom{m}{n} \frac{(t - n)_+^{m-1}}{(m - 1)!}$$

11. Define

$$\frac{d}{dt} b_m(t) = b_m'(t)$$

then

$$b_m'(t) = b_{m-1}(t) - b_{m-1}(t - 1), \qquad m = 2, 3, 4, \ldots$$

12. Define

$$\frac{d^n}{dt^n} b_m(t) = b_m^{(n)}(t), \quad n \in \mathbb{P}$$

then

$$b_1'(t) = \delta(t) - \delta(t - 1)$$

$$b_m^{(m)}(t) = \sum_{n=0}^{m} (-1)^n \binom{m}{n} \delta(t - n)$$

where $\delta(\cdot)$ is Dirac's delta function.

13. For $m = 2, 3, 4, \ldots$

$$b_m(t) = \frac{t}{(m - 1)} b_m'(t) + \frac{m}{(m - 1)} b_{m-1}(t - 1)$$

$$b_m(t) = \frac{t}{(m - 1)} b_{m-1}(t) + \frac{(m - t)}{(m - 1)} b_{m-1}(t - 1)$$

This equation can be used for the recursive computation of $b_m(t)$.

14. $b_{2m}(t+m) \leftrightarrow |B_m(\omega)|^2$.

15. For $t \in \mathbb{R}$

$$\int_{-\infty}^{\infty} b_m(x) b_m(x-t)\, dx = \int_{-\infty}^{\infty} b_m(x) b_m(x+t)\, dx = b_{2m}(t+m)$$

16. $B_m(\omega)$ satisfies the Strang–Fix condition for $m \in \mathbb{P}$.

$$B_m(0) = 1$$

$$\left.\frac{d^j}{d\omega^j} B_m(\omega)\right|_{\omega=2\pi n} = 0, \quad n \in \mathbb{Z}\backslash\{0\}, \text{ and } j \in [0, m-1]$$

17. The m-th-order B-spline $b_m(t)$ has piecewise polynomials of degree $(m-1)$. Further it has $(m-2)$ continuous derivatives. The $(m-1)$-th derivative is a piecewise constant function.

18. The m-th-order B-spline $b_m(t)$ approaches the normal probability density function, as m approaches infinity. □

5.4.2 Examples of B-Splines

Some of the following B-splines are generated by using Properties 9 and 10.

1. First-order B-spline $b_1(t)$, $t \in \mathbb{R}$ is

$$b_1(t) = \begin{cases} 1, & t \in [0, 1) \\ 0, & \text{otherwise} \end{cases}$$

The corresponding two-scale relationship is

$$b_1(t) = b_1(2t) + b_1(2t-1)$$

2. Second-order B-spline $b_2(t)$, $t \in \mathbb{R}$ is

$$b_2(t) = \begin{cases} t, & t \in [0, 1) \\ 2-t, & t \in [1, 2) \\ 0, & \text{otherwise} \end{cases}$$

The corresponding two-scale relationship is

$$b_2(t) = \frac{1}{2}b_2(2t) + b_2(2t-1) + \frac{1}{2}b_2(2t-2)$$

3. Third-order B-spline $b_3(t)$, $t \in \mathbb{R}$ is

$$b_3(t) = \begin{cases} \frac{1}{2}t^2, & t \in [0,1) \\ \frac{3}{4} - \left(t - \frac{3}{2}\right)^2, & t \in [1,2) \\ \frac{1}{2}(3-t)^2, & t \in [2,3) \\ 0, & \text{otherwise} \end{cases}$$

The corresponding two-scale relationship is

$$b_3(t) = \frac{1}{4}b_3(2t) + \frac{3}{4}b_3(2t-1) + \frac{3}{4}b_3(2t-2) + \frac{1}{4}b_3(2t-3)$$

4. Fourth-order B-spline $b_4(t), t \in \mathbb{R}$ is

$$b_4(t) = \begin{cases} \frac{1}{6}t^3, & t \in [0,1) \\ \frac{1}{6}\left(-3t^3 + 12t^2 - 12t + 4\right), & t \in [1,2) \\ \frac{1}{6}\left(3t^3 - 24t^2 + 60t - 44\right), & t \in [2,3) \\ \frac{1}{6}(4-t)^3, & t \in [3,4) \\ 0, & \text{otherwise} \end{cases}$$

The corresponding two-scale relationship is

$$b_4(t) = \frac{1}{8}b_4(2t) + \frac{1}{2}b_4(2t-1) + \frac{3}{4}b_4(2t-2) + \frac{1}{2}b_4(2t-3) + \frac{1}{8}b_4(2t-4)$$

$\square$

5.4.3 Orthogonalization of B-Splines

Observe that $b_1(t)$ and its integer translates trivially form an orthogonal sequence for $t \in \mathbb{R}$. It can be shown using Riesz theory that for $m = 2, 3, 4, \ldots$ the sequence $\{b_m(t-n) \mid n \in \mathbb{Z}, t \in \mathbb{R}\}$ forms a nonorthogonal basis. The mathematicians Battle and Lemarié discovered a procedure to orthogonalize this basis. For $\omega \in \mathbb{R}$, $m \in \mathbb{P}$, let

$$\mathcal{L}_m(\omega) = \sum_{n \in \mathbb{Z}} |B_m(\omega + 2\pi n)|^2$$

$$\Phi(\omega) = \frac{B_m(\omega)}{\sqrt{\mathcal{L}_m(\omega)}}$$

where $\phi(t) \leftrightarrow \Phi(\omega)$. Then $\{\phi(t-n) \mid n \in \mathbb{Z}, t \in \mathbb{R}\}$ forms an orthonormal basis set, because $\sum_{n \in \mathbb{Z}} |\Phi(\omega + 2\pi n)|^2 = 1$. This orthogonalization process is different than the Gram–Schmidt orthogonalization process, where orthogonality is not preserved under translation. Note that $b_m(\cdot)$ satisfies the two-scale relationship (B-spline Property 9 of last subsection). Therefore, $\phi(\cdot)$ computed from the above equation also satisfies the two-scale relationship. It follows from Property 9, that

$$B_m(\omega) = \frac{1}{2} P_m\left(\frac{\omega}{2}\right) B_m\left(\frac{\omega}{2}\right)$$

$$P_m(\omega) = \sum_{n=0}^{m} p_m(n) e^{-i\omega n}$$

From the above equations it can be inferred that

$$\Phi(\omega) = \frac{1}{2} P_m\left(\frac{\omega}{2}\right) \sqrt{\frac{\mathcal{L}_m(\omega/2)}{\mathcal{L}_m(\omega)}} \Phi\left(\frac{\omega}{2}\right)$$

It is also known that

$$\Phi(\omega) = \frac{1}{\sqrt{2}} H\left(\frac{\omega}{2}\right) \Phi\left(\frac{\omega}{2}\right)$$

$$\Psi(\omega) = \frac{1}{\sqrt{2}} G\left(\frac{\omega}{2}\right) \Phi\left(\frac{\omega}{2}\right)$$

$$G(\omega) = -e^{-i\omega} \overline{H(\omega + \pi)}$$

Therefore,

$$H(\omega) = \frac{1}{\sqrt{2}} P_m(\omega) \sqrt{\frac{\mathcal{L}_m(\omega)}{\mathcal{L}_m(2\omega)}}$$

Observe in the above equations that the orthogonalized scaling function and the mother wavelet do not have a compact support. But these have exponential decay. Also observe that $\mathcal{L}_1(\omega) = 1$. The 1-order B-spline yields the Haar wavelet. The 2-order B-spline yields the so-called Franklin wavelet. The above procedure to orthogonalize is summarized in the following observation.

Observation 5.5. The m-th-order B-spline $b_m(t)$ is orthogonalized as

$$\mathcal{L}_m(\omega) = \sum_{n \in \mathbb{Z}} |B_m(\omega + 2\pi n)|^2 = \sum_{n \in \mathbb{Z}} \left| sinc\left(\frac{\omega + 2\pi n}{2}\right) \right|^{2m}$$

$$P_m(\omega) = \sum_{n=0}^{m} p_m(n) e^{-i\omega n}$$

$$p_m(n) = 2^{-m+1} \binom{m}{n}, \qquad 0 \le n \le m$$

Then

$$H(\omega) = \frac{1}{\sqrt{2}} P_m(\omega) \sqrt{\frac{\mathcal{L}_m(\omega)}{\mathcal{L}_m(2\omega)}}$$

□

The following observation is useful in computing $\mathcal{L}_m(\omega)$.

Observation 5.6. Expression for $\mathcal{L}_m(\omega)$, $m \in \mathbb{P}$.

$$\mathcal{L}_m(\omega) = \sum_{n=-(m-1)}^{(m-1)} b_{2m}(m+n) e^{-i\omega n}, \qquad \omega \in \mathbb{R}, \; m \in \mathbb{P}$$

More specifically $\mathcal{L}_1(\omega) = 1$, $\forall \omega \in \mathbb{R}$.   □

The above observation is established in the problem section.

Observations 5.7.

1. As $\mathcal{L}_1(\omega) = 1$, and using the definition of $\mathcal{L}_1(\omega)$, it can be inferred that

$$\sum_{n \in \mathbb{Z}} sinc^2\left(\frac{\omega + 2\pi n}{2}\right) = 1, \quad \forall \, \omega \in \mathbb{R}$$

The above result yields

$$\sum_{n \in \mathbb{Z}} \frac{1}{(\omega + 2\pi n)^2} = \frac{1}{4\sin^2(\omega/2)}, \quad \omega \in \mathbb{R} \backslash 2\pi \mathbb{Z}$$

2. Differentiate both sides of the last result twice. It leads to

$$\sum_{n \in \mathbb{Z}} \frac{1}{(\omega + 2\pi n)^4} = \frac{(2 + \cos\omega)}{48\sin^4(\omega/2)}, \quad \omega \in \mathbb{R} \backslash 2\pi \mathbb{Z}$$

3. As

$$\mathcal{L}_2(\omega) = \sum_{n \in \mathbb{Z}} sinc^4\left(\frac{\omega + 2\pi n}{2}\right)$$

Use of last result leads to

$$\mathcal{L}_2(\omega) = \frac{1}{3}(2 + \cos\omega), \quad \omega \in \mathbb{R} \backslash 2\pi \mathbb{Z}$$

This result is useful in evaluating the $\mathcal{L}(\cdot)$ function of the Battle–Lemarié wavelets.

4. For $\omega \in \mathbb{R} \backslash 2\pi \mathbb{Z}$

$$\sum_{n \in \mathbb{Z}} \frac{1}{(\omega + 2\pi n)^{m+2}} = \frac{(-1)^m}{(m+1)!} \frac{d^m}{d\omega^m} \sum_{n \in \mathbb{Z}} \frac{1}{(\omega + 2\pi n)^2}, \quad m \in \mathbb{P}$$

□

Problems

1. Let $\beta_n(t) = sinc(\omega_c t - n\pi)$, for each $n \in \mathbb{Z}$, $t \in \mathbb{R}$. Prove that the sequence of functions $\{\beta_n(t) \mid n \in \mathbb{Z}\}$ are orthogonal over $t \in \mathbb{R}$.

   Hint: It is proved that

   $$\int_{-\infty}^{\infty} \beta_m(t) \beta_n(t) \, dt = \frac{\pi}{\omega_c} \delta_{mn}, \quad m, n \in \mathbb{Z}$$

   Consider the Fourier transform pair

   $$sinc(\omega_c t - n\pi) \leftrightarrow \frac{\pi}{\omega_c} e^{-in\pi\omega/\omega_c} g_{\omega_c}(\omega),$$

   where $g_{\omega_c}(\cdot)$ is the gate function. In the next step, use Parseval's relation

   $$\int_{-\infty}^{\infty} f_1(t) f_2(t) \, dt = \frac{1}{2\pi} \int_{-\infty}^{\infty} F_1(-\omega) F_2(\omega) \, d\omega$$

   where $f_1(t) \leftrightarrow F_1(\omega)$, and $f_2(t) \leftrightarrow F_2(\omega)$ are Fourier transform pairs. Substitute $f_1(t) = \beta_m(t)$, and $f_2(t) = \beta_n(t)$ in the above equation. The result follows immediately.

2. The scaling function of Shannon's wavelet is $\phi(t) = sinc \, \pi t$, $t \in \mathbb{R}$. Prove that

   $$h(n) = \frac{1}{\sqrt{2}} sinc \, \frac{n\pi}{2}, \quad n \in \mathbb{Z}$$

   Hint: The $h(n)$'s are evaluated as follows.

   $$\phi(t) = \sum_{n \in \mathbb{Z}} h(n) \sqrt{2} \phi(2t - n)$$

   $$h(n) = \sqrt{2} \int_{-\infty}^{\infty} \phi(t) \overline{\phi(2t - n)} dt, \quad n \in \mathbb{Z}$$

   In the above equation, substitute

   $$\phi(2t - n) = sinc \, \pi(2t - n)$$

   This results in

   $$h(n) = \sqrt{2} \int_{-\infty}^{\infty} sinc \, \pi t \, \overline{sinc \, \pi(2t - n)} dt$$

   Note that

$$sinc\ \pi t \leftrightarrow g_\pi(\omega)$$

$$sinc\ \pi(2t-n) \leftrightarrow \frac{1}{2}\exp\left(-i\frac{\omega n}{2}\right) g_\pi\left(\frac{\omega}{2}\right)$$

Use of Parseval's relation results in

$$h(n) = \frac{\sqrt{2}}{4\pi} \int_{-\infty}^{\infty} g_\pi(\omega)\exp\left(i\frac{\omega n}{2}\right) \overline{g_\pi\left(\frac{\omega}{2}\right)} d\omega$$

$$= \frac{\sqrt{2}}{4\pi} \int_{-\pi}^{\pi} \exp\left(i\frac{\omega n}{2}\right) d\omega = \frac{1}{\sqrt{2}} sinc\ \frac{n\pi}{2}$$

3. The mother wavelet function of Shannon's wavelets is $\psi(t)$, $t \in \mathbb{R}$, and its Fourier transform is $\Psi(\omega)$, $\omega \in \mathbb{R}$. Prove that

$$\psi(t) = -2\phi(2t-1) + \phi\left(t-\frac{1}{2}\right), \qquad t \in \mathbb{R}$$

$$= \frac{(\sin 2\pi t - \cos \pi t)}{\pi(t-1/2)}$$

$$\Psi(\omega) = e^{-i\omega/2}(g_\pi(\omega) - g_\pi(\omega/2)), \qquad \omega \in \mathbb{R}$$

Prove these results.

Hint: In the dilation equation

$$\phi(t) = \sum_{n\in\mathbb{Z}} \sqrt{2}\phi(2t-n)h(n)$$

substitute expressions for $h(n)$'s from the last problem. This results in

$$\phi(t) = \phi(2t) + \sum_{n\in\mathbb{Z}} \frac{2}{\pi}\frac{(-1)^n}{(2n+1)}\phi(2t-2n-1)$$

Therefore,

$$\phi\left(t-\frac{1}{2}\right) = \phi(2t-1) + \sum_{n\in\mathbb{Z}} \frac{2}{\pi}\frac{(-1)^n}{(2n+1)}\phi(2t-2n-2)$$

Substituting $g(n) = (-1)^n\, \overline{h(1-n)}$, $n \in \mathbb{Z}$ in the following equation

$$\psi(t) = \sum_{n\in\mathbb{Z}} \sqrt{2}\phi(2t-n)g(n)$$

results in

$$\psi(t) = -\phi(2t-1) + \sum_{k\in\mathbb{Z}} \frac{2}{\pi}\frac{(-1)^k}{(2k+1)}\phi(2t+2k)$$

Substitute $k = -(n+1)$ in the above equation

$$\psi(t) = -\phi(2t-1) + \sum_{n \in \mathbb{Z}} \frac{2}{\pi} \frac{(-1)^n}{(2n+1)} \phi(2t-2n-2)$$

$$= -\phi(2t-1) + \phi\left(t - \frac{1}{2}\right) - \phi(2t-1)$$

$$= -2\phi(2t-1) + \phi\left(t - \frac{1}{2}\right)$$

The trigonometric form of $\psi(t)$ follows easily. The Fourier transform of $\psi(t)$ can then be computed from the above equation, and the definition of the Fourier transform.

4. Establish the following results about Meyer wavelets.
   (a) $|\Phi(\omega)|^2 + |\Phi(2\pi - \omega)|^2 = 1, \forall |\omega| \in [2\pi/3, 4\pi/3]$.
   (b)
   $$\int_{-\infty}^{\infty} |\Phi(\omega)|^2 \, d\omega = 2\pi$$

   (c) $\sum_{n \in \mathbb{Z}} |\Phi(\omega + 2\pi n)|^2 = 1, \forall \omega \in \mathbb{R}$.
   (d) The set of elements $\{\phi(t-n) \mid n \in \mathbb{Z}\}$ are orthonormal.
   (e) $H(\omega) = \sqrt{2} \sum_{n \in \mathbb{Z}} \Phi(2\omega + 4\pi n), \forall \omega \in \mathbb{R}$.
   (f) The Fourier transform of the mother wavelet is

   $$\Psi(\omega) = -e^{-i\omega/2} \Phi\left(\frac{\omega}{2}\right) [\Phi(\omega - 2\pi) + \Phi(\omega + 2\pi)], \qquad \forall \omega \in \mathbb{R}$$

   $$\Psi(\omega) = \begin{cases} -e^{-i\omega/2} \sin\left[\frac{\pi}{2}\varsigma\left(\frac{3}{2\pi}|\omega| - 1\right)\right], & |\omega| \in [2\pi/3, 4\pi/3] \\ -e^{-i\omega/2} \cos\left[\frac{\pi}{2}\varsigma\left(\frac{3}{4\pi}|\omega| - 1\right)\right], & |\omega| \in [4\pi/3, 8\pi/3] \\ 0, & \text{elsewhere} \end{cases}$$

   (g) $\psi(t) = \psi(1-t), t \in \mathbb{R}$.
   Hint: See Vidakovic (1999).
   (a) For $\omega \in [2\pi/3, 4\pi/3]$

   $$|\Phi(\omega)|^2 + |\Phi(2\pi - \omega)|^2$$

   $$= \cos^2\left[\frac{\pi}{2}\varsigma\left(\frac{3}{2\pi}\omega - 1\right)\right] + \cos^2\left[\frac{\pi}{2}\varsigma\left(\frac{3}{2\pi}(2\pi - \omega) - 1\right)\right]$$

   $$= \cos^2\left[\frac{\pi}{2}\varsigma\left(\frac{3}{2\pi}\omega - 1\right)\right] + \cos^2\left[\frac{\pi}{2} - \frac{\pi}{2}\varsigma\left(\frac{3}{2\pi}\omega - 1\right)\right]$$

   $$= \cos^2\left[\frac{\pi}{2}\varsigma\left(\frac{3}{2\pi}\omega - 1\right)\right] + \sin^2\left[\frac{\pi}{2}\varsigma\left(\frac{3}{2\pi}\omega - 1\right)\right]$$

   $$= 1$$

   The result follows similarly for $\omega \in [-4\pi/3, -2\pi/3]$.

(b)

$$\int_{-\infty}^{\infty} |\Phi(w)|^2$$

$$= 2\left[\int_0^{2\pi/3} dw + \int_{2\pi/3}^{4\pi/3} |\Phi(w)|^2 \, dw\right]$$

$$= 2\left[\frac{2\pi}{3} + \int_{2\pi/3}^{\pi} |\Phi(w)|^2 \, dw + \int_{\pi}^{4\pi/3} |\Phi(w)|^2 \, dw\right]$$

Substituting $w = (2\pi - z)$ in the second integral results in

$$\int_{-\infty}^{\infty} |\Phi(w)|^2$$

$$= 2\left[\frac{2\pi}{3} + \int_{2\pi/3}^{\pi} |\Phi(w)|^2 \, dw + \int_{2\pi/3}^{\pi} |\Phi(2\pi - z)|^2 \, dz\right]$$

$$= 2\left[\frac{2\pi}{3} + \frac{\pi}{3}\right]$$

$$= 2\pi$$

(c) The result follows from a pictorial representation of

$$Y(w) \triangleq \sum_{n \in \mathbb{Z}} |\Phi(w + 2\pi n)|^2$$

and use of the identity $|\Phi(w)|^2 + |\Phi(2\pi - w)|^2 = 1$, $|w| \in [2\pi/3, 4\pi/3]$. In particular, observe that $\Phi(w)$ is an even function of w, and its support is $[-4\pi/3, 4\pi/3]$. Further, $Y(w) = |\Phi(w)|^2 = 1$, for $|w| \in [0, 2\pi/3]$. Also $Y(w) = |\Phi(w)|^2 + |\Phi(2\pi - w)|^2 = 1$, for $|w| \in [2\pi/3, 4\pi/3]$. Finally observe that $Y(w)$ is an even function, and periodic with period 2π. Therefore, $Y(w) = 1, \forall w \in \mathbb{R}$.

(d) This result is a consequence of the following fact.

$$\sum_{n \in \mathbb{Z}} |\Phi(w + 2\pi n)|^2 = 1, \quad \forall w \in \mathbb{R}$$

(e) Note that

$$\Phi(2w) = \frac{1}{\sqrt{2}} H(w) \Phi(w)$$

Observe that

$$\Phi(w) = 1, \quad w \in [-2\pi/3, 2\pi/3]$$
$$\Phi(2w) = 0, \quad w \in [-\pi, -2\pi/3] \cup [2\pi/3, \pi]$$

Therefore,

$$H(\omega) = \sqrt{2}\Phi(2\omega), \quad 0 \leq |\omega| \leq 2\pi/3$$

Also $H(\omega) = \sum_{n \in \mathbb{Z}} h(n) e^{-i\omega n}$ has period 2π, as $H(\omega) = H(\omega + 2\pi)$. Consequently

$$H(\omega) = \sqrt{2} \sum_{n \in \mathbb{Z}} \Phi(2\omega + 4\pi n)$$

(f) Recall that if $g(n) = (-1)^n \overline{h(1-n)}$, $n \in \mathbb{Z}$, $G(\omega) = -e^{-i\omega}\overline{H(\omega + \pi)}$, then

$$H(\omega) = \sqrt{2} \sum_{n \in \mathbb{Z}} \Phi(2\omega + 4\pi n)$$

$$G(\omega) = -e^{-i\omega}\sqrt{2} \sum_{n \in \mathbb{Z}} \Phi(2\omega + 2\pi + 4\pi n)$$

Therefore,

$$\Psi(\omega) = \frac{1}{\sqrt{2}} G\left(\frac{\omega}{2}\right) \Phi\left(\frac{\omega}{2}\right)$$

$$= -e^{-i\omega/2}\Phi\left(\frac{\omega}{2}\right) \sum_{n \in \mathbb{Z}} \Phi(\omega + 2\pi + 4\pi n)$$

$$= -e^{-i\omega/2}\Phi\left(\frac{\omega}{2}\right) [\Phi(\omega - 2\pi) + \Phi(\omega + 2\pi)]$$

The last step follows from the observation that

$$supp\ \Phi\left(\frac{\omega}{2}\right) = [-8\pi/3, 8\pi/3]$$

and only $\Phi(\omega - 2\pi)$, $\Phi(\omega + 2\pi)$ overlap with $\Phi(\omega/2)$. First note that

$$\Phi\left(\frac{\omega}{2}\right) \Phi(\omega - 2\pi) = \begin{cases} \Phi(\omega - 2\pi), & \omega \in [2\pi/3, 4\pi/3] \\ \Phi\left(\frac{\omega}{2}\right), & \omega \in [4\pi/3, 8\pi/3] \end{cases}$$

The result follows.

(g) The result follows by observing that

$$\psi(1-t) \leftrightarrow e^{-i\omega}\Psi(-\omega)$$

$$\Psi(\omega) = -e^{-i\omega/2}\Phi\left(\frac{\omega}{2}\right) [\Phi(\omega - 2\pi) + \Phi(\omega + 2\pi)]$$

and part (f) of the problem.

5. Consider a special case of the Meyer wavelet. Let

$$\Phi(\omega) = \begin{cases} 1, & 0 \leq |\omega| \leq 2\pi/3 \\ \sin\left[\frac{3}{4}|\omega|\right], & 2\pi/3 \leq |\omega| \leq 4\pi/3 \\ 0, & \text{elsewhere} \end{cases}$$

Prove the following results.

(a) For $t \in \mathbb{R}$

$$\phi(t) = \frac{2}{3}sinc\left(\frac{2\pi t}{3}\right) + \frac{4}{\pi(9-16t^2)}\left[3\cos\left(\frac{4\pi t}{3}\right) + 4t\sin\left(\frac{2\pi t}{3}\right)\right]$$

(b)

$$h(n) = \frac{\sqrt{2}}{2}\phi\left(\frac{n}{2}\right), \qquad n \in \mathbb{Z}$$

$$= \frac{\sqrt{2}}{3}sinc\left(\frac{\pi n}{3}\right) + \frac{2\sqrt{2}}{\pi(9-4n^2)}\left[3\cos\left(\frac{2\pi n}{3}\right) + 2n\sin\left(\frac{\pi n}{3}\right)\right]$$

Hint:

(a) Note that

$$\phi(t)$$

$$= \frac{1}{2\pi}\int_{-\infty}^{\infty} \Phi(\omega) e^{i\omega t} d\omega$$

$$= \frac{1}{2\pi}\left[\int_{-4\pi/3}^{-2\pi/3} \sin\left(-\frac{3}{4}\omega\right) e^{i\omega t} d\omega + \int_{-2\pi/3}^{2\pi/3} e^{i\omega t} d\omega \right.$$

$$\left. + \int_{2\pi/3}^{4\pi/3} \sin\left(\frac{3}{4}\omega\right) e^{i\omega t} d\omega \right]$$

Also

$$\frac{1}{2\pi}\int_{-2\pi/3}^{2\pi/3} e^{i\omega t} d\omega = \frac{2}{3}sinc\left(\frac{2\pi t}{3}\right)$$

and

$$\int_{-4\pi/3}^{-2\pi/3} \sin\left(-\frac{3}{4}\omega\right) e^{i\omega t} d\omega = \int_{2\pi/3}^{4\pi/3} \sin\left(\frac{3}{4}\omega\right) e^{-i\omega t} d\omega$$

Therefore,

$$\int_{2\pi/3}^{4\pi/3} \sin\left(\frac{3}{4}\omega\right) e^{i\omega t} d\omega + \int_{-4\pi/3}^{-2\pi/3} \sin\left(-\frac{3}{4}\omega\right) e^{i\omega t} d\omega$$

$$= \int_{2\pi/3}^{4\pi/3} \sin\left(\frac{3}{4}\omega\right) e^{i\omega t} d\omega + \int_{2\pi/3}^{4\pi/3} \sin\left(\frac{3}{4}\omega\right) e^{-i\omega t} d\omega$$

$$= 2\int_{2\pi/3}^{4\pi/3} \sin\left(\frac{3}{4}\omega\right) \cos(\omega t) d\omega$$

$$= \int_{2\pi/3}^{4\pi/3} \left[\sin\omega\left(\frac{3}{4}+t\right) + \sin\omega\left(\frac{3}{4}-t\right)\right] d\omega$$

Evaluate the integral

$$\int_{2\pi/3}^{4\pi/3} \sin \omega \left(\frac{3}{4} + t \right) d\omega = \frac{4}{(3+4t)} \left[\cos \frac{4\pi}{3} t - \sin \frac{2\pi}{3} t \right]$$

Consequently

$$\int_{2\pi/3}^{4\pi/3} \sin \omega \left(\frac{3}{4} + t \right) d\omega + \int_{2\pi/3}^{4\pi/3} \sin \omega \left(\frac{3}{4} - t \right) d\omega$$

$$= \frac{8}{(9-16t^2)} \left[3 \cos \left(\frac{4\pi t}{3} \right) + 4t \sin \left(\frac{2\pi t}{3} \right) \right]$$

The final result follows, by putting together all steps.

(b) Observe that

$$h(n) = \sqrt{2} \int_{-\infty}^{\infty} \phi(t) \overline{\phi(2t-n)} dt, \qquad n \in \mathbb{Z}$$

$$\phi(2t-n) \longleftrightarrow \frac{1}{2} e^{-i\omega n/2} \Phi\left(\frac{\omega}{2} \right)$$

Using Parseval's relation

$$h(n) = \frac{\sqrt{2}}{4\pi} \int_{-\infty}^{\infty} \Phi(\omega) \overline{\Phi\left(\frac{\omega}{2} \right)} e^{i\omega n/2} d\omega$$

$$= \frac{\sqrt{2}}{4\pi} \int_{-\infty}^{\infty} \Phi(\omega) e^{i\omega n/2} d\omega$$

$$= \frac{\sqrt{2}}{2} \phi\left(\frac{n}{2} \right)$$

Next use the part (a) result.

6. Establish the following results about spline-wavelets. In this problem $t, \omega \in \mathbb{R}$, and $m \in \mathbb{P}$ unless specified otherwise.

(a) Partition of unity. $\sum_{n\in\mathbb{Z}} b_m (t-n) = 1, \forall t \in \mathbb{R}$.

(b) $b_m(t)$ is symmetric with respect to $t = m/2$.

$$b_m \left(\frac{m}{2} + t \right) = b_m \left(\frac{m}{2} - t \right), \qquad t \in \mathbb{R}$$

(c) The two-scale equation for $b_m(t)$:

$$b_m(t) = \sum_{n=0}^{m} p_m(n) b_m(2t-n)$$

where

$$p_m(n) = 2^{-m+1} \binom{m}{n}, \qquad 0 \le n \le m$$

(d) Define $x_+ = max\,(x, 0)$, $x \in \mathbb{R}$. Then

$$b_m\,(t) = \sum_{n=0}^{m} (-1)^n \binom{m}{n} \frac{(t-n)_+^{m-1}}{(m-1)!}$$

(e) Define

$$\frac{d}{dt} b_m\,(t) = b'_m\,(t)$$

then

$$b'_m\,(t) = b_{m-1}\,(t) - b_{m-1}(t-1), \qquad m = 2, 3, 4, \ldots$$

(f) Define

$$\frac{d^n}{dt^n} b_m\,(t) = b_m^{(n)}(t), \qquad n \in \mathbb{P}$$

then

$$b'_1\,(t) = \delta\,(t) - \delta\,(t-1)$$

$$b_m^{(m)}\,(t) = \sum_{n=0}^{m} (-1)^n \binom{m}{n} \delta\,(t-n)$$

where $\delta\,(\cdot)$ is Dirac's delta function.

(g) For $m = 2, 3, 4, \ldots$

$$b_m\,(t) = \frac{t}{(m-1)} b'_m\,(t) + \frac{m}{(m-1)} b_{m-1}\,(t-1)$$

$$b_m\,(t) = \frac{t}{(m-1)} b_{m-1}\,(t) + \frac{(m-t)}{(m-1)} b_{m-1}\,(t-1)$$

(h) $b_{2m}\,(t+m) \leftrightarrow |B_m\,(\omega)|^2$.

(i) For $t \in \mathbb{R}$

$$\int_{-\infty}^{\infty} b_m\,(x)\, b_m\,(x-t)\, dx = \int_{-\infty}^{\infty} b_m\,(x)\, b_m\,(x+t)\, dx = b_{2m}\,(t+m)$$

Hint:

(a) The proof is by induction on m. It is evident that $\sum_{n \in \mathbb{Z}} b_1\,(t-n) = 1$.
Assume that $\sum_{n \in \mathbb{Z}} b_{m-1}\,(t-n) = 1$. Then

$$\sum_{n \in \mathbb{Z}} b_m\,(t-n) = \sum_{n \in \mathbb{Z}} \int_0^1 b_{m-1}\,(t-n-x)\, dx$$

$$= \int_0^1 \sum_{n \in \mathbb{Z}} b_{m-1}\,(t-n-x)\, dx = \int_0^1 dx = 1$$

(b) The result follows from

$$b_m \left(\frac{m}{2} + t \right) \leftrightarrow \{sinc\,(\omega/2)\}^m, \quad \omega \in \mathbb{R}$$

$$b_m \left(\frac{m}{2} - t \right) \leftrightarrow \{sinc\,(\omega/2)\}^m, \quad \omega \in \mathbb{R}$$

(c) Let $\Im\,(\cdot)$ be the Fourier transform operator, We have

$$b_m\,(2t - n) \leftrightarrow \frac{e^{-i\omega n/2}}{2} \left(\frac{1 - e^{-i\omega/2}}{i\omega/2} \right)^m$$

$$\Im \left[\sum_{n=0}^{m} p_m\,(n)\,b_m\,(2t - n) \right]$$

$$= \frac{1}{2} \left(\frac{1 - e^{-i\omega/2}}{i\omega/2} \right)^m \sum_{n=0}^{m} p_m\,(n)\,e^{-i\omega n/2}$$

$$= \frac{1}{2} \left(\frac{1 - e^{-i\omega/2}}{i\omega/2} \right)^m 2^{-m+1} \left(1 + e^{-i\omega/2} \right)^m$$

$$= \left(\frac{1 - e^{-i\omega}}{i\omega} \right)^m = B_m\,(\omega)$$

(d) Note that

$$\frac{(t - n)_+^{m-1}}{(m - 1)!} \leftrightarrow \frac{e^{-i\omega n}}{(i\omega)^m}, \quad m \in \mathbb{P}, n \in \mathbb{N}$$

then

$$B_m\,(\omega) = \left(\frac{1 - e^{-i\omega}}{i\omega} \right)^m$$

$$= \frac{1}{(i\omega)^m} \sum_{n=0}^{m} (-1)^n \binom{m}{n} e^{-i\omega n}$$

The result follows.

(e) In the integral

$$b_m\,(t) = \int_0^1 b_{m-1}\,(t - x)\,dx$$

substitute $(t - x) = y$. This results in

$$b_m\,(t) = \int_{t-1}^t b_{m-1}\,(y)\,dy$$

Take derivative of both sides with respect to t. This leads to the stated result.

(f) Note that

$$\frac{d}{dt}(t-n)_+ = u(t-n)$$

where $u(\cdot)$ is the unit step function. For $0 \le n \le m$

$$\frac{d^r}{dt^r}\frac{(t-n)_+^{m-1}}{(m-1)!} = \frac{(t-n)_+^{m-r-1}}{(m-r-1)!}, \quad 1 \le r \le (m-2)$$

$$\frac{d^{m-1}}{dt^{m-1}}\frac{(t-n)_+^{m-1}}{(m-1)!} = u(t-n)$$

$$\frac{d^m}{dt^m}\frac{(t-n)_+^{m-1}}{(m-1)!} = \delta(t-n)$$

The result follows by using part (d) of the problem.

(g) We have

$$\Im[b_m(t)] = \left(\frac{1-e^{-i\omega}}{i\omega}\right)^m$$

$$\Im[b'_m(t)] = i\omega\left(\frac{1-e^{-i\omega}}{i\omega}\right)^m$$

$$\Im[tb'_m(t)] = i\frac{d}{d\omega}\left[i\omega\left(\frac{1-e^{-i\omega}}{i\omega}\right)^m\right]$$

After some algebraic manipulations it can be shown that for $m = 2, 3, 4, \ldots$

$$\frac{1}{(m-1)}\Im[tb'_m(t)] = \left(\frac{1-e^{-i\omega}}{i\omega}\right)^{m-1}\left[\left(\frac{1-e^{-i\omega}}{i\omega}\right) - \frac{m}{(m-1)}e^{-i\omega}\right]$$

Taking the Fourier inverse of both sides, results in

$$\frac{t}{(m-1)}b'_m(t) = b_m(t) - \frac{m}{(m-1)}b_{m-1}(t-1)$$

The first result follows from the above equation. The second equation follows by using the equation

$$b'_m(t) = b_{m-1}(t) - b_{m-1}(t-1)$$

(h) It is known that $B_1(\omega) = (1-e^{-i\omega})/(i\omega) = e^{-i\omega/2}\,sinc\,(\omega/2),\ \omega \in \mathbb{R}$. Also

$$B_m(\omega) = \{B_1(\omega)\}^m = e^{-i\omega m/2}\left\{sinc\left(\frac{\omega}{2}\right)\right\}^m$$

Therefore,

$$B_{2m}(\omega) = e^{-i\omega m}\left\{sinc\left(\frac{\omega}{2}\right)\right\}^{2m}$$

Further

$$b_{2m}\left(t+m\right) \leftrightarrow e^{i\omega m}B_{2m}\left(\omega\right)$$
$$= \left\{sinc\left(\frac{\omega}{2}\right)\right\}^{2m}$$
$$= |B_m\left(\omega\right)|^2$$

Consequently $b_{2m}\left(t+m\right) \leftrightarrow |B_m\left(\omega\right)|^2$.

(i) Observe that $b_{2m}\left(t+m\right) \leftrightarrow |B_m\left(\omega\right)|^2$. Also

$$\int_{-\infty}^{\infty} b_m\left(x\right)b_m\left(x-t\right)dx \leftrightarrow B_m\left(\omega\right)B_m\left(-\omega\right) = |B_m\left(\omega\right)|^2$$

$$\int_{-\infty}^{\infty} b_m\left(x\right)b_m\left(x+t\right)dx \leftrightarrow B_m\left(-\omega\right)B_m\left(\omega\right) = |B_m\left(\omega\right)|^2$$

7. Prove that

$$\mathcal{L}_m\left(\omega\right) = \sum_{n=-(m-1)}^{(m-1)} b_{2m}\left(m+n\right)e^{-i\omega n}, \qquad \omega \in \mathbb{R},\ m \in \mathbb{P}$$

More specifically $\mathcal{L}_1\left(\omega\right) = 1, \forall\, \omega \in \mathbb{R}$.

Hint: It is known from Property 14 of B-splines, that $b_{2m}\left(m+t\right) \leftrightarrow |B_m\left(\omega\right)|^2$. Therefore,

$$b_{2m}\left(m+t\right) = \frac{1}{2\pi}\int_{-\infty}^{\infty} |B_m\left(\omega\right)|^2 e^{i\omega t}d\omega$$
$$= \frac{1}{2\pi}\sum_{k\in\mathbb{Z}}\int_{2\pi k}^{2\pi(k+1)} |B_m\left(\omega\right)|^2 e^{i\omega t}d\omega$$
$$= \frac{1}{2\pi}\sum_{k\in\mathbb{Z}}\int_{0}^{2\pi} |B_m\left(\omega+2\pi k\right)|^2 e^{i\omega t}d\omega$$
$$= \frac{1}{2\pi}\int_{0}^{2\pi} \mathcal{L}_m\left(\omega\right)e^{i\omega t}d\omega$$

Consequently

$$b_{2m}\left(m+n\right) = \frac{1}{2\pi}\int_{0}^{2\pi} \mathcal{L}_m\left(\omega\right)e^{i\omega n}d\omega, \qquad n \in \mathbb{Z}$$

In the above equation, $b_{2m}\left(m+n\right)$ can be considered to be the n-th coefficient of the Fourier series of a 2π-periodic function $\mathcal{L}_m\left(\omega\right)$.

$$\mathcal{L}_m\left(\omega\right) = \sum_{n\in\mathbb{Z}} b_{2m}\left(m+n\right)e^{-i\omega n}$$

The result follows because $supp\, b_{2m}\left(m+n\right) = [-m,m]$.

Also observe that $\mathcal{L}_1\left(\omega\right) = b_2\left(1\right) = 1, \forall\, \omega \in \mathbb{R}$.

CHAPTER 6

Applications

6.1 Introduction

Of the several applications of wavelet transforms, only three well-known applications are described. These are: signal denoising, image compression, and wavelet neural networks.

6.2 Signal Denoising via Wavelets

In this section the possibility of using wavelets to remove noise from a signal is explored. This process is called signal denoising. Actually orthogonal transforms, including wavelet transforms, can be used for signal denoising. Nevertheless, wavelet transforms have been found to be good candidates for signal denoising in practice.

A signal is a function, and noise is simply the unwanted part of it. The input signal is a sequence of N points. Let it be $\{X_i \in \mathbb{R} \mid 0 \leq i \leq (N-1)\}$. The pure part of X_i is s_i, and the noise component is N_i. Thus

$$X_i = s_i + N_i, \quad 0 \leq i \leq (N-1)$$

Assume that N_i is normally distributed with mean 0, and variance σ^2. Further, the random variable N_i is independent of random variable N_j, where $i \neq j$, and $0 \leq i, j \leq (N-1)$. Actually $\{N_i \mid 0 \leq i \leq (N-1)\}$ is called a Gaussian white noise process with parameter σ. Observe that s_i is assumed to be deterministic, and N_i and X_i are probabilistic for $0 \leq i \leq (N-1)$. The purpose of denoising is to determine the pure signal s_i, $0 \leq i \leq (N-1)$; or its approximation

$$\{\widehat{s}_i \in \mathbb{R} \mid 0 \leq i \leq (N-1)\}$$

by using wavelet transform technique. The denoising is performed by first computing the discrete wavelet transform of the noisy signal. Then the coefficients are subject to some thresholding operation to remove the coefficients with small magnitude, and finally the coefficients are subject to inverse transform. This procedure implicitly assumes that the noise components contribute very little to the transform coefficients.

That is, if the energy of the pure signal is concentrated in the wavelet coefficients of larger magnitude, then wavelet coefficients with smaller magnitude can be neglected. Thus the recovered (denoised) signal $\{\widehat{s}_i \in \mathbb{R} \mid 0 \leq i \leq (N-1)\}$ can be obtained.

Thresholding Operation

A noise-contaminated signal is transformed via a discrete wavelet transform. Then the transformed coefficients are mapped according to a thresholding operator. The purpose of thresholding is noise removal. Two types of threshold operators (functions) are considered. These are: a hard thresholding operator, and a soft thresholding operator. The hard thresholding operator is $T_h(\cdot)$:

$$T_h(a) = \begin{cases} a, & \text{if } |a| \geq \theta \\ 0, & \text{otherwise} \end{cases}$$

where $\theta \in \mathbb{R}^+$. If this threshold operator is used, then the coefficients greater than or equal to θ in magnitude are used in the reconstruction of the signal. The variable θ is called the threshold level. The hard thresholding is a "keep" or "kill" rule. The soft thresholding operator is $T_s(\cdot)$:

$$T_s(a) = \begin{cases} a - \theta, & \text{if } a \geq \theta \\ 0, & \text{if } |a| < \theta \\ a + \theta, & \text{if } a \leq -\theta \end{cases}$$

where $\theta \in \mathbb{R}^+$. In this case the coefficients greater than or equal to θ in magnitude are used in the reconstruction of the signal, but their absolute values are shrunk by the value θ. The soft thresholding is a "shrink" or "kill" rule. It is not hard to observe that a critical step in using the thresholding operation is the value of the threshold parameter θ. Generally, the value of θ is independent of the scale j of the wavelet coefficient.

Denoising Steps

The following steps specify the denoising steps succinctly. Let

$$X = \begin{bmatrix} X_0 & X_1 & \cdots & X_{N-1} \end{bmatrix}^T$$
$$\mathfrak{N} = \begin{bmatrix} N_0 & N_1 & \cdots & N_{N-1} \end{bmatrix}^T$$
$$S = \begin{bmatrix} s_0 & s_1 & \cdots & s_{N-1} \end{bmatrix}^T$$
$$\widehat{S} = \begin{bmatrix} \widehat{s}_0 & \widehat{s}_1 & \cdots & \widehat{s}_{N-1} \end{bmatrix}^T$$

Further, let A be an orthogonal transform matrix of size N. It is used to transform the random signal vector (contaminated by noise) X to a vector W. The vector W is of size N. We have

$$X = S + \mathfrak{N}$$
$$W = AX, \quad Y = AS, \quad U = A\mathfrak{N}$$
$$\widehat{Y} = \mathfrak{D}(W, \theta)$$
$$\widehat{S} = A^{-1}\widehat{Y}$$

where $\mathfrak{D}(\cdot, \cdot)$ is the denoising operator. More explicitly,

$$\widehat{Y} = \Delta W$$
$$\Delta = diag(\delta_0, \delta_0, \dots, \delta_{N-1})$$
$$W = \begin{bmatrix} w_0 \ w_1 \ \cdots \ w_{N-1} \end{bmatrix}^T$$

If hard thresholding is used

$$\delta_i = \begin{cases} 1, & \text{if } |w_i| \geq \theta \\ 0, & \text{otherwise} \end{cases}$$

where $0 \leq i \leq (N-1)$.

Determination of the Threshold Parameter θ

Donoho and Johnstone (1992) suggested that θ be equal to $\sigma\sqrt{2\ln(N)}$, where σ is the standard deviation of the noise components in the signal. A plausible explanation of this choice of the threshold level θ is next provided. The choice of the parameter θ is based upon the following observations.

Observations 6.1. Relevant observations to determine the threshold level.

1. The elements N_i, $0 \leq i \leq (N-1)$ of the noise vector $\mathfrak{N}$ form a Gaussian white noise process with parameter σ. Also A is the orthogonal transform matrix. Let

$$U = A\mathfrak{N} = \begin{bmatrix} U_0 \ U_1 \ \cdots \ U_{N-1} \end{bmatrix}^T$$

Then U_i is normally distributed with mean 0, and variance σ^2. Further, the random variable U_i is independent of random variable U_j, where $i \neq j$, and $0 \leq i,j \leq (N-1)$. That is, $\{U_i \mid 0 \leq i \leq (N-1)\}$ is a Gaussian white noise process with parameter σ. This statement implies that an orthogonal transform maps a Gaussian white noise process into the same Gaussian white noise process.

2. Let $U_0, U_1, \dots, U_{N-1}$ be independent and identically distributed normal random variables, each with cumulative distribution function $F_U(u)$, $u \in \mathbb{R}$. The mean and variance of the random variables are 0 and σ^2 respectively. Define $V_i = |U_i|$, $0 \leq i \leq (N-1)$, and $Z = \max\{V_0, V_1, \dots, V_{N-1}\}$. Let the cumulative distribution function of Z be $F_Z(z)$, $z \in \mathbb{R}$. Then the complementary cumulative distribution function, $F_Z^c(\cdot)$ of the random variable Z is

$$F_Z^c(z) \simeq \frac{2\sigma N}{\sqrt{2\pi z}} \exp(-z^2/(2\sigma^2)), \qquad z \to \infty$$

Further, if $\theta = \sigma\sqrt{2\ln(N)}$, then

$$F_Z^c(\theta) \simeq \frac{1}{\sqrt{\pi \ln(N)}}$$

□

The above observations are established in the problem section. These essentially imply that if $\theta = \sigma\sqrt{2\ln(N)}$ and the noise is "bounded," then negligible noise is present after thresholding for sufficiently large N. This is true, if the contribution of noise to the magnitude of the transform coefficient is bounded by $\sigma\sqrt{2\ln(N)}$, for $0 \le i \le (N-1)$. The value σ is not known in advance. Therefore, it is determined empirically.

Risk Measure of the Estimator

The goal of the thresholding operation is to minimize the error in the estimated value. The risk measure of the estimator is defined as

$$R\left(\widehat{S}, S\right) = \mathcal{E}\left(\left\|\widehat{S} - S\right\|^2\right)$$

where $\mathcal{E}(\cdot)$ is the expectation operator. Observe that

$$R\left(\widehat{S}, S\right) = \mathcal{E}\left(\left\|\widehat{S} - S\right\|^2\right) = \mathcal{E}\left(\left\|A^{-1}\widehat{Y} - S\right\|^2\right)$$

$$= \mathcal{E}\left(\left\|A^{-1}\left(\widehat{Y} - AS\right)\right\|^2\right) = \mathcal{E}\left(\left\|\left(\widehat{Y} - Y\right)\right\|^2\right)$$

The ideal mean squared-error is

$$R\left(\widehat{S}^{IDEAL}, S\right) = \sum_{i=0}^{N-1} \min\left(s_i^2, \sigma^2\right)$$

The *ideal* mean-squared error is not achievable because it requires a knowledge of the vector S. It is also an indicator of the extent to which the energy is compressed into the transform coefficients of larger magnitude.

6.3 Image Compression

An image can mathematically be considered as a function which takes nonnegative values on a plane. The domain of this function is a set of rectangular lattice points.

Let the size of this rectangle be $M \times N$. The brightness of the image at each of these points on the plane represents the value of the function. The brightness (or luminance) of the image is measured in units of *pixels*. Further, let the precision of this luminance indicator be B bits. It is typically 8 bits for black-and-white pictures, and 24 bits for colored pictures. A bit is a unit of information. It takes values of either 0 or 1. Therefore, the value of a pixel ranges from 0 to $(2^B - 1)$. Thus an image can be directly specified by MNB number of bits.

Industrial applications of imaging do not require an exact replication of an image. Therefore, engineers and computer scientists try to transform the image and represent the image with less than MNB number of bits, while maintaining an acceptable level of distortion. Since network bandwidth and storage are at premium, it is important to compress these images. There are two types of compression techniques. These are lossless and lossy compression. Lossless compression techniques are used for compression of texts. Lossy compression can be used for most images, if a certain allowable degree of error is tolerable in the reconstructed image. However, in certain applications, like medical imaging no error is acceptable.

Lossy compression consists of three steps. These are transformation of the image, quantization of the transformed coefficients, and lastly the encoding of these coefficients. Well-known transforms are the discrete cosine transform, fast Fourier transform, and wavelet transform. Quantization of the coefficients represents the accuracy with which these coefficients are represented. Encoding of the quantized coefficients is an efficient scheme to code these coefficients. Two-dimensional wavelet transforms are a popular and successful method for image compression.

Two-Dimensional Wavelets

Wavelet transform in a single dimension is studied in detail in the rest of the book. As two-dimensional wavelets are used in image compression, only a bird's-eye view of the multiresolution analysis in two dimensions is presented.

The single-dimension wavelet transform discussed in detail in a different chapter, is extended to two dimensions. Denote the two-dimensional function by $f(t_1, t_2) \in L^2(\mathbb{R}^2)$, where $(t_1, t_2) \in \mathbb{R}^2$. That is, the function $f(\cdot, \cdot)$ is square integrable over the real plane. In the following axioms, $\overline{A}$ denotes the closure of the set A.

Axioms: The multiresolution analysis of $L^2(\mathbb{R}^2)$ is a sequence of closed subspaces

$$\{\mathcal{V}_j \mid \mathcal{V}_j \subseteq L^2(\mathbb{R}^2), j \in \mathbb{Z}\}$$

and a function $\Phi(\cdot, \cdot)$ called the scaling function, so that:

1. *Nesting property:* $\mathcal{V}_j \subset \mathcal{V}_{j+1}$, for all values of $j \in \mathbb{Z}$. This hierarchy of approximation spaces is often represented as

$$\ldots \subset \mathcal{V}_{-2} \subset \mathcal{V}_{-1} \subset \mathcal{V}_0 \subset \mathcal{V}_1 \subset \mathcal{V}_2 \subset \ldots$$

2. *Upward completeness*: $\overline{\cup_{j\in\mathbb{Z}}\mathcal{V}_j} = L^2\left(\mathbb{R}^2\right)$. This is the closure property.

3. *Downward completeness*: $\cap_{j\in\mathbb{Z}}\mathcal{V}_j = \{(0,0)\}$.

4. *Scaling property*: $f\left(\cdot,\cdot\right) \in \mathcal{V}_j \Leftrightarrow f\left(2\cdot,2\cdot\right) \in \mathcal{V}_{j+1}$, for all values of $j \in \mathbb{Z}$.

5. *Existence of scaling function*: A scaling function $\varPhi\left(\cdot,\cdot\right) \in \mathcal{V}_0$ exists such that $\{\varPhi\left(t_1 - n_1, t_2 - n_2\right) \mid n_1, n_2 \in \mathbb{Z}\}$ forms an orthonormal basis of $\mathcal{V}_0$.   ☐

Define $\mathcal{V}_j$, $j \in \mathbb{Z}$, as the tensor product of two one-dimensional V_j spaces:

$$\mathcal{V}_j = V_j \otimes V_j, \ j \in \mathbb{Z}$$

where $\otimes$ is the tensor product operator. Also let $\varPhi\left(t_1,t_2\right) = \phi\left(t_1\right)\phi\left(t_2\right)$, $\forall$ $\left(t_1,t_2\right) \in \mathbb{R}^2$. For all values of $j \in \mathbb{Z}$, $\mathcal{V}_j$ is spanned by the orthonormal basis $\{\varPhi_{j,i_1,i_2}\left(t_1,t_2\right) \mid i_1, i_2 \in \mathbb{Z}\}$, where

$$\varPhi_{j,i_1,i_2}\left(t_1,t_2\right) = 2^j\phi\left(2^j t_1 - i_1\right)\phi(2^j t_2 - i_2), \quad j, i_1, i_2 \in \mathbb{Z}$$

Note that $\varPhi_0\left(\cdot,\cdot\right) \triangleq \varPhi\left(\cdot,\cdot\right)$. In the case of single-dimensional wavelets, W_j is the orthogonal complement of V_j in V_{j+1}. Similarly, let $\mathcal{W}_j$ be the orthogonal complement of $\mathcal{V}_j$ in $\mathcal{V}_{j+1}$. That is,

$$\mathcal{V}_j \cap \mathcal{W}_j = \{(0,0)\}, \quad j \in \mathbb{Z}$$
$$\mathcal{V}_{j+1} = \mathcal{V}_j \oplus \mathcal{W}_j, \quad j \in \mathbb{Z}$$

where $\oplus$ is the direct sum operator. The complementary space $\mathcal{W}_j$ is related to its one-dimensional cousin. This relationship is stated in the following lemma.

Lemma 6.1. *For* $j \in \mathbb{Z}$

$$\mathcal{W}_j = \left(V_j \otimes W_j\right) \oplus \left(W_j \otimes V_j\right) \oplus \left(W_j \otimes W_j\right) \tag{6.1}$$

Proof. We have

$$\begin{aligned}
\mathcal{V}_{j+1} &= V_{j+1} \otimes V_{j+1} \\
&= \left(V_j \oplus W_j\right) \otimes \left(V_j \oplus W_j\right) \\
&= \left(V_j \otimes V_j\right) \oplus \left(\left(V_j \otimes W_j\right) \oplus \left(W_j \otimes V_j\right) \oplus \left(W_j \otimes W_j\right)\right) \\
&= \mathcal{V}_j \oplus \left(\left(V_j \otimes W_j\right) \oplus \left(W_j \otimes V_j\right) \oplus \left(W_j \otimes W_j\right)\right)
\end{aligned}$$

As $\mathcal{V}_{j+1} = \mathcal{V}_j \oplus \mathcal{W}_j$, the result follows.   ☐

Note that $\mathcal{W}_j$ is made up of the spaces: $\left(V_j \otimes W_j\right)$, $\left(W_j \otimes V_j\right)$, and $\left(W_j \otimes W_j\right)$. These three spaces are respectively generated as follows. Define

$$\varPsi^{(0,1)}\left(t_1,t_2\right) = \phi\left(t_1\right)\psi\left(t_2\right)$$
$$\varPsi^{(1,0)}\left(t_1,t_2\right) = \psi\left(t_1\right)\phi\left(t_2\right)$$
$$\varPsi^{(1,1)}\left(t_1,t_2\right) = \psi\left(t_1\right)\psi\left(t_2\right)$$

where $(t_1, t_2) \in \mathbb{R}^2$ and $\psi(\cdot)$ is the one-dimensional wavelet associated with the scaling function $\phi(\cdot)$. Define $\sigma = \{(0, 1), (1, 0), (1, 1)\}$. For each $j \in \mathbb{Z}$, the space $\mathcal{W}_j$ is spanned by

$$\left\{ \Psi_{j, i_1, i_2}^n (\cdot, \cdot) \mid i_1, i_2 \in \mathbb{Z}, n \in \sigma \right\}$$

where

$$\Psi_{j, i_1, i_2}^n (t_1, t_2) = 2^j \Psi^n (2^j t_1 - i_1, 2^j t_2 - i_2),$$

$$n \in \sigma, i_1, i_2 \in \mathbb{Z}, \quad \text{and} \quad (t_1, t_2) \in \mathbb{R}^2$$

The two-dimensional fast wavelength transform is computed in two steps.

Step 1: In the first step, each row of the image is decomposed into low-pass filter component (low-frequency) and high-pass filter component (high-frequency). The high-pass filter indeed uses the wavelet filter. Evidently, the high-frequency information refers to the horizontal orientation of the image.

Step 2: The low-pass and high-pass transformed elements are now separately filtered column-wise to obtain the four subcomponents of the transform. These are low-low-pass, low-high-pass, high-low-pass, and high-high-pass subimages. These transform components are the coefficients of the image array with respect to the basis functions:

- The low-low-pass transform components (LL) are the coefficients of the image array with respect to the basis functions $\{\Phi_{j, i_1, i_2}(t_1, t_2) \mid i_1, i_2 \in \mathbb{Z}\}$.

- Similarly, the low-high-pass transform components (LH) are the coefficients of the image array with respect to the basis functions $\left\{ \Psi_{j, i_1, i_2}^{(0,1)}(t_1, t_2) \mid i_1, i_2 \in \mathbb{Z} \right\}$.

- The high-low-pass transform components (HL) are the coefficients of the image array with respect to the basis functions $\left\{ \Psi_{j, i_1, i_2}^{(1,0)}(t_1, t_2) \mid i_1, i_2 \in \mathbb{Z} \right\}$.

- Finally the high-high-pass transform components (HH) are the coefficients of the image array with respect to the basis functions $\left\{ \Psi_{j, i_1, i_2}^{(1,1)}(t_1, t_2) \mid i_1, i_2 \in \mathbb{Z} \right\}$.

The low-low-pass subimage is again subjected to the above two-step process, by decreasing the value of the dilation index j by one. This provides further coarser decomposition of the image. This process is repeated until the desired number of steps, or until the output of low-low-pass filter becomes less interesting.

Note that the wavelets $\Phi(t_1, t_2)$ are the impulse response of a two-dimensional filter that is low-pass in both horizontal and vertical directions. $\Psi^{(0,1)}(t_1, t_2)$ is the impulse response of a two-dimensional filter that is low-pass in the horizontal direction and high-pass in the vertical direction. Therefore, the corresponding wavelet filter coefficients are mostly related to the image content in the horizontal direction. The filter coefficients corresponding to the wavelets $\Psi^{(1,0)}(t_1, t_2)$ are related to the image content in the vertical direction. Lastly, the filter coefficients corresponding to the wavelets $\Psi^{(1,1)}(t_1, t_2)$ are related to the image content in the diagonal direction. See Figure 6.1.

Low-low-pass filter (LL) $\Phi(t_1, t_2)$	High-low-pass filter (HL) $\Psi^{(1,0)}(t_1, t_2)$ Vertical direction
Low–high-pass filter (LH) $\Psi^{(0,1)}(t_1, t_2)$ Horizontal direction	High-high-pass filter (HH) $\Psi^{(1,1)}(t_1, t_2)$ Diagonal orientation

Figure 6.1. Two-dimensional wavelet decomposition.

The reconstruction of the image from the coefficients proceeds as in the case of the one-dimensional wavelets. For a given value of scale, the filters first operate upon the columns and then upon the rows of the subimage. The subimages thus obtained, are added up to obtain low-pass subimage at the next finer scale. This transformation is iterated until the original value of scale (resolution level) is reached.

Compression with Wavelets

First compute wavelet coefficients. Set to zero any coefficients that are close to zero. In the next step quantize the remaining coefficients. Quantization is the process of splitting the dynamic range of the coefficients into a finite number of intervals, and assigning to all the values of an interval the same value. The coefficients can then be output in standard order using arithmetic coding or Huffman coding. Better compression can be achieved by using the so-called zero-tree approach. These later coding techniques are described in any standard textbook on information theory.

6.4 Wavelet Neural Networks

The idea of combining artificial neural networks with wavelet transforms is explored in this section. Such networks are called wavelet neural networks. Wavelet neural networks exploit the properties of both artificial neural networks and wavelet transforms. Wavelet neural networks can be used for function approximation and representation. The use of wavelet neural networks is demonstrated in the classification of data points.

Artificial neural networks are initially introduced in this section. Wavelet neural networks use the method of gradient descent. Therefore, these are next discussed. Finally, the synergy between artificial neural networks and wavelet transforms is explored. Wavelet networks with both scalar and vector inputs are considered.

6.4.1 Artificial Neural Network

The study of artificial neural networks (ANN) originally began with the goal of studying biological neural systems. For our discussion, the human brain consists of *neurons, axons, dendrites*, and *synapses*.

Neurons are nerve cells, which are connected to other neurons via strands of fiber called axons (transmission lines). The purpose of axons is to transmit nerve impulses between two neurons whenever the stimulation of neurons occur. The axons of two different neurons are connected via dendrites. The dendrites are extensions from the cell body of the neurons. The synapse is the contact point between a dendrite and an axon.

Artificial neural networks try to simulate biological neural activity. Using the analogy of biological neurons and their interconnections, an artificial neural network can be considered to be an assemblage of nodes and directed links. The use of ANNs in classification of data points is demonstrated in this subsection. In rest of this subsection, an artificial neuron is simply referred to as a neuron.

Perceptron

The perceptron is a useful model of ANN. It consists of two types of nodes. These are the input nodes and a single output node. The input and output nodes are representations of the input attributes and the model output respectively. The output node of the perceptron simulates a neuron. Each input node is directly connected to the output node via a weighted link. The weighted link simulates the strength of the synaptic connection between the neurons. The output node performs mathematical operations, and generates the classification of the data points. The weights of the input nodes are trained by the learning data points to possibly produce correct classification at the output node. Once the weights are determined, the classification of a test data point can be determined.

The definition of a perceptron is initially provided. This is followed by a description of the perceptron learning algorithm.

Definition 6.1. *Let* $t \in \mathbb{P}$. *The set of data points, and the set of labels of the classes of the data points are* $\mathcal{X} \subseteq \mathbb{R}^t$, *and* $\Omega = \{-1, 1\}$ *respectively. Consider a data point* $(\zeta_1, \zeta_2, \ldots, \zeta_t) \in \mathcal{X}$. *Also let* $(w_1, w_2, \ldots, w_t) \in \mathbb{R}^t$ *be the synaptic weight vector, and* $\beta \in \mathbb{R}$ *be the bias factor, and*

$$v = \sum_{j=1}^{t} w_j \zeta_j + \beta \tag{6.2a}$$

The perceptron is the function $f_{percep} : \mathcal{X} \to \Omega$, *where*

$$f_{percep}(\zeta_1, \zeta_2, \ldots, \zeta_t) = sgn(v) \in \Omega \tag{6.2b}$$

□

The $sgn(\cdot)$ function is defined as: $sgn(x) = 1$ if $x > 0$, and $sgn(x) = -1$ if $x < 0$. In the above definition, the $sgn(\cdot)$ function emulates a neuron. It is one of severable possible such functions which can model a neuron. It is an example of an *activation function*. More such functions are discussed later in this subsection. Also, $v = \sum_{j=1}^{t} w_j \zeta_j + \beta$ is the equation of a hyperplane.

As the name suggests, a hyperplane is simply an extension of the concept of a straight line in two-dimensional space, and a plane in three-dimensional space into a higher-dimensional space.

Consequently, the perceptron can be used to classify linearly separable data points. However, a major challenge is to determine the weight vector and the bias factor of the perceptron.

For simplicity in discussion, let $\zeta_0 \triangleq 1$, $w_0 \triangleq \beta$, $\zeta \triangleq (\zeta_0, \zeta_1, \zeta_2, \ldots, \zeta_t)$ be the extended data point, and $w \triangleq (w_0, w_1, w_2, \ldots, w_t)$ be the extended weight vector. Therefore, $v = w\zeta^T$, and the output of the perceptron is equal to $sgn(v)$.

Assume that the training data set is

$$\mathcal{D} = \left\{ (x_i, y_i) \mid x_i \in \mathcal{X} \subseteq \mathbb{R}^t, y_i \in \Omega, 1 \leq i \leq n \right\}$$

The weight vector and the bias factor are determined by the training data set $\mathcal{D}$. An iterative learning algorithm is proposed to determine the extended weight vector. Let $x_{i0} = 1$, and $x_i = (x_{i1}, x_{i2}, \ldots, x_{it}) \in \mathcal{X}$. The weights are updated as

$$\Delta_i^{(k)} = \left(y_i - y_i^{(k)} \right)$$
$$w_j^{(k+1)} = w_j^{(k)} + \mu \Delta_i^{(k)} x_{ij}, \quad 0 \leq j \leq t$$

After iteration number $k \in \mathbb{P}$; $w_j^{(k)}$ is the weight parameter for $0 \leq j \leq t$, and $w^{(k)}$ is the corresponding weight vector. The parameter μ, is called the *learning rate*. Typically $\mu \in (0, 1]$. Also

$$y_i^{(k)} = sgn\left(\sum_{j=0}^{t} w_j^{(k)} x_{ij} \right)$$

Justification of the above expression for updating the weights is as follows. The new weight is equal to the sum of the old weight and a correctional term. The correctional term is actually proportional to $\Delta_i^{(k)}$. If the prediction of the classification is correct, then the value of the correction term is equal zero, otherwise it is modified as:

- Let $y_i = -1$, and $y_i^{(k)} = +1$. Therefore, $\Delta_i^{(k)} = -2$. To mitigate the error, $w_j^{(k+1)}$ is decreased if x_{ij} is positive; and increased if x_{ij} is negative.

- Let $y_i = +1$, and $y_i^{(k)} = -1$. Therefore, $\Delta_i^{(k)} = 2$. To mitigate the error, $w_j^{(k+1)}$ is increased if x_{ij} is positive; and decreased if x_{ij} is negative.

Note that the argument of the activation function $sgn\,(\cdot)$ in the expression for $y_i^{(k)}$, is a linear function of the weight vector, bias factor, and the data point. Therefore, the assumed decision boundary of the two classes is a hyperplane. If the data points are linearly separable, the iterative training algorithm converges to an optimal solution. However, if the data points are not linearly separable, then the algorithm does not converge.

In the above discussion, the activation function was $sgn\,(\cdot)$. Some other examples of activation function are:

- *Unit step function*: The unit step function is:

$$u\,(x) = \begin{cases} 1, & x > 0 \\ 0, & x < 0 \end{cases}$$

  Thus $u\,(x) = (1 + sgn\,(x))\,/2$.

- *Sigmoid or logistic function*: The sigmoid or logistic function for $a \in \mathbb{R}^+$ is:

$$f\,(x) = \frac{1}{1 + \exp\,(-ax)}, \quad x \in \mathbb{R}$$

  The value, $f\,(x)$ is bounded between 0 and 1, and is differentiable for all $x \in \mathbb{R}$.

- *Hyperbolic tangent function*: The hyperbolic tangent function for $a \in \mathbb{R}^+$ is:

$$f\,(x) = \frac{1 - \exp\,(-ax)}{1 + \exp\,(-ax)} = \tanh\left(\frac{ax}{2}\right), \quad x \in \mathbb{R}$$

  The value, $f\,(x)$ is bounded between -1 and 1, and is differentiable for all $x \in \mathbb{R}$.

6.4.2 Gradient Descent

The gradient of a multivariable function is a generalization of the derivative of a single variable function. Its use in the steepest descent algorithm is discussed in this section. Steepest descent algorithm is a numerical technique to find a minima of a function. Steepest descent is also called gradient descent. Its use in a probabilistic context is also outlined. In this case, the technique is called stochastic gradient descent.

Definitions 6.2. *Gradient of a function. Let $\Omega \subseteq \mathbb{R}^n$, and $f\,(\cdot)$ be a real-valued function; where $f\,:\,\Omega \to \mathbb{R}$, $x = (x_1, x_2, \ldots, x_n)$, and $x \in \Omega$. The gradient of $f(x)$, denoted by $\nabla f\,(x)$, is a vector of partial derivatives*

$$\nabla f\,(x) = \left(\frac{\partial f\,(x)}{\partial x_1}, \frac{\partial f\,(x)}{\partial x_2}, \ldots, \frac{\partial f\,(x)}{\partial x_n}\right) \triangleq \frac{\partial f\,(x)}{\partial x} \tag{6.3}$$

provided the partial derivatives exist. □

In the above definition, gradient is represented as a row vector. The gradient of a three-dimensional function $\phi(x, y, z)$ can also represented as

$$\nabla \phi = \left(\frac{\partial \phi}{\partial x}, \frac{\partial \phi}{\partial y}, \frac{\partial \phi}{\partial z} \right)$$
$$= i \frac{\partial \phi}{\partial x} + j \frac{\partial \phi}{\partial y} + k \frac{\partial \phi}{\partial z}$$

where $(1, 0, 0) \triangleq i$, $(0, 1, 0) \triangleq j$, and $(0, 0, 1) \triangleq k$. The vectors i, j, and k are along the x-axis, y-axis, and z-axis respectively in the space $\mathbb{R}^3$.

Observation 6.2. Let $\phi(x, y, z)$ be a three-dimensional function whose gradient exists. Let $r = (ix + jy + kz)$, and $ds = \left(dx^2 + dy^2 + dz^2 \right)^{1/2}$. Then

$$\frac{d\phi}{ds} = \frac{\partial \phi}{\partial x} \frac{\partial x}{\partial s} + \frac{\partial \phi}{\partial y} \frac{\partial y}{\partial s} + \frac{\partial \phi}{\partial z} \frac{\partial z}{\partial s}$$
$$= \nabla \phi \circ \frac{dr}{ds}$$

where $\circ$ is the dot product operator.   □

Example 6.1. Let $\phi(x, y, z)$ be a differentiable function defined at each point (x, y, z) in a certain region of $\mathbb{R}^3$. Therefore, the gradient of the function ϕ exists in this region. We establish that the greatest rate of change of ϕ takes place in the direction of the vector $\nabla \phi$. Further, its magnitude is equal to $\|\nabla \phi\|$, where $\|\cdot\|$ is the Euclidean norm. Observe that

$$\frac{d\phi}{ds} = \nabla \phi \circ \frac{dr}{ds}$$

is the projection of $\nabla \phi$ in the direction of dr/ds. This projection is maximum when $\nabla \phi$ and dr/ds have the same direction. Then $d\phi/ds$ takes maximum value in the direction of the gradient $\nabla \phi$. Further, its magnitude is

$$\left| \frac{d\phi}{ds} \right| = \|\nabla \phi\| \left\| \frac{dr}{ds} \right\|$$
$$= \|\nabla \phi\|$$

The last result follows because

$$\left\| \frac{dr}{ds} \right\| = \sqrt{\left(dx^2 + dy^2 + dz^2 \right) / ds^2}$$
$$= 1$$

□

Gradient Descent Algorithm

The gradient or steepest descent algorithm is a numerical technique to determine a minima of a function. It is assumed that the minima exists. The main idea of this algorithm is best demonstrated in one dimension. Consider a function $f : \mathbb{R} \to \mathbb{R}$, whose first derivative exists at each point in its domain.

The steepest descent algorithm begins at a point $x_0 \in \mathbb{R}$, and progresses through points $x_1, x_2, x_3, \ldots$ and so on, so that $f(x_0) \geq f(x_1) \geq f(x_2) \geq \ldots$.

Denote the first derivative of $f(x)$ with respect to $x \in \mathbb{R}$ as $f'(x)$. For $x \in \mathbb{R}$ and small ϵ, we have

$$f(x + \epsilon) \simeq f(x) + \epsilon f'(x)$$

In the above relationship, substitute $\epsilon = -\eta f'(x)$, where η is a small positive constant. This leads to

$$f(x - \eta f'(x)) \simeq f(x) - \eta (f'(x))^2$$
$$\leq f(x)$$

Therefore, steepest descent is achieved if we use the recursion

$$x_{k+1} = x_k - \eta f'(x_k), \quad k = 0, 1, 2, \ldots$$

for appropriate small positive value of η. This parameter η is called the *learning rate* or *step size*. If the value of η is high, then it is possible for the algorithm to overshoot the minima and oscillate. However, if it is too small, then the convergence of the algorithm to a minima will be too slow. Therefore, a proper value of η is determined experimentally (trial and error). In order for the algorithm to achieve its true minima, the initial value x_0 should be selected appropriately.

If f is a function of several variables, then the first derivative of a single variable function in the above discussion is replaced by its gradient. In this case, the value of the vector x is updated as

$$x \leftarrow x - \eta \nabla f(x)$$

In practice, the gradient descent algorithm is terminated, if either a prespecified maximum number of iterations have been reached or if the Euclidean norm $\|\nabla f(x_k)\| \leq \delta$, where δ is a prespecified small number.

Stochastic Gradient Descent

In the stochastic gradient descent algorithm, a representative and manageable-sized data set $\mathcal{D}$ is selected. Let this data set be

$$\mathcal{D} = \{z_i \mid 1 \leq i \leq N\}$$

Further, let the nonnegative objective function to be minimized be

$$C\left(\theta\right) = \sum_{z_i \in \mathcal{D}} e\left(\theta, z_i\right)$$

where θ is the vector of unknown variables. The vector θ which minimizes $C\left(\theta\right)$ has to be determined. Then the gradient is computed at each point in the data set $\mathcal{D}$. The gradients thus computed are averaged as

$$\nabla e_{\mathcal{D}}\left(\theta\right) = \frac{1}{|\mathcal{D}|} \sum_{z_i \in \mathcal{D}} \nabla e\left(\theta, z_i\right)$$

The vector θ is updated as

$$\theta \leftarrow \theta - \eta \nabla e_{\mathcal{D}}\left(\theta\right)$$

where $\eta \in (0, 1]$ is the learning rate or step size. The parameter η determines the speed of convergence of the algorithm.

6.4.3 Wavelets and Neural Networks

A wavelet neural network consists of artificial neural networks where the activation functions are wavelets. The neurons which use wavelets as activation functions are called *wavelons*. If a set of observed values of a function is known, then it might be possible to find its representation in terms of activation functions which are members of an orthonormal family of wavelets.

Let $\psi : \mathbb{R} \to \mathbb{R}$ be a mother wavelet function, and

$$\psi_{\alpha, u}\left(x\right) = \frac{1}{\sqrt{\alpha}} \psi\left(\frac{x - u}{\alpha}\right), \quad \text{where } \alpha \in \mathbb{R}^+, \; u \in \mathbb{R}, \; x \in \mathbb{R}$$

In the above expression, α and u represent dilation and translation of the mother wavelet $\psi\left(\cdot\right)$ respectively. Further $\widetilde{\Psi}$ is a denumerable family of wavelet functions of the form

$$\widetilde{\Psi} = \left\{\psi_{\lambda_l, t_l}\left(x\right) \mid \lambda_l \in \mathbb{R}^+, \; t_l \in \mathbb{R}, \; x \in \mathbb{R}, \; l \in \mathbb{Z}\right\}$$

These functions satisfy the frame property. That is, there exist two constants $c_{\min}$ and $c_{\max}$, where $0 < c_{\min} \leq c_{\max} < \infty$, and for all functions $f\left(\cdot\right) \in L^2\left(\mathbb{R}\right)$ we have

$$c_{\min} \|f\|^2 \leq \sum_{\psi \in \widetilde{\Psi}} |\langle x, f \rangle|^2 \leq c_{\max} \|f\|^2$$

where $\langle \cdot, \cdot \rangle$ is the inner product operator in $L^2\left(\mathbb{R}\right)$. A function $f\left(\cdot\right) \in L^2\left(\mathbb{R}\right)$ is approximated as $g\left(\cdot\right)$, where

$$g\left(x\right) = \sum_{j=1}^{M} w_j \psi_{\lambda_j, t_j}\left(x\right) + \overline{g}, \quad x \in \mathbb{R}$$

where $w_j \in \mathbb{R}$, $\lambda_j \in \mathbb{R}^+$, $t_j \in \mathbb{R}$ for $1 \leq j \leq M$; and $\bar{g} \in \mathbb{R}$.

This neural network model has M number of wavelons. Further, the output neuron is simply a *summer* (which performs M number of additions). Observe that the output is a weighted sum of the wavelon outputs and the constant term $\bar{g}$. As the wavelet function $\psi(\cdot)$ has a zero mean, the inclusion of the term $\bar{g}$ in the model accounts for functions with nonzero mean.

The unknowns in the expression for $g(x)$ are: w_j, λ_j, t_j for $1 \leq j \leq M$; and $\bar{g}$. These unknowns in vector notation are:

$$w = (w_1, w_2, \ldots, w_M)$$
$$\lambda = (\lambda_1, \lambda_2, \ldots, \lambda_M)$$
$$t = (t_1, t_2, \ldots, t_M)$$
$$\theta = (w, \lambda, t, \bar{g})$$

Observe that θ is a vector of all the unknowns in the model.

6.4.4 Learning Algorithm

The learning algorithm for the vector parameter θ which uses a set of random data points $\mathcal{D}$, is next described. It is

$$\mathcal{D} = \{(x_i, y_i) \mid x_i \in \mathbb{R}, y_i = f(x_i) \in \mathbb{R}, 1 \leq i \leq N\}$$

Actually $f(x_i) = (h(x_i) + \epsilon_i)$, where ϵ_i is the noise component of $f(x_i)$ for $1 \leq i \leq N$. Further the mean $\mathcal{E}(\epsilon_i) = 0$, and the random variables ϵ_i's are independent of each other for $1 \leq i \leq N$. In order to denote the dependence of $g(\cdot)$ on the unknown vector θ, we denote it as $g_\theta(\cdot)$. The unknown vector θ is determined by minimizing

$$C(\theta) = \frac{1}{2} \mathcal{E} \left\{ \sum_{i=1}^{N} (c(\theta, x_i))^2 \right\}$$
$$c(\theta, x) = (g_\theta(x) - f(x))$$

The optimization is numerically performed by using the method of stochastic gradient descent. This is determined by computing the gradient of

$$e(\theta, x) = \frac{1}{2} (c(\theta, x))^2$$
$$= \frac{1}{2} (g_\theta(x) - f(x))^2$$

with respect to the vector θ at each of the N data points. We denote the first derivative of $\psi_{\lambda_j, t_j}(x)$ with respect to x by $\psi'_{\lambda_j, t_j}(x)$. The required partial derivatives are:

$$\frac{\partial e\left(\theta, x\right)}{\partial w_j} = c\left(\theta, x\right)\psi_{\lambda_j, t_j}(x), \quad 1 \le j \le M$$

$$\frac{\partial e\left(\theta, x\right)}{\partial \lambda_j} = -c\left(\theta, x\right)\frac{w_j}{2\lambda_j}\left\{\psi_{\lambda_j, t_j}(x) - \frac{2t_j}{\lambda_j}\psi'_{\lambda_j, t_j}(x)\right\}, \quad 1 \le j \le M$$

$$\frac{\partial e\left(\theta, x\right)}{\partial t_j} = -c\left(\theta, x\right)\frac{w_j}{\lambda_j}\psi'_{\lambda_j, t_j}(x), \quad 1 \le j \le M$$

$$\frac{\partial e\left(\theta, x\right)}{\partial g} = c\left(\theta, x\right)$$

Using the above partial derivatives, the gradient $\nabla e\left(\theta, x\right)$ can be determined. The stochastic gradient for the set of data points $\mathcal{D}$ is

$$\nabla e_{\mathcal{D}}\left(\theta\right) = \frac{1}{|\mathcal{D}|} \sum_{(x_i, y_i) \in \mathcal{D}} \nabla e\left(\theta, x_i\right)$$

where $|\mathcal{D}| = N$. The vector θ is updated as

$$\theta \leftarrow \theta - \eta \nabla e_{\mathcal{D}}\left(\theta\right)$$

where $\eta \in (0, 1]$ is the learning rate or step size. The parameter η determines the speed of convergence of the algorithm. As θ is determined iteratively, the vector θ in iteration number $k \in \mathbb{N}$ is denoted as θ_k. Thus

$$\theta_{k+1} \leftarrow \theta_k - \eta \nabla e_{\mathcal{D}}(\theta_k), \quad \text{where } k \in \mathbb{N}$$

In order to develop the algorithm further, constraints on adjustable parameters have to be specified. In addition, as the learning algorithm is iterative, initialization of the vector θ (equal to θ_0) has to be described. Further, as the stochastic descent algorithm is numerical, the number of steps in the algorithm also have to be specified.

Constraints on the Adjustable Parameters

Assume that the function $f\left(\cdot\right)$ is approximated, and its domain is $\mathbb{R}_\omega \subset \mathbb{R}$. Let $f : \mathbb{R}_\omega \to \mathbb{R}$. Then

(a) Wavelets should be kept inside or near the domain $\mathbb{R}_\omega$. In order to accomplish this select another domain $\mathbb{R}_W$ such that $\mathbb{R}_\omega \subset \mathbb{R}_W \subset \mathbb{R}$; and let

$$t_j \in \mathbb{R}_W, \quad \text{for } 1 \le j \le M$$

(b) Wavelets should not be excessively compressed. Therefore, select $\epsilon > 0$ so that

$$\lambda_j > \epsilon, \quad \text{for } 1 \le j \le M$$

Initialization of the Vector θ

Initialization of the vector θ_0. Let $\mathbb{R}_\omega = [a, b]$.

(a) Set $w_j = 0$, for $1 \leq j \leq M$.

(b) Initialization of t_j and λ_j, for $1 \leq j \leq M$. Select a point p so that $a < p < b$, and set $t_1 = p$. Let $\lambda_1 = (b - a)\xi$ where $\xi > 0$. A possible value of ξ is 0.5. This initialization procedure is repeated for the intervals $[a, p]$ and $[p, b]$. The interval $[a, p]$ is used for setting t_2 and λ_2, and the interval $[p, b]$ is used for setting t_3 and λ_3. This scheme is repeated recursively until each wavelon is initialized. Note that this scheme is possible, if $M = (2^L - 1)$ for some positive integer L.

If the integer M is not of this form, then the remaining uninitialized wavelons cannot cover the next resolution level. Therefore, these remaining wavelons are initialized to random translations (the t_j's) in the remaining finest scale.

(c) The scalar $\bar{g}$ is initialized to a value equal to the average value of all possible observations.

Stopping Criteria for the Learning Algorithm

The wavelon learning algorithm is stopped when any one of the following conditions is satisfied.

(a) The Euclidean norm of the gradient or of the variation of the gradient, reaches a lower bound.

(b) The number of iterations in the stochastic gradient algorithm reaches a prespecified maximum value.

Performance of the Learning Algorithm

The ultimate performance of the learning algorithm depends upon the following:

(a) The points in the training data set $\mathcal{D}$ are not too noisy.

(b) The size of the data set $|\mathcal{D}|$ is sufficiently large.

(c) The selected wavelet $\psi(\cdot)$ and its modifications are good enough to model the function $f(\cdot)$.

If the performance of the learning algorithm is not good, then it is also possible to examine multidimensional wavelet neural networks. It is also possible to use a combination of scaling functions and artificial neural networks.

6.4.5 Wavelons with Vector Inputs

Preceding subsections considered wavelons with scalar inputs. Wavelons with vector inputs are considered in this subsection. The primary purpose of a wavelet network is to attune the wavelet basis to the training data set. We consider a wavelet network which takes a real-valued vector as input and produces a scalar. That is, this framework is a multi-input/ single-output structure. The wavelet neural network is organized in three layers.

- The first layer is the lower or input layer. It accepts data points, where each data point is a vector of real-valued elements. It transmits the accepted inputs to the second layer.

- The second layer is often called the middle or hidden layer. It is made up of a combination of several wavelons. Therefore, it can also be termed the wavelon layer. Each node in this layer is made up of multidimensional wavelets.

- The third layer is the output layer. It produces a scalar output.

In this subsection x is a vector in space $\mathbb{R}^n$, where $x = (x_1, x_2, \ldots, x_n)$. The function $f(\cdot) \in L^2(\mathbb{R}^n)$ is approximated as $g(\cdot)$, where

$$g(x) = \sum_{j=1}^{M} w_j \widetilde{\psi}_j(x) + \sum_{i=1}^{n} a_i x_i + \overline{g}, \quad x \in \mathbb{R}^n$$

where $w_j \in \mathbb{R}$, for $1 \leq j \leq M$, and $a_i \in \mathbb{R}$, for $1 \leq i \leq n$ are the weights; and $\overline{g} \in \mathbb{R}$. Also $\widetilde{\psi}_j(x) \in \mathbb{R}$, for $1 \leq j \leq M$ are the multidimensional wavelets (wavelons). These wavelets are defined as the product of n number of scalar wavelets. These are

$$\widetilde{\psi}_j(x) = \prod_{i=1}^{n} \psi(z_{ij}), \quad 1 \leq j \leq M$$

$$z_{ij} = \frac{x_i - v_{ij}}{\beta_{ij}}, \quad \beta_{ij} \in \mathbb{R}^+, \quad v_{ij} \in \mathbb{R}, \quad 1 \leq i \leq n, \ 1 \leq j \leq M$$

The vector elements, x_i, for $1 \leq i \leq n$, of the vector x are the data points in the input layer of the artificial neural network. The M number of multidimensional wavelets reside in the second (hidden) layer. Note that the β_{ij}'s and v_{ij}'s are the dilation and translation parameters respectively. The third layer is simply the final value $g(x)$.

The unknowns in the expression for $g(x)$ are: w_j, for $1 \leq j \leq M$; a_i, for $1 \leq i \leq n$, $\overline{g}$; and β_{ij}, v_{ij}, for $1 \leq i \leq n$, and $1 \leq j \leq M$. These unknowns are compactly expressed as:

$$w = (w_1, w_2, \ldots, w_M)$$
$$a = (a_1, a_2, \ldots, a_n)$$
$$\beta = \{\beta_{ij} \mid 1 \leq i \leq n, 1 \leq j \leq M\}$$
$$v = \{v_{ij} \mid 1 \leq i \leq n, 1 \leq j \leq M\}$$
$$\theta = (w, a, \beta, v, \overline{g})$$

Observe that θ is a vector of all the unknowns in the model.

The learning algorithm for the vector parameter θ which uses a set of random data points $\mathcal{D}$, is next described. The set $\mathcal{D}$ is

$$\mathcal{D} = \left\{ \left(x^{(m)}, y^{(m)} \right) \mid x^{(m)} \in \mathbb{R}^n, y^{(m)} = f\left(x^{(m)} \right) \in \mathbb{R}; 1 \le m \le N \right\}$$

Actually

$$f\left(x^{(m)} \right) = \left(h\left(x^{(m)} \right) + \epsilon_m \right),$$

where ϵ_m is the noise component of $f\left(x^{(m)} \right)$ for $1 \le m \le N$. Further, the mean $\mathcal{E}\left(\epsilon_m \right) = 0$, and the random variables ϵ_m's are independent of each other for $1 \le m \le N$. In order to denote the dependence of $g\left(\cdot \right)$ on the unknown vector θ, we denote it as $g_\theta\left(\cdot \right)$. The unknown vector θ is determined by minimizing

$$C\left(\theta \right) = \frac{1}{2}\mathcal{E}\left\{ \sum_{m=1}^{N} \left(c\left(\theta, x^{(m)} \right) \right)^2 \right\}$$

$$c\left(\theta, x \right) = \left(g_\theta\left(x \right) - f\left(x \right) \right)$$

The optimization is numerically performed by using the method of stochastic gradient descent. This is determined by initially computing the gradient of

$$e\left(\theta, x \right) = \frac{1}{2}\left(c\left(\theta, x \right) \right)^2$$

$$= \frac{1}{2}\left(g_\theta\left(x \right) - f\left(x \right) \right)^2$$

with respect to the vector θ at each of the N data points. Denote the derivative of $\psi\left(t \right)$ with respect to t by $\psi'\left(t \right)$. The required partial derivatives evaluated at data point $x = \left(x_1, x_2, \ldots, x_n \right)$ are

$$\frac{\partial e\left(\theta, x \right)}{\partial w_j} = c\left(\theta, x \right) \widetilde{\psi}_j(x), \quad 1 \le j \le M$$

$$\frac{\partial e\left(\theta, x \right)}{\partial a_i} = c\left(\theta, x \right) x_i, \quad 1 \le i \le n$$

$$\frac{\partial e\left(\theta, x \right)}{\partial v_{ij}} = -c\left(\theta, x \right) \frac{w_j}{\beta_{ij}} \psi\left(z_{1j} \right) \cdots \psi'\left(z_{ij} \right) \cdots \psi(z_{nj}),$$

$$1 \le i \le n, \ 1 \le j \le M$$

$$\frac{\partial e\left(\theta, x \right)}{\partial \beta_{ij}} = z_{ij} \frac{\partial e\left(\theta, x \right)}{\partial v_{ij}},$$

$$1 \le i \le n, \ 1 \le j \le M$$

$$\frac{\partial e\left(\theta, x \right)}{\partial \overline{g}} = c\left(\theta, x \right)$$

Using the above partial derivatives, the gradient $\nabla e\left(\theta, x \right)$ can be determined. The stochastic gradient for the set of data points $\mathcal{D}$ can be computed as in the last subsection. A steepest descent iterative algorithm for determining the vector θ can then be used (described in the last subsection). In order to develop the iterative learning algorithm further, initialization of the vector θ has to be specified.

Initialization of the Vector θ

(a) Elements of the vector w and a are initialized by small random numbers in the interval $[0, 1]$.

(b) Initialization of β_{ij} and v_{ij} for $1 \le i \le n$, $1 \le j \le M$. Define $x_i^{\min}$ and $x_i^{\max}$ as the minimum and maximum values of the ith coordinate of the set of data points $\mathcal{D}$, where $i = 1, 2, \ldots, n$. That is,

$$x_i^{\min} = \min_{1 \le m \le N} x_i^{(m)}, \quad 1 \le i \le n$$

$$x_i^{\max} = \max_{1 \le m \le N} x_i^{(m)}, \quad 1 \le i \le n$$

The initialization of the translation and dilation parameters are

$$v_{ij} = \frac{1}{2} \left(x_i^{\max} + x_i^{\min} \right)$$

$$\beta_{ij} = \delta \left(x_i^{\max} - x_i^{\min} \right)$$

respectively, where $1 \le i \le n$, $1 \le j \le M$. Further, the value of δ is typically 0.2. Note that in this scheme, the center of the wavelet j is initialized at the center of the parallelepiped specified by the set of input data points.

(c) The scalar $\overline{g}$ is initialized to a value equal to average value of all possible observations.

Candidate Wavelet Functions

Some possible wavelet functions which can be used for the function $\psi(\cdot)$ are: Mexican-hat wavelet, Morlet, and Gaussian derivative wavelet. Recall that a Mexican-hat wavelet is defined as

$$\psi(t) = \left(1 - t^2\right) e^{-t^2/2}, \quad t \in \mathbb{R}$$

A real-valued Morlet is

$$\psi_c(t) = \frac{e^{-t^2/2}}{\sqrt{2\pi}} \cos \omega_0 t, \quad t \in \mathbb{R}$$

where ω_0 is typically greater than or equal to five. A Gaussian derivative wavelet is

$$\psi(t) = t e^{-t^2/2}, \quad t \in \mathbb{R}$$

Note that, if $g(t) = e^{-t^2/2}$, $t \in \mathbb{R}$; then $\psi(t) = -dg(t)/dt$. Hence the name Gaussian derivative wavelet.

Problems

1. This problem is related to signal denoising via wavelet transforms. Let

$$\mathfrak{N} = \begin{bmatrix} N_0 \; N_1 \; \cdots \; N_{N-1} \end{bmatrix}^T$$

$$U = A\mathfrak{N} = \begin{bmatrix} U_0 \; U_1 \; \cdots \; U_{N-1} \end{bmatrix}^T$$

The elements N_i, $0 \le i \le (N-1)$ of the noise vector $\mathfrak{N}$ form a Gaussian white noise process with parameter σ. Also A is the orthogonal transform matrix.

Prove that U_i is normally distributed with mean 0, and variance σ^2. Further, the random variable U_i is independent of random variable U_j, where $i \ne j$, and $0 \le i, j \le (N-1)$. That is, $\{U_i \mid 0 \le i \le (N-1)\}$ is a Gaussian white noise process with parameter σ. This statement implies that an orthogonal transform maps a Gaussian white noise process into the same Gaussian white noise process.

Establish the above assertion.

Hint: Let

$$t = \begin{bmatrix} t_0 \; t_1 \; \cdots \; t_{N-1} \end{bmatrix}^T$$

The moment-generating function of $\mathfrak{N}$ is

$$\mathcal{M}_{\mathfrak{N}}(t) = \exp\left\{ \frac{1}{2} t^T \Xi t \right\}$$

where the covariance matrix Ξ is a diagonal matrix of size N, and

$$\Xi = diag\left(\sigma^2, \sigma^2, \ldots, \sigma^2\right)$$

Note that $U = A\mathfrak{N}$ is a linear transformation, and its moment-generating function is

$$\mathcal{M}_U(t) = \exp\left\{ \frac{1}{2} t^T \Psi t \right\}$$

where the covariance matrix $\Psi = A\Xi A^T = \Xi$. This is true because $AA^T = I$, where I is an identity matrix of size N. Thus $\{U_i \mid 0 \le i \le (N-1)\}$ is also a Gaussian white noise process with parameter σ.

2. Let $U_0, U_1, \ldots, U_{N-1}$ be independent and identically distributed normal random variables, each with cumulative distribution function $F_U(u)$, $u \in \mathbb{R}$. The mean and variance of the random variables are 0 and σ^2.

Define $V_i = |U_i|$, $0 \le i \le (N-1)$, and $Z = \max\{V_0, V_1, \ldots, V_{N-1}\}$. Let the cumulative distribution function of Z be $F_Z(z)$, $z \in \mathbb{R}$. Then the complementary cumulative distribution function, $F_Z^c(\cdot)$ of the random variable Z is

$$F_Z^c(z) \simeq \frac{2\sigma N}{\sqrt{2\pi} z} \exp(-z^2/(2\sigma^2)), \quad \text{as } z \to \infty$$

Further, if $\theta = \sigma \sqrt{2 \ln (N)}$, then

$$F_Z^c(\theta) \simeq \frac{1}{\sqrt{\pi \ln(N)}}$$

Establish the above assertion.

Hint: This result is established in several steps.

Step 1: Let U be a normally distributed random variable with mean 0, variance σ^2, and cumulative distribution function $F_U(u)$. Let $V = |U|$. Then the tail of the distribution $F_V(\cdot)$ is approximated as

$$F_V^c(v) \simeq \frac{2\sigma \exp\left(-v^2/(2\sigma^2)\right)}{\sqrt{2\pi} v}, \quad \text{as } v \to \infty$$

This result was established in the problem section of the chapter on probability theory and stochastic processes.

Step 2: As per the hypothesis of the problem, it is given that $U_0, U_1, \ldots, U_{N-1}$ are independent and identically distributed random variables.

Therefore, $V_0, V_1, \ldots, V_{N-1}$ are also independent and identically distributed random variables. Denote a generic such random variable by V. If

$$Z = \max\{V_0, V_1, \ldots, V_{N-1}\}$$

then

$$F_Z(z) = (F_V(z))^N$$

This result has been established in the problem section of the chapter on probability theory and stochastic processes.

Step 3: The results of the above steps are next combined. We have for $z \to \infty$

$$F_Z(z) = (1 - F_V^c(z))^N$$

$$\simeq \left(1 - \frac{2\sigma \exp\left(-z^2/(2\sigma^2)\right)}{\sqrt{2\pi} z}\right)^N$$

$$\simeq 1 - \frac{2\sigma N \exp\left(-z^2/(2\sigma^2)\right)}{\sqrt{2\pi} z}$$

That is,

$$F_Z^c(z) \simeq \frac{2\sigma N \exp\left(-z^2/(2\sigma^2)\right)}{\sqrt{2\pi} z}$$

If $\theta = \sigma \sqrt{2 \ln (N)}$, then

$$F_Z^c(\theta) \simeq \frac{1}{\sqrt{\pi \ln(N)}}$$

PART II

Intermediate Topics

CHAPTER 7

Periodic Wavelet Transform

7.1 Introduction

Periodic wavelet transforms are studied in this chapter. In many practical applications, the functions to be transformed are defined on a compact set. An example of a compact set on the real line $\mathbb{R}$ is an interval of finite length. A square or a rectangle of finite dimensions is an example of compact set in the xy-plane $\mathbb{R}^2$.

An immediate solution to this problem of data on a compact set is to pad the data with zeros, and apply the wavelet theory developed on the real line. However, this scheme introduces discontinuities at the end points of the interval. Another possible approach, is to make the data periodic, with period equal to the length of the compact interval. The wavelet theory that is developed in this chapter can then be applied to this periodic data. Nevertheless, assumption of periodicity might introduce edge effects at the end points.

Periodization of a function is initially defined and discussed. This is followed by a discussion of periodization of scaling and wavelet functions, and a periodic multiresolution analysis. These techniques are then applied to periodic series expansions. Finally, a fast periodic wavelet transform is developed.

Notation. Modulo operation: Let $p \in \mathbb{P}$ be the modulus, and $n \in \mathbb{Z}$, $\langle n \rangle_p \equiv n \,(\mathrm{mod}\, p)$, where

$$n \equiv q\,(\mathrm{mod}\, p) \Leftrightarrow n = rp + q, \ \ \forall\, r \in \mathbb{Z}$$

Ceiling operator: For $x \in \mathbb{R}$, $\lceil x \rceil$ = smallest integer greater than or equal to x. Floor operator: For $x \in \mathbb{R}$, $\lfloor x \rfloor$ = greatest integer less than or equal to x. $\qquad \square$

7.2 Periodization of a Function

A procedure for the periodization of a function is outlined in this section. In practical applications a function $f\,(\cdot)$ is defined on a compact support $[a, b] \subset \mathbb{R}$. A compact support is an interval of finite-length. Assume that $f\,(\cdot) \in L^2([a, b])$.

For simplicity assume that the support of the function $f(\cdot)$ is $[0,1]$. Such functions can be expanded in a series with orthogonal basis by periodizing scaling and wavelet functions. Therefore, the period of the function is 1.

Note parenthetically that if the $supp\ f(t) = [a,b]$, then the variable $t \in [a,b]$ can be transformed to τ so that $\tau \in [0,1]$. A modified function $f_m(\cdot)$ is obtained.

$$\tau = \frac{(t-a)}{(b-a)}, \qquad t \in [a,b]$$
$$t = \tau(b-a) + a, \qquad \tau \in [0,1]$$
$$f_m(\tau) = f(t), \qquad \tau \in [0,1]$$

A wavelet series expansion of the function $f_m(\cdot)$ can be obtained as outlined below. It is assumed in the rest of the chapter, that $supp\ f(t) = [0,1]$.

Definition 7.1. *A periodic function with period 1. Let $t \in \mathbb{R}$, and a function $f(\cdot)$*
is

$$f(t) = \begin{cases} f(t), & t \in [0,1] \\ 0, & t \notin [0,1] \end{cases} \tag{7.1a}$$

Let

$$\widehat{f}(t) = \sum_{n \in \mathbb{Z}} f(t+n), \qquad t \in \mathbb{R} \tag{7.1b}$$

It can be observed that $\widehat{f}(\cdot)$ is a periodic function with period 1.   □

7.3 Periodization of Scaling and Wavelet Functions

Periodization of scaling and wavelet functions is introduced in this section. This is followed by a brief discussion of its ramifications. Let $t \in \mathbb{R}$, and assume that the scaling and wavelet functions have a compact support. The compact support is $[0,1]$.

Definition 7.2. *Let $\phi_{jk}(t) = 2^{j/2}\phi(2^j t - k)$, and $\psi_{jk}(t) = 2^{j/2}\psi(2^j t - k)$, $t \in \mathbb{R}$ and $j,k \in \mathbb{Z}$. The periodized scaling and wavelet functions, each with period 1 are*

$$\widehat{\phi}_{jk}(t) = \sum_{n \in \mathbb{Z}} \phi_{jk}(t+n) \tag{7.2a}$$

$$\widehat{\psi}_{jk}(t) = \sum_{n \in \mathbb{Z}} \psi_{jk}(t+n) \tag{7.2b}$$

respectively.   □

Observations 7.1. Let $t \in \mathbb{R}$.

1. The periodic scaling and wavelet functions have a period of 1 each. This implies

$$\widehat{\phi}_{jk}(t+1) = \widehat{\phi}_{jk}(t)$$
$$\widehat{\psi}_{jk}(t+1) = \widehat{\psi}_{jk}(t)$$

2.

$$\widehat{\phi}_{jk}(t) = \sum_{n \in \mathbb{Z}} \phi_{j,k-2^j n}(t)$$
$$\widehat{\psi}_{jk}(t) = \sum_{n \in \mathbb{Z}} \psi_{j,k-2^j n}(t)$$

3.

$$\widehat{\phi}_{jk}(t) = 2^{-j/2}, \quad j \leq 0, \ k \in \mathbb{Z}$$

In particular

$$\widehat{\phi}_{0k}(t) = 1, \quad k \in \mathbb{Z}$$

4.

$$\widehat{\psi}_{jk}(t) = 0, \quad j \leq -1, \ k \in \mathbb{Z}$$

□

See the problem section for proofs of the above observations.

Observation 7.2. Let $j > 0$, then $\widehat{\phi}_{jk}(t)$ and $\widehat{\psi}_{jk}(t)$ are each periodic in the parameter k with period 2^j. Therefore, there are only 2^j distinct periodized scaling functions and only 2^j distinct periodized wavelet functions. These are

$$\left\{ \widehat{\phi}_{jk}(t) \mid j > 0, \ 0 \leq k \leq \left(2^j - 1\right) \right\}$$
$$\left\{ \widehat{\psi}_{jk}(t) \mid j > 0, \ 0 \leq k \leq \left(2^j - 1\right) \right\}$$

□

See the problem section for a proof of the above observation. It implies that $\phi_{jk} = \phi_{jk'}$ if $k \equiv k' \ (\mathrm{mod}\ 2^j)$. Similarly, $\psi_{jk} = \psi_{jk'}$ if $k \equiv k' \ (\mathrm{mod}\ 2^j)$.

Observation 7.3. Recall from the chapter on Daubechies wavelets that, if $\Psi(\omega)$ has a zero of order $N \in \mathbb{P}$ at $\omega = 0$, then

$$supp\ \phi(t) = supp\ h(n) = supp\ g(n) = supp\ \psi(t) = [0, 2N - 1]$$

$$supp\ \phi_{jk}(t) = supp\ \psi_{jk}(t) = \left[\frac{k}{2^j}, \frac{k + 2N - 1}{2^j}\right]$$

Let the length of the support interval of $\phi(t)$ be $M \in \mathbb{P}$. That is, $M = (2N - 1)$ is an odd integer. For Daubechies' wavelets, the length of the support interval of $\psi(t)$ is also M, then the length of the support interval of $\phi_{jk}(t)$ and $\psi_{jk}(t)$ is $2^{-j}M$.

If the j's are chosen such that $2^{-j}M \leq 1$, then the $\phi_{jk}(t+n)$ terms in the series expansion of $\widehat{\phi}_{jk}(t)$ do not overlap. Also the $\psi_{jk}(t+n)$ terms in the series expansion of $\widehat{\psi}_{jk}(t)$ do not overlap. Let the smallest value of j such that $2^{-j}M \leq 1$ be j_0. Then $j_0 = \lceil \log_2 M \rceil$.   □

Observation 7.4. The following orthonormal relationships are preserved for periodic scaling and wavelet functions over the interval $[0, 1]$. Let $j, k, l, m \in \mathbb{N}$, then

$$\int_0^1 \widehat{\phi}_{jk}(t)\overline{\widehat{\phi}_{jl}(t)}dt = \delta_{kl}, \quad k, l \in \left[0, 2^j - 1\right]$$

$$\int_0^1 \widehat{\psi}_{jk}(t)\overline{\widehat{\psi}_{jl}(t)}dt = \delta_{kl}, \quad k, l \in \left[0, 2^j - 1\right]$$

$$\int_0^1 \widehat{\psi}_{jk}(t)\overline{\widehat{\psi}_{ml}(t)}dt = 0, \quad k \in [0, 2^j - 1], \; l \in [0, 2^m - 1], \; j \neq m$$

$$\int_0^1 \widehat{\phi}_{jk}(t)\overline{\widehat{\psi}_{ml}(t)}dt = 0, \quad k \in [0, 2^j - 1], \; l \in [0, 2^m - 1], \; 0 \leq j \leq m$$

□

7.4 Periodic Multiresolution Analysis

Analogous to the multiresolution analysis on the real line $\mathbb{R}$, a periodic multiresolution analysis is described. The periodic multiresolution analysis of $L^2([0, 1])$ is a sequence of closed subspaces $\left\{\widehat{V}_j \mid \widehat{V}_j \subset L^2([0, 1]), \; j \in \mathbb{N}\right\}$, such that:

1. *Nesting property*: $\widehat{V}_j \subset \widehat{V}_{j+1}$, for all values of $j \in \mathbb{N}$. This is the nesting property of the subspaces.

2. *Closure property*: $\overline{\cup_{j \in \mathbb{N}}\widehat{V}_j} = L^2([0, 1])$. This is the closure property.

3. *Constant functions*: $\cap_{j \in \mathbb{Z}}\widehat{V}_j = \{$constant functions$\}$.

4. *Scaling property*: $f(\cdot) \in \widehat{V}_j \Leftrightarrow f(2\cdot) \in \widehat{V}_{j+1}$, for all values of $j \in \mathbb{N}$.

5. Let $\widehat{W}_j$ be the orthogonal complement of $\widehat{V}_j$ in $\widehat{V}_{j+1}$, then

$$\widehat{V}_{j+1} = \widehat{V}_j \oplus \widehat{W}_j, \quad j \in \mathbb{N}$$

This orthogonality relationship is indicated by $\widehat{V}_j \perp \widehat{W}_j$. Observe that $\widehat{V}_j \subset \widehat{V}_{j+1}$, however $\widehat{W}_j \cap \widehat{W}_k = \{0\}, j \neq k$, and $\forall \, j, k \in \mathbb{N}$.

6. Let $j \in \mathbb{N}$.

   (a) $\widehat{V}_j$ is spanned by $\left\{ \widehat{\phi}_{jk}(t), t \in [0,1] \mid 0 \le k \le (2^j - 1) \right\}$.

   (b) $\widehat{W}_j$ is spanned by $\left\{ \widehat{\psi}_{jk}(t), t \in [0,1] \mid 0 \le k \le (2^j - 1) \right\}$.   □

Observe that in the above specifications, the index j takes values in the set $\mathbb{N}$. This is true because functions in the subspace $\widehat{V}_j$ for $j \le 0$ are all constants.

Also let $\widehat{\phi}_{j0}(\cdot) \triangleq \widehat{\phi}_j(\cdot)$, where $j \in \mathbb{N}$. Note that there are some differences between the nonperiodic and periodic MRA. In both cases, there are multiresolution spaces. The basis functions for the spaces V_j's in the nonperiodic MRA are formed by translations and dilations of scaling function $\phi(\cdot)$. However, in the case of periodic MRA, it is generally impossible to determine $\widehat{\phi}_{j+1}(\cdot)$ from $\widehat{\phi}_j(\cdot)$. For example $\widehat{\phi}_0(\cdot)$ is a constant function. Therefore, it is not suitable to specify $\widehat{\phi}_1(\cdot)$.

Observations 7.5. Some observations about the periodic MRA.

1. $\widehat{V}_\infty = L^2([0,1])$.

2. Space $\widehat{W}_j$ is orthogonal to space $\widehat{W}_k$, where $j \ne k, j, k \in \mathbb{N}$

3. Also

$$\widehat{V}_{j+1} = \widehat{V}_0 \oplus \left\{ \bigoplus_{n=0}^{j} \widehat{W}_n \right\}, \qquad j \in \mathbb{N}$$

4. $L^2([0,1]) = \widehat{V}_0 \oplus \widehat{W}_0 \oplus \widehat{W}_1 \oplus \widehat{W}_2 \oplus \ldots = \widehat{V}_0 \oplus \left\{ \bigoplus_{n \in \mathbb{N}} \widehat{W}_n \right\}$.

5. Let $j_0 \in \mathbb{N}$, then $L^2([0,1]) = \widehat{V}_{j_0} \oplus \widehat{W}_{j_0} \oplus \widehat{W}_{j_0+1} \oplus \widehat{W}_{j_0+2} \oplus \ldots$.   □

7.5 Periodic Series Expansions

Based upon the discussion in earlier sections, it can be surmised that a periodic function can be expanded in terms of periodic scaling functions and periodic wavelets. Let $f(t) \in \mathbb{C}, t \in \mathbb{R}$, be a function with compact support on the interval $[0,1]$. Also let $f(\cdot) \in L^2([0,1])$.

1. Let $f(\cdot) \in \widehat{V}_J$, where $J \in \mathbb{P}$. Then its expansion in terms of periodic scaling functions is

$$f(t) = \sum_{k=0}^{(2^J-1)} \widehat{c}(J,k) \widehat{\phi}_{Jk}(t), \qquad t \in [0,1]$$

$$\widehat{c}(J,k) = \int_0^1 f(t) \overline{\widehat{\phi}_{Jk}(t)} dt, \qquad 0 \le k \le (2^J - 1)$$

The corresponding Parseval relation is

$$\int_0^1 |f(t)|^2 \, dt = \sum_{k=0}^{(2^J-1)} |\widehat{c}(J,k)|^2$$

Since $\widehat{f}(\cdot)$ is a periodized version of $f(\cdot)$ and $\widehat{\phi}_{Jk}(t)$ is periodic with period 1

$$\widehat{f}(t) = \sum_{k=0}^{(2^J-1)} \widehat{c}(J,k)\,\widehat{\phi}_{Jk}(t), \qquad t \in \mathbb{R}$$

$$\widehat{c}(J,k) = \int_0^1 f(t)\,\overline{\widehat{\phi}_{Jk}(t)}dt, \qquad 0 \le k \le (2^J-1)$$

Notice that the expression for $\widehat{c}(J,k)$ does not change.

2. The function $f(\cdot) \in \widehat{V}_J$, is expanded in terms of periodic scaling and wavelet functions. Let $0 \le j_0 \le (J-1)$, $J \in \mathbb{N}$ then

$$\widehat{V}_J = \widehat{V}_{j_0} \oplus \widehat{W}_{j_0} \oplus \widehat{W}_{j_0+1} \oplus \widehat{W}_{j_0+2} \oplus \ldots \oplus \widehat{W}_{J-1}$$

The corresponding expansion is

$$f(t) = \sum_{k=0}^{(2^{j_0}-1)} \widehat{c}(j_0,k)\,\widehat{\phi}_{j_0 k}(t) + \sum_{j=j_0}^{(J-1)} \sum_{k=0}^{(2^j-1)} \widehat{d}(j,k)\,\widehat{\psi}_{jk}(t), \qquad t \in [0,1]$$

$$\widehat{c}(j_0,k) = \int_0^1 f(t)\,\overline{\widehat{\phi}_{j_0 k}(t)}dt, \qquad 0 \le k \le (2^{j_0}-1)$$

$$\widehat{d}(j,k) = \int_0^1 f(t)\,\overline{\widehat{\psi}_{jk}(t)}dt, \qquad j_0 \le j \le (J-1), \; 0 \le k \le (2^j-1)$$

The corresponding Parseval relation is

$$\int_0^1 |f(t)|^2 \, dt = \sum_{k=0}^{(2^{j_0}-1)} |\widehat{c}(j_0,k)|^2 + \sum_{j=j_0}^{(J-1)} \sum_{k=0}^{(2^j-1)} \left|\widehat{d}(j,k)\right|^2$$

Once again the expansion of $\widehat{f}(\cdot)$ is

$$\widehat{f}(t) = \sum_{k=0}^{(2^{j_0}-1)} \widehat{c}(j_0,k)\,\widehat{\phi}_{j_0 k}(t) + \sum_{j=j_0}^{(J-1)} \sum_{k=0}^{(2^j-1)} \widehat{d}(j,k)\,\widehat{\psi}_{jk}(t), \qquad t \in \mathbb{R}$$

$$\widehat{c}(j_0,k) = \int_0^1 f(t)\,\overline{\widehat{\phi}_{j_0 k}(t)}dt, \qquad 0 \le k \le (2^{j_0}-1)$$

$$\widehat{d}(j,k) = \int_0^1 f(t)\,\overline{\widehat{\psi}_{jk}(t)}dt, \qquad j_0 \le j \le (J-1), \; 0 \le k \le (2^j-1)$$

Observations 7.6. Properties of the coefficients.

1. For $0 \leq k \leq (2^j - 1)$

$$\widehat{c}(j,k) = \int_{-\infty}^{\infty} \widehat{f}(t) \, \overline{\phi_{jk}(t)} dt$$

$$\widehat{d}(j,k) = \int_{-\infty}^{\infty} \widehat{f}(t) \, \overline{\psi_{jk}(t)} dt$$

2. The scaling and wavelet expansion coefficients of $\widehat{f}(t)$ at scale $j > 0$ have a period 2^j. That is, if $l \in \mathbb{Z}$

$$\widehat{c}(j, k + l2^j) = \widehat{c}(j,k)$$
$$\widehat{d}(j, k + l2^j) = \widehat{d}(j,k)$$

$\square$

See the problem section for a proof of the above observations.

7.6 Fast Periodic Wavelet Transform

A fast periodic wavelet transform is the subject of this section. Computational complexity of the fast periodic wavelet transform is also indicated. Further, a matrix formulation of the fast periodic wavelet transformation is also discussed. Algorithms for fast periodic wavelet transform and its inverse are also provided.

Periodic functions can be expanded in terms of periodic scale functions and periodic wavelets. Let $f(\cdot) \in \widehat{V}_J \subseteq L^2([0,1])$, where $J \in \mathbb{P}$ is a function with compact support on the interval $[0,1]$. Also $supp\ \phi(t) = [0, M]$, where M is an odd positive integer. Consequently $supp\ h(n) = [0, M]$, and $supp\ g(n) = [0, M]$.

The function $f(\cdot)$ is expanded in terms of periodized versions of $\phi_{jk}(\cdot)$ and $\psi_{jk}(\cdot)$. These are $\widehat{\phi}_{jk}(\cdot)$ and $\widehat{\psi}_{jk}(\cdot)$ respectively. Recall that for $t \in \mathbb{R}$, $\widehat{\phi}_{jk}(t) = \sum_{n \in \mathbb{Z}} \phi_{jk}(t + n)$, and $\widehat{\psi}_{jk}(t) = \sum_{n \in \mathbb{Z}} \phi_{jk}(t + n)$. If the j's are chosen such that $2^{-j}M \leq 1$, then the $\phi_{jk}(t + n)$ terms in the series expansion of $\widehat{\phi}_{jk}(t)$ and also the $\psi_{jk}(t + n)$ terms in the series expansion of $\widehat{\psi}_{jk}(t)$ do not overlap. Let the smallest value of j such that $2^{-j}M \leq 1$ be j_0, then $j_0 = \lceil \log_2 M \rceil$.

Let $f(\cdot) \in \widehat{V}_J$, and $0 \leq j_0 \leq (J - 1)$, then the wavelet expansion is

$$f(t) = \sum_{k=0}^{(2^{j_0}-1)} \widehat{c}(j_0, k) \widehat{\phi}_{j_0 k}(t) + \sum_{j=j_0}^{J-1} \sum_{k=0}^{(2^j-1)} \widehat{d}(j,k) \widehat{\psi}_{jk}(t), \quad t \in [0,1]$$

$$\widehat{c}(j_0, k) = \int_0^1 f(t) \overline{\widehat{\phi}_{j_0 k}(t)} dt, \quad 0 \leq k \leq (2^{j_0} - 1)$$

$$\hat{d}(j,k) = \int_0^1 f(t)\overline{\psi_{jk}(t)}dt, \quad j_0 \le j \le (J-1),\ 0 \le k \le (2^j-1)$$

$\hat{c}(j_0,k)$ and $\hat{d}(j,k)$ are periodic in the shift parameter k, with period 2^{j_0} and 2^j respectively. The coefficients in the above series expansion can be expanded as in Mallat's pyramid algorithm.

First compute the sequence $\{\hat{c}(J,k) \mid 0 \le k \le (2^J-1)\}$. If the function $f(\cdot)$ is sufficiently smooth and J is large then

$$\hat{c}(J,k) \simeq 2^{-J/2}f(2^{-J}k), \quad 0 \le k \le (2^J-1)$$

Then for $j = J, J-1, \ldots, (j_0+1)$ compute

$$\{\hat{c}(j-1,k) \mid 0 \le k \le (2^{j-1}-1)\}$$
$$\{\hat{d}(j-1,k) \mid 0 \le k \le (2^{j-1}-1)\}$$

from $\{\hat{c}(j,k) \mid 0 \le k \le (2^j-1)\}$ by using the recursive relationship

$$\hat{c}(j-1,k) = \sum_{n=0}^{M} \overline{h(n)}\hat{c}(j,\langle n+2k \rangle_{2^j}), \quad 0 \le k \le (2^{j-1}-1)$$

$$\hat{d}(j-1,k) = \sum_{n=0}^{M} \overline{g(n)}\hat{c}(j,\langle n+2k \rangle_{2^j}), \quad 0 \le k \le (2^{j-1}-1)$$

Note that at each level-j, 2^j number of $\hat{c}(j,k)$ coefficients produce 2^{j-1} number of $\hat{c}(j-1,k)$ and $\hat{d}(j-1,k)$ coefficients each. At the end of the transformation there will be a total of $(2^{J+1}-2^{j_0})$ number of $\hat{c}(.,.)$ and $(2^J-2^{j_0})$ number of $\hat{d}(.,.)$ coefficients. The inverse of the fast periodic wavelet algorithm is computed as follows. For $j = (j_0+1), (j_0+2), \ldots, J$, and $0 \le k \le (2^j-1)$

$$\hat{c}(j,k) = \sum_{m=l(k)}^{u(k)} \hat{c}(j-1,\langle m \rangle_{2^{j-1}}) h(k-2m)$$
$$+ \sum_{m=l(k)}^{u(k)} \hat{d}(j-1,\langle m \rangle_{2^{j-1}}) g(k-2m)$$

where the limits $l(k)$ and $u(k)$ are determined by noting that $(k-2m) \in [0,M]$. Thus $l(k) = \lceil (k-M)/2 \rceil$, and $u(k) = \lfloor k/2 \rfloor$. The fast periodic wavelet algorithm and its inverse are summarized in the following observations.

Observation 7.7. *Computation of periodic wavelet transform.* Let $t \in \mathbb{R}$, $f(\cdot) \in \hat{V}_J \subseteq L^2([0,1])$, where $J \in \mathbb{P}$, and $supp\ f(t) = [0,1]$. Also let $supp\ \phi(t) = [0,M]$, where M is an odd positive integer. If $j_0 < J$, where $j_0 = \lceil \log_2 M \rceil$, then $\phi_{jk}(\cdot)$

and $\psi_{jk}(\cdot)$ can be periodized with period 1 by non-overlapping segments of $\phi_{jk}(\cdot)$ and $\psi_{jk}(\cdot)$ respectively.

The wavelet series expansion of the function $f(\cdot)$ is given by

$$f(t) = \sum_{k=0}^{(2^{j_0}-1)} \widehat{c}(j_0, k)\,\widehat{\phi}_{j_0 k}(t) + \sum_{j=j_0}^{J-1} \sum_{k=0}^{(2^j-1)} \widehat{d}(j, k)\,\widehat{\psi}_{jk}(t), \qquad t \in [0, 1]$$

The coefficients in the above series are computed as follows. Let

$$\widehat{c}(J, k) \simeq 2^{-J/2} f(2^{-J} k), \qquad 0 \le k \le (2^J - 1)$$

For $j = J, J-1, \ldots, (j_0 + 1)$ compute

$$\left\{ \widehat{c}(j-1, k) \mid 0 \le k \le (2^{j-1} - 1) \right\}$$
$$\left\{ \widehat{d}(j-1, k) \mid 0 \le k \le (2^{j-1} - 1) \right\}$$

from the sequence $\left\{ \widehat{c}(j, k) \mid 0 \le k \le (2^j - 1) \right\}$. These are

$$\widehat{c}(j-1, k) = \sum_{n=0}^{M} \overline{h(n)} \widehat{c}(j, \langle n + 2k \rangle_{2^j}), \qquad 0 \le k \le (2^{j-1} - 1)$$

$$\widehat{d}(j-1, k) = \sum_{n=0}^{M} \overline{g(n)} \widehat{c}(j, \langle n + 2k \rangle_{2^j}), \qquad 0 \le k \le (2^{j-1} - 1)$$

$\square$

Observation 7.8. *Computation of the inverse of periodic wavelet transform.* The following coefficients are given

$$\widehat{c}(j_0, k), \qquad 0 \le k \le (2^{j_0} - 1)$$
$$\widehat{d}(j, k), \qquad j_0 \le j \le (J-1), \; 0 \le k \le (2^j - 1)$$

For $j = (j_0 + 1), (j_0 + 2), \ldots, J$; and $0 \le k \le (2^j - 1)$, compute recursively

$$\widehat{c}(j, k) = \sum_{m=l(k)}^{u(k)} \widehat{c}(j-1, \langle m \rangle_{2^{j-1}})\, h(k - 2m)$$

$$+ \sum_{m=l(k)}^{u(k)} \widehat{d}(j-1, \langle m \rangle_{2^{j-1}})\, g(k - 2m)$$

where $l(k) = \lceil (k - M)/2 \rceil$ and $u(k) = \lfloor k/2 \rfloor$. At the end of the above sequence of operations $\widehat{c}(J, k)$, $0 \le k \le (2^J - 1)$ is obtained. The original function $f(\cdot)$ is recovered from the relationship

$$f(2^{-J} k) = 2^{J/2} \widehat{c}(J, k), \qquad 0 \le k \le (2^J - 1)$$

$\square$

7.6.1 Computational Complexity

Computational complexity of the fast periodic wavelet transform is determined in this subsection. It is assumed that a multiplication operation is more expensive than an addition operation. Note that $f(\cdot) \in \widehat{V}_J \subseteq L^2([0, 1])$, where $J \in \mathbb{P}$. Let $D = 2^J$ be the length of the data vector, and $supp\ \phi(t) = [0, M]$. Typically $M \ll D$. The recursive computations are indexed by $j = J, J - 1, \ldots, (j_0 + 1)$, where $j_0 < J$, and $j_0 = \lceil \log_2 M \rceil$. The first stage $(j = J)$ of the recursion needs

$$2(M + 1)2^{J-1} = (M + 1)D$$

multiplication and modulo operations. The second stage $(j = (J - 1))$ in the recursion requires

$$2^{-1}(M + 1)D$$

multiplication and modulo operations. Furthermore, the last stage of the recursion $(j = (J - (J - j_0 - 1)) = (j_0 + 1))$ requires

$$2^{-(J-j_0-1)}(M + 1)D$$

multiplication and modulo operations. Therefore, the total number of multiplication and modulo operations through $(J - j_0)$ stages is equal to $2(M + 1)D(1 - 2^{j_0-J})$. This expression is bounded by $2(M+1)D$. Since M is a constant, the computational complexity of the periodic fast wavelet transform is equal to $O(D)$. The computational complexity of the corresponding inverse transformation is identical. This result is summarized in the following observation.

Observation 7.9. Let $D = 2^J$, where $J \in \mathbb{P}$, be the length of the data vector in the fast periodic wavelet transform algorithm, then the computational complexity of this algorithm is $O(D)$.   □

7.6.2 A Matrix Formulation

It is instructive to obtain a matrix formulation of the fast periodic wavelet transformation. Let the data vector be of length 2^J, where $J \in \mathbb{P}$ and $\widehat{\mathcal{F}}(J)$ be

$$\widehat{\mathcal{F}}(J) = [f(0), f(2^{-J}), f(2^{-J}2), f(2^{-J}3), \ldots, f(1 - 2^{-J})]^T$$

The fast periodic wavelet transformation is implemented recursively. The equations in the j-th stage of the recursion can be rewritten in terms of the following vectors and matrices.

$\widehat{C}(j)$ and $\widehat{D}(j)$ are column vectors of length 2^j. These are

$$\widehat{C}(j) = [\widehat{c}(j, 0), \widehat{c}(j, 1), \ldots, \widehat{c}(j, 2^j - 1)]^T, \qquad j \in [j_0, J]$$

$$\widehat{D}(j) = [\widehat{d}(j, 0), \widehat{d}(j, 1), \ldots, \widehat{d}(j, 2^j - 1)]^T, \qquad j \in [j_0, J - 1]$$

Note that the recursion is initialized by $\widehat{C}(J)$, which is a vector of length 2^J.

$$\widehat{C}(J) = 2^{-J/2}\widehat{F}(J)$$

$\widehat{\mathcal{H}}(j)$ and $\widehat{\mathcal{G}}(j)$ are matrices of size $2^{j-1} \times 2^j$. Each row of the matrix $\widehat{\mathcal{H}}(j)$ has the entries from the sequence $\{h(n) \mid 0 \le n \le M\}$, where M is an odd positive integer. The remaining entries in the row are all zeros. The matrix $\widehat{\mathcal{H}}(j)$ is constructed as follows. The first row has $h(n)$ in column n, where $0 \le n \le M$. The second row has $h(n)$ in column $(n + 2)$, where $0 \le n \le M$. The third row has $h(n)$ in column $(n + 4)$, $0 \le n \le M$. The fourth, fifth, and the remaining rows are similarly filled. If in any row, the last column of the matrix has been reached, and all the $(M + 1)$ number of $h(n)$'s have not been filled, then these elements wrap around to column number 0, and continue on until the element $h(M)$ has been used in filling up. Recall that if $n \in \mathbb{Z}$, $supp\ h(n) = supp\ g(n) = [0, M]$. That is, $h(n) = g(n) = 0$, for $n \notin [0, M]$. Let

$$\widehat{\mathcal{H}}(j) = [h_{rc}(j)], \quad \text{where} \quad h_{rc}(j) = h(\langle c - 2r \rangle_{2^j})$$

$$0 \le r \le (2^{j-1} - 1), \quad 0 \le c \le (2^j - 1)$$

This procedure is further clarified subsequently via an example. The matrix $\widehat{\mathcal{G}}(j)$ is formed similarly by replacing the $h(n)$'s by $g(n)$'s in the matrix $\widehat{\mathcal{H}}(j)$. In other words

$$\widehat{\mathcal{G}}(j) = [g_{rc}(j)], \quad \text{where} \quad g_{rc}(j) = g(\langle c - 2r \rangle_{2^j})$$

$$0 \le r \le (2^{j-1} - 1), \quad 0 \le c \le (2^j - 1)$$

$$g(n) = \begin{cases} (-1)^n \, \overline{h(M - n)}, & n \in [0, M] \\ 0, & n \notin [0, M] \end{cases}$$

Then as per the recursion for $j = J, J - 1, \ldots, (j_0 + 1)$

$$\widehat{C}(j - 1) = \overline{\widehat{\mathcal{H}}(j)}\widehat{C}(j)$$
$$\widehat{D}(j - 1) = \overline{\widehat{\mathcal{G}}(j)}\widehat{C}(j)$$

Further, because of the orthogonality of the $\widehat{V}_j$ and $\widehat{W}_j$ spaces, and defining $\widehat{\mathcal{I}}(j)$ and $\widehat{\mathcal{O}}(j)$ as an identity matrix and an all-zero matrix of size $2^j \times 2^j$ each respectively,

$$\widehat{\mathcal{H}}(j)\overline{\widehat{\mathcal{H}}(j)}^T = \widehat{\mathcal{I}}(j - 1)$$
$$\widehat{\mathcal{G}}(j)\overline{\widehat{\mathcal{G}}(j)}^T = \widehat{\mathcal{I}}(j - 1)$$
$$\widehat{\mathcal{H}}(j)\overline{\widehat{\mathcal{G}}(j)}^T = \widehat{\mathcal{O}}(j - 1)$$
$$\widehat{\mathcal{G}}(j)\overline{\widehat{\mathcal{H}}(j)}^T = \widehat{\mathcal{O}}(j - 1)$$

Let

$$\widehat{\mathcal{S}}(j) = \begin{bmatrix} \widehat{\mathcal{H}}(j) \\ \widehat{\mathcal{G}}(j) \end{bmatrix}$$

This implies

$$\begin{bmatrix} \widehat{\mathcal{C}}(j-1) \\ \widehat{\mathcal{D}}(j-1) \end{bmatrix} = \overline{\widehat{\mathcal{S}}(j)} \widehat{\mathcal{C}}(j)$$

$$\widehat{\mathcal{S}}(j)\overline{\widehat{\mathcal{S}}(j)}^T = \widehat{\mathcal{I}}(j)$$

The final transformed vector $\widehat{\mathcal{T}}(J)$ is of length 2^J

$$\widehat{\mathcal{T}}(J) = \left[\widehat{\mathcal{C}}(j_0), \widehat{\mathcal{D}}(j_0), \widehat{\mathcal{D}}(j_0+1), \widehat{\mathcal{D}}(j_0+2), \ldots, \widehat{\mathcal{D}}(J-1) \right]^T$$

The inverse of the fast periodic wavelet transform can be computed via

$$\widehat{\mathcal{C}}(j) = \widehat{\mathcal{S}}(j)^T \begin{bmatrix} \widehat{\mathcal{C}}(j-1) \\ \widehat{\mathcal{D}}(j-1) \end{bmatrix}, \qquad j = (j_0+1), (j_0+2), \ldots, J$$

The input to this inverse operation is the vector $\widehat{\mathcal{T}}(J)$. In the last iteration $\widehat{\mathcal{C}}(J)$ is produced. The data vector $\widehat{\mathcal{F}}(J)$ is computed as

$$\widehat{\mathcal{F}}(J) = 2^{J/2}\widehat{\mathcal{C}}(J)$$

The above matrix algorithms are summarized as follows.

Algorithm for Fast Periodic Wavelet Transform

Let $f(\cdot) \in \widehat{V}_J \subseteq L^2([0,1])$, $J \in \mathbb{P}$, M be an odd positive integer, $supp\ \phi(t) = [0, M]$, $j_0 = \lceil \log_2 M \rceil$, where $j_0 < J$. Also, if $n \in \mathbb{Z}$, $supp\ h(n) = supp\ g(n) = [0, M]$. That is, $h(n) = g(n) = 0$, for $n \notin [0, M]$. The data vector of length 2^J is given by $\widehat{\mathcal{F}}(J)$

$$\widehat{\mathcal{F}}(J) = \left[f(0), f(2^{-J}), f(2^{-J}2), f(2^{-J}3), \ldots, f(1-2^{-J}) \right]^T$$

Compute

$$\widehat{\mathcal{C}}(J) = 2^{-J/2}\widehat{\mathcal{F}}(J)$$

For $j = J, J-1, \ldots, (j_0+1)$ define $\widehat{\mathcal{H}}(j)$ and $\widehat{\mathcal{G}}(j)$ as matrices each of size $2^{j-1} \times 2^j$, where

$$\widehat{\mathcal{H}}(j) = [h_{rc}(j)], \quad h_{rc}(j) = h(\langle c - 2r \rangle_{2^j}),$$
$$0 \le r \le (2^{j-1}-1), \ 0 \le c \le (2^j - 1)$$
$$\widehat{\mathcal{G}}(j) = [g_{rc}(j)], \quad g_{rc}(j) = g(\langle c - 2r \rangle_{2^j}),$$
$$0 \le r \le (2^{j-1}-1), \ 0 \le c \le (2^j - 1)$$

$$g(n) = \begin{cases} (-1)^n \, \overline{h(M-n)}, & n \in [0, M] \\ 0, & n \notin [0, M] \end{cases}$$

Next define

$$\widehat{S}(j) = \begin{bmatrix} \widehat{\mathcal{H}}(j) \\ \widehat{\mathcal{G}}(j) \end{bmatrix}, \qquad j = J, J - 1, \ldots, (j_0 + 1)$$

Perform the following recursive operations for $j = J, J - 1, \ldots, (j_0 + 1)$.

$$\begin{bmatrix} \widehat{\mathcal{C}}(j-1) \\ \widehat{\mathcal{D}}(j-1) \end{bmatrix} = \overline{\widehat{S}(j)} \widehat{\mathcal{C}}(j)$$

The transformed vector $\widehat{T}(J)$ is given by

$$\widehat{T}(J) = \begin{bmatrix} \widehat{\mathcal{C}}(j_0), \widehat{\mathcal{D}}(j_0), \widehat{\mathcal{D}}(j_0 + 1), \widehat{\mathcal{D}}(j_0 + 2), \ldots, \widehat{\mathcal{D}}(J - 1) \end{bmatrix}^T$$

□

Algorithm for Inverse of Fast Periodic Wavelet Transform

The transformed vector $\widehat{T}(J)$ is given. It is required to compute the data vector $\widehat{\mathcal{F}}(J)$. For $j = (j_0 + 1), (j_0 + 2), \ldots, J$ perform the following recursive operations

$$\widehat{\mathcal{C}}(j) = \widehat{S}(j)^T \begin{bmatrix} \widehat{\mathcal{C}}(j-1) \\ \widehat{\mathcal{D}}(j-1) \end{bmatrix}$$

After these steps $\widehat{\mathcal{F}}(J)$ is recovered as

$$\widehat{\mathcal{F}}(J) = 2^{J/2} \widehat{\mathcal{C}}(J)$$

□

Example 7.1. Consider Daubechies wavelets where $\Psi(\omega)$ has a zero of order $N = 2$ at $\omega = 0$. This implies that $M = (2N - 1) = 3$. Then

$$supp \, h(n) = [0, 3], \quad supp \, g(n) = [0, 3], \quad supp \, \phi(t) = [0, 3], \quad supp \, \psi(t) = [0, 3]$$

The relationship $g(n) = (-1)^n \, \overline{h(3-n)}$ for $n \in [0, 3]$, implies

$$g(0) = \overline{h(3)}, \; g(1) = -\overline{h(2)}, \; g(2) = \overline{h(1)}, \text{ and } g(3) = -\overline{h(0)}$$

Also $g(n) = 0$ for values of $n \notin [0, 3]$. The value of $j_0 = \lceil \log_2 M \rceil = 2$. Let $J = 4$. That is, the size of the data vector is $2^4 = 16$. The matrices $\widehat{\mathcal{H}}(3)$, $\widehat{\mathcal{H}}(4)$, $\widehat{\mathcal{G}}(3)$, and $\widehat{\mathcal{G}}(4)$ are used in the transformation. The matrices $\widehat{\mathcal{H}}(3)$, and $\widehat{\mathcal{G}}(3)$ are of size 4×8. The matrices $\widehat{\mathcal{H}}(4)$, and $\widehat{\mathcal{G}}(4)$ are of size 8×16. Consider the $\widehat{\mathcal{H}}(3)$, and $\widehat{\mathcal{G}}(3)$ matrices.

$$\widehat{\mathcal{H}}(3) = \begin{bmatrix} h(0) & h(1) & h(2) & h(3) & 0 & 0 & 0 & 0 \\ 0 & 0 & h(0) & h(1) & h(2) & h(3) & 0 & 0 \\ 0 & 0 & 0 & 0 & h(0) & h(1) & h(2) & h(3) \\ h(2) & h(3) & 0 & 0 & 0 & 0 & h(0) & h(1) \end{bmatrix}$$

$$\widehat{\mathcal{G}}(3) = \begin{bmatrix} g(0) & g(1) & g(2) & g(3) & 0 & 0 & 0 & 0 \\ 0 & 0 & g(0) & g(1) & g(2) & g(3) & 0 & 0 \\ 0 & 0 & 0 & 0 & g(0) & g(1) & g(2) & g(3) \\ g(2) & g(3) & 0 & 0 & 0 & 0 & g(0) & g(1) \end{bmatrix}$$

It can be readily checked that

$$\widehat{\mathcal{H}}(3)\overline{\widehat{\mathcal{H}}(3)}^T = \widehat{\mathcal{I}}(2), \quad \widehat{\mathcal{G}}(3)\overline{\widehat{\mathcal{G}}(3)}^T = \widehat{\mathcal{I}}(2),$$
$$\widehat{\mathcal{H}}(3)\overline{\widehat{\mathcal{G}}(3)}^T = \widehat{\mathcal{O}}(2), \quad \widehat{\mathcal{G}}(3)\overline{\widehat{\mathcal{H}}(3)}^T = \widehat{\mathcal{O}}(2)$$

Similar results can be verified for the $\widehat{\mathcal{H}}(4)$, and $\widehat{\mathcal{G}}(4)$ matrices. Using these matrices the fast periodic wavelet transform and its inverse is computed. For clarity, we explicitly outline the steps in matrix notation in the computation of the periodic wavelet transform and its inverse.

Computation of periodic wavelet transform:

The data vector is

$$\widehat{\mathcal{F}}(4) = [f(0), f(1/16), f(2/16), \ldots, f(15/16)]^T$$

The following steps are executed sequentially

$$\widehat{\mathcal{C}}(4) = 2^{-2}\widehat{\mathcal{F}}(4)$$

$$\widehat{\mathcal{C}}(3) = \overline{\widehat{\mathcal{H}}(4)}\widehat{\mathcal{C}}(4), \quad \widehat{\mathcal{D}}(3) = \overline{\widehat{\mathcal{G}}(4)}\widehat{\mathcal{C}}(4)$$

$$\widehat{\mathcal{C}}(2) = \overline{\widehat{\mathcal{H}}(3)}\widehat{\mathcal{C}}(3), \quad \widehat{\mathcal{D}}(2) = \overline{\widehat{\mathcal{G}}(3)}\widehat{\mathcal{C}}(3)$$

The transformed vector $\widehat{\mathcal{T}}(4)$ is given by

$$\widehat{\mathcal{T}}(4) = \left[\widehat{\mathcal{C}}(2), \widehat{\mathcal{D}}(2), \widehat{\mathcal{D}}(3)\right]^T$$

Computation of the inverse periodic wavelet transform:

We are given the transformed vector $\widehat{\mathcal{T}}(4)$

$$\widehat{\mathcal{T}}(4) = \left[\widehat{\mathcal{C}}(2), \widehat{\mathcal{D}}(2), \widehat{\mathcal{D}}(3)\right]^T$$

The following steps are executed sequentially

$$\widehat{C}(3) = \widehat{\mathcal{H}}(3)^T \widehat{C}(2) + \widehat{\mathcal{G}}(3)^T \widehat{D}(2)$$

$$\widehat{C}(4) = \widehat{\mathcal{H}}(4)^T \widehat{C}(3) + \widehat{\mathcal{G}}(4)^T \widehat{D}(3)$$

The data vector $\widehat{\mathcal{F}}(4)$ is

$$\widehat{\mathcal{F}}(4) = 2^2 \widehat{C}(4)$$

$\square$

Problems

1. Let $t \in \mathbb{R}$. Establish the following results.

   (a) The periodic scaling and wavelet functions have a period of 1 each.

   $$\widehat{\phi}_{jk}(t+1) = \widehat{\phi}_{jk}(t)$$
   $$\widehat{\psi}_{jk}(t+1) = \widehat{\psi}_{jk}(t)$$

   (b)

   $$\widehat{\phi}_{jk}(t) = \sum_{n \in \mathbb{Z}} \phi_{j,k-2^j n}(t)$$
   $$\widehat{\psi}_{jk}(t) = \sum_{n \in \mathbb{Z}} \psi_{j,k-2^j n}(t)$$

   (c)

   $$\widehat{\phi}_{jk}(t) = 2^{-j/2}, \quad j \le 0, \ k \in \mathbb{Z}$$

   Consequently

   $$\widehat{\phi}_{0k}(t) = 1, \quad k \in \mathbb{Z}$$

   (d)

   $$\widehat{\psi}_{jk}(t) = 0, \quad j \le -1, \ k \in \mathbb{Z}$$

   Hint:

   (a)

   $$\widehat{\phi}_{jk}(t+1) = \sum_{n \in \mathbb{Z}} \phi_{jk}(t+n+1) = \sum_{n \in \mathbb{Z}} \phi_{jk}(t+n) = \widehat{\phi}_{jk}(t)$$

   The second result is proved similarly.

(b)

$$\widehat{\phi}_{jk}(t) = \sum_{n\in\mathbb{Z}} \phi_{jk}(t+n) = 2^{j/2} \sum_{n\in\mathbb{Z}} \phi\left(2^j t + 2^j n - k\right)$$

$$= \sum_{n\in\mathbb{Z}} \phi_{j,k-2^j n}(t)$$

The second result follows similarly.

(c) It is known from the chapter on discrete wavelet transform that

$$\widehat{\phi}_{j0}(t) = \sum_{n\in\mathbb{Z}} \phi_{j0}(t+n) = 2^{-j/2}, \quad \text{for } j \le 0, \ \forall t \in \mathbb{R}$$

It is next shown that $\widehat{\phi}_{jk}(\cdot) = \widehat{\phi}_{j0}(\cdot)$, from which the result follows.

$$\widehat{\phi}_{jk}(t) = \sum_{n\in\mathbb{Z}} \phi_{jk}(t+n)$$

$$= 2^{j/2} \sum_{n\in\mathbb{Z}} \phi\left(2^j(t+n) - k\right)$$

$$= 2^{j/2} \sum_{n\in\mathbb{Z}} \phi\left(2^j(t+n-k2^{-j})\right)$$

If $j \le 0$, $\left(n - k2^{-j}\right) \in \mathbb{Z}$. Substitute $\left(n - k2^{-j}\right) = m$ in the above equation. This leads to

$$\widehat{\phi}_{jk}(t) = 2^{j/2} \sum_{m\in\mathbb{Z}} \phi\left(2^j(t+m)\right)$$

$$= \widehat{\phi}_{j0}(t)$$

Therefore,

$$\widehat{\phi}_{jk}(t) = 2^{-j/2}, \qquad j \le 0, \ k \in \mathbb{Z}$$

(d) It can be proved that $\widehat{\psi}_{jk}(t) = \widehat{\psi}_{j0}(t)$ if $j \le 0$. However, it is known from the chapter on discrete wavelet transform that $\widehat{\psi}_{j0}(t) = 0$ if $j \le -1$. The result follows.

2. Let $j > 0$, then $\widehat{\phi}_{jk}(t)$ and $\widehat{\psi}_{jk}(t)$ are each periodic in the parameter k with period 2^j. Prove that there are only 2^j distinct periodized scaling functions and only 2^j distinct periodized wavelet functions. These are

$$\left\{\widehat{\phi}_{jk}(t) \mid j > 0, \ 0 \le k \le \left(2^j - 1\right)\right\}$$

$$\left\{\widehat{\psi}_{jk}(t) \mid j > 0, \ 0 \le k \le \left(2^j - 1\right)\right\}$$

Hint: If $j > 0$ and $l \in \mathbb{Z}$ then

$$\widehat{\phi}_{j,k+l2^j}(t) = \sum_{n\in\mathbb{Z}} \phi_{j,k+l2^j}(t+n)$$

$$= 2^{j/2}\sum_{n\in\mathbb{Z}} \phi\left(2^j t + 2^j n - k - l2^j\right)$$

$$= 2^{j/2}\sum_{n\in\mathbb{Z}} \phi\left(2^j(t+n-l) - k\right)$$

In the above equation, let $(n-l) = m \in \mathbb{Z}$.

$$\widehat{\phi}_{j,k+l2^j}(t) = 2^{j/2}\sum_{m\in\mathbb{Z}} \phi\left(2^j(t+m) - k\right)$$

$$= \sum_{m\in\mathbb{Z}} \phi_{jk}(t+m)$$

$$= \widehat{\phi}_{jk}(t)$$

The proof of the periodicity of $\widehat{\psi}_{jk}(t)$ is similar to the proof of the periodicity of $\widehat{\phi}_{jk}(t)$.

3. The following orthonormal relationships are preserved for periodic scaling and wavelet functions over the interval $[0, 1]$. Let $j, k, l, m \in \mathbb{N}$, then

$$\int_0^1 \widehat{\phi}_{jk}(t)\overline{\widehat{\phi}_{jl}(t)}dt = \delta_{kl}, \quad k, l \in [0, 2^j - 1]$$

$$\int_0^1 \widehat{\psi}_{jk}(t)\overline{\widehat{\psi}_{jl}(t)}dt = \delta_{kl}, \quad k, l \in [0, 2^j - 1]$$

$$\int_0^1 \widehat{\psi}_{jk}(t)\overline{\widehat{\psi}_{ml}(t)}dt = 0, \quad k \in [0, 2^j - 1], \ l \in [0, 2^m - 1], \ j \neq m$$

$$\int_0^1 \widehat{\phi}_{jk}(t)\overline{\widehat{\psi}_{ml}(t)}dt = 0, \quad k \in [0, 2^j - 1], \ l \in [0, 2^m - 1], \ 0 \leq j \leq m$$

Prove the above results.

Hint:

$$\int_0^1 \widehat{\phi}_{jk}(t)\overline{\widehat{\phi}_{jl}(t)}dt = \int_0^1 \sum_{n\in\mathbb{Z}} \phi_{jk}(t+n)\overline{\widehat{\phi}_{jl}(t)}dt$$

$$= \sum_{n\in\mathbb{Z}} \int_n^{n+1} \phi_{jk}(x)\overline{\widehat{\phi}_{jl}(x-n)}dx$$

$$= \sum_{n\in\mathbb{Z}} \int_n^{n+1} \phi_{jk}(x)\overline{\widehat{\phi}_{jl}(x)}dx$$

$$= \int_{-\infty}^{\infty} \phi_{jk}(x)\overline{\widehat{\phi}_{jl}(x)}dx$$

Substituting $\widehat{\phi}_{jl}(x) = \sum_{n\in\mathbb{Z}} \phi_{j,l-2^j n}(x)$ results in

$$\int_0^1 \widehat{\phi}_{jk}(t)\,\overline{\widehat{\phi}_{jl}(t)}dt = \int_{-\infty}^{\infty} \phi_{jk}(x)\sum_{n\in\mathbb{Z}}\overline{\phi_{j,l-2^j n}(x)}dx$$

$$= \sum_{n\in\mathbb{Z}}\int_{-\infty}^{\infty} \phi_{jk}(x)\overline{\phi_{j,l-2^j n}(x)}dx$$

$$= \sum_{n\in\mathbb{Z}} \delta_{k,l-2^j n}$$

Note that $\delta_{k,l-2^j n} = 1$ when $n = 0$ and $k = l$, because $k, l \in \left[0, 2^j - 1\right]$; and $\delta_{k,l-2^j n} = 0$ otherwise. Therefore,

$$\int_0^1 \widehat{\phi}_{jk}(t)\,\overline{\widehat{\phi}_{jl}(t)}dt = \delta_{kl}$$

The remaining results follow similarly.

4. Establish the following results about coefficients that occur in the periodic series expansions.

   (a) For $0 \le k \le \left(2^j - 1\right)$

$$\widehat{c}(j, k) = \int_{-\infty}^{\infty} \widehat{f}(t)\,\overline{\phi_{jk}(t)}dt$$

$$\widehat{d}(j, k) = \int_{-\infty}^{\infty} \widehat{f}(t)\,\overline{\psi_{jk}(t)}dt$$

   (b) The scaling and wavelet expansion coefficients of $\widehat{f}(t)$ at scale $j > 0$ have a period 2^j. That is, if $l \in \mathbb{Z}$

$$\widehat{c}\left(j, k + l2^j\right) = \widehat{c}(j, k)$$

$$\widehat{d}\left(j, k + l2^j\right) = \widehat{d}(j, k)$$

Hint:

   (a) We have

$$\widehat{c}(j, k) = \int_0^1 f(t)\,\overline{\widehat{\phi}_{jk}(t)}dt = \int_0^1 \widehat{f}(t)\,\overline{\widehat{\phi}_{jk}(t)}dt$$

$$= \int_0^1 \sum_{n\in\mathbb{Z}} \widehat{f}(t)\,\overline{\phi_{jk}(t+n)}dt$$

$$= \sum_{n\in\mathbb{Z}}\int_n^{n+1} \widehat{f}(x-n)\overline{\phi_{jk}(x)}dx$$

$$= \sum_{n\in\mathbb{Z}}\int_n^{n+1} \widehat{f}(x)\overline{\phi_{jk}(x)}dx$$

$$= \int_{-\infty}^{\infty} \widehat{f}(x)\overline{\phi_{jk}(x)}dx$$

The second result is proved similarly.

(b) We have

$$\widehat{c}\left(j, k + l2^{j}\right) = \int_{-\infty}^{\infty} \widehat{f}\left(t\right) \overline{\phi_{j,k+l2^{j}}\left(t\right)} dt$$

$$= \int_{-\infty}^{\infty} \widehat{f}\left(t\right) 2^{j/2} \overline{\phi\left(2^{j}t - k - l2^{j}\right)} dt$$

Substituting $(t - l) = x$

$$\widehat{c}\left(j, k + l2^{j}\right) = \int_{-\infty}^{\infty} \widehat{f}(x + l) 2^{j/2} \overline{\phi\left(2^{j}x - k\right)} dx$$

$$= \int_{-\infty}^{\infty} \widehat{f}(x) \overline{\phi_{jk}\left(x\right)} dx$$

$$= \widehat{c}\left(j, k\right)$$

The second result is proved similarly.

CHAPTER 8

Biorthogonal Wavelet Transform

8.1 Introduction

Biorthogonal wavelets are studied in this chapter. This is a generalization of the discrete orthogonal wavelets discussed in a different chapter. Functions (signals) are generally expanded in terms of orthogonal basis functions. However in some applications, it is convenient to expand the function in terms of biorthogonal functions. Biorthogonality offers a more versatile tool, if it replaces the condition of orthogonality. Wavelets which use biorthogonality, are often symmetric and have compact support. Symmetricity of the wavelets and scaling functions is one of the reasons to select biorthogonal over orthogonal wavelets.

Biorthogonal systems, as the name implies, use dual basis. This offers more flexibility. However, use of biorthogonality comes with a disadvantage. Parseval's condition is no longer valid for biorthogonal systems. That is, the norm of the spanning function is not equal to the norm of the coefficients which occur in its expansion.

We initially explain the biorthogonal representation of a function. This is followed by an introduction to biorthogonal wavelets. Biorthogonal decomposition and reconstruction of a function in terms of biorthogonal wavelets is next outlined. A procedure for the construction of biorthogonal scaling coefficients is also specified. An example in the form of a B-spline biorthogonal wavelets is subsequently provided. A brief introduction to semi-orthogonal wavelets is also given.

8.2 Biorthogonal Representations of a Function

In order to study biorthogonal representations of a function, first recall its orthogonal representations.

Definition 8.1. *Inner product. Let $L^2(\mathbb{R})$ be the space of all square-integrable functions. Also let $a : \mathbb{R} \to \mathbb{C}$, and $b : \mathbb{R} \to \mathbb{C}$, and $a, b \in L^2(\mathbb{R})$. The inner product of the two functions $a(\cdot)$ and $b(\cdot)$ is*

$$\langle a(\cdot), b(\cdot) \rangle \triangleq \langle a, b \rangle = \int_{-\infty}^{\infty} a(t)\overline{b(t)}dt \tag{8.1}$$

☐

Orthogonal Expansion of a Function

Let $A \subseteq \mathbb{R}$, and $\{f(t) \in \mathbb{C} \mid t \in A\} \in L^2(A)$. Also consider an orthonormal basis set $\{\alpha_n(t) \in \mathbb{C} \mid t \in A, \ n \in \mathbb{Z}\} \subseteq L^2(A)$. That is,

$$\langle \alpha_m, \alpha_n \rangle = \delta_{m,n}, \quad \forall \, m, n \in \mathbb{Z}$$

Then $\forall \, t \in \mathbb{R}$

$$f(t) = \sum_{n \in \mathbb{Z}} c_n \alpha_n(t), \quad \text{where} \quad c_n = \langle f, \alpha_n \rangle, \ n \in \mathbb{Z}$$

It is important to note that the following Parseval's relationship holds for this expansion

$$\int_{t \in A} |f(t)|^2 \, dt = \sum_{n \in \mathbb{Z}} |c_n|^2$$

Biorthogonal Expansion of a Function

Let $A \subseteq \mathbb{R}$, and $\{f(t) \in \mathbb{C} \mid t \in A\} \in L^2(A)$. The biorthogonal expansion of function $f \in L^2(A)$ is as follows. Consider the dual basis sets

$$\{\alpha_n(t) \in \mathbb{C} \mid t \in A, \ n \in \mathbb{Z}\} \subseteq L^2(A)$$
$$\{\tilde{\alpha}_n(t) \in \mathbb{C} \mid t \in A, \ n \in \mathbb{Z}\} \subseteq L^2(A)$$

$$\langle \alpha_m, \tilde{\alpha}_n \rangle = \delta_{mn}, \quad \forall \, m, n \in \mathbb{Z}$$

Note that these sets are not orthonormal. Then $\forall \, t \in \mathbb{R}$,

$$f(t) = \sum_{n \in \mathbb{Z}} c_n \alpha_n(t), \quad \text{where} \quad c_n = \langle f, \tilde{\alpha}_n \rangle, \ n \in \mathbb{Z}$$

Also it is possible to have

$$f(t) = \sum_{n \in \mathbb{Z}} \tilde{c}_n \tilde{\alpha}_n(t), \quad \text{where} \quad \tilde{c}_n = \langle f, \alpha_n \rangle, \ n \in \mathbb{Z}$$

The Parseval-type of relationship is

$$\int_{t \in A} |f(t)|^2 \, dt = \sum_{n \in \mathbb{Z}} c_n \overline{\tilde{c}_n}$$

If the biorthogonal basis sets are orthonormal, then $\alpha_n(\cdot) = \tilde{\alpha}_n(\cdot)$, $\forall \, n \in \mathbb{Z}$. The extension of the concept of biorthogonality to discrete spaces can be made analogously. The concept of biorthogonality is demonstrated via an example from linear algebra.

Example 8.1. Let $\alpha = \{\alpha_1, \alpha_2\}$ be a basis for the two-dimensional space $\mathbb{R}^2$, where $\alpha_1 = (1, 1)$, and $\alpha_2 = (3, 4)$. Form a matrix A with vectors α_1 and α_2 as rows. The corresponding dual basis $\tilde{\alpha} = \{\tilde{\alpha}_1, \tilde{\alpha}_2\}$, is obtained from the columns of the matrix A^{-1}. Thus

$$A = \begin{bmatrix} 1 & 1 \\ 3 & 4 \end{bmatrix}, \quad \text{and} \quad A^{-1} = \begin{bmatrix} 4 & -1 \\ -3 & 1 \end{bmatrix}$$

and $\tilde{\alpha}_1 = (4, -3)$, and $\tilde{\alpha}_2 = (-1, 1)$. Let I be an identity matrix of size 2. The relationship $AA^{-1} = I$ leads to

$$\langle \alpha_1, \tilde{\alpha}_1 \rangle = 1, \ \langle \alpha_1, \tilde{\alpha}_2 \rangle = 0, \ \langle \alpha_2, \tilde{\alpha}_1 \rangle = 0, \ \text{and} \ \langle \alpha_2, \tilde{\alpha}_2 \rangle = 1$$

In the next step, we obtain expansion of a vector $\theta = (a, b)$ in terms of both basis sets. Let

$$\theta = (a, b) = c_1 \alpha_1 + c_2 \alpha_2$$

Then

$$c_1 = (4a - 3b), \ c_2 = (-a + b)$$

Similarly, let

$$\theta = (a, b) = \tilde{c}_1 \tilde{\alpha}_1 + \tilde{c}_2 \tilde{\alpha}_2$$

Then

$$\tilde{c}_1 = (a + b), \ \tilde{c}_2 = (3a + 4b)$$

It can indeed be verified that

$$c_1 = \langle \theta, \tilde{\alpha}_1 \rangle, \ c_2 = \langle \theta, \tilde{\alpha}_2 \rangle, \ \tilde{c}_1 = \langle \theta, \alpha_1 \rangle, \ \tilde{c}_2 = \langle \theta, \alpha_2 \rangle$$

The Parseval-type of relationship is

$$\langle \theta, \theta \rangle = (a^2 + b^2) = c_1 \tilde{c}_1 + c_2 \tilde{c}_2$$

□

8.3 Biorthogonal Wavelets

Biorthogonalized wavelets are a generalization of orthogonalized wavelets. Therefore, there are more degrees of freedom in designing biorthogonal wavelets. Motivation for the use of biorthogonal wavelet basis is initially provided. Biorthogonal spaces and their basis are next introduced. This is followed by a discussion of biorthogonal scaling functions and dual wavelets. Biorthogonal relationships in the frequency domain are also stated. Relationships between scaling and wavelet coefficients are next derived. Finally, the support values of the scaling functions, wavelet functions, scaling function coefficients, and wavelet coefficients are specified.

8.3.1 Motivation for the Use of Biorthogonal Wavelet Bases

Motivation for the use of biorthogonal wavelet basis is provided in this subsection. Let the scaling function ϕ be the generator of the multiresolution analysis (MRA) $\{V_j \mid V_j \subseteq L^2(\mathbb{R}), \ j \in \mathbb{Z}\}$. Consider a function $f \in V_{j+1}$, and let $f \triangleq f_{j+1}$. Therefore,

$$f_{j+1} = \sum_{k \in \mathbb{Z}} c\,(j+1, k)\,\phi_{j+1,k}$$

Let $V_{j+1} = V_j \oplus W_j$, and $f_{j+1} = (f_j + g_j)$, where $f_j \in V_j$ and $g_j \in W_j$. Therefore,

$$f_j = \sum_{k \in \mathbb{Z}} c\,(j, k)\,\phi_{jk}$$

Assume that $\{\phi_{jk} \mid k \in \mathbb{Z}\}$ is not an orthonormal basis. Consequently, $c\,(j, k) \neq \langle f, \phi_{jk}\rangle$. In order to determine $c\,(j, k)$, another scaling function $\widetilde{\phi}$ is introduced so that

$$\left\langle \phi_{jk}, \widetilde{\phi}_{jl} \right\rangle = \delta_{kl}, \quad \forall \, k, l \in \mathbb{Z}$$

$$\left\langle g_j, \widetilde{\phi}_{jl} \right\rangle = 0, \quad \forall \, l \in \mathbb{Z}$$

In this case $c\,(j, k) = \left\langle f, \widetilde{\phi}_{jk} \right\rangle$.

Next consider the subspace W_j. Let the scaling function $\widetilde{\phi}$ be the generator of the MRA $\{\widetilde{V}_j \mid \widetilde{V}_j \subseteq L^2(\mathbb{R}), \ j \in \mathbb{Z}\}$. Note that $g_j \in W_j$, and $\left\langle g_j, \widetilde{\phi}_{jl} \right\rangle = 0$, imply $W_j \perp \widetilde{V}_j$. As $V_{j+1} = V_j \oplus W_j$, there is wavelet ψ such that $\{\psi_{jk} \mid k \in \mathbb{Z}\}$ is a Riesz basis of W_j (not necessarily orthonormal). Expand $g_j \in W_j$ as

$$g_j = \sum_{k \in \mathbb{Z}} d\,(j, k)\,\psi_{jk}$$

In order to determine the coefficients $d\,(j, k)$, a wavelet $\widetilde{\psi} \in \widetilde{V}_0$ is introduced so that

$$\left\langle \psi_{jk}, \widetilde{\psi}_{jl} \right\rangle = \delta_{kl}, \quad \forall \, k, l \in \mathbb{Z}$$

$$\left\langle \phi_{jk}, \widetilde{\psi}_{jl} \right\rangle = 0, \quad \forall \, k, l \in \mathbb{Z}$$

The Riesz basis set $\left\{ \widetilde{\psi}_{jk} \mid k \in \mathbb{Z} \right\}$ generates the space $\widetilde{W}_j$. Consequently, $\widetilde{W}_j \perp V_j$ and let $\widetilde{V}_j \oplus \widetilde{W}_j = \widetilde{V}_{j+1}$.

In this formulation, ϕ and $\widetilde{\phi}$ are called *biorthogonal scaling functions*, or *dual scaling functions*. Further, ψ and $\widetilde{\psi}$ are called *biorthogonal mother wavelets*, or *dual wavelets*. Also $\{\psi_{jk} \mid k \in \mathbb{Z}\}$ and $\left\{ \widetilde{\psi}_{jk} \mid k \in \mathbb{Z} \right\}$ are called *biorthogonal wavelet basis*. The MRAs

$$\{V_j \mid V_j \subseteq L^2(\mathbb{R}), \ j \in \mathbb{Z}\}, \quad \text{and} \quad \{\widetilde{V}_j \mid \widetilde{V}_j \subseteq L^2(\mathbb{R}), \ j \in \mathbb{Z}\}$$

are called *biorthogonal MRAs* or *dual MRAs*.

8.3.2 Biorthogonal Spaces

Biorthogonal spaces are introduced in this subsection. The multiresolution analysis with biorthogonal basis consists of a pair of hierarchies of approximation spaces. Their characteristics are formally outlined as follows. The multiresolution analysis of $L^2(\mathbb{R})$ is a sequence of closed subspaces $\{V_j \mid V_j \subseteq L^2(\mathbb{R}), \ j \in \mathbb{Z}\}$, and $\{\widetilde{V}_j \mid \widetilde{V}_j \subseteq L^2(\mathbb{R}), \ j \in \mathbb{Z}\}$. The V_j and $\widetilde{V}_j$ spaces are called the *primary* and *dual subspaces*. These spaces are qualified as follows.

Observations 8.1. Some observations about biorthogonal spaces.

1. $V_j \subset V_{j+1}$, and $\widetilde{V}_j \subset \widetilde{V}_{j+1}$ for all values of $j \in \mathbb{Z}$. This is the so-called nesting property of the subspaces.

$$\ldots \subset V_{-2} \subset V_{-1} \subset V_0 \subset V_1 \subset V_2 \subset \ldots$$
$$\ldots \subset \widetilde{V}_{-2} \subset \widetilde{V}_{-1} \subset \widetilde{V}_0 \subset \widetilde{V}_1 \subset \widetilde{V}_2 \subset \ldots$$

2. $\overline{\cup_{j \in \mathbb{Z}} V_j} = L^2(\mathbb{R})$, and $\overline{\cup_{j \in \mathbb{Z}} \widetilde{V}_j} = L^2(\mathbb{R})$. This is the closure property.

3. $\cap_{j \in \mathbb{Z}} V_j = \{0\}$, and $\cap_{j \in \mathbb{Z}} \widetilde{V}_j = \{0\}$.

4. It follows that $V_j \cap V_k = V_k$, and $\widetilde{V}_j \cap \widetilde{V}_k = \widetilde{V}_k$, for $k \leq j; \ j, k \in \mathbb{Z}$.

5. $x(\cdot) \in V_j \Leftrightarrow x(2\cdot) \in V_{j+1}$, and $y(\cdot) \in \widetilde{V}_j \Leftrightarrow y(2\cdot) \in \widetilde{V}_{j+1}, \forall j \in \mathbb{Z}$.

6. $x(t) \in V_0 \Leftrightarrow x(t+1) \in V_0$, and $y(t) \in \widetilde{V}_0 \Leftrightarrow y(t+1) \in \widetilde{V}_0; \forall t \in \mathbb{R}$.

7. Let W_j be the complement of V_j in V_{j+1}, and $\widetilde{W}_j$ be the complement of $\widetilde{V}_j$ in $\widetilde{V}_{j+1}$. These complements are not orthogonal complements.

$$V_j \cap W_j = \{0\}, \quad \text{and } V_{j+1} = V_j \oplus W_j, \quad \forall j \in \mathbb{Z}$$
$$\widetilde{V}_j \cap \widetilde{W}_j = \{0\}, \quad \text{and } \widetilde{V}_{j+1} = \widetilde{V}_j \oplus \widetilde{W}_j, \quad \forall j \in \mathbb{Z}$$

The operator $\oplus$, for example implies that, for all $f_{j+1} \in V_{j+1}$, there exists $f_j \in V_j$ and $g_j \in W_j$ so that $f_{j+1} = f_j + g_j$.

Note that it is not required that $V_j \perp W_j$, and $\widetilde{V}_j \perp \widetilde{W}_j$ (as in the case of orthogonal MRA). This is indicated as

$$V_j \not\perp W_j, \quad \text{and } \widetilde{V}_j \not\perp \widetilde{W}_j$$

where $\not\perp$ denotes nonorthogonality. This definition of W_j and $\widetilde{W}_j$ leads to

$$W_n \cap W_m = \{0\}, \quad n \neq m, \text{ and } \forall n, m \in \mathbb{Z}$$
$$\widetilde{W}_n \cap \widetilde{W}_m = \{0\}, \quad n \neq m, \text{ and } \forall n, m \in \mathbb{Z}$$

$$V_j \cap W_k = \{0\}, \quad j \leq k; \ j, k \in \mathbb{Z}$$
$$\widetilde{V}_j \cap \widetilde{W}_k = \{0\}, \quad j \leq k; \ j, k \in \mathbb{Z}$$

$$\cup_{j \in \mathbb{Z}} W_j = L^2(\mathbb{R}), \quad \text{and } \cup_{j \in \mathbb{Z}} \widetilde{W}_j = L^2(\mathbb{R})$$

8. Biorthogonality requires that $V_j \perp \widetilde{W}_j$, and $\widetilde{V}_j \perp W_j$, $\forall j \in \mathbb{Z}$. Consequently

$$W_n \perp \widetilde{W}_m, \quad n \neq m, \quad \text{where } n, m \in \mathbb{Z}$$

$$V_j \perp \widetilde{W}_j \Rightarrow V_s \perp \widetilde{W}_j, \quad s \leq j; \ s, j \in \mathbb{Z}$$
$$\widetilde{V}_j \perp W_j \Rightarrow \widetilde{V}_s \perp W_j, \quad s \leq j; \ s, j \in \mathbb{Z}$$

9. $L^2(\mathbb{R}) = \bigoplus_{n \in \mathbb{Z}} W_n$, and $L^2(\mathbb{R}) = \bigoplus_{n \in \mathbb{Z}} \widetilde{W}_n$. $\qquad\qquad\qquad$ □

8.3.3 Biorthogonal Space Bases

Bases of biorthogonal spaces are introduced. It is also assumed that $\int_{-\infty}^{\infty} \phi(t)\,dt = \int_{-\infty}^{\infty} \widetilde{\phi}(t)\,dt = 1$.

Observations 8.2. Some observations about basis of biorthogonal spaces.

1. The biorthogonal wavelet system is specified by the functions $\phi \in V_0$, $\psi \in W_0$, $\widetilde{\phi} \in \widetilde{V}_0$, and $\widetilde{\psi} \in \widetilde{W}_0$, where:
   (a) ϕ is called the analysis (or primal) scaling function,
   (b) $\widetilde{\phi}$ is called the synthesis (or dual) scaling function,
   (c) $\psi \cdot$ is called the analysis (or primal) wave function,
   (d) $\widetilde{\psi}$ is called the synthesis (or dual) wave function.
   Also

$$\{\phi(\cdot - n) \mid n \in \mathbb{Z}\},$$
$$\{\psi(\cdot - n) \mid n \in \mathbb{Z}\},$$
$$\left\{\widetilde{\phi}(\cdot - n) \mid n \in \mathbb{Z}\right\},$$
$$\left\{\widetilde{\psi}(\cdot - n) \mid n \in \mathbb{Z}\right\}$$

are basis sets of $V_0, W_0, \widetilde{V}_0$, and $\widetilde{W}_0$ respectively. Also note that these basis sets are not orthogonal sets.
Note that $V_0 \perp \widetilde{W}_0$, and $\widetilde{V}_0 \perp W_0$, imply

$$\left\langle \phi(\cdot), \widetilde{\psi}(\cdot - n) \right\rangle = 0, \quad n \in \mathbb{Z}$$
$$\left\langle \psi(\cdot), \widetilde{\phi}(\cdot - n) \right\rangle = 0, \quad n \in \mathbb{Z}$$
$$\left\langle \widetilde{\phi}(\cdot), \psi(\cdot - n) \right\rangle = 0, \quad n \in \mathbb{Z}$$
$$\left\langle \widetilde{\psi}(\cdot), \phi(\cdot - n) \right\rangle = 0, \quad n \in \mathbb{Z}$$

It is a requirement for dual functions that they satisfy the following conditions.

$$\left\langle \phi\left(\cdot\right), \widetilde{\phi}\left(\cdot - n\right) \right\rangle = \delta_{n0}, \quad n \in \mathbb{Z}$$

$$\left\langle \psi\left(\cdot\right), \widetilde{\psi}\left(\cdot - n\right) \right\rangle = \delta_{n0}, \quad n \in \mathbb{Z}$$

2. It is also required that the admissibility conditions be satisfied. That is,

$$\int_{-\infty}^{\infty} \psi\left(t\right) dt = 0, \text{ and } \int_{-\infty}^{\infty} \widetilde{\psi}\left(t\right) dt = 0$$

3. Define $\forall\, t \in \mathbb{R}$

$$\phi_{jk}\left(t\right) = 2^{j/2}\phi(2^j t - k), \qquad j, k \in \mathbb{Z}$$
$$\psi_{jk}\left(t\right) = 2^{j/2}\psi(2^j t - k), \qquad j, k \in \mathbb{Z}$$
$$\widetilde{\phi}_{jk}\left(t\right) = 2^{j/2}\widetilde{\phi}(2^j t - k), \qquad j, k \in \mathbb{Z}$$
$$\widetilde{\psi}_{jk}\left(t\right) = 2^{j/2}\widetilde{\psi}(2^j t - k), \qquad j, k \in \mathbb{Z}$$

Then for all values of $j \in \mathbb{Z}$

$$\{\phi_{jk} \mid k \in \mathbb{Z}\}, \text{ is the basis set of space } V_j$$
$$\{\psi_{jk} \mid k \in \mathbb{Z}\}, \text{ is the basis set of space } W_j$$
$$\{\widetilde{\phi}_{jk} \mid k \in \mathbb{Z}\}, \text{ is the basis set of space } \widetilde{V}_j$$
$$\{\widetilde{\psi}_{jk} \mid k \in \mathbb{Z}\}, \text{ is the basis set of space } \widetilde{W}_j$$

Note that these are not orthogonal sets.

4. It can be shown using the biorthogonality conditions that

$$\left\langle \phi_{jk}, \widetilde{\psi}_{jl} \right\rangle = 0, \qquad \forall\, j, k, l \in \mathbb{Z}$$

$$\left\langle \psi_{jk}, \widetilde{\phi}_{jl} \right\rangle = 0, \qquad \forall\, j, k, l \in \mathbb{Z}$$

$$\left\langle \phi_{jk}, \widetilde{\phi}_{jl} \right\rangle = \delta_{kl}, \qquad \forall\, j, k, l \in \mathbb{Z}$$

$$\left\langle \psi_{jk}, \widetilde{\psi}_{mn} \right\rangle = \delta_{jm}\delta_{kn}, \qquad \forall\, j, k, m, n \in \mathbb{Z}$$

$\square$

8.3.4   Biorthogonal Scaling Functions and Dual Wavelets

Relevant relationships between biorthogonal scaling functions and dual wavelets are derived in this subsection.

Observations 8.3. Some observations about biorthogonal scaling and wavelet functions.

1. As V_1 is a scaled version of V_0, the basis set $\{\sqrt{2}\phi(2\cdot-n)\mid n\in\mathbb{Z}\}$ spans the space V_1. Similarly, the basis set $\left\{\sqrt{2}\,\widetilde{\phi}(2\cdot-n)\mid n\in\mathbb{Z}\right\}$ spans the space $\widetilde{V}_1$. Then $V_0\subset V_1$ and $\widetilde{V}_0\subset\widetilde{V}_1$ imply the following scaling equations.

$$\phi(t)=\sum_{n\in\mathbb{Z}}h(n)\sqrt{2}\phi(2t-n),\quad\forall\,t\in\mathbb{R}$$

$$h(n)=\left\langle\phi(\cdot),\sqrt{2}\,\widetilde{\phi}(2\cdot-n)\right\rangle,\quad\forall\,n\in\mathbb{Z}$$

$$\widetilde{\phi}(t)=\sum_{n\in\mathbb{Z}}\widetilde{h}(n)\sqrt{2}\,\widetilde{\phi}(2t-n),\quad\forall\,t\in\mathbb{R}$$

$$\widetilde{h}(n)=\left\langle\widetilde{\phi}(\cdot),\sqrt{2}\phi(2\cdot-n)\right\rangle,\quad\forall\,n\in\mathbb{Z}$$

The $h(n)$'s and $\widetilde{h}(n)$'s are called the scaling function, and dual scaling function coefficients respectively. Each of these sequences forms a low-pass filter. The biorthogonal wavelet functions are $\psi\in W_0\subset V_1$ and $\widetilde{\psi}\in\widetilde{W}_0\subset\widetilde{V}_1$. Thus

$$\psi(t)=\sum_{n\in\mathbb{Z}}g(n)\sqrt{2}\phi(2t-n),\quad\forall\,t\in\mathbb{R}$$

$$g(n)=\left\langle\psi(\cdot),\sqrt{2}\,\widetilde{\phi}(2\cdot-n)\right\rangle,\quad\forall\,n\in\mathbb{Z}$$

$$\widetilde{\psi}(t)=\sum_{n\in\mathbb{Z}}\widetilde{g}(n)\sqrt{2}\,\widetilde{\phi}(2t-n),\quad\forall\,t\in\mathbb{R}$$

$$\widetilde{g}(n)=\left\langle\widetilde{\psi}(\cdot),\sqrt{2}\phi(2\cdot-n)\right\rangle,\quad\forall\,n\in\mathbb{Z}$$

The $g(n)$'s and $\widetilde{g}(n)$'s are called the wavelet, and dual wavelet coefficients respectively. Each of these sequences forms a high-pass filter.

2. Using the biorthogonality requirements between the functions $\phi,\psi,\widetilde{\phi}$, and $\widetilde{\psi}$, the following results can be obtained.

$$\sum_{n\in\mathbb{Z}}h(n)\overline{\widetilde{g}(n-2m)}=0,\qquad m\in\mathbb{Z}$$

$$\sum_{n\in\mathbb{Z}}g(n)\overline{\widetilde{h}(n-2m)}=0,\qquad m\in\mathbb{Z}$$

$$\sum_{n\in\mathbb{Z}}h(n)\overline{\widetilde{h}(n-2m)}=\delta_{m0},\qquad m\in\mathbb{Z}$$

$$\sum_{n\in\mathbb{Z}}g(n)\overline{\widetilde{g}(n-2m)}=\delta_{m0},\qquad m\in\mathbb{Z}$$

$\square$

8.3.5 Biorthogonal Relationships in the Frequency Domain

Biorthogonal relationships in the frequency domain are stated in this subsection.

Observations 8.4. Some observations about biorthogonal relationships in the frequency domain.

1. Let $\omega \in \mathbb{R}$. Define

$$\phi(t) \leftrightarrow \Phi(\omega), \quad H(\omega) = \sum_{n \in \mathbb{Z}} h(n) e^{-i\omega n}$$

$$\widetilde{\phi}(t) \leftrightarrow \widetilde{\Phi}(\omega), \quad \widetilde{H}(\omega) = \sum_{n \in \mathbb{Z}} \widetilde{h}(n) e^{-i\omega n}$$

$$\psi(t) \leftrightarrow \Psi(\omega), \quad G(\omega) = \sum_{n \in \mathbb{Z}} g(n) e^{-i\omega n}$$

$$\widetilde{\psi}(t) \leftrightarrow \widetilde{\Psi}(\omega), \quad \widetilde{G}(\omega) = \sum_{n \in \mathbb{Z}} \widetilde{g}(n) e^{-i\omega n}$$

Use of the scaling relationships results in

$$\Phi(\omega) = \frac{1}{\sqrt{2}} H\left(\frac{\omega}{2}\right) \Phi\left(\frac{\omega}{2}\right)$$

$$\widetilde{\Phi}(\omega) = \frac{1}{\sqrt{2}} \widetilde{H}\left(\frac{\omega}{2}\right) \widetilde{\Phi}\left(\frac{\omega}{2}\right)$$

$$\Psi(\omega) = \frac{1}{\sqrt{2}} G\left(\frac{\omega}{2}\right) \Phi\left(\frac{\omega}{2}\right)$$

$$\widetilde{\Psi}(\omega) = \frac{1}{\sqrt{2}} \widetilde{G}\left(\frac{\omega}{2}\right) \widetilde{\Phi}\left(\frac{\omega}{2}\right)$$

Observing that $\Psi(0) = \widetilde{\Psi}(0) = 0$, the above equations yield

$$H(0) = \widetilde{H}(0) = \sqrt{2}$$
$$G(0) = \widetilde{G}(0) = 0$$

Consequently

$$\sum_{n \in \mathbb{Z}} h(n) = \sum_{n \in \mathbb{Z}} \widetilde{h}(n) = \sqrt{2}$$

$$\sum_{n \in \mathbb{Z}} g(n) = \sum_{n \in \mathbb{Z}} \widetilde{g}(n) = 0$$

2.

$$\Phi(\omega) = \prod_{k \in \mathbb{P}} \left\{ \frac{1}{\sqrt{2}} H\left(\frac{\omega}{2^k}\right) \right\} \Phi(0)$$

$$\widetilde{\Phi}(\omega) = \prod_{k \in \mathbb{P}} \left\{ \frac{1}{\sqrt{2}} \widetilde{H}\left(\frac{\omega}{2^k}\right) \right\} \widetilde{\Phi}(0)$$

$$\Psi\left(\omega\right) = \left\{\frac{1}{\sqrt{2}}G\left(\frac{\omega}{2}\right)\right\} \prod_{k\in\mathbb{P}}\left\{\frac{1}{\sqrt{2}}H\left(\frac{\omega}{2^{k+1}}\right)\right\}\Phi\left(0\right)$$

$$\widetilde{\Psi}\left(\omega\right) = \left\{\frac{1}{\sqrt{2}}\widetilde{G}\left(\frac{\omega}{2}\right)\right\} \prod_{k\in\mathbb{P}}\left\{\frac{1}{\sqrt{2}}\widetilde{H}\left(\frac{\omega}{2^{k+1}}\right)\right\}\widetilde{\Phi}\left(0\right)$$

3. The biorthogonality conditions in the frequency domain translate to

$$\sum_{n\in\mathbb{Z}}\Phi\left(\omega+2\pi n\right)\overline{\widetilde{\Psi}\left(\omega+2\pi n\right)} = 0, \qquad \forall\,\omega\in\mathbb{R}$$

$$\sum_{n\in\mathbb{Z}}\Psi\left(\omega+2\pi n\right)\overline{\widetilde{\Phi}\left(\omega+2\pi n\right)} = 0, \qquad \forall\,\omega\in\mathbb{R}$$

$$\sum_{n\in\mathbb{Z}}\Phi\left(\omega+2\pi n\right)\overline{\widetilde{\Phi}\left(\omega+2\pi n\right)} = 1, \qquad \forall\,\omega\in\mathbb{R}$$

$$\sum_{n\in\mathbb{Z}}\Psi\left(\omega+2\pi n\right)\overline{\widetilde{\Psi}\left(\omega+2\pi n\right)} = 1, \qquad \forall\,\omega\in\mathbb{R}$$

4. It can be shown that

$$H(\omega)\overline{\widetilde{G}(\omega)} + H(\omega+\pi)\overline{\widetilde{G}(\omega+\pi)} = 0, \qquad \forall\,\omega\in\mathbb{R}$$
$$G(\omega)\overline{\widetilde{H}(\omega)} + G(\omega+\pi)\overline{\widetilde{H}(\omega+\pi)} = 0, \qquad \forall\,\omega\in\mathbb{R}$$
$$H(\omega)\overline{\widetilde{H}(\omega)} + H(\omega+\pi)\overline{\widetilde{H}(\omega+\pi)} = 2, \qquad \forall\,\omega\in\mathbb{R}$$
$$G(\omega)\overline{\widetilde{G}(\omega)} + G(\omega+\pi)\overline{\widetilde{G}(\omega+\pi)} = 2, \qquad \forall\,\omega\in\mathbb{R}$$

Substitution of $\omega = 0$ results in

$$H(\pi)\overline{\widetilde{G}(\pi)} = 0$$
$$G(\pi)\overline{\widetilde{H}(\pi)} = 0$$
$$H(\pi)\overline{\widetilde{H}(\pi)} = 0$$
$$G(\pi)\overline{\widetilde{G}(\pi)} = 2$$

The last equation implies that $G(\pi) \neq 0$, and $\widetilde{G}(\pi) \neq 0$. Therefore, $H(\pi) = \widetilde{H}(\pi) = 0$. This results in

$$\sum_{n\in\mathbb{Z}}h\left(2n\right) = \sum_{n\in\mathbb{Z}}h\left(2n+1\right) = \frac{1}{\sqrt{2}}$$

$$\sum_{n\in\mathbb{Z}}\widetilde{h}\left(2n\right) = \sum_{n\in\mathbb{Z}}\widetilde{h}\left(2n+1\right) = \frac{1}{\sqrt{2}}$$

$\square$

8.3.6 Relationships between Scaling Coefficients

Relationships between scaling coefficients are obtained in this subsection.

Observations 8.5. Certain useful relationships about scaling coefficients.

1. Define I to be a 2×2 identity matrix, and matrices $M(\omega), \widetilde{M}(\omega)$ as follows.

$$M(\omega) = \begin{bmatrix} H(\omega) & H(\omega + \pi) \\ G(\omega) & G(\omega + \pi) \end{bmatrix}$$

$$\widetilde{M}(\omega) = \begin{bmatrix} \widetilde{H}(\omega) & \widetilde{H}(\omega + \pi) \\ \widetilde{G}(\omega) & \widetilde{G}(\omega + \pi) \end{bmatrix}$$

Then

$$M(\omega)\overline{\widetilde{M}(\omega)}^T = 2I, \qquad \forall \, \omega \in \mathbb{R}$$

The matrices $M(\omega)$ and $\widetilde{M}(\omega)$ are called the modulation matrices.

2. The above matrix equations can be split into

$$\begin{bmatrix} H(\omega) & H(\omega + \pi) \\ G(\omega) & G(\omega + \pi) \end{bmatrix} \begin{bmatrix} \overline{\widetilde{H}(\omega)} \\ \overline{\widetilde{H}(\omega + \pi)} \end{bmatrix} = \begin{bmatrix} 2 \\ 0 \end{bmatrix}$$

$$\begin{bmatrix} H(\omega) & H(\omega + \pi) \\ G(\omega) & G(\omega + \pi) \end{bmatrix} \begin{bmatrix} \overline{\widetilde{G}(\omega)} \\ \overline{\widetilde{G}(\omega + \pi)} \end{bmatrix} = \begin{bmatrix} 0 \\ 2 \end{bmatrix}$$

Define

$$\Delta(\omega) = H(\omega) G(\omega + \pi) - G(\omega) H(\omega + \pi)$$

where $\Delta(\omega) \neq 0$ because, the wavelets form a basis for the complementary spaces. Then

$$\overline{\widetilde{H}(\omega)} = \frac{2G(\omega + \pi)}{\Delta(\omega)}$$

$$\overline{\widetilde{H}(\omega + \pi)} = \frac{-2G(\omega)}{\Delta(\omega)}$$

$$\overline{\widetilde{G}(\omega)} = \frac{-2H(\omega + \pi)}{\Delta(\omega)}$$

$$\overline{\widetilde{G}(\omega + \pi)} = \frac{2H(\omega)}{\Delta(\omega)}$$

Let $\Delta(\omega) = ce^{-il\omega}, l \in \mathbb{Z}$, and $c \in \mathbb{R} \setminus \{0\}$ be a constant. The above equations yield

$$\overline{\widetilde{H}(\omega)} = \frac{2e^{il\omega}G(\omega + \pi)}{c}$$

$$\overline{\widetilde{H}\left(\omega+\pi\right)}=\frac{-2e^{il\omega}G\left(\omega\right)}{c}$$

These equations imply that $l=L$, is an odd integer. Let $c=\pm2$, then

$$G\left(\omega\right)=\mp e^{-iL\omega}\overline{\widetilde{H}\left(\omega+\pi\right)}$$
$$\widetilde{G}\left(\omega\right)=\mp e^{-iL\omega}\overline{H\left(\omega+\pi\right)}$$

Therefore,

$$G\left(\pi\right)=\pm\sqrt{2}$$
$$\widetilde{G}\left(\pi\right)=\pm\sqrt{2}$$

3. For $n\in\mathbb{Z}$, and L an odd integer, the above equations imply

$$g(n)=\pm\left(-1\right)^{n}\overline{\widetilde{h}\left(L-n\right)}$$
$$\widetilde{g}(n)=\pm\left(-1\right)^{n}\overline{h\left(L-n\right)}$$

Substituting $L=1$, as a particular case results in

$$g(n)=\pm\left(-1\right)^{n}\overline{\widetilde{h}\left(1-n\right)}$$
$$\widetilde{g}(n)=\pm\left(-1\right)^{n}\overline{h\left(1-n\right)}$$

$\square$

8.3.7 Support Values

Support values of both primal and dual: scaling functions, wavelet functions, scaling function coefficients, and wavelet coefficients are next obtained. Recall that, if $supp$ $f\left(t\right)=[L_1,L_2],L_1,L_2\in\mathbb{Z}$ where $t\in\mathbb{R}$, then the diameter of the support of the function is $diam\ supp\ f\left(t\right)=\left(L_2-L_1\right)$.

Observation 8.6. Let

$$supp\ \phi\left(t\right)=[L_1,L_2],\ \ \text{and}\ \ supp\ \widetilde{\phi}\left(t\right)=\left[\widetilde{L}_1,\widetilde{L}_2\right]$$

Then

$$supp\ \{h\left(n\right)\}=[L_1,L_2],\ \ \text{and}\ \ supp\left\{\widetilde{h}\left(n\right)\right\}=\left[\widetilde{L}_1,\widetilde{L}_2\right]$$

$$supp\ \{g\left(n\right)\}=[1-\widetilde{L}_2,1-\widetilde{L}_1],\ \ \text{and}\ \ supp\ \{\widetilde{g}\left(n\right)\}=[1-L_2,1-L_1]$$

$$supp\ \psi\left(t\right)=\left[\frac{L_1-\widetilde{L}_2+1}{2},\frac{L_2-\widetilde{L}_1+1}{2}\right]$$

$$supp \, \widetilde{\psi} \, (t) = \left[\frac{\widetilde{L}_1 - L_2 + 1}{2}, \frac{\widetilde{L}_2 - L_1 + 1}{2} \right]$$

$$diam \; supp \; \psi \, (t) = diam \; supp \; \widetilde{\psi} \, (t) = \frac{\left(L_2 - L_1 + \widetilde{L}_2 - \widetilde{L}_1 \right)}{2}$$

$\square$

The above results can be proved as in the case of orthogonal wavelets.

8.4 Decomposition and Reconstruction of Functions

The biorthogonal decomposition and reconstruction of a function is studied in this section. A digital filter interpretation of this process is also provided. Consequences of symmetric $h(n)$'s and $\widetilde{h}(n)$'s are also explored. Moments of biorthogonal scaling and wavelets are also defined. These are useful in the construction of biorthogonal scaling coefficients.

8.4.1 Basics

Let $f \in L^2 (\mathbb{R})$. Also let P_j be the projection operator into subspace V_j. That is,

$$f_j \triangleq P_j f = \sum_{k \in \mathbb{Z}} \left\langle f, \widetilde{\phi}_{jk} \right\rangle \phi_{jk}$$

Thus f_j is an approximation of the function f at scale 2^{-j}. Similarly, let Q_j be the projection operator into subspace W_j. That is,

$$g_j \triangleq Q_j f = \sum_{k \in \mathbb{Z}} \left\langle f, \widetilde{\psi}_{jk} \right\rangle \psi_{jk}$$

Therefore, $V_j \cap W_j = \{0\}$, and $V_{j+1} = V_j \oplus W_j$ imply

$$f_{j+1} = f_j + g_j$$

The following observations readily follow from the above discussion. These are similar to the corresponding observations for orthogonal expansions of functions.

Observations 8.7. About decomposition and reconstruction of a function.

1. The result $L^2 (\mathbb{R}) = \bigoplus_{n \in \mathbb{Z}} W_n$ implies $f = \sum_{j \in \mathbb{Z}} g_j$.

2. Let $j_0 \in \mathbb{Z}$, and $L^2(\mathbb{R}) = V_{j_0} \oplus W_{j_0} \oplus W_{j_0+1} \oplus W_{j_0+2} \oplus \ldots$. Therefore,

$$f = f_{j_0} + \sum_{j=j_0}^{\infty} g_j$$

3. As $V_{j_0} = \bigoplus_{j \le (j_0-1)} W_j$

$$f_{j_0} = \sum_{j \le (j_0-1)} g_j$$

□

Let $f : \mathbb{R} \to \mathbb{C}$, and $f \in L^2(\mathbb{R})$. Then

$$f(t) = \sum_{j,k \in \mathbb{Z}} d(j,k) \psi_{jk}(t) = \sum_{j,k \in \mathbb{Z}} \tilde{d}(j,k) \tilde{\psi}_{jk}(t)$$

$$d(j,k) = \langle f, \tilde{\psi}_{jk} \rangle, \qquad j,k \in \mathbb{Z}$$

$$\tilde{d}(j,k) = \langle f, \psi_{jk} \rangle, \qquad j,k \in \mathbb{Z}$$

Biorthogonal multiresolution analysis is similar to the orthogonal multiresolution analysis. Let $f \in V_J$, and $j_0 < J$, then the biorthogonal wavelet expansion is

$$f(t) = \sum_{k \in \mathbb{Z}} c(j_0,k) \phi_{j_0 k}(t) + \sum_{j=j_0}^{J-1} \sum_{k \in \mathbb{Z}} d(j,k) \psi_{jk}(t)$$

$$c(j_0,k) = \langle f, \tilde{\phi}_{j_0 k} \rangle = \int_{-\infty}^{\infty} f(t) \overline{\tilde{\phi}_{j_0 k}}(t) dt, \qquad k \in \mathbb{Z}$$

$$d(j,k) = \langle f, \tilde{\psi}_{jk} \rangle = \int_{-\infty}^{\infty} f(t) \overline{\tilde{\psi}_{jk}}(t) dt, \qquad j,k \in \mathbb{Z}$$

Initially compute the sequence $\{c(J,k) \mid k \in \mathbb{Z}\}$. If the function $f(t)$ is sufficiently smooth then

$$c(J,k) \simeq 2^{-J/2} f(2^{-J} k)$$

Then for $j = J, J-1, \ldots, (j_0+1)$ compute

$$\{c(j-1,k) \mid k \in \mathbb{Z}\} \quad \text{and} \quad \{d(j-1,k) \mid k \in \mathbb{Z}\}$$

from $\{c(j,k) \mid k \in \mathbb{Z}\}$ by using the recursive relationship

$$c(j-1,k) = \sum_{m \in \mathbb{Z}} \overline{\tilde{h}(m-2k)} c(j,m), \qquad k \in \mathbb{Z}$$

$$d(j-1,k) = \sum_{m \in \mathbb{Z}} \overline{\tilde{g}(m-2k)} c(j,m), \qquad k \in \mathbb{Z}$$

The above steps constitute the decomposition algorithm. The inverse fast biorthogonal wavelet transform is obtained recursively from

$$c(j,k) = \sum_{m \in \mathbb{Z}} c(j-1,m)\, h(k-2m) + \sum_{m \in \mathbb{Z}} d(j-1,m)\, g(k-2m), \quad k \in \mathbb{Z}$$

for $j = (j_0+1), (j_0+2), \ldots, J$. These are the reconstruction steps.   □

8.4.2 Digital Filter Interpretation

A digital filter interpretation of the biorthogonal decomposition and reconstruction of a function is provided. Let $\mathcal{H}(z)$, $\widetilde{\mathcal{H}}(z)$, $\mathcal{G}(z)$, and $\widetilde{\mathcal{G}}(z)$ be the z-transforms of the sequences $\{h(n) \mid n \in \mathbb{Z}\}$, $\{\widetilde{h}(n) \mid n \in \mathbb{Z}\}$, $\{g(n) \mid n \in \mathbb{Z}\}$, and $\{\widetilde{g}(n) \mid n \in \mathbb{Z}\}$ respectively.

For $j = j_0, (j_0 + 1), (j_0 + 2), \ldots, J$ define the z-transforms of the sequences $\{c(j,k) \mid k \in \mathbb{Z}\}$, and $\{d(j,k) \mid k \in \mathbb{Z}\}$ to be $\mathcal{C}(j,z)$ and $\mathcal{D}(j,z)$ respectively.

Lemma 8.1. *For $j = J, J - 1, \ldots, (j_0 + 1)$*

$$\mathcal{C}\left(j-1, z^2\right) = \frac{1}{2}\left[\overline{\widetilde{\mathcal{H}}(z)}\mathcal{C}(j,z) + \overline{\widetilde{\mathcal{H}}(-z)}\mathcal{C}(j,-z)\right] \tag{8.2a}$$

$$\mathcal{D}\left(j-1, z^2\right) = \frac{1}{2}\left[\overline{\widetilde{\mathcal{G}}(z)}\mathcal{C}(j,z) + \overline{\widetilde{\mathcal{G}}(-z)}\mathcal{C}(j,-z)\right] \tag{8.2b}$$

and for $j = (j_0 + 1), (j_0 + 2), \ldots, J$

$$\mathcal{C}(j,z) = \left[\mathcal{H}(z)\mathcal{C}\left(j-1, z^2\right) + \mathcal{G}(z)\mathcal{D}\left(j-1, z^2\right)\right] \tag{8.2c}$$

These equations correspond to decomposition and reconstruction of a function.   □

8.4.3 Symmetric $h(n)$'s and $\widetilde{h}(n)$'s

Consequences of symmetric $h(n)$'s and $\widetilde{h}(n)$'s are explored in this subsection. It is possible for $\{h(n) \mid n \in \mathbb{Z}\}$ and $\{\widetilde{h}(n) \mid n \in \mathbb{Z}\}$ to be symmetric in the case of biorthogonal wavelets. In this case, these sequences correspond to linear phase filters. Assume that the support of these sequences is compact and identical. Consider two cases. In one case, the sequences $\{h(n) \mid n \in \mathbb{Z}\}$ and $\{\widetilde{h}(n) \mid n \in \mathbb{Z}\}$ have even number of terms, and in the other case, there are odd number of terms.

Case 1: Let the number of terms in the sequences

$$\{h(n) \mid n \in \mathbb{Z}\} \quad \text{and} \quad \{\widetilde{h}(n) \mid n \in \mathbb{Z}\}$$

be an even number. Then it is possible to express $H(\omega)$ and $\widetilde{H}(\omega)$ as

$$H(\omega) = e^{-ik\omega+i\omega/2} \cos\left(\frac{\omega}{2}\right) p(\cos\omega), \qquad k \in \mathbb{Z}$$

$$\widetilde{H}(\omega) = e^{-il\omega+i\omega/2} \cos\left(\frac{\omega}{2}\right) \widetilde{p}(\cos\omega), \qquad l \in \mathbb{Z}$$

where $p(\cos\omega)$ and $\widetilde{p}(\cos\omega)$ are polynomials in $\cos\omega$. Also $k = l$, as the support of the two sequences is identical. Substituting the above relationships the following equation

$$H(\omega)\overline{\widetilde{H}(\omega)} + H(\omega + \pi)\overline{\widetilde{H}(\omega + \pi)} = 2, \qquad \forall\, \omega \in \mathbb{R}$$

results in

$$(1 + x)\, p(x)\, \widetilde{p}(x) + (1 - x)\, p(-x)\, \widetilde{p}(-x) = 4$$

where $x = \cos\omega$. Therefore, the above relationship has to exist for biorthogonality of basis, if the scaling coefficients have an even number of significant terms.

Case 2: Let the number of terms in the sequences

$$\{h(n) \mid n \in \mathbb{Z}\} \quad \text{and} \quad \left\{\widetilde{h}(n) \mid n \in \mathbb{Z}\right\}$$

be an odd number. Then it is possible to express $H(\omega)$ and $\widetilde{H}(\omega)$ as

$$H(\omega) = e^{-ik\omega} p(\cos\omega), \qquad k \in \mathbb{Z}$$

$$\widetilde{H}(\omega) = e^{-il\omega} \widetilde{p}(\cos\omega), \qquad l \in \mathbb{Z}$$

where $p(\cos\omega)$ and $\widetilde{p}(\cos\omega)$ are polynomials in $\cos\omega$. The support of the sequences is identical. This implies $k = l$. Substitution of the above relationships the following equation

$$H(\omega)\overline{\widetilde{H}(\omega)} + H(\omega + \pi)\overline{\widetilde{H}(\omega + \pi)} = 2, \qquad \forall\, \omega \in \mathbb{R}$$

results in

$$p(x)\, \widetilde{p}(x) + p(-x)\, \widetilde{p}(-x) = 2$$

where $x = \cos\omega$. Therefore, the above relationship has to exist for biorthogonality of basis, if the scaling coefficients have odd number of significant terms.

These observations are used in the construction of biorthogonal scaling coefficients.

8.4.4 Moments

Definitions of moments of biorthogonal scaling and wavelets are given in this subsection. These are useful in the construction of biorthogonal scaling functions.

While discussing orthogonal wavelets, the moments of the scaling and wavelet functions were defined as

$$M_j = \int_{-\infty}^{\infty} t^j \phi(t)\, dt, \qquad j \in \mathbb{N}$$

$$N_j = \int_{-\infty}^{\infty} t^j \psi(t)\, dt, \qquad j \in \mathbb{N}$$

Note that $M_0 = \Phi(0)$, and $N_0 = \Psi(0)$. Moments for their biorthogonal counterpart are defined similarly.

Definition 8.2 *Moments of biorthogonal scaling function* $\widetilde{\phi}(\cdot)$, *and wavelet function* $\widetilde{\psi}(\cdot)$.

$$\widetilde{M}_j = \int_{-\infty}^{\infty} t^j \widetilde{\phi}(t)\, dt, \qquad j \in \mathbb{N} \tag{8.3a}$$

$$\widetilde{N}_j = \int_{-\infty}^{\infty} t^j \widetilde{\psi}(t)\, dt, \qquad j \in \mathbb{N} \tag{8.3b}$$

$\square$

Also $\widetilde{M}_0 = \widetilde{\Phi}(0)$, and $\widetilde{N}_0 = \widetilde{\Psi}(0)$, it is required that $\Psi(0) = \int_{-\infty}^{\infty} \psi(t)\, dt = 0$. For the smoothness of the wavelet function, it is required that $N_j = 0$, $j = 0, 1, 2, \ldots, N$. Once again recall that if the first through the Nth moments of the wavelet function $\psi(\cdot)$ vanish, and $\Phi(0) \neq 0$, then

$$\left. \frac{d^j}{d\omega^j} \Psi(\omega) \right|_{\omega=0} = 0, \quad j = 0, 1, 2, \ldots, N$$

$$\left. \frac{d^j}{d\omega^j} G(\omega) \right|_{\omega=0} = 0, \quad j = 0, 1, 2, \ldots, N$$

$$\left. \frac{d^j}{d\omega^j} H(\omega) \right|_{\omega=\pi} = 0, \quad j = 0, 1, 2, \ldots, N$$

Similar results are noted in the following observation.

Observation 8.8. If $\widetilde{N}_j = 0$, $j = 0, 1, 2, \ldots, N$, and $\widetilde{\Phi}(0) \neq 0$, then

$$\left. \frac{d^j}{d\omega^j} \widetilde{\Psi}(\omega) \right|_{\omega=0} = 0, \quad j = 0, 1, 2, \ldots, N$$

$$\left. \frac{d^j}{d\omega^j} \widetilde{G}(\omega) \right|_{\omega=0} = 0, \quad j = 0, 1, 2, \ldots, N$$

$$\left. \frac{d^j}{d\omega^j} \widetilde{H}(\omega) \right|_{\omega=\pi} = 0, \quad j = 0, 1, 2, \ldots, N$$

The proofs of these results are similar to the proofs in the case of orthogonal wavelets. $\square$

8.5 Construction of Biorthogonal Scaling Coefficients

The construction of compactly supported biorthogonal wavelets is studied. Assume that $\Phi(0) \neq 0$, and $\widetilde{\Phi}(0) \neq 0$, and $\omega \in \mathbb{R}$. Also assume that the mother wavelet function $\psi(\cdot)$ is so that

$$\int_{-\infty}^{\infty} t^k \psi(t) dt = 0, \quad \text{for } k = 0, 1, 2, \ldots, \left(\widetilde{N} - 1\right)$$

which implies

$$\Psi^{(k)}(0) = 0, \quad \text{for } k = 0, 1, 2, \ldots, \left(\widetilde{N} - 1\right)$$

In addition assume that the biorthogonal wavelet function $\widetilde{\psi}(\cdot)$ is so that

$$\int_{-\infty}^{\infty} t^k \widetilde{\psi}(t) dt = 0, \quad \text{for } k = 0, 1, 2, \ldots, (N - 1)$$

which implies

$$\widetilde{\Psi}^{(k)}(0) = 0, \quad \text{for } k = 0, 1, 2, \ldots, (N - 1)$$

Then $\Psi(\omega)$ and $\widetilde{\Psi}(\omega)$ have zeros of order $\widetilde{N}$ and N respectively at $\omega = 0$. As

$$\Psi(\omega) = \mp \frac{1}{\sqrt{2}} e^{-iL\omega/2} \overline{\widetilde{H}\left(\frac{\omega}{2} + \pi\right)} \Phi\left(\frac{\omega}{2}\right), \qquad L \text{ is an odd integer}$$

$$\widetilde{\Psi}(\omega) = \mp \frac{1}{\sqrt{2}} e^{-iL\omega/2} \overline{H\left(\frac{\omega}{2} + \pi\right)} \widetilde{\Phi}\left(\frac{\omega}{2}\right), \qquad L \text{ is an odd integer}$$

$H(\omega)$ and $\widetilde{H}(\omega)$ have zeros of order N and $\widetilde{N}$ respectively at $\omega = \pi$. Then $H(\omega)$, and $\widetilde{H}(\omega)$ are divisible by $R(\omega)$ and $\widetilde{R}(\omega)$ respectively, where $R(\omega)$ and $\widetilde{R}(\omega)$ have N and $\widetilde{N}$ zeros respectively at $\omega = \pi$, and $R(0) = \widetilde{R}(0) = 1$.

$$R(\omega) = \left(\frac{1 + e^{-i\omega}}{2}\right)^N$$

$$\widetilde{R}(\omega) = \left(\frac{1 + e^{-i\omega}}{2}\right)^{\widetilde{N}}$$

Next consider two cases. In the first case, let each N and $\widetilde{N}$ be even numbers. In the second case N and $\widetilde{N}$ are allowed to be odd numbers.

   Case 1: N and $\widetilde{N}$ are both even numbers. Let $N = 2K$ and $\widetilde{N} = 2\widetilde{K}$. Then $R(\omega) = e^{-i\omega K}(\cos \omega/2)^{2K}$, and $\widetilde{R}(\omega) = e^{-i\omega \widetilde{K}}(\cos \omega/2)^{2\widetilde{K}}$. Let

$$H\left(\omega\right) = R\left(\omega\right)Q\left(\cos\omega\right)$$
$$= e^{-i\omega K}\left(\cos\omega/2\right)^{2K}Q\left(\cos\omega\right)$$
$$\widetilde{H}\left(\omega\right) = \widetilde{R}\left(\omega\right)\widetilde{Q}\left(\cos\omega\right)$$
$$= e^{-i\omega\widetilde{K}}\left(\cos\omega/2\right)^{2\widetilde{K}}\widetilde{Q}\left(\cos\omega\right)$$

Also the following restrictions are placed: $Q\left(-1\right)\neq 0$ and $\widetilde{Q}\left(-1\right)\neq 0$. These are linear phase filters with an odd number of significant $h(n)$'s and $\widetilde{h}(n)$'s respectively. As $H\left(\omega\right)$ is 2π-periodic, by introducing suitable integer translations in the indices of $h(n)$'s, the $e^{-i\omega K}$ term in it can be ignored. This will occur, if the support of $h(n)$'s is symmetric around $n = 0$. Similarly, $e^{-i\omega\widetilde{K}}$ factor will be ignored in $\widetilde{H}(\omega)$. That is, the support of $\widetilde{h}(n)$'s is also symmetric around $n = 0$. Therefore, assume

$$H\left(\omega\right) = \left(\cos\omega/2\right)^{2K}Q\left(\cos\omega\right)$$
$$\widetilde{H}\left(\omega\right) = \left(\cos\omega/2\right)^{2\widetilde{K}}\widetilde{Q}\left(\cos\omega\right)$$

Substitute the above values in the following equation

$$H(\omega)\overline{\widetilde{H}(\omega)} + H(\omega+\pi)\overline{\widetilde{H}(\omega+\pi)} = 2, \qquad \forall\,\omega\in\mathbb{R}$$

It results in

$$\left(\cos\omega/2\right)^{\left(N+\widetilde{N}\right)}Q\left(\cos\omega\right)\widetilde{Q}\left(\cos\omega\right)$$
$$+\left(\sin\omega/2\right)^{\left(N+\widetilde{N}\right)}Q\left(\cos\left(\omega+\pi\right)\right)\widetilde{Q}\left(\cos\left(\omega+\pi\right)\right) = 2$$

In the above equation, let $y = \sin^2\omega/2$, and define $P(y)$ as

$$P(y) = Q\left(\cos\omega\right)\widetilde{Q}\left(\cos\omega\right)/2$$
$$P(1-y) = Q\left(\cos\left(\omega+\pi\right)\right)\widetilde{Q}\left(\cos\left(\omega+\pi\right)\right)/2$$

Therefore,

$$(1-y)^{K+\widetilde{K}}P(y) + y^{K+\widetilde{K}}P(1-y) = 1, \qquad y\in[0,1]$$

This is Bezout's equation. It has also occurred in the study of orthogonal wavelet basis. One of its solutions is

$$P(y) = \sum_{k=0}^{K+\widetilde{K}-1}\binom{K+\widetilde{K}+k-1}{k}y^k$$

Case 2: N and $\widetilde{N}$ are both odd numbers. Let $N = (2K+1)$ and $\widetilde{N} = (2\widetilde{K}+1)$. Then

$$R\left(\omega\right) = e^{-i\omega K - i\omega/2}\left(\cos\omega/2\right)^{2K+1}, \quad\text{and}\quad \widetilde{R}\left(\omega\right) = e^{-i\omega\widetilde{K}-i\omega/2}\left(\cos\omega/2\right)^{2\widetilde{K}+1}$$

Let

$$H(\omega) = R(\omega) Q(\cos\omega)$$
$$= e^{-i\omega K - i\omega/2} (\cos\omega/2)^{2K+1} Q(\cos\omega)$$
$$\widetilde{H}(\omega) = \widetilde{R}(\omega) \widetilde{Q}(\cos\omega)$$
$$= e^{-i\omega\widetilde{K} - i\omega/2} (\cos\omega/2)^{2\widetilde{K}+1} \widetilde{Q}(\cos\omega)$$

Also the following restrictions are placed: $Q(-1) \neq 0$ and $\widetilde{Q}(-1) \neq 0$. These are linear phase filters with an even number of significant $h(n)$'s and $\widetilde{h}(n)$'s. Once again, as in the previous case, $e^{-i\omega K - i\omega/2}$ and $e^{-i\omega\widetilde{K} - i\omega/2}$ factors can be modified by shifting the support of $h(n)$'s and $\widetilde{h}(n)$'s so that they each become equal to $e^{-i\omega/2}$. This will occur, if the support of $h(n)$'s and $\widetilde{h}(n)$'s is symmetric around $n = 1/2$. Therefore, assume

$$H(\omega) = e^{-i\omega/2} (\cos\omega/2)^{2K+1} Q(\cos\omega)$$
$$\widetilde{H}(\omega) = e^{-i\omega/2} (\cos\omega/2)^{2\widetilde{K}+1} \widetilde{Q}(\cos\omega)$$

Substitute the above values in the following equation

$$H(\omega)\overline{\widetilde{H}(\omega)} + H(\omega + \pi)\overline{\widetilde{H}(\omega + \pi)} = 2, \qquad \forall \omega \in \mathbb{R}$$

It results in

$$(\cos\omega/2)^{(N+\widetilde{N})} Q(\cos\omega) \widetilde{Q}(\cos\omega)$$
$$+ (\sin\omega/2)^{(N+\widetilde{N})} Q(\cos(\omega + \pi)) \widetilde{Q}(\cos(\omega + \pi)) = 2$$

In the above equation, let $y = \sin^2\omega/2$, and define $P(y)$ as

$$P(y) = Q(\cos\omega) \widetilde{Q}(\cos\omega) /2$$
$$P(1 - y) = Q(\cos(\omega + \pi)) \widetilde{Q}(\cos(\omega + \pi)) /2$$

Therefore,

$$(1 - y)^{K+\widetilde{K}+1} P(y) + y^{K+\widetilde{K}+1} P(1 - y) = 1, \qquad y \in [0, 1]$$

A solution of the above equation is

$$P(y) = \sum_{k=0}^{K+\widetilde{K}} \binom{K + \widetilde{K} + k}{k} y^k$$

This construction is summarized in the following observation.

Observation 8.9. Assume that biorthogonal wavelets are compactly supported. Let $\Phi(0) \neq 0$, $\widetilde{\Phi}(0) \neq 0$, and $\omega \in \mathbb{R}$. Also let the mother wavelet function $\psi(\cdot)$ be so that

$$\int_{-\infty}^{\infty} t^k \psi(t)dt = 0, \quad \text{for } k = 0, 1, 2, \ldots, \left(\widetilde{N} - 1\right)$$

In addition assume that the biorthogonal wavelet function $\widetilde{\psi}(\cdot)$ is so that

$$\int_{-\infty}^{\infty} t^k \widetilde{\psi}(t)dt = 0, \quad \text{for } k = 0, 1, 2, \ldots, (N - 1)$$

Let $y = \sin^2 \omega/2$, and define

$$P(y) = Q\left(\cos \omega\right) \widetilde{Q}\left(\cos \omega\right)/2$$

The relationship between $Q(\cos \omega)$, $\widetilde{Q}(\cos \omega)$, and $P(y)$ is shown in the following two cases.

Case 1: N and $\widetilde{N}$ are both even numbers. Let $N = 2K$ and $\widetilde{N} = 2\widetilde{K}$. Let the support of $h(n)$'s and $\widetilde{h}(n)$'s be symmetric around $n = 0$. Therefore,

$$H\left(\omega\right) = \left(\cos \frac{\omega}{2}\right)^N Q\left(\cos \omega\right)$$

$$\widetilde{H}\left(\omega\right) = \left(\cos \frac{\omega}{2}\right)^{\widetilde{N}} \widetilde{Q}\left(\cos \omega\right)$$

These are linear phase filters with an odd number of significant $h(n)$'s and $\widetilde{h}(n)$'s. Then

$$P(y) = \sum_{k=0}^{K+\widetilde{K}-1} \binom{K + \widetilde{K} + k - 1}{k} y^k$$

Case 2: N and $\widetilde{N}$ are both odd numbers. Let $N = (2K + 1)$ and $\widetilde{N} = (2\widetilde{K}+1)$. Let the support of $h(n)$'s and $\widetilde{h}(n)$'s be symmetric around $n = 1/2$. Therefore,

$$H\left(\omega\right) = e^{-i\omega/2} \left(\cos \frac{\omega}{2}\right)^N Q\left(\cos \omega\right)$$

$$\widetilde{H}\left(\omega\right) = e^{-i\omega/2} \left(\cos \frac{\omega}{2}\right)^{\widetilde{N}} \widetilde{Q}\left(\cos \omega\right)$$

These are linear phase filters with an even number of significant $h(n)$'s and $\widetilde{h}(n)$'s. Then

$$P(y) = \sum_{k=0}^{K+\widetilde{K}} \binom{K + \widetilde{K} + k}{k} y^k$$

□

B-spline-based biorthogonal wavelets are discussed in the next section.

8.6 B-Spline-Based Biorthogonal Wavelets

B-spline-based biorthogonal wavelets can be constructed, using the results from the last section. Let $\tilde{Q}(\cos \omega) = \sqrt{2}$, then $Q(\cos \omega) = \sqrt{2}P(y)$. Also let $z = e^{i\omega}$. Once again consider the two cases, when N and $\tilde{N}$ are both either even numbers, or odd numbers.

Case 1: N and $\tilde{N}$ are even numbers, where $N = 2K$ and $\tilde{N} = 2\tilde{K}$.

$$H(\omega) = \sqrt{2}\left(\cos\frac{\omega}{2}\right)^N \sum_{k=0}^{K+\tilde{K}-1}\binom{K+\tilde{K}+k-1}{k}\left(\sin^2\frac{\omega}{2}\right)^k$$

$$\tilde{H}(\omega) = \sqrt{2}\left(\cos\frac{\omega}{2}\right)^{\tilde{N}} = \frac{\sqrt{2}z^{\tilde{K}}}{2^{\tilde{N}}}\sum_{k=0}^{\tilde{N}}\binom{\tilde{N}}{k}z^{-k}$$

It follows from the expressions for $H(\omega)$ and $\tilde{H}(\omega)$ that

$$supp\ \{h(n)\} = \left[-\left(N+\frac{\tilde{N}}{2}-1\right), \left(N+\frac{\tilde{N}}{2}-1\right)\right]$$

$$supp\ \{\tilde{h}(n)\} = \left[-\frac{\tilde{N}}{2}, \frac{\tilde{N}}{2}\right]$$

Therefore,

$$supp\ \phi(t) = supp\ \{h(n)\} = \left[-\left(N+\frac{\tilde{N}}{2}-1\right), \left(N+\frac{\tilde{N}}{2}-1\right)\right]$$

$$supp\ \tilde{\phi}(t) = supp\ \{\tilde{h}(n)\} = \left[-\frac{\tilde{N}}{2}, \frac{\tilde{N}}{2}\right]$$

Also

$$g(n) = \pm(-1)^n\overline{\tilde{h}(1-n)}, \qquad n \in \left[-\frac{(\tilde{N}-2)}{2}, \frac{(\tilde{N}+2)}{2}\right]$$

$$\tilde{g}(n) = \pm(-1)^n\overline{h(1-n)}, \qquad n \in \left[-\left(N+\frac{\tilde{N}}{2}-2\right), \left(N+\frac{\tilde{N}}{2}\right)\right]$$

Consequently

$$supp\ \{g(n)\} = \left[-\frac{\left(\widetilde{N}-2\right)}{2}, \frac{\left(\widetilde{N}+2\right)}{2}\right]$$

$$supp\ \{\widetilde{g}(n)\} = \left[-\left(N+\frac{\widetilde{N}}{2}-2\right), \left(N+\frac{\widetilde{N}}{2}\right)\right]$$

Further

$$supp\ \psi(t) = supp\ \widetilde{\psi}(t) = \left[\frac{-\left(N+\widetilde{N}-2\right)}{2}, \frac{\left(N+\widetilde{N}\right)}{2}\right]$$

$$diam\ supp\ \psi(t) = diam\ supp\ \widetilde{\psi}(t) = \left(N+\widetilde{N}-1\right)$$

It follows from the expression $\widetilde{H}(\omega) = \sqrt{2}\left(\cos\omega/2\right)^{\widetilde{N}}$ and

$$\widetilde{\Phi}(\omega) = \frac{1}{\sqrt{2}}\widetilde{H}\left(\frac{\omega}{2}\right)\widetilde{\Phi}\left(\frac{\omega}{2}\right)$$

that

$$\widetilde{\Phi}(\omega) = \left(sinc\ \frac{\omega}{2}\right)^{\widetilde{N}}$$

$$\widetilde{\phi}(t) = b_{\widetilde{N}}\left(t+\widetilde{K}\right), \qquad t \in \mathbb{R}$$

where $b_{\widetilde{N}}(\cdot)$ is a B-spline function of order $\widetilde{N}$.

Case 2: N and $\widetilde{N}$ are odd numbers, where $N = (2K+1)$ and $\widetilde{N} = \left(2\widetilde{K}+1\right)$.

$$H(\omega) = \sqrt{2}e^{-i\omega/2}\left(\cos\frac{\omega}{2}\right)^{N}\sum_{k=0}^{K+\widetilde{K}}\binom{K+\widetilde{K}+k}{k}\left(\sin^2\frac{\omega}{2}\right)^{k}$$

$$\widetilde{H}(\omega) = \sqrt{2}e^{-i\omega/2}\left(\cos\frac{\omega}{2}\right)^{\widetilde{N}} = \frac{\sqrt{2}z^{\widetilde{K}}}{2^{\widetilde{N}}}\sum_{k=0}^{\widetilde{N}}\binom{\widetilde{N}}{k}z^{-k}$$

It follows from the expressions for $H(\omega)$ and $\widetilde{H}(\omega)$ that

$$supp\ \{h(n)\} = \left[-\left(N+\frac{\widetilde{N}}{2}-\frac{3}{2}\right), \left(N+\frac{\widetilde{N}}{2}-\frac{1}{2}\right)\right]$$

$$supp\ \left\{\widetilde{h}(n)\right\} = \left[-\frac{\left(\widetilde{N}-1\right)}{2}, \frac{\left(\widetilde{N}+1\right)}{2}\right]$$

Therefore,

$$supp\, \phi\,(t) = supp\,\{h\,(n)\} = \left[-\left(N + \frac{\widetilde{N}}{2} - \frac{3}{2}\right), \left(N + \frac{\widetilde{N}}{2} - \frac{1}{2}\right)\right]$$

$$supp\, \widetilde{\phi}\,(t) = supp\,\left\{\widetilde{h}\,(n)\right\} = \left[-\frac{\left(\widetilde{N} - 1\right)}{2}, \frac{\left(\widetilde{N} + 1\right)}{2}\right]$$

Also

$$g(n) = \pm(-1)^n \,\overline{\widetilde{h}\,(1-n)}, \qquad n \in \left[-\frac{\left(\widetilde{N} - 1\right)}{2}, \frac{\left(\widetilde{N} + 1\right)}{2}\right]$$

$$\widetilde{g}(n) = \pm(-1)^n \,\overline{h\,(1-n)}, \qquad n \in \left[-\left(N + \frac{\widetilde{N}}{2} - \frac{3}{2}\right), \left(N + \frac{\widetilde{N}}{2} - \frac{1}{2}\right)\right]$$

Consequently

$$supp\,\{g\,(n)\} = \left[-\frac{\left(\widetilde{N} - 1\right)}{2}, \frac{\left(\widetilde{N} + 1\right)}{2}\right]$$

$$supp\,\{\widetilde{g}\,(n)\} = \left[-\left(N + \frac{\widetilde{N}}{2} - \frac{3}{2}\right), \left(N + \frac{\widetilde{N}}{2} - \frac{1}{2}\right)\right]$$

Further

$$supp\, \psi\,(t) = supp\, \widetilde{\psi}\,(t) = \left[\frac{-\left(N + \widetilde{N} - 2\right)}{2}, \frac{\left(N + \widetilde{N}\right)}{2}\right]$$

$$diam\, supp\, \psi\,(t) = diam\, supp\, \widetilde{\psi}\,(t) = \left(N + \widetilde{N} - 1\right)$$

It follows from the expression $\widetilde{H}\,(\omega) = \sqrt{2}e^{-i\omega/2}\,(\cos\omega/2)^{\widetilde{N}}$ and

$$\widetilde{\Phi}\,(\omega) = \frac{1}{\sqrt{2}}\widetilde{H}\left(\frac{\omega}{2}\right)\widetilde{\Phi}\left(\frac{\omega}{2}\right)$$

that

$$\widetilde{\Phi}\,(\omega) = e^{-i\omega/2}\left(sinc\,\frac{\omega}{2}\right)^{\widetilde{N}}$$

$$\widetilde{\phi}\,(t) = b_{\widetilde{N}}\left(t + \widetilde{K}\right), \qquad t \in \mathbb{R}$$

where $b_{\widetilde{N}}\,(\cdot)$ is a B-spline function of order $\widetilde{N}$.

In each of the two cases, the functions $\phi(\cdot)$, $\psi(\cdot)$, and $\widetilde{\psi}(\cdot)$ are obtained numerically.

Example 8.2. Let $N = \tilde{N} = 1$. Then

$$\tilde{H}(\omega) = \frac{\sqrt{2}}{2}\left(1 + z^{-1}\right)$$

$$H(\omega) = \frac{\sqrt{2}}{2}\left(1 + z^{-1}\right)$$

$$\tilde{\Phi}(\omega) = e^{-i\omega/2}\left(sinc\frac{\omega}{2}\right)$$

$$\tilde{\phi}(t) = b_1(t), \qquad t \in \mathbb{R}$$

$$g(n) = \pm(-1)^n\,\overline{\tilde{h}(1-n)}, \qquad n \in [0, 1]$$
$$\tilde{g}(n) = \pm(-1)^n\,\overline{h(1-n)}, \qquad n \in [0, 1]$$

$$supp\,\{h(n)\} = supp\,\phi(t) = [0, 1]$$
$$supp\,\left\{\tilde{h}(n)\right\} = supp\,\tilde{\phi}(t) = [0, 1]$$
$$supp\,\{g(n)\} = [0, 1]$$
$$supp\,\{\tilde{g}(n)\} = [0, 1]$$
$$supp\,\psi(t) = supp\,\tilde{\psi}(t) = [0, 1]$$
$$diam\,supp\,\psi(t) = diam\,supp\,\tilde{\psi}(t) = 1$$

□

Example 8.3. Let $N = \tilde{N} = 2$. Then

$$\tilde{H}(\omega) = \frac{\sqrt{2}}{4}\left(z + 2 + z^{-1}\right)$$

$$H(\omega) = \frac{\sqrt{2}}{8}\left(-z^2 + 2z + 6 + 2z^{-1} - z^{-2}\right)$$

$$\tilde{\Phi}(\omega) = \left(sinc\frac{\omega}{2}\right)^2$$

$$\tilde{\phi}(t) = b_2(t + 1), \qquad t \in \mathbb{R}$$

$$g(n) = \pm(-1)^n\,\overline{\tilde{h}(1-n)}, \qquad n \in [0, 2]$$
$$\tilde{g}(n) = \pm(-1)^n\,\overline{h(1-n)}, \qquad n \in [-1, 3]$$

$$supp\,\{h(n)\} = supp\,\phi(t) = [-2, 2]$$
$$supp\,\left\{\tilde{h}(n)\right\} = supp\,\tilde{\phi}(t) = [-1, 1]$$
$$supp\,\{g(n)\} = [0, 2]$$
$$supp\,\{\tilde{g}(n)\} = [-1, 3]$$

$$supp\ \psi\ (t) = supp\ \widetilde{\psi}\ (t) = [-1, 2]$$
$$diam\ supp\ \psi\ (t) = diam\ supp\ \widetilde{\psi}\ (t) = 3$$

□

Example 8.4. Let $N = \widetilde{N} = 3$. Then

$$\widetilde{H}\ (\omega) = \frac{\sqrt{2}}{8} \left(z + 3 + 3z^{-1} + z^{-2}\right)$$

$$H\ (\omega) = \frac{\sqrt{2}}{64} \left(3z^3 - 9z^2 - 7z + 45 + 45z^{-1} - 7z^{-2} - 9z^{-3} + 3z^{-4}\right)$$

$$\widetilde{\Phi}\ (\omega) = e^{-i\omega/2} \left(sinc\ \frac{\omega}{2}\right)^3$$

$$\widetilde{\phi}\ (t) = b_3(t + 1), \qquad t \in \mathbb{R}$$

$$g(n) = \pm(-1)^n\ \overline{\widetilde{h}\ (1-n)}, \qquad n \in [-1, 2]$$
$$\widetilde{g}(n) = \pm(-1)^n\ \overline{h\ (1-n)}, \qquad n \in [-3, 4]$$

$$supp\ \{h\ (n)\} = supp\ \phi\ (t) = [-3, 4]$$
$$supp\ \left\{\widetilde{h}\ (n)\right\} = supp\ \widetilde{\phi}\ (t) = [-1, 2]$$
$$supp\ \{g\ (n)\} = [-1, 2]$$
$$supp\ \{\widetilde{g}\ (n)\} = [-3, 4]$$
$$supp\ \psi\ (t) = supp\ \widetilde{\psi}\ (t) = [-2, 3]$$
$$diam\ supp\ \psi\ (t) = diam\ supp\ \widetilde{\psi}\ (t) = 5$$

□

8.7 Semi-Orthogonal Wavelets

Semi-orthogonal wavelets are actually a special case of biorthogonal wavelets. Initially consider the biorthogonal MRA

$$\{V_j \mid V_j \subseteq L^2(\mathbb{R}),\ j \in \mathbb{Z}\}, \quad \text{and} \quad \left\{\widetilde{V}_j \mid \widetilde{V}_j \subseteq L^2(\mathbb{R}),\ j \in \mathbb{Z}\right\}$$

where $V_{j+1} = V_j \oplus W_j$, $\widetilde{V}_{j+1} = \widetilde{V}_j \oplus \widetilde{W}_j$, $V_j \not\perp W_j$, $\widetilde{V}_j \not\perp \widetilde{W}_j$, $V_j \perp \widetilde{W}_j$, and $\widetilde{V}_j \perp W_j\ \forall\ j \in \mathbb{Z}$. Further $W_n \perp \widetilde{W}_m$, $n \neq m$, where $n, m \in \mathbb{Z}$.

The corresponding biorthogonal scaling and wavelet functions are ϕ, and $\widetilde{\phi}$. Also the biorthogonal wavelet functions are ψ, and $\widetilde{\psi}$. Further

V_j spanned by $\{\phi_{jk} \mid k \in \mathbb{Z}\}$, $\widetilde{V}_j$ spanned by $\left\{\widetilde{\phi}_{jk} \mid k \in \mathbb{Z}\right\}$

W_j spanned by $\{\psi_{jk} \mid k \in \mathbb{Z}\}$, $\widetilde{W}_j$ spanned by $\left\{\widetilde{\psi}_{jk} \mid k \in \mathbb{Z}\right\}$

Next consider the possibility, where $V_0 = \widetilde{V}_0$, but ϕ and $\widetilde{\phi}$ are different. In this case $V_j = \widetilde{V}_j$, $\forall\, j \in \mathbb{Z}$. Further, $V_j \perp W_j$, and $\widetilde{V}_j \perp W_j$ imply $W_j = \widetilde{W}_j$ $\forall$ $j \in \mathbb{Z}$. Furthermore, $W_n \perp W_m$, $n \neq m$, $\forall\, n, m \in \mathbb{Z}$. This scenario is indeed an orthogonal MRA. However, the basis functions do not form an orthogonal set. Therefore, this is called *semi-orthogonal* wavelet analysis.

Note that orthogonality requires that the extra conditions, the two biorthogonal scaling functions and the dual wavelets, be identical. That is, $\phi = \widetilde{\phi}$ and $\psi = \widetilde{\psi}$.

Problems

1. Consider the sequence $\{h(n) \mid n \in \mathbb{Z}\}$. This sequence has a compact support, with diameter N. Further, this sequence is symmetric. The z-transform of this sequence is

$$\mathcal{H}(z) = \sum_{n=0}^{N-1} h(n)\, z^{-n}$$

Assuming $z = e^{i\omega}$, prove that:

(a) If N is an even number, then

$$\mathcal{H}(z) = 2e^{-i\omega(N-1)/2} \sum_{n=0}^{N/2-1} h(n) \cos\omega \left\{ n - \frac{(N-1)}{2} \right\}$$

(b) If N is an odd number, then

$$\mathcal{H}(z) =$$

$$e^{-i\omega(N-1)/2} \left[h\left(\frac{N-1}{2}\right) + 2 \sum_{n=0}^{(N-3)/2} h(n) \cos\omega \left\{ n - \frac{(N-1)}{2} \right\} \right]$$

Hint: See Oppenheim and Schafer (1975). The symmetry property of the sequence implies

$$h(n) = h(N-1-n), \quad n \in \{0, 1, 2, \ldots, (N-1)\}$$

Unit-sample response of a causal finite impulse response systems with linear phase have the above property of symmetry.

CHAPTER 9

Coiflets

9.1 Introduction

Coiflets are a system of orthogonal wavelets with compact support. In addition, both the corresponding wavelet and scaling functions have vanishing moments. Wavelets with such characteristics were first analyzed by Ingrid Daubechies. She named these wavelets "coiflets" after Ronald Coifman, who requested her to analyze such wavelets. It turns out that coiflets are more symmetric than Daubechies' wavelets. However these are achieved at the expense of larger support diameter. Preliminaries to develop coiflets are initially outlined. This is followed by a scheme to construct coiflets.

9.2 Preliminaries

Certain basic concepts required to develop coiflets are specified in this section. Let the moments of the scaling function $\phi(\cdot)$ and the wavelet function $\psi(\cdot)$ be

$$\mathcal{M}_j = \int_{-\infty}^{\infty} t^j \phi(t)\, dt, \quad j \in \mathbb{N}$$

$$\mathcal{N}_j = \int_{-\infty}^{\infty} t^j \psi(t)\, dt, \quad j \in \mathbb{N}$$

respectively. In coiflets, the wavelet function $\psi(\cdot)$ and the scaling function $\phi(\cdot)$ observe the following properties:

$$\mathcal{M}_j = \delta_{j0}, \quad j = 0, 1, 2, \ldots, (L-1)$$
$$\mathcal{N}_j = 0, \quad j = 0, 1, 2, \ldots, (L-1)$$

where δ_{j0} is equal to 1 for $j = 0$, and zero otherwise. Also L is a positive integer, that is $L \in \mathbb{P}$. This wavelet system is designated to be of order (or degree) L. In design of such systems, it is often required that the diameter of the support of the scaling function filter $h(\cdot)$ be minimum.

One of the important reasons for the use of coiflets is next examined. Assume that $\phi\left(\cdot\right)$ is real-valued. Recall that for representing a function $f(\cdot) \in V_J$, where $J \in \mathbb{Z}$, the scaling-function expansion of $f\left(\cdot\right)$ is

$$f(t) = \sum_{k \in \mathbb{Z}} c\left(J, k\right) \phi_{Jk}(t), \quad \forall t \in \mathbb{R}$$

$$c\left(J, k\right) = \langle f, \phi_{Jk} \rangle = \int_{-\infty}^{\infty} f(t) \overline{\phi_{Jk}\left(t\right)} dt, \qquad \forall k \in \mathbb{Z}$$

It can be shown that in a coiflet system of order $L \in \mathbb{P}$,

$$\left| c\left(J, k\right) - 2^{-J/2} f\left(2^{-J}k\right) \right| = O\left(2^{-J(L+1/2)}\right)$$

where it is assumed that the Lth derivative of $f\left(\cdot\right)$ is uniformly bounded. This implies that if the function $f\left(\cdot\right)$ has L continuous derivatives, then its sampled values can be efficiently used to approximate the scaling coefficients.

Scaling- and Wavelet-Function Vanishing Moments

Immediate consequences of vanishing moments of scaling and wavelet functions are examined. Some of these results were derived in developing Daubechies wavelets. These are reproduced here for completeness.

Definition 9.1. *The Fourier transforms of $\phi\left(\cdot\right)$ and $\psi\left(\cdot\right)$, are $\Phi\left(\cdot\right)$ and $\Psi\left(\cdot\right)$ respectively. That is, $\phi\left(t\right) \leftrightarrow \Phi\left(\omega\right)$ and $\psi\left(t\right) \leftrightarrow \Psi\left(\omega\right)$.*
Also, $H\left(\omega\right) = \sum_{n \in \mathbb{Z}} h\left(n\right) e^{-i\omega n}$, and $G\left(\omega\right) = \sum_{n \in \mathbb{Z}} g\left(n\right) e^{-i\omega n}$.
The jth derivative of $\Phi\left(\omega\right)$, $\Psi\left(\omega\right)$, $H\left(\omega\right)$, and $G\left(\omega\right)$, with respect to ω are denoted by $\Phi^{(j)}\left(\omega\right)$, $\Psi^{(j)}\left(\omega\right)$, $H^{(j)}\left(\omega\right)$, and $G^{(j)}\left(\omega\right)$ respectively, where $j \in \mathbb{N}$. Also, $\Phi^{(0)}\left(\omega\right) = \Phi\left(\omega\right)$, $\Psi^{(0)}\left(\omega\right) = \Psi\left(\omega\right)$, $H^{(0)}\left(\omega\right) = H\left(\omega\right)$, and $G^{(0)}\left(\omega\right) = G\left(\omega\right)$. □

Observations 9.1. Relationships between moments and derivatives.

1. Let the first through the $(L-1)$th moment of the wavelet function $\psi\left(\cdot\right)$ vanish. Thus $\mathcal{N}_j = 0$, for $j = 0, 1, 2, \ldots, (L-1)$. Recall that $\mathcal{N}_0 = 0$ is the admissibility condition. This implies
   (a)
   $$\Psi^{(j)}\left(0\right) = 0, \quad j = 0, 1, 2, \ldots, (L-1)$$

   This result implies that $\Psi\left(\omega\right)$ has a root of multiplicity L at $\omega = 0$.
   (b)
   $$G^{(j)}\left(0\right) = 0, \quad j = 0, 1, 2, \ldots, (L-1)$$

   This result implies that $G\left(\omega\right)$ has a root of multiplicity L at $\omega = 0$.

   $$H^{(j)}\left(\pi\right) = 0, \quad j = 0, 1, 2, \ldots, (L-1)$$

This result implies that $H(\omega)$ has a root of multiplicity L at $\omega = \pi$.

(c)

$$\sum_{n \in \mathbb{Z}} n^j g(n) = 0, \quad j = 0, 1, 2, \ldots, (L-1)$$

$$\sum_{n \in \mathbb{Z}} (-1)^n n^j h(n) = 0, \quad j = 0, 1, 2, \ldots, (L-1)$$

The above results were established in the chapter on Daubechies wavelets with a slightly different notation.

2. Let the first through the $(L-1)$th moment of the scaling function $\phi(\cdot)$ vanish. That is, $\mathcal{M}_j = 0$, for $j = 1, 2, \ldots, (L-1)$. This implies

   (a)

   $$\Phi^{(j)}(0) = \delta_{j0}, \quad j = 0, 1, 2, \ldots, (L-1)$$

   where δ_{j0} is equal to 1 for $j = 0$, and zero otherwise. This result implies that $\Phi(\omega)$ has a root of multiplicity $(L-1)$ at $\omega = 0$.

   (b)

   $$H^{(j)}(0) = 0, \quad j = 1, 2, \ldots, (L-1)$$

   This result implies that $H(\omega)$ has a root of multiplicity $(L-1)$ at $\omega = 0$.
   Let $\varrho = -i(2m+1)$, where $m \in \mathbb{Z}$

   $$G^{(j)}(\pi) = \pm\sqrt{2}\varrho^j, \quad j = 1, 2, \ldots, (L-1)$$

   (c)

   $$\sum_{n \in \mathbb{Z}} n^j h(n) = 0, \quad j = 1, 2, \ldots, (L-1)$$

   $$\sum_{n \in \mathbb{Z}} (-1)^n n^j g(n) = \pm\sqrt{2}(2m+1)^j, \quad j = 1, 2, \ldots, (L-1)$$

   This observation is established in the problem section.   □

9.3 Construction of Coiflets

Construction of coiflets is similar to that of the Daubechies wavelets. A scheme for the construction of coiflets is provided in several steps. That is, the filter $H(\omega)$, $\omega \in \mathbb{R}$ is determined. This will lead to the determination of the scaling and wavelet functions, and the filter $G(\cdot)$.

Step 0: For convenience, define

$$\xi\left(\omega\right) = \frac{1}{\sqrt{2}}H(\omega), \quad \forall\, \omega \in \mathbb{R}$$

Therefore, the orthogonality condition

$$|H\left(\omega\right)|^2 + |H\left(\omega + \pi\right)|^2 = 2$$

implies

$$|\xi\left(\omega\right)|^2 + |\xi\left(\omega + \pi\right)|^2 = 1$$

Step 1: Two conditions related to the vanishing moments of the wavelet and scaling functions are specified.

Condition A: Let the first through the $(L-1)$th moment of the wavelet function $\psi\left(\cdot\right)$ vanish. Thus $\mathcal{N}_j = 0$, for $j = 0, 1, 2, \ldots, (L-1)$. Recall that $\mathcal{N}_0 = 0$ is the admissibility condition. Thus $H^{(j)}\left(\pi\right) = \xi^{(j)}\left(\pi\right) = 0$, for $j = 0, 1, 2, \ldots, (L-1)$.
Therefore, $H\left(\omega\right)$, and in turn $\xi\left(\omega\right)$, has a zero of order L at $\omega = \pi$.

Condition B: Also assume that the first $(L-1)$ moments of the scaling function $\phi\left(\cdot\right)$ vanish. That is, $\mathcal{M}_j = 0$, for $j = 1, 2, \ldots, (L-1)$. Thus $H^{(j)}\left(0\right) = \xi^{(j)}\left(0\right) = 0$, for $j = 1, 2, \ldots, (L-1)$.
Therefore, $H\left(\omega\right)$, and in turn $\xi\left(\omega\right)$, has a zero of order $(L-1)$ at $\omega = 0$. Recall that $\mathcal{M}_0 = 1$. This implies $\xi\left(0\right) = 1$.

Step 2: From Step 1 - Condition A, observe that $\xi\left(\omega\right)$ has a zero of order L at $\omega = \pi$. Therefore, let

$$\xi(\omega) = \left(\frac{1 + e^{-i\omega}}{2}\right)^L \mathcal{L}\left(\omega\right)$$

where $\mathcal{L}$ is a trigonometric polynomial.

Step 3: From Step 1 - Condition B, observe that $\xi\left(0\right) = 1$. and $\xi^{(j)}\left(0\right) = 0$, for $j = 1, 2, \ldots, (L-1)$. Therefore, let

$$\xi(\omega) = 1 + \left(\frac{1 - e^{-i\omega}}{2}\right)^L \widetilde{\mathcal{L}}\left(\omega\right)$$

where $\widetilde{\mathcal{L}}$ is a trigonometric polynomial.

Step 4: For simplicity assume that L is an even integer. That is, let $L = 2K$, where $K \in \mathbb{P}$. The case of an odd L can be similarly analyzed. From Step 2, we have

$$\xi(\omega) = \left\{\cos^2\left(\frac{\omega}{2}\right)\right\}^K \mathcal{P}(\omega), \quad \text{where} \quad \mathcal{P}\left(\omega\right) = e^{-i\omega K}\mathcal{L}\left(\omega\right)$$

From Step 3 we have

$$\xi(\omega) = 1 + \left\{ \sin^2 \left(\frac{\omega}{2} \right) \right\}^K \widetilde{\mathcal{P}}(\omega), \quad \text{where} \quad \widetilde{\mathcal{P}}(\omega) = i^L e^{-i\omega K} \widetilde{\mathcal{L}}(\omega)$$

Step 5: Let $y = \sin^2(\omega/2)$, $\mathcal{P}(\omega) \triangleq P_1(y)$, and $\widetilde{\mathcal{P}}(\omega) \triangleq P_2(y)$. From Step 4 we have

$$(1-y)^K P_1(y) = 1 + y^K P_2(y)$$

This leads to

$$(1-y)^K P_1(y) + y^K \{-P_2(y)\} = 1$$

Substitute $(1-y)$ for y in the above equation. We have

$$y^K P_1(1-y) + (1-y)^K \{-P_2(1-y)\} = 1$$

As the polynomials y^K and $(1-y)^K$ are relatively prime, comparison of the multipliers of y^K in the last two equations lead to $P_1(1-y) = -P_2(y)$. Therefore,

$$(1-y)^K P_1(y) + y^K P_1(1-y) = 1, \quad \text{where} \quad y \in [0,1]$$

Using Bezout's theorem, a general solution of the above equation has been derived in the chapter on Daubechies wavelets. It is

$$P_1(y) = \sum_{k=0}^{K-1} \binom{K+k-1}{k} y^k + y^K R\left(\frac{1}{2} - y \right)$$

where $R(y)$ is a polynomial of odd degree. Also

$$P_2(y) = -P_1(1-y)$$

$$= -\left\{ \sum_{k=0}^{K-1} \binom{K+k-1}{k} (1-y)^k + (1-y)^K R\left(y - \frac{1}{2} \right) \right\}$$

Step 6: From Step 5, we obtain

$$P(\omega) = \sum_{k=0}^{K-1} \binom{K+k-1}{k} \left\{ \sin^2 \left(\frac{\omega}{2} \right) \right\}^k + \left\{ \sin^2 \left(\frac{\omega}{2} \right) \right\}^K f(\omega)$$

where $f(\cdot)$ is a trigonometric polynomial. Use of Step 4 leads to

$$\xi(\omega) = \left\{ \cos^2 \left(\frac{\omega}{2} \right) \right\}^K P(\omega)$$

$$= \left\{ \cos^2 \left(\frac{\omega}{2} \right) \right\}^K \left[\sum_{k=0}^{K-1} \binom{K+k-1}{k} \left\{ \sin^2 \left(\frac{\omega}{2} \right) \right\}^k \right.$$

$$\left. + \left\{ \sin^2 \left(\frac{\omega}{2} \right) \right\}^K f(\omega) \right]$$

Step 7: Assume that the polynomial $f(\cdot)$ is of the form

$$f(\omega) = \sum_{n=0}^{2K-1} f_n e^{-in\omega}$$

where $f_n \in \mathbb{R}$ for $0 \le n \le (2K-1)$. This polynomial is determined by using results from Step 6, and by the orthogonality condition

$$|\xi(\omega)|^2 + |\xi(\omega + \pi)|^2 = 1$$

The results of the above construction are summarized in the following theorem due to Daubechies.

Theorem 9.1. *Coiflet filter.* $H(\omega), \omega \in \mathbb{R}$. *Let* $K \in \mathbb{P}$, *and* $L = 2K$. *Assume that the first* $(L-1)$ *moments of the wavelet function* $\psi(\cdot)$ *vanish. That is,* $\mathcal{N}_j = 0$, *for* $j = 0, 1, 2, \dots, (L-1)$. *Also let the first* $(L-1)$ *moments of the scaling function* $\phi(\cdot)$ *vanish. That is,* $\mathcal{M}_j = 0$, *for* $j = 1, 2, \dots, (L-1)$. *It is also known that* $\mathcal{M}_0 = 1$. *Define* $\xi(\omega) = H(\omega)/\sqrt{2}, \forall \, \omega \in \mathbb{R}$. *Then*

$$\xi(\omega) = \left\{\cos^2\left(\frac{\omega}{2}\right)\right\}^K \left[\sum_{k=0}^{K-1} \binom{K+k-1}{k} \left\{\sin^2\left(\frac{\omega}{2}\right)\right\}^k\right.$$
$$\left. + \left\{\sin^2\left(\frac{\omega}{2}\right)\right\}^K f(\omega)\right] \tag{9.1a}$$

Also the function $\xi(\cdot)$ *satisfies*

$$\xi(0) = 1 \tag{9.1b}$$
$$\xi^{(j)}(\pi) = 0, \quad for \quad j = 0, 1, \dots, (L-1) \tag{9.1c}$$
$$\xi^{(j)}(0) = 0, \quad for \quad j = 1, 2, \dots, (L-1) \tag{9.1d}$$

Further, the polynomial $f(\cdot)$ *is of the form*

$$f(\omega) = \sum_{n=0}^{2K-1} f_n e^{-in\omega}, \quad f_n \in \mathbb{R} \quad for \quad 0 \le n \le (2K-1) \tag{9.1e}$$

The coefficients $f_n \in \mathbb{R}$, *for* $0 \le n \le (2K-1)$ *are determined from the relationship*

$$|\xi(\omega)|^2 + |\xi(\omega + \pi)|^2 = 1 \tag{9.1f}$$

$\square$

Once the coiflet filter $H(\cdot)$ is determined, the scaling and wavelet functions, and the filter $G(\cdot)$ can be determined. The coiflet filter $H(\cdot)$ is generally determined numerically. Nevertheless, this filter is determined explicitly for $K = 1$.

Example 9.1. Coiflet filter is determined in this example for $K = 1$. The coefficients of this filter are determined in several steps.

Step 1: Substitute $K = 1$ in the statement of the above theorem. This leads to

$$H(\omega) = \sqrt{2}\cos^2\left(\frac{\omega}{2}\right)\left\{1 + \sin^2\left(\frac{\omega}{2}\right)\left(f_0 + f_1 e^{-i\omega}\right)\right\}$$

Let $z = e^{i\omega}$, then

$$\cos^2\left(\frac{\omega}{2}\right) = \frac{1}{4}\left(z + 2 + z^{-1}\right)$$

$$\cos^2\left(\frac{\omega}{2}\right)\sin^2\left(\frac{\omega}{2}\right) = \frac{1}{4}\sin^2\omega$$

$$= -\frac{1}{16}\left(z^2 - 2 + z^{-2}\right)$$

Therefore,

$$H(\omega) = \frac{\sqrt{2}}{4}\left(z + 2 + z^{-1}\right) - \frac{\sqrt{2}}{16}\left(z^2 - 2 + z^{-2}\right)\left(f_0 + f_1 z^{-1}\right)$$

Note that $H(\omega)$ can be expressed as

$$H(\omega) = \sum_{n=-2}^{3} h(n) z^{-n}$$

Use of the last two equations, result in

$$h(-2) = -\frac{\sqrt{2}}{16}f_0, \quad h(-1) = \frac{\sqrt{2}(4 - f_1)}{16}, \quad h(0) = \frac{\sqrt{2}(8 + 2f_0)}{16}$$

$$h(1) = \frac{\sqrt{2}(4 + 2f_1)}{16}, \quad h(2) = -\frac{\sqrt{2}}{16}f_0, \quad h(3) = -\frac{\sqrt{2}}{16}f_1$$

It remains to determine f_0 and f_1.

Step 2: Consequences of the result $|H(\omega)|^2 + |H(\omega + \pi)|^2 = 2$ are explicitly stated. These are

$$h(-2)^2 + h(-1)^2 + h(0)^2 + h(1)^2 + h(2)^2 + h(3)^2 = 1$$
$$h(-2)h(0) + h(-1)h(1) + h(0)h(2) + h(1)h(3) = 0$$
$$h(-2)h(2) + h(-1)h(3) = 0$$

Step 3: The coefficients f_0 and f_1 are determined by using results from Steps 1 and 2. Thus

$$3f_0^2 + 3f_1^2 + 16f_0 + 4f_1 - 16 = 0$$
$$f_0^2 + f_1^2 + 4f_0 - 4 = 0$$
$$f_0^2 + f_1^2 - 4f_1 = 0$$

The last two equations yield $(f_0 + f_1) = 1$. Substituting $f_1 = (1 - f_0)$ in any one of the above equations yields

$$f_0 = \frac{1}{2}\left(-1 \pm \sqrt{7}\right), \quad \text{and} \quad f_1 = \frac{1}{2}\left(3 \mp \sqrt{7}\right)$$

Step 4: Observe that the coiflet filter can have two sets of values. Substitution of

$$f_0 = \frac{1}{2}\left(-1 + \sqrt{7}\right), \quad \text{and} \quad f_1 = \frac{1}{2}\left(3 - \sqrt{7}\right)$$

in results of Step 1 yield

$$h(-2) = \frac{\sqrt{2}}{32}\left(1 - \sqrt{7}\right), \quad h(-1) = \frac{\sqrt{2}\left(5 + \sqrt{7}\right)}{32},$$

$$h(0) = \frac{\sqrt{2}\left(7 + \sqrt{7}\right)}{16}, \quad h(1) = \frac{\sqrt{2}\left(7 - \sqrt{7}\right)}{16},$$

$$h(2) = \frac{\sqrt{2}}{32}\left(1 - \sqrt{7}\right), \quad h(3) = \frac{\sqrt{2}}{32}\left(-3 + \sqrt{7}\right)$$

As a quick check, observe that indeed $H(0) = \sum_{n=-2}^{3} h(n) = \sqrt{2}$.   □

Observation 9.2. The support diameter of the coiflet filter $H(\cdot)$ is $6K$. The coefficients of this filter are

$$(h(l), h(l+1), \ldots, h(m-1), h(m))$$

where $l = -2K$, and $m = (4K - 1)$.   □

Problems

1. Let $\mathcal{M}_j = \int_{-\infty}^{\infty} t^j \phi(t)\, dt$, $j \in \mathbb{N}$, and $\mathcal{M}_0 = 1$. Also let

$$\mathcal{M}_j = 0, \quad \text{for } j = 1, 2, \ldots, (L - 1)$$

Assume for simplicity that $\phi(\cdot)$ is real-valued, $f(\cdot) \in V_n$, and

$$c(n, k) = \langle f, \phi_{nk} \rangle = \int_{-\infty}^{\infty} f(t) \phi_{nk}(t)\, dt, \qquad \forall\, k \in \mathbb{Z}$$

For a coiflet system of order $L \in \mathbb{P}$ show that

$$\left| c(n, k) - 2^{-n/2} f\left(2^{-n} k\right) \right| = O\left(2^{-n(L+1/2)}\right)$$

Hint: We have

$$c(n, k) = \int_{-\infty}^{\infty} f(t) 2^{n/2} \phi\left(2^n t - k\right) dt$$

$$= 2^{n/2} \int_{-\infty}^{\infty} f(y + 2^{-n} k) \phi\left(2^n y\right) dy$$

Expand $f(y + 2^{-n} k)$ into a Taylor's series about $2^{-n} k$. The ith derivative of $f(\cdot)$ is denoted by $f^{(i)}(\cdot)$. This leads to

$$f(y + 2^{-n} k) = \sum_{i=0}^{L-1} f^{(i)}\left(2^{-n} k\right) \frac{y^i}{i!} + \frac{y^L}{L!} f^{(L)}(\xi)$$

where $\xi \in (2^{-n} k, y + 2^{-n} k)$. Substitute the above expansion in the expression for $c(n, k)$. This results in

$$c(n, k) = 2^{n/2} \int_{-\infty}^{\infty} \left\{ \sum_{i=0}^{L-1} f^{(i)}\left(2^{-n} k\right) \frac{y^i}{i!} + \frac{y^L}{L!} f^{(L)}(\xi) \right\} \phi\left(2^n y\right) dy$$

Observe that

$$\int_{-\infty}^{\infty} y^i \phi\left(2^n y\right) dy = 2^{-n(i+1)} \int_{-\infty}^{\infty} z^i \phi(z)\, dz = 2^{-n(i+1)} \mathcal{M}_i, \quad i \in \mathbb{N}$$

Therefore,

$$c(n, k) = 2^{n/2} \left\{ f\left(2^{-n} k\right) + \sum_{i=1}^{L-1} f^{(i)}\left(2^{-n} k\right) \frac{2^{-n(i+1)}}{i!} \mathcal{M}_i \right.$$

$$\left. + f^{(L)}(\xi) \frac{2^{-n(L+1)}}{L!} \mathcal{M}_L \right\}$$

$$= 2^{n/2} \left\{ f\left(2^{-n} k\right) + O\left(2^{-n(L+1)}\right) \right\}$$

The last step used the fact: $\mathcal{M}_0 = 1$, $\mathcal{M}_j = 0$, $j = 1, 2, \ldots, (L-1)$. The result follows.

2. Let the first $(L-1)$ moments of the scaling function $\phi(\cdot)$ vanish. That is, $\mathcal{M}_j = 0$, for $j = 1, 2, \ldots, (L-1)$. Then prove:

(a)
$$\Phi^{(j)}(0) = \delta_{j0}, \quad j = 0, 1, 2, \ldots, (L-1)$$

where δ_{j0} is equal to 1 for $j = 0$, and zero otherwise. This result implies that $\Phi(\omega)$ has a root of multiplicity $(L-1)$ at $\omega = 0$.

(b)
$$H^{(j)}(0) = 0, \quad j = 1, 2, \ldots, (L-1)$$

This result implies that $H(\omega)$ has a root of multiplicity $(L-1)$ at $\omega = 0$. Let $\varrho = -i(2m+1)$, where $m \in \mathbb{Z}$

$$G^{(j)}(\pi) = \pm\sqrt{2}\varrho^j, \quad j = 1, 2, \ldots, (L-1)$$

(c)
$$\sum_{n \in \mathbb{Z}} n^j h(n) = 0, \quad j = 1, 2, \ldots, (L-1)$$

$$\sum_{n \in \mathbb{Z}} (-1)^n n^j g(n) = \pm\sqrt{2}(2m+1)^j, \quad j = 1, 2, \ldots, (L-1)$$

Hint:

(a) As $\phi(t) \leftrightarrow \Phi(\omega)$, we have

$$\Phi^{(j)}(\omega) = (-i)^j \int_{-\infty}^{\infty} t^j \phi(t) e^{-i\omega t} dt, \quad j = 0, 1, 2, \ldots, (L-1)$$

The result follows.

(b) The following results are used.

$$\Phi(\omega) = \frac{1}{\sqrt{2}} H\left(\frac{\omega}{2}\right) \Phi\left(\frac{\omega}{2}\right)$$

$$G(\omega) = \mp e^{-i(2m+1)\omega} \overline{H(\omega + \pi)}, \quad m \in \mathbb{Z}$$

$$\overline{H(\omega + \pi)} = \sum_{n \in \mathbb{Z}} \overline{h(n)} e^{i(\omega + \pi)n}$$

$$\Phi(0) = 1, \quad H(0) = \sqrt{2}, \quad \text{and} \quad H(\pi) = 0$$

Therefore, $G(0) = 0$. We also have

$$\frac{d}{d\omega}\Phi(\omega) = \frac{1}{\sqrt{2}}\left\{\frac{d}{d\omega}H\left(\frac{\omega}{2}\right)\right\}\Phi\left(\frac{\omega}{2}\right) + \frac{1}{\sqrt{2}}H\left(\frac{\omega}{2}\right)\left\{\frac{d}{d\omega}\Phi\left(\frac{\omega}{2}\right)\right\}$$

Substitute $\omega = 0$ in the above equation. This yields

$$\left.\frac{d}{d\omega}H(\omega)\right|_{\omega=0} = 0$$

Also

$$\frac{d}{d\omega}G\left(\omega\right) = \mp e^{-i(2m+1)\omega}\left\{\varrho\overline{H\left(\omega + \pi\right)} + \frac{d}{d\omega}\overline{H\left(\omega + \pi\right)}\right\}$$

Substitute $\omega = \pi$ in the above equation. This yields

$$\left.\frac{d}{d\omega}G\left(\omega\right)\right|_{\omega=\pi} = \pm\varrho\sqrt{2}$$

Subsequent results can be proved similarly by using induction on j, where $j = 1, 2, \ldots, (L-1)$.

(c) These relationships follow by using the definition of $H(\cdot)$, $G(\cdot)$, and results from part (b).

CHAPTER 10

The Lifting Technique

10.1 Introduction

The lifting scheme is a technique to compute classical wavelet transforms efficiently. Its time and space complexity is relatively small, when compared to the classical techniques. Further, it does not use Fourier transform techniques in its analysis. The efficiency in the lifting scheme occurs due to factorization of specific polynomials judiciously.

The lifting scheme of generating wavelets is explained via the theory of Laurent polynomials. It is used in specifying the polyphase matrix of biorthogonal wavelet with compact support. This polyphase matrix is in turn factored via the use of Euclidean algorithm for finding the greatest common divisor of two Laurent polynomials. The factorization of the polyphase matrix, leads to improvement in the efficiency of the wavelet transform algorithm. This technique can also be extended to the implementation of the so-called second-generation of wavelets.

10.2 Laurent Polynomials

Laurent polynomials are special polynomials named after the French mathematician Pierre Alphonse Laurent (1813–1854).

Definitions 10.1. *Laurent polynomial.*

1. *Consider the sequence $\{f(n) \in \mathbb{C} \mid n \in \mathbb{Z}\}$. Let $\operatorname{supp}\{f(n)\} = [n_l, n_u]$, where $n_l \leq n_u$, $f(n_l) \neq 0$, and $f(n_u) \neq 0$. Also $\mathcal{F}(z)$ is*

$$\mathcal{F}(z) = \sum_{n=n_l}^{n_u} f(n) z^{-n}, \qquad z \in \mathbb{C} \qquad (10.1)$$

$\mathcal{F}(z)$ is said to be the Laurent polynomial associated with this sequence.

2. *The degree of Laurent polynomial $\mathcal{F}(z)$ is $\deg[\mathcal{F}(z)] = (n_u - n_l)$.*

3. *Let $A_i, 1 \leq i \leq n$ be square matrices of the same size. Then the product $A_1 A_2 A_3 \ldots A_n$ is denoted by $\prod_{i=1}^{n} A_i$.*
   Note that in this product the sequence of matrix multiplication is preserved. Recall that matrix multiplication is not commutative.   □

Observations 10.1. Basic observations about Laurent polynomials.

1. The zero Laurent polynomial is defined to have degree $-\infty$.

2. The notion of degree of a Laurent polynomial, is different than that of degree of a regular polynomial. For example, the degree of a regular polynomial z^n, is n, while the Laurent degree of the Laurent polynomial z^n, is 0.

3. The diameter of the sequence $\{f(n) \mid n \in \mathbb{Z}\}$ is equal to $(\deg[\mathcal{F}(z)] + 1)$.

4. Consider Laurent polynomials with real coefficients. The sum or difference of two Laurent polynomials is a Laurent polynomial. The product of two Laurent polynomials of degrees d_1 and d_2 is a Laurent polynomial of degree $(d_1 + d_2)$. The division operation among Laurent polynomials is defined as follows. Consider Laurent polynomials $\mathcal{F}(z)$ and $\mathcal{G}(z)$, such that $\mathcal{G}(z) \neq 0$ and $\deg[\mathcal{F}(z)] \geq \deg[\mathcal{G}(z)]$, then there exist quotient and remainder Laurent polynomials $\mathcal{Q}(z)$ and $\mathcal{R}(z)$ respectively such that

$$\mathcal{F}(z) = \mathcal{G}(z)\,\mathcal{Q}(z) + \mathcal{R}(z)$$
$$\deg[\mathcal{F}(z)] = \deg[\mathcal{Q}(z)] + \deg[\mathcal{G}(z)]$$
$$\deg[\mathcal{R}(z)] < \deg[\mathcal{G}(z)]$$

Observe that if $\mathcal{G}(z)$ is a monomial, that is $\deg[\mathcal{G}(z)] = 0$, then $\mathcal{R}(z) = 0$. In this case division is exact. It is worth noting that the Laurent polynomials, $\mathcal{Q}(z)$ and $\mathcal{R}(z)$ are not unique. That is, division of Laurent polynomials is not necessarily unique. Also a Laurent polynomial is invertible if and only if it is of zero degree. That is, when it is a mononomial.   □

Example 10.1. Let

$$\mathcal{F}(z) = 2z^{-1} + 6 + 8z, \text{ and } \mathcal{G}(z) = 2 + 3z$$

$\mathcal{F}(z)$ has to be divided by $\mathcal{G}(z)$. Note that $\deg[\mathcal{F}(z)] = 2$, $\deg[\mathcal{G}(z)] = 1$, then $\deg[\mathcal{R}(z)] < 1$. That is, $\deg[\mathcal{R}(z)] = 0$ and $\deg[\mathcal{Q}(z)] = 2$. Consequently, $\mathcal{R}(z)$ has to be of the form cz^{-1}, or c, or cz, where c is a constant. All these remainders have degree equal to 0. As

$$\mathcal{F}(z) = \mathcal{G}(z)\,\mathcal{Q}(z) + \mathcal{R}(z)$$

it is possible to have:

(a) $\mathcal{R}(z) = cz^{-1}$, then

$$Q(z) = \frac{2}{9}z^{-1} + 2\frac{2}{3}$$

$$R(z) = 1\frac{5}{9}z^{-1}$$

(b) $R(z) = c$, then

$$Q(z) = z^{-1} + 2\frac{2}{3}$$

$$R(z) = -2\frac{1}{3}$$

(c) $R(z) = cz$, then

$$Q(z) = z^{-1} + 1\frac{1}{2}$$

$$R(z) = 3\frac{1}{2}z$$

□

10.3 Greatest Common Divisor of Two Laurent Polynomials

The determination of greatest common divisor of two Laurent polynomials is similar to the determination of the greatest common divisor (gcd) of two integers, with few differences. The gcd of two Laurent polynomials is not unique. These are only unique to within a factor z^n, $n \in \mathbb{Z}$. Two Laurent polynomials $\mathcal{F}(z)$ and $\mathcal{G}(z)$ are relatively prime if the degree of their gcd polynomial is zero. Further, these relatively prime Laurent polynomials can have common roots at zero and infinity.

The gcd of two Laurent polynomials, $\mathcal{F}(z)$ and $\mathcal{G}(z)$ is determined as follows. Assume that $\mathcal{G}(z) \neq 0$, and $\deg[\mathcal{F}(z)] \geq \deg[\mathcal{G}(z)]$. The algorithm is analogous to the Euclidean algorithm for finding the gcd of two integers. The algorithm is split into the following steps.

- *Initialization*: Let $\mathcal{F}_0(z) = \mathcal{F}(z)$, and $\mathcal{G}_0(z) = \mathcal{G}(z)$.
- *First step*: As

$$\mathcal{G}_0(z) \neq 0, \mathcal{F}_0(z) = \mathcal{G}_0(z)\mathcal{Q}_1(z) + \mathcal{R}_0(z), \text{ where } \deg[\mathcal{R}_0(z)] < \deg[\mathcal{G}_0(z)]$$

Let $\mathcal{F}_1(z) = \mathcal{G}_0(z)$, and $\mathcal{G}_1(z) = \mathcal{R}_0(z)$. In matrix notation, this is

$$\begin{bmatrix} \mathcal{F}_1(z) \\ \mathcal{G}_1(z) \end{bmatrix} = \begin{bmatrix} 0 & 1 \\ 1 & -\mathcal{Q}_1(z) \end{bmatrix} \begin{bmatrix} \mathcal{F}_0(z) \\ \mathcal{G}_0(z) \end{bmatrix}$$

- *Second step*: Let

  $\mathcal{G}_1(z) \neq 0, \mathcal{F}_1(z) = \mathcal{G}_1(z) \mathcal{Q}_2(z) + \mathcal{R}_1(z)$, where $\deg[\mathcal{R}_1(z)] < \deg[\mathcal{G}_1(z)]$

  That is, $\deg[\mathcal{R}_1(z)] < \deg[\mathcal{R}_0(z)]$. Let $\mathcal{F}_2(z) = \mathcal{G}_1(z)$, and $\mathcal{G}_2(z) = \mathcal{R}_1(z)$. Thus

  $$\begin{bmatrix} \mathcal{F}_2(z) \\ \mathcal{G}_2(z) \end{bmatrix} = \begin{bmatrix} 0 & 1 \\ 1 & -\mathcal{Q}_2(z) \end{bmatrix} \begin{bmatrix} \mathcal{F}_1(z) \\ \mathcal{G}_1(z) \end{bmatrix}$$

- *N-th step* (*final step*): Let $\mathcal{G}_{N-1}(z) \neq 0$, $\mathcal{F}_{N-1}(z) = \mathcal{G}_{N-1}(z) \mathcal{Q}_N(z) + \mathcal{R}_{N-1}(z)$, where $\deg[\mathcal{R}_{N-1}(z)] < \deg[\mathcal{G}_{N-1}(z)]$. That is, $\deg[\mathcal{R}_{N-1}(z)] < \deg[\mathcal{R}_{N-2}(z)]$. Let $\mathcal{F}_N(z) = \mathcal{G}_{N-1}(z)$, and $\mathcal{G}_N(z) = \mathcal{R}_{N-1}(z)$. Thus

  $$\begin{bmatrix} \mathcal{F}_N(z) \\ \mathcal{G}_N(z) \end{bmatrix} = \begin{bmatrix} 0 & 1 \\ 1 & -\mathcal{Q}_N(z) \end{bmatrix} \begin{bmatrix} \mathcal{F}_{N-1}(z) \\ \mathcal{G}_{N-1}(z) \end{bmatrix}$$

  $\mathcal{G}_N(z) = 0$. The gcd of the Laurent polynomials $\mathcal{F}(z)$ and $\mathcal{G}(z)$ is $\mathcal{F}_N(z) = \mathcal{G}_{N-1}(z)$.

Notice that the above algorithm terminates for a value of j for which $\mathcal{G}_j(z) = 0$. In the above algorithm notice that $\mathcal{R}_{N-1}(z) = 0$, and

$$\deg[\mathcal{R}_{N-1}(z)] < \deg[\mathcal{R}_{N-2}(z)] < \deg[\mathcal{R}_{N-3}(z)] < $$
$$\ldots \deg[\mathcal{R}_0(z)] < \deg[\mathcal{G}(z)]$$

This algorithm is encapsulated in the following observations.

Observations 10.2. Euclidean algorithm for gcd of Laurent polynomials.

1. Consider, two Laurent polynomials $\mathcal{F}(z)$ and $\mathcal{G}(z)$, such that $\mathcal{G}(z) \neq 0$, and $\deg[\mathcal{F}(z)] \geq \deg[\mathcal{G}(z)]$. Initialize $\mathcal{F}_0(z) = \mathcal{F}(z)$, and $\mathcal{G}_0(z) = \mathcal{G}(z)$, and iterate through the following steps for $j = 1, 2, \ldots, N$.

$$\mathcal{F}_j(z) = \mathcal{G}_{j-1}(z)$$
$$\mathcal{G}_j(z) = \mathcal{F}_{j-1}(z) - \mathcal{G}_{j-1}(z)\mathcal{Q}_j(z)$$

where $\mathcal{G}_N(z) = 0$, and the gcd of the Laurent polynomials $\mathcal{F}(z)$ and $\mathcal{G}(z)$ is $\mathcal{F}_N(z)$. In this algorithm, N is the smallest value of j for which $\mathcal{G}_j(z) = 0$. The number of steps N in the above algorithm is bounded by $(1 + \deg[\mathcal{G}(z)])$. If $\mathcal{F}_N(z)$ is a monomial, then the polynomials $\mathcal{F}(z)$ and $\mathcal{G}(z)$ are relatively prime.

2. The above algorithm in matrix notation is stated as follows. First define

$$\mathcal{M}_j(z) = \begin{bmatrix} 0 & 1 \\ 1 & -\mathcal{Q}_j(z) \end{bmatrix}, \quad 1 \leq j \leq N$$

$$\mathcal{N}_j(z) = \begin{bmatrix} \mathcal{Q}_j(z) & 1 \\ 1 & 0 \end{bmatrix}, \quad 1 \leq j \leq N$$

$$\mathcal{M}_j(z)\mathcal{N}_j(z) = 1, \quad 1 \leq j \leq N$$

Then

$$\begin{bmatrix} \mathcal{F}_N(z) \\ 0 \end{bmatrix} = \left(\prod_{j=N}^{1} M_j(z) \right) \begin{bmatrix} \mathcal{F}(z) \\ \mathcal{G}(z) \end{bmatrix}$$

$$\begin{bmatrix} \mathcal{F}(z) \\ \mathcal{G}(z) \end{bmatrix} = \left(\prod_{j=1}^{N} N_j(z) \right) \begin{bmatrix} \mathcal{F}_N(z) \\ 0 \end{bmatrix}$$

At this point, the reader should be aware of the notation for a sequence of matrix multiplications. This notation (or interpretation) was introduced at the beginning of the chapter.   □

Example 10.2. Let $\mathcal{F}(z)$ and $\mathcal{G}(z)$ be two Laurent polynomials, where $\mathcal{F}(z) = 2z^{-1} + 6 + 8z$, and $\mathcal{G}(z) = 2 + 3z$. The gcd of the two polynomials is obtained. In this process, the matrix $\begin{bmatrix} \mathcal{F}(z) & \mathcal{G}(z) \end{bmatrix}^T$ is factorized. For the first division

$$\mathcal{F}_0(z) = 2z^{-1} + 6 + 8z$$
$$\mathcal{G}_0(z) = 2 + 3z$$

$$\mathcal{Q}_1(z) = z^{-1} + 2\frac{2}{3}$$
$$\mathcal{R}_0(z) = -2\frac{1}{3}$$

For the second division

$$\mathcal{F}_1(z) = 2 + 3z$$
$$\mathcal{G}_1(z) = -2\frac{1}{3}$$

$$\mathcal{Q}_2(z) = -\frac{6}{7} - 1\frac{2}{7}z$$
$$\mathcal{R}_1(z) = 0$$

The gcd is equal to $-2\frac{1}{3}$. Therefore, the polynomials are relatively prime. Also

$$\begin{bmatrix} 2z^{-1} + 6 + 8z \\ 2 + 3z \end{bmatrix} = \begin{bmatrix} z^{-1} + 2\frac{2}{3} & 1 \\ 1 & 0 \end{bmatrix} \begin{bmatrix} -\frac{6}{7} - 1\frac{2}{7}z & 1 \\ 1 & 0 \end{bmatrix} \begin{bmatrix} -2\frac{1}{3} \\ 0 \end{bmatrix}$$

□

10.4 Biorthogonal Wavelet Transform

This section uses results from the chapter on biorthogonal wavelet transform. The biorthogonal wavelet transform is interpreted in terms of its associated polyphase matrix. A polyphase matrix is a convenient way to express the special structure of the modulation matrices (discussed in the chapter on biorthogonal wavelet transform). A technique to factorize this polyphase matrix via the lifting scheme is specified in the next section. The goal is to achieve efficient implementation of the biorthogonal wavelet transform. The biorthogonal wavelet transform is essentially defined by the following:

- Scaling and wavelet functions, and their duals. That is,

$$\left\{ \phi(t), \psi(t), \widetilde{\phi}(t), \widetilde{\psi}(t) \mid t \in \mathbb{R} \right\}$$

- The scaling and wavelet coefficients, and their duals. These express relationships among the above functions. These are

$$\left\{ h(n), g(n), \widetilde{h}(n), \widetilde{g}(n) \mid n \in \mathbb{Z} \right\}$$

These sequences are also referred to as filters.

- The sequences $\{h(n) \mid n \in \mathbb{Z}\}$, and $\{g(n) \mid n \in \mathbb{Z}\}$ are called the primary low-pass and high-pass filters respectively.

- The sequences $\left\{ \widetilde{h}(n) \mid n \in \mathbb{Z} \right\}$, and $\{\widetilde{g}(n) \mid n \in \mathbb{Z}\}$ are called the dual low-pass and high-pass filters respectively.

Note that, for orthogonal transforms $h(n) = \widetilde{h}(n)$, and $g(n) = \widetilde{g}(n), \forall n \in \mathbb{Z}$. Let $z = e^{i\omega}$, and define

$$\mathcal{H}(z) = \sum_{n \in \mathbb{Z}} h(n) z^{-n}, \quad \widetilde{\mathcal{H}}(z) = \sum_{n \in \mathbb{Z}} \widetilde{h}(n) z^{-n}$$

$$\mathcal{G}(z) = \sum_{n \in \mathbb{Z}} g(n) z^{-n}, \quad \widetilde{\mathcal{G}}(z) = \sum_{n \in \mathbb{Z}} \widetilde{g}(n) z^{-n}$$

Assume that the filters $\left\{ h(n), g(n), \widetilde{h}(n), \widetilde{g}(n) \mid n \in \mathbb{Z} \right\}$ have finite support, then $\mathcal{H}(z)$, $\widetilde{\mathcal{H}}(z)$, $\mathcal{G}(z)$, and $\widetilde{\mathcal{G}}(z)$ are Laurent polynomials. For biorthogonality, the following conditions have to hold

$$\mathcal{G}(z) = \mp z^{-L} \overline{\widetilde{\mathcal{H}}(-z)}, \qquad L \text{ is an odd integer}$$
$$\widetilde{\mathcal{G}}(z) = \mp z^{-L} \overline{\mathcal{H}(-z)}, \qquad L \text{ is an odd integer}$$

The forward and inverse biorthogonal wavelet transformations consist of several stages. The forward direction is associated with the deconstruction of a sequence, while the inverse direction is associated with the reconstruction of the corresponding sequence.

Conditions for perfect deconstruction and reconstruction of a sequence is initially summarized. Filtering at a single stage of the forward (deconstructing operation) and inverse (reconstructing operation) directions of the transformation are subsequently described.

10.4.1 Perfect Deconstruction and Reconstruction

Conditions for perfect deconstruction and reconstruction of a sequence are specified in terms of the polyphase matrices.

Definition 10.2. *Consider a sequence* $\{x(n) \in \mathbb{C} \mid n \in \mathbb{Z}\}$. *Let its z-transform be denoted by* $\mathcal{X}(z)$. *Also let its even and odd components,* $\mathcal{X}_e(z)$ *and* $\mathcal{X}_o(z)$ *respectively be*

$$\mathcal{X}_e(z) = \sum_{n \in \mathbb{Z}} x(2n) z^{-n} \tag{10.2a}$$

$$\mathcal{X}_o(z) = \sum_{n \in \mathbb{Z}} x(2n+1) z^{-n} \tag{10.2b}$$

$\square$

It follows from the above definition that

$$\mathcal{X}(z) = \mathcal{X}_e(z^2) + z^{-1}\mathcal{X}_o(z^2)$$
$$\mathcal{X}(-z) = \mathcal{X}_e(z^2) - z^{-1}\mathcal{X}_o(z^2)$$
$$\mathcal{X}_e(z^2) = \frac{(\mathcal{X}(z) + \mathcal{X}(-z))}{2}$$
$$\mathcal{X}_o(z^2) = \frac{(\mathcal{X}(z) - \mathcal{X}(-z))}{2z^{-1}}$$

The above results are encapsulated in terms of matrices in the following observation.

Observation 10.3. About perfect deconstruction and reconstruction of a sequence.

$$\begin{bmatrix} \mathcal{X}_e(z^2) \\ \mathcal{X}_o(z^2) \end{bmatrix} = \frac{1}{2}\mathcal{Y}(z) \begin{bmatrix} \mathcal{X}(z) \\ \mathcal{X}(-z) \end{bmatrix}$$

where

$$\mathcal{Y}(z) = \begin{bmatrix} 1 & 1 \\ z & -z \end{bmatrix}$$

Note that

$$\mathcal{Y}(z)\overline{\mathcal{Y}(z)}^T = 2\mathcal{I}$$

where $\mathcal{I}$ is a 2×2 identity matrix. Therefore,

$$\begin{bmatrix} \mathcal{X}(z) \\ \mathcal{X}(-z) \end{bmatrix} = \overline{\mathcal{Y}(z)}^T \begin{bmatrix} \mathcal{X}_e(z^2) \\ \mathcal{X}_o(z^2) \end{bmatrix}$$

$\square$

After a sequence is transformed (deconstructed), it should be possible to reconstruct the signal back from its transformed sequence. This requirement was stated in terms of the modulation matrix and its dual in the chapter on biorthogonal wavelet transform. This concept can also be elaborated in terms of polyphase matrices.

Definitions 10.3. *Modulation and polyphase matrices in z-notation. Let the z-transform of the primary filters be $\mathcal{H}(z)$, and $\mathcal{G}(z)$. The z-transform of the dual filters are $\widetilde{\mathcal{H}}(z)$, and $\widetilde{\mathcal{G}}(z)$ respectively.*

1. *The modulation matrix $\mathcal{M}(z)$, and its dual $\widetilde{\mathcal{M}}(z)$ are*

$$\mathcal{M}(z) = \begin{bmatrix} \mathcal{H}(z) & \mathcal{H}(-z) \\ \mathcal{G}(z) & \mathcal{G}(-z) \end{bmatrix}, \quad \widetilde{\mathcal{M}}(z) = \begin{bmatrix} \widetilde{\mathcal{H}}(z) & \widetilde{\mathcal{H}}(-z) \\ \widetilde{\mathcal{G}}(z) & \widetilde{\mathcal{G}}(-z) \end{bmatrix} \quad (10.3)$$

2. *Polyphase matrices. Let the even and odd components of $\mathcal{H}(z)$ be $\mathcal{H}_e(z)$, and $\mathcal{H}_o(z)$ respectively; and also the even and odd components of $\mathcal{G}(z)$ be $\mathcal{G}_e(z)$, and $\mathcal{G}_o(z)$ respectively. Similarly, the even and odd components of $\widetilde{\mathcal{H}}(z)$ are $\widetilde{\mathcal{H}}_e(z)$, and $\widetilde{\mathcal{H}}_o(z)$ respectively; and the even and odd components of $\widetilde{\mathcal{G}}(z)$ are $\widetilde{\mathcal{G}}_e(z)$, and $\widetilde{\mathcal{G}}_o(z)$ respectively. The polyphase matrix $\mathcal{P}(z)$ and its dual $\widetilde{\mathcal{P}}(z)$ are*

$$\mathcal{P}(z) = \begin{bmatrix} \mathcal{H}_e(z) & \mathcal{H}_o(z) \\ \mathcal{G}_e(z) & \mathcal{G}_o(z) \end{bmatrix}, \quad \widetilde{\mathcal{P}}(z) = \begin{bmatrix} \widetilde{\mathcal{H}}_e(z) & \widetilde{\mathcal{H}}_o(z) \\ \widetilde{\mathcal{G}}_e(z) & \widetilde{\mathcal{G}}_o(z) \end{bmatrix} \quad (10.4)$$

$\square$

Observation 10.4. The relationship between modulation and polyphase matrices. As $\overline{\mathcal{Y}(z)}^T \mathcal{Y}(z) = 2\mathcal{I}$, we have

$$\mathcal{P}(z^2) = \frac{1}{2}\mathcal{M}(z)\mathcal{Y}(z)^T, \quad \text{and} \quad \widetilde{\mathcal{P}}z^2) = \frac{1}{2}\widetilde{\mathcal{M}}(z)\mathcal{Y}(z)^T$$

$$\mathcal{M}(z) = \mathcal{P}(z^2)\overline{\mathcal{Y}(z)}, \quad \text{and} \quad \widetilde{\mathcal{M}}(z) = \widetilde{\mathcal{P}}(z^2)\overline{\mathcal{Y}(z)}$$

$\square$

The original sequence should be recoverable from the transformed sequence. The condition for perfect reconstruction of the original sequence from the transformed sequence can be stated in terms of the modulation and polyphase matrices. The condition for perfect reconstruction in terms of the modulation matrices was derived in the chapter on biorthogonal wavelet transform.

Observation 10.5. Condition for perfect reconstruction in terms of the modulation matrices in z-notation is:

$$M(z)\overline{\widetilde{M}(z)}^T = 2\mathcal{I}$$

Condition for perfect reconstruction in terms of the polyphase matrices is:

$$P(z)\overline{\widetilde{P}(z)}^T = \mathcal{I}$$

We also have

$$M(z)^T\overline{\widetilde{M}(z)} = 2\mathcal{I}, \quad \text{and} \quad P(z)^T\overline{\widetilde{P}(z)} = \mathcal{I}$$

□

The word polyphase has been used in filter theory literature to denote splitting of signals into several streams, and processing them in parallel. Note that the elements of the matrix $P(z)$ are Laurent polynomials. Therefore, the determinants of the matrices $P(z)$ and $\widetilde{P}(z)$ are Laurent polynomials. From the above equations it can be concluded that the determinants of the inverses of matrices $P(z)$ and $\widetilde{P}(z)$ are also Laurent polynomials. This is possible if the determinants of the matrices $P(z)$ and $\widetilde{P}(z)$ are mononomials. Hence these determinants are of the form cz^n, $c \in \mathbb{R}\setminus\{0\}$, and $n \in \mathbb{Z}$. The polynomials $\mathcal{G}(z)$ and $\widetilde{\mathcal{G}}(z)$ are normalized such that the determinants of $P(z)$ and $\widetilde{P}(z)$ are each equal to 1. Therefore, since the determinant of $P(z)$ is equal to 1, inverting the $P(z)$ matrix yields

$$\overline{\widetilde{P}(z)}^T = \begin{bmatrix} \mathcal{G}_o(z) & -\mathcal{H}_o(z) \\ -\mathcal{G}_e(z) & \mathcal{H}_e(z) \end{bmatrix}$$

Thus

$$\widetilde{P}(z) = \begin{bmatrix} \widetilde{\mathcal{H}}_e(z) & \widetilde{\mathcal{H}}_o(z) \\ \widetilde{\mathcal{G}}_e(z) & \widetilde{\mathcal{G}}_o(z) \end{bmatrix} = \begin{bmatrix} \overline{\mathcal{G}_o(z)} & -\overline{\mathcal{G}_e(z)} \\ -\overline{\mathcal{H}_o(z)} & \overline{\mathcal{H}_e(z)} \end{bmatrix}$$

The above equations lead to

$$\widetilde{\mathcal{G}}(z) = z^{-1}\overline{\mathcal{H}(-z)}, \quad \text{and} \quad \widetilde{\mathcal{H}}(z) = -z^{-1}\overline{\mathcal{G}(-z)}$$

A similar and more general result was stated at the beginning of the section. Further, if the filter coefficients are real numbers then

$$\widetilde{\mathcal{G}}(z) = z^{-1}\mathcal{H}(-z^{-1}), \quad \text{and} \quad \widetilde{\mathcal{H}}(z) = -z^{-1}\mathcal{G}(-z^{-1})$$

As mentioned earlier $\det P(z) = \det \widetilde{P}(z) = 1$. This implies

$$\mathcal{H}_e(z)\mathcal{G}_o(z) - \mathcal{H}_o(z)\mathcal{G}_e(z) = 1$$
$$\widetilde{\mathcal{H}}_e(z)\widetilde{\mathcal{G}}_o(z) - \widetilde{\mathcal{H}}_o(z)\widetilde{\mathcal{G}}_e(z) = 1$$

The above discussion is condensed in the following observation.

Observations 10.6. Assume that the polynomials $\mathcal{G}(z)$ and $\widetilde{\mathcal{G}}(z)$ are normalized such that the determinants of $P(z)$ and $\widetilde{P}(z)$ are each equal to 1. Then

1. $\det P(z) = \det \widetilde{P}(z) = 1$.
2. If the filter coefficients are real numbers, then $\widetilde{\mathcal{G}}(z) = z^{-1}\mathcal{H}(-z^{-1})$, and $\widetilde{\mathcal{H}}(z) = -z^{-1}\mathcal{G}(-z^{-1})$.   □

10.4.2   Single-Stage Deconstruction and Reconstruction

The deconstruction and reconstruction of a sequence for only a single stage of a biorthogonal transformation is analyzed in this subsection.

Deconstruction of a Sequence: Single Stage

The deconstruction of a sequence via a biorthogonal transformation for only a single stage is analyzed. Let $\mathcal{F}(z)$ be the z-transform of the input signal (sequence). It generates two sequences. Let the z-transforms of these sequences be specified as $\mathcal{U}(z)$ and $\mathcal{V}(z)$ respectively. The $\mathcal{U}(z)$ and $\mathcal{V}(z)$ transforms corresponds to the low- and high-frequency components respectively.

$$\mathcal{U}(z^2) = \frac{1}{2}\left[\widetilde{\mathcal{H}}(z)\mathcal{F}(z) + \overline{\widetilde{\mathcal{H}}(-z)}\mathcal{F}(-z)\right]$$
$$\mathcal{V}(z^2) = \frac{1}{2}\left[\widetilde{\mathcal{G}}(z)\mathcal{F}(z) + \overline{\widetilde{\mathcal{G}}(-z)}\mathcal{F}(-z)\right]$$

The above result is taken from the digital filter representation of the biorthogonal wavelet transform (from the chapter on biorthogonal wavelet transform). Define $\mathcal{F}_e(z)$, and $\mathcal{F}_o(z)$ as the even and odd components of $\mathcal{F}(z)$ respectively. Then

$$\begin{bmatrix} \mathcal{U}(z^2) \\ \mathcal{V}(z^2) \end{bmatrix} = \frac{1}{2}\overline{\widetilde{\mathcal{M}}(z)}\begin{bmatrix} \mathcal{F}(z) \\ \mathcal{F}(-z) \end{bmatrix}$$
$$= \frac{1}{2}\overline{\widetilde{\mathcal{M}}(z)}\overline{\mathcal{Y}(z)}^{-T}\begin{bmatrix} \mathcal{F}_e(z^2) \\ \mathcal{F}_o(z^2) \end{bmatrix}$$
$$= \overline{\widetilde{\mathcal{P}}(z^2)}\begin{bmatrix} \mathcal{F}_e(z^2) \\ \mathcal{F}_o(z^2) \end{bmatrix}$$

Therefore,

$$\begin{bmatrix} \mathcal{U}(z) \\ \mathcal{V}(z) \end{bmatrix} = \widetilde{\mathcal{P}(z)} \begin{bmatrix} \mathcal{F}_e(z) \\ \mathcal{F}_o(z) \end{bmatrix}$$

Reconstruction of a Sequence: Single Stage

The reconstruction of a sequence via the inverse biorthogonal transformation for only a single stage is analyzed. In the inverse transformation stage, the low- and high-frequency contents are specified as $\mathcal{U}(z)$ and $\mathcal{V}(z)$ respectively. The aim is to recover the signal information $\mathcal{F}(z)$ from the row vector $\begin{bmatrix} \mathcal{U}(z) & \mathcal{V}(z) \end{bmatrix}$, which is

$$\mathcal{F}(z) = \mathcal{H}(z)\mathcal{U}(z^2) + \mathcal{G}(z)\mathcal{V}(z^2)$$

That the above operation is indeed correct, is demonstrated below. We have

$$\mathcal{H}(z)\mathcal{U}(z^2) + \mathcal{G}(z)\mathcal{V}(z^2) = \begin{bmatrix} \mathcal{H}(z) & \mathcal{G}(z) \end{bmatrix} \begin{bmatrix} \mathcal{U}(z^2) \\ \mathcal{V}(z^2) \end{bmatrix}$$

$$= \begin{bmatrix} 1 & 0 \end{bmatrix} \mathcal{M}(z)^T \begin{bmatrix} \mathcal{U}(z^2) \\ \mathcal{V}(z^2) \end{bmatrix}$$

$$= \frac{1}{2} \begin{bmatrix} 1 & 0 \end{bmatrix} \mathcal{M}(z)^T \widetilde{\mathcal{M}(z)} \begin{bmatrix} \mathcal{F}(z) \\ \mathcal{F}(-z) \end{bmatrix}$$

$$= \begin{bmatrix} 1 & 0 \end{bmatrix} \begin{bmatrix} \mathcal{F}(z) \\ \mathcal{F}(-z) \end{bmatrix}$$

$$= \mathcal{F}(z)$$

Thus

$$\mathcal{H}(z)\mathcal{U}(z^2) + \mathcal{G}(z)\mathcal{V}(z^2) = \mathcal{F}(z)$$

We also have

$$\begin{bmatrix} \mathcal{F}_e(z) \\ \mathcal{F}_o(z) \end{bmatrix} = \mathcal{P}(z)^T \begin{bmatrix} \mathcal{U}(z) \\ \mathcal{V}(z) \end{bmatrix}$$

The next observation summarizes the results of forward and inverse biorthogonal wavelet transformation for a single stage.

Observation 10.7. Summary of forward and inverse biorthogonal wavelet transformation for a single stage. The z-transform of the sequence to be deconstructed is $\mathcal{F}(z)$.

The forward wavelet transform (deconstruction) generates two sequences. Let the z-transforms of these sequences be $\mathcal{U}(z)$ and $\mathcal{V}(z)$ respectively. The $\mathcal{U}(z)$ and $\mathcal{V}(z)$ transforms correspond to the low- and high-frequency components respectively. Thus:

Forward transformation:

$$\begin{bmatrix} \mathcal{U}(z) \\ \mathcal{V}(z) \end{bmatrix} = \widetilde{\mathcal{P}}\,(z) \begin{bmatrix} \mathcal{F}_e\,(z) \\ \mathcal{F}_o\,(z) \end{bmatrix}$$

Inverse transformation:

$$\mathcal{F}(z) = \mathcal{H}\,(z)\,\mathcal{U}(z^2) + \mathcal{G}\,(z)\,\mathcal{V}(z^2)$$

$$\begin{bmatrix} \mathcal{F}_e\,(z) \\ \mathcal{F}_o\,(z) \end{bmatrix} = \mathcal{P}\,(z)^T \begin{bmatrix} \mathcal{U}(z) \\ \mathcal{V}(z) \end{bmatrix}$$

$\square$

Observe in the above summary, that the implementation of the forward and inverse transformation would significantly improve if the polyphase matrices are factorized. This is indeed the subject of the next section. The factorization technique of the polyphase matrices is called the lifting scheme.

Example 10.3. A simple example of polyphase matrix results in the so-called *lazy wavelet transform*. It is obtained by defining $\mathcal{P}\,(z) = \mathcal{I}$, the 2×2 identity matrix. This gives

$$\mathcal{H}\,(z) = \widetilde{\mathcal{H}}\,(z) = 1$$
$$\mathcal{G}\,(z) = \widetilde{\mathcal{G}}\,(z) = z^{-1}$$

This transform splits the sequence into its even and odd components. This operation is also called polyphase decomposition. $\square$

10.5 The Lifting Technique

The lifting scheme has been largely developed by Wim Sweldens and his colleagues. The lifting technique is a scheme for building wavelets and wavelet transforms. It actually builds larger filters from very simple filters via a sequence of *lifting steps*.

10.5.1 Lifting Technique via Polyphase Matrix

A technique is developed to generate new biorthogonal wavelet filters from old biorthogonal wavelet filters. A primary artifice to accomplish this is the judicious use of the polyphase matrix.

Definition 10.4. *The filter pair* $\{h(n), g(n) \in \mathbb{C} \mid n \in \mathbb{Z}\}$ *is complementary, if the determinant of its corresponding polyphase matrix* $\mathcal{P}\,(z)$ *is equal to unity.* $\square$

Observation 10.8. If the filter pair $\{h(n), g(n) \mid n \in \mathbb{Z}\}$ is complementary, then the filter pair $\left\{ \widetilde{h}(n), \widetilde{g}(n) \mid n \in \mathbb{Z} \right\}$ is also complementary.   □

Use of the lifting technique is demonstrated via the use of dual and primary lifting. The following terminology is used in describing these lifting techniques.

- Consider a set of filters which perform biorthogonal wavelet transformation. These are:
$$\left\{ h(n), g(n), \widetilde{h}(n), \widetilde{g}(n) \mid n \in \mathbb{Z} \right\}$$
  Assume that these filters have a compact support. The z-transforms of these filters are $\mathcal{H}(z)$, $\widetilde{\mathcal{H}}(z)$, $\mathcal{G}(z)$, and $\widetilde{\mathcal{G}}(z)$ respectively.

- The filters $\{h(n), g(n) \mid n \in \mathbb{Z}\}$ are a complementary filter pair. The corresponding polyphase matrix is $\mathcal{P}(z)$, and its dual polyphase matrix is $\widetilde{\mathcal{P}}(z)$. The determinant of the polyphase matrix corresponding to a complementary filter pair is unity.

- A new polyphase matrix $\mathcal{P}_{new}(z)$ is formed. Let its corresponding complementary filter pair be $\{h_{new}(n), g_{new}(n) \mid n \in \mathbb{Z}\}$.

- Thus a new set of filters
$$\left\{ h_{new}(n), g_{new}(n), \widetilde{h}_{new}(n), \widetilde{g}_{new}(n) \mid n \in \mathbb{Z} \right\}$$
  is formed. Let the corresponding z-transforms of the filters be
$$\mathcal{H}_{new}(z), \mathcal{G}_{new}(z), \widetilde{\mathcal{H}}_{new}(z), \text{ and } \widetilde{\mathcal{G}}_{new}(z)$$
  respectively.

- The new dual polyphase matrix is $\widetilde{\mathcal{P}}_{new}(z)$.

Dual Lifting

In dual lifting $\widetilde{\mathcal{H}}(z)$ and $\mathcal{G}(z)$ are modified, however $\mathcal{H}(z)$ and $\widetilde{\mathcal{G}}(z)$ remain unchanged. A new polyphase matrix of a new filter pair is obtained via a transformation of the old polyphase matrix $\mathcal{P}(z)$. Let $\{h_{new}(n), g_{new}(n) \mid n \in \mathbb{Z}\}$ be a new complementary pair, and its polyphase matrix be $\mathcal{P}_{new}(z)$, where

$$\mathcal{P}_{new}(z) = \begin{bmatrix} 1 & 0 \\ T(z) & 1 \end{bmatrix} \mathcal{P}(z)$$

In the above equation, $T(z)$ is a Laurent polynomial. Note that the first matrix is lower-triangular, and its determinant is equal to unity. Therefore, the determinant of $\mathcal{P}_{new}(z)$ is also unity. The next observation determines the relationships between the old and new filters. Its proof is provided in the problem section.

Observation 10.9. Dual lifting. If $\mathcal{T}(z)$ is a Laurent polynomial, then the following relationships hold. The dual polyphase matrix of the dual complementary filter pair

$$\left\{ \widetilde{h}_{new}(n), \widetilde{g}_{new}(n) \mid n \in \mathbb{Z} \right\}$$

is

$$\widetilde{\mathcal{P}}_{new}(z) = \begin{bmatrix} 1 & -\overline{\mathcal{T}(z)} \\ 0 & 1 \end{bmatrix} \widetilde{\mathcal{P}}(z)$$

and

$$\mathcal{H}_{new}(z) = \mathcal{H}(z)$$
$$\mathcal{G}_{new}(z) = \mathcal{G}(z) + \mathcal{T}(z^2)\,\mathcal{H}(z)$$
$$\widetilde{\mathcal{H}}_{new}(z) = \widetilde{\mathcal{H}}(z) - \overline{\mathcal{T}(z^2)}\widetilde{\mathcal{G}}(z)$$
$$\widetilde{\mathcal{G}}_{new}(z) = \widetilde{\mathcal{G}}(z)$$

$\square$

Primary Lifting

In primary lifting $\mathcal{H}(z)$ and $\widetilde{\mathcal{G}}(z)$ are modified, however $\widetilde{\mathcal{H}}(z)$ and $\mathcal{G}(z)$ remain unchanged. A new polyphase matrix of a new filter pair is obtained via a transformation of the old polyphase matrix $\mathcal{P}(z)$. Let $\{h_{new}(n), g_{new}(n) \mid n \in \mathbb{Z}\}$ be a new complementary pair, and its polyphase matrix be $\mathcal{P}_{new}(z)$, where

$$\mathcal{P}_{new}(z) = \begin{bmatrix} 1 & S(z) \\ 0 & 1 \end{bmatrix} \mathcal{P}(z)$$

In the above equation, $S(z)$ is a Laurent polynomial. Note that the first matrix is upper-triangular, and its determinant is equal to unity. Therefore, the determinant of $\mathcal{P}_{new}(z)$ is also unity. The next observation determines the relationships between the old and new filters. Its proof is provided in the problem section.

Observation 10.10. Primary lifting. If $S(z)$ is a Laurent polynomial, then the following relationships hold. The dual polyphase matrix of the dual complementary filter pair

$$\left\{ \widetilde{h}_{new}(n), \widetilde{g}_{new}(n) \mid n \in \mathbb{Z} \right\}$$

is

$$\widetilde{\mathcal{P}}_{new}(z) = \begin{bmatrix} 1 & 0 \\ -\overline{S(z)} & 1 \end{bmatrix} \widetilde{\mathcal{P}}(z)$$

and

$$\mathcal{H}_{new}(z) = \mathcal{H}(z) + \mathcal{S}(z^2)\mathcal{G}(z)$$
$$\mathcal{G}_{new}(z) = \mathcal{G}(z)$$
$$\widetilde{\mathcal{H}}_{new}(z) = \widetilde{\mathcal{H}}(z)$$
$$\widetilde{\mathcal{G}}_{new}(z) = \widetilde{\mathcal{G}}(z) - \overline{\mathcal{S}(z^2)}\widetilde{\mathcal{H}}(z)$$

$\square$

10.5.2 Polyphase Matrix Factorization

A scheme to factorize a polyphase matrix associated with a pair of complementary filters $\{h(n), g(n) \mid n \in \mathbb{Z}\}$ is outlined. The Euclidean algorithm is used in factorization of the polyphase matrix.

The even and odd components of $\mathcal{H}(z)$ are $\mathcal{H}_e(z)$ and $\mathcal{H}_o(z)$ have to be relatively prime. If these are not relatively prime, then any common factor of $\mathcal{H}_e(z)$ and $\mathcal{H}_o(z)$ will also divide the determinant of matrix $\mathcal{P}(z)$, which is actually 1.

The division process that is required in the Euclidean algorithm is not unique. Therefore, the greatest common divisor of $\mathcal{H}_e(z)$ and $\mathcal{H}_o(z)$ will be a mononomial. The greatest common divisor of $\mathcal{H}_e(z)$ and $\mathcal{H}_o(z)$ is chosen to be a constant $K \in \mathbb{R} \setminus \{0\}$. Then

$$\begin{bmatrix} \mathcal{H}_e(z) \\ \mathcal{H}_o(z) \end{bmatrix} = \left(\prod_{i=1}^{m} \mathcal{N}_i(z) \right) \begin{bmatrix} K \\ 0 \end{bmatrix}$$
$$\mathcal{N}_i(z) = \begin{bmatrix} \mathcal{Q}_i(z) & 1 \\ 1 & 0 \end{bmatrix}, \quad 1 \leq i \leq m$$

In the above equation $\mathcal{Q}_i(z)$, for $1 \leq i \leq m$ are Laurent polynomials. Also $\mathcal{Q}_1(z)$ is equal to zero, if $\deg[\mathcal{H}_e(z)] < \deg[\mathcal{H}_o(z)]$. Observe that if m is an even integer, then the determinant of the product of m matrices is 1. However, if m is an odd integer, then the value of this determinant is equal to -1.

Assume m to be an even integer. A filter $\{g'(n) \mid n \in \mathbb{Z}\}$ is generated which is complementary to $\{h(n) \mid n \in \mathbb{Z}\}$.

Let the z-transform of the sequence $\{g'(n) \mid n \in \mathbb{Z}\}$ be $\mathcal{G}'(z)$. Its even and odd parts are $\mathcal{G}'_e(z)$ and $\mathcal{G}'_o(z)$ respectively, and the corresponding polyphase matrix is $\mathcal{P}'(z)$. As the determinant of $\mathcal{P}'(z)$ is equal to 1, we have

$$\mathcal{P}'(z)^T = \begin{bmatrix} \mathcal{H}_e(z) & \mathcal{G}'_e(z) \\ \mathcal{H}_o(z) & \mathcal{G}'_o(z) \end{bmatrix} = \left(\prod_{i=1}^{m} \mathcal{N}_i(z) \right) \begin{bmatrix} K & 0 \\ 0 & 1/K \end{bmatrix}$$

It can be verified that

$$\begin{bmatrix} \mathcal{Q}_i(z) & 1 \\ 1 & 0 \end{bmatrix} = \begin{bmatrix} 1 & \mathcal{Q}_i(z) \\ 0 & 1 \end{bmatrix} \begin{bmatrix} 0 & 1 \\ 1 & 0 \end{bmatrix} = \begin{bmatrix} 0 & 1 \\ 1 & 0 \end{bmatrix} \begin{bmatrix} 1 & 0 \\ \mathcal{Q}_i(z) & 1 \end{bmatrix}$$

The above artifice is used several times in the rest of this chapter. Define

$$\mathcal{O}_i\left(z\right) = \begin{bmatrix} 1 & \mathcal{Q}_{2i-1}\left(z\right) \\ 0 & 1 \end{bmatrix}, \qquad i = 1, 2, \ldots, \frac{m}{2}$$

$$\mathcal{E}_i\left(z\right) = \begin{bmatrix} 1 & 0 \\ \mathcal{Q}_{2i}\left(z\right) & 1 \end{bmatrix}, \qquad i = 1, 2, \ldots, \frac{m}{2}$$

Then

$$\mathcal{P}'(z)^T = \left(\prod_{i=1}^{m/2} \mathcal{O}_i\left(z\right) \mathcal{E}_i\left(z\right) \right) \begin{bmatrix} K & 0 \\ 0 & 1/K \end{bmatrix}$$

The high-pass filter $\{g\left(n\right) \mid n \in \mathbb{Z}\}$ is recovered from the filter $\{g'\left(n\right) \mid n \in \mathbb{Z}\}$ via the transformation

$$\mathcal{P}\left(z\right) = \begin{bmatrix} 1 & 0 \\ \mathcal{T}\left(z\right) & 1 \end{bmatrix} \mathcal{P}'(z)$$

for some Laurent polynomial $\mathcal{T}\left(z\right)$. Another possible transformation could be

$$\mathcal{P}\left(z\right) = \mathcal{P}'(z) \begin{bmatrix} 1 & \mathcal{S}\left(z\right) \\ 0 & 1 \end{bmatrix}$$

Define

$$n = (m/2 + 1), \quad \mathcal{S}_n\left(z\right) = 0, \quad \mathcal{T}_n\left(z\right) = K^2 \mathcal{T}\left(z\right)$$
$$\mathcal{S}_i\left(z\right) = \mathcal{Q}_{2i}(z), \quad \mathcal{T}_i\left(z\right) = \mathcal{Q}_{2i-1}(z), \quad \text{for} \ \ 1 \leq i \leq (n-1)$$

Further the primary and dual lifting matrices $\mathcal{A}_i\left(z\right)$ and $\mathcal{B}_i\left(z\right)$ respectively for $1 \leq i \leq n$ are

$$\mathcal{A}_i\left(z\right) = \begin{bmatrix} 1 & \mathcal{S}_i\left(z\right) \\ 0 & 1 \end{bmatrix}, \quad \mathcal{B}_i\left(z\right) = \begin{bmatrix} 1 & 0 \\ \mathcal{T}_i\left(z\right) & 1 \end{bmatrix}$$

Note that $\mathcal{S}_i\left(z\right)$ and $\mathcal{T}_i\left(z\right)$ for $1 \leq i \leq n$ are Laurent polynomials. Thus

$$\mathcal{P}\left(z\right) = \begin{bmatrix} \mathcal{H}_e\left(z\right) & \mathcal{H}_o\left(z\right) \\ \mathcal{G}_e\left(z\right) & \mathcal{G}_o\left(z\right) \end{bmatrix}$$

$$= \begin{bmatrix} K & 0 \\ 0 & 1/K \end{bmatrix} \left(\prod_{i=n}^{1} \mathcal{A}_i\left(z\right) \mathcal{B}_i\left(z\right) \right)$$

The above discussion essentially describes the factorization process of the matrix $\mathcal{P}\left(z\right)$ when m is an even integer. The above details are summarized in the following observation.

Observation 10.11. The goal is to obtain a factorization of the polyphase matrix $\mathcal{P}(z)$ associated with a pair of complementary filters $\{h(n), g(n) \mid n \in \mathbb{Z}\}$. Let the even and odd components of $\mathcal{H}(z)$ be $\mathcal{H}_e(z)$ and $\mathcal{H}_o(z)$ respectively, and let the greatest common divisor of the polynomials $\mathcal{H}_e(z)$ and $\mathcal{H}_o(z)$ be $K \in \mathbb{R} \backslash \{0\}$. Using the Euclidean algorithm, obtain

$$\begin{bmatrix} \mathcal{H}_e(z) \\ \mathcal{H}_o(z) \end{bmatrix} = \left(\prod_{i=1}^{m} \mathcal{N}_i(z) \right) \begin{bmatrix} K \\ 0 \end{bmatrix}$$

$$\mathcal{N}_i(z) = \begin{bmatrix} \mathcal{Q}_i(z) & 1 \\ 1 & 0 \end{bmatrix}, \quad 1 \le i \le m$$

In the above equation $\mathcal{Q}_i(z)$, for $1 \le i \le m$ are Laurent polynomials. Observe that if m is an *even integer*, then the determinant of the product of m matrices is 1. Assume that m is an even integer.

Generate a filter $\{g'(n) \mid n \in \mathbb{Z}\}$ which is complementary to $\{h(n) \mid n \in \mathbb{Z}\}$. Let the z-transform of the sequence $\{g'(n) \mid n \in \mathbb{Z}\}$ be $\mathcal{G}'(z)$. Its even and odd parts are $\mathcal{G}'_e(z)$ and $\mathcal{G}'_o(z)$ respectively, and the corresponding polyphase matrix is $\mathcal{P}'(z)$. Thus

$$\mathcal{P}'(z)^T = \begin{bmatrix} \mathcal{H}_e(z) & \mathcal{G}'_e(z) \\ \mathcal{H}_o(z) & \mathcal{G}'_o(z) \end{bmatrix} = \left(\prod_{i=1}^{m} \mathcal{N}_i(z) \right) \begin{bmatrix} K & 0 \\ 0 & 1/K \end{bmatrix}$$

The high-pass filter $\{g(n) \mid n \in \mathbb{Z}\}$ is recovered from the filter $\{g'(n) \mid n \in \mathbb{Z}\}$ via the transformation

$$\mathcal{P}(z) = \begin{bmatrix} 1 & 0 \\ \mathcal{T}(z) & 1 \end{bmatrix} \mathcal{P}'(z)$$

Define

$$n = (m/2 + 1), \quad \mathcal{S}_n(z) = 0, \quad \mathcal{T}_n(z) = K^2 \mathcal{T}(z)$$
$$\mathcal{S}_i(z) = \mathcal{Q}_{2i}(z), \quad \mathcal{T}_i(z) = \mathcal{Q}_{2i-1}(z), \quad \text{for } 1 \le i \le (n-1)$$

and the primary and dual lifting matrices $\mathcal{A}_i(z)$ and $\mathcal{B}_i(z)$, for $1 \le i \le n$ respectively as

$$\mathcal{A}_i(z) = \begin{bmatrix} 1 & \mathcal{S}_i(z) \\ 0 & 1 \end{bmatrix}, \quad \mathcal{B}_i(z) = \begin{bmatrix} 1 & 0 \\ \mathcal{T}_i(z) & 1 \end{bmatrix}$$

Note that $\mathcal{S}_i(z)$ and $\mathcal{T}_i(z)$ for $1 \le i \le n$ are Laurent polynomials. Finally

$$\mathcal{P}(z) = \begin{bmatrix} K & 0 \\ 0 & 1/K \end{bmatrix} \left(\prod_{i=n}^{1} \mathcal{A}_i(z) \mathcal{B}_i(z) \right)$$

$\square$

Next consider the case when m is an odd integer. As polyphase matrices should have a determinant value of 1, write $\left[\mathcal{H}_e(z)\ \mathcal{H}_o(z) \right]^T$ as

$$\begin{bmatrix} \mathcal{H}_e(z) \\ \mathcal{H}_o(z) \end{bmatrix} = \left(\prod_{i=1}^{m+1} \mathcal{N}_i(z) \right) \begin{bmatrix} K \\ 0 \end{bmatrix}$$

$$\mathcal{N}_{m+1}(z) = \begin{bmatrix} 1 & 0 \\ 0 & -1 \end{bmatrix}$$

Notice that $(m+1)$ is an even integer, and the matrix $\mathcal{P}(z)$ can now be factorized as in the case when m is an even integer. The factorization of the polyphase matrix $\mathcal{P}(z)$ is summarized in the following theorem.

Theorem 10.1. *The polyphase matrix $\mathcal{P}(z)$ associated with a pair of complementary filters $\{h(n), g(n) \mid n \in \mathbb{Z}\}$ can be factorized by using the Euclidean algorithm for polynomials.*   □

The dual polyphase matrix $\widetilde{\mathcal{P}}(z)$ is next obtained. Define $\tilde{\mathcal{A}}_i(z)$ and $\tilde{\mathcal{B}}_i(z)$ such that

$$\mathcal{A}_i(z)\overline{\tilde{\mathcal{A}}_i(z)}^T = \mathcal{I}, \quad \text{for } 1 \le i \le n$$

$$\mathcal{B}_i(z)\overline{\tilde{\mathcal{B}}_i(z)}^T = \mathcal{I}, \quad \text{for } 1 \le i \le n$$

Then

$$\tilde{\mathcal{A}}_i(z) = \begin{bmatrix} 1 & 0 \\ -\mathcal{S}_i(z) & 1 \end{bmatrix}, \quad \tilde{\mathcal{B}}_i(z) = \begin{bmatrix} 1 & -\overline{\mathcal{T}_i(z)} \\ 0 & 1 \end{bmatrix}, \quad \text{for } 1 \le i \le n$$

As $\mathcal{P}(z)\overline{\widetilde{\mathcal{P}}(z)}^T = \mathcal{I}$, observe that

$$\widetilde{\mathcal{P}}(z) = \begin{bmatrix} \tilde{\mathcal{H}}_e(z) & \tilde{\mathcal{H}}_o(z) \\ \tilde{\mathcal{G}}_e(z) & \tilde{\mathcal{G}}_o(z) \end{bmatrix}$$

$$= \begin{bmatrix} 1/K & 0 \\ 0 & K \end{bmatrix} \left(\prod_{i=n}^{1} \tilde{\mathcal{A}}_i(z)\tilde{\mathcal{B}}_i(z) \right)$$

10.5.3 Examples

The theoretical details developed in the last subsection are clarified via examples.

Example 10.4. Daubechies orthonormal filter with 2 vanishing moments: In this example, the $\{h(n) \mid n = 0, 1, 2, 3\}$ filter is given by

$$h(0) = \frac{(\sqrt{3}+1)}{4\sqrt{2}}, \quad h(1) = \frac{(3+\sqrt{3})}{4\sqrt{2}},$$

$$h(2) = \frac{(3-\sqrt{3})}{4\sqrt{2}}, \quad h(3) = \frac{(1-\sqrt{3})}{4\sqrt{2}}$$

The relationship

$$g(n) = (-1)^n \, \overline{h\,(3-n)}, \quad n \in [0,3]$$

implies

$$g(0) = \overline{h(3)}, \quad g(1) = -\overline{h(2)}, \quad g(2) = \overline{h(1)}, \quad \text{and} \quad g(3) = -\overline{h(0)}$$

Also $g(n) = 0$ for values of $n \notin [0,3]$.

$$\mathcal{H}_e\,(z) = h(0) + h(2)z^{-1}$$
$$\mathcal{H}_o\,(z) = h(1) + h(3)z^{-1}$$
$$\mathcal{G}_e\,(z) = g(0) + g(2)z^{-1} = h(3) + h(1)z^{-1}$$
$$\mathcal{G}_o\,(z) = g(1) + g(3)z^{-1} = -h(2) - h(0)z^{-1}$$

From the above equations, it follows that the determinant of the matrix

$$\begin{bmatrix} \mathcal{H}_e\,(z) & \mathcal{H}_o\,(z) \\ \mathcal{G}_e\,(z) & \mathcal{G}_o\,(z) \end{bmatrix}$$

is $-z^{-1}$. Since a polyphase matrix is required to have a unit value for its determinant, factorize the matrix

$$P\,(z) = \begin{bmatrix} \mathcal{H}_e\,(z) & \mathcal{H}_o\,(z) \\ -z\mathcal{G}_e\,(z) & -z\mathcal{G}_o\,(z) \end{bmatrix} = \begin{bmatrix} (h(0)+h(2)z^{-1}) & (h(1)+h(3)z^{-1}) \\ -(h(3)z+h(1)) & (h(2)z+h(0)) \end{bmatrix}$$

Its determinant is unity. The first step of the factorization process requires the use of the Euclidean algorithm. Thus

$$\begin{bmatrix} \mathcal{H}_e\,(z) \\ \mathcal{H}_o\,(z) \end{bmatrix} = \begin{bmatrix} -\sqrt{3} & 1 \\ 1 & 0 \end{bmatrix} \begin{bmatrix} \frac{\sqrt{3}}{4} + \frac{(\sqrt{3}-2)}{4}z^{-1} & 1 \\ 1 & 0 \end{bmatrix} \begin{bmatrix} \frac{(1+\sqrt{3})}{\sqrt{2}} \\ 0 \end{bmatrix}$$

It is rewritten as

$$\begin{bmatrix} \mathcal{H}_e\,(z) \\ \mathcal{H}_o\,(z) \end{bmatrix} = \begin{bmatrix} 1 & -\sqrt{3} \\ 0 & 1 \end{bmatrix} \begin{bmatrix} 1 & 0 \\ \frac{\sqrt{3}}{4} + \frac{(\sqrt{3}-2)}{4}z^{-1} & 1 \end{bmatrix} \begin{bmatrix} \frac{(1+\sqrt{3})}{\sqrt{2}} \\ 0 \end{bmatrix}$$

Consider an auxiliary filter $\mathcal{G}'\,(z)$ complementary to $\mathcal{H}\,(z)$. Its even and odd parts are $\mathcal{G}'_e(z)$ and $\mathcal{G}'_o(z)$ respectively. These are obtained from the following equation.

$$\mathcal{P}'(z)^T = \begin{bmatrix} \mathcal{H}_e(z) & \mathcal{G}'_e(z) \\ \mathcal{H}_o(z) & \mathcal{G}'_o(z) \end{bmatrix}$$

$$= \begin{bmatrix} 1 & -\sqrt{3} \\ 0 & 1 \end{bmatrix} \begin{bmatrix} 1 & 0 \\ \frac{\sqrt{3}}{4} + \frac{(\sqrt{3}-2)}{4} z^{-1} & 1 \end{bmatrix} \begin{bmatrix} \frac{(1+\sqrt{3})}{\sqrt{2}} & 0 \\ 0 & \frac{(-1+\sqrt{3})}{\sqrt{2}} \end{bmatrix}$$

$\mathcal{G}'_e(z)$ and $\mathcal{G}'_o(z)$ are found to be

$$\begin{bmatrix} \mathcal{G}'_e(z) \\ \mathcal{G}'_o(z) \end{bmatrix} = \begin{bmatrix} \frac{(-3+\sqrt{3})}{\sqrt{2}} \\ \frac{(-1+\sqrt{3})}{\sqrt{2}} \end{bmatrix}$$

Since

$$\mathcal{P}(z) = \begin{bmatrix} 1 & 0 \\ \mathcal{T}(z) & 1 \end{bmatrix} \mathcal{P}'(z)$$

The above equations yield

$$-z\mathcal{G}_e(z) = \mathcal{G}'_e(z) + \mathcal{T}(z)\mathcal{H}_e(z)$$
$$-z\mathcal{G}_o(z) = \mathcal{G}'_o(z) + \mathcal{T}(z)\mathcal{H}_o(z)$$

Consequently, $\mathcal{T}(z) = (2 - \sqrt{3})z$. The final matrix factorization is

$$\mathcal{P}(z) = \begin{bmatrix} \mathcal{H}_e(z) & \mathcal{H}_o(z) \\ -z\mathcal{G}_e(z) & -z\mathcal{G}_o(z) \end{bmatrix}$$

$$= \begin{bmatrix} \frac{(1+\sqrt{3})}{\sqrt{2}} & 0 \\ 0 & \frac{(-1+\sqrt{3})}{\sqrt{2}} \end{bmatrix} \begin{bmatrix} 1 & 0 \\ z & 1 \end{bmatrix} \begin{bmatrix} 1 & \frac{\sqrt{3}}{4} + \frac{(\sqrt{3}-2)}{4} z^{-1} \\ 0 & 1 \end{bmatrix} \begin{bmatrix} 1 & 0 \\ -\sqrt{3} & 1 \end{bmatrix}$$

□

Example 10.5. Consider the biorthogonal wavelets due to Cohen, Daubechies, and Feauveau (1992). Assume that the first two moments of the primary and dual wavelet functions vanish. Then

$$\mathcal{H}(z) = \frac{\sqrt{2}}{8}\left(-z^2 + 2z + 6 + 2z^{-1} - z^{-2}\right)$$

$$\mathcal{G}(z) = \mp\frac{\sqrt{2}}{4}\left(-z^{-2} + 2z^{-1} - 1\right)$$

We shall use the positive sign in the expression for $G(z)$. That is, we use

$$\mathcal{G}(z) = \frac{\sqrt{2}}{4}\left(-z^{-2} + 2z^{-1} - 1\right)$$

The above equations yield

$$\mathcal{H}_e(z) = \frac{\sqrt{2}}{8}(-z + 6 - z^{-1})$$

$$\mathcal{H}_o(z) = \frac{\sqrt{2}}{8}(2z + 2)$$

$$\mathcal{G}_e(z) = \frac{\sqrt{2}}{4}(-z^{-1} - 1)$$

$$\mathcal{G}_o(z) = \frac{\sqrt{2}}{2}$$

It can be verified that the determinant of the polyphase matrix is 1. As the Euclidean factorization process is not unique, the following two factorizations are possible:

$$\begin{bmatrix} \mathcal{H}_e(z) \\ \mathcal{H}_o(z) \end{bmatrix} = \begin{bmatrix} -\frac{1}{2} + \frac{7}{2}z^{-1} & 1 \\ 1 & 0 \end{bmatrix} \begin{bmatrix} -\frac{z}{4} - \frac{z^2}{4} & 1 \\ 1 & 0 \end{bmatrix} \begin{bmatrix} -\sqrt{2}z^{-1} \\ 0 \end{bmatrix}$$

and

$$\begin{bmatrix} \mathcal{H}_e(z) \\ \mathcal{H}_o(z) \end{bmatrix} = \begin{bmatrix} -\frac{1}{2} - \frac{1}{2}z^{-1} & 1 \\ 1 & 0 \end{bmatrix} \begin{bmatrix} \frac{z}{4} + \frac{1}{4} & 1 \\ 1 & 0 \end{bmatrix} \begin{bmatrix} \sqrt{2} \\ 0 \end{bmatrix}$$

Note that in the first factorization, the gcd $-\sqrt{2}z^{-1}$ is not a constant. The z^{-1} factor of the gcd is removed by suitably modifying the polynomial $\mathcal{H}(z)$. Further, the magnitude of the coefficients of Laurent polynomials in the first factorization have larger values. Notice the 7/2 factor. Therefore, the second factorization is used. It is modified as

$$\begin{bmatrix} \mathcal{H}_e(z) \\ \mathcal{H}_o(z) \end{bmatrix} = \begin{bmatrix} 1 & -\frac{1}{2} - \frac{1}{2}z^{-1} \\ 0 & 1 \end{bmatrix} \begin{bmatrix} 1 & 0 \\ \frac{z}{4} + \frac{1}{4} & 1 \end{bmatrix} \begin{bmatrix} \sqrt{2} \\ 0 \end{bmatrix}$$

Let $\mathcal{G}'(z)$ be a filter complementary to $\mathcal{H}(z)$. Its even and odd parts are $\mathcal{G}'_e(z)$ and $\mathcal{G}'_o(z)$ respectively. These are obtained from the following equation.

$$\mathcal{P}'(z)^T = \begin{bmatrix} \mathcal{H}_e(z) & \mathcal{G}'_e(z) \\ \mathcal{H}_o(z) & \mathcal{G}'_o(z) \end{bmatrix}$$

$$= \begin{bmatrix} 1 & -\frac{1}{2} - \frac{1}{2}z^{-1} \\ 0 & 1 \end{bmatrix} \begin{bmatrix} 1 & 0 \\ \frac{z}{4} + \frac{1}{4} & 1 \end{bmatrix} \begin{bmatrix} \sqrt{2} & 0 \\ 0 & \frac{\sqrt{2}}{2} \end{bmatrix}$$

Consequently $\mathcal{G}'_e(z)$ and $\mathcal{G}'_o(z)$ are

$$\begin{bmatrix} \mathcal{G}'_e(z) \\ \mathcal{G}'_o(z) \end{bmatrix} = \begin{bmatrix} \frac{\sqrt{2}}{4}(-z^{-1} - 1) \\ \frac{\sqrt{2}}{2} \end{bmatrix}$$

Notice that

$$\begin{bmatrix} \mathcal{G}'_e(z) \\ \mathcal{G}'_o(z) \end{bmatrix} = \begin{bmatrix} \mathcal{G}_e(z) \\ \mathcal{G}_o(z) \end{bmatrix}$$

Finally

$$\mathcal{P}(z) = \begin{bmatrix} \mathcal{H}_e(z) & \mathcal{H}_o(z) \\ \mathcal{G}_e(z) & \mathcal{G}_o(z) \end{bmatrix}$$

$$= \begin{bmatrix} \sqrt{2} & 0 \\ 0 & \frac{\sqrt{2}}{2} \end{bmatrix} \begin{bmatrix} 1 & \frac{z}{4} + \frac{1}{4} \\ 0 & 1 \end{bmatrix} \begin{bmatrix} 1 & 0 \\ -\frac{1}{2} - \frac{1}{2}z^{-1} & 1 \end{bmatrix}$$

□

Example 10.6. Consider the Haar wavelet. Then

$$\mathcal{H}(z) = \frac{1}{\sqrt{2}}(1 + z^{-1}), \ \mathcal{G}(z) = \frac{1}{\sqrt{2}}(1 - z^{-1})$$

$$h(0) = h(1) = g(0) = \frac{1}{\sqrt{2}}, \ g(1) = -\frac{1}{\sqrt{2}}$$

$$\mathcal{H}_e(z) = \mathcal{H}_o(z) = \mathcal{G}_e(z) = \frac{1}{\sqrt{2}}, \ \mathcal{G}_o(z) = -\frac{1}{\sqrt{2}}$$

Notice that the determinant of the matrix

$$\begin{bmatrix} \mathcal{H}_e(z) & \mathcal{H}_o(z) \\ \mathcal{G}_e(z) & \mathcal{G}_o(z) \end{bmatrix}$$

is -1. Since a polyphase matrix is required to have a unit value for its determinant, factorize the matrix

$$\mathcal{P}(z) = \begin{bmatrix} \mathcal{H}_e(z) & \mathcal{H}_o(z) \\ -\mathcal{G}_e(z) & -\mathcal{G}_o(z) \end{bmatrix} = \begin{bmatrix} \frac{1}{\sqrt{2}} & \frac{1}{\sqrt{2}} \\ -\frac{1}{\sqrt{2}} & \frac{1}{\sqrt{2}} \end{bmatrix}$$

It is observed that the determinant of the matrix $\mathcal{P}(z)$ is indeed equal to 1. Use of the Euclidean algorithm results in

$$\begin{bmatrix} \mathcal{H}_e(z) \\ \mathcal{H}_o(z) \end{bmatrix} = \begin{bmatrix} 1 & 1 \\ 1 & 0 \end{bmatrix} \begin{bmatrix} \frac{1}{\sqrt{2}} \\ 0 \end{bmatrix}$$

The factorization algorithm terminates in only a single (odd integer) step. Therefore, let

$$\mathcal{P}'(z)^T = \begin{bmatrix} \mathcal{H}_e(z) & \mathcal{G}'_e(z) \\ \mathcal{H}_o(z) & \mathcal{G}'_o(z) \end{bmatrix}$$

$$= \begin{bmatrix} 1 & 1 \\ 1 & 0 \end{bmatrix} \begin{bmatrix} 1 & 0 \\ 0 & -1 \end{bmatrix} \begin{bmatrix} \frac{1}{\sqrt{2}} & 0 \\ 0 & \sqrt{2} \end{bmatrix}$$

$$= \begin{bmatrix} 1 & -1 \\ 1 & 0 \end{bmatrix} \begin{bmatrix} \frac{1}{\sqrt{2}} & 0 \\ 0 & \sqrt{2} \end{bmatrix}$$

Note that the determinant of the matrix $\mathcal{P}'(z)$ is equal to 1, and $\mathcal{G}'_e(z) = -\sqrt{2}$ and $\mathcal{G}'_o(z) = 0$. Use of the relationship

$$\mathcal{P}(z) = \begin{bmatrix} 1 & 0 \\ \mathcal{T}(z) & 1 \end{bmatrix} \mathcal{P}'(z)$$

results in $\mathcal{T}(z) = 1$. The final factorization is

$$\mathcal{P}(z) = \begin{bmatrix} \mathcal{H}_e(z) & \mathcal{H}_o(z) \\ -\mathcal{G}_e(z) & -\mathcal{G}_o(z) \end{bmatrix} = \begin{bmatrix} \frac{1}{\sqrt{2}} & \frac{1}{\sqrt{2}} \\ -\frac{1}{\sqrt{2}} & \frac{1}{\sqrt{2}} \end{bmatrix}$$

$$= \begin{bmatrix} 1 & 0 \\ 1 & 1 \end{bmatrix} \begin{bmatrix} \frac{1}{\sqrt{2}} & 0 \\ 0 & \sqrt{2} \end{bmatrix} \begin{bmatrix} 1 & 1 \\ -1 & 0 \end{bmatrix}$$

$$= \begin{bmatrix} \frac{1}{\sqrt{2}} & 0 \\ 0 & \sqrt{2} \end{bmatrix} \begin{bmatrix} 1 & 0 \\ \frac{1}{2} & 1 \end{bmatrix} \begin{bmatrix} 1 & 1 \\ -1 & 0 \end{bmatrix}$$

$\square$

10.6 Second-Generation Wavelets

The first generation of wavelets were typically dyadic dilates and translates of a specific function in $L^2(\mathbb{R})$. These were developed using Fourier transforms. Use of the lifting scheme in generating wavelets of the first generation was demonstrated in the last section.

Second-generation wavelets are a generalization and a more powerful scheme to generate wavelets. These use the lifting scheme. The theory of second-generation wavelets is developed directly in time or spatial domain. This technique can also be used on complex domains and irregular sampling. It can also be conveniently extended to multi-dimensional data. The following discussion follows the presentation of Uytterhoeven (1999).

The wavelet transformation of a one-dimensional signal is a multiresolution specification of it in terms of wavelet basis functions. At each multiresolution level of the signal, the signal is made up of two parts. These are the low-pass part, and the high-pass part. The low-pass part is obtained via a low-pass wavelet filter. It specifies the low-resolution part of the signal at that specific multiresolution level. The high-pass part is obtained via a high-pass wavelet filter. It specifies the high-resolution part of the signal at that specific multiresolution level.

The lifting scheme provides an efficient implementation of these filtering operations. Let λ_{j+1} and γ_{j+1} be data sets at level $(j+1)$ which represent the low-resolution and high-resolution part respectively. As per the wavelet transformation algorithm, the data set λ_{j+1} is transformed into two data sets, λ_j and γ_j at level j. The data set λ_j is the low-resolution part and γ_j is the high-resolution part. In general, this is accomplished via several iterations of the lifting operations.

The basic lifting operations are: splitting, prediction, and update.

- This *splitting* operation is achieved via the lazy wavelet transform. This step partitions the initial data set λ_{j+1} into two data sets. This is actually the separation of the data set into two sets of even and odd samples.

- The prediction operation is also called the *dual lifting* step. At level j, the data γ'_j is predicted from the data set λ'_j. This is done via the prediction operator $P(\cdot)$. If the signal samples have a high degree of correlation, then the prediction will be successful. That is, $\left|\gamma'_j - P\left(\lambda'_j\right)\right|$ will be small. Then, it will be only necessary to store $\left(\gamma'_j - P\left(\lambda'_j\right)\right)$. Therefore, in this step, γ'_j is replaced by $\left(\gamma'_j - P\left(\lambda'_j\right)\right)$. Thus dual lifting performs the decorrelation operation.

- In the dual lifting operation, certain information is lost. For example, the mean value of the signal is lost. The lost information is recovered in the *primal lifting* step. This is done via the updating operator $U(\cdot)$. The data set λ'_j is updated from the new data set γ'_j. Therefore, in this step λ'_j is replaced by $\left(\lambda'_j + U\left(\gamma'_j\right)\right)$.

Typically, the above lifting operations are executed several times before the data sets λ_j and γ_j are obtained. The use of the above steps is demonstrated below for only a pair of lifting steps. The low-resolution data set λ_{j+1} at level $(j+1)$ is transformed to data sets λ_j and γ_j at level j.

- *Splitting*: The data set λ_{j+1} is split into the data sets λ_j and γ_j via the use of lazy wavelet transform.

- *Prediction*, or *dual lifting*: Predict the data set γ_j from the data set λ_j, and perform the operation: $\gamma_j \leftarrow \left(\gamma_j - P\left(\lambda_j\right)\right)$.

- *Update*, or *primal lifting*: Update the data set λ_j by using the latest data set γ_j as: $\lambda_j \leftarrow \lambda_j + U\left(\gamma_j\right)$.

The above elementary steps can be similarly executed on the data set λ_j. Several such steps will lead to a multiresolution decomposition of the original data set. The above steps constitute the *forward transform*.

The above recursive formulation will not be useful, unless the original data is recoverable. This is achieved via the *inverse transform*. Its main steps are: the inverse update step, inverse prediction step, and the merge operation.

- *Inverse update:* $\lambda_j \leftarrow \lambda_j - U\left(\gamma_j\right)$.
- *Inverse prediction:* $\gamma_j \leftarrow \left(\gamma_j + P\left(\lambda_j\right)\right)$.
- *Merge:* $\lambda_{j+1} \leftarrow \lambda_j \cup \gamma_j$.

Example 10.7. Consider a one-dimensional signal $x = \{x_k\}$. We demonstrate a second-generation wavelet transform via linear prediction operation.

Splitting: The signal x, that is λ_{j+1}, is split into even (that is λ_j) and odd (that is γ_j) samples as:

$$s_i \leftarrow x_{2i}, \quad \text{and} \quad d_i \leftarrow x_{2i+1}$$

Prediction: The odd samples are predicted using linear interpolation:

$$d_i \leftarrow \left\{d_i - \frac{1}{2}\left(s_i + s_{i+1}\right)\right\}$$

Update: The even samples are updated to maintain the mean value of the samples. This is:

$$s_i \leftarrow \left\{s_i + \frac{1}{4}\left(d_{i-1} + d_i\right)\right\}$$

In the above transformations, the data sets $\{s_i\}$ and $\{d_i\}$ represent the low- and high-resolution components respectively, of the source signal at multiresolution level-j. $\square$

Problems

1. In dual lifting, the new polyphase matrix $\mathcal{P}_{new}\left(z\right)$ is

$$\mathcal{P}_{new}\left(z\right) = \begin{bmatrix} 1 & 0 \\ \mathcal{T}\left(z\right) & 1 \end{bmatrix} \mathcal{P}\left(z\right)$$

Prove the following results.

(a)

$$\widetilde{\mathcal{P}}_{new}\left(z\right) = \begin{bmatrix} 1 & -\overline{\mathcal{T}\left(z\right)} \\ 0 & 1 \end{bmatrix} \widetilde{\mathcal{P}}\left(z\right)$$

(b)

$$\mathcal{H}_{new}\left(z\right) = \mathcal{H}(z), \quad \text{and} \quad \mathcal{G}_{new}\left(z\right) = \mathcal{G}\left(z\right) + \mathcal{T}\left(z^2\right)\mathcal{H}\left(z\right)$$

(c)

$$\widetilde{\mathcal{H}}_{new}\left(z\right) = \widetilde{\mathcal{H}}\left(z\right) - \overline{\mathcal{T}\left(z^2\right)}\widetilde{\mathcal{G}}(z), \quad \text{and} \quad \widetilde{\mathcal{G}}_{new}\left(z\right) = \widetilde{\mathcal{G}}\left(z\right)$$

Hint:

(a) Use of the relationship $P(z)\overline{\tilde{P}(z)}^T = I$ yields

$$\tilde{P}(z) = \left(P(z)^{-1}\right)^T$$

Also

$$P_{new}(z)^{-1} = P(z)^{-1}\begin{bmatrix} 1 & 0 \\ -T(z) & 1 \end{bmatrix}$$

and $P_{new}(z)\overline{\tilde{P}_{new}(z)}^T = I$ results in

$$\tilde{P}_{new}(z) = \left(P_{new}(z)^{-1}\right)^T$$

The result follows.

(b) It is known that the modulation matrix $M(z)$, and the polyphase matrix $P(z)$ are related as

$$M(z) = P(z^2)\mathcal{Y}(z)$$

where

$$\mathcal{Y}(z) = \begin{bmatrix} 1 & 1 \\ z & -z \end{bmatrix}$$

The new modulation matrix is

$$M_{new}(z) = P_{new}(z^2)\mathcal{Y}(z)$$

Use of the above relationships yield

$$M_{new}(z) = \begin{bmatrix} 1 & 0 \\ T(z^2) & 1 \end{bmatrix} P(z^2)\,\overline{\mathcal{Y}(z)}$$

$$= \begin{bmatrix} 1 & 0 \\ T(z^2) & 1 \end{bmatrix} M(z)$$

This yields the stated result.

(c) The dual of the new modulation matrix is $\widetilde{M}_{new}(z)$. It is

$$\widetilde{M}_{new}(z) = \tilde{P}_{new}(z^2)\overline{\mathcal{Y}(z)}$$

Use of the part (a) result yields

$$\widetilde{M}_{new}(z) = \begin{bmatrix} 1 & -\overline{T(z^2)} \\ 0 & 1 \end{bmatrix} \tilde{P}(z^2)\,\overline{\mathcal{Y}(z)}$$

$$= \begin{bmatrix} 1 & -\overline{T(z^2)} \\ 0 & 1 \end{bmatrix} \widetilde{M}(z)$$

This yields the stated result.

2. In primary lifting, the new polyphase matrix $\mathcal{P}_{new}(z)$ is

$$\mathcal{P}_{new}(z) = \begin{bmatrix} 1 & S(z) \\ 0 & 1 \end{bmatrix} P(z)$$

Prove the following results.

(a)

$$\tilde{\mathcal{P}}_{new}(z) = \begin{bmatrix} 1 & 0 \\ -\overline{S(z)} & 1 \end{bmatrix} \tilde{P}(z)$$

(b)

$$\mathcal{H}_{new}(z) = \mathcal{H}(z) + S(z^2)\mathcal{G}(z), \text{ and } \mathcal{G}_{new}(z) = \mathcal{G}(z)$$

(c)

$$\tilde{\mathcal{H}}_{new}(z) = \tilde{\mathcal{H}}(z), \text{ and } \tilde{\mathcal{G}}_{new}(z) = \tilde{\mathcal{G}}(z) - \overline{S(z^2)}\tilde{\mathcal{H}}(z)$$

Hint:

(a) Use of the relationship $P(z)\overline{\tilde{P}(z)}^T = \mathcal{I}$ yields

$$\tilde{P}(z) = \overline{\left(P(z)^{-1}\right)^T}$$

Also

$$\mathcal{P}_{new}(z)^{-1} = P(z)^{-1} \begin{bmatrix} 1 & -S(z) \\ 0 & 1 \end{bmatrix}$$

and $\mathcal{P}_{new}(z)\overline{\tilde{\mathcal{P}}_{new}(z)}^T = \mathcal{I}$ results in

$$\tilde{\mathcal{P}}_{new}(z) = \overline{\left(\mathcal{P}_{new}(z)^{-1}\right)^T}$$

The result follows.

(b) It is known that the modulation matrix $\mathcal{M}(z)$, and the polyphase matrix $P(z)$ are related as

$$\mathcal{M}(z) = P(z^2)\overline{\mathcal{Y}(z)}$$

where

$$\mathcal{Y}(z) = \begin{bmatrix} 1 & 1 \\ z & -z \end{bmatrix}$$

A new polyphase matrix $\mathcal{P}_{new}(z)$ is defined, where

$$\mathcal{P}_{new}(z) = \begin{bmatrix} 1 & S(z) \\ 0 & 1 \end{bmatrix} P(z)$$

where $S(z)$ is a Laurent polynomial. The corresponding new modulation matrix is

$$\mathcal{M}_{new}(z) = \mathcal{P}_{new}(z^2)\overline{\mathcal{Y}}(z)$$

Use of the above relationships yield

$$\mathcal{M}_{new}(z) = \begin{bmatrix} 1 & S(z^2) \\ 0 & 1 \end{bmatrix} P(z^2)\overline{\mathcal{Y}}(z)$$

$$= \begin{bmatrix} 1 & S(z^2) \\ 0 & 1 \end{bmatrix} \mathcal{M}(z)$$

This yields the stated result.

(c) The dual of the new modulation matrix is $\widetilde{\mathcal{M}}_{new}(z)$. That is,

$$\widetilde{\mathcal{M}}_{new}(z) = \widetilde{\mathcal{P}}_{new}(z^2)\overline{\mathcal{Y}}(z)$$

Use of the part (a) result yields

$$\widetilde{\mathcal{M}}_{new}(z) = \begin{bmatrix} 1 & 0 \\ -S(z^2) & 1 \end{bmatrix} \widetilde{P}(z^2)\overline{\mathcal{Y}}(z)$$

$$= \begin{bmatrix} 1 & 0 \\ -S(z^2) & 1 \end{bmatrix} \widetilde{\mathcal{M}}(z)$$

This yields the stated result.

CHAPTER 11

Wavelet Packets

11.1 Introduction

Wavelet packets are a natural and versatile extension of wavelet bases to extract useful and interesting information from signals. With the use of wavelet packets a very large class of bases can be constructed. In this type of transformation, the basis selection for a given application is made based upon a collection (library) of functions. The wavelet-packet transforms offer more flexibility than the classical fast wavelet transform algorithm, albeit at the cost of a more computationally expensive algorithm.

Let the number of data points to be transformed be N. Then the computational complexity of wavelet packet transformation is $O(N \log N)$. This is in contrast to the computational complexity of the fast wavelet transform algorithm, which is $O(N)$.

Wavelet packet generation uses the concept of graph-theoretic trees. Therefore, relevant graph theory is explained in the next section. This is followed by a description of elementary properties of wavelet packets. The wavelet packet transformation and a best basis selection algorithm is subsequently described.

11.2 Elements of Graph Theory

Graph-theoretic language of trees is used in describing the wavelet packet transform. Therefore, some terminology related to trees is initially introduced.

Language of Trees

In order to describe an algorithm to compute wavelet-packet transform, familiarity with the language of trees is necessary. Some of the terminology used in describing this algorithm is defined. Terms like, graph, connected graph, binary tree, and leaves of a tree are used.

- A *graph* G is defined as $G = (V, E)$, where V is the set of *vertices* (also called *nodes*), and E is the set of *edges* (also called *arcs*). Ordered pairs of elements belonging to the set V, form the set of edges E.

- An edge $e \in E$ is specified as (v_i, v_j), where $v_i, v_j \in V$.

- A *path* of length k from vertex w to vertex w', in a graph is a sequence of distinct vertices $\{v_0, v_1, v_2, \ldots, v_k\}$, such that $v_0 = w, v_k = w'$, and $(v_{j-1}, v_j) \in E$ for $1 \leq j \leq k$.

- A path is *closed*, if the path length is greater than one, and $v_0 = v_k$.

- A closed path with no repeated nodes, except the first and the last one in a path is called a *circuit* or *cycle*.

- A graph is said to be *connected* if there is a path between every pair of vertices in it.

- A *tree* is a connected graph without cycles. Note that, if a tree has p nodes, then it has $(p - 1)$ edges in it.

- A graph is said to be a *binary tree* (or dyadic tree) if it has the following structure:
  - A binary tree has a special vertex called the *root node*. It lies on two edges.
  - It has a set of nodes, called *internal vertices*, which lie on three edges.
  - It also has a set of nodes, called *leaves* which lie only on a single edge.

Terminology Used in Describing a Binary Tree

In order to effectively use binary trees, related terminology is introduced.

- The vertices of a binary tree are generally arranged on successive *levels*.

- The root node is said to be at level 0.

- Any non-leaf node is joined to a pair of *successor nodes* (*child or offspring nodes*) on the next level.

- The leaf nodes do not have child nodes. For convenience, the children of a non-leaf node will be called the *left-child* and the *right-child*.

- All vertices except the root node have a single *predecessor* (*parent node*).

- The length of the path from the root of a tree to a specific vertex, is called the *height* (*depth*) of the vertex. As it turns out, this is also equal to the level in which the node is located.

- The height of a root node is 0. The largest value of the depth of a vertex in a binary tree is called the *depth of the binary tree*. Denote it by $M \in \mathbb{N}$.

- If the number of nodes at each height m of a tree is 2^m, then the tree is called a *complete binary tree*; where $m = 0, 1, 2, \cdots, M$.

- The nodes of a binary tree can be identified recursively by its coordinates. Denote the root node by $(0,0)$. Let the depth of a non-root node be $m \in \mathbb{P}$, and the coordinates of its parent node be $(m-1, l)$. Then the coordinates of the node are either $(m, 2l)$ if it is a left-child, or $(m, 2l+1)$ if it is a right-child. Note that the level $m = 0, 1, 2, \cdots, M$; and a node is labeled as (m, l) where $l = 0, 1, 2, \ldots, (2^m - 1)$.

- An alternative indexing of the nodes of a binary tree is to map the node (m, l) to $n = (2^m + l)$, where $l = 0, 1, 2, \ldots, (2^m - 1)$ and $m = 0, 1, 2, \cdots, M$.

Figure 11.1 clarifies the scheme for labeling the nodes of a binary tree. The tree has been drawn horizontally for clarity.

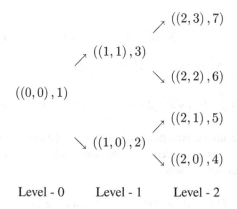

Level - 0   Level - 1   Level - 2

Figure 11.1. Labeling of the nodes of a binary tree.

11.3 Elementary Properties of Wavelet Packets

There are two types of wavelet packets. These are the *basic* and *general wavelet packets*. Basic wavelet packets are a collection of wavelet and scaling functions, which are generated recursively. A more general form of wavelet packets are generated in turn by dilation and translation of the basic wavelet packets. Wavelet packets allow the splitting of certain subspaces of $L^2(\mathbb{R})$ into a plethora of orthogonally-complement subspaces. This presents an opportunity for a function belonging to the space $L^2(\mathbb{R})$ to be represented by multiple sets of basis functions, of which the classical wavelet bases is a particular case. In classical multiresolution analysis, the space $L^2(\mathbb{R})$ is approximated by a sequence of closed subspaces

$$\{V_j \mid V_j \subseteq L^2(\mathbb{R}),\ j \in \mathbb{Z}\}, \quad \text{where } V_j \subset V_{j+1},\ \forall\, j \in \mathbb{Z}$$

It is also known that $V_{j+1} = V_j \oplus W_j$, where W_j is called the detail space. Further, the spaces $W_j, j \in \mathbb{Z}$ are mutually orthogonal. In wavelet packet transform, the space W_j is further decomposed for values of $j \in \mathbb{P}$.

11.3.1 Basic Wavelet Packets

Recall that $\phi(\cdot) \in V_0$ is a scaling function, and $\{\phi(\cdot - n) \mid n \in \mathbb{Z}\}$ is an orthonormal basis of V_0. Further W_0 is the orthogonal complement of V_0 in V_1. The space W_0 is spanned by an orthonormal basis $\{\psi(\cdot - n) \mid n \in \mathbb{Z}\}$. For $t \in \mathbb{R}$, the following relations were also observed

$$\phi(t) = \sum_{n \in \mathbb{Z}} \sqrt{2}\phi(2t - n) h(n),$$

$$h(n) = \left\langle \phi(\cdot), \sqrt{2}\phi(2 \cdot - n) \right\rangle, \quad h(n) \in l^2(\mathbb{Z}), \ \forall\, n \in \mathbb{Z}$$

$$\psi(t) = \sum_{n \in \mathbb{Z}} \sqrt{2}\phi(2t - n) g(n),$$

$$g(n) = \left\langle \psi(\cdot), \sqrt{2}\phi(2 \cdot - n) \right\rangle, \quad g(n) \in l^2(\mathbb{Z}), \ \forall\, n \in \mathbb{Z}$$

In analogy with the above equations, the sequence $\{\lambda_n(\cdot) \mid n \in \mathbb{N}\}$ is defined as follows. These functions are called basic wavelet packets. These in turn are used to generate general wavelet packets.

Definition 11.1. *The basic wavelet packet sequence* $\{\lambda_n(\cdot) \mid n \in \mathbb{N}\}$ *is defined recursively as*

$$\lambda_0(t) = \phi(t) \quad and \quad \lambda_1(t) = \psi(t) \tag{11.1a}$$

$$\lambda_{2n}(t) = \sum_{k \in \mathbb{Z}} \sqrt{2}\lambda_n(2t - k) h(k), \quad n \in \mathbb{N} \tag{11.1b}$$

$$\lambda_{2n+1}(t) = \sum_{k \in \mathbb{Z}} \sqrt{2}\lambda_n(2t - k) g(k), \quad n \in \mathbb{N} \tag{11.1c}$$

where $t \in \mathbb{R}$.   □

This generation of wavelet packets can be visualized by considering a binary tree. The wavelet packet $\{\lambda_1(\cdot)\}$ is at the root node $(0,0)$ of a binary tree. At level 1 of the binary tree, the basic wavelet packets $\{\lambda_2(\cdot)\}$ and $\{\lambda_3(\cdot)\}$ are at nodes $(1,0)$ and $(1,1)$ respectively. Similarly at level 2 of the binary tree, $\{\lambda_4(\cdot)\}$, $\{\lambda_5(\cdot)\}$, $\{\lambda_6(\cdot)\}$, and $\{\lambda_7(\cdot)\}$ are at nodes $(2,0)$, $(2,1)$, $(2,2)$, and $(2,3)$ respectively. In general, if the label of a wavelet packet $\{\lambda_n(\cdot)\}$, $n \in \mathbb{P}$ are (m,l), then $n = (2^m + l)$, where $l = 0, 1, 2, \ldots, (2^m - 1)$. This explanation is further clarified via Figure 11.2. The tree is drawn horizontally for clarity.

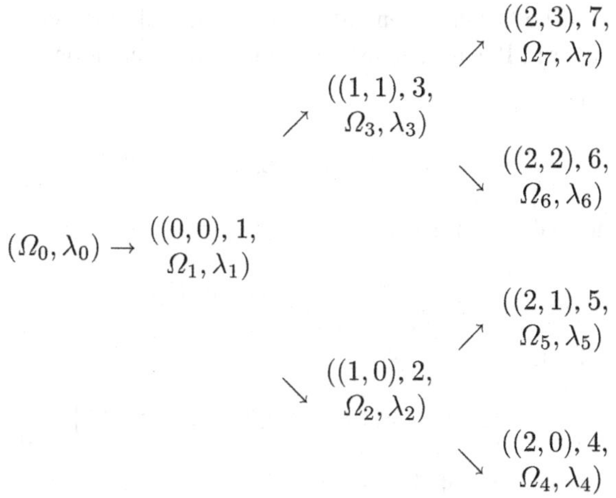

$$((2,3), 7, \quad \Omega_7, \lambda_7)$$
$$\nearrow$$

$$((1,1), 3, \quad \Omega_3, \lambda_3)$$
$$\nearrow$$

$$((2,2), 6, \quad \Omega_6, \lambda_6)$$
$$\searrow$$

$$(\Omega_0, \lambda_0) \rightarrow \quad ((0,0), 1, \quad \Omega_1, \lambda_1)$$

$$((2,1), 5, \quad \Omega_5, \lambda_5)$$
$$\nearrow$$

$$((1,0), 2, \quad \Omega_2, \lambda_2)$$
$$\searrow$$

$$((2,0), 4, \quad \Omega_4, \lambda_4)$$
$$\searrow$$

Figure 11.2. Wavelet packets on a tree.

Some observations regarding basic wavelet packets are listed below.

Definition 11.2. *The sequence of functions* $\{\lambda_n (\cdot - k) \mid k \in \mathbb{Z}\}$ *spans the space* Ω_n*, where* $n \in \mathbb{N}$*.* □

Use of the above definition results in $\Omega_0 = V_0$, and $\Omega_1 = W_0$.

Observations 11.1. Some results related to the Ω_n spaces.

1. For all values of $j \in \mathbb{Z}$, $V_{j+1} = V_j \oplus W_j$. Further the spaces V_j and W_j are orthogonal to each other. The orthonormal basis sets of the spaces V_j, W_j, and V_{j+1} are

$$\{\phi_{jk}(\cdot) \mid k \in \mathbb{Z}\}, \ \{\psi_{jk}(\cdot) \mid k \in \mathbb{Z}\}, \ \text{and} \ \{\phi_{j+1,k}(\cdot) \mid k \in \mathbb{Z}\}$$

respectively.

$$\phi_{jk}(t) = \sum_{n \in \mathbb{Z}} h(n - 2k)\, \phi_{j+1,n}(t), \qquad \forall\, k \in \mathbb{Z}$$

$$= \sum_{n \in \mathbb{Z}} h(n - 2k)\, \sqrt{2}\phi_{jn}(2t), \qquad \forall\, k \in \mathbb{Z}$$

$$\psi_{jk}(t) = \sum_{n \in \mathbb{Z}} g(n - 2k)\, \phi_{j+1,n}(t), \qquad \forall\, k \in \mathbb{Z}$$

$$= \sum_{n \in \mathbb{Z}} g(n - 2k)\, \sqrt{2}\phi_{jn}(2t), \qquad \forall\, k \in \mathbb{Z}$$

$$g(n) = \pm (-1)^n\, \overline{h(2l + 1 - n)}, \qquad l \in \mathbb{Z}, \ \forall\, n \in \mathbb{Z}$$

where $t \in \mathbb{R}$. The last equation has been established in the chapter on discrete wavelet transform. It is used to establish the next observation.

2. Let $m \in \mathbb{N}$. Then

$$\{\lambda_n \left(\cdot - k\right) \mid k \in \mathbb{Z}, 0 \leq n < 2^m\}$$

is an orthonormal basis for V_m. Also

$$V_m = \Omega_0 \oplus \Omega_1 \oplus \cdots \oplus \Omega_{2^m - 1}$$

3. Let $m \in \mathbb{N}$. Then

$$\{\lambda_n \left(\cdot - k\right) \mid k \in \mathbb{Z}, 2^m \leq n < 2^{m+1}\}$$

is an orthonormal basis of W_m. Also

$$W_m = \Omega_{2^m} \oplus \Omega_{2^m+1} \oplus \cdots \oplus \Omega_{2^{m+1} - 1}$$

4. The sequence of functions

$$\{\lambda_n \left(\cdot - k\right) \mid k \in \mathbb{Z}, \text{ and } n \in \mathbb{N}\}$$

is an orthonormal basis of the space $L^2 \left(\mathbb{R}\right)$. Also

$$L^2 \left(\mathbb{R}\right) = \bigoplus_{n \in \mathbb{N}} \Omega_n$$

□

Examples 11.1. Some illustrative examples.

1. Orthonormal basis of V_0 is $\{\lambda_0 \left(\cdot - k\right) \mid k \in \mathbb{Z}\}$. Also $V_0 = \Omega_0$.

2. Orthonormal basis of W_0 is $\{\lambda_1 \left(\cdot - k\right) \mid k \in \mathbb{Z}\}$. Also $W_0 = \Omega_1$.

3. Orthonormal basis of V_1 is $\{\lambda_n \left(\cdot - k\right) \mid k \in \mathbb{Z}, \text{ and } n = 0, 1\}$. Also $V_1 = \Omega_0 \oplus \Omega_1$.

4. Orthonormal basis of W_1 is $\{\lambda_n \left(\cdot - k\right) \mid k \in \mathbb{Z}, \text{ and } n = 2, 3\}$. Also $W_1 = \Omega_2 \oplus \Omega_3$.

5. Orthonormal basis of V_2 is $\{\lambda_n \left(\cdot - k\right) \mid k \in \mathbb{Z}, \text{ and } n = 0, 1, 2, 3\}$. Also $V_2 = \Omega_0 \oplus \Omega_1 \oplus \Omega_2 \oplus \Omega_3$.

6. Orthonormal basis of W_2 is $\{\lambda_n \left(\cdot - k\right) \mid k \in \mathbb{Z}, \text{ and } n = 4, 5, 6, 7\}$. Also $W_2 = \Omega_4 \oplus \Omega_5 \oplus \Omega_6 \oplus \Omega_7$.

□

The recursive definition of $\lambda_n \left(\cdot\right)$'s can be examined in the frequency domain. Let

$$\phi(t) \leftrightarrow \Phi(\omega), \quad \text{and} \quad \psi(t) \leftrightarrow \Psi(\omega)$$

$$H(\omega) = \sum_{k \in \mathbb{Z}} h(k) e^{-i\omega k}, \quad \text{and} \quad G(\omega) = \sum_{k \in \mathbb{Z}} g(k) e^{-i\omega k}$$

Note that

$$G(\omega) = \sum_{k \in \mathbb{Z}} \pm(-1)^k \overline{h(2l+1-k)} e^{-i\omega k}, \quad l \in \mathbb{Z}$$

Definition 11.3. *Fourier transform of* $\lambda_n(\cdot)$. *Let* $\lambda_n(t) \leftrightarrow \Lambda_n(\omega)$ *for* $n \in \mathbb{N}$. $\square$

Observation 11.2. Results related to $\Lambda(\cdot)$'s.

$$\Lambda_{2n}(\omega) = \frac{1}{\sqrt{2}} H\left(\frac{\omega}{2}\right) \Lambda_n\left(\frac{\omega}{2}\right), \quad n \in \mathbb{N}$$

$$\Lambda_{2n+1}(\omega) = \frac{1}{\sqrt{2}} G\left(\frac{\omega}{2}\right) \Lambda_n\left(\frac{\omega}{2}\right), \quad n \in \mathbb{N}$$

This result is obtained by using the recursive definitions of $\lambda_n(\cdot)$'s. $\square$

It is also possible to derive an explicit expression for $\Lambda_n(\omega)$. The following relationships which were derived in the chapter on discrete wavelet transform are summarized for ready reference.

$$\Phi(0) = \int_{-\infty}^{\infty} \phi(t)\, dt = 1$$

$$\Phi(\omega) = \frac{1}{\sqrt{2}} H\left(\frac{\omega}{2}\right) \Phi\left(\frac{\omega}{2}\right)$$

$$\Psi(\omega) = \frac{1}{\sqrt{2}} G\left(\frac{\omega}{2}\right) \Phi\left(\frac{\omega}{2}\right)$$

$$\Phi(\omega) = \prod_{k \in \mathbb{P}} \left\{\frac{1}{\sqrt{2}} H\left(\frac{\omega}{2^k}\right)\right\}$$

$$\Psi(\omega) = \left\{\frac{1}{\sqrt{2}} G\left(\frac{\omega}{2}\right)\right\} \prod_{k \in \mathbb{P}} \left\{\frac{1}{\sqrt{2}} H\left(\frac{\omega}{2^{k+1}}\right)\right\}$$

Further, $\Lambda_0(\omega) = \Phi(\omega)$ and $\Lambda_1(\omega) = \Psi(\omega)$. Therefore,

$$\Lambda_0(\omega) = \frac{1}{\sqrt{2}} H\left(\frac{\omega}{2}\right) \Phi\left(\frac{\omega}{2}\right)$$

$$\Lambda_1(\omega) = \frac{1}{\sqrt{2}} G\left(\frac{\omega}{2}\right) \Phi\left(\frac{\omega}{2}\right)$$

$\Lambda_2(\omega)$ can be expanded as

$$\Lambda_2(\omega) = \frac{1}{\sqrt{2}} H\left(\frac{\omega}{2}\right) \Lambda_1\left(\frac{\omega}{2}\right)$$

$$= \left\{\frac{1}{\sqrt{2}} H\left(\frac{\omega}{2}\right)\right\} \left\{\frac{1}{\sqrt{2}} G\left(\frac{\omega}{4}\right)\right\} \Phi\left(\frac{\omega}{4}\right)$$

Infinite product expansions of $\Lambda_0(\omega)$, $\Lambda_1(\omega)$, and $\Lambda_2(\omega)$ now readily follow.

$$\Lambda_0(\omega) = \prod_{k \in \mathbb{P}} \left\{ \frac{1}{\sqrt{2}} H\left(\frac{\omega}{2^k}\right) \right\}$$

$$\Lambda_1(\omega) = \frac{1}{\sqrt{2}} G\left(\frac{\omega}{2}\right) \prod_{k \in \mathbb{P}} \left\{ \frac{1}{\sqrt{2}} H\left(\frac{\omega}{2^{k+1}}\right) \right\}$$

$$\Lambda_2(\omega) = \left\{ \frac{1}{\sqrt{2}} H\left(\frac{\omega}{2}\right) \right\} \left\{ \frac{1}{\sqrt{2}} G\left(\frac{\omega}{4}\right) \right\} \prod_{k \in \mathbb{P}} \left\{ \frac{1}{\sqrt{2}} H\left(\frac{\omega}{2^{k+2}}\right) \right\}$$

A convenient infinite product expansion of $\Lambda_n(\omega)$ can now be developed.

Observation 11.3. Let

$$n = \sum_{j \in \mathbb{P}} \zeta_j 2^{j-1}, \quad \zeta_j \in \{0, 1\}, \quad j \in \mathbb{P}, \ n \in \mathbb{N}$$

The above expression for n provides its binary expansion. Define a function $I_{\zeta_j}(\cdot)$, $j \in \mathbb{P}$ as

$$I_{\zeta_j}(\omega) = \begin{cases} \dfrac{1}{\sqrt{2}} H(\omega), & \text{if } \zeta_j = 0 \\[2mm] \dfrac{1}{\sqrt{2}} G(\omega), & \text{if } \zeta_j = 1 \end{cases}$$

Then

$$\Lambda_n(\omega) = \prod_{j \in \mathbb{P}} I_{\zeta_j}\left(\frac{\omega}{2^j}\right), \quad n \in \mathbb{N}$$

$\square$

11.3.2 General Wavelet Packets

General wavelet packets are obtained from the basic wavelet packets by scaling and dilating these later functions.

Definition 11.4. *General wavelet packet (functions) are obtained by scaling and translation of the basic wavelet packets (functions)* $\lambda_n(\cdot)$, $n \in \mathbb{N}$

$$\lambda_{n,j,k}(\cdot) = 2^{j/2} \lambda_n(2^j \cdot - k), \quad j, k \in \mathbb{Z} \ \text{and} \ n \in \mathbb{N} \tag{11.2}$$

where j and k are the scaling and translation parameters respectively, and n is called the modulation or oscillation parameter. $\square$

The above definition yields

$$\lambda_{0,j,k}\left(\cdot\right) = \phi_{jk}(\cdot), \text{ and } \lambda_{1,j,k}(\cdot) = \psi_{jk}\left(\cdot\right)$$

It immediately follows that the space V_j is spanned by the orthonormal basis

$$\left\{\lambda_{0,j,k}\left(\cdot\right) = 2^{j/2}\lambda_0(2^j \cdot -k), \ j, k \in \mathbb{Z}\right\}$$

The space W_j is spanned by the orthonormal basis

$$\left\{\lambda_{1,j,k}\left(\cdot\right) = 2^{j/2}\lambda_1(2^j \cdot -k), \ j, k \in \mathbb{Z}\right\}$$

The function $\lambda_{n,j,k}\left(\cdot\right) = 2^{j/2}\lambda_n\left(2^j \cdot -k\right)$ is roughly centered at $2^{-j}k$, has an approximate support of size 2^{-j}, and oscillates approximately n times.

Observation 11.4. For a fixed value of $m \in \mathbb{N}$, the set of functions

$$\lambda_{n,j,k}\left(\cdot\right) = 2^{j/2}\lambda_n(2^j \cdot -k), \quad j, k \in \mathbb{Z}$$
$$2^m \leq n < 2^{m+1}$$

form an orthonormal basis of the space $L^2(\mathbb{R})$.   □

There are several other orthonormal bases of the space $L^2\left(\mathbb{R}\right)$ which can be obtained by using special combinations of the indices n, j, and k. In short, the complete collection of general wavelet packet functions is an over-complete system for the space $L^2\left(\mathbb{R}\right)$.

Observation 11.5. Define an index set

$$\mathbb{I} = \{(n, j) \mid n \in \mathbb{N} \text{ and } j \in \mathbb{Z}\}$$

and an interval

$$I_{nj} = [2^j n, 2^j\left(n+1\right)), \text{ where } (n, j) \in \mathbb{I}$$

such that these intervals form a disjoint and countable covering of the interval $[0, \infty)$. That is,

$$\cup_{m\in\mathbb{N}} I_{n_m, j_m} = [0, \infty)$$

Then the set of wavelet packets $\{\lambda_{n,j,k}(\cdot), (n, j) \in \mathbb{I}, k \in \mathbb{Z}\}$ is a complete orthonormal basis of the space $L^2(\mathbb{R})$. Consequently, if $f\left(\cdot\right) \in L^2(\mathbb{R})$, then

$$f\left(t\right) = \sum_{(n,j)\in\mathbb{I}} \sum_{k\in\mathbb{Z}} \alpha_{n,j,k}\lambda_{n,j,k}\left(t\right)$$
$$\alpha_{n,j,k} = \langle f, \lambda_{n,j,k}\rangle, \quad (n, j) \in \mathbb{I}, \text{ and } k \in \mathbb{Z}$$

□

Note that the classical wavelet bases cover $[0, \infty)$ by intervals which use the indices $(n_0, j_0) = (0, 0)$, and $\{(n_m, j_m) \mid m \in \mathbb{P}, n_m = 1, \text{ and } j_m = (m - 1)\}$.

There are several candidates for a complete orthonormal basis among the family of general wavelet packet functions $\{\lambda_{n,j,k}(\cdot), j, k \in \mathbb{Z} \text{ and } n \in \mathbb{N}\}$. The collection of all basis functions is called a library of bases. The best possible basis for a given function $f(\cdot)$ is chosen based upon an optimal cost function.

11.4 Wavelet Packet Transformation

An algorithm to compute wavelet packet transformation is discussed in this section. However for pedagogical purposes, the classical fast wavelet transform algorithm is initially recalled.

Review of Classical Fast Wavelet Transform

Let the input signal $f(\cdot)$ be of compact support. The sampled data vector is assumed to be of size $N = 2^J$, where $J \in \mathbb{N}$. Let

$$\widehat{C}(J) = 2^{-J/2} \left[f(0), f(2^{-J}), f(2^{-J}2), f(2^{-J}3), \ldots, f(1 - 2^{-J}) \right]^T$$

be the data vector. For simplicity in notation let $\widehat{C}(J) \triangleq F_d$. The data vector F_d is passed through $\{h(n) \mid n \in \mathbb{Z}\}$ (low-pass) and $\{g(n) \mid n \in \mathbb{Z}\}$ (high-pass) filters. Let the low-pass and high-pass filters be denoted by H_f and G_f respectively. The outputs of the H_f and G_f filters, each contain $N/2$ number of coefficients. Denote these outputs by $H_f F_d$ and $G_f F_d$ respectively. The data vector $H_f F_d$ is again passed through the low-pass and high-pass filters. Denote these outputs by $H_f H_f F_d$ and $G_f H_f F_d$. The outputs $H_f H_f F_d$ and $G_f H_f F_d$, each contain $N/4$ number of coefficients. The output of the low-pass filter $H_f H_f F_d$ is then again passed though the filters H_f and G_f. This process is repeated until a predetermined number of levels of iterations (S) has been reached.

Note that the number of levels in the transformation cannot exceed J. At each level of the transformation the number of points is halved. Therefore, the size of the original data vector and the transformed vector are identical. This transformation is illustrated more precisely via a binary tree. Note that this binary tree is different than the binary tree used in describing the generation of basic wavelet packets.

For simplicity assume that there are three stages in the transformation. That is, S is equal to three. Also let $J \geq 3$, because the number of data points has to be larger than or equal to 2^S. See Figure 11.3.

- Initially, scaled data vector F_d is at the root node $(0, 0)$ of a binary tree.

- In the first level of transformation the outputs are $H_f F_d$ and $G_f F_d$. Assume that these outputs reside at the nodes $(1,0)$ and $(1,1)$ respectively. The high-frequency output $G_f F_d$ is a part of the final fast wavelet transform. The low-frequency output $H_f F_d$ is used in the next iteration.

- In the second level of transformation the outputs are $H_f H_f F_d$ (node $(2,0)$) and $G_f H_f F_d$ (node $(2,1)$). The high-frequency output $G_f H_f F_d$ is a part of the final fast wavelet transform. Once again the low-frequency output $H_f H_f F_d$ is used in the next iteration.

- In the third and final level of transformation the outputs are $H_f H_f H_f F_d$ (node $(3,0)$) and $G_f H_f H_f F_d$ (node $(3,1)$). Both the low- and high-frequency output of the final stage (level) $H_f H_f H_f F_d$ and $G_f H_f H_f F_d$ respectively are a part of the final fast wavelet transform.

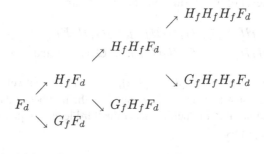

Figure 11.3. A binary tree representation of fast wavelet transformation.

The final transformed vector is $H_f H_f H_f F_d, G_f H_f H_f F_d, G_f H_f F_d$, and $G_f F_d$. At each successive iteration, improved localization in frequency at the expense of localization in time is obtained. Further, the size of the transformed vector is the same as the size of the data vector. The corresponding binary tree is called either a *fast wavelet tree*, or simply a *decomposition tree*.

Wavelet Packet Transformation

A description of wavelet packet transformation is provided. In the classical fast wavelet transformation, the high-frequency output of an iteration level is not subject to high- and low-frequency transformation. In contrast, the high-frequency output is subject to both low- and high-frequency transformation when wavelet packets are used. At each level of iteration, there are a total of 2^J data points. Therefore, if the original data is transformed through S number of stages, there will be $2^J S$ coefficients. As in the case of fast wavelet transform, the wavelet packet transform can be pictorially illustrated in the form of a binary tree. This tree is often termed a *wavelet packet tree*, or a *binary splitting tree*.

This idea is best illustrated by an example. Once again assume that there are three stages in the transformation.

- Begin with the data vector F_d. The corresponding associated node is the root node $(0,0)$ of a binary tree.

- In the first level of transformation the outputs are $H_f F_d$ at node $(1,0)$, and $G_f F_d$ at node $(1,1)$. The number of coefficients at each node is equal to half the number of data points. Therefore, the total number of coefficients at the first level is equal to the number of original data points.

- In the second level of transformation, both $H_f F_d$ and $G_f F_d$ are each passed though the filters H_f and G_f. The outputs are $H_f H_f F_d$ at node $(2,0)$, and $G_f H_f F_d$ at node $(2,1)$; and $H_f G_f F_d$ at node $(2,2)$ and $G_f G_f F_d$ at node $(2,3)$. The number of coefficients at each of these four nodes is equal to one-fourth the number of data points. Therefore, the total number of coefficients at the second level is equal to the number of original data points.

- In the third level of transformation, the outputs are

$$H_f H_f H_f F_d, \, G_f H_f H_f F_d, \, H_f G_f H_f F_d, \, G_f G_f H_f F_d,$$
$$H_f H_f G_f F_d, \, G_f H_f G_f F_d, \, H_f G_f G_f F_d, \text{ and } G_f G_f G_f F_d$$

These are at nodes $(3,0)$, $(3,1)$, $(3,2),\ldots,(3,7)$ respectively. The number of coefficients at each node is equal to one-eight the number of data points. Therefore, the total number of coefficients at the third level is equal to the number of original data points.

As the number of stages in the transformations is 3, then there are 3 times 2^J number of coefficients. Therefore, this is an inefficient way to represent the original data, if all the 3 times 2^J number of coefficients are used.

Therefore, in actual implementation of the wavelet transform, at each iteration, each output of a filter can either be split into two parts (low- and high-frequency components), or retain a single component (either low- or high-frequency component), or not split at all. This process is called the pruning of the tree. The decision to prune or not to prune at a particular node of the tree is based upon a certain cost function. Based upon these decisions, a *best basis* for a given data vector is obtained. An algorithm to select the best basis is called the *best basis selection algorithm*. These concepts are discussed next.

11.5 Best Basis Selection Algorithm

For a successful implementation of the wavelet packet transformation, an algorithm is specified to select the best possible basis from a library of basis functions. The choice is made by assigning a cost to each set of basis functions. In this section requirements of a cost function, and some candidates for a cost function are discussed.

Admissibility conditions for the pruned tree are also specified. Finally an algorithm to implement the best basis selection is outlined.

11.5.1 Cost Function and Measures

Cost function and some measures to evaluate the worth of a basis are specified.

Definition 11.5. *Let the data vector be F_d and B be a basis. Then BF_d is a representation of F_d with respect to the basis B. The cost of this basis is specified as $\Theta(BF_d)$.* $\square$

Following are the requirements of a cost functional. Let $X = (x_1, x_2, \ldots, x_N)$ and $Y = (y_1, y_2, \ldots, y_{N'})$ be two vectors. Define Z to be a vector obtained by concatenating vectors X and Y. That is, $Z = (x_1, x_2, \ldots, x_N, y_1, y_2, \ldots, y_{N'})$. Then

- The cost function should be additive. That is, $\Theta(Z) = (\Theta(X) + \Theta(Y))$.
- The cost of the zero vector ϖ, should be equal to 0. That is, $\Theta(\varpi) = 0$.

Cost Measures

Some useful cost functionals (measures) are next defined. These cost functionals are:

- Threshold cost functional.
- Entropy-based cost functional.
- l^p-norm cost functional $(0 < p < 2)$.

Threshold Cost Functional: The cost of a vector X is defined as the number of elements $x_j, 1 \leq j \leq N$ whose absolute value is greater than a threshold value $T > 0$. Thus

$$I(x) = \begin{cases} 1, & \text{if } |x| \geq T \\ 0, & \text{if } |x| < T \end{cases}$$

$$\Theta(X) = \sum_{j=1}^{N} I(x_j)$$

Entropy-based cost functional: The entropy-based cost functional is defined as

$$\Theta(X) = -\sum_{j=1}^{N} |x_j|^2 \log\left(|x_j|^2\right)$$

where it is assumed that $0 \log(0) = 0$. Define

$$p_j = \frac{|x_j|^2}{\sum_{j=1}^{N} |x_j|^2}, \quad 1 \le j \le N$$

Consequently, minimizing this cost functional is the same as minimizing the value $-\sum_{j=1}^{N} p_j \log(p_j)$. This later expression has been traditionally called Shannon's entropy. The entropy-based cost functional is generally used in practice because of its good discriminating characteristics.

l^p-**norm cost functional** $(0 < p < 2)$**:** This cost functional is defined as

$$\Theta(X) = \sum_{j=1}^{N} |x_j|^p$$

Observe that if $p = 2$, costs are identical because of the energy preserving property of the transformation.

11.5.2 Characteristics of Wavelet Packet Trees

Some observations related to wavelet packet trees are listed.

Observations 11.6.

1. A wavelet packet tree should be such that the intervals $I_{nj} = [2^j n, 2^j (n + 1))$, where $(n, j) \in \mathbb{I}$, corresponding to the index set $\mathbb{I} = \{(n, j) \mid n \in \mathbb{N} \text{ and } j \in \mathbb{Z}\}$ form a disjoint and countable covering of the interval $[0, \infty)$.

2. The binary tree corresponding to wavelet packet transformation is said to be an *admissible tree*, if each node of the tree has either 0 or 2 children. The wavelet packets generated by an admissible tree should cover the interval $[0, \infty)$ and create an orthonormal basis of space $L^2(\mathbb{R})$.

3. If the number of data points to be transformed is $N = 2^J$, then the depth, S of the wavelet packet tree is at most J.

4. Let the number of admissible wavelet packet trees of depth $S \in \mathbb{N}$, be N_S. Then

$$N_0 = 1$$
$$N_{S+1} = N_S^2 + 1$$

This value also gives the number of wavelet packet bases in a complete binary tree of depth S.   □

Note that $N_1 = 2, N_2 = 5, N_3 = 26, N_4 = 677$, and $N_5 = 458330$. Therefore, it can easily be concluded that the number of wavelet packet bases increases quickly. Consequently an efficient algorithm is indeed necessary to find the best basis.

11.5.3 Algorithm for Selection of Best Basis

An algorithm to select best basis is described. Assume that the data to be transformed has length $N = 2^J$. The number of transformation stages is S, where $S \leq J$. The wavelet packet transformation is performed in two steps. In the first step the decomposition tree of depth S for the given data vector is generated. Then the cost of the coefficients is computed for each of the nodes of the tree. The computational complexity of this step is $O(NS)$.

In the second step of the transformation, an algorithm is developed to prune the decomposition tree. Pruning is required, because the total number of possible candidates for the best basis is N_S. Even for moderately small values of S, this number grows to be a very large value. However, the binary tree structure of the coefficient representation can be utilized to develop an efficient algorithm for best basis selection.

The algorithm is a bottom-up search of the binary tree. The algorithm starts at the bottom level (S) of the tree and decides if it is cheaper to retain a pair of offspring nodes or the parent node. The algorithm performs this selection process exhaustively at this level of the tree, and then moves to the level $(S - 1)$. The selection process is again repeated at this level. The algorithm terminates until the root node of the tree has been examined. These steps are next outlined more precisely.

The nodes of the binary tree are labeled as (m, l), where $0 \leq l < 2^m$, and $0 \leq m \leq S$. The data vector resides at the node $(0, 0)$. Coefficient vectors reside at all other nodes. As mentioned earlier, the cost of a coefficient vector is computed by using an appropriate cost function. Denote the cost of these vectors at each of its node by $C(m, l)$, where $0 \leq l < 2^m$, and $0 \leq m \leq S$. For convenience a new variable $M(m, l)$ is introduced which takes a value of either 0 or 1, where $0 \leq l < 2^m$, and $0 \leq m \leq S$. Before the algorithm is described, a notation is introduced.

Notation: The assignment operator is denoted by $\leftarrow$. In this notation $a \leftarrow b$, implies that the value of b is assigned to a.   □

Algorithm: Selection of best wavelet packet basis.

Input: J, where $N = 2^J$ is the number of points in the data vector. $S \in \mathbb{P}$, where $S \leq J$ is the number of transformation stages. The cost of the coefficient vector at node (m, l) of the tree is $C(m, l)$ where $0 \leq l < 2^m, 0 \leq m \leq S$.

Output: The algorithm determines if $M(m, l)$ is equal to either 0 or 1, where $0 \leq m \leq S, 0 \leq l < 2^m$. The nodes (m, l)'s for which $M(m, l) = 1$ correspond to the best basis.

Step 1: Initialize $M(S, l) \leftarrow 1, 0 \leq l < 2^S$.

Step 2: Let $m \leftarrow S$.

Step 3: Let $l \leftarrow 0$.

Step 4: This step compares the cost of a parent node with sum of the costs of its offspring-nodes.

- If $C\left(m-1,l\right) \leq \left(C\left(m,2l\right) + C\left(m,2l+1\right)\right)$ then let $M\left(m-1,l\right) \leftarrow 1$, and all the $M(.,.)$ values of the nodes below the node $(m-1,l)$ in the decomposition tree are assigned a value of 0. That is, the $M(.,.)$ values of the successor nodes of $(m-1,l)$ and their successor nodes and so on are each assigned a value of 0. That is,

$$M\left(a,b\right) \leftarrow 0, \quad m \leq a \leq S, \quad 2^{a-m+1}l \leq b \leq \left(2^{a-m+1}l + 2^{a-m+1} - 1\right)$$

- If $C\left(m-1,l\right) > \left(C\left(m,2l\right) + C\left(m,2l+1\right)\right)$ then let

$$C\left(m-1,l\right) \leftarrow \left(C\left(m,2l\right) + C\left(m,2l+1\right)\right)$$
$$M\left(m-1,l\right) \leftarrow 0$$

Step 5: Let $l \leftarrow (l+1)$. If $l < \left(2^{m-1}-1\right)$ then **go to** Step 4.

Step 6: Let $m \leftarrow (m-1)$.

- If $m \geq 1$, **go to** Step 3.
- If $m = 0$, algorithm terminates.

$\square$

The nodes (m,l) for which $M(m,l) = 1$ correspond to the best basis. The net cost of this basis is equal to

$$\sum_{m=0}^{S} \sum_{l=0}^{(2^m-1)} M(m,l)C(m,l)$$

It can be observed from this algorithm, that the best basis is not unique. Further the complexity of the selection process is $O\left(2^S\right)$, where $\left(2^{S+1}-1\right)$ is the number of nodes in the binary tree.

Problems

1. Establish the following results.
   (a) For all values of $j \in \mathbb{Z}$, $V_{j+1} = V_j \oplus W_j$. Further the spaces V_j and W_j are orthogonal to each other. The orthonormal basis sets of the spaces V_j, W_j, and V_{j+1} are $\left\{\phi_{jk}\left(\cdot\right) \mid k \in \mathbb{Z}\right\}$, $\left\{\psi_{jk}\left(\cdot\right) \mid k \in \mathbb{Z}\right\}$, and $\left\{\phi_{j+1,k}\left(\cdot\right) \mid k \in \mathbb{Z}\right\}$ respectively.

$$\phi_{jk}(t) = \sum_{n \in \mathbb{Z}} h(n - 2k) \phi_{j+1,n}(t), \qquad \forall k \in \mathbb{Z}$$

$$= \sum_{n \in \mathbb{Z}} h(n - 2k) \sqrt{2} \phi_{jn}(2t), \qquad \forall k \in \mathbb{Z}$$

$$\psi_{jk}(t) = \sum_{n \in \mathbb{Z}} g(n - 2k) \phi_{j+1,n}(t), \qquad \forall k \in \mathbb{Z}$$

$$= \sum_{n \in \mathbb{Z}} g(n - 2k) \sqrt{2} \phi_{jn}(2t), \qquad \forall k \in \mathbb{Z}$$

where $t \in \mathbb{R}$.

(b) Let $m \in \mathbb{N}$. Then

$$\{\lambda_n(\cdot - k) \mid k \in \mathbb{Z}, 0 \le n < 2^m\}$$

is an orthonormal basis for V_m. Also

$$V_m = \Omega_0 \oplus \Omega_1 \oplus \cdots \oplus \Omega_{2^m - 1}$$

(c) Let $m \in \mathbb{N}$. Then

$$\{\lambda_n(\cdot - k) \mid k \in \mathbb{Z}, 2^m \le n < 2^{m+1}\}$$

is an orthonormal basis of W_m. Also

$$W_m = \Omega_{2^m} \oplus \Omega_{2^m + 1} \oplus \cdots \oplus \Omega_{2^{m+1} - 1}$$

(d) The sequence of functions

$$\{\lambda_n(\cdot - k) \mid k \in \mathbb{Z}, \text{ and } n \in \mathbb{N}\}$$

is an orthonormal basis of the space $L^2(\mathbb{R})$. Also

$$L^2(\mathbb{R}) = \bigoplus_{n \in \mathbb{N}} \Omega_n$$

Hint: See Vidakovic (1999).

(a) The first result is established in two steps.

Step 1: We have $\phi_{jk}(t) = 2^{j/2} \phi(2^j t - k), \forall k \in \mathbb{Z}, \forall t \in \mathbb{R}$. Therefore,

$$\phi_{j+1,k}(t) = 2^{(j+1)/2} \phi(2^{j+1} t - k) = \sqrt{2} 2^{j/2} \phi(2^j 2t - k) = \sqrt{2} \phi_{jk}(2t)$$

Step 2: In this step, the result $\phi(t) = \sum_{n \in \mathbb{Z}} h(n) \sqrt{2} \phi(2t - n), t \in \mathbb{R}$ is used. Note that

$$\phi_{jk}(t) = 2^{j/2}\phi\left(2^j t - k\right)$$

$$= 2^{j/2}\sum_{n\in\mathbb{Z}} h(n)\,\sqrt{2}\phi\left(2\left(2^j t - k\right) - n\right)$$

$$= \sum_{n\in\mathbb{Z}} h(n)\,2^{(j+1)/2}\phi\left(2^{j+1}t - 2k - n\right)$$

$$= \sum_{n\in\mathbb{Z}} h(n-2k)\,2^{(j+1)/2}\phi\left(2^{j+1}t - n\right)$$

$$= \sum_{n\in\mathbb{Z}} h(n-2k)\,\phi_{j+1,n}(t)$$

$$= \sum_{n\in\mathbb{Z}} h(n-2k)\,\sqrt{2}\phi_{jn}(2t), \quad \text{via Step 1}$$

The second result is proved similarly.

(b) The proof is obtained by induction on m. By definition $\lambda_0(\cdot) = \phi(\cdot)$ and the orthonormal basis of V_0 is $\{\lambda_0(\cdot - k) \mid k \in \mathbb{Z}\}$. Assume that

$$\{\lambda_n(\cdot - k) \mid k \in \mathbb{Z}, 0 \le n < 2^m\}$$

is an orthonormal basis of V_m, $m \in \mathbb{P}$. Then

$$\left\{\sqrt{2}\lambda_n(2\cdot - k) \mid k \in \mathbb{Z}, 0 \le n < 2^m\right\}$$

is an orthonormal basis of V_{m+1}. From the recursive definition of $\lambda_n(\cdot)$'s

$$\lambda_{2n}(t-l) = \sum_{k\in\mathbb{Z}} \sqrt{2}\lambda_n(2t-k)\,h(k-2l), \quad l \in \mathbb{Z},\ n \in \mathbb{P}$$

$$\lambda_{2n+1}(t-l) = \sum_{k\in\mathbb{Z}} \sqrt{2}\lambda_n(2t-k)\,g(k-2l), \quad l \in \mathbb{Z},\ n \in \mathbb{P}$$

is obtained for $t \in \mathbb{R}$. The sets of functions $\{\lambda_{2n}(\cdot - k) \mid k \in \mathbb{Z}\}$ and $\{\lambda_{2n+1}(\cdot - k) \mid k \in \mathbb{Z}\}$ for $n \in \mathbb{P}$ are orthogonal to each other. This follows from part (a) of the problem. The union of the space spanned by these functions is the same as that spanned by the set of basis functions $\{\sqrt{2}\lambda_n(2\cdot - k) \mid k \in \mathbb{Z}, 0 \le n < 2^m\}$. Therefore, from the above equations it can be concluded that the orthonormal basis of V_{m+1} is

$$\{\lambda_n(\cdot - k) \mid k \in \mathbb{Z}, 0 \le n < 2^{m+1}\}$$

This completes the induction step.

(c) The result follows from part (b) of the problem, and the fact $V_{m+1} = V_m \oplus W_m$.

(d) The result follows by letting $m \to \infty$ in part (c) of the problem.

2. For a fixed value of $m \in \mathbb{N}$, the set of functions

$$\lambda_{n,j,k}(\cdot) = 2^{j/2}\lambda_n(2^j \cdot -k), \quad j,k \in \mathbb{Z}$$
$$2^m \leq n < 2^{m+1}$$

form an orthonormal basis of the space $L^2(\mathbb{R})$. Establish this result.
Hint: See Vidakovic (1999). For $m = 0$, the value of $n = 1$, and $\lambda_1(\cdot) = \psi(\cdot)$, $\{\psi_{jk}(\cdot) \mid j,k \in \mathbb{Z}\}$ is an orthonormal basis of the space $L^2(\mathbb{R})$. For $m \in \mathbb{P}$, and part (c) of the last problem it follows that

$$\{\lambda_n(\cdot - k) \mid 2^m \leq n < 2^{m+1}, k \in \mathbb{Z}\}$$

is an orthonormal basis of W_m. It is known that $L^2(\mathbb{R}) = \bigoplus_{n \in \mathbb{Z}} W_n$. Therefore, by dilating these basis functions with 2^j, where $j \in \mathbb{Z}$, and normalizing by $2^{j/2}$ the conclusion of this observation is obtained.

3. Prove the following assertion. Define an index set

$$\mathbb{I} = \{(n,j) \mid n \in \mathbb{N} \text{ and } j \in \mathbb{Z}\}$$

and an interval

$$I_{nj} = [2^j n, 2^j(n+1)), \text{ where } (n,j) \in \mathbb{I}$$

such that these intervals form a disjoint and countable covering of the interval $[0, \infty)$. That is,

$$\cup_{m \in \mathbb{N}} I_{n_m, j_m} = [0, \infty)$$

Then the set of wavelet packets $\{\lambda_{n,j,k}(\cdot), (n,j) \in \mathbb{I}, k \in \mathbb{Z}\}$ is a complete orthonormal basis of the space $L^2(\mathbb{R})$. Consequently, if $f(\cdot) \in L^2(\mathbb{R})$, then

$$f(t) = \sum_{(n,j) \in \mathbb{I}} \sum_{k \in \mathbb{Z}} \alpha_{n,j,k} \lambda_{n,j,k}(t)$$
$$\alpha_{n,j,k} = \langle f, \lambda_{n,j,k} \rangle, \quad (n,j) \in \mathbb{I}, \text{ and } k \in \mathbb{Z}$$

Hint: See Coifman, Meyer, and Wickerhauser in Ruskai, et al. (1992); or Wickerhauser (1994).

4. Let the number of admissible wavelet packet trees of depth $S \in \mathbb{N}$, be N_S. Then prove that

$$N_0 = 1$$
$$N_{S+1} = N_S^2 + 1$$

This value also gives the number of wavelet packet bases in a complete binary tree of depth S.
Hint: See Mallat (2009). The observation, that each node of a wavelet packet tree has either 0 or 2 children. The stated result is proved by induction on S. For $S = 0$, $N_0 = 1$. The family of trees of depth at most $(S + 1)$ are made

up of trees of depth 0 (root node) and trees of depth 1 through $(S + 1)$. Then from each of the nodes $(1, 0)$ and $(1, 1)$ there will be N_S admissible binary trees. Therefore, N_{S+1} is equal to N_S times N_S plus one tree of depth 0. Therefore, $N_{S+1} = N_S^2 + 1$.

CHAPTER 12

Lapped Orthogonal Transform

12.1 Introduction

Lapped orthogonal transforms (LOTs) are good candidates for processing signals from several engineering disciplines, including speech and image. The goal of transformations is to achieve data compression. These transforms were introduced by H. S. Malvar and D. H. Staelin in 1988. Yves Meyer termed LOTs *Malvar wavelets*. LOTs actually complement wavelet packet analyses.

Jean Ville suggested in 1948 that signals can be studied in two different ways. In one technique, the signal is split into several successive blocks in time domain, and then each block is individually analyzed in the frequency domain. In the other technique, the complete signal is split into successive frequency bands, and then the components in each frequency band are analyzed in time domain. Yves Meyer opined that the first technique is a precursor to Malvar wavelets, and the second technique to wavelet packets. Only a simplified and discrete version of Malvar wavelets, called LOT is discussed in this chapter.

Motivation for the use of orthogonal transforms is initially provided. As mentioned earlier, these transforms are essentially used for data compression. Metrics which quantify the efficiency of the orthogonal transform are also described. This is followed by a description of the autoregressive process of order one, which is specified as $AR(1)$. This process is studied, because it is a simple and effective model for speech and image signals. Karhunen and Loève transforms (KLT) are next introduced. This transform is data dependent, and therefore it is computationally inefficient. KLT is studied, because it provides a template for introducing computationally efficient transforms.

Discrete cosine transforms (DCT) are next studied. This is a computationally efficient transform. Further, this is an asymptotically efficient transform if the signal samples are highly correlated, and can be modeled by an $AR(1)$ process. Block transforms, by themselves, introduce discontinuities between successive blocks of the recovered signals. In order to overcome this phenomenon, overlapping between successive blocks is used. The transforms that use overlapping are called lapped orthogonal transforms. Study of this transform is the main goal of this chapter. Earlier sections in the chapter simply provide a foundation for its study.

Notation. $\mathcal{E}(\cdot)$, $Var(\cdot)$, and $Cov(\cdot, \cdot)$ are the expectation, variance, and covariance operators respectively.   □

12.2 Orthogonal Transforms

Orthogonal transforms are a valuable tool in the art and science of data compression. The goal of data compression is to represent discrete signals with a small *expected* number of bits per sample. This can be done with either a low distortion (called lossy compression), or without any distortion (lossless compression) in the recovered signal.

In the method of data compression via orthogonal transforms, blocks of discrete signals of fixed length are transformed. The goal of these techniques is to eliminate correlations between adjacent samples of signals in the transformed domain, and achieve data compression.

A motivation for the use of orthogonal transforms is provided in this section. The goal of using orthogonal transformations is to map a sequence of data samples (data vector or data block) into another sequence (also called the transformed or spectral vector) of the same length. Let us call the elements of the transformed vector, spectral coefficients. It is hoped that these spectral coefficients are decorrelated. Further, if some of these spectral coefficients have a relatively smaller magnitude than other coefficients, then these can be neglected (eliminated). This property is called compaction. That is, the number of spectral coefficients required to recover the original signal-vector approximately is smaller. If the inverse transformation of the modified spectral vector is performed, then an approximation of the original data vector occurs. Such operations can lead to data compression. Data compression in turn, helps in achieving efficient transmission and/or storage of transformed signals.

Basics of Orthogonal Transformation

The matrix A of size N is said to be orthogonal if $AA^T = A^T A = I$, where I is an identity matrix of size N. Observe that the matrix A is invertible. That is,

$$A^{-1} = A^T$$

Further the columns the matrix A are orthonormal. Consequently, these column vectors are also linearly independent of each other. Note that the rows of the matrix A are also orthonormal.

Let $x \in \mathbb{R}^N$ be a data vector, $y \in \mathbb{R}^N$ be the transformed vector, and A be the orthogonal transformation matrix of size N. Also let

$$x = \begin{bmatrix} x_0 & x_1 & \cdots & x_{N-1} \end{bmatrix}^T$$
$$y = \begin{bmatrix} y_0 & y_1 & \cdots & y_{N-1} \end{bmatrix}^T$$

and

$$y = A^T x$$

Therefore,

$$x = Ay$$

Note that the term $x^T x$ is often said to represent the "energy" of the input signal vector. This leads to

$$x^T x = y^T y$$

Thus orthogonal transforms preserve energy in the data and transformed vectors. The goal of the orthogonal transformation is to make sure that the energy of the signal vector is concentrated in as few spectral coefficients as possible. In this case the less significant spectral coefficients may be assigned a zero value. Let the transformed vector be approximated as $\widehat{y}$, and the reconstructed data vector be $\widehat{x}$, where

$$\widehat{x} = A\widehat{y}$$

The squared error in the block x is ε^2, where

$$
\begin{aligned}
\varepsilon^2 &= (\widehat{x} - x)^T (\widehat{x} - x) \\
&= (A\widehat{y} - Ay)^T (A\widehat{y} - Ay) = (A(\widehat{y} - y))^T (A(\widehat{y} - y)) \\
&= (\widehat{y} - y)^T A^T A (\widehat{y} - y) = (\widehat{y} - y)^T (\widehat{y} - y)
\end{aligned}
$$

Thus

$$\varepsilon^2 = (\widehat{x} - x)^T (\widehat{x} - x) = (\widehat{y} - y)^T (\widehat{y} - y)$$

The last result implies that the squared error in the reconstructed data vector is the same as the squared error in the approximated spectral vector.

Assume that only $L \leq (N - 1)$ of the spectral coefficients are retained. For simplicity let the first L spectral coefficients be retained, and the rest be initialized to zero. That is,

$$
\widehat{y}_i = \begin{cases} y_i, & 0 \leq i \leq (L - 1) \\ 0, & L \leq i \leq (N - 1) \end{cases}
$$

Then

$$\varepsilon^2 = \sum_{i=0}^{N-1} (\widehat{y}_i - y_i)^2 = \sum_{i=L}^{N-1} y_i^2$$

Therefore, in order to minimize the squared error, only the $(N - L)$ spectral coefficients with the smallest magnitude are initialized to zero. This also essentially reduces the dimensionality of the transformed vector, which in turn leads to data compression.

As is usually the case, several successive blocks of data have to be compressed. Therefore, the value of L may vary from block to block. That is, the value of L is not fixed in general.

A well-known example of orthogonal transform is the discrete cosine transform. Further, if the data vector is complex, then the matrix A can be unitary. The very versatile discrete Fourier transform is an example of a unitary transform.

12.3 Transform Efficiency

Efficiency of an orthogonal transform is studied in this section. Orthogonal transforms by themselves do not imply that data compression has been achieved. In order to achieve data compression, the spectral coefficients are quantized, and then encoded for a more efficient representation. Quantization process is essentially nonlinear, and hence irreversible. That is, if quantization is used, then it is not possible to recover in general the original signal vector after the inverse transformation.

For efficient data compression, it is important to remove correlation among the data samples. Further, it would be nice to have only a few dominant spectral coefficients. The transform efficiency can be evaluated via the following metrics.

- Decorrelation efficiency
- Compaction efficiency
- Coding gain

The decorrelation efficiency is defined in terms of the elements of the covariance matrices of the data and transformed vectors. The compaction efficiency and coding gain are defined in terms of the variances of the elements of the signal and transformed random vectors. Therefore, these are initially developed.

12.3.1 Covariance Matrices

Covariance matrices of the signal and transformed vectors are developed in this subsection. Let X be the signal random vector, and Y be the transformed random vector. The orthogonal transformation matrix is A.

Signal Random Vector X

Let the real-valued samples of a signal be specified by the vector

$$x = [x_0, x_1, \ldots, x_{N-1}]^T$$

These can also be interpreted in terms of a random process. Let the corresponding random variables be represented via a random vector X as

$$X = \begin{bmatrix} X_0 & X_1 & \cdots & X_{N-1} \end{bmatrix}^T$$

Therefore, $X = x$ is an instance of the random vector X. The mean vector is

$$\mu_X \triangleq \mathcal{E}(X) = \begin{bmatrix} \mathcal{E}(X_0) & \mathcal{E}(X_1) & \cdots & \mathcal{E}(X_{N-1}) \end{bmatrix}^T$$

Its covariance matrix is

$$\Xi_X = \mathcal{E}\left((X - \mu_X)(X - \mu_X)^T\right) = \mathcal{E}\left(XX^T\right) - \mu_X\mu_X^T$$

Let

$$\Xi_X = [\alpha_{ij}]$$

Note that $Var(X_k) = \alpha_{kk}$, for $0 \le k \le (N - 1)$.

Transformation of the Vector X to Vector Y

Next consider an orthogonal matrix A of size N. That is,

$$AA^T = I, \quad \text{and} \quad A^T A = I$$

where I is an identity matrix of size N. Also

$$A^{-1} = A^T$$

The matrix A^T transforms the random vector X into another random vector Y. That is,

$$Y = A^T X$$

The corresponding mean vector and the covariance matrix are μ_Y and Ξ_Y respectively, where

$$\mu_Y = A^T \mu_X$$

$$\Xi_Y = \mathcal{E}\left((Y - \mu_Y)(Y - \mu_Y)^T\right) = \mathcal{E}\left(YY^T\right) - \mu_Y\mu_Y^T$$

Thus

$$\begin{aligned}
\Xi_Y &= \mathcal{E}\left((Y - \mu_Y)(Y - \mu_Y)^T\right) \\
&= \mathcal{E}\left((A^T X - A^T \mu_X)(A^T X - A^T \mu_X)^T\right) \\
&= \mathcal{E}\left((A^T(X - \mu_X))(A^T(X - \mu_X))^T\right) \\
&= A^T \mathcal{E}\left((X - \mu_X)(X - \mu_X)^T\right) A \\
&= A^{-1}\Xi_X A
\end{aligned}$$

That is,

$$\Xi_Y = A^{-1}\Xi_X A$$

Let

$$\Xi_Y = [\sigma_{ij}]$$

Therefore, $Var(Y_k) = \sigma_{kk} \triangleq \sigma_k^2$, for $0 \le k \le (N - 1)$.

Observation 12.1. It can be established that $tr(\Xi_Y) = tr(\Xi_X)$ where $\Xi_Y = A^{-1}\Xi_X A$. This implies

$$\sum_{k=0}^{N-1} \alpha_{kk} = \sum_{k=0}^{N-1} \sigma_{kk}$$

That is, the sum of variances of the elements of the data vector is equal to the sum of the variances of the spectral coefficient.   □

The above observation is established in the problem section.

12.3.2 Transform Metrics

Metrics for the efficiency of orthogonal transform are defined. These are: decorrelation efficiency, compaction efficiency, and coding gain.

Decorrelation Efficiency

One of the goals of orthogonal transformation is to have the spectral coefficients as much decorrelated as possible. In this case, the quantization of a specific spectral coefficient will not affect the quantization of other spectral coefficients. That is, the σ_{ij}'s for $i \neq j$ should be as small as possible in magnitude. Thus the decorrelation efficiency of the transform η_d is defined as

$$\eta_d = 1 - \frac{\sum_{0 \leq i,j \leq (N-1), i \neq j} \sigma_{ij}}{\sum_{0 \leq i,j \leq (N-1), i \neq j} \alpha_{ij}}$$

It is established in a subsequent section, that η_d is equal to unity for the Karhunen–Loève transform.

Compaction Efficiency

The orthogonal transform A, is selected so that the transform has energy compaction property. Index the variances of the spectral coefficients in descending order. That is, $\sigma_0^2 \geq \sigma_1^2 \geq \cdots \geq \sigma_{N-1}^2$. Let

$$\sigma^2 = \frac{1}{N} \sum_{k=0}^{N-1} \sigma_k^2$$

The compaction efficiency of the transform $\eta_c\,(L)$, for a specific value of L is defined as

$$\eta_c\,(L) = \frac{\sum_{k=0}^{L-1} \sigma_k^2}{\sum_{k=0}^{N-1} \sigma_k^2}, \quad L = 1, 2, \ldots, N$$

The above expression can also be expressed as

$$\eta_c\,(L) = \frac{\sum_{k=0}^{L-1} \sigma_k^2}{N\sigma^2}, \quad L = 1, 2, \ldots, N$$

As the KLT diagonalizes the data covariance matrix Ξ_X uniquely, and the sum of the variances of the components of the signal vector is equal to the sum of variances of the spectral coefficients, $\eta_c(L)$ is maximized. That is, KLT achieves maximum energy compaction of any orthogonal transform for a specific value of L. This assertion can be carefully established via the method of Lagrange multipliers.

Coding Gain

The coding gain C_{GAIN} of the transform is defined as the ratio of the arithmetic and the geometric mean of the variances of the spectral coefficients. Let

$$C_{AM} = \frac{1}{N} \sum_{k=0}^{N-1} \sigma_k^2 = \sigma^2, \text{ and } C_{GM} = \left\{ \prod_{k=0}^{N-1} \sigma_k^2 \right\}^{1/N}$$

$$C_{GAIN} = \frac{C_{AM}}{C_{GM}}$$

Note that the arithmetic mean $C_{AM} = \sigma^2$ is a constant for a given signal vector. Also observe that it is independent of the orthogonalization matrix A. For a given signal vector, the variances are typically same. Therefore, in the transform domain, an increase in the variance of a specific spectral coefficient should be matched by a decrease in the variances of one or more spectral coefficients. This is true because, the sum of variances of the signal components and those of the spectral coefficients are identical. This results in a decrease in the geometric mean C_{GM}. Consequently the coding gain C_{GAIN} increases, when the orthogonal matrix A is used in the transformation process. This definition of coding gain also has an information-theoretic interpretation. This is not discussed in this chapter.

12.4 AR(1) Process

The $AR(1)$ stochastic process is a useful model for several physical scenarios. The $AR(1)$ process is initially defined and then some of its basic properties are listed.

Definition 12.1. $AR(1)$ *process. The* $AR(1)$ *process is an autoregressive process of order one. The* $AR(1)$ *process is a stochastic process* $X = \{X_n \mid n \in \mathbb{Z}\}$ *where*

$$X_n = \rho X_{n-1} + \xi_n + \eta \tag{12.1}$$

and

(a) *The random variable* X_n *takes values in the set* $\mathbb{R}$ *for all values of* n

(b) $\eta \in \mathbb{R}, \rho \in (-1, 1) \setminus \{0\}$

(c) ξ_n is a normally distributed random variable with $\mathcal{E}(\xi_n) = 0$, $Var(\xi_n) = \sigma_\xi^2$, and ξ_n is independent of ξ_m for all $m \neq n$. The process $\{\xi_n \mid n \in \mathbb{Z}\}$ is sometimes called a white noise process.

(d) $\mathcal{E}(X_n) = \mu$, $Var(X_n) = \sigma^2$ for each value of n. That is, the mean and variance of the random variable X_n are independent of n.   □

Based upon the above definition, the following observations are obtained.

Observations 12.2. Some useful observations about the $AR(1)$ process.

1. We have

$$\mu = \frac{\eta}{1 - \rho}$$

$$\sigma^2 = \frac{\sigma_\xi^2}{1 - \rho^2}$$

2. Let $Cov(X_n, X_{n+k}) \triangleq \gamma_k$, then $\gamma_k = \sigma^2 \rho^{|k|}$, for $k \in \mathbb{Z}$.
   Note that $Cov(X_n, X_{n+k})$ is independent of n. Therefore, the $AR(1)$ process is stationary in the wide sense.

3. The correlation coefficient is $\varrho_k = \gamma_k/\gamma_0 = \rho^{|k|}$, for $k \in \mathbb{Z}$. Further, ρ is called a single-step correlation coefficient of the data samples.

4. The correlation coefficient matrix R_N of size N is $R_N = [r_{ij}]$, where

$$r_{ij} = \gamma_0^{-1} Cov(X_i, X_j) = \rho^{|i-j|}, \quad 0 \le i, j \le (N-1)$$

□

Some of the above observations are established in the problem section. The $AR(1)$ process is also called the stationary Markov-1 process.

Observations 12.3. Some observations about the correlation coefficient matrix R_N.

1. The matrix R_N of size N is

$$R_N = \begin{bmatrix} 1 & \rho & \rho^2 & \cdots & \rho^{N-2} & \rho^{N-1} \\ \rho & 1 & \rho & \cdots & \rho^{N-3} & \rho^{N-2} \\ \vdots & \vdots & \vdots & \ddots & \vdots & \vdots \\ \rho^{N-2} & \rho^{N-3} & \rho^{N-4} & \cdots & 1 & \rho \\ \rho^{N-1} & \rho^{N-2} & \rho^{N-3} & \cdots & \rho & 1 \end{bmatrix}$$

The above matrix has a special structure. Each element in a diagonal descending from left to right (north-west to south-east) is a constant. Such matrices are called Toeplitz matrices in honor of the mathematician Otto Toeplitz (1881–1940).

The matrix R_N is symmetric, therefore all of its eigenvalues are all real-valued. Further, the eigenvectors are mutually orthogonal, and can be made orthonormal.

2. Inverse of the matrix R_N is a tridiagonal Toeplitz matrix

$$R_N^{-1} = \beta^{-2} \begin{bmatrix} 1-\rho\alpha & -\alpha & 0 & 0 & \cdots & 0 & 0 & 0 & 0 \\ -\alpha & 1 & -\alpha & 0 & \cdots & 0 & 0 & 0 & 0 \\ 0 & -\alpha & 1 & -\alpha & \cdots & 0 & 0 & 0 & 0 \\ \vdots & \vdots & \vdots & \vdots & \ddots & \vdots & \vdots & \vdots & \vdots \\ 0 & 0 & 0 & 0 & \cdots & -\alpha & 1 & -\alpha & 0 \\ 0 & 0 & 0 & 0 & \cdots & 0 & -\alpha & 1 & -\alpha \\ 0 & 0 & 0 & 0 & \cdots & 0 & 0 & -\alpha & 1-\rho\alpha \end{bmatrix}$$

where

$$\alpha = \frac{\rho}{1+\rho^2}, \quad \beta^2 = \frac{1-\rho^2}{1+\rho^2}, \quad \rho \neq \pm 1$$

3. Consider a matrix B_N.

$$B_N = \begin{bmatrix} 1-\alpha & -\alpha & 0 & 0 & \cdots & 0 & 0 & 0 & 0 \\ -\alpha & 1 & -\alpha & 0 & \cdots & 0 & 0 & 0 & 0 \\ 0 & -\alpha & 1 & -\alpha & \cdots & 0 & 0 & 0 & 0 \\ \vdots & \vdots & \vdots & \vdots & \ddots & \vdots & \vdots & \vdots & \vdots \\ 0 & 0 & 0 & 0 & \cdots & -\alpha & 1 & -\alpha & 0 \\ 0 & 0 & 0 & 0 & \cdots & 0 & -\alpha & 1 & -\alpha \\ 0 & 0 & 0 & 0 & \cdots & 0 & 0 & -\alpha & 1-\alpha \end{bmatrix}$$

This matrix resembles the matrix R_N^{-1}. It turns out that its eigenvalue-eigenvector pairs are (λ_k, c_k), where $\lambda_k = (1 - 2\alpha \cos(k\pi/n))$, and c_k is the basis vector of discrete cosine transform for $0 \leq k \leq (N-1)$. The discrete cosine transform is discussed later in the chapter.   □

12.5 Karhunen–Loéve Transform

We study a special transform in this section. It is called the Karhunen–Loéve transform (KLT). It is named after K. Karhunen (1915–1992) and M. Loéve (1907–1979). It transforms a random vector via an orthogonal matrix. However, unlike DFT and DCT, this orthogonal transform matrix is actually data dependent. The KLT uses the representation of a random vector in terms of the eigenvectors of its covariance matrix.

It should be noted that the KLT is also sometimes termed the Kosambi–Karhunen–Loéve transform. The first name is after the Harvard-educated mathematician D. D. Kosambi (1907–1966).

It is demonstrated in this section that the KLT decorrelates the spectral coefficients (elements of the transformed vector) in the transform domain. This decorrelation is important for data compression.

The KLT also provides the so-called "energy compaction." This implies that only a small number of the spectral coefficients have a significant magnitude. Consequently, the spectral coefficients with smaller magnitude can essentially be ignored.

As mentioned earlier, the KLT is data dependent. Hence it is inconvenient to design a fast KLT algorithm. Nevertheless, it might be possible to design its close approximations. One such transformation is the DCT. Fast and efficient algorithms exist for the computation of the DCT. Proper use of the DCT assumes that the data is derived from an autoregressive process of order one.

12.5.1 KLT Matrix

Consider a random data vector X, where

$$X = \begin{bmatrix} X_0 & X_1 & \cdots & X_{N-1} \end{bmatrix}^T$$

The mean vector is

$$\mu_X \triangleq \mathcal{E}(X) = \begin{bmatrix} \mathcal{E}(X_0) & \mathcal{E}(X_1) & \cdots & \mathcal{E}(X_{N-1}) \end{bmatrix}^T$$

Its covariance matrix is

$$\Xi_X = \mathcal{E}\left((X - \mu_X)(X - \mu_X)^T\right) = \mathcal{E}(XX^T) - \mu_X\mu_X^T$$

Observe that the matrix Ξ_X is symmetric. That is, $\Xi_X = \Xi_X^T$. In addition, it is also positive semidefinite. Thus all of its eigenvalues are nonnegative, and the eigenvectors are orthogonal. Nevertheless, these eigenvectors can be made orthonormal. Let the eigenvalue-eigenvector pairs be (λ_k, ϕ_k), where $0 \leq k \leq (N-1)$. Thus $\lambda_k \in \mathbb{R}_0^+$ for $0 \leq k \leq (N-1)$. Also

$$\phi_i^T \phi_j = \delta_{ij}, \quad 0 \leq i, j \leq (N-1)$$

where $\delta_{ij} = 1$ if $i = j$ and zero otherwise. Further

$$\Xi_X \phi_k = \lambda_k \phi_k, \quad 0 \leq k \leq (N-1)$$

The above results can also be represented compactly as follows. Let

$$\Phi = \begin{bmatrix} \phi_0 & \phi_1 & \cdots & \phi_{N-1} \end{bmatrix}$$

and Λ be a diagonal matrix with the λ_k's on its main diagonal. That is,

$$\Lambda = diag\left(\lambda_0, \lambda_1, \ldots, \lambda_{N-1}\right)$$

We have

$$\Phi^T \Phi = I$$

That is, Φ is an orthogonal matrix. This implies

$$\Phi^{-1} = \Phi^T$$

Further

$$\Xi_X \Phi = \Phi \Lambda$$

Therefore,

$$\Phi^{-1} \Xi_X \Phi = \Lambda$$

We next transform the vector X by the orthogonal matrix Φ^T to obtain a vector Y. That is,

$$Y = \Phi^T X$$

Thus Φ^T is the KLT matrix.

12.5.2 Properties of the KLT Matrix

Properties of the KLT matrix, Φ^T are described. Consider the transformed vector Y. The corresponding mean vector and the covariance matrix are μ_Y and Ξ_Y respectively, where

$$\mu_Y = \Phi^T \mu_X$$

$$\Xi_Y = \mathcal{E}\left((Y - \mu_Y)(Y - \mu_Y)^T\right) = \mathcal{E}\left(YY^T\right) - \mu_Y \mu_Y^T$$

Thus

$$\Xi_Y = \mathcal{E}\left((Y - \mu_Y)(Y - \mu_Y)^T\right) = \Phi^{-1} \Xi_X \Phi$$

Therefore,

$$\Xi_Y = \Phi^{-1} \Xi_X \Phi = \Lambda$$

Observe that, as $\Xi_Y = \Lambda$, and the variance

$$Var\left(Y_k\right) = \sigma_{Y_k}^2 = \lambda_k, \quad \text{for } 0 \le k \le (N-1)$$

12.5.3 Karhunen–Loéve Transform of Vector x

The Karhunen–Loéve transform (KLT) of the vector $x \in \mathbb{R}^N$ is defined as

$$y = \Phi^T x$$

Thus

$$x = \Phi y = \sum_{k=0}^{N-1} \phi_k y_k$$

That is, a signal vector x is represented in an N-dimensional vector space spanned by the N eigenvectors $\{\phi_k \mid 0 \leq 0 \leq (N-1)\}$.

Observations 12.4. Some useful observations about KLT.

1. Decorrelation of the spectral coefficients. The transformation $y = \Phi^T x$ is said to decorrelate the vector x, because the nondiagonal terms in the matrix Ξ_Y are all zeros. That is, elements of the vector y are decorrelated. Note that the decorrelation efficiency η_d of KLT is unity, as all off-diagonal terms in the covariance matrix Ξ_Y of the transformed vector are zeros.

2. Preservation of energy. The term $x^T x$ is said to represent the energy of the input signal vector. We have

$$x^T x = y^T y$$

Therefore, the KLT is said to preserve energy under the transformation.

3. KLT achieves maximum energy compaction of any orthogonal transform.

4. Assume that, for energy compaction we want to maximize energy via only $L < N$ components. We select these L components which correspond to the L largest eigenvalues. Recall that all the eigenvalues of the matrix Ξ_X are nonnegative. The eigenvalues of matrix Ξ_X are first sorted in descending order, so that $\lambda_0 \geq \lambda_1 \geq \cdots \geq \lambda_{N-1}$, and then the L largest values are selected. The value L is determined by first selecting a threshold value $\tau \in (0, 1]$. It is the smallest integer L so that

$$\frac{\sum_{i=0}^{L-1} \lambda_i}{\sum_{i=0}^{N-1} \lambda_i} \geq \tau$$

The recovered signal vector $\hat{x}$ is

$$\hat{x} = \sum_{k=0}^{L-1} \phi_k y_k$$

The fraction of lost information is $\sum_{i=L}^{N-1} \lambda_i / \sum_{i=0}^{N-1} \lambda_i$.

5. Relationship between the KLT and DCT. It has been discussed in the section on the $AR(1)$ (autoregressive process of order one) process, that its covariance matrix is symmetric and Toeplitz. Further, if the single-step correlation coefficient ρ of the process tends to unity, the eigenvectors of this matrix turn out to be the basis vectors of the DCT matrix. Thus the DCT matrix is a good candidate to transform signals modeled via the $AR(1)$ process. In this case the DCT transform would decorrelate the elements of the transformed vector efficiently if $\rho \simeq 1$. This transform is also convenient for achieving energy compaction.   □

12.6 Discrete Cosine Transform

The discrete cosine transform (DCT) is described in this section. As we shall see, the DCT is not the real part of the discrete Fourier transform.

As in the case of the DFT, the DCT helps in representing a discrete-time signal (of finite length) as a weighted sum of its basis vectors. However, the DCT is more advantageous than the DFT for two significant reasons. The DCT is a real-valued transform, while the DFT is complex-valued. Further, the DFT introduces discontinuity in time. This is because the DFT assumes that the truncated time signal is periodic. This in turn introduces spurious frequencies in the transformed (frequency) domain due to edge discontinuities. In contrast, the DCT assumes even symmetry when the time signal is truncated. Consequently, no discontinuity is introduced. This in turn avoids the introduction of unwanted frequencies in the transformed domain. The Figures 12.1a and b demonstrate these differences pictorially.

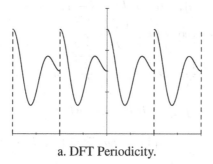

a. DFT Periodicity.

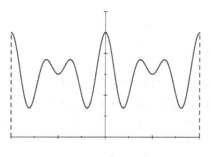

b. DCT Periodicity.

Figures 12.1 a and b. Periodicities assumed by the DFT and DCT.

Basics of the DCT are initially described in this section. This is followed by a description of some techniques to compute the DCT of a given data vector. It is also

indicated that the basis vectors that are used in the DCT also occur as the eigenvectors
of some special matrices.

The DCT is an ideal transform if the source signals can be effectively modeled as
an $AR(1)$ process. That is, if the single-step correlation coefficient ρ of the $AR(1)$
process tends towards unity, then the DCT will be identical to the KLT. Some of its
possible applications are in speech and image processing. Hence the popularity of
the DCT for processing such signals.

12.6.1 Basics of the DCT

Elements of the DCT are discussed in this subsection. The DCT is initially defined.
This is followed by a listing of some of its important properties.

Definitions 12.2. *Discrete cosine transform (DCT).*

1. *The DCT matrix C is a square matrix of size $N \in \mathbb{P}$, where*

$$C = [c_{kl}], \quad 0 \le k, l \le (N-1) \tag{12.2a}$$

$$c_{kl} = \sigma_k \cos\left\{\left(l + \frac{1}{2}\right)\frac{k\pi}{N}\right\} \tag{12.2b}$$

$$\sigma_0 = \frac{1}{\sqrt{N}}, \quad and \quad \sigma_k = \sqrt{\frac{2}{N}}, \ for \ 1 \le k \le (N-1) \tag{12.2c}$$

2. *The DCT of a vector $f \in \mathbb{R}^N$ is $F = Cf$, where*

$$f \triangleq \begin{bmatrix} f_0 & f_1 & \cdots & f_{N-1} \end{bmatrix}^T, \quad and \quad F \triangleq \begin{bmatrix} F_0 & F_1 & \cdots & F_{N-1} \end{bmatrix}^T \tag{12.3}$$

$\square$

Some useful observations about the DCT.

Observations 12.5.

1. The matrix C is not symmetric. That is, $C \neq C^T$.

2. The DCT is a linear transformation. Let $\alpha, \beta \in \mathbb{R}$, and $f, g \in \mathbb{R}^N$. Also let
   the DCT of the vectors f and g be F and G respectively. Then the DCT of
   $(\alpha f + \beta g)$ is $(\alpha F + \beta G)$.

3. The DCT of the vector f can be explicitly stated as

$$F_k = \sigma_k \sum_{l=0}^{N-1} \cos\left\{\left(l + \frac{1}{2}\right)\frac{k\pi}{N}\right\} f_l, \quad where \ \ 0 \le k \le (N-1)$$

4. $CC^T = C^T C = I$, where I is the identity matrix of size N. Thus the matrix C
   is orthogonal.

5. $C^{-1} = C^T = [c_{lk}]$.

6. The *inverse DCT* of the vector F is $f = C^T F$, where $C^T = [c_{lk}]$. That is,

$$f_l = \sum_{k=0}^{N-1} \sigma_k \cos\left\{\left(l + \frac{1}{2}\right)\frac{k\pi}{N}\right\} F_k, \quad \text{where} \quad 0 \le l \le (N-1)$$

7. Let

$$c_k = \begin{bmatrix} c_{k0} & c_{k1} & \cdots & c_{k,N-1} \end{bmatrix}^T, \quad 0 \le k \le (N-1)$$

Then $\{c_k \mid 0 \le k \le (N-1)\}$ is the orthogonal basis set of the transform.

8. Energy conservation. We have $f^T f = F^T F$. That is,

$$\sum_{l=0}^{N-1} f_l^2 = \sum_{k=0}^{N-1} F_k^2$$

The term $f^T f = \sum_{l=0}^{N-1} f_l^2$ is often said to be the "energy" of the signal block.

9. For a specific $l \in 0, 1, \ldots, (N-1)$, let $\cos\left\{\left(l + \frac{1}{2}\right)\frac{k\pi}{N}\right\} \triangleq b_k$ for $0 \le k \le (N-1)$. Then

$$b_{-k} = b_k$$
$$b_{k+2N} = -b_k$$
$$b_{k+4N} = -b_{k+2N} = b_k$$

$\square$

Some of the above observations are proved in the problem section. It should be noted that there are several versions of the DCTs. These are: DCT-1, DCT-2, DCT-3, and DCT-4. Similar to the DCTs there are discrete sine transforms (DSTs). The different versions of the DSTs are: DST-1, DST-2, DST-3, and DST-4. The DCT discussed in this section is the DCT-2. It also happens to be the most useful and popular DCT in practice.

12.6.2   Computation of the DCT

Three illustrative methods for the computation of the DCT are described in this subsection. These methods use the DFT to compute the DCT. Therefore, the FFT methods can be used to compute the DCT of a given real data vector.

Method 1

Let $\mathbb{C}$ be the set of complex numbers. Also let $z \in \mathbb{C}$. If $z = (a + ib)$, where $a, b \in \mathbb{R}$ and $i = \sqrt{-1}$, then the real part of z is a, and its imaginary part is b. Denote $a \triangleq \text{Re}(z)$ and $b \triangleq \text{Im}(z)$. Thus

$$c_{kl} = \sigma_k \cos\left\{\left(l+\frac{1}{2}\right)\frac{k\pi}{N}\right\} = \sigma_k \operatorname{Re}\left\{\exp\left\{i\left(l+\frac{1}{2}\right)\frac{k\pi}{N}\right\}\right\}$$

$$= \sigma_k \operatorname{Re}\left\{\exp\left\{\frac{\pi i}{2N}k\right\}\exp\left\{\frac{2\pi i}{2N}kl\right\}\right\}$$

Let

$$\omega_{2N} = \exp\left(\frac{2\pi i}{2N}\right)$$

Therefore,

$$F_k = \sigma_k \sum_{l=0}^{N-1}\cos\left\{\left(l+\frac{1}{2}\right)\frac{k\pi}{N}\right\}f_l$$

$$= \sigma_k \operatorname{Re}\left\{\exp\left\{\frac{\pi i}{2N}k\right\}\sum_{l=0}^{2N-1}\omega_{2N}^{kl}f_l\right\}$$

where $f_l = 0$, for $N \le l \le (2N-1)$; and $0 \le k \le (N-1)$. Thus an N-point DCT can be computed from a $2N$-point DFT. Thus this method is amenable to a $2N$-point FFT algorithm.

Method 2

Define

$$\widehat{f}_l = \begin{cases} f_l, & 0 \le l \le (N-1) \\ f_{2N-1-l}, & N \le l \le (2N-1) \end{cases}$$

Observe that $\widehat{f}_N = \widehat{f}_{N-1}$, and $\widehat{f}_{2N-1} = \widehat{f}_0$. Thus the sequence $\widehat{f}_0, \widehat{f}_1, \ldots, \widehat{f}_{2N-1}$ is symmetric about $(N-1/2)$, and no discontinuities are introduced in it. Let the DFT of the sequence $\left\{\widehat{f}_l \mid 0 \le l \le (2N-1)\right\}$ be $\left\{\widehat{F}_k \mid 0 \le k \le (2N-1)\right\}$. Let

$$\omega_{2N} = \exp\left(\frac{2\pi i}{2N}\right)$$

Then

$$\widehat{F}_k = \frac{1}{\sqrt{2N}}\sum_{l=0}^{2N-1}\widehat{f}_l\omega_{2N}^{lk}, \quad \text{where } 0 \le k \le (2N-1)$$

It is established in the problem section that

$$F_0 = \frac{1}{\sqrt{2}}\widehat{F}_0$$

$$F_k = \omega_{2N}^{k/2}\widehat{F}_k, \quad 1 \le k \le (N-1)$$

Note that this method is amenable to a $2N$-point FFT algorithm. In addition, the modified input sequence $\widehat{f}_l$'s has no discontinuities in it.

Method 3

Recall that

$$F_k = \sigma_k \sum_{l=0}^{N-1} \cos\left\{\left(l + \frac{1}{2}\right)\frac{k\pi}{N}\right\} f_l, \quad \text{where } 0 \le k \le (N-1)$$

Observe that

$$\left(l + \frac{1}{2}\right)\frac{k\pi}{N} = (2l+1)\frac{k\pi}{2N} = \frac{2\pi}{4N}k(2l+1)$$

Thus

$$\omega_{4N} = \exp\left(\frac{2\pi i}{4N}\right)$$

$$\cos\left\{\left(l + \frac{1}{2}\right)\frac{k\pi}{N}\right\} = \frac{1}{2}\left\{\omega_{4N}^{k(2l+1)} + \omega_{4N}^{-k(2l+1)}\right\}$$

$$= \frac{1}{2}\left\{\omega_{4N}^{k(2l+1)} + \omega_{4N}^{4N-k(2l+1)}\right\}$$

and

$$F_k = \frac{\sigma_k}{2}\left\{\sum_{l=0}^{N-1} \omega_{4N}^{k(2l+1)} f_l + \sum_{l=0}^{N-1} \omega_{4N}^{4N-k(2l+1)} f_l\right\}$$

$$\triangleq \frac{\sigma_k}{2}\sum_{l=0}^{4N-1} \omega_{4N}^{kl}\widetilde{f}_l$$

We next need to define $\widetilde{f}_l, 0 \le l \le (4N-1)$ in terms of $f_l, 0 \le l \le (N-1)$. Write

$$\sum_{l=0}^{4N-1} \omega_{4N}^{kl}\widetilde{f}_l = \sum_{l=0}^{2N-1} \omega_{4N}^{k(2l)}\widetilde{f}_{2l} + \sum_{l=0}^{2N-1} \omega_{4N}^{k(2l+1)}\widetilde{f}_{2l+1}$$

Let $\widetilde{f}_{2l} = 0$ for $0 \le l \le (2N-1)$. Therefore,

$$\sum_{l=0}^{4N-1} \omega_{4N}^{kl}\widetilde{f}_l = \sum_{l=0}^{2N-1} \omega_{4N}^{k(2l+1)}\widetilde{f}_{2l+1}$$

$$= \sum_{l=0}^{N-1} \omega_{4N}^{k(2l+1)}\widetilde{f}_{2l+1} + \sum_{l=N}^{2N-1} \omega_{4N}^{k(2l+1)}\widetilde{f}_{2l+1}$$

In the second summation on the right-hand side of the expression, substitute

$$2l + 1 = 4N - (2j+1)$$

Thus

$$\sum_{l=0}^{4N-1} \omega_{4N}^{kl} \widetilde{f}_l = \sum_{l=0}^{N-1} \omega_{4N}^{k(2l+1)} \widetilde{f}_{2l+1} + \sum_{j=0}^{N-1} \omega_{4N}^{k(4N-(2j+1))} \widetilde{f}_{4N-(2j+1)}$$

$$= \sum_{l=0}^{N-1} \omega_{4N}^{k(2l+1)} \widetilde{f}_{2l+1} + \sum_{l=0}^{N-1} \omega_{4N}^{-k(2l+1)} \widetilde{f}_{4N-(2l+1)}$$

Therefore, let

$$\widetilde{f}_{2l+1} = f_l, \quad 0 \le l \le (N-1)$$
$$\widetilde{f}_{4N-(2l+1)} = f_l, \quad 0 \le l \le (N-1)$$

This leads to

$$\sum_{l=0}^{4N-1} \omega_{4N}^{kl} \widetilde{f}_l = 2 \sum_{l=0}^{N-1} \cos\left\{\left(l+\frac{1}{2}\right)\frac{k\pi}{N}\right\} f_l$$

and

$$F_k = \frac{\sigma_k}{2} \sum_{l=0}^{4N-1} \omega_{4N}^{kl} \widetilde{f}_l$$

$$= \sigma_k \sum_{l=0}^{N-1} \cos\left\{\left(l+\frac{1}{2}\right)\frac{k\pi}{N}\right\} f_l$$

The above discussion is summarized in the following observation.

Observation 12.6. For the given input vector $f \in \mathbb{R}^N$, we describe a technique to determine the DCT vector $F \in \mathbb{R}^N$. This is done via the computation of a $4N$-point DFT of vector $\widetilde{f} \in \mathbb{R}^{4N}$, where

$$\widetilde{f}_{2l} = 0, \qquad\qquad 0 \le l \le (2N-1)$$
$$\widetilde{f}_{2l+1} = f_l, \qquad\qquad 0 \le l \le (N-1)$$
$$\widetilde{f}_{4N-(2l+1)} = f_l, \qquad 0 \le l \le (N-1)$$

Therefore, the $4N$-point DFT of vector $\widetilde{f}$ is $\widetilde{F}$ where

$$\widetilde{F}_k = \frac{1}{\sqrt{4N}} \sum_{l=0}^{4N-1} \omega_{4N}^{kl} \widetilde{f}_l, \quad 0 \le k \le (4N-1)$$

and

$$F_k = \sqrt{N} \sigma_k \widetilde{F}_k, \quad 0 \le k \le (N-1)$$

Therefore, this method is amenable to a $4N$-point FFT algorithm.   □

12.6.3 DCT Basis Vectors as Eigenvectors of Special Matrices

It is demonstrated in this subsection, that the basis vectors of DCT occur as eigenvectors of some special matrices. That is, the DCT basis vectors c_k, $0 \leq k \leq (N-1)$ are also the eigenvectors of some special matrices. Consider the tridiagonal matrix A_N of size N, where

$$A_N = \begin{bmatrix} 1 & -1 & 0 & 0 \cdots & 0 & 0 & 0 & 0 \\ -1 & 2 & -1 & 0 \cdots & 0 & 0 & 0 & 0 \\ 0 & -1 & 2 & -1 \cdots & 0 & 0 & 0 & 0 \\ \vdots & \vdots & \vdots & \vdots \ddots & \vdots & \vdots & \vdots & \vdots \\ 0 & 0 & 0 & 0 \cdots & -1 & 2 & -1 & 0 \\ 0 & 0 & 0 & 0 \cdots & 0 & -1 & 2 & -1 \\ 0 & 0 & 0 & 0 \cdots & 0 & 0 & -1 & 1 \end{bmatrix}$$

It can be shown that the eigenvalues of this matrix are $\lambda_k = 2\left(1 - \cos\left(k\pi/N\right)\right)$, where $0 \leq k \leq (N-1)$, and $N \geq 3$. Further, the eigenvector corresponding to the eigenvalue λ_k is indeed the DCT basis vector c_k for $0 \leq k \leq (N-1)$. This conclusion should actually be transparent from the trigonometric identity

$$-\cos\left(j-1\right)\theta + 2\cos j\theta - \cos\left(j+1\right)\theta = \left(2 - 2\cos\theta\right)\cos j\theta$$

Also consider a matrix B_N, where $N \geq 2$. It is described in the section on the $AR\left(1\right)$ process. It turns out that its eigenvalue-eigenvector pairs are $\left(\lambda_k, c_k\right)$, where

$$\lambda_k = \left(1 - 2\alpha \cos\left(k\pi/N\right)\right)$$

and c_k is the basis vector of the DCT for $0 \leq k \leq (N-1)$.

Next consider an all-1 matrix D_N of size N, where $N \geq 2$. That is,

$$D_N = [d_{kl}], \quad \text{where } d_{kl} = 1, \quad \text{for } 0 \leq k, l \leq (N-1)$$

Thus the matrix D_N is singular. It can be shown that its characteristic polynomial is

$$\det\left(\lambda I_N - D_N\right) = \lambda^{N-1}\left(\lambda - N\right)$$

where I_N is an identity matrix of size N. The eigenvector corresponding to the eigenvalue $\lambda_0 = N$ is c_0. Further, the eigenvector corresponding to the eigenvalue $\lambda_k = 0$ is c_k for $1 \leq k \leq (N-1)$. The results in this subsection are established (verified) in the problem section. This result implies that, if the single-step correlation coefficient ρ of the $AR\left(1\right)$ process tends towards unity, then the DCT is identical to the KLT.

12.7 Lapped Transform

Lapped orthogonal transforms (LOT) find application in multiple engineering disciplines, including image and speech. The reason for its use is next elaborated upon. Let $X_i \in \mathbb{R}^N$ be a block (vector) of N contiguous signal samples, where $i = 0, 1, 2, \ldots, (M - 1)$. The data block X_i is transformed into a vector $Y_i \in \mathbb{R}^N$ via an orthogonal matrix A of size N. Thus

$$AA^T = A^T A = I$$
$$A^{-1} = A^T$$

$$Y_i = AX_i \quad \text{and} \quad X_i = A^T Y_i$$

where $0 \leq i \leq (M - 1)$. Therefore, the M number of blocks are transformed as follows. Let

$$X = \begin{bmatrix} X_0 & X_1 & \cdots & X_{M-1} \end{bmatrix}^T$$
$$Y = \begin{bmatrix} Y_0 & Y_1 & \cdots & Y_{M-1} \end{bmatrix}^T$$

$$Y = \begin{bmatrix} A & 0 & \cdots & 0 \\ 0 & A & \cdots & 0 \\ \vdots & \vdots & \ddots & \vdots \\ 0 & 0 & \cdots & 0 \\ 0 & 0 & \cdots & A \end{bmatrix} X, \quad X = \begin{bmatrix} A^T & 0 & \cdots & 0 \\ 0 & A^T & \cdots & 0 \\ \vdots & \vdots & \ddots & \vdots \\ 0 & 0 & \cdots & 0 \\ 0 & 0 & \cdots & A^T \end{bmatrix} Y$$

That is, Y is obtained by transforming each block independently of all other blocks. Typically Y_i is approximated (quantized) as $\widehat{Y}_i$, where $\widehat{Y}_i$ has a smaller *expected* number of bits in its representation than for the vector Y_i. The reconstructed vector is $\widehat{X}_i$, where

$$\widehat{X}_i = A^T \widehat{Y}_i$$

Next consider the data vector $X_i \in \mathbb{R}^N$, for which the corresponding transformed vector is $Y_i \in \mathbb{R}^N$, the approximated transformed vector is $\widehat{Y}_i \in \mathbb{R}^N$, and the recovered data vector is $\widehat{X}_i \in \mathbb{R}^N$, where $i = 0, 1, 2, \ldots, (M - 1)$.

Due to the different levels of quantizations in the $\widehat{Y}_i$-sequence there might be discontinuities between the vector $\widehat{X}_i$ and its adjacent vectors, which are $\widehat{X}_{i-1}$ and $\widehat{X}_{i+1}$ (artifacts at block boundaries). In order to avoid this phenomenon of blockiness, overlapping of adjacent blocks is used in computing the spectral coefficients. The transforms which use overlapping are called lapped transforms.

Block artifact-effects can be mitigated by using basis functions which decay smoothly to zero. This necessitates the basis functions of neighboring blocks to overlap. The basis functions would then have a length $L > N$. However, the number of transformed coefficients per block would still be N. Thus the square orthogonal matrix A is replaced by an $N \times L$ matrix P. For simplicity, we shall assume that $L = 2N$. The matrix P is called a *lapped orthogonal transform* (LOT) matrix. Let this $N \times 2N$ matrix be

$$P = \begin{bmatrix} A & B \end{bmatrix}$$

where A and B are square matrices of size N each. The transformed vector Y_i is

$$Y_i = P \begin{bmatrix} X_i \\ X_{i+1} \end{bmatrix} = AX_i + BX_{i+1}$$

For implementing LOT we have

$$Y = TX$$

In order to recover the original vector X from the vector Y, we should have $X = T^{-1}Y$. That is, the matrix T should be invertible. Generally, the matrix T is selected so that $T^{-1} = T^T$. Therefore, the requirement for the orthogonal transformation matrix T is $TT^T = T^TT = I$, where I is an identity matrix of appropriate size.

Example 12.1. The matrix T for $M = 4$ is

$$T = \begin{bmatrix} A & B & 0 & 0 \\ 0 & A & B & 0 \\ 0 & 0 & A & B \\ B & 0 & 0 & A \end{bmatrix}$$

Notice the wrap-around placement of matrix B in the fourth row of matrix T. The corresponding transform of the block-vector

$$X = \begin{bmatrix} X_0 & X_1 & X_2 & X_3 \end{bmatrix}^T$$

is

$$Y = \begin{bmatrix} Y_0 & Y_1 & Y_2 & Y_3 \end{bmatrix}^T$$

Thus

$$\begin{bmatrix} Y_0 \\ Y_1 \\ Y_2 \\ Y_3 \end{bmatrix} = \begin{bmatrix} A & B & 0 & 0 \\ 0 & A & B & 0 \\ 0 & 0 & A & B \\ B & 0 & 0 & A \end{bmatrix} \begin{bmatrix} X_0 \\ X_1 \\ X_2 \\ X_3 \end{bmatrix}$$

The matrix T^T for $M = 4$ is

$$T^T = \begin{bmatrix} A^T & 0 & 0 & B^T \\ B^T & A^T & 0 & 0 \\ 0 & B^T & A^T & 0 \\ 0 & 0 & B^T & A^T \end{bmatrix}$$

Further

- $T^TT = I$ implies $\left(A^TA + B^TB\right) = I$, and $A^TB = B^TA = 0$.
- $TT^T = I$ implies $\left(AA^T + BB^T\right) = I$, and $AB^T = BA^T = 0$.   □

In general, the result $X = T^TY$ leads to

$$X_i = \begin{bmatrix} B^T & A^T \end{bmatrix} \begin{bmatrix} Y_{i-1} \\ Y_i \end{bmatrix}$$

$$= B^T Y_{i-1} + A^T Y_i$$

The above expression for X_i and the relationship $Y_i = (AX_i + BX_{i+1})$ together imply

$$A^T A + B^T B = I, \text{ and } A^T B = B^T A = 0$$

Note that $A^T B = 0$ implies $B^T A = 0$. Observe that

$$P^T P = A^T A + B^T B = I$$
$$PP^T = \left(AA^T + BB^T\right) = I$$

Observations 12.7.

1. This observation specifies the requirement for $P = \begin{bmatrix} A & B \end{bmatrix}$ to be a LOT matrix. Let

$$V = \begin{bmatrix} 0 & I_N \\ 0 & 0 \end{bmatrix}$$

be a square matrix of size $2N$, and I_N be an identity matrix of size N. The requirements $\left(AA^T + BB^T\right) = PP^T = I_N$, and $AB^T = 0$, can be stated compactly as

$$PV^m P^T = \delta_{m0} I_N$$

where $m = 0$ or 1, and

(a) If $m = 0$, then $\delta_{m0} = 1$
(b) If $m = 1$, then $\delta_{m0} = 0$

Therefore, if the above conditions are satisfied, then the matrix P is called a LOT matrix.

2. If P_0 is a LOT matrix, and Z is an orthogonal matrix, then $P = ZP_0$ is also a LOT matrix.   □

A Special LOT

Malvar constructed a special LOT matrix. This transform assumes that it is used for compressing data which can reasonably be modeled by $AR\,(1)$ processes with single-step correlation coefficient $\rho \simeq 1$. Malvar uses the DCT matrix C of size N. It is assumed in this subsection, that N is an even integer. Recall that the basis vectors of the DCT are the rows of the matrix C. Let

$$C = [c_{kl}]$$

$$c_k = \begin{bmatrix} c_{k0} & c_{k1} & \cdots & c_{k,N-1} \end{bmatrix}^T, \quad 0 \le k \le (N-1)$$

Therefore,

$$C^T = \begin{bmatrix} c_0 & c_1 & \cdots & c_{N-1} \end{bmatrix}$$

Malvar defined two matrices D_e and D_0, each of size $N/2 \times N$. These are defined as

$$D_e^T = \begin{bmatrix} c_0 & c_2 & \cdots & c_{N-2} \end{bmatrix}$$
$$D_o^T = \begin{bmatrix} c_1 & c_3 & \cdots & c_{N-1} \end{bmatrix}$$

A LOT matrix P_0 is defined in terms of the matrices $Q = (D_e - D_o)$, and J. The matrix J is a square matrix of size N. Its a diagonal matrix with all 1's on the north-east to south-west diagonal. All other elements in this matrix are 0's. This matrix is also called the *counter-identity matrix*. Note that the size of the matrix Q is $N/2 \times N$. The LOT matrix P_0 is defined as

$$P_0 = \frac{1}{2} \begin{bmatrix} Q & QJ \\ Q & -QJ \end{bmatrix}$$

Observe that the matrix P_0 is of size $N \times 2N$. It is shown in the problem section that $P_0 V^m P_0^T = \delta_{m0} I_N$, where $m = 0$ or 1, and I_N is an identity matrix of size N. This confirms that P_0 is indeed a LOT matrix.

It should be noted that the $N \times 2N$ LOT matrix P_0 may not be optimal (from the perspective of data compression). For example, consider a model covariance matrix C_X for the data of size $2N$. A possible candidate for the matrix C_X would be the covariance (or correlation) matrix of the $AR(1)$ process. Let it be $R_{2N} = [r_{ij}]$ where $r_{ij} = \rho^{|i-j|}$, $0 \le i, j \le (2N-1)$, and ρ is the single-step correlation coefficient of the data samples. Therefore, $P_0 C_X P_0^T \triangleq S_0$ may not be diagonal. Recall that the matrix S_0 should be diagonal for the coding gain C_{GAIN} of the transform to be maximum. In order to achieve this goal, consider the matrix

$$P = ZP_0$$

where Z is an orthogonal matrix. Note that P is also a LOT matrix via an earlier observation. The matrix Z is determined so that $PC_X P^T \triangleq S$ is a diagonal matrix. Thus

$$\begin{aligned} S = PC_X P^T &= ZP_0 C_X (ZP_0)^T \\ &= ZP_0 C_X P_0^T Z^T \\ &= ZS_0 Z^T \end{aligned}$$

Therefore, the matrix S is a diagonal matrix, if the rows of matrix Z are the eigenvectors of the matrix $S_0 = P_0 C_X P_0^T$. The matrix Z is usually determined via iterative computations. Malvar outlined a technique to determine the orthogonal matrix Z efficiently.

Problems

1. Prove that $tr\,(\Xi_Y) = tr\,(\Xi_X)$, where $\Xi_Y = A^{-1}\Xi_X A$.
   Hint: This result follows by using the properties of the trace of a square matrix.
   Let A and B be square matrices, then it is known that $tr\,(AB) = tr\,(BA)$.
   Therefore,

   $$tr\,(\Xi_Y) = tr\,(A^{-1}\Xi_X A) = tr\,(A^{-1}\,(\Xi_X A)) = tr\,((\Xi_X A)\,A^{-1}) = tr\,(\Xi_X)$$

2. Consider the autoregressive process $AR\,(1)$. It is $X = \{X_n \mid n \in \mathbb{Z}\}$ where

   $$X_n = \rho X_{n-1} + \xi_n + \eta$$

   Prove that
   (a) $\mathcal{E}\,(X_n) = \mu = \eta/\,(1-\rho)$, for each value of n.
   (b) $Var\,(X_n) = \sigma^2 = \sigma_\xi^2/\,(1-\rho^2)$ for each value of n.
   (c) Let $Cov\,(X_n, X_{n+k}) \triangleq \gamma_k$, then $\gamma_k = \sigma^2\rho^{|k|}$, for $k \in \mathbb{Z}$.
   Hint:
   (a) We have

   $$\mathcal{E}\,(X_n) = \rho\mathcal{E}\,(X_{n-1}) + \mathcal{E}\,(\xi_n) + \eta$$
   $$\mu = \rho\mu + \eta$$

   The result follows.
   (b) As ξ_n is independent of X_{n-1} we have

   $$Var\,(X_n) = Var\,(\rho X_{n-1}) + Var\,(\xi_n) + Var\,(\eta)$$
   $$\sigma^2 = \rho^2\sigma^2 + \sigma_\xi^2$$

   The result follows.
   (c) Using the expression

   $$X_n = \rho X_{n-1} + \xi_n + \eta$$

   we have

   $$(X_n - \mu) = \rho\,(X_{n-1} - \mu) + \xi_n + \eta - \mu\,(1-\rho)$$

   That is,

   $$(X_n - \mu) = \rho\,(X_{n-1} - \mu) + \xi_n$$

Multiply both sides of the above expression by $(X_{n-1} - \mu)$. This leads to

$$(X_n - \mu)(X_{n-1} - \mu) = \rho(X_{n-1} - \mu)^2 + \xi_n(X_{n-1} - \mu)$$

Take expectations on both sides of the above expression, and noting that ξ_n is independent of X_{n-1} we have

$$\gamma_1 = Cov(X_n, X_{n-1}) = \sigma^2 \rho$$

We also have

$$(X_{n-1} - \mu) = \rho(X_{n-2} - \mu) + \xi_{n-1}$$

Using the above expression for $(X_{n-1} - \mu)$ leads to

$$(X_n - \mu) = \rho(X_{n-1} - \mu) + \xi_n$$
$$(X_n - \mu) = \rho^2(X_{n-2} - \mu) + \rho\xi_{n-1} + \xi_n$$

Multiply both sides of the above expression by $(X_{n-2} - \mu)$. This leads to

$$(X_n - \mu)(X_{n-2} - \mu) = \rho^2(X_{n-2} - \mu)^2 + (\rho\xi_{n-1} + \xi_n)(X_{n-2} - \mu)$$

Take expectations on both sides of the above expression, and noting that ξ_{n-1} and ξ_n are each independent of X_{n-2}, and also of each other, we have

$$\gamma_2 = Cov(X_n, X_{n-2}) = \sigma^2 \rho^2$$

It can similarly be established that

$$\gamma_k = Cov(X_n, X_{n-k}) = \sigma^2 \rho^k, \quad \text{for } k \geq 0$$

Further $Cov(X_{n-k}, X_n) = Cov(X_n, X_{n-k}) \; \forall \; k, n \in \mathbb{Z}$. The result follows.

3. Let $C = [c_{kl}]$ be the DCT matrix. Prove that $CC^T = I$.
   Hint: Let

$$c_k = \begin{bmatrix} c_{k0} & c_{k1} & \cdots & c_{k,N-1} \end{bmatrix}^T$$
$$c_m = \begin{bmatrix} c_{m0} & c_{m1} & \cdots & c_{m,N-1} \end{bmatrix}^T$$

We have to show that $c_k^T c_m = \delta_{km}$, where $\delta_{km} = 1$ if $k = m$, and $\delta_{km} = 0$ otherwise; and $0 \leq k, m \leq (N-1)$. Observe that

$$\cos\left\{\left(l + \frac{1}{2}\right)\frac{k\pi}{N}\right\} = \frac{1}{2}\left[\exp\left\{i\left(l + \frac{1}{2}\right)\frac{k\pi}{N}\right\} + \exp\left\{-i\left(l + \frac{1}{2}\right)\frac{k\pi}{N}\right\}\right]$$

Let $a \triangleq \exp(ik\pi/N)$ and $b \triangleq \exp(im\pi/N)$. Therefore,

$$(ab)^N = \exp\{i(k + m)\pi\}, \quad \text{and} \quad (a/b)^N = \exp\{i(k - m)\pi\}$$

Thus

$$c_k^T c_m = \sum_{l=0}^{N-1} c_{kl} c_{ml}$$

$$= \frac{1}{4} \sigma_k \sigma_m \sum_{l=0}^{N-1} \left\{ a^{(l+1/2)} + a^{-(l+1/2)} \right\} \left\{ b^{(l+1/2)} + b^{-(l+1/2)} \right\}$$

$$= \frac{1}{4} \sigma_k \sigma_m \sum_{l=0}^{N-1} \left\{ (ab)^{(l+1/2)} + (ab)^{-(l+1/2)} + (a/b)^{(l+1/2)} + (a/b)^{-(l+1/2)} \right\}$$

Consider three cases.

Case (i): Let $k = m = 0$. Then $a = b = 1$. Thus

$$c_0^T c_0 = \frac{1}{4} \sigma_0^2 (4N) = 1$$

Case (ii): Let $k = m \neq 0$. Then

$$c_k^T c_k = \frac{1}{4} \sigma_k^2 \sum_{l=0}^{N-1} \left\{ a^{(2l+1)} + a^{-(2l+1)} + 2 \right\}$$

Observe that $a \neq 1$. Further

$$\sum_{l=0}^{N-1} a^{(2l+1)} = \frac{a \left(a^{2N} - 1 \right)}{(a^2 - 1)} = 0$$

$$\sum_{l=0}^{N-1} a^{-(2l+1)} = \frac{a^{-1} \left(a^{-2N} - 1 \right)}{(a^{-2} - 1)} = 0$$

Thus

$$c_k^T c_k = \frac{1}{4} \sigma_k^2 (2N) = 1$$

Case (iii): Let $k \neq m$, where $0 \leq k, m \leq (N - 1)$. This implies $a \neq b$. This in turn implies $a/b \neq 1$, and $b/a \neq 1$. Also if $a = 1$, then $b \neq 1$; and if $b = 1$, then $a \neq 1$. This implies that $ab \neq 1$. Let

$$S_1 = \sum_{l=0}^{N-1} (ab)^{(l+1/2)} = (ab)^{1/2} \frac{\left\{ (ab)^N - 1 \right\}}{\{ab - 1\}}$$

$$S_2 = \sum_{l=0}^{N-1} (ab)^{-(l+1/2)} = (ab)^{-1/2} \frac{\left\{ (ab)^{-N} - 1 \right\}}{\left\{ (ab)^{-1} - 1 \right\}} = \frac{S_1}{(ab)^N}$$

$$S_3 = \sum_{l=0}^{N-1} (a/b)^{(l+1/2)} = (a/b)^{1/2} \frac{\left\{(a/b)^N - 1\right\}}{\left\{(a/b) - 1\right\}}$$

$$S_4 = \sum_{l=0}^{N-1} (a/b)^{-(l+1/2)} = (a/b)^{-1/2} \frac{\left\{(a/b)^{-N} - 1\right\}}{\left\{(a/b)^{-1} - 1\right\}} = \frac{S_3}{(a/b)^N}$$

Four subcases occur for unequal k and m. These are:

Subcase (a): k and m are both even integers or zero. Then $(k + m)$ and $|k - m|$ are both even integers. This implies

$$S_1 = S_2 = S_3 = S_4 = 0 \Rightarrow c_k^T c_m = 0$$

Subcase (b): k and m are both odd integers. Then $(k + m)$ and $|k - m|$ are both even integers. This implies

$$S_1 = S_2 = S_3 = S_4 = 0 \Rightarrow c_k^T c_m = 0$$

Subcase (c): k is either an even integer or zero, and m is an odd integer. Then $(k + m)$ and $|k - m|$ are both odd integers. This implies

$$S_1 + S_2 = 0, \quad \text{and} \quad S_3 + S_4 = 0 \Rightarrow c_k^T c_m = 0$$

Subcase (d): k is an odd integer, and m is an even integer or zero. Then $(k + m)$ and $|k - m|$ are both odd integers. This implies

$$S_1 + S_2 = 0, \quad \text{and} \quad S_3 + S_4 = 0 \Rightarrow c_k^T c_m = 0$$

Thus $c_k^T c_m = 0$ in each of the four subcases.

4. Let C be the DCT matrix. Prove that $C^T C = I$.

   Hint: Let $C = [c_{kl}]$ and $C^T = [c_{lk}]$. We have to show that

$$\sum_{k=0}^{N-1} c_{kl} c_{km} = \delta_{lm}$$

where $\delta_{lm} = 1$ if $l = m$, and $\delta_{lm} = 0$ otherwise; and $0 \leq l, m \leq (N - 1)$. Observe that

$$\cos\left\{\left(l + \frac{1}{2}\right)\frac{k\pi}{N}\right\}$$

$$= \frac{1}{2}\left[\exp\left\{i\left(l + \frac{1}{2}\right)\frac{k\pi}{N}\right\} + \exp\left\{-i\left(l + \frac{1}{2}\right)\frac{k\pi}{N}\right\}\right]$$

$$\cos\left\{\left(m + \frac{1}{2}\right)\frac{k\pi}{N}\right\}$$

$$= \frac{1}{2}\left[\exp\left\{i\left(m + \frac{1}{2}\right)\frac{k\pi}{N}\right\} + \exp\left\{-i\left(m + \frac{1}{2}\right)\frac{k\pi}{N}\right\}\right]$$

We introduce the notation

$$g \triangleq \exp(i\,(l + 1/2)\,\pi/N), \quad \text{and} \quad h \triangleq \exp\left(i\,(m + 1/2)\,\pi/N\right)$$

Thus

$$(gh)^N = \exp\{i\,(l + m + 1)\,\pi\}, \quad \text{and} \quad (g/h)^N = \exp\{i\,(l - m)\,\pi\}$$

Therefore,

$$\cos\left\{\left(l + \frac{1}{2}\right)\frac{k\pi}{N}\right\} = \frac{1}{2}\left(g^k + g^{-k}\right)$$

$$\cos\left\{\left(m + \frac{1}{2}\right)\frac{k\pi}{N}\right\} = \frac{1}{2}\left(h^k + h^{-k}\right)$$

Thus

$$\sum_{k=0}^{N-1} c_{kl} c_{km} = \frac{1}{4}\sum_{k=0}^{N-1} \sigma_k^2 \left(g^k + g^{-k}\right)\left(h^k + h^{-k}\right)$$

$$= \frac{1}{4}\sum_{k=0}^{N-1} \sigma_k^2 \left\{(gh)^k + (gh)^{-k} + (g/h)^k + (g/h)^{-k}\right\}$$

$$\triangleq \frac{1}{4}\left(T_1 + T_2 + T_3 + T_4\right)$$

where

$$T_1 = \sum_{k=0}^{N-1} \sigma_k^2 \,(gh)^k, \quad T_2 = \sum_{k=0}^{N-1} \sigma_k^2 \,(gh)^{-k},$$

$$T_3 = \sum_{k=0}^{N-1} \sigma_k^2 \,(g/h)^k, \quad T_4 = \sum_{k=0}^{N-1} \sigma_k^2 \,(g/h)^{-k}$$

Simplification of T_1, where $gh \neq 1$:

$$T_1 = \sum_{k=0}^{N-1} \sigma_k^2 \,(gh)^k = \frac{1}{N} + \frac{2}{N}\sum_{k=1}^{N-1} (gh)^k = -\frac{1}{N} + \frac{2}{N}\frac{\left\{(gh)^N - 1\right\}}{\{gh - 1\}}$$

$$= -\frac{1}{N} + \frac{2}{N}\frac{\left\{\exp\{i\,(l + m + 1)\,\pi\} - 1\right\}}{\{gh - 1\}}$$

Simplification of T_2, where $gh \neq 1$:

$$T_2 = \sum_{k=0}^{N-1} \sigma_k^2 \,(gh)^{-k} = \frac{1}{N} + \frac{2}{N}\sum_{k=1}^{N-1} (gh)^{-k} = -\frac{1}{N} + \frac{2}{N}\frac{\left\{(gh)^{-N} - 1\right\}}{\left\{(gh)^{-1} - 1\right\}}$$

$$= -\frac{1}{N} + \frac{2}{N}\frac{gh}{\{1 - gh\}}\left\{\exp\{-i\,(l + m + 1)\,\pi\} - 1\right\}$$

Simplification of T_3, where $g \neq h$:

$$T_3 = \sum_{k=0}^{N-1} \sigma_k^2 \, (g/h)^k = \frac{1}{N} + \frac{2}{N} \sum_{k=1}^{N-1} (g/h)^k = -\frac{1}{N} + \frac{2}{N} \frac{\left\{ (g/h)^N - 1 \right\}}{\{g/h - 1\}}$$

$$= -\frac{1}{N} + \frac{2}{N} \frac{\{\exp\{i\,(l - m)\,\pi\} - 1\}}{\{(g/h) - 1\}}$$

Simplification of T_4, where $h \neq g$:

$$T_4 = \sum_{k=0}^{N-1} \sigma_k^2 \, (h/g)^k = \frac{1}{N} + \frac{2}{N} \sum_{k=1}^{N-1} (h/g)^k = -\frac{1}{N} + \frac{2}{N} \frac{\left\{ (h/g)^N - 1 \right\}}{\{(h/g) - 1\}}$$

$$= -\frac{1}{N} + \frac{2}{N} \frac{\{\exp\{i\,(m - l)\,\pi\} - 1\}}{\{(h/g) - 1\}}$$

We consider two cases.

Case (i): Let $l = m$. Thus $g = h = \exp\left(i \,(l + 1/2)\, \pi/N \right)$. This leads to

$$T_1 = -\frac{1}{N} + \frac{2}{N} \frac{\{\exp\{i\pi\} - 1\}}{\{gh - 1\}} = -\frac{1}{N} - \frac{4}{N} \frac{1}{\{gh - 1\}}$$

$$T_2 = -\frac{1}{N} + \frac{2}{N} \frac{gh}{\{1 - gh\}} \{\exp\{-i\pi\} - 1\} = -\frac{1}{N} - \frac{4}{N} \frac{gh}{\{1 - gh\}}$$

Consequently

$$T_1 + T_2 = \frac{2}{N}$$

Also

$$T_3 = T_4 = \sum_{k=0}^{N-1} \sigma_k^2 = \frac{1}{N} + \frac{2\,(N - 1)}{N} = \frac{(2N - 1)}{N}$$

Therefore,

$$\sum_{k=0}^{N-1} c_{kl} c_{kl} = \frac{1}{4} \left(T_1 + T_2 + T_3 + T_4 \right) = 1$$

Case (ii): Let $l \neq m$. Four subcases occur. These are:

Subcase (a): l and m are both either even integers or zeros. Then $(l + m)$ and $|l - m|$ are both even integers. Therefore,

$$T_1 = -\frac{1}{N} - \frac{4}{N\,\{gh - 1\}}$$

$$T_2 = -\frac{1}{N} - \frac{4}{N} \frac{gh}{\{1 - gh\}}$$

Consequently

$$T_1 + T_2 = \frac{2}{N}$$

Also
$$T_3 = T_4 = -\frac{1}{N}$$

Therefore,
$$\sum_{k=0}^{N-1} c_{kl}c_{km} = \frac{1}{4}(T_1 + T_2 + T_3 + T_4) = 0$$

Subcase (b): l and m are both odd integers. Then $(l+m)$ and $|l-m|$ are both even integers. This subcase is like Subcase (a). Therefore, $\sum_{k=0}^{N-1} c_{kl}c_{km} = 0$.

Subcase (c): l is either an even integer or zero, and m is an odd integer. Then $(l+m)$ and $|l-m|$ are both odd integers. Therefore,
$$T_1 = T_2 = -\frac{1}{N}$$

Consequently
$$T_1 + T_2 = -\frac{2}{N}$$

Also
$$T_3 = -\frac{1}{N} - \frac{4}{N\{(g/h) - 1\}}$$
$$T_4 = -\frac{1}{N} - \frac{4}{N\{(h/g) - 1\}}$$

Consequently
$$T_3 + T_4 = \frac{2}{N}$$

Therefore,
$$\sum_{k=0}^{N-1} c_{kl}c_{km} = \frac{1}{4}(T_1 + T_2 + T_3 + T_4) = 0$$

Subcase (d): l is an odd integer, and m is either an even integer or zero. Then $(l+m)$ and $|l-m|$ are both odd integers. This subcase is similar to Subcase (c).

Therefore, the Subcases (a), (b), (c), and (d) each yield $\sum_{k=0}^{N-1} c_{kl}c_{km} = 0$.

Finally, the Cases (i) and (ii) together imply $\sum_{k=0}^{N-1} c_{kl}c_{km} = \delta_{lm}$.

5. Justify Method 2 of the computation of the DCT.
   Hint: For $0 \le k \le (2N - 1)$

$$\widehat{F}_k = \frac{1}{\sqrt{2N}} \sum_{l=0}^{2N-1} \widehat{f}_l \omega_{2N}^{lk}$$

$$= \frac{1}{\sqrt{2N}} \sum_{l=0}^{N-1} \widehat{f}_l \omega_{2N}^{lk} + \frac{1}{\sqrt{2N}} \sum_{l=N}^{2N-1} \widehat{f}_l \omega_{2N}^{lk}$$

$$= \frac{1}{\sqrt{2N}} \sum_{l=0}^{N-1} f_l \omega_{2N}^{lk} + \frac{1}{\sqrt{2N}} \sum_{l=N}^{2N-1} f_{2N-1-l} \omega_{2N}^{lk}$$

$$= \frac{1}{\sqrt{2N}} \sum_{l=0}^{N-1} f_l \omega_{2N}^{lk} + \frac{1}{\sqrt{2N}} \sum_{j=0}^{N-1} f_j \omega_{2N}^{-(j+1)k}$$

$$= \frac{1}{\sqrt{2N}} \omega_{2N}^{-k/2} \sum_{l=0}^{N-1} f_l \left\{ \omega_{2N}^{k(l+1/2)} + \omega_{2N}^{-k(l+1/2)} \right\}$$

$$= \frac{2}{\sqrt{2N}} \omega_{2N}^{-k/2} \sum_{l=0}^{N-1} f_l \cos \left\{ \left(l + \frac{1}{2} \right) k \frac{2\pi}{2N} \right\}$$

$$= \sqrt{\frac{2}{N}} \omega_{2N}^{-k/2} \frac{F_k}{\sigma_k}$$

Therefore,

$$F_k = \sigma_k \sqrt{\frac{N}{2}} \omega_{2N}^{k/2} \widehat{F}_k, \quad 0 \le k \le (N-1)$$

6. Verify that the eigenvalue and eigenvector pairs of the matrix A_N are (λ_k, c_k), where $\lambda_k = 2 (1 - \cos (k\pi/N))$, c_k is a basis vector in the DCT for $0 \le k \le (N-1)$, and $N \ge 3$. The matrix A_N is defined in the section on the DCT. Hint: For $N \ge 3$, we need to verify that $A_N c_k = \lambda_k c_k$, for $0 \le k \le (N-1)$. Recall that

$$c_k = \begin{bmatrix} c_{k0} \ c_{k1} & \cdots & c_{k,N-1} \end{bmatrix}^T, \quad \text{for } 0 \le k \le (N-1)$$

$$c_{kl} = \sigma_k \cos \left\{ \left(l + \frac{1}{2} \right) \frac{k\pi}{N} \right\}, \quad \text{for } 0 \le l \le (N-1)$$

$$\sigma_0 = \frac{1}{\sqrt{N}}, \quad \text{and} \quad \sigma_k = \sqrt{\frac{2}{N}}, \quad \text{for } 1 \le k \le (N-1)$$

In these verifications the following trigonometric identities are used

$$\cos a + \cos b = 2 \cos \left(\frac{a+b}{2} \right) \cos \left(\frac{a-b}{2} \right)$$

$$\cos (a + b) = \cos a \cos b - \sin a \sin b$$

We consider the following cases:

Case (i): It needs to be checked that

$$A_N c_0 = \lambda_0 c_0$$

Note that $\lambda_0 = 0$, and c_0 is a column vector whose elements are each equal to σ_0. The result follows.

Case (ii): It needs to be checked that

$$A_N c_k = \lambda_k c_k, \ \lambda_k = 2(1 - \cos (k\pi/N)), \quad \text{for } 1 \le k \le (N-1)$$

Consider the following subcases.

Subcase (a): It needs to be checked that

$$c_{k0} - c_{k1} = \lambda_k c_{k0} = 2 \left(1 - \cos\left(k\pi/N\right)\right) c_{k0}$$

That is, it needs to be checked that

$$c_{k0} + c_{k1} = 2c_{k0} \cos\left(k\pi/N\right)$$

This is verifiable via the first trigonometric identity.

Subcase (b): It needs to be checked that

$$-c_{k,(l-1)} + 2c_{kl} - c_{k,(l+1)}$$
$$= \lambda_k c_{kl}$$
$$= 2 \left(1 - \cos\left(k\pi/N\right)\right) c_{kl}, \quad 1 \leq l \leq (N-2)$$

That is, it needs to be checked that

$$c_{k,(l-1)} + c_{k,(l+1)} = 2c_{kl} \cos(k\pi/N), \quad 1 \leq l \leq (N-2)$$

This is also verifiable via the first trigonometric identity.

Subcase (c): It needs to be checked that

$$-c_{k,(N-2)} + c_{k,(N-1)} = \lambda_k c_{k,(N-1)} = 2 \left(1 - \cos\left(k\pi/N\right)\right) c_{k,(N-1)}$$

That is, it needs to be checked that

$$c_{k,(N-2)} + c_{k,(N-1)} = 2c_{k,(N-1)} \cos\left(k\pi/N\right)$$

This is also verifiable via the two trigonometric identities.
The result follows.

7. Verify that the eigenvalue and eigenvector pairs of the matrix B_N are (λ_k, c_k), where $\lambda_k = (1 - 2\alpha \cos\left(k\pi/N\right))$, c_k is a basis vector in the DCT for $0 \leq k \leq (N-1)$, and $N \geq 2$. The matrix B_N is defined in the section on $AR(1)$ process.

Hint: The result can easily be checked for matrix B_2. We next concentrate on matrix B_N, where $N \geq 3$. We need to verify that $B_N c_k = \lambda_k c_k$, for $0 \leq k \leq (N-1)$. Recall that

$$c_k = \begin{bmatrix} c_{k0} & c_{k1} & \cdots & c_{k,N-1} \end{bmatrix}^T, \quad \text{for } 0 \leq k \leq (N-1)$$
$$c_{kl} = \sigma_k \cos\left\{\left(l + \frac{1}{2}\right)\frac{k\pi}{N}\right\},$$
$$\sigma_0 = \frac{1}{\sqrt{N}}, \quad \text{and } \sigma_k = \sqrt{\frac{2}{N}}, \quad \text{for } 1 \leq k \leq (N-1)$$

In these verifications the following trigonometric identities are used

$$\cos a + \cos b = 2 \cos \left(\frac{a+b}{2}\right) \cos \left(\frac{a-b}{2}\right)$$

$$\cos (a + b) = \cos a \cos b - \sin a \sin b$$

We consider the following cases:
Case (i): It needs to be checked that

$$B_N c_0 = \lambda_0 c_0$$

Note that $\lambda_0 = (1 - 2\alpha)$, and c_0 is a column vector whose elements are each equal to σ_0. The result follows.
Case (ii): It needs to be checked that

$$B_N c_k = \lambda_k c_k, \quad \lambda_k = (1 - 2\alpha \cos(k\pi/N)), \quad \text{for } 1 \le k \le (N-1)$$

Consider the following subcases.
Subcase (a): It needs to be checked that

$$(1 - \alpha) c_{k0} - \alpha c_{k1} = \lambda_k c_{k0} = (1 - 2\alpha \cos(k\pi/N)) c_{k0}$$

That is, it needs to be checked that

$$c_{k0} + c_{k1} = 2 c_{k0} \cos(k\pi/N)$$

This is verifiable via the first trigonometric identity.
Subcase (b): It needs to be checked that

$$-\alpha c_{k,(l-1)} + c_{kl} - \alpha c_{k,(l+1)}$$
$$= \lambda_k c_{kl}$$
$$= (1 - 2\alpha \cos(k\pi/N)) c_{kl}, \quad 1 \le l \le (N-2)$$

That is, it needs to be checked that

$$c_{k,(l-1)} + c_{k,(l+1)} = 2 c_{kl} \cos(k\pi/N), \quad 1 \le l \le (N-2)$$

This is also verifiable via the first trigonometric identity.
Subcase (c): It needs to be checked that

$$-\alpha c_{k,(N-2)} + (1 - \alpha) c_{k,(N-1)}$$
$$= \lambda_k c_{k,(N-1)}$$
$$= (1 - 2\alpha \cos(k\pi/N)) c_{k,(N-1)}$$

That is, it needs to be checked that

$$c_{k,(N-2)} + c_{k,(N-1)} = 2 c_{k,(N-1)} \cos(k\pi/N)$$

This is also verifiable via the two trigonometric identities.
The result follows.

8. Let D_N be an all-1 matrix of size N. Show that the characteristic polynomial of:

(a) Matrix D_2 is $\lambda(\lambda - 2)$.
(b) Matrix D_3 is $\lambda^2(\lambda - 3)$.
(c) Matrix D_4 is $\lambda^3(\lambda - 4)$.
(d) Matrix D_N is $\lambda^{N-1}(\lambda - N)$.

9. Verify that the eigenvalue and eigenvector pairs of the matrix D_N are (λ_k, c_k), where $0 \leq k \leq (N-1)$ and $N \geq 2$. Also, $\lambda_0 = N$, and its corresponding eigenvector is c_0. Further, if $\lambda_k = 0$, then c_k is the corresponding eigenvector for $1 \leq k \leq (N-1)$.

Hint: We need to verify that $D_N c_k = \lambda_k c_k$, for $0 \leq k \leq (N-1)$. Recall that

$$c_k = \begin{bmatrix} c_{k0} & c_{k1} & \cdots & c_{k,N-1} \end{bmatrix}^T, \qquad 0 \leq k \leq (N-1)$$

$$c_{kl} = \sigma_k \cos\left\{\left(l + \frac{1}{2}\right)\frac{k\pi}{N}\right\},$$

$$\sigma_0 = \frac{1}{\sqrt{N}}, \quad \text{and } \sigma_k = \sqrt{\frac{2}{N}}, \quad \text{for } 1 \leq k \leq (N-1)$$

In these verifications the following trigonometric identity is used

$$\cos a + \cos b = 2 \cos\left(\frac{a+b}{2}\right) \cos\left(\frac{a-b}{2}\right)$$

We consider the following cases:

Case (i): It needs to be checked that

$$D_N c_0 = \lambda_0 c_0$$

Note that $\lambda_0 = N$, and c_0 is a column vector whose elements are each equal to σ_0. The result follows.

Case (ii): It needs to be checked that

$$D_N c_k = \lambda_k c_k, \quad \lambda_k = 0, \quad \text{for } 1 \leq k \leq (N-1)$$

This statement is true if

$$S_k = \sum_{l=0}^{N-1} c_{kl} = 0, \quad \text{for } 1 \leq k \leq (N-1)$$

Observe that

$$S_k = \sum_{l=0}^{N-1} c_{kl} = \sigma_k \sum_{l=0}^{N-1} \cos\left\{\left(l + \frac{1}{2}\right)\frac{k\pi}{N}\right\}$$

and

$$\left(l+\frac{1}{2}\right)\frac{k\pi}{N} = (2l+1)\frac{k\pi}{2N} = \frac{2\pi}{4N}k\,(2l+1)$$

Therefore, letting

$$\omega_{4N} = \exp\left(\frac{2\pi i}{4N}\right)$$

$$\cos\left\{\left(l+\frac{1}{2}\right)\frac{k\pi}{N}\right\} = \frac{1}{2}\left\{\omega_{4N}^{k(2l+1)} + \omega_{4N}^{-k(2l+1)}\right\}$$

For simplicity in notation, let

$$\omega_{4N}^{k} \triangleq a$$

Therefore,

$$\cos\left\{\left(l+\frac{1}{2}\right)\frac{k\pi}{N}\right\} = \frac{1}{2}\left\{a^{(2l+1)} + a^{-(2l+1)}\right\}$$

and

$$S_k = \frac{\sigma_k}{2}\sum_{l=0}^{N-1}\left\{a^{(2l+1)} + a^{-(2l+1)}\right\}$$

Note that

$$S_k^+ \triangleq \sum_{l=0}^{N-1} a^{(2l+1)} = \frac{a\left(1-a^{2N}\right)}{(1-a^2)}$$

$$S_k^- \triangleq \sum_{l=0}^{N-1} a^{-(2l+1)} = \frac{a^{-1}\left(1-a^{-2N}\right)}{(1-a^{-2})} = \frac{S_k^+}{a^{2N}}$$

Therefore,

$$S_k^+ + S_k^- = S_k^+\left\{1+\frac{1}{a^{2N}}\right\} = \frac{a\left(1-a^{4N}\right)}{a^{2N}\left(1-a^2\right)}$$

As $a^{4N} = 1$, we have

$$S_k = \frac{\sigma_k}{2}\left\{S_k^+ + S_k^-\right\} = 0$$

Finally

$$S_k = \sum_{l=0}^{N-1} c_{kl} = 0, \qquad 1 \le k \le (N-1)$$

as required.

10. Malvar describes an efficient algorithm for the construction of a LOT matrix P_0. It is required to prove that $P_0 V^m P_0^T = \delta_{m0} I_N$, where I_N is an identity matrix of size N. Also, if $m = 0$ then $\delta_{m0} = 1$, and if $m = 1$ then $\delta_{m0} = 0$.
Hint: We have

$$P_0 = \frac{1}{2}\begin{bmatrix} Q & QJ \\ Q & -QJ \end{bmatrix}$$

where $Q = (D_e - D_o)$, and J is a counter-identity matrix of size N. In order to prove the stated result, it needs to be established that

(a) $P_0 P_0^T = I_N$

(b) If

$$A = \frac{1}{2}\begin{bmatrix} Q \\ Q \end{bmatrix} \quad \text{and} \quad B = \frac{1}{2}\begin{bmatrix} QJ \\ -QJ \end{bmatrix}$$

Then $AB^T = 0$.

The stated results are established in several steps.

Step 1: In this step, it is shown that $QQ^T = 2I_{N/2}$.

$$QQ^T = (D_e - D_o)(D_e - D_o)^T$$
$$= D_e D_e^T - D_e D_o^T - D_o D_e^T + D_o D_o^T$$
$$= I_{N/2} - 0 - 0 + I_{N/2} = 2I_{N/2}$$

Step 2: The matrix P_0 can be expressed as

$$P_0 = \frac{1}{2}UV$$

where

$$U = \begin{bmatrix} Q & 0 \\ 0 & Q \end{bmatrix} \quad \text{and} \quad V = \begin{bmatrix} I_N & J \\ I_N & -J \end{bmatrix}$$

Therefore, $UU^T = 2I_N$. Note that $J^T = J$, and $JJ^T = J^T J = J^2 = I_N$. Consequently $VV^T = 2I_{2N}$.

Step 3: We have

$$P_0 P_0^T = \frac{1}{4}(UV)(UV)^T = \frac{1}{4}UVV^T U^T$$
$$= \frac{1}{4}U(2I_{2N})U^T = \frac{1}{2}UU^T = I_N$$

This proves part (a) of the requirement.

Step 4: Consider the following substeps.

Substep (*a*): We have

$$AB^T = \frac{1}{4}\begin{bmatrix} Q \\ Q \end{bmatrix}\begin{bmatrix} QJ \\ -QJ \end{bmatrix}^T = \frac{1}{4}\begin{bmatrix} Q \\ Q \end{bmatrix}\left[(QJ)^T \quad -(QJ)^T \right]$$
$$= \frac{1}{4}\begin{bmatrix} S & -S \\ S & -S \end{bmatrix}$$

where $S = Q(QJ)^T$.

Substep (*b*): It can be established that

$$c_{kl} = (-1)^k c_{k,N-1-l}, \quad \text{for } 0 \le k, l \le (N-1)$$

where c_{kl} is an element of the DCT matrix C.

Substep (c): If W is a row vector of size N, then WJ is also a row vector, in which the order of the elements (of row W) is reversed.

Substep (d): Note that the matrix D_e has the zeroth and even numbered rows, and the matrix D_o has the odd numbered rows of the DCT matrix C. Therefore, use of results from Substeps (b) and (c) lead to

$$D_e J = D_e, \text{ and } D_o J = -D_o$$

Thus

$$QJ = (D_e - D_o) J = D_e + D_o$$

Substep (*e*): Therefore,

$$\begin{aligned} S = Q(QJ)^T &= (D_e - D_o)(D_e + D_o)^T \\ &= D_e D_e^T + D_e D_o^T - D_o D_e^T - D_o D_o^T \\ &= I_{N/2} + 0 - 0 - I_{N/2} = 0 \end{aligned}$$

Thus $S = 0$, and $AB^T = 0$. This proves part (b) of the requirement.

PART III

Signal Processing

CHAPTER 13

Discrete Fourier Transform

13.1 Introduction

The discrete Fourier transform (DFT) is an important tool in the study of signals. It is an alternate representation of a periodic sequence of discrete set of points by finite sums of weighted trigonometric (sine and cosine) functions. Techniques for the fast computation of the DFT are called fast Fourier transforms (FFTs). These techniques are also described in this chapter.

Elements of the DFT are initially provided. This is followed by a description of a novel technique to compute the DFT via Ramanujan numbers. These numbers help in computing the DFT of a sequence of numbers via only shift and addition (and subtraction) operations; and a very small number of division operations.

13.2 Elements of the DFT

Basics of the DFT are provided in this section. Important properties of the DFT are also listed. This is followed by a description of efficient techniques to compute the DFT. The Cooley–Tukey and the coprime-factorization FFT algorithms are also outlined.

Definition 13.1. *Discrete Fourier transform.*
Let $N \in \mathbb{P}$, $\pi = 3.1415926535897\ldots$, $\omega_N = e^{2\pi i/N}$, and $i = \sqrt{-1}$. The discrete Fourier transform of the sequence of complex numbers

$$\{y(0), y(1), \ldots, y(N-1)\} \tag{13.1a}$$

is a sequence of complex numbers

$$\{Y(0), Y(1), \ldots, Y(N-1)\} \tag{13.1b}$$

where

$$Y(m) = \frac{1}{\sqrt{N}} \sum_{n=0}^{(N-1)} y(n)\,\omega_N^{mn}, \quad \forall\, m \in \mathbb{Z}_N \tag{13.1c}$$

and $\mathbb{Z}_N = \{0, 1, 2, \ldots, N-1\}$.   □

In the above definition, the arguments of $y(\cdot)$ and $Y(\cdot)$ are computed modulo N.

Observation 13.1. The inverse of the DFT is

$$y(n) = \frac{1}{\sqrt{N}} \sum_{m=0}^{(N-1)} Y(m) \, w_N^{-mn}, \quad \forall n \in \mathbb{Z}_N \qquad (13.2)$$

□

The DFT and its inverse are also sometimes denoted by $\Im_N [y(n)] \triangleq Y(m)$, and $\Im_N^{-1} [Y(m)] \triangleq y(n)$ respectively. Some elementary properties of the DFT are summarized below.

13.2.1 Properties of the DFT

Let $N \in \mathbb{P}, \alpha_1, \alpha_2 \in \mathbb{C}$, and

$$\Im_N [y(n)] = Y(m), \quad \Im_N [y_1(n)] = Y_1(m), \quad \Im_N [y_2(n)] = Y_2(m)$$

1. Periodicity: $Y(m) = Y(m+N)$
2. Linearity: $\Im_N [\alpha_1 y_1(n) + \alpha_2 y_2(n)] = \alpha_1 Y_1(m) + \alpha_2 Y_2(m)$
3. Time reversal: $\Im_N [y(-n)] = Y(-m)$
4. Conjugate function: $\Im_N \left[\overline{y(n)} \right] = \overline{Y(-m)}$
5. Symmetry or duality: $\Im_N [Y(n)] = y(-m)$
6. Time shift: $\Im_N [y(n - n_0)] = w_N^{mn_0} Y(m), \quad \forall n_0 \in \mathbb{Z}$
7. Frequency shift: $\Im_N \left[w_N^{nk} y(n) \right] = Y(m+k), \quad \forall k \in \mathbb{Z}$
8. Circular convolution: Let

$$\{x(0), x(1), \ldots, x(N-1)\} \quad \text{and} \quad \{y(0), y(1), \ldots, y(N-1)\}$$

be two periodic complex sequences of period N each. The circular convolution of these two sequences is a periodic sequence of period N. Let this convolved sequence be $\{w(0), w(1), \ldots, w(N-1)\}$, where

$$w(n) = \sum_{k=0}^{(N-1)} x(k) y(n-k), \quad \forall n \in \mathbb{Z}_N$$

In the above equation, $(n-k)$ is computed modulo N. Therefore, this convolution is circular. It can be shown that if $\Im_N [x(n)] = X(m), \Im_N [y(n)] = Y(m)$, and $\Im_N [w(n)] = W(m)$ then

$$W(m) = \sqrt{N} X(m) Y(m), \quad \forall m \in \mathbb{Z}_N$$

Similarly the discrete Fourier transform of the sequence $x(n) y(n)$, $n \in \mathbb{Z}_N$ is the sequence

$$\frac{1}{\sqrt{N}} \sum_{k=0}^{(N-1)} X(k) Y(m-k), \quad m \in \mathbb{Z}_N$$

9. Parseval's relationships:

$$\sum_{k=0}^{(N-1)} x(k) \overline{y(k)} = \sum_{k=0}^{(N-1)} \overline{y(k)} \frac{1}{\sqrt{N}} \sum_{j=0}^{(N-1)} X(j) \omega_N^{-jk}$$

$$= \frac{1}{\sqrt{N}} \sum_{j=0}^{(N-1)} X(j) \sum_{k=0}^{(N-1)} \overline{y(k)} \omega_N^{-jk}$$

Thus

$$\sum_{k=0}^{(N-1)} x(k) \overline{y(k)} = \sum_{j=0}^{(N-1)} X(j) \overline{Y(j)}$$

Therefore,

$$\sum_{k=0}^{(N-1)} |x(k)|^2 = \sum_{j=0}^{(N-1)} |X(j)|^2$$

□

13.2.2 Computation of the DFT

Note that a direct computation of the DFT of the complex sequence

$$\{y(0), y(1), \ldots, y(N-1)\} \triangleq \{y(n) \mid y(n) \in \mathbb{C}, \; n \in \mathbb{Z}_N\}$$

requires up to N^2 complex multiplication and addition operations. Thus the computational complexity of a direct computation of DFT of a size-N sequence is $\Theta(N^2)$ operations.

Computationally efficient algorithms to compute DFT algorithms are called fast Fourier transforms (FFTs). It is assumed in these algorithms, that it is more expensive to perform multiplication, than either an addition or subtraction operation. Two computationally efficient algorithms to compute the DFT are outlined below. These are:

(a) A fast Fourier transform algorithm originally due to the celebrated German mathematician J. C. F. Gauss, and later rediscovered independently by James W. Cooley (1926–2016) and John W. Tukey (1915–2000); and others. Cooley and Tukey developed an efficient computerized algorithm to implement the discrete Fourier transform.

(b) A prime factor fast Fourier transform algorithm, which uses the number-theoretic Chinese remainder theorem.

These families of FFT algorithms are generally regarded as some of the most influential algorithms developed in the last century.

Cooley–Tukey FFT Algorithm

The Cooley-Tukey FFT algorithm achieves reduction in the number of computations by using the principle of divide and conquer. The origin of the FFT algorithm is first given. Let $N = 2D$, and split the sequence

$$\{y(n) \mid y(n) \in \mathbb{C}, n = 0, 1, \ldots, (N - 1)\}$$

into two sequences:

$$\{p(n) \mid p(n) = y(2n), n = 0, 1, \ldots, (D - 1)\}$$
$$\{q(n) \mid q(n) = y(2n + 1), n = 0, 1, \ldots, (D - 1)\}$$

These are the sequences with even and odd indices respectively. Let $\Im_D[p(n)] = P(m), \Im_D[q(n)] = Q(m)$, then

$$\omega_N^{2km} = \omega_D^{km}$$
$$\omega_N^{(2k+1)m} = \omega_D^{km}\omega_N^m$$

Consequently

$$Y(m) = P(m) + \omega_N^m Q(m), \quad 0 \le m \le (N - 1)$$

Note that in the computation of $Y(m)$'s, $P(m)$ and $Q(m)$ are each periodic in m with period D. Also we have

$$P(m + D) = P(m), \quad \forall m \in \mathbb{Z}_D$$
$$Q(m + D) = Q(m), \quad \forall m \in \mathbb{Z}_D$$
$$\omega_N^{D+m} = -\omega_N^m, \quad \forall m \in \mathbb{Z}_D$$

The transform coefficients $Y(m)$ for $0 \le m \le (N - 1)$ can be expressed as

$$Y(m) = P(m) + \omega_N^m Q(m), \quad \forall m \in \mathbb{Z}_D$$
$$Y(m + D) = P(m) - \omega_N^m Q(m), \quad \forall m \in \mathbb{Z}_D$$

Observe that the computation of $P(m)$ and $Q(m)$, $\forall m \in \mathbb{Z}_D$, each requires $(D - 1)^2$ multiplications. The computation of $Y(m)$'s after this splitting requires $2(D - 1)^2 + (D - 1)$ multiplication operations, while a direct computation requires

$(2D - 1)^2$ such operations. Consequently there is a reduction in the multiplicative complexity, approximately by a factor of two. Let the complexity of computing DFT of size N be $C(N)$. Therefore, if such splitting operations are used, then $C(N) \sim 2C(N/2) + N/2$, and $C(2) = 1$.

Let $N = 2^K$, and successively use the splitting operation to compute $P(m)$'s and $Q(m)$'s, and so on. It can then be shown that $C(N) \sim NK/2$. Therefore, the computational complexity of the Cooley-Tukey FFT algorithm is $\Theta(N \log N)$.

Coprime-Factorization FFT Algorithm

A fast algorithm to compute DFT can be obtained by factorizing N into its coprime factors. This FFT algorithm is based upon the Chinese remainder theorem. The Chinese remainder theorem is discussed in the chapter on set and number theory. Let

$$N = \prod_{k=1}^{K} N_k, \quad \text{where } N_k \in \mathbb{P}, \ 1 \le k \le K$$

and $\gcd(N_k, N_j) = 1, \ k \ne j, \ 1 \le k, j \le K$. That is, the factors N_k's are relatively prime in pairs. Define

$$P_k = \frac{N}{N_k}, \quad 1 \le k \le K$$

Also let $Q_1, Q_2, \dots, Q_K \in \mathbb{P}$ such that

$$(P_k Q_k) \equiv 1 (\text{mod } N_k), \quad 1 \le k \le K$$

Let $n \equiv n_k \ (\text{mod } N_k), \ 1 \le k \le K$, where $n \in \mathbb{P}$, then $n \ (\text{mod } N)$ is mapped into $(n_1, n_2, \dots, n_K)$. This is called Map-1 mapping. That is,

$$n \ (\text{mod } N) \rightarrow (n_1, n_2, \dots, n_K), \quad 0 \le n \le (N-1)$$

$$n \equiv \sum_{k=1}^{K} n_k P_k Q_k \ (\text{mod } N)$$

Let $\eta_k \equiv n_k Q_k \ (\text{mod } N_k), \ 1 \le k \le K$, then $n \ (\text{mod } N)$ is mapped into $(\eta_1, \eta_2, \dots, \eta_K)$. This is called Map-2 mapping. That is,

$$n \ (\text{mod } N) \rightarrow (\eta_1, \eta_2, \dots, \eta_K), \quad 0 \le n \le (N-1)$$

$$n \equiv \sum_{k=1}^{K} \eta_k P_k \ (\text{mod } N)$$

Observe that in the definition of the DFT, the data and frequency elements are indexed by n and m respectively, where $0 \le m, n \le (N-1)$. The maps for the frequency indexing variable are as follows. If $m \equiv m_k \ (\text{mod } N_k), 1 \le k \le K$, then $m \ (\text{mod } N)$ is mapped into $(m_1, m_2, \dots, m_K)$. This is Map-1 mapping. Thus

$$m \ (\mathrm{mod}\, N) \rightarrow (m_1, m_2, \ldots, m_K), \quad 0 \le m \le (N-1)$$

$$m \equiv \sum_{k=1}^{K} m_k P_k Q_k \ (\mathrm{mod}\, N)$$

Let $\mu_k \equiv m_k Q_k \ (\mathrm{mod}\, N_k)$, $1 \le k \le K$, then $m \ (\mathrm{mod}\, N)$ is mapped into $(\mu_1, \mu_2, \ldots, \mu_K)$. This is Map-2 mapping. Thus

$$m \ (\mathrm{mod}\, N) \rightarrow (\mu_1, \mu_2, \ldots, \mu_K), \quad 0 \le m \le (N-1)$$

$$m \equiv \sum_{k=1}^{K} \mu_k P_k \ (\mathrm{mod}\, N)$$

These maps would result in four different implementations of DFT computation. These are:

(a) Indexing variables m and n are both mapped as per Map-1.

(b) Indexing variable m is mapped as Map-1, and indexing variable n is mapped as Map-2.

(c) Indexing variable m is mapped as Map-2, and indexing variable n is mapped as Map-1.

(d) Indexing variables m and n are both mapped as per Map-2.

The above four implementations are conceptually similar. Therefore, only the coprime-factorization algorithm for a fast implementation of the DFT via scheme number (b) is demonstrated. In this scheme the indexing variables m are mapped as per Map-1, and indexing variable n are mapped as per Map-2. Then for $0 \le m, n \le (N-1)$

$$(mn) \ (\mathrm{mod}\, N) \equiv \left\{ \sum_{k=1}^{K} m_k \eta_k P_k^2 Q_k \right\} \ (\mathrm{mod}\, N)$$

$$\equiv \left\{ \sum_{k=1}^{K} \frac{N m_k \eta_k}{N_k} P_k Q_k \right\} \ (\mathrm{mod}\, N)$$

Therefore,

$$\omega_N^{mn} = \prod_{k=1}^{K} \omega_{N_k}^{m_k \eta_k}$$

And for $m_k = 0, 1, \ldots, (N_k - 1)$, $1 \le k \le K$,

$$Y(m_1, m_2, \ldots, m_K) = \frac{1}{\sqrt{N_K}} \sum_{\eta_K=0}^{(N_K-1)} \cdots$$

$$\cdots \left\{ \frac{1}{\sqrt{N_2}} \sum_{\eta_2=0}^{(N_2-1)} \left[\frac{1}{\sqrt{N_1}} \sum_{\eta_1=0}^{(N_1-1)} y(\eta_1, \eta_2, \ldots, \eta_K) \omega_{N_1}^{m_1 \eta_1} \right] \omega_{N_2}^{m_2 \eta_2} \right\} \cdots \omega_{N_K}^{m_K \eta_K}$$

Observe that this scheme converts the DFT in a single dimension into a multidimensional DFT. Furthermore, the success of this implementation depends upon efficient implementation of DFTs of size N_k's. This can be made true by having optimized DFTs for small values of N_k's. Also if N_k's are composite numbers, then using Cooley–Tukey type implementation of the DFT of size N_k gives further improvement in its computational efficiency.

In addition to the Cooley–Tukey and coprime-factorization FFT algorithms, there are other computationally efficient discrete Fourier transform algorithms. Nevertheless, the salient features of the Cooley–Tukey and coprime-factorization FFT algorithms are the basis of these other algorithms.

Furthermore, there are useful families of discrete transforms which are related to the discrete Fourier transform. A prominent example is the discrete cosine transform. This transform is used extensively in signal processing. Several fast versions of this transform are related to the FFT algorithms. Discrete cosine transform is discussed in a different chapter.

13.3 DFT Computation for Ramanujan Numbers

For special values of N, a method of computing the DFT with zero multiplications is presented. The complexity of the proposed algorithm is $O\left(N^2\right)$ shift and addition operations; and N division operations. A shift operation is a multiplication (or division) by integral powers of 2. Computation of the DFT involves evaluation of sine and cosine of angles which are multiples of $2\pi/N$. If N is chosen such that $2\pi/N$ is approximately 2^{-a}, $a \in \mathbb{P}$, then the trigonometric functions can be evaluated recursively by simple shift and addition operations. Such integers are called *Ramanujan numbers*, after the mathematician Srinivasa Iyengar Ramanujan (1887–1920). His approximations to π have recently been used to compute it to more than one billion digits. Multiplication of a real number by these trigonometric functions can be computed by shifts and additions. In this section, addition and subtraction operations are simply referred to as an addition operation.

In this scheme of computation, the DFT can be computed by $O\left(N^2\right)$ addition operations; and N division operations. It is assumed that shift operations take negligible time. The algorithms are also amenable to parallelization. If the computations are allowed in parallel, the DFT can be accomplished with: N adders, in $O\left(N\right)$ addition times; and N dividers in a single division time.

The DFT transforms a sequence

$$\{y\left(n\right) \mid y\left(n\right) \in \mathbb{C}, n = 0, 1, \ldots, (N-1)\}$$

to a sequence

$$\{Y\left(m\right) \mid Y\left(m\right) \in \mathbb{C}, m = 0, 1, \ldots, (N-1)\}$$

Let $y(n) = y_r(n) + iy_i(n)$, where $y_r(n) \in \mathbb{R}$ and $y_i(n) \in \mathbb{R}$ are respectively the real and imaginary parts of $y(n)$. Then computation of the transform elements $Y(m)$'s will involve computations of the form $u(n) = p\cos(2\pi n/N)$ and $v(n) = p\sin(2\pi n/N)$, where $p \in \mathbb{R}$, and $0 \leq n \leq (N-1)$. Define

$$U(N,p) = \{u(n) \mid u(n) = p\cos(2\pi n/N),\ 0 \leq n \leq (N-1),\ p \in \mathbb{R}\}$$
$$V(N,p) = \{v(n) \mid v(n) = p\sin(2\pi n/N),\ 0 \leq n \leq (N-1),\ p \in \mathbb{R}\}$$

The sequences $U(N,p)$ and $V(N,p)$ can be evaluated recursively by using the trigonometric identity:

$$\cos(n+1)\rho = 2\cos\rho\cos(n\rho) - \cos(n-1)\rho, \quad n = 0,1,2,3,\ldots$$

where ρ is any angle. For small values of ρ, $\cos\rho$ can be approximated by $(1-\rho^2/2)$. If $\rho^2/2$ is equal to 2^{-d}, $d \in \mathbb{P}$, then this trigonometric sequence can be evaluated recursively using shift and addition operations via the following set of equations. Let $\lambda = (1 - 2^{-d})$, then

$$\cos 0 = 1$$
$$\cos\rho \simeq \lambda$$
$$\cos(n+1)\rho \simeq 2\lambda\cos(n\rho) - \cos(n-1)\rho, \quad n = 1,2,3,\ldots$$

where $\simeq$ denotes approximation. This cosine sequence can be evaluated by shift and addition operations recursively. If ρ is chosen properly, $U(N,p)$ and $V(N,p)$, and therefore the DFT can be computed recursively by using shift and addition operations. Observe that with the use of these numbers, this approximation has replaced a multiplication operation by two shift and two addition operations. Consequently, for this approximation to occur, $2\pi/N$ has to be approximated by numbers of the form 2^{-a}, where $a \in \mathbb{P}$.

13.3.1 Ramanujan Numbers

In the computation of the DFT, a multiplication operation has been replaced by a shift and an addition operation by the use of these numbers. N is a Ramanujan number of order-1, if $2\pi/N \simeq 2^{-a}, a \in \mathbb{P}$. More precisely Ramanujan numbers of order-1, $\mathcal{R}_1(a)$ are defined as follows:

$$\mathcal{R}_1(a) = \left[\frac{2\pi}{\mathcal{I}_1(a)}\right]$$
$$\mathcal{I}_1(a) = 2^{-a}, \quad a \in \mathbb{P}$$

where $[\cdot]$ is a function which rounds off its argument to its nearest integer. Ramanujan numbers of order-1 can be computed simply as follows. Consider the binary expansion of π. It is $11.00100100001111\ldots$. If a is chosen to be 3, then $\mathcal{I}_1(3) = 2^{-3}$, and $\mathcal{R}_1(3) = [110010.0100001111\ldots] = 110010$. That is, $\mathcal{R}_1(3)$ is equal to 50. Similarly it can be shown that $\mathcal{R}_1(7) = 804$. Observe that in the above equations, the value of π is implicitly approximated. Denote this approximate value of π by $\widehat{\pi}$. Let the relative error in this approximation be ϵ. Then

$$\widehat{\pi} = \frac{1}{2}\mathcal{R}_1(a)\,\mathcal{I}_1(a)$$
$$\widehat{\pi} = \pi(1+\epsilon)$$

These error terms will be used to evaluate error-estimates in the computation of the sequences $U(N,p)$ and $V(N,p)$. These in turn will be used to evaluate the degree of accuracy obtained in the computation of DFT. It follows from the above discussion that ϵ is equal to $O(N^{-1})$. Ramanujan numbers of order-1, and their properties are listed in the Table 13.1.

a	$\mathcal{R}_1(a)$	$\widehat{\pi}$	ϵ
0	6	3.00	-4.5070×10^{-2}
1	13	3.25	3.4507×10^{-2}
2	25	3.125	-5.2816×10^{-3}
3	50	3.125	-5.2816×10^{-3}
4	101	3.15625	4.6656×10^{-3}
5	201	3.140625	-3.0801×10^{-4}
6	402	3.140625	-3.0801×10^{-4}
7	804	3.140625	-3.0801×10^{-4}
8	1608	3.140625	-3.0801×10^{-4}
9	3217	3.1416015625	2.8358×10^{-6}

Table 13.1. Ramanujan numbers - $\mathcal{R}_1(a)$

Ramanujan numbers of order-2 are defined as follows. These numbers are defined such that $2\pi/N$ is approximated by a sum or difference of two numbers which are negative powers of 2. More precisely, Ramanujan numbers of order-2, $\mathcal{R}_{21}(l,m)$ and $\mathcal{R}_{22}(l,m)$ are defined as

$$\mathcal{R}_{2j}(l,m) = \left[\frac{2\pi}{\mathcal{I}_{2j}(l,m)}\right], \quad j = 1,2$$
$$\mathcal{I}_{21}(l,m) = 2^{-l} + 2^{-m}, \quad m > l \geq 0$$
$$\mathcal{I}_{22}(l,m) = 2^{-l} - 2^{-m}, \quad (m-1) > l \geq 0$$

where $l, m \in \mathbb{N}$. For example, $\mathcal{R}_{21}(3,5) = 40$, and $\mathcal{R}_{21}(1,3) = 10$. In general, these higher-order numbers give better accuracy at the expense of additional shifts and addition operations. Recursive algorithms to evaluate sequences of type $\{u(n) \mid 0 \leq n \leq (N-1)\}$ and $\{v(n) \mid 0 \leq n \leq (N-1)\}$ is next developed. These in turn will be used to compute DFTs the size of a Ramanujan number.

13.3.2 Recursive Computations

In order to compute the DFT, an algorithm to compute the sequences $U(N,p)$ and $V(N,p)$ is initially developed. Define

$$W(M,p) = \{w(n) \mid w(n) = p\cos(2\pi n/M), 0 \le n \le \Psi, \ p \in \mathbb{R}\}$$

$$\Psi = \left(\frac{M}{4} - 1\right)$$
$$M = \beta N$$

$$\beta = \begin{cases} 1, & 4 \mid N \\ 2, & 2 \mid N, \text{ and } 4 \nmid N \\ 4, & 2 \nmid N \end{cases}$$

That is, β is equal to 1, if N is divisible by 4. It is equal to 2, if N is divisible by 2, and not by 4. Otherwise, it is equal to 4 (N is not divisible by 2). Note that M is divisible by 4. The use of the variable β facilitates the computation of $W(M,p)$ by considering cosine values in the first quadrant of the circle. Then $u(n)$'s and $v(n)$'s can be evaluated by computing the members of the sequence $W(M,p)$. Note that, if β is equal to 1, then comparatively a smaller number of computations have to be performed. If N is divisible by 4, for example $N = \mathcal{R}_1(7) = 804$, then the elements of the set $U(N,p)$ and $V(N,p)$ can be obtained from $W(N,p)$. If N is even, but not divisible by 4, for example $N = \mathcal{R}_1(6) = 402$, then $U(N,p)$ and $V(N,p)$ can be obtained from $W(2N,p)$. For odd values of N, for example $N = \mathcal{R}_1(2) = 205$, then $U(N,p)$ and $V(N,p)$ can be obtained from $W(4N,p)$. In summary, the elements of the sequences $U(N,p)$ and $V(N,p)$ can be obtained from $W(M,p)$.

The sequence $W(M,p)$ can be evaluated by any of the following three algorithms. The algorithms A, B, and C are next outlined. Algorithms B and C are computationally more superior and more expensive than algorithm A. In these algorithms, "←" is the assignment operator. Let

$$x = \frac{2\pi}{M}, \quad \widehat{x} = \frac{2\widehat{\pi}}{M}, \quad \alpha = \frac{\widehat{x}^2}{2}$$

Approximate

$$\sin x = 2\sin(x/2)\cos(x/2) \simeq x\left(1 - x^2/8\right)$$
$$\sin \widehat{x} \simeq (\widehat{x} - \sigma), \sigma = \widehat{x}^3/8$$

Algorithm A: Simple trigonometric technique.

The $W(M,p)$ is estimated as follows.

$$w\left(0\right) \leftarrow p$$
$$w\left(1\right) \leftarrow \left(1 - \alpha\right)p$$
$$w\left(n + 1\right) \leftarrow 2\left(1 - \alpha\right)w\left(n\right) - w(n - 1), \quad 1 \leq n \leq \left(\Psi - 1\right)$$

Observe that $w\left(n\right)$'s can be computed by shift and addition operations. If N is a Ramanujan number of order-1, then the computation of $w\left(n\right)$'s requires $\left(2\Psi - 1\right) = \left(M/2 - 3\right)$ additions. Shift operations take negligible time.

Algorithm B: Refined trigonometric technique.

Define

$$Q\left(M, p\right) = \{q(n) \mid q(n) = p\cos nx, \ 0 \leq n \leq J_c, \ p \in \mathbb{R}\}$$
$$R\left(M, p\right) = \{r(n) \mid r(n) = p\sin nx, \ 0 \leq n \leq J_s, \ p \in \mathbb{R}\}$$

$$J_c = \begin{cases} \frac{M}{8}, & 8 \mid M \\ \left(\frac{M}{8} - \frac{1}{2}\right), & 8 \nmid M \end{cases}$$

$$J_s = \begin{cases} \left(\frac{M}{8} - 1\right), & 8 \mid M \\ \left(\frac{M}{8} - \frac{1}{2}\right), & 8 \nmid M \end{cases}$$

Note that M is always divisible by 4. Then the $W\left(M, p\right)$ sequence and therefore the DFT can be evaluated from $Q\left(M, p\right)$ and $R\left(M, p\right)$ sequences. This algorithm uses the results

$$\cos nx = \cos x \cos \left(n - 1\right)x - \sin x \sin \left(n - 1\right)x, \quad n \in \mathbb{P}$$
$$\sin nx = \sin x \cos \left(n - 1\right)x + \cos x \sin \left(n - 1\right)x, \quad n \in \mathbb{P}$$

Then

$$q\left(0\right) \leftarrow p, \quad r\left(0\right) \leftarrow 0$$
$$q\left(1\right) \leftarrow \left(1 - \alpha\right)p, \quad r\left(1\right) \leftarrow \left(\hat{x} - \sigma\right)p$$
$$q\left(n\right) \leftarrow \left(1 - \alpha\right)q\left(n - 1\right) - \left(\hat{x} - \sigma\right)r(n - 1), \quad 2 \leq n \leq J_c$$
$$r\left(n\right) \leftarrow \left(\hat{x} - \sigma\right)q\left(n - 1\right) + \left(1 - \alpha\right)r(n - 1), \quad 2 \leq n \leq J_s$$

Once again, if N is a Ramanujan number, $Q\left(M, p\right)$ and $R\left(M, p\right)$ sequences can be estimated by shift and addition operations. The number of addition and shift operations is $O(M)$.

Algorithm C: Refined trigonometric technique.

This algorithm uses the results

$$\cos(n+1)x + \cos(n-1)x = 2\cos nx \cos x, \quad n \in \mathbb{P}$$
$$\sin(n+1)x + \sin(n-1)x = 2\sin nx \cos x, \quad n \in \mathbb{P}$$

Then

$$q(0) = p, \quad r(0) = 0$$
$$\Delta q(1) = -\alpha p, \quad \Delta r(1) = (\hat{x} - \sigma)p$$
$$q(n) = q(n-1) + \Delta q(n), \quad 1 \le n \le J_c$$
$$\Delta q(n+1) = \Delta q(n) - 2\alpha q(n), \quad 1 \le n \le (J_c - 1)$$
$$r(n) = r(n-1) + \Delta r(n), \quad 1 \le n \le J_s$$
$$\Delta r(n+1) = \Delta r(n) - 2\alpha r(n), \quad 1 \le n \le (J_s - 1)$$

The number of addition and shift operations is $O(M)$.

It can be noticed that both the algorithms B and C can be parallelized.

13.3.3 Discrete Fourier Transform Computation

The recursive computations developed in algorithms A, B, and C can now be used in the computation of DFT. The DFT can be evaluated by computing sequences $W(M, y_r(n))$ and $W(M, y_i(n))$ for $0 \le n \le (N-1)$.

At the end of each of the Algorithms A, B, and C the sums $\sum_{n=0}^{(N-1)} y(n) \omega_N^{mn}$, $m \in \mathbb{Z}_N$ are obtained. These sums are normalized by $\sqrt{N}$ to obtain the DFT coefficients $Y(m)$, $m \in \mathbb{Z}_N$.

It is now evident that the DFT can be evaluated by $O(N^2)$ addition operations, and N division operations. The division operations are actually normalizations by $\sqrt{N}$. The error in the computation of the DFT, due to approximation of these trigonometric operations, is next evaluated. Let the approximated value of $Y(m)$ be $\hat{Y}(m)$. Define the error as

$$\hat{Y}(m) - Y(m) = \Delta Y(m), \quad \text{for } 0 \le m \le (N-1)$$

Let the average magnitude square of the transformed sequence be $E(N)$, and the average magnitude squared error in the transformed sequence be $\Delta E(N)$. Then the error in the computation of the DFT, due to the approximation can be characterized by the ratio of $\Delta E(N)$ and $E(N)$. Denote it by $A(N)$. The above definitions yield

$$E(N) = \frac{1}{N} \sum_{m=0}^{(N-1)} |Y(m)|^2$$

$$\Delta E(N) = \frac{1}{N} \sum_{m=0}^{(N-1)} |\Delta Y(m)|^2$$

$$A(N) = \frac{\Delta E(N)}{E(N)}$$

Using the Bunyakovsky–Cauchy–Schwartz inequality, it can be shown that

$$A(N) \leq \frac{D(N)}{N}$$

where

$$D(N) = \sum_{m=0}^{(N-1)} \sum_{n=0}^{(N-1)} |\widehat{\omega}_N^{mn} - \omega_N^{mn}|^2$$

$$\widehat{\omega}_N = e^{i2\widehat{\pi}/N}$$

$\sqrt{D(N)}$ is the so-called Frobenius norm of the matrix, whose elements are

$$(\widehat{\omega}_N^{mn} - \omega_N^{mn}), \quad 0 \leq m, n \leq (N-1)$$

An upper bound of $A(N)$ is now easily computable. These upper bound values are tabulated for Ramanujan numbers of order-1, for algorithms A, B, and C in Table 13.2. These upper bound estimates are much less than unity. Based upon this table, the following general observations can be made. Algorithms B and C outperform algorithm A. And the performance of algorithms B and C are comparable.

a	$\mathcal{R}_1(a)$	Algorithm A	Algorithm B	Algorithm C
0	6	2.81895×10^{-3}	8.65824×10^{-4}	8.65824×10^{-4}
1	13	1.71361×10^{-2}	3.03621×10^{-3}	3.03613×10^{-3}
2	25	7.31063×10^{-4}	1.28404×10^{-4}	1.28305×10^{-4}
3	50	1.46213×10^{-3}	2.56607×10^{-4}	2.56610×10^{-4}
4	101	2.84300×10^{-3}	4.49498×10^{-4}	4.49498×10^{-4}
5	201	2.41653×10^{-5}	3.83272×10^{-6}	3.83272×10^{-6}
6	402	4.83306×10^{-5}	7.66545×10^{-6}	7.66545×10^{-6}
7	804	9.66611×10^{-5}	1.53309×10^{-5}	1.53309×10^{-5}
8	1608	1.96878×10^{-4}	3.11903×10^{-5}	3.11903×10^{-5}
9	3217	3.44284×10^{-8}	5.35502×10^{-9}	5.35502×10^{-9}

Table 13.2. Upper bound of $A(N)$ for Ramanujan numbers - $\mathcal{R}_1(a)$

Problems

1. Develop a fast Fourier transform algorithm.
   Hint: See Briggs and Henson (1995).

CHAPTER 14

The z-Transform and Discrete-Time Fourier Transform

14.1 Introduction

Some properties of the z-transform, and discrete-time Fourier transform of discrete-time sequences are summarized. These are useful in the study of discrete-time signal processing.

14.2 z-Transform

In this section the z-transform is defined. Some of its important properties are also studied. Finally some examples are given. In addition, an expression for the inversion of the z-transform is stated. The field $\mathbb{F}$ is either the set of real numbers $\mathbb{R}$, or the set of complex numbers $\mathbb{C}$.

Definition 14.1. *The z-transform of a sequence* $\{f(n) \in \mathbb{F} \mid n \in \mathbb{Z}\}$ *is*

$$\mathcal{Z}\{f(n)\} = \mathcal{F}(z) = \sum_{n \in \mathbb{Z}} f(n) z^{-n}, \quad z \in R_f \subset \mathbb{C} \qquad (14.1)$$

where R_f is the region of convergence. It is a region in the set $\mathbb{C}$ for which the series converges. □

Let $z = re^{i\omega}$, where $r \in \mathbb{R}_0^+$, $i = \sqrt{-1}$, and $\omega \in \mathbb{R}$. Then the region of convergence of $\mathcal{F}(z)$ can be determined from values of r for which $\sum_{n \in \mathbb{Z}} |f(n) r^{-n}| < \infty$.

Region of Convergence

Some useful properties of the region of convergence of a sequence are summarized.

1. The convergent region is at least a ring of the form $0 \leq \alpha < |z| < \beta \leq \infty$. The values α and β depend upon the behavior of $f(n)$ as $n \to +\infty$ and $-\infty$ respectively.

2. If $f(n) = 0$ for $n < 0$, then $\beta \to \infty$, because $\mathcal{F}(z)$ has only negative powers of z. And R_f is the exterior of the circle $|z| = \alpha$.

3. If $f(n) = 0$ for $n > 0$, then $\alpha = 0$, because $\mathcal{F}(z)$ has only positive powers of z. And R_f is the interior of the circle $|z| = \beta$.

14.2.1 Properties

Properties of the z-transform are discussed in this subsection. Let $\mathcal{F}(z)$, $\mathcal{F}_1(z)$, and $\mathcal{F}_2(z)$ be the z-transforms of the sequences

$$\{f(n) \in \mathbb{F} \mid n \in \mathbb{Z}\},$$
$$\{f_1(n) \in \mathbb{F} \mid n \in \mathbb{Z}\},$$
$$\{f_2(n) \in \mathbb{F} \mid n \in \mathbb{Z}\}$$

respectively. Their regions of convergence are R_f, R_{f_1} and R_{f_2} respectively. Let

$$R_f = \{z \mid 0 \leq \alpha < |z| < \beta \leq \infty\}$$
$$R_{f_1} = \{z \mid 0 \leq \alpha_1 < |z| < \beta_1 \leq \infty\}$$
$$R_{f_2} = \{z \mid 0 \leq \alpha_2 < |z| < \beta_2 \leq \infty\}$$

Basic properties of the z-transform:

1. Linearity: Let $a_1, a_2 \in \mathbb{C}$.

$$f(n) = a_1 f_1(n) + a_2 f_2(n), \quad n \in \mathbb{Z}$$
$$\mathcal{Z}\{f(n)\} = \mathcal{F}(z) = a_1 \mathcal{F}_1(z) + a_2 \mathcal{F}_2(z), \quad z \in R_f$$
$$R_{f_1} \cap R_{f_2} \subset R_f$$

$$R_{f_1} \cap R_{f_2} = \{z \mid 0 \leq \max(\alpha_1, \alpha_2) < |z| < \min(\beta_1, \beta_2) \leq \infty\}$$

Note that R_f is larger than or equal to $R_{f_1} \cap R_{f_2}$.

2. Time reversal:

$$\mathcal{Z}\{f(-n)\} = \mathcal{F}(z^{-1}), \quad \left\{z \mid 0 \leq \frac{1}{\beta} < |z| < \frac{1}{\alpha} \leq \infty\right\}$$

3. Conjugate function:

$$\mathcal{Z}\left\{\overline{f(n)}\right\} = \overline{\mathcal{F}(\bar{z})}, \quad z \in R_f$$

4. Translation:

$$\mathcal{Z}\left\{f\left(n-k\right)\right\} = z^{-k}\mathcal{F}(z), \quad k \in \mathbb{Z},\ z \in R_f$$

5. Multiplication by exponential: Let $|a| \in \mathbb{R}^{+}$.

$$\mathcal{Z}\left\{a^n f\left(n\right)\right\} = \mathcal{F}(z/a), \quad \{z \mid 0 \le |a|\,\alpha < |z| < |a|\,\beta \le \infty\}$$

6. Multiplication by n:

$$\mathcal{Z}\left\{nf\left(n\right)\right\} = -z\frac{d\mathcal{F}(z)}{dz}, \quad z \in R_f$$

7. Convolution:

$$f\left(n\right) = \sum_{k \in \mathbb{Z}} f_1\left(k\right) f_2(n-k), \quad n \in \mathbb{Z}$$
$$\mathcal{F}\left(z\right) = \mathcal{F}_1\left(z\right) \mathcal{F}_2(z), \quad z \in R_{f_1} \cap R_{f_2}$$

$\qquad\qquad\qquad\qquad\qquad\qquad\qquad\qquad\qquad\qquad\qquad\qquad$ □

Examples of the z-Transform

Some useful z-transforms are given.

1. Let

$$\delta\left(n\right) = \begin{cases} 1, & n = 0 \\ 0, & n \in \mathbb{Z}\backslash\{0\} \end{cases}$$
$$\mathcal{Z}\left\{\delta\left(n\right)\right\} = 1$$

This sequence is called the unit sample.

2. Define for $k \in \mathbb{Z}$

$$\delta\left(n-k\right) = \begin{cases} 1, & n = k \\ 0, & n \in \mathbb{Z}\backslash\{k\} \end{cases}$$
$$\mathcal{Z}\left\{\delta\left(n-k\right)\right\} = z^{-k}$$

3. Let $\alpha \in \mathbb{C}$

$$f\left(n\right) = \begin{cases} \alpha^n, & n \in \mathbb{N} \\ 0, & \text{otherwise} \end{cases}$$

$$\mathcal{Z}\left\{f\left(n\right)\right\} = \sum_{n=0}^{\infty} \alpha^n z^{-n}$$

$$= \frac{1}{(1 - \alpha z^{-1})}, \quad |\alpha z^{-1}| < 1$$

Therefore, $\mathcal{Z}\left\{f\left(n\right)\right\} = \left(1 - \alpha z^{-1}\right)^{-1}$ for $|\alpha| < |z|$. The region of convergence is the exterior of the circle $|z| = |\alpha|$. $\qquad\qquad$ □

14.2.2 Down-Sampled and Up-Sampled Sequences

The z-transforms of down-sampled and up-sampled sequences are obtained in this subsection. Down-sampling a sequence by a factor of two contracts the original sequence. Up-sampling by a factor of two expands the time scale by a factor of two, and inserts a zero between each sample of the signal.

Definitions 14.2. *The down-sampled and up-sampled sequences. Let*

$$\{f(n) \in \mathbb{F} \mid n \in \mathbb{Z}\}$$

be a sequence.

1. *The down-sampled sequence $\{a(n) \in \mathbb{F} \mid n \in \mathbb{Z}\}$ is*

$$a(n) = f(2n), \quad n \in \mathbb{Z} \tag{14.2}$$

2. *The up-sampled sequence $\{b(n) \in \mathbb{F} \mid n \in \mathbb{Z}\}$ is*

$$b(n) = \begin{cases} f(\frac{n}{2}), & \text{if } n \text{ is divisible by 2} \\ 0, & \text{otherwise} \end{cases}, \quad n \in \mathbb{Z} \tag{14.3}$$

$\square$

Observation 14.1. Let the z-transforms of the sequences

$$\{f(n) \in \mathbb{F} \mid n \in \mathbb{Z}\}, \quad \{a(n) \in \mathbb{F} \mid n \in \mathbb{Z}\}, \text{ and } \{b(n) \in \mathbb{F} \mid n \in \mathbb{Z}\}$$

in the above definitions be $\mathcal{F}(z)$, $\mathcal{A}(z)$, and $\mathcal{B}(z)$ respectively. Then

$$\mathcal{A}(z^2) = \frac{1}{2}(\mathcal{F}(z) + \mathcal{F}(-z))$$
$$\mathcal{A}(z) = \frac{1}{2}(\mathcal{F}(\sqrt{z}) + \mathcal{F}(-\sqrt{z}))$$
$$\mathcal{B}(z) = \mathcal{F}(z^2)$$

$\square$

14.2.3 Inversion

The z-transform of a sequence can be inverted by using the theory of complex variables. It can be shown that

$$f(n) = \frac{1}{2\pi i} \oint_C \mathcal{F}(z) z^{n-1} dz$$

where the contour integration is counterclockwise along a closed contour C. Further-more, the contour integration is performed in the z-plane containing the origin, and the contour lies within the region of convergence. If

$$\mathcal{F}(z) = \sum_{n \in \mathbb{N}} f(n) z^{-n}$$

and d/dz^{-1} is the differential operator with respect to z^{-1}, then

$$f(n) = \frac{1}{n!} \frac{d^n \mathcal{F}(z)}{d(z^{-1})^n} \bigg|_{z^{-1}=0}, \quad n \in \mathbb{N}$$

There are several other techniques available to invert a z-transform. Some of these are: inversion using Fourier series, inversion using series representation, and inversion using partial fraction expansion.

14.3 Discrete-Time Fourier Transform

The discrete-time Fourier transform of a sequence $\{f(n) \in \mathbb{F} \mid n \in \mathbb{Z}\}$ is simply defined by letting $r = 1$ in its definition of the z-transform. That is, we let $z = e^{i\omega}$ in the definition of the z-transform of the sequence. Therefore, the discrete-time Fourier transform of this sequence is $\sum_{n \in \mathbb{Z}} f(n) e^{-i\omega n}$. If the region of convergence includes the unit circle, then the discrete-time Fourier transform of the sequence exists.

Let $\mathcal{F}(z)$ be the z-transform of the sequence $\{f(n) \in \mathbb{F} \mid n \in \mathbb{Z}\}$, where $\mathbb{F}$ is either the set of real numbers $\mathbb{R}$, or the set of complex numbers $\mathbb{C}$. The discrete-time Fourier transform of this sequence is $\mathcal{F}(e^{i\omega})$.

Definition 14.3. *The discrete-time Fourier transform of the sequence*

$$\{f(n) \in \mathbb{F} \mid n \in \mathbb{Z}\} \tag{14.4a}$$

is

$$\mathcal{D}\{f(n)\} = \mathcal{F}(e^{i\omega})$$
$$= \sum_{n \in \mathbb{Z}} f(n) e^{-i\omega n}, \quad \omega \in \mathbb{R} \tag{14.4b}$$

provided

$$\sum_{n \in \mathbb{Z}} |f(n)| < \infty \tag{14.4c}$$

For convenience and ease in notation, $\mathcal{F}(e^{i\omega})$ is sometimes denoted by $F(\omega)$. $\square$

The discrete-time Fourier transform $\mathcal{F}\left(e^{i\omega}\right)$ can be inverted as

$$f\left(n\right) = \frac{1}{2\pi} \int_{\omega_0}^{\omega_0+2\pi} \mathcal{F}\left(e^{i\omega}\right) e^{in\omega} d\omega, \quad \omega_0 \in \mathbb{R}, \quad n \in \mathbb{Z}$$

Properties of the Discrete-Time Fourier Transform

The study of the discrete-time Fourier transform is analogous to the study of z-transforms. Therefore, only some of its properties are summarized briefly. Let $a_1, a_2 \in \mathbb{C}$. Consider the following sequences and their respective discrete-time Fourier transforms.

$$\{f\left(n\right) \in \mathbb{F} \mid n \in \mathbb{Z}\}, \quad \mathcal{D}\{f\left(n\right)\} = \mathcal{F}(e^{i\omega}), \quad \omega \in \mathbb{R}$$
$$\{f_1\left(n\right) \in \mathbb{F} \mid n \in \mathbb{Z}\}, \quad \mathcal{D}\{f_1\left(n\right)\} = \mathcal{F}_1(e^{i\omega}), \quad \omega \in \mathbb{R}$$
$$\{f_2\left(n\right) \in \mathbb{F} \mid n \in \mathbb{Z}\}, \quad \mathcal{D}\{f_2\left(n\right)\} = \mathcal{F}_2(e^{i\omega}), \quad \omega \in \mathbb{R}$$

Some of its properties are:

1. Linearity:

$$f\left(n\right) = a_1 f_1\left(n\right) + a_2 f_2(n), \quad n \in \mathbb{Z}$$
$$\mathcal{D}\{f\left(n\right)\} = \mathcal{F}\left(e^{i\omega}\right) = a_1 \mathcal{F}_1\left(e^{i\omega}\right) + a_2 \mathcal{F}_2\left(e^{i\omega}\right)$$

2. Time reversal:

$$\mathcal{D}\{f\left(-n\right)\} = \mathcal{F}\left(e^{-i\omega}\right)$$

3. Conjugation:

$$\mathcal{D}\left\{\overline{f\left(n\right)}\right\} = \overline{\mathcal{F}\left(e^{-i\omega}\right)}$$

4. Translation:

$$\mathcal{D}\{f\left(n-k\right)\} = e^{-i\omega k} \mathcal{F}(e^{i\omega}), \quad k \in \mathbb{Z}$$

5. Modulation:

$$\mathcal{D}\left\{e^{i\omega_0 n} f\left(n\right)\right\} = \mathcal{F}(e^{i(\omega-\omega_0)}), \quad \omega_0 \in \mathbb{R}$$

6. Periodicity:

$$\mathcal{F}(e^{i\omega}) = \mathcal{F}(e^{i(\omega+2\pi)})$$

7. Multiplication by n:

$$\mathcal{D}\{nf\left(n\right)\} = i\frac{d\mathcal{F}(e^{i\omega})}{d\omega}$$

8. Convolution:

$$f\left(n\right) = \sum_{k \in \mathbb{Z}} f_1\left(k\right) f_2(n-k), \quad n \in \mathbb{Z}$$
$$\mathcal{F}\left(e^{i\omega}\right) = \mathcal{F}_1\left(e^{i\omega}\right) \mathcal{F}_2\left(e^{i\omega}\right)$$

9. Sequence multiplication:

$$f(n) = f_1(n) f_2(n), \qquad n \in \mathbb{Z}$$

$$\mathcal{D}\{f(n)\} = \frac{1}{2\pi} \int_0^{2\pi} \mathcal{F}_1\left(e^{i\theta}\right) \mathcal{F}_2\left(e^{i(\omega-\theta)}\right) d\theta \triangleq \frac{1}{2\pi} \mathcal{F}_1\left(e^{i\omega}\right) * \mathcal{F}_2\left(e^{i\omega}\right)$$

where $*$ is the convolution operation.

10. Parseval's relationships:

$$\sum_{n \in \mathbb{Z}} f_1(n) f_2(n) = \frac{1}{2\pi} \int_0^{2\pi} \mathcal{F}_1\left(e^{i\omega}\right) \mathcal{F}_2\left(e^{-i\omega}\right) d\omega$$

$$\sum_{n \in \mathbb{Z}} f_1(n) \overline{f_2(n)} = \frac{1}{2\pi} \int_0^{2\pi} \mathcal{F}_1\left(e^{i\omega}\right) \overline{\mathcal{F}_2\left(e^{i\omega}\right)} d\omega$$

$$\sum_{n \in \mathbb{Z}} |f(n)|^2 = \frac{1}{2\pi} \int_0^{2\pi} \left|\mathcal{F}\left(e^{i\omega}\right)\right|^2 d\omega$$

$\square$

Problems

1. Prove that the discrete-time Fourier transform of the sequence

$$f(n) = f_1(n) f_2(n), \ n \in \mathbb{Z}$$

is

$$\mathcal{D}\{f(n)\} = \frac{1}{2\pi} \mathcal{F}_1\left(e^{i\omega}\right) * \mathcal{F}_2\left(e^{i\omega}\right)$$

where $*$ is the convolution operation.

Hint:

$$\mathcal{F}\left(e^{i\omega}\right) = \sum_{n \in \mathbb{Z}} f(n) e^{-i\omega n} = \sum_{n \in \mathbb{Z}} f_1(n) f_2(n) e^{-i\omega n}$$

Substitute

$$f_1(n) = \frac{1}{2\pi} \int_0^{2\pi} \mathcal{F}_1\left(e^{i\theta}\right) e^{in\theta} d\theta$$

Then

$$\mathcal{F}\left(e^{i\omega}\right) = \sum_{n\in\mathbb{Z}} \left\{ \frac{1}{2\pi} \int_0^{2\pi} \mathcal{F}_1\left(e^{i\theta}\right) e^{in\theta} d\theta \right\} f_2\left(n\right) e^{-i\omega n}$$

$$= \frac{1}{2\pi} \int_0^{2\pi} \mathcal{F}_1\left(e^{i\theta}\right) \left\{ \sum_{n\in\mathbb{Z}} f_2\left(n\right) e^{-i(\omega-\theta)n} \right\} d\theta$$

$$= \frac{1}{2\pi} \int_0^{2\pi} \mathcal{F}_1\left(e^{i\theta}\right) \mathcal{F}_2\left(e^{i(\omega-\theta)}\right) d\theta$$

The result follows.

2. Establish the following Parseval relationships

$$\sum_{n\in\mathbb{Z}} f_1\left(n\right) f_2\left(n\right) = \frac{1}{2\pi} \int_0^{2\pi} \mathcal{F}_1\left(e^{i\omega}\right) \mathcal{F}_2\left(e^{-i\omega}\right) d\omega$$

$$\sum_{n\in\mathbb{Z}} f_1\left(n\right) \overline{f_2\left(n\right)} = \frac{1}{2\pi} \int_0^{2\pi} \mathcal{F}_1\left(e^{i\omega}\right) \overline{\mathcal{F}_2\left(e^{i\omega}\right)} d\omega$$

$$\sum_{n\in\mathbb{Z}} \left| f\left(n\right) \right|^2 = \frac{1}{2\pi} \int_0^{2\pi} \left| \mathcal{F}\left(e^{i\omega}\right) \right|^2 d\omega$$

CHAPTER 15

Elements of Continuous-Time Signal Processing

15.1 Introduction

Elements of continuous-time signal processing techniques are discussed in this chapter. Note that a signal is simply a function. A continuous-time Fourier-transform pair is denoted as $f(t) \leftrightarrow F(\omega)$, and $i = \sqrt{-1}$.

15.2 Continuous-Time Signal Processing

The mathematical language used in describing continuous-time signals is explained. Terms such as linearity, time-invariance, impulse response, causality, and stability are introduced. These terms are explained within the context of continuous-time signal processing. Certain filter characteristics are also specified. A filter specifies a mapping of an input signal to an output signal.

A system (filter) can actually be specified via an input function and a corresponding output function. In other words, a system is a mapping of the input signal $f(t)$ to an output signal $g(t)$, where $t \in \mathbb{R}$.

Definitions 15.1. *The system is continuous in time.*

1. *System description: A system is a mapping of the input signal $f(t)$ to an output signal $g(t)$, where $t \in \mathbb{R}$. This is expressed as*

$$g(t) = \mathcal{L}_C(f(t)), \qquad \forall\, t \in \mathbb{R} \tag{15.1}$$

and $\mathcal{L}_C$ is the continuous-time system operator. The functions $f(\cdot)$ and $g(\cdot)$ can be either real or complex-valued.

2. *Linear system: A system is linear, if its operator satisfies the following equations. If for each $a_1, a_2 \in \mathbb{C}$, and $g_1(t) = \mathcal{L}_C(f_1(t))$ and $g_2(t) = \mathcal{L}_C(f_2(t))$ then*

$$\mathcal{L}_C(a_1 f_1(t) + a_2 f_2(t)) = a_1 g_1(t) + a_2 g_2(t), \qquad \forall\, t \in \mathbb{R} \tag{15.2}$$

3. *Time-invariant system*: *A system is time-invariant if*

$$\mathcal{L}_C \left(f \left(t - t_0 \right) \right) = g(t - t_0), \qquad \forall \, t_0, \, t \in \mathbb{R} \tag{15.3}$$

4. *Impulse response of the system*: *If the input function is Dirac's delta function* $\delta(t), \, t \in \mathbb{R}$, *then the output function is the impulse response function* $p(t)$, $t \in \mathbb{R}$. *That is,*

$$\mathcal{L}_C \left(\delta \left(t \right) \right) = p(t), \qquad \forall \, t \in \mathbb{R} \tag{15.4}$$

5. *Causal-system*: *A system is causal (nonanticipative), if the output* $g \left(t_0 \right)$ *of the system for each* $t_0 \in \mathbb{R}$ *depends only on the input* $f \left(t \right)$ *for* $t \leq t_0$.
   Alternate definition of a causal system. Consider any two inputs $f_1 \left(t \right)$ *and* $f_2 \left(t \right)$ *to the system* $\mathcal{L}_C$, *where* $t \in \mathbb{R}$. *The corresponding outputs are* $g_1 \left(t \right)$, *and* $g_2 \left(t \right)$ *respectively. The system* $\mathcal{L}_C$ *is causal, if* $f_1 \left(t \right) = f_2 \left(t \right)$, $\forall \, t < t_0$, *then* $g_1 \left(t \right) = g_2 \left(t \right)$, $\forall \, t < t_0$.

6. *Stability*: *A function* $f \left(t \right)$ *is bounded if* $\left| f \left(t \right) \right| \leq A < \infty$, $\forall \, t \in \mathbb{R}$, *for some nonnegative real number* A. *A system is stable if a bounded input produces a bounded output.* □

Responses (outputs) for different types of inputs for linear and time-invariant systems is next determined.

Observations 15.1. Let the continuous-time system be linear and time-invariant, and the system operator be $\mathcal{L}_C$. Also let the input and output functions be $f \left(\cdot \right)$ and $g \left(\cdot \right)$ respectively. The corresponding impulse response function is $p \left(\cdot \right)$.

1. We have $\mathcal{L}_C \left(\delta \left(t - \tau \right) \right) = p(t - \tau); \, t, \tau \in \mathbb{R}$.

2. The impulse response $p \left(\cdot \right)$ is stable if $\int_{-\infty}^{\infty} \left| p \left(t \right) \right| dt < \infty$.

3. Response to an arbitrary input. The output response $g(\cdot)$ of a linear time-invariant system to an input $f(\cdot)$ is

$$g \left(t \right) = \int_{-\infty}^{\infty} f \left(\tau \right) p \left(t - \tau \right) d\tau \triangleq f(t) * p(t), \quad t \in \mathbb{R}$$

where $*$ is the continuous-time convolution operator. That is, the response of a linear system due to an arbitrary input is determined by its impulse response function and the input function.

4. Response of a causal system to an arbitrary input. For a linear time-invariant causal system, for $t \in \mathbb{R}$

$$g(t) = \int_{-\infty}^{t} f \left(\tau \right) p \left(t - \tau \right) d\tau$$
$$= \int_{0}^{\infty} f \left(t - \tau \right) p \left(\tau \right) d\tau$$

5. If a system $\mathcal{L}_C$ is specified via a linear constant-coefficient differential equation, the system is causal if and only if $p(t) = 0$ for $\forall\, t < 0$.

6. Response of a causal system to a step function. Let the input function be defined as $u(t)$, where

$$u(t) = \begin{cases} 1, & t > 0 \\ 0, & \text{otherwise} \end{cases}$$

Its response $v(t)$ is given by

$$v(t) = \int_0^t p(\tau)\, d\tau, \quad t > 0$$

7. Exponential input. Let

$$f(t) = e^{i\omega t}, \quad \omega, t \in \mathbb{R}, \text{ and } i = \sqrt{-1}$$

The corresponding output function is

$$g(t) = k e^{i\omega t}, \quad t \in \mathbb{R}$$

and k is a constant.   □

See the problem section for a proof of some of these results. The system transfer function of a linear and time-invariant system is next defined. This is the characterization of a system in the frequency domain.

Definition 15.2. *System transfer function. Consider a linear and time-invariant system. Also let the input and output functions be $f(\cdot)$ and $g(\cdot)$ respectively. The corresponding impulse response function is $p(\cdot)$.*
Let $f(t) \leftrightarrow F(\omega)$, $g(t) \leftrightarrow G(\omega)$, and $p(t) \leftrightarrow P(\omega)$; $\omega, t \in \mathbb{R}$. As

$$g(t) = f(t) * p(t), \tag{15.5}$$

it follows that $G(\omega) = P(\omega)F(\omega)$. $P(\omega)$ is called the system transfer function, or the frequency response of the system.   □

A system is next examined from the perspective of energy. Energy of a signal $a(t), t \in \mathbb{R}$ is defined as

$$E = \int_{-\infty}^{\infty} |a(t)|^2\, dt$$

Signals in real life have finite energy, because the function $a(t)$ typically has finite support, and the values $a(t)$ are finite. Therefore, the space of finite-energy signals is the space $L^2(\mathbb{R})$. If $a(t) \leftrightarrow A(\omega)$ then via Parseval's relationship, we have

$$E = \int_{-\infty}^{\infty} |a(t)|^2\, dt = \frac{1}{2\pi} \int_{-\infty}^{\infty} |A(\omega)|^2\, d\omega < \infty$$

Note that $a(t)$ can be either $f(t)$ or $g(t)$.

Continuous-Time Filters

A filter is simply a system. It transforms an input signal to its output signal. Filters are generally classified in terms of their frequency characteristics. Let $P(\omega)$ be the Fourier transform of its impulse response. Commonly used filters are low-pass, high-pass, band-pass, and band-stop filters. The system transfer function $P(\omega)$ of these filters is specified as follows.

The band-pass and band-stop filters in the frequency domain are specified in terms of the interval $I_\omega \subset \mathbb{R}$, where

$$I_\omega = [-\omega_1, -\omega_0] \cup [\omega_0, \omega_1], \quad \text{where } 0 < \omega_0 < \omega_1$$

Note that

$$\omega \in I_\omega \iff \omega_0 \leq |\omega| \leq \omega_1$$

1. *Low-pass filter.*

$$P(\omega) = \begin{cases} P(\omega), & |\omega| \leq \omega_{low} \\ 0, & \text{otherwise} \end{cases}$$

ω_{low} is called the cut-off frequency of the continuous-time low-pass filter. Also, $|P(\omega)| \in \mathbb{R}_0^+$, $\forall\, |\omega| \leq \omega_{low}$.

2. *High-pass filter.*

$$P(\omega) = \begin{cases} P(\omega), & |\omega| \geq \omega_{high} \\ 0, & \text{otherwise} \end{cases}$$

ω_{high} is called the cut-off frequency of the continuous-time high-pass filter. Also, $|P(\omega)| \in \mathbb{R}_0^+$, $\forall\, |\omega| \geq \omega_{high}$.

3. *Band-pass filter.*

$$P(\omega) = \begin{cases} P(\omega), & \omega \in I_\omega \\ 0, & \text{otherwise} \end{cases}$$

ω_0 and ω_1 are called the band-pass frequencies of the continuous-time band-pass filter. Also, $|P(\omega)| \in \mathbb{R}_0^+$, $\forall\, \omega \in I_\omega$.

4. *Band-stop filter.*

$$P(\omega) = \begin{cases} P(\omega), & \omega \in \mathbb{R}\backslash I_\omega \\ 0, & \omega \in I_\omega \end{cases}$$

ω_0 and ω_1 are called the band-stop frequencies of the continuous-time band-stop filter. Also, $|P(\omega)| \in \mathbb{R}_0^+$, $\forall\, \omega \in \mathbb{R}\backslash I_\omega$.

Problems

1. Let the continuous-time system be linear and time-invariant. Also let the input and output functions be $f\left(\cdot\right)$ and $g\left(\cdot\right)$ respectively. The corresponding impulse response function is $p\left(\cdot\right)$. Show that

$$g\left(t\right) = \int_{-\infty}^{\infty} f\left(\tau\right) p\left(t - \tau\right) d\tau \triangleq f(t) * p(t), \quad t \in \mathbb{R}$$

where $*$ is the convolution operator.

Hint: Note that

$$f(t) = \int_{-\infty}^{\infty} f\left(\tau\right) \delta\left(t - \tau\right) d\tau$$

Then

$$g\left(t\right) = \mathcal{L}_C\left[f\left(t\right)\right] = \mathcal{L}_C\left(\int_{-\infty}^{\infty} f\left(\tau\right) \delta\left(t - \tau\right) d\tau\right)$$

$$= \int_{-\infty}^{\infty} f\left(\tau\right) \mathcal{L}_C\left(\delta\left(t - \tau\right)\right) d\tau$$

The last step follows from the linearity of the system. Since $\mathcal{L}_C\left(\delta\left(t - \tau\right)\right) = p\left(t - \tau\right)$

$$g\left(t\right) = \int_{-\infty}^{\infty} f\left(\tau\right) p\left(t - \tau\right) d\tau \triangleq f(t) * p(t)$$

2. Let the continuous-time system be linear, time-invariant, and causal. Also let the input and output functions be $f\left(\cdot\right)$ and $g\left(\cdot\right)$ respectively. The corresponding impulse response function is $p\left(\cdot\right)$. Show that

$$g(t) = \int_{-\infty}^{t} f\left(\tau\right) p\left(t - \tau\right) d\tau = \int_{0}^{\infty} f\left(t - \tau\right) p\left(\tau\right) d\tau, \quad t \in \mathbb{R}$$

Hint: We have

$$g\left(t\right) = \int_{-\infty}^{\infty} f\left(\tau\right) p\left(t - \tau\right) d\tau = \int_{-\infty}^{t} f\left(\tau\right) p\left(t - \tau\right) d\tau$$

$$= \int_{0}^{\infty} f\left(t - \tau\right) p\left(\tau\right) d\tau$$

3. Consider a continuous-time, linear, time-invariant, and causal system. Let the input function be defined as $u(t)$, as

$$u(t) = \begin{cases} 1, & t > 0 \\ 0, & \text{otherwise} \end{cases}$$

Show, that its response $v(t)$ is given by

$$v(t) = \int_0^t p(\tau)\, d\tau, \quad t > 0$$

Hint: Observe that

$$v(t) = \int_{-\infty}^t u(\tau)\, p(t - \tau)\, d\tau = \int_0^t p(t - \tau)\, d\tau = \int_0^t p(\tau)\, d\tau$$

4. Consider a continuous-time, linear and time-invariant system. Also let the input and output functions be $f(\cdot)$ and $g(\cdot)$ respectively. Let $f(t) = e^{i\omega t}$, where $w, t \in \mathbb{R}$ and $i = \sqrt{-1}$. Show that the output function $g(t) = ke^{i\omega t}$, where k is a constant, and $t \in \mathbb{R}$.

Hint: It is given that $g(t) = \mathcal{L}_C\left(e^{i\omega t}\right)$. Since the system is time-invariant, for a fixed value of $\tau \in \mathbb{R}$,

$$g(t + \tau) = \mathcal{L}_C\left(e^{i\omega(t+\tau)}\right) = \mathcal{L}_C\left(e^{i\omega\tau} e^{i\omega t}\right)$$
$$= e^{i\omega\tau} \mathcal{L}_C\left(e^{i\omega t}\right)$$

The last step follows because the system is linear and $e^{i\omega\tau}$ is a constant. Therefore,

$$g(t + \tau) = e^{i\omega\tau} g(t)$$

Substituting $t = 0$ in the above equation results in $g(\tau) = ke^{i\omega\tau}$, where $k = g(0)$. Replacing τ by t yields the required result.

CHAPTER 16

Elements of Discrete-Time Signal Processing

16.1 Introduction

Elements of discrete-time signal processing techniques are discussed in this chapter. Basics of the z-transform analysis of discrete-time linear systems, and properties of certain relevant discrete-time filters are also specified.

16.2 Discrete-Time Signal Processing

Mathematical language used in describing discrete-time signals is outlined in this section. Typically signals found in nature are continuous. However, in order to process continuous-time signals on a computer, these signals have to be discretized. Discretization takes place by sampling continuous-time signals at regular intervals of length T_s. The optimal value of T_s is determined by the frequency content of a real-valued signal $f(t)$, where $t \in \mathbb{R}$. Optimality implies the recoverability of the signal $f(t)$ from its sampled values at $f(nT_s)$, $n \in \mathbb{Z}$. The inverse of T_s is called the sampling frequency (or sampling rate) f_s.

Let $f(t) \leftrightarrow F(\omega)$, and $F(\omega) = 0$ for $\omega_c \le |\omega|$. Then as per the celebrated Shannon's sampling theorem,

$$T_s \le \frac{\pi}{\omega_c}$$

$$\frac{\omega_c}{\pi} \le f_s$$

Minimum sampling frequency f_s is called the Nyquist rate, and its inverse is called the Nyquist interval. Therefore, the Nyquist frequency is equal to ω_c/π, and the Nyquist interval is equal to π/ω_c. We denote $f(nT_s)$ by $f(n)$, where $n \in \mathbb{Z}$, if the context is clear. Having determined the conversion process of a continuous-time signal to a discrete-time signal, we are ready to study discrete-time signal processing. Discrete-time signal processing is the study of sequences $\{f(n) \mid n \in \mathbb{Z}\}$.

Definitions 16.1. *The system is discrete in time.*

1. *System description. A discrete-time system is a mapping that transforms a sequence of input signal to a sequence of output signal. Let the input and output sequences be given by $\{x(n) \mid n \in \mathbb{Z}\}$ and $\{y(n) \mid n \in \mathbb{Z}\}$ respectively. The relationship or the mapping between these two sequences is expressed as*

$$y(n) = \mathcal{L}_D(x(n)), \qquad \forall n \in \mathbb{Z} \tag{16.1}$$

and $\mathcal{L}_D$ is the system operator. The sequences $x(\cdot)$ and $y(\cdot)$ can either be real- or complex-valued.

2. *Linear system. A system is linear, if its operator satisfies the following condition. If for each $a_1, a_2 \in \mathbb{C}$, and $y_1(n) = \mathcal{L}_D(x_1(n))$ and $y_2(n) = \mathcal{L}_D(x_2(n))$ then*

$$\mathcal{L}_D(a_1 x_1(n) + a_2 x_2(n)) = a_1 y_1(n) + a_2 y_2(n), \qquad \forall n \in \mathbb{Z} \tag{16.2}$$

3. *Time-invariant or shift-invariant system. A system is shift-invariant if*

$$y(n - n_0) = \mathcal{L}_D(x(n - n_0)), \qquad \forall n_0, n \in \mathbb{Z} \tag{16.3}$$

4. *Unit sample input response of the system. The unit sample input sequence is*

$$\delta(n) = \begin{cases} 1, & n = 0 \\ 0, & n \in \mathbb{Z} \setminus \{0\} \end{cases} \tag{16.4a}$$

The response of the system to the unit sample is called the unit sample response $\{h(n) \mid n \in \mathbb{Z}\}$. That is,

$$\mathcal{L}_D(\delta(n)) = h(n), \qquad \forall n \in \mathbb{Z} \tag{16.4b}$$

5. *Causal system. A system $\mathcal{L}_D$ is causal (nonanticipative), if the output $y(n_0)$ of the system for each $n_0 \in \mathbb{Z}$ depends only on the input $x(n)$ for $n \leq n_0$.*
   Alternate definition of a causal system. Consider any two inputs $x_1(n)$ and $x_2(n)$ to the system $\mathcal{L}_D$, where $n \in \mathbb{Z}$. The corresponding outputs are $y_1(n)$, and $y_2(n)$ respectively. The system $\mathcal{L}_D$ is causal, if $x_1(n) = x_2(n), \forall n < n_0$, then $y_1(n) = y_2(n), \forall n < n_0$.

6. *Stability. A sequence $\{a(n) \mid n \in \mathbb{Z}\}$ is bounded if $|a(n)| \leq A < \infty, \forall n \in \mathbb{Z}$, for some nonnegative real number A. A system is stable if a bounded input produces a bounded output (BIBO).*   □

An important observation about BIBO systems is made.

Observation 16.1. A linear and time-invariant discrete-time system $\mathcal{L}_D$ is guaranteed to be stable if $\sum_{n \in \mathbb{Z}} |h(n)| < \infty$.   □

Responses (outputs) for different types of inputs for linear and time-invariant systems is next determined.

Observations 16.2. Let the discrete-time system be linear and time-invariant, and the system operator be $\mathcal{L}_D$. Also let the input and output sequences be $x(n)$ and $y(n)$, $n \in \mathbb{Z}$ respectively. Let the corresponding unit sample input response be $h(n)$, $n \in \mathbb{Z}$.

1. We have $\mathcal{L}_D \left(\delta \left(n - n_0 \right) \right) = h \left(n - n_0 \right); \ n, n_0 \in \mathbb{Z}$.

2. Response to an arbitrary input. The output response $y(n)$, $n \in \mathbb{Z}$ of a discrete-time, and linear time-invariant system to an input $x(n)$, $n \in \mathbb{Z}$ is given by

$$y(n) = \sum_{k \in \mathbb{Z}} x(k) h(n-k) \triangleq x(n) * h(n), \qquad n \in \mathbb{Z}$$

where $*$ is the discrete-time convolution operator. That is, the response of a linear system due to an arbitrary input is determined by its unit sample response sequence and the input sequence.
Observe that, $\sum_{k \in \mathbb{Z}} x(k) h(n-k)$ is convolution in discrete space. Its functionality is similar to the convolution operation in continuous-time.

3. Response of a causal system to an arbitrary input. For a linear time-invariant causal system

$$y(n) = \sum_{k=-\infty}^{n} x(k) h(n-k) = \sum_{k=0}^{\infty} x(n-k) h(k), \qquad n \in \mathbb{Z}$$

4. If a system $\mathcal{L}_D$ is specified via a linear constant-coefficient difference equation, the system $\mathcal{L}_D$ is causal if and only if $h(n) = 0$ for $\forall \, n < 0$.

5. Response of a causal system to a unit sample input sequence. Let the input sequence be defined as $u(n)$, $n \in \mathbb{Z}$, as

$$u(n) = \begin{cases} 1, & n \geq 0 \\ 0, & \text{otherwise} \end{cases}$$

Its response $w(n)$ is given by

$$w(n) = \sum_{k=0}^{n} h(k), \qquad n \geq 0$$

6. Exponential input. Let the input sequence be $x(n) = e^{i\omega n}$, $i = \sqrt{-1}$, $n \in \mathbb{Z}$, $\omega \in \mathbb{R}$. The corresponding output sequence $y(n) = e^{i\omega n} \mathcal{H}\left(e^{i\omega}\right)$, where $\mathcal{H}\left(e^{i\omega}\right) = \sum_{k \in \mathbb{Z}} e^{-i\omega k} h(k)$ and $\omega \in \mathbb{R}$. $\qquad \square$

A system can also be characterized based upon the length of its response to a unit sample.

Definitions 16.2.

1. *Let $A \subset \mathbb{Z}$ be a set of finite cardinality. If the unit sample input response of a system is $\{h(n) \mid n \in A\}$, then the filter is said to be a finite-length impulse response (FIR) system.*

2. *If the unit sample input response of a system is infinite in length, that is $\{h(n) \mid n \in \mathbb{Z}\}$, then the filter is said to be an infinite-length impulse response (IIR) system.* □

16.3 z-Transform Analysis of a Discrete-Time Linear System

System function, and systems specified via linear constant-coefficient difference equations are described. In addition, frequency domain analysis of discrete-time linear systems is also studied.

System Function

Let $\{x(n) \in \mathbb{R} \mid n \in \mathbb{Z}\}$ and $\{y(n) \in \mathbb{R} \mid n \in \mathbb{Z}\}$ be the input and output sequences of a linear time-invariant system. The unit sample response of this system is given by $\{h(n) \in \mathbb{R} \mid n \in \mathbb{Z}\}$. The system is described via the equation

$$y(n) = \sum_{k \in \mathbb{Z}} x(k) \, h(n-k), \qquad n \in \mathbb{Z}$$

These sequences are best studied via their z-transforms. Define

$$\mathcal{X}(z) = \sum_{n \in \mathbb{Z}} x(n) \, z^{-n}$$

$$\mathcal{Y}(z) = \sum_{n \in \mathbb{Z}} y(n) \, z^{-n}$$

$$\mathcal{H}(z) = \sum_{n \in \mathbb{Z}} h(n) \, z^{-n}$$

Then

$$\mathcal{Y}(z) = \mathcal{H}(z) \, \mathcal{X}(z)$$

The function $\mathcal{H}(z)$ is referred to as the system transfer function, or simply the system function.

Systems Described via Linear Constant-Coefficient Difference Equation

Let a system be described via the following linear constant-coefficient difference equation

$$\sum_{k=0}^{N} d(k) y(n-k) = \sum_{k=0}^{M} c(k) x(n-k)$$

where $M, N \in \mathbb{P}$. In order to solve this difference equation, initial conditions also have to be specified.

In general, systems described by such class of difference equations are not necessarily causal. For simplicity, we shall assume that the difference equation describes a linear, time-invariant, and causal system. The difference equation leads to

$$\mathcal{H}(z) = \frac{\sum_{k=0}^{M} c(k) z^{-k}}{\sum_{k=0}^{N} d(k) z^{-k}}$$

The rational transfer function $\mathcal{H}(z)$ is also called a filter. It can be expressed as

$$\mathcal{H}(z) = K \frac{\prod_{k=1}^{M} \left(1 - \lambda_k z^{-1}\right)}{\prod_{k=1}^{N} \left(1 - \mu_k z^{-1}\right)} = K z^{N-M} \frac{\prod_{k=1}^{M} \left(z - \lambda_k\right)}{\prod_{k=1}^{N} \left(z - \mu_k\right)}$$

Note that in the transfer function $\mathcal{H}(z)$, the roots of the numerator polynomial are called the zeros, and the roots of the denominator polynomial are called the poles. In the above equation, K is a constant, $\lambda_k \in \mathbb{C}$, $1 \le k \le M$ is the set of zeros, and $\mu_k \in \mathbb{C}$, $1 \le k \le N$ is the set of poles of the system function. Also observe that if $(N - M)$ is positive, then in addition to the M zeros, there are $(N - M)$ zeros of $\mathcal{H}(z)$ at $z = 0$. However, if $(N - M)$ is negative, then in addition to the N poles, there are $(M - N)$ poles of $\mathcal{H}(z)$ at $z = 0$. In these two cases, and also when $M = N$, the number of zeros and poles of $\mathcal{H}(z)$ are equal in number.

The region of convergence of the transfer function $\mathcal{H}(z)$ should exclude its poles. Furthermore, the region of convergence is generally an annulus of the form

$$\alpha < |z| < \beta$$

Observe that if the denominator is equal to $d(j) z^{-j}$, where $j \in [0, N]$, and $d(j) \ne 0$, then $\mathcal{H}(z)$ is the transfer function of a FIR filter. This is true because, in this case $\mathcal{H}(z)$ can be written as a polynomial in z^{-1} with a finite number of terms.

Observations 16.3. Consider a discrete-time linear time-invariant system.

1. The system is guaranteed to be stable if $\sum_{n \in \mathbb{Z}} |h(n)| < \infty$. This condition is equivalent to

$$\sum_{n \in \mathbb{Z}} |h(n)| |z|^{-n} < \infty$$

evaluated at $|z| = 1$. Therefore, for $\mathcal{H}(z)$ to exist, its region of convergence has to include the unit circle $|z| = 1$.

2. Consider a causal system, where $h(n) = a^n$, $n \geq 0$ and $a \in \mathbb{C}$ is a constant. Its transfer function is

$$H(z) = \frac{1}{1 - az^{-1}}$$

This system is stable, if $|a| < 1$. That is, the pole a of the transfer function $H(z)$ should be inside the unit circle.

3. For a discrete-time, linear, time-invariant, and causal ($h(n) = 0$, $\forall\, n < 0$) system:

   (a) The region of convergence of $\mathcal{H}(z)$ has to be $|z| > r_0$, where r_0 is a positive real number.

   (b) Since it is required for guaranteed filter stability that $\sum_{n \in \mathbb{N}} |h(n)| < \infty$, the region of convergence has to include the unit circle $|z| = 1$.

   (c) The poles of $H(z)$ should be inside the unit circle for stability.

   (d) Furthermore, the region of convergence has to exclude the poles of the transfer function $\mathcal{H}(z)$.   □

Frequency Domain Analysis of Discrete-Time Linear Systems

Discrete-time linear systems can sometimes be effectively studied in the frequency domain.

Definitions 16.3.

1. *The frequency response of a system $\mathcal{H}(e^{i\omega})$ is*

$$\mathcal{H}(e^{i\omega}) = \mathcal{H}(z)|_{z=e^{i\omega}} \tag{16.5a}$$

Let

$$\mathcal{H}(e^{i\omega}) = |\mathcal{H}(e^{i\omega})| e^{i\phi_h(\omega)} \tag{16.5b}$$

then $|\mathcal{H}(e^{i\omega})|$ and $\phi_h(\omega)$ are called the magnitude and phase of the function $\mathcal{H}(e^{i\omega})$ respectively.

2. *Assume $\phi_h(\omega)$ to be a continuous and differentiable function of ω. The group delay $\delta_h(\omega)$ of the filter is*

$$\delta_h(\omega) = -\frac{d\phi_h(\omega)}{d\omega} \tag{16.6}$$

□

Bandwidth Characterization

A discrete-time filter, similar to its continuous-time analog, transforms an input signal to its output signal. Filters are generally classified in terms of their frequency response. Let $\mathcal{H}(e^{i\omega})$ be the unit-sample frequency response of a linear discrete-time time-invariant system. Note that $\mathcal{H}(e^{i\omega})$ is a periodic function, with period 2π. Therefore, the function $\mathcal{H}(e^{i\omega})$ needs to be studied for only $\omega \in [-\pi, \pi]$.

The band-pass and band-stop filters in the frequency domain are specified in terms of the interval $I_\omega \subset [-\pi, \pi]$, where $I_\omega = [-\omega_1, -\omega_0] \cup [\omega_0, \omega_1]$ and $0 < \omega_0 < \omega_1$. Note that $\omega \in I_\omega \iff \omega_0 \leq |\omega| \leq \omega_1$.

Commonly used filters are low-pass, high-pass, band-pass, and band-stop filters. The system transfer function $\mathcal{H}(e^{i\omega})$ of these filters is specified as follows.

1. *Low-pass filter,* $\omega \in [-\pi, \pi]$.

$$\mathcal{H}(e^{i\omega}) = \begin{cases} \mathcal{H}(e^{i\omega}), & |\omega| \leq \omega_{low} < \pi \\ 0, & \text{otherwise} \end{cases}$$

ω_{low} is called the cut-off frequency of the discrete-time low-pass filter. Also, $|\mathcal{H}(e^{i\omega})| \in \mathbb{R}_0^+$ for $|\omega| \leq \omega_{low} < \pi$.

2. *High-pass filter,* $\omega \in [-\pi, \pi]$.

$$\mathcal{H}(e^{i\omega}) = \begin{cases} \mathcal{H}(e^{i\omega}), & |\omega_{high}| \leq \omega \leq \pi \\ 0, & \text{otherwise} \end{cases}$$

ω_{high} is called the cut-off frequency of the discrete-time high-pass filter. Also, $|\mathcal{H}(e^{i\omega})| \in \mathbb{R}_0^+$ for $|\omega_{high}| \leq \omega \leq \pi$.

3. *Band-pass filter,* $\omega \in [-\pi, \pi]$.

$$\mathcal{H}(e^{i\omega}) = \begin{cases} \mathcal{H}(e^{i\omega}), & \omega \in I_\omega \\ 0, & \text{otherwise} \end{cases}$$

ω_0 and ω_1 are called the band-pass frequencies of the discrete-time band-pass filter. Also, $|\mathcal{H}(e^{i\omega})| \in \mathbb{R}_0^+$ for $\forall \omega \in I_\omega$.

4. *Band-stop filter.*

$$\mathcal{H}(e^{i\omega}) = \begin{cases} \mathcal{H}(e^{i\omega}), & \omega \in [-\pi, \pi] \setminus I_\omega \\ 0, & \omega \in I_\omega \end{cases}$$

ω_0 and ω_1 are called the band-stop frequencies of the discrete-time band-stop filter. Also, $|\mathcal{H}(e^{i\omega})| \in \mathbb{R}_0^+$ for $\forall \omega \in [-\pi, \pi] \setminus I_\omega$.

16.4 Special Filters

Special filters like the linear phase filter, all-pass filter, and minimum-phase filter are studied. Subband coding is also discussed.

16.4.1 Linear Phase Filter

Characteristics of the linear phase filter are described.

Definition 16.4. *A linear time-invariant filter has a linear phase if*

$$\mathcal{H}(e^{i\omega}) = \mathcal{B}(e^{i\omega})e^{-i(\beta\omega-\alpha)} \tag{16.7}$$

where $\mathcal{B}(e^{i\omega})$, α, $\beta \in \mathbb{R}$.   □

Observations 16.4.

1. The group delay of a linear phase filter is $\delta_h(\omega) = \beta = $ a real constant.

2. Let $\{h(n) \in \mathbb{R} \mid n = 0, 1, 2, \ldots, (N-1)\}$ be the unit sample input response of a FIR filter of length N. Then the filter has linear phase if

$$h(n) = \pm h(N-1-n),$$

where the group delay $\beta = (N-1)/2$.   □

The second observation is established in the problem section.

Observation 16.5. The sequence $\{h(n) \in \mathbb{R} \mid n = 0, 1, 2, \ldots, (N-1)\}$ is the unit sample input response of a FIR filter such that $h(n) = \pm h(N-1-n)$. Then

(a) $\mathcal{H}(z) = \pm z^{-(N-1)}\mathcal{H}(z^{-1})$.

(b) If $\mathcal{H}(z)$ has a zero at ζ $(\neq 0)$ then $\mathcal{H}(z)$ has a zero at ζ^{-1}. Also since $h(n)$'s are real, $\overline{\zeta}$ and $\overline{\zeta}^{-1}$ are also zeros of $\mathcal{H}(z)$. Thus complex zeros of $\mathcal{H}(z)$ occur in conjugate reciprocal pairs.

(c) It is possible for $\mathcal{H}(z)$ to have zeros at $z = \pm 1$.   □

16.4.2 All-Pass Filter

Characteristics of the all-pass filter are described.

Definition 16.5. *A stable system $\mathcal{H}(e^{i\omega})$ is an all-pass filter if*

$$\left|\mathcal{H}(e^{i\omega})\right| = 1, \qquad \forall\,\omega \in \mathbb{R} \tag{16.8}$$

□

Observations 16.6. Characterization of the all-pass filter.

1. The zero λ_k and pole μ_k of an all-pass filter are related as $\lambda_k = \overline{\mu_k}^{-1}$, where $k = 1, 2, \ldots, M$.

$$\mathcal{H}(z) = e^{i\theta} \prod_{k=1}^{M} \frac{\left(\lambda_k^{-1} z - 1\right)}{(z - \mu_k)}$$

That is, the poles and zeros of an all-pass filter are constrained to occur in conjugate reciprocal pairs. This is true, as

$$\left|\lambda_k^{-1} z - 1\right| = \left|\overline{\mu_k} z - 1\right| = \left|\mu_k z^{-1} - 1\right| = \left|\mu_k - z\right| = \left|z - \mu_k\right|,$$

$$k = 1, 2, \ldots, M$$

If $h(n)$'s are real numbers, then $\theta = 0$ or π, and any complex pole μ_k is accompanied by a complex conjugate pole $\overline{\mu_k}$.

2. Let $\{x(n) \mid n \in \mathbb{N}\}$ and $\{y(n) \mid n \in \mathbb{N}\}$ be the input and output sequences of an all-pass filter. Use of Parseval's relation results in

$$\sum_{k \in \mathbb{N}} |x(k)|^2 = \sum_{k \in \mathbb{N}} |y(k)|^2$$

3. Let $z = e^{i\omega}$ and $\alpha = re^{i\theta}$, where r is a positive real number then:

   a) The group delay of filter $\mathcal{H}(z) = (z - \alpha)^{-1}$ is

   $$\delta_h(\omega) = \frac{(1 - r\cos(\omega - \theta))}{(1 + r^2 - 2r\cos(\omega - \theta))}$$

   b) The group delay of filter $\mathcal{H}(z) = (\overline{\alpha} z - 1)$ is

   $$\delta_h(\omega) = \frac{\left(r\cos(\omega - \theta) - r^2\right)}{(1 + r^2 - 2r\cos(\omega - \theta))}$$

   c) The group delay of the all-pass filter $\mathcal{H}(z) = (\overline{\alpha} z - 1) / (z - \alpha)$ is

   $$\delta_h(\omega) = \frac{\left(1 - r^2\right)}{|z - \alpha|^2}$$

   If $0 < r < 1$, the group delay of this filter is positive.
   Thus, if the poles of the filter lie inside the unit circle, then the group delay $\delta_h(\omega) > 0$, $\forall \omega \in \mathbb{R}$.   □

16.4.3 Minimum-Phase Filter

If a causal discrete-time linear and time-invariant filter has a rational transfer function $\mathcal{H}(z)$, then all of its poles are inside the unit circle for the system to be stable. A minimum-phase filter has an additional property where the poles of the function

$1/\mathcal{H}(z)$ are also required to be inside the unit circle. Following is the formal definition of a minimum-phase filter.

Definition 16.6. *A filter is minimum-phase if all its zeros λ_j's and poles μ_k's are inside the unit circle. That is, $|\lambda_j| < 1$, and $|\mu_k| < 1$.*   □

Observations 16.7. Some observations regarding minimum phase filters.

1. A minimum-phase filter with transfer function $\mathcal{H}(z)$ is uniquely determined from $|\mathcal{H}(z)|$.
   Observe that $|\mathcal{H}(z)|^2$ is a function of $\cos n\omega$, as $\cos n\omega = (z^n + z^{-n})/2$, determine $|\mathcal{H}(z)|^2$. As $|\mathcal{H}(z)|^2 = \mathcal{H}(z)\mathcal{H}(z^{-1})$, the minimum-phase system is formed from the poles and zeros of $|\mathcal{H}(z)|^2$ that are inside the unit circle.

2. Let $\mathcal{H}(z)$ be the transfer function of any causal stable filter, then

$$\mathcal{H}(z) = \mathcal{M}(z)\mathcal{A}(z)$$

   where $\mathcal{M}(z)$ and $\mathcal{A}(z)$ are the transfer functions of a minimum-phase filter and an all-pass filter respectively. Therefore, $|\mathcal{H}(z)| = |\mathcal{M}(z)|$.

3. Let the group delay of the filters $\mathcal{H}(z)$, $\mathcal{M}(z)$, and $\mathcal{A}(z)$ be $\delta_h(\omega)$, $\delta_m(\omega)$, and $\delta_a(\omega)$ respectively. Then

$$\delta_h(\omega) = \delta_m(\omega) + \delta_a(\omega)$$

   As the all-pass filter is stable and $\delta_a(\omega) > 0$. Therefore, filters that have the same value of $|\mathcal{H}(e^{i\omega})|$ for all values of ω, the minimum-phase filter has the minimum group delay. Consequently, the minimum-phase sequences are also called minimum-delay sequences.

4. Let the phase of the filters $\mathcal{H}(z)$, $\mathcal{M}(z)$, and $\mathcal{A}(z)$ be $\phi_h(\omega)$, $\phi_m(\omega)$, and $\phi_a(\omega)$ respectively. Then

$$\phi_h(\omega) = \phi_m(\omega) + \phi_a(\omega)$$

   As $\delta_a(\omega) > 0$, we have $\phi_a(\omega) < 0$. Therefore,

$$\phi_h(\omega) < \phi_m(\omega)$$

   Next define the negative of the phase of a filter as the phase-lag. Then minimum-phase filters are actually *minimum-phase-lag* filters.

5. Let $\{h(n) \in \mathbb{R} \mid n \in \mathbb{N}\}$ be the unit sample response sequence of a causal filter with transfer functions $\mathcal{H}(z)$. The unit sample response sequence of the corresponding minimum-phase filter is $\{m(n) \in \mathbb{R} \mid n \in \mathbb{N}\}$. The z-transform of this later sequence is $\mathcal{M}(z)$. Then

$$\sum_{k\in\mathbb{N}} h^2(k) = \sum_{k\in\mathbb{N}} m^2(k)$$

It can also be shown that the following stronger result holds.

$$\sum_{k=0}^{n} h^2(k) < \sum_{k=0}^{n} m^2(k), \quad \forall\, n \in \mathbb{N}$$

This implies that the net energy of the two filters is identical. However the energy of the minimum-phase filter $m(n)$ is concentrated at lower values of n, when compared to the filter $h(n)$. This property is also called the minimum energy delay. □

16.4.4 Subband Coding

Consider a data stream $\{f(n) \in \mathbb{R} \mid n \in \mathbb{Z}\}$ with z-transform $\mathcal{F}(z)$. This stream of data has to be transmitted from its originating point to a destination point. The basic aim of communication engineering is the efficient transmission of information from the originating point to its destination (receiver). In order to achieve this goal data compression is required. Subband coding is a technique to implement efficient data transmission. In this scheme, the original data stream is passed through several approximated band-pass filters. The output of certain important filters are allocated more transmission resources than the less important filters. Furthermore filters at the transmitting and receiving end have to be designed such that the original signal (or data stream) is recovered at the receiving end. This scheme is called subband coding. Note that a subband is a contiguous range of frequencies.

To illustrate this technique, it is assumed that the original sequence

$$\{f(n) \in \mathbb{R} \mid n \in \mathbb{Z}\} \triangleq S$$

is split into two streams:

1. The first data stream is $\{f_{low}(n) \in \mathbb{R} \mid n \in \mathbb{Z}\}$. It is obtained by passing the sequence S through a low-pass filter, with transfer function $\mathcal{H}(z)$. Let the z-transform of $\{f_{low}(n) \in \mathbb{R} \mid n \in \mathbb{Z}\}$ be $\mathcal{F}_{low}(z)$. Then $\mathcal{F}_{low}(z) = \mathcal{H}(z)\mathcal{F}(z)$.

2. The second data stream is $\{f_{high}(n) \in \mathbb{R} \mid n \in \mathbb{Z}\}$. It is obtained by passing the sequence S through a high-pass filter, with transfer function $\mathcal{G}(z)$. Let the z-transform of $\{f_{high}(n) \in \mathbb{R} \mid n \in \mathbb{Z}\}$ be $\mathcal{F}_{high}(z)$. Then $\mathcal{F}_{high}(z) = \mathcal{G}(z)\mathcal{F}(z)$.

Observe that now there are two data streams instead of a single data stream to be transmitted. To circumvent this problem, the outputs of low-pass and high-pass filters are each down-sampled and then transmitted. The down-sampling is done by a factor of two. Let the z-transform of the two down-sampled outputs be $\mathcal{F}_1(z)$ and $\mathcal{F}_2(z)$ respectively. Then

$$\mathcal{F}_1(z) = \frac{1}{2}\left[\mathcal{F}_{low}\left(\sqrt{z}\right) + \mathcal{F}_{low}\left(-\sqrt{z}\right)\right]$$

$$= \frac{1}{2}\left[\mathcal{H}\left(\sqrt{z}\right)\mathcal{F}\left(\sqrt{z}\right) + \mathcal{H}\left(-\sqrt{z}\right)\mathcal{F}\left(-\sqrt{z}\right)\right]$$

$$\mathcal{F}_2(z) = \frac{1}{2}\left[\mathcal{F}_{high}\left(\sqrt{z}\right) + \mathcal{F}_{high}\left(-\sqrt{z}\right)\right]$$

$$= \frac{1}{2}\left[\mathcal{G}\left(\sqrt{z}\right)\mathcal{F}\left(\sqrt{z}\right) + \mathcal{G}\left(-\sqrt{z}\right)\mathcal{F}\left(-\sqrt{z}\right)\right]$$

This decomposition-operation of the original stream into two such streams is called the *analysis-operation*. At the receiving end these two streams are processed as follows. Each of these two streams are up-sampled. Recall that up-sampling consists of inserting a zero-valued sample between two successive samples. After up-sampling, the first stream is passed through a filter with transfer function $\widetilde{\mathcal{H}}(z)$. Similarly, after up-sampling, the second stream is passed through a filter with transfer function $\widetilde{\mathcal{G}}(z)$. Let the z-transform of these outputs be $\mathcal{E}_1(z)$ and $\mathcal{E}_2(z)$ respectively. Finally the two streams are merged together to obtain a sequence with z-transform $\mathcal{E}(z)$. That is,

$$\mathcal{E}_1(z) = \widetilde{\mathcal{H}}(z)\mathcal{F}_1(z^2)$$
$$\mathcal{E}_2(z) = \widetilde{\mathcal{G}}(z)\mathcal{F}_2(z^2)$$
$$\mathcal{E}(z) = \mathcal{E}_1(z) + \mathcal{E}_2(z)$$

Then it is hoped that $\mathcal{E}(z) = \mathcal{F}(z)$. This is called perfect reconstruction. It is also reasonable to accept that $\mathcal{E}(z) = z^{-m}\mathcal{F}(z)$, where m is some positive integer. The factor z^{-m} accounts for delay of m units. The filter operation at the receiver is called the *synthesis-operation*. Combination of the above equations yields

$$\mathcal{E}(z) = \frac{1}{2}\left[\mathcal{H}(z)\widetilde{\mathcal{H}}(z) + \mathcal{G}(z)\widetilde{\mathcal{G}}(z)\right]\mathcal{F}(z)$$

$$+ \frac{1}{2}\left[\mathcal{H}(-z)\widetilde{\mathcal{H}}(z) + \mathcal{G}(-z)\widetilde{\mathcal{G}}(z)\right]\mathcal{F}(-z)$$

For perfect reconstruction, the following requirements are necessary.

$$\mathcal{H}(-z)\widetilde{\mathcal{H}}(z) + \mathcal{G}(-z)\widetilde{\mathcal{G}}(z) = 0$$
$$\mathcal{H}(z)\widetilde{\mathcal{H}}(z) + \mathcal{G}(z)\widetilde{\mathcal{G}}(z) = 2z^{-m}, \quad m \in \mathbb{N}$$

The first requirement is satisfied, if

$$\widetilde{\mathcal{H}}(z) = \mathcal{G}(-z), \quad \text{and} \quad \widetilde{\mathcal{G}}(z) = -\mathcal{H}(-z)$$

Substituting these values in the second requirement for perfect reconstruction of the signal gives

$$\mathcal{H}(z)\mathcal{G}(-z) - \mathcal{H}(-z)\mathcal{G}(z) = 2z^{-m}, \quad m \in \mathbb{N}$$

Two solutions are described for this equation.

Solution 1:

Let $\mathcal{G}(z) = \mathcal{H}(-z)$, then

$$\mathcal{H}(z)^2 - \mathcal{H}(-z)^2 = 2z^{-m}, \quad m \in \mathbb{N}$$

If the filter $\mathcal{H}(z)$ is symmetric, that is $h(n) = h(-n)$, $n \in \mathbb{Z}$, then $\mathcal{H}(z) = \mathcal{H}(z^{-1})$. Consequently $\mathcal{G}(z) = \mathcal{H}(-z^{-1})$. As $z = e^{i\omega}$, this implies $\mathcal{G}(e^{i\omega}) = \mathcal{H}(e^{i(\pi-\omega)})$. Next make the transformation $\omega = \alpha + \pi/2$, and observe that

$$\mathcal{G}\left(e^{i(\pi/2+\alpha)}\right) = \mathcal{H}\left(e^{i(\pi/2-\alpha)}\right)$$

This equation implies that the frequency response of the filters $\mathcal{G}(z)$ and $\mathcal{H}(z)$ are symmetric with respect to each other at frequency $\pi/2$. Therefore, the filters with transfer functions $\mathcal{G}(z)$ and $\mathcal{H}(z)$ are termed *quadrature mirror filters* (QMF).
If $m = 1$, then $\mathcal{H}(z) = (1 + z^{-1})/\sqrt{2}$. This is the Haar filter.

Solution 2:

Let $\mathcal{G}(z) = -z^{-N}\mathcal{H}(-z^{-1})$, where N is an odd number, then

$$\widetilde{\mathcal{H}}(z) = z^{-N}\mathcal{H}(z^{-1}), \quad \text{and} \quad \widetilde{\mathcal{G}}(z) = -\mathcal{H}(-z)$$

$$z^{-N}\left[\mathcal{H}(z)\mathcal{H}(z^{-1}) + \mathcal{H}(-z)\mathcal{H}(-z^{-1})\right] = 2z^{-m}$$

Next let $N = m$, and $\mathcal{H}(e^{i\omega}) \triangleq H(\omega)$. If it is assumed that the coefficients of the low pass filter $\mathcal{H}(z)$ are real numbers, then

$$|H(\omega)|^2 + |H(\omega + \pi)|^2 = 2$$

A solution of this equation is not provided. However, note that a similar equation is encountered while analyzing discrete wavelets. Without elaborating further, observe that the results of subband coding can be interpreted in terms of wavelet theory and vice versa.

Problems

1. Let the discrete-time system be linear and time-invariant. Also let the input and output sequences be $x(\cdot)$ and $y(\cdot)$ respectively. The corresponding unit-sample input response sequence is $h(\cdot)$. Show that

$$y(n) = \sum_{k \in \mathbb{Z}} x(k) h(n-k) \triangleq x(n) * h(n), \qquad n \in \mathbb{Z}$$

where $*$ is the discrete-time convolution operator.

Hint: Note that for $n \in \mathbb{Z}$

$$x(n) = \sum_{k \in \mathbb{Z}} x(k) \delta(n-k)$$

Then

$$y(n) = \mathcal{L}_D(x(n)) = \mathcal{L}_D\left(\sum_{k \in \mathbb{Z}} x(k) \delta(n-k)\right)$$

$$= \sum_{k \in \mathbb{Z}} x(k) \mathcal{L}_D(\delta(n-k))$$

The last step follows from the linearity of the system. Since $\mathcal{L}_D(\delta(n-k)) = h(n-k)$

$$y(n) = \sum_{k \in \mathbb{Z}} x(k) h(n-k)$$

Therefore, the response of a linear system due to an arbitrary input is determined by its unit sample response and the input sequence.

2. Let the discrete-time system be linear, time-invariant, and causal. Also let the input and output sequences be $x(\cdot)$ and $y(\cdot)$ respectively. The corresponding unit sample input response sequence is $h(\cdot)$. Show that

$$y(n) = \sum_{k=-\infty}^{n} x(k) h(n-k) = \sum_{k=0}^{\infty} x(n-k) h(k), \qquad n \in \mathbb{Z}$$

Hint: For a causal system $h(n) = 0$ for $n < 0$. Then

$$y(n) = \sum_{k \in \mathbb{Z}} x(k) h(n-k) = \sum_{k=-\infty}^{n} x(k) h(n-k)$$

$$= \sum_{k=0}^{\infty} x(n-k) h(k)$$

3. Let the discrete-time system be linear, time-invariant, and causal. Also, let the input sequence be defined as $u(n), n \in \mathbb{Z}$, as

$$u(n) = \begin{cases} 1, & n \geq 0 \\ 0, & \text{otherwise} \end{cases}$$

Show that, its response $w(n)$ is given by

$$w\left(n\right) = \sum_{k=0}^{n} h(k), \qquad n \in \mathbb{Z}$$

Hint: Observe that

$$w\left(n\right) = \sum_{k=-\infty}^{n} u\left(k\right) h\left(n - k\right) = \sum_{k=0}^{n} h\left(n - k\right)$$

$$= \sum_{k=0}^{n} h\left(k\right)$$

4. Let the discrete-time system be linear, and time-invariant. Also let the input sequence be $x\left(n\right) = e^{i\omega n}$, $i = \sqrt{-1}$, $n \in \mathbb{Z}$, $\omega \in \mathbb{R}$. Show that, the output sequence $y\left(n\right) = e^{i\omega n} \mathcal{H}\left(e^{i\omega}\right)$, where $\mathcal{H}\left(e^{i\omega}\right) = \sum_{k \in \mathbb{Z}} e^{-i\omega k} h\left(k\right)$ and $\omega \in \mathbb{R}$.

Hint: It is known that

$$y\left(n\right) = \sum_{k \in \mathbb{Z}} x\left(k\right) h(n - k), \qquad n \in \mathbb{Z}$$

$$= \sum_{k \in \mathbb{Z}} x\left(n - k\right) h\left(k\right) = \sum_{k \in \mathbb{Z}} e^{i\omega(n-k)} h\left(k\right)$$

$$= e^{i\omega n} \sum_{k \in \mathbb{Z}} e^{-i\omega k} h\left(k\right) = e^{i\omega n} \mathcal{H}\left(e^{i\omega}\right)$$

5. Prove that, the filter $\{h\left(n\right) \in \mathbb{R} \mid n = 0, 1, 2, \ldots, \left(N - 1\right)\}$ has linear phase property, if

$$h\left(n\right) = \pm h(N - 1 - n), \quad n = 0, 1, 2, \ldots, \left(N - 1\right)$$

Hint: The above assertion is proved for the positive sign. Let

$$\mathcal{H}\left(z\right) = \sum_{n=0}^{\left(N-1\right)} h\left(n\right) z^{-n}$$

If N is even then

$$\mathcal{H}\left(e^{i\omega}\right) = 2e^{-i\omega(N-1)/2} \left[\sum_{n=0}^{\left(N-2\right)/2} h\left(n\right) \cos \omega \left\{ n - \frac{\left(N - 1\right)}{2} \right\} \right]$$

If N is odd then

$$\mathcal{H}\left(e^{i\omega}\right)$$

$$= e^{-i\omega(N-1)/2} \left[h\left(\frac{N - 1}{2}\right) + 2 \sum_{n=0}^{\left(N-3\right)/2} h\left(n\right) \cos \omega \left\{ n - \frac{\left(N - 1\right)}{2} \right\} \right]$$

In both cases, the sum inside the square brackets is real, implying a group delay of $\left(N - 1\right)/2$.

Note that if $N = 2M$, $\mathcal{H}(z)$ can be written as $e^{-i\omega M + i\omega/2} \cos(\omega/2) b(\cos\omega)$, where $b(\cos\omega)$ is a polynomial in $\cos\omega$. However, if $N = (2M - 1)$, $\mathcal{H}(z)$ can be written as $e^{-i\omega(M-1)} c(\cos\omega)$, where $c(\cos\omega)$ is a polynomial in $\cos\omega$. This observation will be useful in analyzing biorthogonal wavelets.

6. Let $z = e^{i\omega}$ and $\alpha = re^{i\theta}$, where r is a positive real number. Prove that the group delay of the all-pass filter $\mathcal{H}(z) = (\bar{\alpha}z - 1)/(z - \alpha)$ is

$$\delta_h(\omega) = \frac{\left(1 - r^2\right)}{|z - \alpha|^2}$$

7. Let $\{x(n) \mid n \in \mathbb{N}\}$ and $\{y(n) \mid n \in \mathbb{N}\}$ be the input and output sequences of an all-pass filter. Prove that

$$\sum_{k \in \mathbb{N}} |x(k)|^2 = \sum_{k \in \mathbb{N}} |y(k)|^2$$

Hint: Let the z-transform of the input and output sequences of the all-pass filter be $\mathcal{X}(z)$ and $\mathcal{Y}(z)$ respectively. Also let its transfer function be $\mathcal{H}(z)$, where $\left|\mathcal{H}(e^{i\omega})\right| = 1$, $\forall\, \omega \in \mathbb{R}$. We also have $\mathcal{Y}(z) = \mathcal{H}(z)\mathcal{X}(z)$. For an all-pass filter

$$\left|\mathcal{Y}(e^{i\omega})\right|^2 = \left|\mathcal{H}(e^{i\omega})\right|^2 \left|\mathcal{X}(e^{i\omega})\right|^2 = \left|\mathcal{X}(e^{i\omega})\right|^2$$

Use of Parseval's relationship leads to

$$\sum_{k \in \mathbb{N}} |y(k)|^2 = \frac{1}{2\pi} \int_{-\infty}^{\infty} \left|\mathcal{Y}(e^{i\omega})\right|^2 d\omega$$

$$= \frac{1}{2\pi} \int_{-\infty}^{\infty} \left|\mathcal{X}(e^{i\omega})\right|^2 d\omega = \sum_{k \in \mathbb{N}} |x(k)|^2$$

8. Let $\{h(n) \in \mathbb{R} \mid n \in \mathbb{N}\}$ be the unit sample response sequence of a causal filter with transfer functions $\mathcal{H}(z)$. The unit sample response sequence of the corresponding minimum-phase filter is $\{m(n) \in \mathbb{R} \mid n \in \mathbb{N}\}$. The z-transform of this later sequence is $\mathcal{M}(z)$. Prove the following results.

(a)
$$\sum_{k \in \mathbb{N}} h^2(k) = \sum_{k \in \mathbb{N}} m^2(k)$$

(b) A stronger result:

$$\sum_{k=0}^{n} h^2(k) < \sum_{k=0}^{n} m^2(k), \qquad \forall\, n \in \mathbb{N}$$

Hint: See Hayes (1999).

(a) The statement implies that the net energy of the two filters is identical. It follows from Parseval's relation (as in the last problem).

(b) Let

$$M(z) = \left(1 - \alpha_j z^{-1}\right) C(z)$$

where $|\alpha_j| < 1$ and $C(z)$ is the transfer function of another minimum phase sequence. Let

$$\mathcal{H}(z) = \left(z^{-1} - \overline{\alpha}_j\right) C(z)$$

Then

$$\mathcal{H}(z) = \frac{\left(z^{-1} - \overline{\alpha}_j\right)}{\left(1 - \alpha_j z^{-1}\right)} M(z)$$

Observe that

$$|\mathcal{H}(z)| = |\mathcal{M}(z)|$$

Let $C(z)$ be the z-transform of the sequence $\{c(n) \in \mathbb{R} \mid n \in \mathbb{N}\}$. These imply

$$m(n) = c(n) - \alpha_j c(n-1)$$
$$h(n) = c(n-1) - \overline{\alpha}_j c(n)$$

Thus

$$\sum_{k=0}^{n} |m(k)|^2 - \sum_{k=0}^{n} |h(k)|^2$$

$$= \sum_{k=0}^{n} |c(k) - \alpha_j c(k-1)|^2 - \sum_{k=0}^{n} |c(k-1) - \overline{\alpha}_j c(k)|^2$$

$$= \sum_{k=0}^{n} \left(1 - |\alpha_j|^2\right) |c(k)|^2 - \sum_{k=0}^{n} \left(1 - |\alpha_j|^2\right) |c(k-1)|^2$$

$$= \left(1 - |\alpha_j|^2\right) \left\{|c(n)|^2 - |c(-1)|^2\right\}$$

Note that $c(-1) = 0$, because of causality. Thus

$$\sum_{k=0}^{n} |m(k)|^2 - \sum_{k=0}^{n} |h(k)|^2 = \left(1 - |\alpha_j|^2\right) |c(n)|^2$$

The right-hand side of the above expression is greater than zero as α_j lies inside the unit circle. The result follows.

PART IV

Mathematical Concepts

CHAPTER 17

Set-Theoretic Concepts and Number Theory

17.1 Introduction

Certain mathematical preliminaries are discussed in this chapter. Sets, functions, and basic number-theoretic topics like countability, divisibility, prime numbers, and greatest common divisor are defined and discussed. Basics of congruence arithmetic and the Chinese remainder theorem are also examined.

17.2 Sets

Basic concepts and notation relating to sets is summarized in this section.

Definitions 17.1. *Concerning sets.*

1. *A set is a well-defined list or collection of objects. A set can be specified by listing all the objects in it. A set S with elements x, and property $\alpha(x)$ is written as $S = \{x \mid \alpha(x)\}$.*

2. *An element or member of a set is an object which belongs to the list of objects of the set. If S is a set, and b is an element of this set, then it is denoted as $b \in S$. The Greek symbol $\in$ is called the membership symbol. If an element b does not belongs to a set, then it is denoted by $b \notin S$.*

3. *An empty or null set is a set with no objects in it. It is denoted by $\varnothing$.*

4. *Let A and B be two sets such that, every element of A is also an element of B, then the set A is said to be a subset of the set B. This is denoted symbolically by $A \subseteq B$. It is also possible for these two sets A and B to be equal.*

5. *Let A and B be two sets such that, A is a subset of the set B. Furthermore, there exists an element in the set B that is not in the set A. Then the set A is said to be a proper subset of the set B. This is denoted by $A \subset B$.*

6. *Two sets U and V are equal, if they contain identical elements. It is written as* $U = V$.

7. *The cardinality $|A|$ of a set A is the number of elements in A. Sets can either have a finite or an infinite number of objects. Thus $|A|$ can be either finite or infinite.*   □

The set of positive even numbers x less than 13 is written as:

$$\{x \mid x \text{ is a positive even number}, x < 13\}$$

This set is indeed equal to $\{2, 4, 6, 8, 10, 12\}$. This set has 6 elements. Therefore, its cardinality is 6. Two sets U and V are equal if and only if $U \subseteq V$ and $V \subseteq U$.

Examples 17.1. A list of some sets of infinite size.

1. The set of positive natural numbers $\mathbb{P} = \{1, 2, 3, \ldots\}$.

2. The set of natural numbers $\mathbb{N} = \{0, 1, 2, 3, \ldots\}$.

3. The set of integers $\mathbb{Z} = \{\ldots, -2, -1, 0, 1, 2, \ldots\}$.

4. Integers divisible by 2 are called even numbers, and integers not divisible by 2 are called odd numbers. The set of positive even numbers is $\{2, 4, 6, \ldots\}$. The set of positive odd numbers is $\{1, 3, 5, \ldots\}$.

5. The set of rational numbers $\mathbb{Q}$ is the set of all fractions m/n, where m is any integer, and n is any integer except 0.

6. The set of all real numbers is denoted by $\mathbb{R}$. These numbers can be written either as terminating or as nonterminating decimal numbers.

7. The set of irrational numbers is the set of real numbers which are not rational. Some examples are: $e, \pi, \sqrt{2}$, and $3^{1/5}$.

8. The set of positive real numbers is $\mathbb{R}^+$. That is,

$$\mathbb{R}^+ = \{r \mid r > 0 \text{ and } r \in \mathbb{R}\}$$

9. The set of nonnegative real numbers is denoted by $\mathbb{R}_0^+$. Thus $\mathbb{R}_0^+ = \mathbb{R}^+ \cup \{0\}$.

10. The set of all complex numbers is denoted by $\mathbb{C}$. Complex numbers are of the form $(p + iq)$, where $p, q \in \mathbb{R}$ and $i = \sqrt{-1}$. Complex numbers of the form $(p + iq)$ where $p, q \in \mathbb{Z}$ are called Gaussian integers.   □

Note that $\mathbb{P} \subset \mathbb{N} \subset \mathbb{Z} \subset \mathbb{Q} \subset \mathbb{R} \subset \mathbb{C}$.

17.2.1 Set Operations

Set operations such as union, intersection, complement, and Cartesian product are defined.

Definitions 17.2. *Set operations.*

1. *The union of two sets A and B is written as $A \cup B$. It is the set of elements which belong to either A or B.*

$$A \cup B = \{x \mid x \in A \ \text{or} \ x \in B\} \tag{17.1}$$

2. *The intersection of two sets A and B is written as $A \cap B$. It is the set of elements which belong to both A and B.*

$$A \cap B = \{x \mid x \in A \ \text{and} \ x \in B\} \tag{17.2}$$

If $A \cap B = \emptyset$, then the sets A and B are said to be disjoint. This intersection operation is sometimes simply denoted by AB.

3. *All studied sets are usually subsets of some large fixed set U. This set is generally called a universal set, or universe of discourse, or space.*

4. *Let A be a subset of some universal set U. Then the complement of the set A is the set of all elements which do not belong to A. The complement of the set A is denoted by A^c.*

$$A^c = \{x \mid x \in U \ \text{and} \ x \notin A\} \tag{17.3}$$

Therefore, $A \cup A^c = U$, and $A \cap A^c = \emptyset$. Alternate ways of denoting the set A^c are $(U - A)$, $\overline{A}$, and A'.

5. *The difference of sets A and B is denoted by $A \backslash B$. It is the relative complement of set B with respect to A. That is, $A \backslash B$ is the set of elements which belong to set A, but not to set B.*

$$A \backslash B = \{x \mid x \in A \ \text{and} \ x \notin B\} \tag{17.4}$$

This set is sometimes denoted by $(A - B)$. Actually $(A - B) = AB^c$.

6. *Let A and B be any two sets. The Cartesian product of sets A and B, denoted by $A \times B$ is the set of all ordered pairs (a, b) where $a \in A$ and $b \in B$.*

$$A \times B = \{(a, b) \mid a \in A, b \in B\} \tag{17.5}$$

The product of a set with itself, $A \times A$, is denoted by $A^{(2)}$ or A^2. Similarly

$$A^{(n)} \triangleq A^n = \underbrace{A \times A \times \cdots \times A}_{n \ \text{times}} \tag{17.6a}$$

The Cartesian product of the sets $A_1, A_2, \ldots, A_n$ is denoted by

$$\times_{i=1}^{n} A_i \tag{17.6b}$$

7. *Let A and B be any two sets. A relation (or binary relation or binary operation) R from A to B is a subset of $A \times B$. The set R is a set of ordered pairs, that is: $R = \{(a, b) \mid a \in A \ \text{and} \ b \in B\} \subseteq A \times B$.* □

17.2.2 Interval Notation

Intervals on the real line are defined below. The set of points on the real line is denoted by $\mathbb{R}$.

Definitions 17.3. *Let $a, b \in \mathbb{R}$, where $a < b$.*

1. *Open interval $(a, b) = \{x \mid a < x < b\}$.*

2. *Closed interval $[a, b] = \{x \mid a \leq x \leq b\}$, where a and b are called the end-points of the interval.*

3. *Open-closed interval $(a, b] = \{x \mid a < x \leq b\}$, where b is the end-point of the interval.*

4. *Closed-open interval $[a, b) = \{x \mid a \leq x < b\}$, where a is the end-point of the interval.*

5. *The intervals $(a, b]$ or $[a, b)$ are half-open (or half-closed) intervals in $\mathbb{R}$.*

6. *A single point in $\mathbb{R}$ is defined as a closed interval.*   □

An infinite interval is best defined via examples. Let $a \in \mathbb{R}$. Some examples of infinite intervals are:

$$(a, \infty) = \{x \mid a < x, x \in \mathbb{R}\}$$
$$[a, \infty) = \{x \mid a \leq x, x \in \mathbb{R}\}$$

and $(-\infty, \infty) = \mathbb{R}$.

17.3 Functions and Sequences

In this section, basic definitions of functions and sequences are given.

Definitions 17.4. *Concerning functions.*

1. *Let A and B be any two sets. Assign to each element a of the set A, a unique element b of the set B. The set of such assignments is called a function or mapping from A into B. It is indicated as $f : A \to B$. The function f is sometimes denoted by $f(\cdot)$.*
   The specific element $b \in B$ assigned to $a \in A$ is denoted by $f(a)$. It is written as $f(a) = b$, or simply $a \mapsto b$. Furthermore, $f(a)$ is sometimes called the image of a or the value of f at a. Also a is called the preimage of b. The set A is called the domain of f and the set B is called the codomain of f. The range of f is denoted by $f(A)$. It is the set of images $f(A) = \{f(a) \mid a \in A \text{ and } f(a) \in B\}$. Sometimes "codomain" and "range" are used synonymously. Note that $\{(a, b) \mid a \in A \text{ and } f(a) = b\} \subseteq A \times B$.

2. *Types of functions*:

   (a) *A function $f : A \to B$ is surjective or onto if every element $b \in B$ is the image of at least one element $a \in A$. That is, $f(A) = B$.*

   (b) *A function $f : A \to B$ is injective or one-to-one if different elements of the domain A are mapped to different elements of the codomain B. Therefore, if $a_1, a_2 \in A$, then $f(a_1) = f(a_2) \Rightarrow a_1 = a_2$.*

   (c) *A function $f : A \to B$ is bijective if it is both surjective and injective. If the sets A and B are finite, then $|A| = |B|$.*

3. *Inverse function: Let $f : A \to B$ be a bijective function. Its inverse is a function $f^{-1} : B \to A$ such that $f^{-1}(b)$ is equal to a unique $a \in A$ for each $b \in B$, and $f(a) = b$. Therefore, a bijective function is said to be invertible.*

4. *Support of a function: Let $f : X \to \mathbb{R}$ be a real-valued function, defined on an arbitrary set X. The support of function f is $\text{supp}(f) = \{x \in X \mid f(x) \neq 0\}$.*

$\square$

17.3.1 Sequences

A sequence of objects from a set S is a list of objects from it, where repetitions are permitted.

Definitions 17.5. *Concerning sequences.*

1. *An infinite sequence from a set S is a function $f : A \to S$, where A is generally the set of positive integers $\mathbb{P}$, or the set of natural numbers $\mathbb{N}$. If $A = \mathbb{P}$, the sequence is generally represented as $s_1, s_2, s_3, \ldots$, such that each $s_j \in S$. If $A = \mathbb{N}$, the infinite sequence is represented as $s_0, s_1, s_2, \ldots$, such that each $s_j \in S$.*

2. *A finite sequence from a set S is a function $f : A \to S$, where $A = \{1, 2, \ldots, n\}$. A finite sequence is generally represented as $\{s_1, s_2, \ldots, s_n\}$, or $(s_1, s_2, \ldots, s_n)$, or $\langle s_1, s_2, \ldots, s_n \rangle$, or simply $s_1, s_2, \ldots, s_n$, where each $s_j \in S$.*

   The value $n \in \mathbb{P}$ is said to be the length of the sequence.

3. *Consider a sequence, $S = \{s_1, s_2, s_3, \ldots\}$. If $\{i_1, i_2, i_3, \ldots\}$ is a sequence of positive integers such that $i_1 < i_2 < i_3 < \cdots$, then $\{s_{i_1}, s_{i_2}, s_{i_3}, \ldots\}$ is a subsequence of the sequence S.* $\square$

If there is no ambiguity, a sequence is sometimes denoted as $\{s_i \mid i \in A\}$ or simply $\{s_i\}$. An example of the set S is the set of real numbers $\mathbb{R}$.

17.4 Elementary Number-Theoretic Concepts

Elementary concepts of number theory such as countability, divisibility, prime numbers, and greatest common divisor are defined and discussed. The notion of greatest common divisor of integers is also extended to polynomials.

17.4.1 Countability

Definitions 17.6.

1. *Consider two sets A and B. These two sets are said to be equivalent if there is a one-to-one correspondence between A and B. Equivalent sets A and B are denoted by $A \sim B$.*

2. *A set A which is equivalent to the set of numbers $\{1, 2, \ldots, n\}$ for some $n \in \mathbb{P}$ is a finite set, otherwise it is called an infinite set.*

3. *Let A be an infinite set, such that $A \sim \mathbb{P}$, then the set A is denumerable, otherwise it is nondenumerable.*

4. *Empty, finite, or denumerable sets are called countable sets. A set which is not countable is called noncountable.*   □

   Examples 17.2. Some useful examples.

1. The set of real numbers between -1 and 1 is nondenumerable and therefore noncountable.

2. If $A \sim B$ and $A \sim C$, then $B \sim C$.

3. The set of rational numbers $\mathbb{Q}$ is denumerable and therefore countable.

4. The set of real numbers $\mathbb{R}$ is nondenumerable and therefore noncountable.   □

17.4.2 Divisibility

Let $m \in \mathbb{Z}$, and $a \in \mathbb{Z} \setminus \{0\}$. Then a is said to *divide* m if $m = ab$, where b is an integer. Furthermore, if a divides m, then a is said to be a *divisor* of m, and m is called a *multiple* of a. This is denoted by $a \mid m$. If m is not divisible by a, then this is denoted by $a \nmid m$.

Also if a and b are positive integers, such that $b \leq a$, then $a = bq + r$, where $0 \leq r < b$. The positive integer a is called the *dividend*, b the *divisor*, q the *quotient*, and r the *remainder*. It is customary to denote q by $\lfloor a/b \rfloor$, where $\lfloor \cdot \rfloor$ is called the *floor function* (or floor operator).

More formally, if $r \in \mathbb{R}$ then its floor $\lfloor r \rfloor$ is defined as the largest integer less than or equal to r. For example, $\lfloor 8.65 \rfloor = 8$, and $\lfloor -8.65 \rfloor = -9$. Similarly $\lfloor 8 \rfloor = 8$, $\lfloor -8 \rfloor = -8$, and $\lfloor 0 \rfloor = 0$.

17.4.3 Prime Numbers

A positive integer $p \in \mathbb{P}$ is said to be a *prime* number, if it is divisible by only two distinct positive integers. The two integers are 1 and itself. Note that by convention, the number 1 is not considered to be a prime number. Some examples of prime numbers are: $2, 3, 5, 7, 11, \ldots$.

A *composite* number is a positive integer, that has at least one factor besides the number one and itself. That is, a positive integer which is not one and a prime number is a composite number. Some examples are $4, 6, 8, 9, 10, \ldots$. Thus, any number which can be factored into prime numbers is called a composite number. In this case any number, greater than 1 but less than n, which divides n is called its proper factor. The next theorem is called the *fundamental theorem of arithmetic*.

Theorem 17.1. *Every integer* $n \in \mathbb{P} \backslash \{1\}$ *can be represented as a product of prime factors. This representation is unique up to the order of the factors.*

Proof. See the problem section.   □

17.4.4 Greatest Common Divisor

The greatest common divisor of two positive integers and the associated well-known Euclidean algorithm are next elucidated. This algorithm is named after the great ancient geometer, Euclid of Alexandria (325 BC-265 BC). The extended Euclidean algorithm is also outlined

Definitions 17.7. *Common divisor, greatest common divisor, and relatively prime integers.*

1. *Let d divide two positive integers a and b, then d is called a common divisor of a and b.*

2. *Let a and b be two positive integers. The largest positive integer d, that divides both a and b is called the greatest common divisor (gcd) of a and b. It is written as* $d = \gcd(a, b)$.

3. *Let a and b be positive integers such that* $\gcd(a, b) = 1$. *This implies that the integers a and b have no factors in common, except* 1. *Then a and b are said to be relatively prime (or coprime) to each other.*   □

Example 17.3. The integer 15 is a common divisor of 30 and 90. Note that $\gcd(30, 90) = 30$. The integers 8 and 17 are relatively prime to each other, because $\gcd(8, 17) = 1$.   □

Observations 17.1. Let $a, b, c \in \mathbb{P}$, and $\gcd(a, b) = d$.

1. $d \mid a$ and $d \mid b$.

2. $c \mid a$ and $c \mid b \Rightarrow c \mid d$.

3. There exist integers $\alpha, \beta \in \mathbb{Z}$, such that $\alpha a + \beta b = d$. □

The integers α and β are determined via the extended Euclidean algorithm. We can also have integers $\alpha', \beta' \in \mathbb{Z}$, such that $\alpha'a + \beta'b = d$; where $\alpha' = (\alpha + kb/d)$, $\beta' = (\beta - ka/d)$, and $k \in \mathbb{Z}$.

Euclidean and Extended Euclidean Algorithms

The Euclidean algorithm finds the greatest common divisor of two positive integers. The *extended Euclidean algorithm* finds the greatest common divisor of two positive integers a and b, and expresses it in the form $\gcd(a, b) = (\alpha a + \beta b)$, where α and β are some integers.

Let $a, b \in \mathbb{P}$, and $b < a$. The greatest common divisor, d of the integers a and b is computed via an iterative procedure called the Euclidean algorithm. The procedure is as follows.

$$a_0 = a, \; b_0 = b$$

$$a_0 = b_0 q_1 + b_1, \; q_1 = \left\lfloor \frac{a_0}{b_0} \right\rfloor, \; 0 < b_1 < b_0, \; a_1 = b_0$$

$$a_1 = b_1 q_2 + b_2, \; q_2 = \left\lfloor \frac{a_1}{b_1} \right\rfloor, \; 0 < b_2 < b_1, \; a_2 = b_1$$

$$\cdots$$

$$\cdots$$

$$a_{n-1} = b_{n-1} q_n + b_n, \; q_n = \left\lfloor \frac{a_{n-1}}{b_{n-1}} \right\rfloor, \; 0 < b_n < b_{n-1}, \; a_n = b_{n-1}$$

$$a_n = b_n q_{n+1} + b_{n+1}, \; q_{n+1} = \left\lfloor \frac{a_n}{b_n} \right\rfloor, \; 0 = b_{n+1} < b_n, \; a_{n+1} = b_n$$

Note that the procedure terminates when the remainder b_{n+1}, is equal to zero. The last nonzero remainder, b_n, is the greatest common divisor of the integers a and b. That is, $d = \gcd(a, b) = b_n$. This procedure terminates in a finite number of steps, because $0 = b_{n+1} < b_n < b_{n-1} < \ldots < b_2 < b_1 < b_0 = b$ and b is finite in value.

Since $a = bq_1 + b_1$ it can be inferred that $d \mid b_1$. The relationship $a_1 = b_1 q_2 + b_2$ shows that $d \mid b_2$. It can be similarly shown that $d \mid b_3$. By induction d divides each b_i, so $d \mid b_n$. Therefore, $d \leq b_n$.

Since $b_{n+1} = 0$, we have $b_n \mid a_n$ which is equal to $b_n \mid b_{n-1}$. Therefore, $b_n \mid a_{n-1}$, that is $b_n \mid b_{n-2}$. It follows by induction that b_n divides each b_i and a_i. Thus $b_n \mid b_0$ and $b_n \mid a_0$, that is $b_n \mid b$ and $b_n \mid a$. Therefore, b_n divides both a and b. This implies $b_n \leq d$.

That is, b_n is the gcd of a and b. This is the end of the description of the Euclidean algorithm.

As mentioned earlier, the extended Euclidean algorithm implicitly uses the Euclidean algorithm. If two positive integers a and b are given such that $b \leq a$, and

$\gcd (a, b) = d$, the extended Euclidean algorithm expresses the greatest common divisor as $d = (\alpha a + \beta b)$, where $\alpha, \beta \in \mathbb{Z}$. This result is called Bezout's theorem for integers. It is named after Étíenne Bézout (1730–1753). The extended Euclidean algorithm is not described in this chapter. These concepts are best illustrated via an example.

Example 17.4. Using the Euclidean algorithm it can be shown that the greatest common divisor of 24 and 160 is 8. Using the extended Euclidean algorithm it can be shown that $7 \cdot 24 + (-1) \cdot 160 = 8 = \gcd (24, 160)$. □

17.4.5 Polynomials

The concept of greatest common divisor of two positive integers is extended to polynomials. Terminology related to polynomials is initially introduced.

Definitions 17.8. *Polynomials over the field of complex numbers.*

1. *A polynomial in the variable (or indeterminate) x over the field $\mathbb{C}$ is an expression of type*
$$f(x) = a_n x^n + a_{n-1} x^{n-1} + \ldots + a_1 x + a_0 \qquad (17.7)$$
where $n \in \mathbb{N}$, $a_m \in \mathbb{C}$ for $0 \leq m \leq n$. Such polynomials are also termed univariate polynomials.

2. *The element a_m is called the coefficient of x^m in $f(x)$, for $0 \leq m \leq n$.*

3. *The largest integer m for which $a_m \neq 0$ is called the degree of the polynomial $f(x)$. It is usually written as $\deg f(x)$, or as simply $\deg f$.*

4. *If $\deg f(x) = m$, and $a_m = 1$, then the polynomial $f(x)$ is a monic polynomial.*

5. *If $f(x) = a_0$, and $a_0 \neq 0$, then the polynomial is said to be a constant polynomial. Its degree is equal to 0.*

6. *If all the coefficients of a polynomial are equal to 0, then the polynomial $f(x)$ is said to be a zero polynomial. Its degree is said to be equal to $-\infty$.*

7. *The value of a polynomial at $b \in \mathbb{C}$ is equal to $f(b) \in \mathbb{C}$.*

8. *The element $b \in \mathbb{C}$ is a root of the equation $f(x) = 0$, if $f(b) = 0$.*

9. *The element $b \in \mathbb{C}$ is a zero of the polynomial $f(x)$, if $f(b) = 0$.*

10. *The set of polynomials in variable x defined over the field $\mathbb{C}$ is denoted as $\mathbb{C}[x]$.*
□

Sometimes, the terms root and zero are used interchangeably. The set of polynomials in variable x defined over the field $\mathbb{R}$ is denoted as $\mathbb{R}[x]$.

Definition 17.9. *Greatest common divisor of nonzero polynomials.*

Let $f(x), g(x) \in \mathbb{C}[x]$; where $f(x) \neq 0$ and $g(x) \neq 0$. The greatest common divisor of $f(x)$ and $g(x)$ is a monic polynomial of greatest degree in $\mathbb{C}[x]$ which divides both $f(x)$ and $g(x)$. It is denoted by $\gcd(f(x), g(x))$.   □

It should be noted that the Euclidean algorithm and extended Euclidean algorithm were developed for integers. There is an analogous Euclidean algorithm and an extended Euclidean algorithm for polynomials. Thus the greatest common divisor of two nonzero polynomials can simply be computed as in the case of integers, which is the Euclidean algorithm. An extended Euclidean algorithm also exists for polynomials. This implies the existence of a Bézout's type of result for polynomials. These in turn are useful in developing Daubechies wavelets and coiflets.

17.5 Congruence Arithmetic

Congruence arithmetic is introduced in this section. The Chinese remainder theorem is also established. It finds use in the computation of discrete Fourier transform.

Definition 17.10. *Let $a, b \in \mathbb{Z}$, and $m \in \mathbb{Z} \setminus \{0\}$. The integer a is congruent to b modulo m, if m divides the difference $(a - b)$. Equivalently $a \pmod{m} \equiv b \pmod{m}$. The integer m is called the modulus. The modulo operation is denoted by $a \equiv b \pmod{m}$.*

However, if m does not divide $(a - b)$, then a and b are incongruent modulo m. This relationship is denoted by $a \not\equiv b \pmod{m}$.

Typically m is a positive integer.   □

Example 17.5. $8 \equiv 3 \pmod{5}$, $18 \equiv 7 \pmod{11}$, and $24 \equiv 4 \pmod{5}$.   □

Some observations about congruences are listed below.

Observations 17.2. Let $a, b, c, a_1, a_2, b_1, b_2 \in \mathbb{Z}$, and $n \in \mathbb{P}$.

1. $a \equiv b \pmod{n}$, if the remainder obtained by dividing a by n is the same as the remainder obtained by dividing b by n.

2. Reflexive property: $a \equiv a \pmod{n}$.

3. Symmetry property: If $a \equiv b \pmod{n}$, then $b \equiv a \pmod{n}$.

4. Transitive property: If $a \equiv b \pmod{n}$ and $b \equiv c \pmod{n}$, then $a \equiv c \pmod{n}$.

5. Let $a_1 \equiv a_2 \pmod{n}$, and $b_1 \equiv b_2 \pmod{n}$. Then

$$(a_1 + b_1) \equiv (a_2 + b_2) \pmod{n}, \quad \text{and} \quad a_1 b_1 \equiv (a_2 b_2) \pmod{n}$$

☐

Definition 17.11. $\mathbb{Z}_m$ *is the set of integers* $\{0, 1, 2, \ldots, (m-1)\}$, $m \in \mathbb{P} \setminus \{1\}$.

☐

Modular arithmetical operations are well defined on the set of integers $\mathbb{Z}_m$. This arithmetic is done by performing the usual real arithmetical operations, followed by the modulo operation.

Examples 17.6. The above ideas are illustrated via the following examples.

1. Addition and multiplication of integers 21 and 13 modulo 5 are performed. Note that 21 (mod 5) $\equiv$ 1 (mod 5), and 13 (mod 5) $\equiv$ 3 (mod 5).
   Addition operation:

$$(21 + 13) \ (\text{mod } 5) \equiv 34 \ (\text{mod } 5) \equiv 4 \ (\text{mod } 5)$$

or

$$(21 + 13) \ (\text{mod } 5) \equiv (21 \ (\text{mod } 5)) + (13 \ (\text{mod } 5))$$
$$\equiv (1 \ (\text{mod } 5)) + (3 \ (\text{mod } 5))$$
$$\equiv 4 \ (\text{mod } 5)$$

Multiplication operation:

$$(21 \times 13) \ (\text{mod } 5) \equiv 273 \ (\text{mod } 5) \equiv 3 \ (\text{mod } 5)$$

or

$$(21 \times 13) \ (\text{mod } 5) \equiv (21 \ (\text{mod } 5)) \times (13 \ (\text{mod } 5))$$
$$\equiv (1 \ (\text{mod } 5)) \times (3 \ (\text{mod } 5))$$
$$\equiv 3 \ (\text{mod } 5)$$

2. The modulo 5 operation partitions the set of integers $\mathbb{Z}$ into 5 classes (or sets). These are:

$$\{\ldots, -10, -5, 0, 5, 10, \ldots\}, \ \{\ldots, -9, -4, 1, 6, 11, \ldots\},$$
$$\{\ldots, -8, -3, 2, 7, 12, \ldots\}, \ \{\ldots, -7, -2, 3, 8, 13, \ldots\},$$
$$\text{and } \{\ldots, -6, -1, 4, 9, 14, \ldots\}$$

☐

The elements $a, b \in \mathbb{Z}_m \setminus \{0\}$, are said to be multiplicative inverses of each other if $ab \equiv 1 \ (\text{mod } m)$. If multiplicative inverse of an element exists, then it is unique. However, it is possible for the multiplicative inverse of $a \in \mathbb{Z}_m$ to not exist.

Definition 17.12. *Let m be a positive integer greater than 1, $a \in \mathbb{Z}_m \setminus \{0\}$, and* $\gcd(a, m) = 1$. *Then $b \in \mathbb{Z}_m$ is an inverse of a modulo m if $ab \equiv 1 \pmod{m}$. The element b is sometimes denoted by a^{-1}.*   □

Example 17.7. The multiplicative inverse of $7 \in \mathbb{Z}_{10}$ is 3, but the multiplicative inverse of $2 \in \mathbb{Z}_{10}$ does not exist.   □

The so-called Chinese remainder theorem is next discussed. It is generally regarded as one of the numerous pearls in number theory. It has found widespread application in diverse fields such as signal processing, coding theory, and cryptography.

Chinese Remainder Theorem

Following is the statement of the Chinese remainder theorem.

Theorem 17.2. *Let $m_1, m_2, \ldots, m_n \in \mathbb{P}$, be n positive integers, which are coprime in pairs, that is $\gcd(m_k, m_j) = 1$, $k \neq j, 1 \leq k, j \leq n$. Also let $m = \prod_{k=1}^{n} m_k$, and $x \in \mathbb{P}$. The n integers $a_1, a_2, \ldots, a_n \in \mathbb{Z}$, with the congruences*

$$x \equiv a_k \pmod{m_k}, \quad 1 \leq k \leq n \tag{17.8a}$$

are also given. These congruences have a single common solution

$$x \equiv \sum_{k=1}^{n} a_k M_k N_k \pmod{m}, \quad M_k = \frac{m}{m_k}, \quad (M_k N_k) \equiv 1 \pmod{m_k}, 1 \leq k \leq n$$

$$\tag{17.8b}$$

Proof. Note that M_k is mutually prime with m_k, that is, $\gcd(m_k, M_k) = 1$, for $1 \leq k \leq n$. Consequently there exist integers $N_1, N_2, \ldots, N_n \in \mathbb{P}$ such that

$$(M_k N_k) \equiv 1 \pmod{m_k}, \quad 1 \leq k \leq n$$

That is, each M_k has a unique reciprocal N_k modulo m_k. Define

$$x = a_1 M_1 N_1 + a_2 M_2 N_2 + \ldots + a_n M_n N_n$$

Since $M_k \equiv 0 \pmod{m_j}$, if $k \neq j, 1 \leq k, j \leq n$, we have

$$x \pmod{m_k} \equiv (a_k M_k N_k) \pmod{m_k} \equiv a_k \pmod{m_k}, \quad 1 \leq k \leq n$$

Therefore, x satisfies all congruences in the hypothesis of the theorem. If x and y are two solutions which satisfy the set of congruence equations, then $x \pmod{m_k} \equiv y \pmod{m_k}$ for $1 \leq k \leq n$. Also since the m_k's are relatively prime in pairs, x

$(\bmod\, m) \equiv y\,(\bmod\, m)$. Therefore, the given system of congruences have a single solution.   □

Example 17.8. The solution to the simultaneous congruences

$$x \equiv 2\,(\bmod\,3), \quad x \equiv 1\,(\bmod\,4),$$
$$x \equiv 3\,(\bmod\,5), \quad \text{and} \quad x \equiv 6\,(\bmod\,7)$$

is determined. Let $m_1 = 3, m_2 = 4, m_3 = 5$, and $m_4 = 7$. Then $m = 3 \cdot 4 \cdot 5 \cdot 7 = 420$,

$$M_1 = \frac{m}{m_1} = 140, \quad M_2 = \frac{m}{m_2} = 105,$$
$$M_3 = \frac{m}{m_3} = 84, \quad \text{and} \quad M_4 = \frac{m}{m_4} = 60$$

Also $(M_1 N_1) \equiv 1\,(\bmod\,3)$ implies $(140 N_1) \equiv 1\,(\bmod\,3)$, that is $(2 N_1) \equiv 1$ $(\bmod\,3)$ gives $N_1 = 2$. Similarly $N_2 = 1, N_3 = 4$, and $N_4 = 2$. Therefore,

$$x \equiv \{(2 \cdot 140 \cdot 2) + (1 \cdot 105 \cdot 1) + (3 \cdot 84 \cdot 4) + (6 \cdot 60 \cdot 2)\}\,(\bmod\,420)$$
$$\equiv 2393\,(\bmod\,420) \equiv 293\,(\bmod\,420)$$

The solution to the given congruences is $x \equiv 293\,(\bmod\,420)$.   □

The Chinese remainder theorem is used in the implementation of a fast version of the discrete Fourier transform. It uses a mapping of a positive integer x modulo m, into $(a_1, a_2, \ldots, a_n)$ where n is the number of relatively prime factors of $m \in \mathbb{P}$. The number x and its representation are related as follows. Let $m_1, m_2, \ldots, m_n \in \mathbb{P}$ be coprime factors of m, where $m = \prod_{k=1}^{n} m_k$. Then $x \equiv a_k\,(\bmod\, m_k)$, for $1 \leq k \leq n$.

Another simpler decomposition of x can be obtained. Define $M_k = m/m_k$, for $1 \leq k \leq n$, and also find integers $N_1, N_2, \ldots, N_n \in \mathbb{P}$ such that $(M_k N_k) \equiv 1$ $(\bmod\, m_k)$, for $1 \leq k \leq n$. Note that a_k's span the set $\{0, 1, 2, \ldots, (m_k - 1)\}$, for $1 \leq k \leq n$. Let $b_k \equiv (a_k N_k)\,(\bmod\, m_k)$, then b_k's also span the set $\{0, 1, 2, \ldots, (m_k - 1)\}$, because $\gcd\,(m_k, N_k) = 1$. It might help reiterating that the numbers a_k, b_k, M_k, and N_k are all computed modulo m_k. Thus another representation of x modulo m, is $(b_1, b_2, \ldots, b_n)$. These observations are summarized in the following lemma.

Lemma 17.1. *Let* $m_1, m_2, \ldots, m_n \in \mathbb{P}$, *be* n *positive integers, which are coprime in pairs, that is* $\gcd\,(m_k, m_j) = 1, k \neq j, 1 \leq k, j \leq n$. *Furthermore, let* $m = \prod_{k=1}^{n} m_k$. *Define* $M_k = m/m_k$, *for* $1 \leq k \leq n$, *and also let* $N_1, N_2, \ldots, N_n \in \mathbb{P}$ *be such that* $(M_k N_k) \equiv 1\,(\bmod\, m_k)$, *for* $1 \leq k \leq n$. *Let* $x \in \mathbb{P}$.

If $x \equiv a_k\,(\bmod\, m_k), 1 \leq k \leq n$, *then*

$$x \pmod{m} \mapsto (a_1, a_2, \ldots, a_n) \tag{17.9a}$$

An alternate map is obtained by defining $b_k \equiv (a_k N_k) \pmod{m_k}, 1 \leq k \leq n$. *Then*

$$x \pmod{m} \mapsto (b_1, b_2, \ldots, b_n) \tag{17.9b}$$

□

Problems

1. Establish the following results about prime numbers.
   (a) Every number $n \in \mathbb{P} \setminus \{1\}$ is either a prime number or a product of prime numbers.
   (b) Let p be a prime number, and $a \in \mathbb{P}$. If $p \nmid a$ then $\gcd(p, a) = 1$.
   (c) Let p be a prime number, and $a, b \in \mathbb{P}$. If $p \mid ab$ then $p \mid a$ and/or $p \mid b$. If the prime number p divides $a_1 a_2 \ldots a_n$ where $a_i \in \mathbb{P}$ for $1 \leq i \leq n$, then p divides at least one a_i.

   Hint: See Apostol (1976).

2. Establish the fundamental theorem of arithmetic. It asserts that, every integer $n \in \mathbb{P} \setminus \{1\}$ can be represented as a product of prime factors. This representation is unique up to the order of its factors.

   Hint: See Apostol (1976). This result is proved by using induction on n. The theorem is true for $n = 2$. In the induction hypothesis, assume that the theorem is true for all integers greater than 1 but less than n. Our goal is to establish the correctness of the theorem for n. If n is a prime integer, then the theorem is true. However, if n is not a prime integer, then it is a composite number. Assume that it has two representations in factored form. Let these be

   $$n = p_1 p_2 \cdots p_i \cdots p_s = q_1 q_2 \cdots q_j \cdots q_t$$

   It is next shown that $s = t$ and each p_i is equal to some q_j. Observe that p_1 must divide the product $q_1 q_2 \cdots q_t$. Consequently, it must divide at least one factor. Relabel $q_1, q_2, \cdots, q_t$ such that $p_1 \mid q_1$. Therefore, $p_1 = q_1$ as the integers p_1 and q_1 are both prime. In the next step, we write

   $$n/p_1 = p_2 \cdots p_i \cdots p_s = q_2 \cdots q_j \cdots q_t$$

   If $s > 1$ or $t > 1$, then $1 < n/p_1 < n$. Invocation of the induction hypothesis implies that the two factorizations of n/p_1 must be identical, except for the order of the factors. Thus $s = t$, and the factorizations $n = p_1 p_2 \cdots p_i \cdots p_s = q_1 q_2 \cdots q_j \cdots q_t$ are identical, except for the order.

3. Prove that there are infinitely many prime numbers.

Hint: See Apostol (1976), and Baldoni, Ciliberto, and Cattaneo (2009). Assume that there are only a finite number of prime numbers $p_1 < p_2 < \cdots < p_n$. Let $N = p_1 p_2 \cdots p_n + 1$. Observe that N is either a prime or a product of prime numbers. The number N is not a prime number as it exceeds each p_i, where $1 \leq i \leq n$. However, if p_i divides N, then p_i also divides $(N - p_1 p_2 \cdots p_n) = 1$. This is not possible since $p_i > 1$.

CHAPTER 18

Matrices and Determinants

18.1 Introduction

Definitions and elementary properties of matrices and determinants are briefly discussed in this chapter. Matrices as an example of linear mappings or transformations (operators) are also explored. In addition, spectral analysis of matrices is also outlined.

18.2 Elements of Matrix Theory

Elements of matrices are discussed in this section. Matrix notation is initially introduced. This is followed by a description of different matrix operations. Different types of matrices are next defined. The concept of a matrix norm is also discussed.

Definitions 18.1. *Let* $m, n \in \mathbb{P}$.

1. *Matrix: A* $m \times n$ *matrix* B *is a rectangular array of* mn *real or complex numbers arranged into* m *rows and* n *columns. The array elements are called its elements. A matrix of* m *rows and* n *columns is of order (size)* $m \times n$ *(read as* m *by* n*).*
   The matrix element in the i*-th row and* j*-th column is* b_{ij}*, where* $1 \leq i \leq m$ *and* $1 \leq j \leq n$*. The matrix* B *is also written as* $[b_{ij}]$*.*

$$
B = \begin{bmatrix}
b_{11} & b_{12} & \cdots & b_{1j} & \cdots & b_{1n} \\
b_{21} & b_{22} & \cdots & b_{2j} & \cdots & b_{2n} \\
\vdots & \vdots & \ddots & \vdots & \ddots & \vdots \\
b_{i1} & b_{i2} & \cdots & b_{ij} & \cdots & b_{in} \\
\vdots & \vdots & \ddots & \vdots & \ddots & \vdots \\
b_{m1} & b_{m2} & \cdots & b_{mj} & \cdots & b_{mn}
\end{bmatrix}
\tag{18.1}
$$

2. *Column vector: A column vector is an* $m \times 1$ *matrix. It is a matrix with* m *rows and a single column. The size or length of this vector is equal to* m*.*

The $m \times n$ matrix B is said to be an array of n column vectors, where the length of each column vector is m.

3. *Row vector: A row vector is a $1 \times n$ matrix. It is a matrix with a single row and n columns. The size or length of this vector is equal to n.*
   The $m \times n$ matrix B is said to be an array of m row vectors, where the length of each row vector is n.

4. *Square matrix: An $n \times n$ matrix with the same number of rows and columns is called a square matrix. It is sometimes simply said to be of order n, or of size n.*

5. *Diagonal elements of a matrix: If a matrix B is of size $n \times n$, then the matrix elements $b_{ii}, 1 \leq i \leq n$ are called its diagonal elements. The elements b_{ij}, with $i \neq j$ and $1 \leq i, j \leq n$ are called its off-diagonal elements.*

6. *Diagonal matrix: An $n \times n$ matrix D is called a diagonal matrix, if all its off-diagonal elements are equal to zero. If the diagonal matrix D has diagonal entries $d_1, d_2, \ldots, d_n$ then the matrix D is represented as $\mathrm{diag}\,(d_1, d_2, \ldots, d_n)$.*

7. *Identity matrix: An $n \times n$ matrix B is called an identity matrix, if all its diagonal elements $b_{ii}, 1 \leq i \leq n$ are each equal to unity, and all other elements are each equal to zero. It is usually denoted by either I or I_n.*

8. *Trace of a square matrix: The trace of a square matrix B is the sum of its diagonal elements. The trace of an $n \times n$ matrix $B = [b_{ij}]$, denoted by $\mathrm{tr}\,(B)$, is equal to $\sum_{i=1}^{n} b_{ii}$.*

9. *Zero or null matrix: If all the elements of a matrix are equal to zero, then it is called a zero or a null matrix. If there is no ambiguity and the context is clear, then it is simply represented as 0 (not to be confused with the real number 0).*

10. *Equal matrices: Let $A = [a_{ij}]$ and $B = [b_{ij}]$ be two $m \times n$ matrices. The matrix A is equal to matrix B, iff $a_{ij} = b_{ij}$, for all values of i and j, where $1 \leq i \leq m$, and $1 \leq j \leq n$. This equality of matrices is simply represented (denoted) as $A = B$.*

11. *Submatrix: The submatrix of a matrix B is a matrix obtained by deleting from it a specified set of rows and columns.* ☐

Occasionally, a row vector $\begin{bmatrix} x_1 & x_2 & \cdots & x_n \end{bmatrix}$ is represented as $(x_1, x_2, \ldots, x_n)$. This is in conformance with the vector notation described in the chapter on applied analysis. In general, if a vector is specified as $x \geq 0$, then the vector is allowed to take a 0 value. Also, the zero vector 0 is simply $\begin{bmatrix} 0 & 0 & \cdots & 0 \end{bmatrix}$.

18.2.1 Basic Matrix Operations

Following are the basic operations of matrix algebra.

Addition and subtraction of matrices: Let the matrices $A = [a_{ij}]$ and $B = [b_{ij}]$ be each of order $m \times n$. The matrices A and B of the same order are said to be conformable (compatible) for addition and subtraction.

The sum of matrices A and B is a matrix $C = [c_{ij}]$, where $c_{ij} = (a_{ij} + b_{ij})$, $1 \leq i \leq m$ and $1 \leq j \leq n$. The matrix C is also of order $m \times n$. This addition operation is denoted by $C = (A + B)$.

Similarly the subtraction of matrices A and B is a matrix $C = [c_{ij}]$, where $c_{ij} = (a_{ij} - b_{ij})$, $1 \leq i \leq m$ and $1 \leq j \leq n$. The matrix C is also of order $m \times n$. This subtraction operation is denoted by $C = (A - B)$.

Matrix multiplication by a constant: Let $\alpha \in \mathbb{C}$ and $A = [a_{ij}]$ be a matrix of order $m \times n$. Then $\alpha A = C = [c_{ij}]$, where $c_{ij} = \alpha a_{ij}$, $1 \leq i \leq m$ and $1 \leq j \leq n$. The matrix C is also of order $m \times n$.

Scalar product of row vectors: Let x and y be row vectors, each with n columns,

$$x = \begin{bmatrix} x_1 & x_2 & \cdots & x_n \end{bmatrix}, \quad \text{and} \quad y = \begin{bmatrix} y_1 & y_2 & \cdots & y_n \end{bmatrix}$$

The scalar product of the two row vectors is $x \circ y = \sum_{i=1}^{n} x_i y_i$. If the elements of these two row vectors are real numbers, then this definition is identical to the *dot* or *inner product* of the two vectors.

Multiplication of matrices: Let $A = [a_{ij}]$ be a matrix of order $m \times k$, and $B = [b_{ij}]$ be a matrix of order $k \times n$. Then the product of matrices A and B is a matrix $C = [c_{ij}]$ of order $m \times n$, where $c_{ij} = \sum_{l=1}^{k} a_{il} b_{lj}$, $1 \leq i \leq m$ and $1 \leq j \leq n$. In other words c_{ij} is the scalar product of row i of the matrix A and column j of matrix B. The matrix A is said to be conformable (compatible) to matrix B for multiplication when the number of columns of A is equal to the number of rows of B. The matrix C is denoted by AB.

Inverse of a matrix: If A and B are square matrices such that $AB = BA = I$, then the matrix B is called the inverse matrix of A. Generally B is denoted by A^{-1}. Conversely, the inverse of matrix A^{-1} is A. If the inverse of a matrix A exists, then the matrix A is called a *nonsingular matrix*. If the inverse does not exist, then A is called a *singular matrix*.

Conjugate of a matrix: If $B = [b_{ij}]$, where $b_{ij} \in \mathbb{C}$, then the conjugate of matrix B is $\overline{B} = [\overline{b}_{ij}]$.

Transpose of a matrix: If $B = [b_{ij}]$ is a matrix of order $m \times n$, then a matrix obtained by interchanging the rows and columns of the matrix B is called the transpose of B. It is of order $n \times m$. It is generally denoted by B^T. Note that $B^T = [b_{ji}]$.

Hermitian transpose of a matrix: If $B = [b_{ij}]$ is a complex matrix of order $m \times n$, then a matrix obtained by interchanging the rows and columns of the matrix B and taking the complex conjugate of the elements is called the Hermitian transpose of B. It is of order $n \times m$, and denoted by $B^\dagger$ († is the dagger symbol). Note that $B^\dagger = [\overline{b}_{ji}] = \overline{B}^T$. The Hermitian transpose of a matrix is named after the mathematician Charles Hermite (1822–1901).

18.2.2   Different Types of Matrices

The power of matrix algebra is further illustrated in this subsection.

Definitions 18.2. *Different types of matrices are defined below.*

1. *Similar matrices: Let A and B be square matrices of order n. Let P be an invertible matrix of order n such that $A = P^{-1}BP$. Then the matrices A and B are termed similar matrices. The operation $P^{-1}BP$ is the similarity transformation of the matrix B.*

2. *Symmetric matrix: B is a symmetric matrix if $B = B^T$.*

3. *Orthogonal matrix: A real square matrix B is orthogonal, if $B^T B = BB^T = I$, that is if $B^T = B^{-1}$.*

4. *Hermitian matrix: A complex square matrix B is Hermitian if $B^\dagger = B$.*

5. *Unitary matrix: A complex square matrix B is unitary, if $B^\dagger B = BB^\dagger = I$, that is if $B^\dagger = B^{-1}$.*

6. *Orthogonal vectors: Two complex row vectors A and B of the same size are orthogonal to each other, if $AB^\dagger = 0$*

7. *Orthonormal set of vectors: The complex row vectors $x_1, x_2, \ldots, x_n$ are an orthonormal set, if the length of vectors $x_j, 1 \le j \le n$ are normalized to unity, and $x_i x_j^\dagger = 0$, for all $i \ne j$ and $1 \le i, j \le n$. A similar definition can be extended to a set of complex column vectors.*

8. *Quadratic forms and definiteness: Let B be a Hermitian matrix of order n, and x is a complex column vector of size n. Let $f(x) = x^\dagger Bx$. The Hermitian matrix B and the quadratic form $f(x)$ associated with matrix B are said to be:*
   (a) *Negative definite if $f(x) < 0$, for all $x \ne 0$.*
   (b) *Negative semidefinite if $f(x) \le 0$, for all x; and $f(x) = 0$, for some $x \ne 0$.*
   (c) *Positive definite if $f(x) > 0$, for all $x \ne 0$.*
   (d) *Positive semidefinite if $f(x) \ge 0$, for all x; and $f(x) = 0$, for some $x \ne 0$.*
   (e) *Indefinite if $f(x) > 0$, for some x; and $f(x) < 0$, for some x.*

9. *Diagonalizable matrix: A square matrix B is diagonalizable, if there exists an invertible matrix P such that $PBP^{-1} = \Lambda$, where Λ is a diagonal matrix.*

10. *Toeplitz matrix: The square matrix $B = [b_{ij}]$ of size n is Toeplitz, if the matrix element $b_{ij} = a_{i-j}$, where $1 \le i, j \le n$.* □

Observations 18.1. Some properties of matrix operations.

1. Transposition properties.
   (a) $(\alpha B)^T = \alpha B^T, \alpha \in \mathbb{C}$
   (b) $\left(B^T\right)^T = B$
   (c) $(\alpha A + \beta B)^T = \alpha A^T + \beta B^T; \alpha, \beta \in \mathbb{C}$
   (d) $(AB)^T = B^T A^T$
   (e) $B^T B$ and BB^T are symmetric matrices.

2. Let the matrices A, B and C be conformable, and $\alpha \in \mathbb{C}$. Then
   (a) $A + B = B + A$
   (b) $A + (B + C) = (A + B) + C$
   (c) $\alpha(A + B) = \alpha A + \alpha B$
   (d) $A(B + C) = AB + AC$, and $(B + C)A = BA + CA$

3. Matrix multiplication is not commutative in general. That is, if A and B are compatible matrices, then AB is not equal to BA in general.

4. Properties of the trace operator. Let A and B be square matrices of the same order.
   (a) Cyclic property of trace: $tr\,(AB) = tr\,(BA)$
   (b) Linearity of trace: $tr\,(A + B) = tr\,(A) + tr\,(B)$
   (c) $tr\,(zA) = z\,tr\,(A)$, $z \in \mathbb{C}$
   (d) $tr\,\left(B^{-1}AB\right) = tr\,(A)$

5. Properties of Hermitian operators and matrices.
   (a) $\left(A^{\dagger}\right)^{\dagger} = A$
   (b) $(AB)^{\dagger} = B^{\dagger}A^{\dagger}$
   (c) Let B be a Hermitian matrix, and R be another matrix of the same order, then $R^{\dagger}BR$ is a Hermitian matrix.

6. Orthogonal expansions and linearly independent vectors. The concept of independence of a set of vectors is also discussed in the chapter on applied analysis.
   (a) The set of vectors which are orthogonal to each other are linearly independent.
   (b) A set of n orthogonal column vectors $x_i \neq 0, 1 \leq i \leq n$ is given. Let u be a column vector of size n. Then the column vector u can be expressed uniquely as a linear combination of the given orthogonal set of vectors.

   $$u = \sum_{i=1}^{n} \beta_i x_i; \quad \beta_i \in \mathbb{C}, \quad 1 \leq i \leq n$$

   $$\overline{\beta}_i = \frac{u^{\dagger} x_i}{x_i^{\dagger} x_i}, \quad 1 \leq i \leq n$$

   If the column vectors $x_i, 1 \leq i \leq n$ are normalized to unity, then $\overline{\beta}_i = u^{\dagger}x_i, 1 \leq i \leq n$.

7. Properties of inverse matrices.
   (a) $B^{-1}B = BB^{-1} = I$, where B is a nonsingular matrix.
   (b) $\left(B^{-1}\right)^{-1} = B$, where B is a nonsingular matrix.
   (c) The inverse of a nonsingular matrix is unique.
   (d) If A and B are nonsingular matrices, then $(AB)^{-1} = B^{-1}A^{-1}$.
   (e) If B is a nonsingular matrix, then B^T is also a nonsingular matrix. Also $\left(B^T\right)^{-1} = \left(B^{-1}\right)^T$.

(f) The inverse of a matrix B exists, if its rows (or columns) form a linearly independent set of vectors.

(g) The inverse of a matrix B exists, if there is no nonzero x such that $Bx = 0$.

□

18.2.3 Matrix Norm

The concept of matrix norm is analogous to the concept of vector norm. Vector norms are discussed in the chapter on applied analysis. Since matrices and vectors generally occur together, it is desirable that the matrix and vector norms be in consonance with each other. For example, if $\|\cdot\|$ is the norm operator, then we should have

$$\|Ax\| \leq \|A\|\,\|x\|$$

where A and x are compatible matrix and vector respectively. Similarly, we should have

$$\|AB\| \leq \|A\|\,\|B\|$$

where A and B are compatible matrices.

Definition 18.3. *Norm of a matrix: The norm function $\|\cdot\|$ assigns a nonnegative real number, to each complex matrix A, subject to the following axioms.*

(a) $\|B\| = 0$ *if and only if $B = 0$.*

(b) $\|B\| > 0$ *for $B \neq 0$.*

(c) $\|\beta B\| = |\beta|\,\|B\|$, *where $|\beta|$ is the magnitude of $\beta \in \mathbb{C}$.*

(d) $\|A + B\| \leq \|A\| + \|B\|$, *where the matrices A and B are of the same size. This is the triangle inequality.*

(e) $\|AB\| \leq \|A\|\,\|B\|$, *where the matrices A and B are compatible.*   □

The most commonly used norm in matrix analysis is the Frobenius norm.

Definitions 18.4. *Frobenius norm of a matrix. Let $B = [b_{ij}]$ be an $m \times n$ complex matrix. The Frobenius norm, also called the F-norm of matrix B is*

$$\|B\|_F = \left\{ \sum_{i=1}^{m} \sum_{j=1}^{n} |b_{ij}|^2 \right\}^{1/2}$$

$$= \sqrt{tr\,(BB^\dagger)} \tag{18.2}$$

Alternate names are: ℓ_2, Euclidean, Hilbert–Schmidt, or Schur norm.   □

18.3 Determinants

A square matrix has a very special number associated with it. It is called its determinant. These are introduced in this section. The notion of the determinant of a
square matrix is initially introduced. This is followed by a summary of some basic
properties of determinants.

Definitions 18.5. *Let* $B = [b_{ij}]$ *be an* $n \times n$ *square matrix of either real or*
complex numbers.

1. *Determinant of a matrix: The determinant* $\det B$ *of the matrix* B *is defined re-*
   cursively as follows:
   (a) *If* $n = 1$, $B = [b]$, *then* $\det B = b$.
   (b) *Let* $n > 1$, *and* B_{ij} *be an* $(n-1) \times (n-1)$ *matrix obtained by deleting*
       row i *and column* j *of matrix* B. *Then* $\det B = \sum_{j=1}^{n} (-1)^{j+1} b_{1j} \det B_{1j}$.
   The value n *is called the order of the determinant. This definition is due to*
   Laplace.

2. *Minor, and cofactor:* B_{ij} *is the submatrix obtained from* B *by deleting the* ith
   row and the jth *column. The minor of the element* b_{ij} *is the determinant of the*
   matrix B_{ij}. *It is denoted by* M_{ij}. *Therefore,* $M_{ij} = \det B_{ij}$.
   The order of this minor is $(n-1)$. *The cofactor of* b_{ij} *is defined by* $(-1)^{i+j} M_{ij}$.
   Denote this cofactor by β_{ij}.

3. *Notation: It is customary to denote the determinant of the matrix* B *as*

$$\det B = |B| = \begin{vmatrix} b_{11} & b_{12} & \cdots & b_{1n} \\ b_{21} & b_{22} & \cdots & b_{2n} \\ \vdots & \vdots & \ddots & \vdots \\ b_{n1} & b_{n2} & \cdots & b_{nn} \end{vmatrix} \tag{18.3}$$

   The vertical lines in the above definition are not related to the absolute value or
   the modulus of a complex number.   □

Observations 18.2.

1. The determinant of the identity matrix I is equal to $\det I = 1$.

2. The determinant of matrix $B = [b_{ij}]$ in terms of its cofactors is

$$\det B = \sum_{k=1}^{n} b_{ik}\beta_{ik} = \sum_{k=1}^{n} b_{kj}\beta_{kj}; \quad \text{for each } i, j, \text{ where } 1 \leq i, j \leq n$$

   The above representation of a determinant is called the *Laplace expansion* of the
   determinant, after the mathematician Pierre-Simon Laplace.

3. $\det B = \det B^T$, where B is any square matrix.

4. $\det AB = \det A \det B = \det BA$, where matrices A and B are any $n \times n$ matrices.

5. Let B be an invertible matrix, then $\det B^{-1} = (\det B)^{-1}$.

6. Let $D = [d_{ij}]$ be an $n \times n$ diagonal matrix. Then $\det D = \prod_{i=1}^{n} d_{ii}$.

7. Let B be a matrix with at least two identical rows (or columns), then $\det B = 0$.

8. If two columns (or two rows) of a matrix are interchanged, then the sign of the determinant changes.

9. If a column (or row) of a matrix is multiplied by $\alpha \in \mathbb{C}$, then the determinant is multiplied by α.

10. If a multiple of a column (row) is added to another column (row), then the value of the determinant remains unchanged.

11. If the determinant of a matrix is equal to zero, then it is a singular matrix; otherwise it is a nonsingular matrix.

12. Let $B = [b_{ij}]$ be a 2×2 matrix, then $\det B = b_{11}b_{22} - b_{12}b_{21}$.

13. The determinant of an orthogonal matrix is equal to either 1 or -1.   □

18.4 More Matrix Theory

Some more concepts from matrix theory are defined and discussed in this section. These are the rank of a matrix, and matrices as linear transformations.

18.4.1 Rank of a Matrix

The concept of the rank of a matrix is introduced.

Definitions 18.6. *Let B be an $m \times n$ matrix. Let the elements of the matrix be complex numbers. The rank of the matrix B is the size of the largest square nonsingular (invertible) submatrix of B. It is denoted by $rank\ B$, or r_B.*   □

Observations 18.3.

1. The rank of a matrix B is equal to its maximum number of linearly independent rows (or columns).

2. Let B be an $n \times n$ matrix. Then $r_B = n$ if and only if the matrix B is nonsingular. That is, the inverse of a matrix exists if and only if $r_B = n$.   □

18.4.2 Matrices as Linear Transformations

Matrices can be viewed as examples of linear mappings.

Definition 18.7. *A matrix transformation is a function $T : \mathbb{C}^n \to \mathbb{C}^m$ for which there exists a complex $m \times n$ matrix B such that $T(x) = Bx$ where $x \in \mathbb{C}^n$ and $T(x) \in \mathbb{C}^m$.* □

Lemma 18.1. *Each and every matrix transformation is a linear transformation.*
Proof. The proof is left to the reader. □

18.5 Spectral Analysis of Matrices

Properties of a square matrix can be studied via its *eigenvalues* and *eigenvectors*. Eigenvalue is also sometimes referred to as *characteristic value*, or *proper value*, or *latent value*. Similarly, eigenvector is also referred to as *characteristic vector*, or *proper vector*, or *latent vector*. This body of knowledge associated with square matrices is called its *spectral analysis*.

Definitions 18.8. *Let B be a square matrix of size n. Its elements can possibly be complex numbers.*

1. *Eigenvalue and eigenvector: A scalar λ is an eigenvalue of matrix B, if $Bx = \lambda x$, where x is a nonzero column vector of size n. The vector x is called an eigenvector of the matrix B. The vector x is unique to within a constant. Also (λ, x) is called an eigenpair of B.*

2. *Simple eigenvalue: An eigenvalue which occurs only once is called a simple eigenvalue.*

3. *Multiple eigenvalue: An eigenvalue which is not simple is a multiple eigenvalue.*

4. *Eigenspace: It is the set of all column vectors $\{x \in \mathbb{C}^n \mid Bx = \lambda x\}$ associated with λ. The vectors which belong to an eigenspace constitute a vector space.*

5. *Spectrum: The set of distinct eigenvalues of B is called its spectrum.*

6. *Characteristic polynomial: The characteristic polynomial $p_B(\lambda)$ of matrix B is equal to $\det(\lambda I - B)$, where I is an $n \times n$ identity matrix.*

7. *Characteristic equation: The characteristic equation of matrix B is specified by $p_B(\lambda) = 0$.* □

Observations 18.4. Let B be a square matrix of size n. Its elements are permitted to be complex numbers.

1. The characteristic polynomial $p_B(\lambda)$ of matrix B is a monic polynomial of degree n in λ.

2. The zeros of the characteristic equation are the eigenvalues of the matrix B. Consequently, the eigenvalues are also called the characteristic roots of B. Therefore, the number of eigenvalues of B is equal to n. Even if the elements of the matrix B are real numbers, the λ's can be imaginary. Furthermore, the n eigenvalues of the matrix B are not necessarily all distinct.

3. The coefficient of λ^{n-1} in the polynomial $p_B(\lambda)$ is equal to negative of the trace of matrix B.

4. The trace of matrix B is equal to the sum of all the eigenvalues.

5. The constant term in the polynomial $p_B(\lambda)$ is equal to $(-1)^n \det B$.

6. The determinant of a matrix B is equal to the product of all eigenvalues.

7. The $\det B = 0$ if and only if 0 is an eigenvalue of the matrix B.

8. If $p_B(\lambda)$ is a characteristic polynomial of a matrix B, then $p_B(B) = 0$. This statement is the so-called Cayley–Hamilton theorem.

9. The eigenvalues of the matrices B and B^T are identical.

10. Let S be a nonsingular matrix, then the eigenvalues of the matrix SBS^{-1} and the matrix B are identical. That is, similar matrices have identical spectra.

11. Let B be a square matrix of order n. Let its distinct eigenvalues be $\lambda_1, \lambda_2, \ldots, \lambda_k$, and the corresponding eigenvectors be $x_1, x_2, \ldots, x_k$ respectively, where $k \le n$. Then the set of vectors $x_1, x_2, \ldots, x_k$ are linearly independent. If $k = n$,

$$R = \begin{bmatrix} x_1 & x_2 & \cdots & x_n \end{bmatrix}, \quad \text{and} \quad \Lambda = diag(\lambda_1, \lambda_2, \ldots, \lambda_n)$$

then

$$R^{-1}BR = \Lambda, \quad \text{and} \quad B = R\Lambda R^{-1}$$

Therefore, the matrix B is diagonalizable, if it has n linearly independent eigenvectors. If in addition R is unitary, then

$$R^\dagger BR = \Lambda, \quad \text{and} \quad B = R\Lambda R^\dagger$$

Note that the matrices B and Λ are similar.   □

Example 18.1. Consider the matrix

$$B = \begin{bmatrix} -4 & 6 \\ -1 & 3 \end{bmatrix}$$

Its characteristic polynomial is

$$p_B(\lambda) = \begin{vmatrix} \lambda + 4 & -6 \\ 1 & \lambda - 3 \end{vmatrix}$$

Therefore, $p_B(\lambda) = \lambda^2 + \lambda - 6 = (\lambda + 3)(\lambda - 2)$. Thus the eigenvalues are $\lambda = -3$ and $\lambda = 2$. It can be verified that the sum of the eigenvalues is equal to the trace of the matrix B, which is equal to -1. Furthermore, the product of the eigenvalues is equal to $\det B$, which is equal to -6.

An eigenvector associated with the eigenvalue -3 is $\begin{bmatrix} 6 & 1 \end{bmatrix}^T$. Similarly, an eigenvector associated with the eigenvalue 2 is $\begin{bmatrix} 1 & 1 \end{bmatrix}^T$. Also check that

$$p_B(B) = B^2 + B - 6I$$
$$= \begin{bmatrix} 10 & -6 \\ 1 & 3 \end{bmatrix} + \begin{bmatrix} -4 & 6 \\ -1 & 3 \end{bmatrix} + \begin{bmatrix} -6 & 0 \\ 0 & -6 \end{bmatrix}$$
$$= \begin{bmatrix} 0 & 0 \\ 0 & 0 \end{bmatrix}$$

Thus $p_B(B) = 0$. $\qquad\qquad\qquad\qquad\qquad\qquad\qquad\qquad\qquad\qquad$ □

Observations 18.5. Some properties of real symmetric matrices are:

1. The eigenvalues of a real symmetric matrix are all real numbers.

2. The eigenvectors corresponding to distinct eigenvalues of a real symmetric matrix are mutually orthogonal.

3. If B is a real symmetric matrix, then there exists a real orthogonal matrix P such that $P^T B P$ is a diagonal matrix, with eigenvalues on the diagonal. □

Observations 18.6. Some properties of unitary matrices are:

1. If a matrix R is unitary, then it is nonsingular, and $R^{-1} = R^\dagger$.

2. The rows of a unitary matrix form an orthonormal set of vectors. Similarly, the columns of a unitary matrix form an orthonormal set of vectors.

3. The product of two unitary matrices is a unitary matrix.

4. If a matrix R is unitary, then $|\det(R)| = 1$.

5. All eigenvalues of a unitary matrix have a unit modulus (magnitude).

6. Let R be a unitary matrix. If matrices A and B are related to each other via a unitary transformation, that is if $A = R^\dagger B R$, then the matrices A and B have the same eigenvalues. □

Problems

1. Let A and B be $n \times n$ square matrices. Establish the following results.

(a) $\det A^T = \det A$.

(b) If the matrix A has either two identical columns (or rows) then $\det A = 0$.

(c) $\det AB = \det A \det B = \det BA$.

2. A is a 2×2 matrix

$$A = \begin{bmatrix} a & b \\ c & d \end{bmatrix}$$

such that $\det A = (ad - bc) \neq 0$. Prove that

$$A^{-1} = \frac{1}{(ad - bc)} \begin{bmatrix} d & -b \\ -c & a \end{bmatrix}$$

CHAPTER 19

Applied Analysis

19.1 Introduction

Analysis is the source of several powerful techniques in applied mathematics. The mathematical concepts defined and developed in this chapter find a variety of applications. Basic concepts in analysis, and complex analysis, are discussed in some depth in this chapter. Asymptotic behavior of algorithms is also outlined.

Concepts such as fields, vector spaces over fields, linear mappings, and tensor products are introduced. Dot product, vector product, and normed and complete vector spaces are defined. Concepts such as completeness, compactness, and orthogonality are also presented. Further, Hilbert spaces, nonorthogonal expansion of functions, and biorthogonal bases are also introduced.

19.2 Basic Concepts

Certain basic concepts in analysis are outlined in this section. These are: point sets, limits, continuous functions, derivatives, monotonicity, partial derivatives, and singularities.

19.2.1 Point Sets

Notions such as neighborhoods, interior points, interior of a set, exterior point, boundary points, limit points, open set, closure of a set, closed set, dense set, and compact set are introduced. These concepts are defined on subsets of the real line $\mathbb{R}$. These in turn can be conveniently extended to other spaces.

Definitions 19.1. *All the defined points and sets are on the real line $\mathbb{R}$.*

1. *The absolute value of $a \in \mathbb{R}$ is denoted by $|a|$. It is equal to a if $a \geq 0$ and $-a$ if $a < 0$.*

2. *δ-neighborhood: Let δ be a positive number. A δ-neighborhood of a point x_0 is the set of all points x such that $|x - x_0| < \delta$.*

3. *Deleted δ-neighborhood: A deleted δ-neighborhood of a point x_0 is the set of all points x such that $0 < |x - x_0| < \delta$. It excludes the point x_0 itself.*

4. *Interior point: A point $x_0 \in X$ is an interior point of the set X if and only if there exists a δ-neighborhood of the point x_0, such that all the points in this neighborhood belong to the set X.*

5. *Interior of a set X : The interior of a set is the set of all its interior points.*

6. *Exterior point: A point $x_0 \in X$ is an exterior point of set X if and only if all the δ-neighborhoods of the point x_0, belong to the complement of the set X.*

7. *Boundary point: A point $x_0 \in X$ is a boundary point of set X if and only if all the δ-neighborhoods of the point x_0, belong to both the set X and its complement.*

8. *Limit points: A point $x_0 \in X$ is a limit point of a set X if and only if all deleted δ-neighborhoods of x_0 contain points which belong to X.*

9. *Open set: A set is open, if every point in it is an interior point.*

10. *Closure of a set: The union of a set of points X and all its limit points is called its closure.*

11. *Closed set: A set X is closed, if it contains all its limit points.*

12. *Dense set: Let $\widetilde{X}$ be a subset of X. The subset $\widetilde{X}$ is dense if the closure of the set $\widetilde{X}$ is equal to X.*

13. *Compact set: A set of points is compact, if and only if it is closed and bounded.*

14. *Let $x \in \mathbb{R}$ and $\epsilon \in \mathbb{R}^{+}$. As $\epsilon \to 0$ then:*
    (a) *$(x + \epsilon)$ is denoted by x_+. Thus x_+ is the right limiting value of x.*
    (b) *$(x - \epsilon)$ is denoted by x_-. Thus x_- is the left limiting value of x.* $\square$

Note that a finite union of closed sets is also closed. However, an infinite union of closed sets is not necessarily closed. For example, let $I_n = [1/n, 1]$. Then $\bigcup_{n=1}^{\infty} I_n = (0, 1]$. This infinite union is not closed, since 0 is a limit point of this union, which is not in this set. Note that an empty set is closed by definition. Intersection of closed sets yields a closed set.

Infinite unions of open intervals are open sets in $\mathbb{R}$. In contrast, infinite intersections of open intervals are not open sets. For example if $J_n = (-1/n, 1/n)$, then $\bigcap_{n=1}^{\infty} J_n = \{0\}$ is closed.

An open set X is dense in its closure. The set of rational numbers $\mathbb{Q}$ is dense in $\mathbb{R}$. The set of irrational numbers is also dense in $\mathbb{R}$.

19.2.2 Limits, Continuity, Derivatives, and Monotonicity

Notions of limits, continuity, and derivative are interlinked. Monotonic functions of different types are also described.

Definitions 19.2.

1. *Limit of a function: A function $f : \mathbb{R} \to \mathbb{R}$ has a limit L at a point $\tilde{x}$, if for every real number $\epsilon > 0$ there exists a real number $\delta > 0$ such that for all $x \in \mathbb{R}$ with*

$$0 < |x - \tilde{x}| < \delta \quad \Rightarrow \quad |f(x) - L| < \epsilon \tag{19.1a}$$

   The limit is denoted by $\lim_{x \to \tilde{x}} f(x) = L$.

2. *Right-hand limit of a function: A function $f : \mathbb{R} \to \mathbb{R}$ has a right-hand limit L at a point $\tilde{x}$, if for every real number $\epsilon > 0$ there exists a real number $\delta > 0$ such that for all $x \in \mathbb{R}$ with*

$$\tilde{x} < x < \tilde{x} + \delta \quad \Rightarrow \quad |f(x) - L| < \epsilon \tag{19.1b}$$

   The limit is denoted by $\lim_{x \to \tilde{x}_+} f(x) = L$.

3. *Left-hand limit of a function: A function $f : \mathbb{R} \to \mathbb{R}$ has a left-hand limit L at a point $\tilde{x}$, if for every real number $\epsilon > 0$ there exists a real number $\delta > 0$ such that for all $x \in \mathbb{R}$ with*

$$\tilde{x} - \delta < x < \tilde{x} \quad \Rightarrow \quad |f(x) - L| < \epsilon \tag{19.1c}$$

   The limit is denoted by $\lim_{x \to \tilde{x}_-} f(x) = L$.

4. *Limit superior and limit inferior of a sequence of real numbers: Consider a sequence of real numbers $\ldots, x_{-2}, x_{-1}, x_0, x_1, x_2, \ldots$. Let ϵ be any positive real number.*

   (a) *A real number $\bar{x}$ is called a limit superior, or greatest limit, or upper limit (lim sup) of the sequence, if infinite number of terms of the sequence are greater than $(\bar{x} - \epsilon)$ and only a finite number of terms are greater than $(\bar{x} + \epsilon)$.*

   (b) *A real number $\underline{x}$ is called a limit inferior, or least limit, or lower limit (lim inf) of the sequence, if infinite number of terms of the sequence are less than $(\underline{x} + \epsilon)$ and only a finite number of terms are less than $(\underline{x} - \epsilon)$.* $\square$

Thus $f(x)$ has a limit L at $x = \tilde{x}$, if for the numbers x near $\tilde{x}$, the value of $f(x)$ is close to L. The right-hand and left-hand limits are generally called the one-sided limits, and $\lim_{x \to \tilde{x}} f(x)$ is called the two-sided limit. These three limits are related by the following lemma.

Lemma 19.1. *A function $f : \mathbb{R} \to \mathbb{R}$ has a limit L at a point $\tilde{x}$ if and only if the right-hand and left-hand limits at the point $\tilde{x}$ exist and are equal. That is,*

$$\lim_{x \to \tilde{x}} f(x) = L \iff \lim_{x \to \tilde{x}_+} f(x) = L \text{ and } \lim_{x \to \tilde{x}_-} f(x) = L \tag{19.2}$$

$\square$

A sequence of real numbers converges if and only if its limit superior and limit inferior are equal and finite. A continuous function is next defined.

Definitions 19.3. *On continuity.*

1. *Right-hand continuity. A function $f : \mathbb{R} \to \mathbb{R}$ is continuous on the right at point $\widetilde{x}$ if: both $\lim_{x \to \widetilde{x}_+} f(x)$ and $f(\widetilde{x})$ exist, and $\lim_{x \to \widetilde{x}_+} f(x) = f(\widetilde{x})$.*

2. *Left-hand continuity. A function $f : \mathbb{R} \to \mathbb{R}$ is continuous on the left at point $\widetilde{x}$ if: both $\lim_{x \to \widetilde{x}_-} f(x)$ and $f(\widetilde{x})$ exist, and $\lim_{x \to \widetilde{x}_-} f(x) = f(\widetilde{x})$.*

3. *A function $f : \mathbb{R} \to \mathbb{R}$ is continuous at point $\widetilde{x}$ if: both $\lim_{x \to \widetilde{x}} f(x)$ and $f(\widetilde{x})$ exist, and $\lim_{x \to \widetilde{x}} f(x) = f(\widetilde{x})$.*
   Equivalently, a function $f : \mathbb{R} \to \mathbb{R}$ is continuous at point $\widetilde{x}$ if for every $\epsilon > 0$, there exists $\delta_{\widetilde{x},\epsilon} > 0$ such that $x \in \mathbb{R}$ and $|x - \widetilde{x}| < \delta_{\widetilde{x},\epsilon} \Rightarrow |f(x) - f(\widetilde{x})| < \epsilon$.
   A function $f(\cdot)$ which is not continuous at $\widetilde{x}$ is said to be discontinuous at $\widetilde{x}$.

4. *A function $f : \widetilde{S} \to \mathbb{R}$ is a continuous function on a set $\widetilde{S} \subseteq \mathbb{R}$, if $f(\cdot)$ is continuous at every point of $\widetilde{S}$.*

5. *Piecewise-continuous functions: A function $f : \mathbb{R} \to \mathbb{R}$ is piecewise-continuous in a finite interval $I \subseteq \mathbb{R}$, if:*
   (a) *The interval I can be divided into a finite number of subintervals. Furthermore, in each such subinterval the function $f(\cdot)$ is continuous.*
   (b) *The limits of $f(x)$ as x approaches the end-points of each subinterval are finite.*
   Thus a piecewise-continuous function is one which has at most a finite number of finite discontinuities in every finite subinterval of $\mathbb{R}$.

6. *A function $f : \mathbb{R} \to \mathbb{R}$ is uniformly continuous on a set $H \subseteq \mathbb{R}$ if for every $\epsilon > 0$ there exists a $\delta > 0$ such that $|x - y| < \delta \Rightarrow |f(x) - f(y)| < \epsilon$ where $x, y \in H$.*   □

It can be demonstrated that, if a real-valued function $f(\cdot)$ is continuous on a closed bounded set H, then it is also uniformly continuous on the set H. The derivative of a function is next defined.

Definitions 19.4. *Let $f : \mathbb{R} \to \mathbb{R}$ be a function.*

1. *Let $a, b \in \mathbb{R}$ such that $a < b$, and $f(\cdot)$ is defined at any point $x_0 \in (a, b)$. The first derivative of $f(x)$ at $x = x_0$ is defined as*

$$f'(x_0) = \lim_{h \to 0} \frac{f(x_0 + h) - f(x_0)}{h} \tag{19.3a}$$

if the limit exists. Other convenient notations for the first derivative of $f(x)$ at x_0 are

$$\frac{df\left(x\right)}{dx}\Bigg|_{x=x_0} \quad and \quad \dot{f}\left(x_0\right) \qquad (19.3b)$$

If there is no ambiguity, the first derivative of $f\left(x\right)$ is simply referred to as the derivative of $f\left(x\right)$.

2. *A function $f\left(\cdot\right)$ is differentiable at a point $x = x_0$ if $f'\left(x_0\right)$ exists.*

3. *If the first derivative of a function exists at all points of an interval, then it is said to be differentiable in the interval.*

4. *Second derivative: The second derivative of $f\left(x\right)$ at $x = x_0$, if it exists is the first derivative of $f'\left(x\right)$. This second derivative is denoted by either $f''\left(x_0\right)$ or $\ddot{f}\left(x_0\right)$.*

5. *Higher derivatives: Higher-order derivatives can be defined recursively. The nth derivative of $f\left(x\right)$ at $x = x_0$, if it exists is the first derivative of the $(n-1)$th derivative of $f\left(x\right)$. It is denoted by $f^{(n)}\left(x_0\right), n \in \mathbb{P}$. The nth derivative of $f\left(x\right)$ at x_0 is also denoted by*

$$\frac{d^n f\left(x\right)}{dx^n}\Bigg|_{x=x_0} \qquad (19.3c)$$

Note that the notation $f^{(0)}\left(x\right) \triangleq f\left(x\right)$ is often used. $\qquad\square$

Observe that if $f\left(x\right)$ is differentiable at $x = x_0$ then it is continuous at that point. Functions can also be classified based upon the existence of its derivatives.

Definitions 19.5. *Consider a function $f : I \to \mathbb{R}$, where I is a closed interval in $\mathbb{R}$.*

1. *The function $f\left(\cdot\right)$ is of class C^0 on I if $f\left(x\right)$ is continuous at all $x \in I$.*

2. *The function $f\left(\cdot\right)$ is of class C^r on I if $f^{(r)}\left(x\right)$ exists and is continuous at all $x \in I$, where r is a positive integer.*

3. *The function $f\left(\cdot\right)$ is smooth (or continuously differentiable) on the closed interval I, if it belongs to class C^1.*

4. *The function $f\left(\cdot\right)$ is of class C^∞ on the closed interval, if all its derivatives exist and are continuous.* $\qquad\square$

A function $f\left(\cdot\right)$ which is infinitely differentiable (that is all its derivatives exist) has a Taylor's series expansion. It is named after the mathematician Brook Taylor (1685–1731).

Theorem 19.1. *Taylor's theorem of the mean. Let $f\left(x\right)$ and its first n derivatives $f'\left(x\right), f''\left(x\right), \ldots, f^{(n)}\left(x\right)$ be continuous in $[a, b]$ and differentiable in (a, b), then there exists a point $\xi \in (a, b)$ such that*

$$f(b) = \sum_{m=0}^{n} \frac{(b-a)^m}{m!} f^{(m)}(a) + R_n \tag{19.4a}$$

$$R_n = \frac{(b-a)^{n+1}}{(n+1)!} f^{(n+1)}(\xi), \quad a < \xi < b \tag{19.4b}$$

where R_n is called the remainder.

Proof. The proof can be found in any standard textbook on calculus.   □

An alternate and well-known representation of the above result is as follows. Let $x, (x+h) \in (a,b)$, then

$$f(x+h) = \sum_{m=0}^{n} \frac{h^m}{m!} f^{(m)}(x) + \frac{h^{n+1}}{(n+1)!} f^{(n+1)}(\xi), \quad a < \xi < b \tag{19.5a}$$

The above result is called Taylor's series for $f(x)$ with a remainder. If the limit $\lim_{n\to\infty} R_n \to 0$, an infinite series is obtained.

$$f(x+h) = \sum_{m\in\mathbb{N}} \frac{h^m}{m!} f^{(m)}(x) \tag{19.5b}$$

The Taylor series is an example of a *power series*. If the power series exists in some interval, then it is a *convergent series* in that interval. Furthermore, the corresponding interval is called the *interval of convergence*.

Example 19.1. A useful binomial series expansion.

$$(1+x)^\alpha = 1 + \alpha x + \frac{\alpha(\alpha-1)}{2!}x^2 + \ldots + \frac{\alpha(\alpha-1)\ldots(\alpha-n+1)}{n!}x^n + \ldots$$

for $|x| < 1$, and any $\alpha \in \mathbb{R}$.   □

Different types of monotonic functions are described below.

Definition 19.6. *Monotonic functions: Let $f : \mathbb{R} \to \mathbb{R}$, $S \subseteq \mathbb{R}$, and $x_1, x_2 \in S$.*

(a) *The function $f(\cdot)$ is monotonically increasing on the set S iff for each pair of numbers x_1, x_2, $x_1 < x_2$ implies $f(x_1) < f(x_2)$.*

(b) *The function $f(\cdot)$ is monotonically nondecreasing on the set S iff for each pair of numbers x_1, x_2, $x_1 < x_2$ implies $f(x_1) \leq f(x_2)$.*

(c) *The function $f(\cdot)$ is monotonically decreasing on the set S iff for each pair of numbers x_1, x_2, $x_1 < x_2$ implies $f(x_1) > f(x_2)$.*

(d) *The function $f(\cdot)$ is monotonically nonincreasing on the set S iff for each pair of numbers x_1, x_2, $x_1 < x_2$ implies $f(x_1) \geq f(x_2)$.*   □

19.2.3 Partial Derivatives

Functions of two or more variables are defined and discussed in this subsection. The difference between dependent and independent variables is also stated. Neighborhoods, limits, continuity, and partial derivatives are defined.

Definitions 19.7. *All the defined points and sets are on the real line* $\mathbb{R}$.

1. *Real-valued function of two real-variables. Let* $I, J, K \subseteq \mathbb{R}$. *A function of two variables is* $f : I \times J \to K$, *where* $(x, y) \in I \times J$ *is assigned a unique element* $z \in K$. *The assignment of the specific pair* (x, y) *to* z *is denoted as* $f(x, y) = z$. *This function is sometimes denoted by* $f(\cdot, \cdot)$.

2. *Dependent and independent variables. If* $z = f(x, y)$, *then* x *and* y *are called the independent variables, and* z *the dependent variable.*

3. *Neighborhoods. Let* δ *be a positive real number. A rectangular* δ-*neighborhood of a point* (x_0, y_0) *is the set of all points* (x, y) *such that* $|x - x_0| < \delta$, *and* $|y - y_0| < \delta$.
   A circular δ-*neighborhood of a point* (x_0, y_0) *is the set of all points* (x, y) *such that* $(x - x_0)^2 + (y - y_0)^2 < \delta^2$.
   A deleted δ-*neighborhood is the set of all points in the* δ-*neighborhood, except the point* (x_0, y_0).

4. *Limits. Consider a real-valued function* $f : \mathbb{R}^2 \to \mathbb{R}$ *defined in a deleted* δ-*neighborhood of* (x_0, y_0). *The limit of the function* $f(x, y)$ *as* (x, y) *approaches* (x_0, y_0) *is* L, *if for every real number* $\epsilon > 0$ *there exists a real number* $\delta > 0$ *such that for all* $x, y \in \mathbb{R}$ *with*

$$0 < |x - x_0| < \delta \quad and \quad 0 < |y - y_0| < \delta \quad \Rightarrow \quad |f(x, y) - L| < \epsilon \quad (19.6a)$$

In general, δ *depends upon* ϵ *and* (x_0, y_0). *The above condition can also be replaced by an alternate condition. It is called the deleted circular* δ-*neighborhood of the point* (x_0, y_0). *This is*

$$0 < (x - x_0)^2 + (y - y_0)^2 < \delta^2 \quad \Rightarrow \quad |f(x, y) - L| < \epsilon \quad (19.6b)$$

The limit is denoted by $\lim_{(x,y) \to (x_0, y_0)} f(x, y) = L$.

5. *Continuity. Let* $f(\cdot, \cdot)$ *be a real-valued function of two real variables. It is defined at* (x_0, y_0) *and also in a* δ-*neighborhood of* (x_0, y_0), *where* $\delta > 0$. *The function* $f(\cdot, \cdot)$ *is continuous at* (x_0, y_0), *if the following three conditions hold:*
   (i) $\lim_{(x,y) \to (x_0, y_0)} f(x, y) = L$. *That is, the limit exists as* $(x, y) \to (x_0, y_0)$.
   (ii) $f(x_0, y_0)$ *is defined at* (x_0, y_0).
   (iii) $L = (x_0, y_0)$.

   If the function is not continuous at $f(x_0, y_0)$, *then it is said to be discontinuous at* $f(x_0, y_0)$. *In this case* (x_0, y_0) *is called a point of discontinuity.* $\qquad \square$

Consider the limits

$$\lim_{x \to x_0} \left\{ \lim_{y \to y_0} f(x, y) \right\} \triangleq L_1, \quad \text{and} \quad \lim_{y \to y_0} \left\{ \lim_{x \to x_0} f(x, y) \right\} \triangleq L_2$$

Note that $L_1 \neq L_2$ in general. However, it is necessary that $L_1 = L_2$ for L to exist. Furthermore, the equality $L_1 = L_2$ does not guarantee that L exists.

Next consider a function of two variables. These variables are assumed to be independent of each other. The ordinary derivative of the function with respect to a single variable, while keeping all other variables fixed, is called the partial derivative of the function with respect to this variable.

Definitions 19.8. *Partial derivatives. Let $f : \mathbb{R}^2 \to \mathbb{R}$ be a function.*

1. *Let $a, b, c, d \in \mathbb{R}$ such that $a < b$ and $c < d$, and $f(\cdot, \cdot)$ is defined at any point $x_0 \in (a, b)$, and $y_0 \in (c, d)$. The first partial derivative of $f(x, y)$ at (x_0, y_0) with respect to x is defined as*

$$\frac{\partial f(x_0, y_0)}{\partial x} = \lim_{\Delta x \to 0} \frac{f(x_0 + \Delta x, y_0) - f(x_0, y_0)}{\Delta x} \qquad (19.7a)$$

if the limit exists. Similarly, the first partial derivative of $f(x, y)$ at (x_0, y_0) with respect to y is defined as

$$\frac{\partial f(x_0, y_0)}{\partial y} = \lim_{\Delta y \to 0} \frac{f(x_0, y_0 + \Delta y) - f(x_0, y_0)}{\Delta y} \qquad (19.7b)$$

if the limit exists. Other convenient notation for the first partial derivative of $f(x, y)$ with respect to x at (x_0, y_0) are

$$\left. \frac{\partial f(x, y)}{\partial x} \right|_{(x=x_0, y=y_0)}, \text{ and } f_x(x_0, y_0) \qquad (19.7c)$$

Similarly, the other convenient notation for the first partial derivative of $f(x, y)$ with respect to y at (x_0, y_0) are

$$\left. \frac{\partial f(x, y)}{\partial y} \right|_{(x=x_0, y=y_0)}, \text{ and } f_y(x_0, y_0) \qquad (19.7d)$$

If f_x and f_y are also continuous in a region $\mathcal{R} \subseteq \mathbb{R}^2$ then f is continuously differentiable in region $\mathcal{R}$.

2. *Higher-order partial derivatives. If the partial derivatives $f_x(x, y)$ and $f_y(x, y)$ exist at all points in a region $\mathcal{R} \subseteq \mathbb{R}^2$ then these partial derivatives are also functions of x and y. Therefore, both $f_x(x, y)$ and $f_y(x, y)$ may have partial derivatives with respect to x and y. If these exist, then they are called the second-order partial derivatives of $f(x, y)$. These are specified as*

$$\frac{\partial}{\partial x}\left(\frac{\partial f(x,y)}{\partial x}\right) = \frac{\partial^2 f(x,y)}{\partial x^2} = f_{xx}(x,y) \tag{19.8a}$$

$$\frac{\partial}{\partial y}\left(\frac{\partial f(x,y)}{\partial y}\right) = \frac{\partial^2 f(x,y)}{\partial y^2} = f_{yy}(x,y) \tag{19.8b}$$

$$\frac{\partial}{\partial y}\left(\frac{\partial f(x,y)}{\partial x}\right) = \frac{\partial^2 f(x,y)}{\partial y \partial x} = f_{xy}(x,y) \tag{19.8c}$$

$$\frac{\partial}{\partial x}\left(\frac{\partial f(x,y)}{\partial y}\right) = \frac{\partial^2 f(x,y)}{\partial x \partial y} = f_{yx}(x,y) \tag{19.8d}$$

If $f_{xy}(\cdot,\cdot)$ and $f_{yx}(\cdot,\cdot)$ are continuous functions, then $f_{yx}(\cdot,\cdot) = f_{yx}(\cdot,\cdot)$.
Third, fourth, and other high-ordered derivatives can similarly be defined. □

19.2.4 Singularity and Related Topics

Bounded function, bounded variation of a function, and singularities of a function are next defined. Singularity of a function is next defined as follows.

Definitions 19.9.

1. *A real-valued function $f(\cdot)$ is bounded in an interval (a,b) if there exists $M \in \mathbb{R}^+$ such that $|f(x)| < M$ for all $x \in (a,b)$.*

2. *A real-valued function $f(\cdot)$ is of bounded variation in an interval (a,b) if and only if there exists $M \in \mathbb{R}^+$ such that $\sum_{i=1}^{m}|f(x_i) - f(x_{i-1})| < M$ for all partitions $a = x_0 < x_1 < x_2 < \cdots < x_m = b$.*

3. *If a function $f(\cdot)$ is unbounded at one or more points of the interval $a \le x \le b$, then such points are called the singularities of $f(\cdot)$.* □

A function $f(\cdot)$ is of bounded variation in every finite open interval if and only if $f(x)$ is bounded and possesses a finite number of relative maximum and minimum values and discontinuities. That is, the function can be represented as a curve of finite length in any finite interval.

19.3 Complex Analysis

A complex number is specified as an ordered pair (a,b) where $a, b \in \mathbb{R}$, and the operations $+$ (addition) and $\times$ (multiplication) are defined by

$$(a,b) + (c,d) = (a+c, b+d) \tag{19.9a}$$

$$(a,b) \times (c,d) = (ac - bd, ad + bc) \tag{19.9b}$$

$$m(a,b) = (ma, mb), \quad m \in \mathbb{R} \tag{19.9c}$$

In addition,

$$(a, b) = (c, d) \quad \Leftrightarrow \quad a = c \text{ and } b = d \tag{19.9d}$$

The set of all complex numbers is denoted by $\mathbb{C}$. It can be checked that this definition satisfies all the axioms of a field. The notion of a field is developed in a subsequent section. Also, $(0, 0)$ and $(1, 0)$ are additive and multiplicative identities respectively. Furthermore, the additive and multiplicative inverses of (a, b) are $(-a, -b)$ and $(a/(a^2 + b^2), -b/(a^2 + b^2))$ respectively. The existence of the multiplicative inverse assumes that a and b are not simultaneously equal to 0.

Also if $(a, 0)$ is represented by a and $(0, b)$ by ib, where $i = \sqrt{-1}$ and $i^2 = -1$, then

$$(a, b) = (a, 0) + (0, b) = a + ib$$

Thus an alternate representation of the complex number (a, b) is $(a + ib)$. It can be checked that the definition of complex addition and multiplication operations are consistent in this representation. The existence of additive and multiplicative identities can be similarly verified.

Definitions 19.10. *Let* $a, b \in \mathbb{R}, i = \sqrt{-1}$ *and* $(a, b) = (a + ib) = z \in \mathbb{C}$ *be a complex number.*

1. *a and b are the real and imaginary parts of z respectively. The real component of z is denoted by $\mathrm{Re}\,(z) = a$. Similarly, the imaginary component of z is denoted by $\mathrm{Im}\,(z) = b$.*

2. *$|z| = (a^2 + b^2)^{1/2}$ is the absolute value or modulus of z.*

3. *$\bar{z} = (a - ib) \in \mathbb{C}$ is the complex conjugate or simply conjugate of z.* $\square$

Observations 19.1. Some elementary observations.

1. $a = (z + \bar{z})/2$, and $b = (z - \bar{z})/(2i)$.

2. $|z| = |\bar{z}|$.

3. If $z_1, z_2 \in \mathbb{C}$ then $|z_1 z_2| = |z_1| |z_2|$.

4. The triangle inequality:

$$|z_1 + z_2| \leq |z_1| + |z_2|$$

Also

$$|z_1| - |z_2| \leq |z_1 - z_2|$$

$\square$

Topics such as De Moivre and Euler identities, limits, continuity, derivatives, analyticity, contours, integration, and infinite series are also stated.

19.3.1 De Moivre and Euler Identities

The celebrated De Moivre and Euler identities are discussed in this subsection.

De Moivre's Identity

Observe that if $z_1, z_2 \in \mathbb{C}, r_1, r_2, \theta_1, \theta_2 \in \mathbb{R}$; where

$$z_1 = r_1 \left(\cos \theta_1 + i \sin \theta_1 \right)$$
$$z_2 = r_2 \left(\cos \theta_2 + i \sin \theta_2 \right)$$

then

$$z_1 z_2 = r_1 r_2 \left\{ \cos \left(\theta_1 + \theta_2 \right) + i \sin \left(\theta_1 + \theta_2 \right) \right\}$$
$$\frac{z_1}{z_2} = \frac{r_1}{r_2} \left\{ \cos \left(\theta_1 - \theta_2 \right) + i \sin \left(\theta_1 - \theta_2 \right) \right\}, \quad r_2 \neq 0$$

Extension of these results yields De Moivre's theorem. It is named after the mathematician Abraham de Moivre (1667–1754).

Theorem 19.2. *Let* $z = r(\cos \theta + i \sin \theta)$, *where* $r, \theta \in \mathbb{R}$, *then for any* $n \in \mathbb{Z}$

$$z^n = r^n \left(\cos n\theta + i \sin n\theta \right) \tag{19.10}$$

Proof. The result can be established by induction.   □

Definition 19.11. *Let* $u, z \in \mathbb{C}$. *The number* u *is called an* nth *root of* z *if* $z = u^n$.   □

If $z = r(\cos \theta + i \sin \theta)$, where $r, \theta \in \mathbb{R}$, the above definition for the nth root of a complex number and De Moivre's theorem yields

$$u = z^{1/n} = \left\{ r \left(\cos \theta + i \sin \theta \right) \right\}^{1/n} \tag{19.11a}$$
$$= r^{1/n} \left\{ \cos \left(\frac{\theta + 2\pi k}{n} \right) + i \sin \left(\frac{\theta + 2\pi k}{n} \right) \right\}, \ \forall \, k \in \mathbb{Z}_n \tag{19.11b}$$

Therefore, it can be concluded that there are n different values of the nth root of z iff $z \neq 0$.

Euler's Identity

The following series expansions are well known.

$$e^x = \sum_{j \in \mathbb{N}} \frac{x^j}{j!}; \qquad e = 2.718281828\ldots, \qquad x \in \mathbb{R} \qquad (19.12\text{a})$$

$$\sin x = \sum_{j \in \mathbb{N}} (-1)^j \frac{x^{2j+1}}{(2j+1)!}, \qquad x \in \mathbb{R} \qquad (19.12\text{b})$$

$$\cos x = \sum_{j \in \mathbb{N}} (-1)^j \frac{x^{2j}}{(2j)!}, \qquad x \in \mathbb{R} \qquad (19.12\text{c})$$

The number e is called Euler's number, after the mathematician Leonhard Euler (1707–1783). The series expansion of $e^x \triangleq \exp(x)$ is also valid if x is a complex number. Substituting $x = i\theta$ in the series expansion of e^x, yields the well-known Euler identity.

$$e^{i\theta} = \cos\theta + i\sin\theta \qquad (19.13)$$

Observations 19.2. Euler's identity leads to the following results.

1. If $z = x + iy$, then $e^z = e^x (\cos y + i \sin y)$.
2. $\sin x = (e^{ix} - e^{-ix}) / (2i)$, and $\cos x = (e^{ix} + e^{-ix}) / 2$.
3. An alternative proof of De Moivre's theorem.

$$(\cos\theta + i\sin\theta)^n = (e^{i\theta})^n = e^{in\theta} = \cos n\theta + i\sin n\theta$$

4. The *nth roots of unity*: Let $z^n = 1$, then the n roots are

$$z = \cos\left(\frac{2\pi k}{n}\right) + i\sin\left(\frac{2\pi k}{n}\right) = e^{2\pi ik/n}, \quad k \in \mathbb{Z}_n$$

Let

$$\cos\left(\frac{2\pi}{n}\right) + i\sin\left(\frac{2\pi}{n}\right) = e^{2\pi i/n} \triangleq \omega$$

Thus the n roots of unity are $1, \omega, \omega^2, \ldots, \omega^{n-1}$.   □

19.3.2 Limits, Continuity, Derivatives, and Analyticity

The definitions of neighborhoods, limit points, closed sets, bounded sets, interior and exterior points, boundary points, and open sets in the complex plane are similar to those defined on the real line. The definitions of limits, and continuity in the complex domain are also similar to those of in the real number domain. Consequently, these are not repeated.

Definitions 19.12. *Let $z \in \mathbb{C}$.*

1. *Assume that $f(z)$ is single-valued in some region $\mathcal{R}$ of the z-plane. The derivative of $f(z)$ is defined as*

$$f'(z) = \lim_{\Delta z \to 0} \frac{f(z + \Delta z) - f(z)}{\Delta z} \qquad (19.14)$$

2. *A function $f(\cdot)$ is analytic at a point $z_0 \in \mathbb{C}$, if its first derivative $f'(z)$ exists at all points in the neighborhood of z_0. That is, $f'(z)$ exists at all points in the region $|z - z_0| < \delta$, where $\delta > 0$.*

3. *If the derivative $f'(z)$ exists at all points z of a region $\mathcal{R}$, then the function $f(\cdot)$ is analytic in $\mathcal{R}$.*

4. *A function which is analytic over the entire complex plane (except at infinity) is called an entire function.* $\square$

A necessary and sufficient condition for a function to be analytic in a region is specified by the Cauchy–Riemann theorem.

Theorem 19.3. *Let $z = x + iy$, where $x, y \in \mathbb{R}$ and $w = f(z) = u(x,y) + iv(x,y)$. The necessary and sufficient conditions that the function $f(\cdot)$ be analytic in a region $\mathcal{R}$, is that functions $u(\cdot, \cdot)$ and $v(\cdot, \cdot)$ satisfy the Cauchy–Riemann equations*

$$\frac{\partial u}{\partial x} = \frac{\partial v}{\partial y}, \qquad (19.15a)$$

$$\frac{\partial u}{\partial y} = -\frac{\partial v}{\partial x} \qquad (19.15b)$$

and these partial derivatives be continuous in the region $\mathcal{R}$.

Proof. See the problem section. $\square$

Observation 19.3. Let $w = f(z) = u(x,y) + iv(x,y)$ be analytic in a region $\mathcal{R}$. Then

$$f'(z) \triangleq \frac{dw}{dz} = \frac{\partial u}{\partial x} + i\frac{\partial v}{\partial x} = \frac{\partial v}{\partial y} - i\frac{\partial u}{\partial y} \qquad (19.16)$$

$\square$

19.3.3 Contours or Curves

A contour is a curve in the complex z-plane. It can be either smooth or piecewise-smooth.

Definitions 19.13. *Let $\alpha(\cdot)$ and $\beta(\cdot)$ be real functions of a real variable t, defined over the interval $t_1 \leq t \leq t_2$, such that $z(t) = \alpha(t) + i\beta(t)$, where $t_1 \leq t \leq t_2$.*

1. *If the functions $\alpha(\cdot)$ and $\beta(\cdot)$ are continuous in the interval $[t_1, t_2]$, then the complex function $z(\cdot)$ is a continuous curve or arc in the complex plane, which starts at $a = z(t_1)$ and ends at $b = z(t_2)$. Therefore, an orientation can also be assigned to the curve, as it moves from $t = t_1$ to $t = t_2$.*

2. *If $t_1 \neq t_2$ but $a = b$, that is, the end-points coincide, then the curve is closed.*

3. *A closed curve which does not intersect itself at any point in the complex plane is called a simple closed curve.*

4. *If $\alpha(t)$ and $\beta(t)$, and consequently $z(t)$, have continuous derivatives in the specified interval, then the curve is called a smooth curve or arc.*

5. *A curve which consists of a finite number of smooth arcs is called a sectionally or piecewise-smooth curve or a contour.*   □

19.3.4 Integration

It is possible to integrate a complex function $f(\cdot)$ along a curve C in the complex plane. Denote this integral by $\int_C f(z)\, dz$. The integral can be defined as the limit of a sum. Let $f(\cdot)$ be a continuous function at all points on the curve C. The end points of the curve C are a and b. Divide C arbitrarily into n parts via points $z_1, z_2, \ldots, z_{n-1}$, and call $a = z_0$, and $b = z_n$. Let

$$\Delta z_k = (z_k - z_{k-1}), \quad 1 \leq k \leq n$$

If ξ_k is a point on the curve C between z_{k-1} and z_k, then

$$\int_a^b f(z)\, dz = \lim_{\substack{n \to \infty \\ \max|\Delta z_k| \to 0}} \sum_{k=1}^{n} f(\xi_k)\, \Delta z_k$$

Thus, if a function $f(\cdot)$ is analytic at all points in a region $\mathcal{R}$ of the complex plane, and C is a curve lying in the region $\mathcal{R}$, then $f(\cdot)$ is integrable along the curve C. The integration around the boundary C of a region $\mathcal{R}$ is denoted by

$$\oint_C f(z)\, dz$$

19.3.5 Infinite Series

Terminology about infinite series is introduced via the following definitions.

Definitions 19.14. *Let $f_1(\cdot), f_2(\cdot), \ldots, f_n(\cdot), \ldots$, be a sequence of functions defined on some region $\mathcal{R}$ of the complex z-plane. Denote this sequence by $\{f_n(\cdot)\}$.*

1. *Limit of a sequence of functions: The function $f(\cdot)$ is the limit of $f_n(\cdot)$ as $n \to \infty$. That is, $\lim_{n \to \infty} f_n(z) = f(z)$, iff for any positive number ϵ there is a number N such that*

$$|f_n(z) - f(z)| < \epsilon, \quad \forall n > N \qquad (19.17a)$$

If this condition is satisfied, the sequence is said to converge to $f(z)$. In general, the number N can be a function of both ϵ and z. If this convergence occurs for all points in the region $\mathcal{R}$, then $\mathcal{R}$ is called the region of convergence.

If the sequence does not converge at some point z, then it is called divergent at z.

2. *Convergence of a series of functions: Using the sequence of functions $\{f_n(\cdot)\}$, generate a new sequence of functions $\{g_n(\cdot)\}$, where $g_n(z) = \sum_{i=1}^{n} f_i(z)$, $g_n(z)$ is called the nth partial sum, and*

$$f_1(z) + f_2(z) + \ldots = \sum_{n \in \mathbb{P}} f_n(z) \qquad (19.17b)$$

is called an infinite series. If $\lim_{n \to \infty} g_n(z) = g(z)$, the infinite series is called convergent, otherwise the series is divergent. If this series converges for all points in the region $\mathcal{R}$, then $\mathcal{R}$ is called the region of convergence of the series.

If the series does not converge at some point z, then it is called divergent at z.

3. *Absolute convergence of a series: The series $\sum_{n \in \mathbb{P}} f_n(z)$ is said to be absolutely convergent, if $\sum_{n \in \mathbb{P}} |f_n(z)|$ converges.*

4. *Conditional convergence of a series: The series $\sum_{n \in \mathbb{P}} f_n(z)$ is said to be conditionally convergent, if $\sum_{n \in \mathbb{P}} f_n(z)$ converges, but $\sum_{n \in \mathbb{P}} |f_n(z)|$ does not converge.*

5. *Uniform convergence of a sequence of functions: In the definition of the limit of a sequence of functions, if the number N depends only on ϵ, and is independent of $z \in \mathcal{R}$, then $\{f_n(z)\}$ is said to converge uniformly to $f(z)$ for all points $z \in \mathcal{R}$.*

6. *Uniform convergence of a series of functions: In the definition of the convergence of a series of functions, if the sequence of partial sums $\{g_n(z)\}$ converges uniformly, for all points $z \in \mathcal{R}$, then the infinite series $\sum_{n \in \mathbb{P}} f_n(z)$ converges uniformly for all points $z \in \mathcal{R}$.* $\square$

19.4 Asymptotics

Basics of asymptotic behavior of functions, and different algorithmic-complexity classes are studied in this section. An algorithm is a finite step-by-step procedure to execute a computational task on a computer. Such steps are known as an *algorithm*. Asymptotic behavior of functions is usually used to describe the computational complexity of algorithms, and also the amount of computer memory needed to execute

them. Study of algorithmic-complexity classes helps in classifying the algorithms
based upon their complexity.

Asymptotic Behavior

It is instructive to specify the asymptotic behavior of continuous functions, convergence of series and sequences, or the computational complexity of algorithms.
These provide comprehensive insight into the behavior of functions. There are several different measures (and corresponding notations) to describe their asymptotic
behavior.

Definitions 19.15. *The asymptotic behavior of a sequence of real numbers a_n
and b_n as $n \to \infty$ is defined below. Let $b_n > 0$ for sufficiently large n.*

1. *O-Notation: It is also called the big-oh notation. For a specified sequence b_n,
   $O(b_n)$ is a set of sequences*

   $$O(b_n) = \{a_n \mid \text{there exist positive constants } K \text{ and } n_0 \text{ such that}$$
   $$0 \leq |a_n| \leq K b_n \text{ for all } n \geq n_0\} \tag{19.18a}$$

   *The O-notation provides an asymptotic upper bound for a sequence to within a
   constant factor.*

2. *Ω-Notation: For a specified sequence b_n, $\Omega(b_n)$ is a set of sequences*

   $$\Omega(b_n) = \{a_n \mid \text{there exist positive constants } k \text{ and } n_0 \text{ such that}$$
   $$0 \leq k b_n \leq |a_n| \text{ for all } n \geq n_0\} \tag{19.18b}$$

   *Therefore, $\Omega(b_n)$ is the set of sequences that grow at least as rapidly as a pos-
   itive multiple of b_n. This notation provides an asymptotic lower bound for a
   sequence to within a constant factor.*

3. *Θ-Notation: For a specified sequence b_n, $\Theta(b_n)$ is a set of sequences*

   $$\Theta(b_n) = \{a_n \mid \text{there exists positive constants } K, k, \text{ and } n_0 \text{ such that}$$
   $$0 \leq k b_n \leq |a_n| \leq K b_n \text{ for all } n \geq n_0\} \tag{19.18c}$$

   *That is, $a_n \in O(b_n)$ and $a_n \in \Omega(b_n)$ iff $a_n \in \Theta(b_n)$. This notation implies
   that the sequences a_n and b_n have the same order of magnitude. Therefore,
   $\Theta(b_n)$ is the set of sequences that grow at the same rate as a positive multiple
   of b_n.*

4. *o-Notation: It is also called the little-oh (or small-oh) notation. For a specified
   sequence b_n, $o(b_n)$ is a set of sequences*

   $$o(b_n) = \{a_n \mid \text{for any } k > 0, \text{ there exists a positive number } n_0 \text{ such that}$$
   $$0 \leq |a_n| < k b_n \text{ for all } n \geq n_0\} \tag{19.18d}$$

That is, $a_n \in o\,(b_n)$ if $\lim_{n\to\infty} |a_n/b_n| = 0$. Thus the sequences a_n becomes insignificant relative to b_n as n gets larger.   □

The O-notation gives an upper bound to within a constant factor. The set of functions that grow no more rapidly than a positive multiple of b_n is called $O\,(b_n)$. This notation is often used in stating the running time of an algorithm. Even though $O\,(b_n)$ is a set, and a_n belongs to this set, it is customary to write $a_n = O\,(b_n)$. This convention is extended to all other notations: $\Omega\,(\cdot), \Theta\,(\cdot)$, and $o\,(\cdot)$.

If a positive sequence b_n is given, then:

(a) $O\,(b_n)$ is the set of all a_n such that $|a_n/b_n|$ is bounded from above as $n \to \infty$. Therefore, this notation is a convenient way to express an upper bound of a sequence within a constant.

(b) $\Omega\,(b_n)$ is the set of all a_n such that $|a_n/b_n|$ is bounded from below by a strictly positive number as $n \to \infty$. This notation is used in expressing a lower bound of a sequence within a constant.

(c) $\Theta\,(b_n)$ is the set of all a_n such that $|a_n/b_n|$ is bounded from both above and below as $n \to \infty$. This notation is used to express matching upper and lower bounds.

(d) $o\,(b_n)$ is the set of all a_n such that $|a_n/b_n| \to 0$ as $n \to \infty$. This notation is used to express bound which is not asymptotically tight.

The above definitions about asymptotic sequences have been defined in terms of sequences. However, these can easily be extended to continuous functions. Alternate simplified notation is given below.

Definitions 19.16. *More notation.*

1. *As $n \to \infty$:*
   a) *$a_n \ll b_n$ or $b_n \gg a_n$ iff $a_n \geq 0$ and $a_n = o\,(b_n)$.*
   b) *Asymptotically equivalent sequences: $a_n \sim b_n$ iff $a_n/b_n \to 1$.*

2. *Asymptotic equality (approximation) between two functions is denoted by $\simeq$.*

3. *Approximation between numbers is denoted by $\approx$.*   □

Examples 19.2. Let $n \in \mathbb{P}$.

1. $f\,(n) = \sum_{j=0}^{m} a_j n^j$, $a_m \neq 0$. Then $f(n) \in O\,(n^m)$.
2. $\cos\,(x) \in O\,(1)$.
3. $\sum_{j=1}^{n} j \in O\,(n^2)$.
4. If $a_n \in O\,(1)$, then the sequence a_n is bounded.
5. $\pi \approx 3.14$. However, it is incorrect to state $\pi \simeq 3.14$.   □

Binomial Coefficients

Binomial coefficients are defined in terms of factorials.

Definitions 19.17. *Let* $n \in \mathbb{N}$.

1. *Factorial of a nonnegative integer* n *is denoted by* $n!$. *It is:*

$$0! = 1 \tag{19.19a}$$

$$n! = (n-1)!n, \quad n = 1, 2, 3, \ldots \tag{19.19b}$$

2. *Binomial coefficients arise in the expansion of the series*

$$(x+y)^n = \sum_{k=0}^{n} \binom{n}{k} x^k y^{n-k} \tag{19.20a}$$

$$\binom{n}{k} = \frac{n!}{k!\,(n-k)!}, \quad 0 \le k \le n \tag{19.20b}$$

The coefficients $\binom{n}{k}$, *of the above polynomial in two variables* x *and* y *are called the binomial coefficients. The above series expansion is often referred to as the binomial theorem.* □

A useful approximation for the factorial of an integer is Stirling's result: $n! \sim \sqrt{2\pi n}\,(n/e)^n$.

19.5 Fields

The notion of a field is introduced in this section. Examples of fields are also provided.

Definition 19.18. *Field. A field* $(F, +, \cdot)$ *is a triple, where* F *is a set, and* $+$ *and* $\cdot$ *are two binary operations, such that the following properties are satisfied for all* $a, b, c \in F$:

(a) *Associativity:* $(a+b)+c = a+(b+c)$; $(a \cdot b) \cdot c = a \cdot (b \cdot c)$

(b) *Commutativity:* $a+b = b+a$; $a \cdot b = b \cdot a$

(c) *Distributivity:* $a \cdot (b+c) = (a \cdot b) + (a \cdot c)$

(d) *Identities: There exists* $0 \in F$ *such that* $a+0 = a$. *The element* 0 (*zero*) *is called an additive identity. There exists* $1 \in F$ *such that* $a \cdot 1 = a$. *The element* 1 *is called a multiplicative identity* (*or unit element*).

(e) *Inverses: For every $a \in F$, there exists an element $b \in F$ such that $a + b = 0$.
The element b is called the additive inverse of the element a. For every nonzero
$a \in F$, there exists an element $b \in F$ such that $a \cdot b = 1$. The element b is called
the multiplicative inverse of the element a.*   □

Generally the additive inverse of $a \in F$ is denoted by $-a \in F$, and the multiplicative inverse of nonzero $a \in F$ is denoted by $a^{-1} \in F$.

Examples 19.3.

1. Some well-known examples of fields:

$$(\mathbb{Q}, +, \times), (\mathbb{R}, +, \times), \text{ and } (\mathbb{C}, +, \times)$$

In these fields, $+$ and $\times$ are the usual addition and multiplication operations.
The order of these fields is infinite. The additive and multiplicative inverses of
an element a are, $-a$ and a^{-1} respectively. Note that a^{-1} is defined, only if
$a \neq 0$. The characteristic of each of these fields is equal to 0.

2. $(\mathbb{Z}_m, +, \times)$ is a field, iff m is a prime number. The addition and multiplication
is modulo m in this field. Furthermore, if the number m is prime and there is no
ambiguity, then this field of numbers is simply denoted by $\mathbb{Z}_p$.   □

19.6 Vector Spaces over Fields

A vector space over a field is defined in this section. Notions related to vector subspaces and direct sum of vector spaces are also introduced. The concept of a linear
combination of vectors, basis vectors, independence of vectors, and dimension of a
vector space are also expounded upon. A formal definition of vector space over fields
is initially given.

Definition 19.19. *Vector space over a field. Let $\mathcal{F} = (F, +, \times)$ be a field. A
vector space is $\mathcal{V} = (V, \mathcal{F}, \boxplus, \boxtimes)$, where V is a nonempty set of vector elements,
and $\boxplus$ and $\boxtimes$ are binary operations.*

(a) *The operation $\boxplus$ is called vector addition, where $\boxplus : V \times V \to V$. For any
$u, v \in V$, the sum $u \boxplus v \in V$.*

(b) *The operation $\boxtimes$ is called vector multiplication by a scalar, where $\boxtimes : F \times V \to
V$. For any $k \in F$ and $u \in V$, the product $k \boxtimes u \in V$.*

The algebraic structure, $\mathcal{V}$, is called a vector space over $\mathcal{F}$ if the following axioms hold.

[*Axiom A1*] $\forall\, u, v, w \in V$, $(u \boxplus v) \boxplus w = u \boxplus (v \boxplus w)$.

[*Axiom A2*] *There is a vector $0 \in V$, called the zero vector, such that $u \boxplus 0 = u$ for each $u \in V$.*

[*Axiom A3*] *For each $u \in V$, there is a vector in V, denoted by $-u$, such that $u \boxplus (-u) = 0$. The vector $-u$ is called the inverse vector of u.*

[*Axiom A4*] *Vector addition is commutative. $\forall\, u, v \in V$, $u \boxplus v = v \boxplus u$.*

[*Axiom M1*] *For any $k \in F$, and any vectors $u, v \in V$, $k \boxtimes (u \boxplus v) = (k \boxtimes u) \boxplus (k \boxtimes v)$.*

[*Axiom M2*] *For any $a, b \in F$, and any vector $u \in V$, $(a + b) \boxtimes u = (a \boxtimes u) \boxplus (b \boxtimes u)$.*

[*Axiom M3*] *For any $a, b \in F$, and any vector $u \in V$, $(a \times b) \boxtimes u = a \boxtimes (b \boxtimes u)$.*

[*Axiom M4*] $\forall u \in V$, *and for the unit element $1 \in F$, $1 \boxtimes u = u$.*   □

The first set of four of the above axioms describes the additive structure of $\mathcal{V}$. The next set of four axioms describes the action of the field $\mathcal{F}$ on V.

The vector addition $\boxplus$ and the field addition $+$ are quite different, but they are both typically denoted by $+$. Similarly, if $a \in F$, and $u \in V$; $(a \boxtimes u)$ is denoted by au. The symbol 0 is used to denote the additive identities of both $\mathcal{V}$ and $\mathcal{F}$.

A vector space is sometimes called a linear vector space or simply a linear space. The reader should be aware that occasionally it is convenient to specify (sometimes) unambiguously the vector space $\mathcal{V}$ and the field $\mathcal{F}$ by the symbols V and F respectively.

Observations 19.4. Assume that $\mathcal{V}$ is a vector space over a field $\mathcal{F}$.

1. For all $a \in F$ and $0 \in V$, $a0 = 0$.

2. For $0 \in F$ and any vector $u \in V$, $0u = 0$.

3. If $a \in F$, $u \in V$, and $au = 0$, then either $a = 0$ or $u = 0$, or both are equal to 0.

4. For all $u \in V$, $(-1)\, u = -u$.

5. The difference of two vectors u and v is $u \boxplus (-v) \triangleq (u - v)$, where $-v$ is the negative of v.

6. For all $a \in F$ and $u, v \in V$, $a(u - v) = au - av$.

7. For all $u, v, w \in V$, if $u + w = v + w$ then $u = v$.   □

Examples 19.4. Certain well-known examples of vector spaces are listed.

1. The set of all n-tuples of real numbers

$$\mathbb{R}^n = \{(x_1, x_2, \ldots, x_n) \mid x_j \in \mathbb{R}, 1 \leq j \leq n\}$$

Note that $\mathbb{R}^1 = \mathbb{R}$. The zero vector in $\mathbb{R}^n$ is simply $(0, 0, \ldots, 0) \triangleq 0$.

2. The set of n-tuples of complex numbers

$$\mathbb{C}^n = \{(x_1, x_2, \ldots, x_n) \mid x_j \in \mathbb{C}, 1 \leq j \leq n\}$$

Note that $\mathbb{C}^1 = \mathbb{C}$. The zero vector in $\mathbb{C}^n$ is simply $(0, 0, \ldots, 0) \triangleq 0$.

3. The set of polynomials of degree less than n with real coefficients. In this case the scalars belong to the set $\mathbb{R}$. Addition is ordinary polynomial addition and scalar multiplication is the usual scalar-by-polynomial multiplication.   □

It is possible to write a vector as a single-column matrix or as a single-row matrix without any ambiguity. In such cases it is called a column vector or a row vector respectively. With a little misuse of notation, the same symbol for the vector and the corresponding row or column vector is used. Also by convention, if a vector is specified as $u \geq 0$ then the vector u is allowed to take a 0 value.

Definitions 19.20. *Let* $\mathcal{U} = (U, \mathcal{F}, \boxplus, \boxtimes)$, $\mathcal{V} = (V, \mathcal{F}, \boxplus, \boxtimes)$, *and* $\mathcal{W} = (W, \mathcal{F}, \boxplus, \boxtimes)$ *be vector spaces defined over the same field. These spaces also have same addition and multiplication operations.*

1. *Let* $U \neq \varnothing$ *and* $U \subseteq V$, *then* $\mathcal{U}$ *is said to be a vector subspace of* $\mathcal{V}$.

2. *Let* U *and* W *be subsets of the set* V. *The sum of two sets* U *and* W *is the set* $\{u + w \mid u \in U, w \in W\}$. *This sum is denoted by* $U + W$. *The corresponding vector space is denoted by* $\mathcal{U} + \mathcal{W}$.

3. *If* $U \cap W = \{0\}$, *then* $U + W$ *is denoted by* $U \oplus W$. *The corresponding vector space is denoted by* $\mathcal{U} \oplus \mathcal{W}$. *This sum is called the direct sum.*   □

Observations 19.5. Some useful observations about the vector space $\mathcal{V}$ and the field $\mathcal{F}$. Also let $\mathcal{U}$ and $\mathcal{W}$ be vector subspaces of $\mathcal{V}$.

1. $\mathcal{U}$ is a vector subspace of $\mathcal{V}$ if and only if $U \neq \varnothing$ and for all $a, b \in F$ and $u, v \in U$, $(au + bv) \in U$.
   Equivalently, $\mathcal{U}$ is a vector subspace of $\mathcal{V}$ if and only if $U \neq \varnothing$ and for all $a \in F$ and $u, v \in U$, $(u + v) \in U$ and $au \in U$.

2. The vector space $\mathcal{V}$ is a vector subspace of itself.

3. The vector space $(\{0\}, \mathcal{F}, \boxplus, \boxtimes)$ is a vector subspace of $\mathcal{V}$.

4. All vector subspaces of $\mathcal{V}$ contain the zero vector 0.

5. The sum of a collection of subspaces is a subspace.

6. The intersection of a collection of subspaces is a subspace.

7. If $U \subseteq V$, and $W \subseteq V$ then $(U + W) \subseteq V$.

8. Each element of the set $U \oplus W$ can be expressed as $u + w$, where $u \in U$ is unique and $w \in W$ is unique.   □

The concept of linear combination of vectors, basis vectors, independence of vectors, and dimension of a vector space is introduced below.

Definitions 19.21. V *is a vector space over a field* $\mathcal{F}$.

1. *If* $u_1, u_2, \ldots, u_n \in V$, *then a vector* $u \in V$ *is a linear combination of* $u_1, u_2, \ldots, u_n$ *if* $u = \sum_{j=1}^{n} b_j u_j$, *where* $b_j \in F$ *for* $1 \le j \le n$.

2. *Let S be a subset of V. The set of all finite linear combinations of vectors in S is the span of the set S. Denote it by $L(S)$. Note that $L(S) \subseteq V$.*
   $L(S)$ is called the space spanned or generated by the set S. Observe that $L(\varnothing) = \{0\}$.

3. *If $S \subseteq V$, and $L(S) = V$ then the set S is called the spanning set of V.*

4. *Vectors of a subset $S \subseteq V$ are said to be linearly independent, if for every finite subset $\{u_1, u_2, \ldots, u_n\}$ of S, $\sum_{j=1}^{n} b_j u_j = 0$ where $b_j \in F$ implies $b_j = 0$, for all $j = 1, 2, \ldots, n$.*
   In other words, the set of vectors $\{u_1, u_2, \ldots, u_n\}$ are linearly independent if and only if the vector u_j cannot be represented as a linear combination of the other vectors of the set, where $j = 1, 2, \ldots, n$.

5. *A subset $S \subseteq V$ is said to be linearly dependent, if it is not linearly independent. In other words, S is linearly dependent if there exists a finite number of distinct vectors $\{u_1, u_2, \ldots, u_n\}$ in S such that $\sum_{j=1}^{n} b_j u_j = 0$ for some combination of $b_j \in F, 1 \le j \le n$, not all zero.*

6. *An independent spanning set of V is called the basis of V.*

7. *The cardinality of any basis set of V is called the dimension of V, or $\dim(V)$. The dimension of the vector space V is finite, if it has a finite basis; or else V is infinite-dimensional. The dimension of V is sometimes denoted by $\dim(V)$.*

8. *Let $B = (u_1, u_2, \ldots, u_n)$ be an ordered basis set of the vector space V, then the coordinates of $u \in V$ with respect to B are $b_1, b_2, \ldots, b_n$, where $u = \sum_{j=1}^{n} b_j u_j$ and $b_j \in F, 1 \le j \le n$. The coordinate-vector $[u]_B$ of u with respect to the ordered basis set B is $(b_1, b_2, \ldots, b_n)$. Note that a basis is an ordered basis, if it is specified as an ordered set.*

9. *Let $x = (x_1, x_2, \ldots, x_n)$ and $y = (y_1, y_2, \ldots, y_n)$ be vectors defined over the field $\mathcal{F}$. The inner product of the vectors x and y is $x \circ y = \sum_{j=1}^{n} x_j y_j \in F$. The vectors x and y are said to be orthogonal, if $x \circ y = 0$. A convenient notation to indicate the orthogonality of two vectors x and y is $x \perp y$.* ☐

A more specific definition of inner product is given later in this chapter.

Observations 19.6. Let the algebraic structures $\mathcal{T} = (T, \mathcal{F}, \boxplus, \boxtimes)$, $\mathcal{U} = (U, \mathcal{F}, \boxplus, \boxtimes)$, $V = (V, \mathcal{F}, \boxplus, \boxtimes)$, and $W = (W, \mathcal{F}, \boxplus, \boxtimes)$ be vector spaces.

1. Let T be a nonempty subset of V. If $T \subseteq W \subseteq V$, then $L(T) \subseteq W$.

2. Let $U \subseteq V$, and $W \subseteq V$ then $(U + W) = L(U \cup W)$.

3. Let $U \subseteq V$, and $W \subseteq V$. If $\{u_j\}$ generates U, and $\{w_j\}$ generates W; then $\{u_j\} \cup \{w_j\} = \{u_j, w_j\}$ generates $U + W$.

4. Let V be a finite-dimensional vector space, such that $\dim(V) = n$.
    (a) Every basis set of V has n elements.
    (b) Any linearly independent set of vectors with n elements is a basis.
    (c) Any set of $m \geq (n + 1)$ vectors is linearly dependent.
    (d) Any set of $m < n$ linearly independent vectors, can be a part of a basis, and can be extended to form a basis of the vector space.
    (e) This vector space is sometimes denoted by $V^{(n)}$ or V^n.

5. Let V be a finite-dimensional vector space, where $\dim(V) = n$. If $W \subseteq V$, then $\dim(W) \leq n$.

6. Let V be a vector space, and $U \subseteq V$, and $W \subseteq V$. If the subspaces U and W are finite-dimensional, then $U + W$ has finite-dimension. Also

$$\dim(U + W) = \dim(U) + \dim(W) - \dim(U \cap W)$$

where $U \cap W \triangleq (U \cap W, \mathcal{F}, \boxplus, \boxtimes)$. If $V = U \oplus W$ then

$$\dim(V) = \dim(U) + \dim(W)$$

□

Some well-known examples of vector spaces are given below.

Examples 19.5. Examples of vector spaces and basis sets.

1. The set of complex numbers $\mathbb{C}$ is a two-dimensional vector space over $\mathbb{R}$. It has the ordered basis $(1, \sqrt{-1})$. Any pair of complex numbers which are not a real multiple of the other form a basis.

2. Consider the set of polynomials in x. Also assume that these polynomials have degree less than or equal to n. The dimension of space of such polynomials is $(n + 1)$. Its ordered basis set is $(1, x, x^2, \ldots, x^n)$.

3. The vector space $F[x]$ defined over the field $\mathcal{F} = (F, +, \times)$ has infinite dimension. Its ordered basis set is $(1, x, x^2, x^3, \ldots)$.

4. In the space $\mathbb{R}^n$, the set of vectors $\{e_1, e_2, e_3, \ldots, e_n\}$ form a basis. These vectors are $e_1 = (1, 0, 0, \ldots, 0, 0)^T$, $e_2 = (0, 1, 0, \ldots, 0, 0)^T, \ldots$, and $e_n = (0, 0, 0, \ldots, 0, 1)^T$. This set is called the standard basis of $\mathbb{R}^n$ and the vectors are called unit vectors. Note that each of these unit vectors has n elements, and $\dim(\mathbb{R}^n) = n$.
   The vector of all ones is called an all-1 vector. It is $e = (1, 1, 1, \ldots, 1, 1)^T$. Also $e = \sum_{i=1}^{n} e_i$.

5. The subspace of $\mathbb{R}^3$ with all 3-tuples of the form $(a, b, a + b)$ has dimension 2. A possible basis of this vector subspace is $\{(1, 0, 1), (0, 1, 1)\}$. Note that the vector $v = (2, -4, -2)$ is in this subspace. This is true, because $v = 2(1, 0, 1) - 4(0, 1, 1)$. Thus the coordinate-vector of v with respect to this basis is $(2, -4)$.

$\square$

19.7 Linear Mappings

Linear mappings or transformations or operators are functions that map one vector space to another.

Definitions 19.22. *Let* $\mathcal{U} = (U, \mathcal{F}, \boxplus, \boxtimes)$, *and* $\mathcal{V} = (V, \mathcal{F}, \boxplus, \boxtimes)$ *be vector spaces over the same field* $\mathcal{F} = (F, +, \times)$.

1. *Linear mapping: A mapping* $f : V \to U$ *is called a linear mapping (or linear transformation or vector space homomorphism) provided the following two conditions are true:*
   (a) $f(x \boxplus y) = f(x) \boxplus f(y)$ *for all* $x, y \in V$.
   (b) $f(k \boxtimes x) = k \boxtimes f(x)$ *for all* $x \in V$ *and all* $k \in F$.
   Therefore, the mapping f *is linear if it preserves the two basic operations of vector addition and scalar multiplication.*

2. *Image (or range) and kernel of linear mapping: Let* $f : V \to U$ *be a linear mapping.*
   (a) *Image: The image of* f *denoted by* im f, *is the set of image points in* U. *Thus*
$$\text{im } f = \{u \in U \mid f(v) = u \text{ for some } v \in V\} \qquad (19.21a)$$
   (b) *Kernel: The kernel of* f, *denoted by* ker f *is the set of points in* V *which map into* $0 \in U$. *Thus*
$$\text{ker } f = \{v \in V \mid f(v) = 0\} \qquad (19.21b)$$

3. *Rank and nullity of a linear mapping: Let the vector space* V *be of finite dimension and* $f : V \to U$ *be a linear mapping.*
   (a) *Rank of a linear mapping* f *is equal to the dimension of its image. Thus*
$$\text{rank } (f) = \dim (\text{im } f) \qquad (19.22a)$$
   (b) *Nullity of a linear mapping* f *is equal to the dimension of its kernel. Thus*
$$\text{nullity } (f) = \dim (\text{ker } f) \qquad (19.22b)$$

□

Observations 19.7. Let $\mathcal{U} = (U, \mathcal{F}, \boxplus, \boxtimes)$, and $\mathcal{V} = (V, \mathcal{F}, \boxplus, \boxtimes)$ be vector spaces over the same field $\mathcal{F} = (F, +, \times)$.

1. Let $f : V \to U$ be a linear mapping.

   (a) Let dim $(\mathcal{V})$ be finite, then the relationships between different dimensions are

   $$\dim (\mathcal{V}) = \dim (\operatorname{im} f) + \dim (\ker f) = \operatorname{rank} (f) + \operatorname{nullity} (f) \quad (19.23)$$

   (b) The image of f is a subset of U, and the kernel of f is a subset of V.
   (c) Let $\{v_1, v_2, \ldots, v_n\}$ be a set of basis vectors of $\mathcal{V}$. Then the vectors $f(v_i) = u_i \in U$, for $1 \le i \le n$ generate im f.
   (d) $f(0) = 0$.

2. Let $\{v_1, v_2, \ldots, v_n\}$ be a set of basis vectors of $\mathcal{V}$. Also let $\{u_1, u_2, \ldots, u_n\}$ be any vectors in U. Then there exists a unique linear mapping $f : V \to U$ such that $f(v_i) = u_i \in U$, for $1 \le i \le n$.   □

Linear mappings are also discussed in the chapter on matrices and determinants. Use of matrices to describe linear mappings makes the above abstract description more concrete.

19.8 Tensor Products

The artifice of tensor products enables the extension of signal processing in a single dimension to more than one dimension. For example, use of tensor products enables operations of two-dimensional functions to inherit properties of operations of single-dimensional functions. Further, use of tensor products provide insight into designing computationally efficient transforms. The tensor product of vector spaces is defined in terms of bilinear maps.

Definition 19.23. *Bilinear map. Let $V = (V, \mathcal{F}, \boxplus, \boxtimes)$ and $W = (W, \mathcal{F}, \boxplus, \boxtimes)$ be vector spaces defined over a field $\mathcal{F} = (F, +, \times)$. A map $f : V \times W \to Z$ is bilinear if*

$$f(a_1 u_1 + a_2 u_2, v) = a_1 f(u_1, v) + a_2 f(u_2, v) \qquad (19.24a)$$
$$f(u, b_1 v_1 + b_2 v_2) = b_1 f(u, v_1) + b_2 f(u, v_2) \qquad (19.24b)$$

where $u, u_1, u_2 \in U$, $v, v_1, v_2 \in V$, and $a_1, a_2, b_1, b_2 \in F$. As usual, the vector addition operator $\boxplus$ is denoted as $+$, and the scalar-vector multiplication operator $\boxtimes$ is simply denoted as dot $\cdot$.   □

Observation 19.8. The conditions for the bilinear map f can alternately be stated as:

(a) $f(u_1 + u_2, v) = f(u_1, v) + f(u_2, v)$

(b) $f(u, v_1 + v_2) = f(u, v_1) + f(u, v_2)$

(c) $f(\lambda u, v) = \lambda f(u, v)$

(d) $f(u, \lambda v) = \lambda f(u, v)$

where $u, u_1, u_2 \in U$, $v, v_1, v_2 \in V$, and $\lambda \in F$.   □

Definition 19.24. *Tensor product of vector spaces. Let* $V = (V, \mathcal{F}, \boxplus, \boxtimes)$ *and* $W = (W, \mathcal{F}, \boxplus, \boxtimes)$ *be vector spaces defined over a field* $\mathcal{F} = (F, +, \times)$. *The tensor product* $V \otimes W$ *is a vector space over field* $\mathcal{F}$ *has a map*

$$\phi : V \times W \to V \otimes W$$

If $v \in V$, *and* $w \in W$, *then* $\phi(v, w) \in V \otimes W$. *Further,* $\phi(v, w) \triangleq v \otimes w$. *As usual, the vector addition operator* $\boxplus$ *is denoted as* +, *and the scalar-vector multiplication operator* $\boxtimes$ *is simply denoted as dot* ·. *Also*

(a) *The map* ϕ *is bilinear.*

(b) *Whenever* $(v_1, v_2, \ldots, v_n)$ *is a basis set of* V, *and* $(w_1, w_2, \ldots, w_m)$ *is a basis set of* W *then*

$$\{\phi(v_i, w_j) = v_i \otimes w_j \mid 1 \leq i \leq n, 1 \leq j \leq m\}$$

is also a basis set of $V \otimes W$.   □

It should be mentioned that, not every element of the form

$$\sum_{i=1}^{n} \sum_{j=1}^{m} c_{ij} v_i \otimes w_j$$

can be expressed as

$$\sum_{i=1}^{n} \sum_{j=1}^{m} a_i b_j v_i \otimes w_j$$

This is true because there are mn number of c_{ij}'s. However, there are only n number of a_i's and m number of b_j's, for a total of only $(m + n)$ scalars. This is similar to the fact that every polynomial in two variables x, y cannot be expressed as a product of type

$$\left(a_{n-1} x^{n-1} + a_{n-2} x^{n-2} + \cdots + a_1 x + a_0\right)$$
$$\times \left(b_{m-1} y^{m-1} + b_{m-2} y^{m-2} + \cdots + b_1 y + b_0\right)$$

For example, the polynomial $xy + 1$ cannot be expressed in the above manner.

Also note informally that, an element in $V \otimes W$ can be considered as an $n \times m$ matrix with elements in the set F.

Examples 19.6. Some illustrative examples.

1. Let $V = \mathbb{R}^n$ and $W = \mathbb{R}^m$. Also let the standard basis set of the space V be $(e_1, e_2, \ldots, e_n)$, and that of space W be $(f_1, f_2, \ldots, f_m)$. Then the basis set of space $V \otimes W$ is $\{e_i \otimes f_j \mid 1 \leq i \leq n, 1 \leq j \leq m\}$.

2. Let $A = [a_{ij}]$ and B be square matrices of size n and m respectively.

   a) Tensor or Kronecker product of matrices:

   $$A \otimes B = \begin{bmatrix} a_{11}B & a_{12}B & \cdots & a_{1n}B \\ a_{21}B & a_{22}B & \cdots & a_{2n}B \\ \vdots & \vdots & \ddots & \vdots \\ a_{n1}B & a_{n2}B & \cdots & a_{nn}B \end{bmatrix}$$

   b) Recall that the rank of a matrix A is denoted as r_A. We have $r_{A \otimes B} = r_A r_B$.

   c)
   $$\det(A \otimes B) = (\det(A))^m (\det(B))^n$$

   d)
   $$(A \otimes B)^T = A^T \otimes B^T$$

   e) Recall that the trace of a matrix A is denoted as $tr(A)$, then
   $$tr(A \otimes B) = tr(A)\, tr(B)$$

   f) If the matrices A and B are diagonalizable, then so is $A \otimes B$.

3. Let A and C be square matrices of size n each, and B and D be square matrices of size m each. Then

   $$(A \otimes B)(C \otimes D) = AC \otimes BD$$

4. Let V be a vector space over the field $\mathbb{F}$. Then $V \otimes \mathbb{F} = V$. Note that $\otimes$ is simply the scalar multiplication operator.

5. Let $V = \mathbb{F}[x]$ be a vector space of polynomials. Then $V \otimes V$ is a vector space of polynomials in two variables, which is $\mathbb{F}[x_1, x_2]$. Further, $f(x) \otimes g(x) = f(x_1) g(x_2)$. Let $\theta = \{1, x, x^2, \ldots\}$ be a basis set of V, then

   $$\theta \otimes \theta = \{x_1^i x_2^j \mid i, j = 0, 1, 2, \ldots\}$$

   is a basis set of $\mathbb{F}[x_1, x_2]$.

It can be parenthetically noted that $f(x) \otimes g(x) \neq g(x) \otimes f(x)$ in general. Observe that

$$f(x) \otimes g(x) = f(x_1) g(x_2) \neq g(x_1) f(x_2) = g(x) \otimes f(x)$$

$\square$

Example 19.7. Evaluate

$$(1, -1) \otimes (2, 3) + (1, 1) \otimes (-1, 2)$$

Let $x = (1, 0)$ and $y = (0, 1)$. Therefore, the given expression is

$$(x, -y) \otimes (2x, 3y) + (x, y) \otimes (-x, 2y)$$
$$= 2(x \otimes x) + 3(x \otimes y) - 2(y \otimes x) - 3(y \otimes y)$$
$$\quad - (x \otimes x) + 2(x \otimes y) - (y \otimes x) + 2(y \otimes y)$$
$$= (x \otimes x) + 5(x \otimes y) - 3(y \otimes x) - (y \otimes y)$$

More explicitly, the above expression can be stated as

$$((1, 0) \otimes (1, 0)) + 5((1, 0) \otimes (0, 1)) - 3((0, 1) \otimes (1, 0)) - ((0, 1) \otimes (0, 1))$$

$\square$

19.9 Vector Algebra

Basic notions from vector algebra are summarized in this section. A vector is a quantity which has both *magnitude* and *direction*. Vectors can themselves be added, and multiplied by scalars. We shall assume that the elements of a vector are real numbers.

A vector in 3-dimensional space $\mathbb{R}^3$ is represented as a point $u = (u_1, u_2, u_3)$, where $u_1, u_2, u_3 \in \mathbb{R}$. That is, u_1, u_2, and u_3 are the *coordinates* of a point specified by u in three-dimensional space. These are also called the *components* of vector u. A vector is represented as a row in this section. We shall use the notation: $(1, 0, 0) \triangleq i$, $(0, 1, 0) \triangleq j$, and $(0, 0, 1) \triangleq k$. The vectors i, j, and k are along the x-axis, y-axis, and z-axis respectively. Also the set of vectors $\{i, j, k\}$ form a basis of the 3-dimensional vector space $\mathbb{R}^3$. The vector u is also written as

$$u = u_1 i + u_2 j + u_3 k$$

Note that the vector u is also called the *position vector* or *radius vector* from the origin $(0, 0, 0)$ to the point (u_1, u_2, u_3). The magnitude or length or Euclidean norm of this vector is

$$\|u\| = \sqrt{u_1^2 + u_2^2 + u_3^2}$$

where $\|u\|$ is the distance from the point $u = (u_1, u_2, u_3)$, to the origin $0 = (0, 0, 0)$. The vector $(0, 0, 0)$ is often called the *null vector*. A *unit vector* is a vector of unit length. The *direction* of a nonnull vector u is specified by $u/\|u\|$. Two vectors u and v are said to be *parallel* to each other, if their directions are identical. There are two kinds of vector products. These are the dot product and cross product. Only the vector dot product is of concern to us in this book.

Dot Product

The *dot (or inner) product* of two vectors $u = (u_1, u_2, u_3)$ and $v = (v_1, v_2, v_3)$ is defined as

$$u \circ v = u_1 v_1 + u_2 v_2 + u_3 v_3$$

It can readily be inferred that

$$|u \circ v| \le \|u\| \cdot \|v\|$$

For the purpose of visual clarity, the symbol "·" is used for denoting scalar multiplication. The above inequality yields

$$-1 \le \frac{u \circ v}{\|u\| \cdot \|v\|} \le 1$$

Therefore, we can also specify the dot product of the two vectors u and v as

$$u \circ v = \|u\| \cdot \|v\| \cdot \cos \theta, \quad \text{where } \theta \in [0, \pi]$$

It can also be shown that θ is the angle between the line segments $0u$ and $0v$.

Observations 19.9. Some useful results related to dot products of vectors are listed. Let u, v, and w be vectors; and $a \in \mathbb{R}$.

1. Commutative law for dot products: $u \circ v = v \circ u$

2. Distributive law for dot products: $u \circ (v + w) = u \circ v + u \circ w$

3. $a(u \circ v) = (au) \circ v = u \circ (av) = (u \circ v)a$

4. $i \circ i = j \circ j = k \circ k = 1$, and $i \circ j = j \circ k = k \circ i = 0$

5. Let $u = u_1 i + u_2 j + u_3 k$, then

$$u_1 = u \circ i, \quad u_2 = u \circ j, \quad u_3 = u \circ k$$

6. If $u \circ v = 0$, and u and v are not null vectors, then u and v are *orthogonal* or *perpendicular* or *normal* to each other.   □

In a three-dimensional coordinate system, the basis vectors are ordered as (i, j, k). These basis vectors form an orthonormal basis because: $i \circ i = j \circ j = k \circ k = 1$, and $i \circ j = j \circ k = k \circ i = 0$. Let the basis vectors i, j, and k be ordered as (i, j, k).

19.10 Vector Spaces Revisited

The following topics are discussed in this section. Normed vector space, complete vector space, concept of compactness of a set, inner product space, orthogonality, and Gram–Schmidt orthogonalization process.

19.10.1 Normed Vector Space

It is possible to introduce a metric related to the size (length) of the vector. This is done by introducing the concept of a norm. A representation of the distance between any two vectors can also be defined by the notion of norm.

Definitions 19.25. *Let* $V = (V, \mathcal{F}, +, \times)$ *be a vector space over a field* $\mathcal{F} = (F, +, \times)$.

1. *Norm of a vector: The norm of a vector is a function* $\|\cdot\| : V \to \mathbb{R}_0^+$. *The norm of the vector* $u \in V$ *is a nonnegative real number, denoted by* $\|u\|$. *It is subject to the following conditions.*
   $[N1]$ $\|u\| \geq 0$, *with equality if and only if* $u = 0$. *That is, the norm of a vector is a nonnegative number.*
   $[N2]$ $\|au\| = |a| \cdot \|u\|$, *where* $|a|$ *is the magnitude of* a, *and* $a \in F$. *This is the homogeneity property of the norm.*
   $[N3]$ $\|u + v\| \leq \|u\| + \|v\|$. *This is the triangle inequality.*
   This vector space V, *along with its norm* $\|\cdot\|$ *is called a normed vector space. That is, the two-tuple* $(V, \|\cdot\|)$ *is called a normed space.*

2. *Distance function: For* $u, v \in V$, *the distance or metric function from* u *to* v *is* $d(u, v)$. *That is,* $d : V \times V \to \mathbb{R}$. *Let* $u, v, w \in V$, *then the distance function satisfies the following axioms:*
   $[D1]$ $d(u, v) \geq 0$, *with equality if and only if* $u = v$.
   $[D2]$ $d(u, v) = d(v, u)$. *This is the symmetry of the distance function.*
   $[D3]$ $d(u, w) \leq d(u, v) + d(v, w)$. *This is the triangle inequality.*

3. *Let* V *be a normed vector space, and* $d(\cdot, \cdot)$ *be a distance function. The two-tuple* (V, d) *is called a metric space.*
   Also let $u, v \in V$. *The function* $d(\cdot, \cdot)$ *defined by* $d(u, v) = \|u - v\|$ *is called the induced metric on* V.

4. *Let the vector space be* $\mathbb{C}^n$. *Also let* $x = (x_1, x_2, \ldots, x_n) \in \mathbb{C}^n$. *Then the Euclidean norm is given by*

$$\|x\|_2 = \left(\sum_{j=1}^{n} |x_j|^2 \right)^{1/2} \tag{19.25}$$

If the norm is Euclidean and the context is unambiguous, the subscript 2 in the above equation is generally dropped.

5. *Matrix norm: A matrix A is a rectangular array of complex numbers. The matrix norm induced by the vector norm $\|\cdot\|_2$ is defined by $\|A\|_2 = \sup_{\|x\|_2=1} \|Ax\|_2$.* □

In a misuse of notation, the vector space $\mathcal{V}$, and the field $\mathcal{F}$ are generally denoted by V and F respectively. Matrix norms are also discussed in the chapter on matrices and determinants.

19.10.2 Complete Vector Space and Compactness

The notion of convergence, complete vector space, and compactness are introduced in this subsection. This enables us to extend concepts from finite-dimensional spaces to infinite-dimensional spaces. Let $\mathcal{V} = (V, \mathcal{F}, +, \times)$ be a normed vector space over a field $\mathcal{F} = (F, +, \times)$, where $\|\cdot\|$ is the norm function of a vector. Also let $\{g_n\}$ denote a sequence of vectors $g_1, g_2, \ldots, g_n, \ldots$, which belong to the vector space $\mathcal{V}$. This sequence converges to g if $\|g_n - g\|$ tends to 0 for very large values of n.

A sequence $\{g_n\}$ is called a *Cauchy sequence* if $\|g_n - g_m\|$ tends to 0 for very large values of m and n. More precisely, a sequence $\{g_n\}$ in a normed vector space $\mathcal{V}$ is said to be a Cauchy sequence if for each $\epsilon > 0$, there exists n_0 such that $\|g_n - g_m\| < \epsilon$ for all $m, n > n_0$.

Definition 19.26. *A normed vector space $\mathcal{V}$ is complete, if every Cauchy sequence in the vector space converges.* □

Examples of normed vector spaces are presented below. All the vector spaces in these examples are complete.

Examples 19.8. Some illustrative examples.

1. Let the vector space be $\mathbb{R}^n$. Also let $x = (x_1, x_2, \ldots, x_n) \in \mathbb{R}^n$. Then the p-norm of vector x is defined as

$$\|x\|_p = \left(\sum_{j=1}^{n} |x_j|^p \right)^{1/p}, \quad 1 \le p < \infty \tag{19.26}$$

(a) $p = 1$: $\|x\|_1 = \sum_{j=1}^{n} |x_j|$.

(b) $p = 2$: This is the Euclidean norm. $\|x\|_2 = \left(\sum_{j=1}^{n} x_j^2 \right)^{1/2}$.

(c) As p tends towards ∞, $\|x\|_p$ tends towards $\|x\|_\infty = \max_{1 \le j \le n} \{|x_j|\}$.

The extension of the definition of the p-norm to $x \in \mathbb{C}^n$ should be immediately evident.

2. *Sequence space l^p, $1 \leq p < \infty$: Let the sequence $x = (x_1, x_2, \ldots, x_n, \ldots)$,*
   $x_j \in \mathbb{R}$, $j = 1, 2, 3, \ldots$ satisfy

$$\sum_{j \in \mathbb{P}} |x_j|^p < \infty \qquad (19.27a)$$

Sequences which satisfy the above condition belong to the space l^p. The following norm can be defined, for $x = (x_1, x_2, \ldots, x_n, \ldots) \in l^p$.

$$\|x\|_p = \left(\sum_{j \in \mathbb{P}} |x_j|^p \right)^{1/p}, \qquad 1 \leq p < \infty \qquad (19.27b)$$

This norm is commonly referred to as the l^p-*norm*.
The sequence $(x_1, x_2, \ldots, x_n, \ldots)$ is bounded if there exists a finite $M \in \mathbb{R}$
such that $|x_j| < M$ for all values $j = 1, 2, 3, \ldots$... The space l^∞ consists of
bounded sequences.

3. *Function space L^p, $1 \leq p < \infty$: Let the function $f(t)$, $t \in \mathbb{R}$, satisfy*
   $\int_{-\infty}^{\infty} |f(t)|^p \, dt < \infty$. *This function $f(\cdot)$ is said to be p-integrable. Then L^p*
   is a function space in which the following norm can be defined

$$\|f\|_p = \left(\int_{-\infty}^{\infty} |f(t)|^p \, dt \right)^{1/p}, \ 1 \leq p < \infty. \qquad (19.28)$$

This norm is commonly referred to as L^p or $L^p(\mathbb{R})$ *norm.*   □

The concept of compactness on a metric space is next introduced.

Definitions 19.27. *Bounded metric space, and compact metric space.*

1. *A subset $A \subseteq V$ of the metric space is said to be totally bounded, if for every*
   $\epsilon > 0$, *A contains a finite set A_ϵ such that for each $x \in V$, there is a $y \in A_\epsilon$*
   such that $d(x, y) < \epsilon$.

2. *A metric space (V, d) is said to be compact, if it is complete and totally bounded.*
                                                                                              □

19.10.3 Inner Product Space

The inner product of two vectors within a specific setting has been discussed earlier
in the chapter. Using the same ideas, but different notation, this concept is revisited.
Inner product space can be defined by placing additional structure on vector space
$\mathcal{V} = (V, \mathcal{F}, +, \times)$ over a field $\mathcal{F} = (F, +, \times)$. The concept of angle between two
vectors is introduced via the concept of inner product. This is followed by the concept
of orthogonality of vectors.

Definition 19.28. *Inner product space*: *A complex inner product on a vector space $\mathcal{V}$ over field $\mathbb{C}$ is a function $\langle \cdot, \cdot \rangle : V \times V \to \mathbb{C}$ such that for all $u, v, w \in V$ and $a, b \in \mathbb{C}$ the following axioms hold:*

[I1] $\langle u, u \rangle \geq 0$, where $\langle u, u \rangle = 0$ if and only if $u = 0$.

[I2] $\langle u, v \rangle = \overline{\langle v, u \rangle}$ (the bar indicates complex conjugation).

[I3] $\langle au + bv, w \rangle = a \langle u, w \rangle + b \langle v, w \rangle$. That is, the inner product function $\langle \cdot, \cdot \rangle$ is linear in the first argument.

The inner product vector space is denoted by the two-tuple $(\mathcal{V}, \langle \cdot, \cdot \rangle)$. □

The axioms [I1] and [I2] imply that $\langle u, u \rangle$ is real. Observe that the axiom [I2] implies that the inner product is commutative over its two components, except for the conjugacy. Furthermore, axiom [I3] implies that the inner product is linear in its first component. The vector space $\mathcal{V}$ along with the defined inner product is called an *inner product vector space*. It can easily be shown that the inner product, as defined is also linear in its second component, except for conjugacy.

$$\langle u, av + bw \rangle = \overline{a} \langle u, v \rangle + \overline{b} \langle u, w \rangle$$

Some textbooks define the axiom [I3] alternately. Let us call this modified axiom [I3′]. It is $\langle u, av + bw \rangle = a \langle u, v \rangle + b \langle u, w \rangle$. That is, the inner product $\langle \cdot, \cdot \rangle$ is linear in the second argument. This definition is equally valid, if its usage is consistent with it. Also observe that this distinction is unnecessary, if the inner product space is defined over the set of real numbers $\mathbb{R}$. Unless stated otherwise, the axioms [I1], [I2], and [I3] are used in this chapter to define the inner product vector space. Some of its useful properties are summarized below.

Observations 19.10. $(\mathcal{V}, \langle \cdot, \cdot \rangle)$ is an inner product vector space.

1. Bunyakovsky–Cauchy–Schwartz inequality: If $u, v \in V$, then $|\langle u, v \rangle| \leq \|u\| \cdot \|v\|$. Equality is obtained if $u = 0$, or $v = 0$, or $u = \alpha v$, where $\alpha \in \mathbb{C}$. The last condition shows linear dependence.

2. The inner product $\langle \cdot, \cdot \rangle$ defined on the vector space $\mathcal{V}$ induces a norm $\|\cdot\|$ on $\mathcal{V}$. The norm is given by the relationship $\|u\| = \sqrt{\langle u, u \rangle}$ for all $u \in V$. Thus every inner product space is a normed space, but not vice versa. The nonnegative number $\|u\|$ is called the *length* of the vector u.

3. The norm on an inner product space satisfies the parallelogram equality. Let $u, v \in V$, then

$$\|u + v\|^2 + \|u - v\|^2 = 2 \left(\|u\|^2 + \|v\|^2 \right)$$

This result derives its name from a similar result about parallelograms in plane geometry.

4. If a norm does not satisfy the above parallelogram equality, it cannot be obtained from an inner product by the use of relationship $\|u\| = \sqrt{\langle u, u \rangle}$. Therefore, it can be inferred that not all normed spaces are inner product spaces. Conversely, all inner product spaces are normed.   □

The above set of observations are further clarified by the following examples.

Examples 19.9.

1. Let V be a vector space such that $V = \mathbb{R}^n$. Also let $x, y \in V$, where $x = (x_1, x_2, \ldots, x_n)$ and $y = (y_1, y_2, \ldots, y_n)$. The function defined by $x \circ y \triangleq \langle x, y \rangle = \sum_{j=1}^n x_j y_j$ is an inner product on V. This is actually the definition of the *dot product* in $\mathbb{R}^n$. It is also reminiscent of the dot product operation introduced in the section on vector algebra. This function is also called the *real* or *standard* or *Euclidean inner product* on $V = \mathbb{R}^n$.
   Note that $\langle x, x \rangle = \sum_{j=1}^n x_j^2 = \|x\|_2^2$, where $\|\cdot\|_2$ is the Euclidean norm on $\mathbb{R}^n$. This space is called *real Euclidean space*. If $n = 2$, then the space is called Euclidean plane.

2. Let V be a vector space such that $V = \mathbb{C}^n$. Let $x, y \in V$, where $x = (x_1, x_2, \ldots, x_n)$ and $y = (y_1, y_2, \ldots, y_n)$. The function defined by $\langle x, y \rangle = \sum_{j=1}^n x_j \overline{y}_j$ is an inner product on V. This representation of the inner product is also called the dot product. The function $\langle \cdot, \cdot \rangle$ is also called the *standard inner product* on $V = \mathbb{C}^n$. This space is called *complex Euclidean space.*

3. The inner product $\langle \cdot, \cdot \rangle$ defined on a vector space V is also an inner product on any vector subspace $\mathcal{U}$ of V.   □

One of the most important inner-product spaces is the Hilbert space. The two most well-known examples of Hilbert spaces are the l^2 and L^2 spaces. Hilbert space is a natural extension of the Euclidean space. These spaces were extensively studied by the mathematician David Hilbert (1862–1943).

Definitions 19.29. *Some definitions related to Hilbert space.*

1. *An inner-product space $\mathcal{H}$ is called a Hilbert space, if it is complete with respect to the norm induced by the inner product.*

2. *A Hilbert space of finite dimension n, is denoted by $\mathcal{H}_n$.*   □

19.10.4 Orthogonality

The notion of orthogonality of two vectors is next introduced. In a real inner product space, the angle between two nonzero vectors $u, v \in V$ is the real number θ, such that

$$\cos \theta = \frac{\langle u, v \rangle}{\|u\| \cdot \|v\|}, \quad 0 \leq \theta \leq \pi \tag{19.29}$$

Therefore, two vectors u and v are orthogonal to each other, if $\langle u, v \rangle = 0$. This concept of orthogonality can be extended to any inner product vector space.

Definitions 19.30. $(\mathcal{V}, \langle \cdot, \cdot \rangle)$ *is an inner product vector space.*

1. *Orthogonal vectors: Two vectors $u, v \in V$ are orthogonal if and only if $\langle u, v \rangle = 0$. This relationship is sometimes denoted by $u \perp v$.*

2. *Orthogonal set: A subset $S \subseteq V$ is an orthogonal set, if all the vectors in the set S are mutually orthogonal. That is, for all vectors $u, v \in S$, $\langle u, v \rangle = 0$, where $u \neq v$.*

3. *Orthonormal set: A subset $S \subseteq V$ is an orthonormal set if S is an orthogonal set and all vectors of the set S have unit length.*

4. *Orthogonal complement: If $U \subseteq V$, then the orthogonal complement of the subset U is the set of all vectors $v \in V$, where v is orthogonal to all the vectors in U. Denote this set by $U^\perp = \{v \in V \mid \langle u, v \rangle = 0, \ \forall\, u \in U\}$. The sets U and $U^\perp$ are said to be orthogonal to each other, and this relationship is indicated by $U \perp U^\perp$.* □

Observations 19.11. $(\mathcal{V}, \langle \cdot, \cdot \rangle)$ is an inner product vector space.

1. Let $u, v \in V$, then $\langle u, v \rangle = 0$ if and only if $\|u + v\|^2 = \|u\|^2 + \|v\|^2$. This is the Pythagorean theorem.

2. If $u \neq v$, and $u, v \in V$, then $\|u\| = \|v\| \Leftrightarrow \langle u + v, u - v \rangle = 0$. This result is reminiscent of a property of a rhombus in plane geometry, which is: The diagonals of a rhombus are orthogonal to each other.

3. An orthogonal set S of nonzero vectors, is independent. That is, all the vectors in the set S are independent of each other. The concept of independence of vectors has been discussed in the chapter on matrices and determinants.

4. If the inner product space is defined over real numbers, then two nonzero vectors are orthogonal if and only if the angle between them is equal to $\pi/2$.

5. Let the dimension of the vector space be $\dim(\mathcal{V}) = n$. Then:
   (a) Any orthonormal set contains at most n vectors.
   (b) Any orthonormal set of n vectors is a basis of $\mathcal{V}$.

6. Let $U \subseteq V, u \in U$, and $(u_1, u_2, \ldots, u_n)$ be an orthonormal basis of U. Then $u = \sum_{j=1}^{n} \langle u, u_j \rangle\, u_j$.

7. If $U \subseteq V$, then the orthogonal complement $U^\perp$ is a subset of V. Also V is a direct sum of the sets U and $U^\perp$, that is $V = U \oplus U^\perp$. □

19.10.5 Gram–Schmidt Orthogonalization Process

The Gram–Schmidt orthogonalization process is a procedure for constructing an orthonormal set of vectors from an arbitrary linearly independent set of vectors. This construction follows from the following observation. Let $(V, \langle \cdot, \cdot \rangle)$ be an inner product vector space over the field $\mathbb{C}$. Also let $\{u_1, u_2, \ldots, u_r\}$ be an orthonormal set of vectors which belong to the set V. These vectors are linearly independent. Furthermore, for any $v \in V$, the vector w given by

$$w = v - \langle v, u_1 \rangle u_1 - \langle v, u_2 \rangle u_2 - \cdots - \langle v, u_r \rangle u_r$$

is orthogonal to each $u_j, 1 \leq j \leq r$. This observation is used in the Gram–Schmidt orthonormalization process. It is summarized in the following theorem.

Theorem 19.4. *Let $(V, \langle \cdot, \cdot \rangle)$ be an inner product vector space over $\mathbb{C}$. Also let*

$$\{u_1, u_2, \ldots, u_m\}$$

be a linearly independent set of vectors which belong to V. Define

$$w_1 = u_1, \quad v_1 = \frac{w_1}{\|w_1\|} \tag{19.30a}$$

$$w_r = u_r - \sum_{j=1}^{r-1} \langle u_r, v_j \rangle v_j, \quad v_r = \frac{w_r}{\|w_r\|}, \quad 2 \leq r \leq m \tag{19.30b}$$

Then the set $\{v_1, v_2, \ldots, v_m\}$ is an orthonormal set in V, and the space spanned by the set of vectors $\{u_1, u_2, \ldots, u_m\}$ and $\{v_1, v_2, \ldots, v_m\}$ are identical for all values of m.

Proof. The proof is left to the reader.   □

19.11 More Hilbert Spaces

Recall that the concept of norm assigns length and size to vectors. It also enables us to speak about convergence in a vector space. The concept of inner product introduces concepts such as angles, and orthogonality. These spaces are important because their geometry is similar to the Euclidean spaces.

Definition 19.31. *An inner product space which is complete is called a Hilbert space.*   □

Alternately, an inner product space in which every Cauchy sequence converges with respect to the norm induced by the inner product space is called a Hilbert space. Some examples are the spaces $\mathbb{R}^n$; and $l^p, L^p, 1 \leq p < \infty$.

More concretely, H is a complete inner product space, then $\{u_n \mid n \in \mathbb{Z}\}$ is an orthonormal basis (or Hilbert basis) of the space H subject to the following conditions:

- Orthogonality: $\langle u_n, u_m \rangle = 0$, if $n, m \in \mathbb{Z}, n \neq m$.
- Normalization: $\langle u_n, u_n \rangle = 1$, for all values of $n \in \mathbb{Z}$.
- Completeness: Given $x \in H$ and $\langle x, u_n \rangle = 0$, $\forall n \in \mathbb{Z}$, then $x = 0$.
  For every $x, y \in H$ the following expansions are valid.

$$x = \sum_{n \in \mathbb{Z}} \alpha_n u_n, \quad \text{where} \quad \alpha_n = \langle x, u_n \rangle, \quad n \in \mathbb{Z}$$

$$\langle x, x \rangle = \|x\|^2 = \sum_{n \in \mathbb{Z}} |\alpha_n|^2$$

$$\langle x, y \rangle = \sum_{n \in \mathbb{Z}} \alpha_n \langle u_n, y \rangle = \sum_{n \in \mathbb{Z}} \alpha_n \overline{\langle y, u_n \rangle}$$

19.11.1 Non-Orthogonal Expansion

A non-orthogonal expansion for x in a Hilbert space H is $x = \sum_{n \in \mathbb{Z}} \alpha_n u_n$, where $\{u_n \mid n \in \mathbb{Z}\}$ is a complete set of vectors. The sequence of vectors $\{u_n \mid n \in \mathbb{Z}\}$ need not be orthogonal, nor linearly independent (recall that orthogonality implies linear independence) for some applications.

Definition 19.32. *Frame. The set of functions $C = \{u_n \mid n \in \mathbb{Z}\}$ belonging to the Hilbert space H is a frame if there exist two constants A and B such that for every $x \in H$ we have:*

$$A \|x\|^2 \leq \sum_{n \in \mathbb{Z}} |\langle x, u_n \rangle|^2 \leq B \|x\|^2 \tag{19.31}$$

A and B are called the frame bounds. In other words, A and B "frame" the value $\sum_{n \in \mathbb{Z}} |\langle x, u_n \rangle|^2 / \|x\|^2$. Under this interpretation a frame is a spanning set, where the set of functions can be dependent.
If $A = B$, then the frame is said to be tight.   □

An orthonormal basis is a tight frame for which $A = B = 1$. But the converse is not true. That is, if $A = B = 1$, then we do not necessarily have an orthonormal basis. Therefore, if the frame is tight we have

$$A \|x\|^2 = \sum_{n \in \mathbb{Z}} |\langle x, u_n \rangle|^2$$

In this case, for $x \in H$:

$$x = A^{-1} \sum_{n \in \mathbb{Z}} \alpha_n u_n, \quad \text{where} \quad \alpha_n = \langle x, u_n \rangle, \quad n \in \mathbb{Z}$$

As noted earlier, the set of functions $\{u_n \mid n \in \mathbb{Z}\}$ can be linearly dependent, hence the above expansion need not be unique. Frames do not necessarily satisfy Parseval's relationship. Also observe that frames are complete, since if $\langle x, u_n \rangle = 0, \forall n \in \mathbb{Z}$, then

$$A \|x\|^2 = \sum_{n \in \mathbb{Z}} |\langle x, u_n \rangle|^2 = 0$$

which implies $x = 0$.

Definition 19.33. *If the set of functions $\{e_n \mid n \in \mathbb{Z}\}$, which belong to the Hilbert space H form a frame, and are also linearly independent, then the set is a Riesz basis.*
□

If $\{e_n \mid n \in \mathbb{Z}\}$ is a Riesz basis for Hilbert space H, and for any $x \in H$ we have

$$A \|x\|^2 \leq \sum_{n \in \mathbb{Z}} |\langle x, e_n \rangle|^2 \leq B \|x\|^2$$

For each $x \in L^2(\mathbb{R})$ its representation is

$$\sum_{n \in \mathbb{Z}} \langle x, e_n \rangle e_n$$

Riesz bases are named after the Hungarian mathematician Frigyes Riesz (1880–1956). Since frames are complete, so is the Riesz basis. Any Riesz basis can be made into a Hilbert basis by the Gram–Schmidt orthogonalization process.

19.11.2 Biorthogonal Bases

An exclusive chapter describes biorthogonal wavelets. Therefore, a definition of biorthogonal bases is in order.

Definition 19.34. *Biorthogonal bases. The sequences*

$$\{u_n \mid n \in \mathbb{Z}\} \quad \text{and} \quad \{\tilde{u}_n \mid n \in \mathbb{Z}\}$$

are a pair of biorthogonal bases of a Hilbert space H if and only if:

(a) $\langle u_m, \tilde{u}_n \rangle = \delta_{mn}, \quad \forall m, n \in \mathbb{Z}$

(b) *There exist strictly positive constants $A, B, \tilde{A}, \tilde{B}$ such that $\forall x \in H$*

$$A \|x\|^2 \leq \sum_{n \in \mathbb{Z}} |\langle x, u_n \rangle|^2 \leq B \|x\|^2 \qquad (19.32a)$$

$$\tilde{A} \|x\|^2 \leq \sum_{n \in \mathbb{Z}} |\langle x, \tilde{u}_n \rangle|^2 \leq \tilde{B} \|x\|^2 \qquad (19.32b)$$

□

We have $\forall\ x, y \in H$

$$x = \sum_{n \in \mathbb{Z}} \langle x, u_n \rangle\ \tilde{u}_n = \sum_{n \in \mathbb{Z}} \langle x, \tilde{u}_n \rangle\ u_n$$

$$\|x\|^2 = \sum_{n \in \mathbb{Z}} \langle x, u_n \rangle\ \overline{\langle x, \tilde{u}_n \rangle}$$

$$\langle x, y \rangle = \sum_{n \in \mathbb{Z}} \langle x, u_n \rangle\ \overline{\langle y, \tilde{u}_n \rangle}$$

$$= \sum_{n \in \mathbb{Z}} \langle x, \tilde{u}_n \rangle\ \overline{\langle y, u_n \rangle}$$

Note that if the set $\{u_n \mid n \in \mathbb{Z}\}$ is orthogonal, then it is its own dual.

Problems

1. Let $\mathcal{U} = (U, \mathcal{F}, \boxplus, \boxtimes)$, and $\mathcal{V} = (V, \mathcal{F}, \boxplus, \boxtimes)$ be vector spaces over the same field $\mathcal{F} = (F, +, \times)$. Also let $f : V \to U$ be a linear mapping, and $\dim (\mathcal{V})$ finite. Prove that $\dim (\mathcal{V}) = \dim (\operatorname{im} f) + \dim (\ker f)$.

   Hint: See Lipschutz (1968). As per the hypothesis $\dim (\mathcal{V}) = n$. Let the image of the mapping be $\tilde{I}$ and the kernel be $\tilde{K}$. That is, $\tilde{I} \subseteq U$ and $\tilde{K} \subseteq V$. Since $\dim (\mathcal{V}) = n$ is finite, assume that $\dim (\ker f) = s \leq n$. Therefore, we need to establish that $\dim (\operatorname{im} f) = (n - s)$. Let $\{k_1, k_2, \dots, k_s\}$ be a basis of the kernel space $\tilde{K}$. This basis set can be extended to form a basis for V. Let this basis set of V be

$$\tilde{C} = \{k_1, k_2, \dots, k_s, v_1, v_2, \dots, v_{n-s}\}$$

   Next define $\tilde{D} = \{f(v_1), f(v_2), \dots, f(v_{n-s})\}$. It remains to prove that the set $\tilde{D}$ is a basis of the image $\tilde{I}$. This is done in two steps. In the first step it is proved that the set $\tilde{D}$ generates the image and in the second step it is established that the members of the set $\tilde{D}$ are linearly independent.

   Step 1: Assume that $u \in \tilde{I}$. Thus there exists $v \in V$ such that $u = f(v)$. As the set $\tilde{C}$ generates V, we have

$$v = \sum_{i=1}^{s} a_i k_i + \sum_{i=1}^{n-s} b_i v_i, \quad \forall\ a_i, b_i \in F$$

$$u = f(v) = \sum_{i=1}^{s} a_i f(k_i) + \sum_{i=1}^{n-s} b_i f(v_i)$$

Note that the $f(k_i)$'s are each equal to zero, since $k_i \in \widetilde{K}$. Consequently $u = \sum_{i=1}^{n-s} b_i f(v_i)$. Thus the set $\widetilde{D}$ generates the image of f.

Step 2: Define $d = \sum_{i=1}^{n-s} d_i v_i$ where all $d_i \in F$, and assume $\sum_{i=1}^{n-s} d_i f(v_i) = 0$, then $f(d) = 0$, thus $d \in \widetilde{K}$. Therefore, $d = \sum_{i=1}^{s} c_i k_i$, where all $c_i \in F$. This yields

$$\sum_{i=1}^{n-s} d_i v_i - \sum_{i=1}^{s} c_i k_i = 0$$

Since the set $\widetilde{C}$ generates V, the members of the set $\widetilde{C}$ are linearly independent. Hence the coefficients d_i's and c_i's are all equal to zero. That is, $d_i = 0$ for $1 \le i \le (n-s)$. Thus the $f(v_i)$'s are linearly independent. Consequently the set $\widetilde{D}$ is a basis of the image $\widetilde{I}$. Therefore, dim $(\text{im } f) = (n-s)$.

2. Let $u, v \in \mathbb{R}^n$. Prove the famous Minkowski inequality.

$$\|u + v\|_2 \le \|u\|_2 + \|v\|_2$$

Hint: This inequality is named after Hermann Minkowski (1864–1909). To get insight into this problem, first establish the above result in the two-dimensional space $\mathbb{R}^2$.

3. Establish the Bunyakovsky–Cauchy–Schwartz inequality, $|\langle u, v \rangle| \le \|u\| \cdot \|v\|$, where $u, v \in V$.
   Hint: Let $(\mathcal{V}, \langle \cdot, \cdot \rangle)$ be an inner product vector space. If $v = 0$, then the inequality is valid since $\langle u, 0 \rangle = 0$. Let $v \ne 0$. For all $\alpha \in \mathbb{C}$

$$0 \le \|u - \alpha v\|^2 = \langle u - \alpha v, u - \alpha v \rangle$$
$$= \langle u, u \rangle - \overline{\alpha} \langle u, v \rangle - \alpha [\langle v, u \rangle - \overline{\alpha} \langle v, v \rangle]$$

The expression inside the $[\cdots]$ brackets is zero if $\overline{\alpha} = \langle v, u \rangle / \langle v, v \rangle$. Consequently

$$0 \le \langle u, u \rangle - \frac{\langle v, u \rangle}{\langle v, v \rangle} \langle u, v \rangle = \|u\|^2 - \frac{|\langle u, v \rangle|^2}{\|v\|^2}$$

where the equality $\langle v, u \rangle = \overline{\langle u, v \rangle}$ is used. The result follows. In the above derivation, equality holds if $u = \alpha v$, which shows a linear dependence.

4. Let $(\mathcal{V}, \langle \cdot, \cdot \rangle)$ be an inner product vector space. Prove that the inner product $\langle \cdot, \cdot \rangle$ defined on the vector space $\mathcal{V}$ induces a norm $\|\cdot\|$ on V. This norm is given by the relationship $\|u\| = \sqrt{\langle u, u \rangle}$ for all $u \in V$.
   Hint: Essentially it needs to be established that the induced norm $\|\cdot\|$ satisfies the norm defining properties, $[N1]$ through $N[3]$. The property $[N1]$ follows from $[I1]$. Furthermore, $\|au\|^2 = \langle au, au \rangle = a \langle u, au \rangle = a\overline{a} \langle u, u \rangle = |a|^2 \langle u, u \rangle$. After taking the square root of both sides, $[N2]$ is obtained. The property $[N3]$ follows directly from the Bunyakovsky–Cauchy–Schwartz inequality. As

$$\|u + v\|^2 = \langle u + v, u + v \rangle = \langle u, u \rangle + \langle u, v \rangle + \langle v, u \rangle + \langle v, v \rangle$$
$$= \|u\|^2 + 2\operatorname{Re}\left(\langle u, v \rangle\right) + \|v\|^2$$
$$\leq \|u\|^2 + 2\left|\langle u, v \rangle\right| + \|v\|^2$$
$$\leq \|u\|^2 + 2\|u\|\,\|v\| + \|v\|^2 = \left(\|u\| + \|v\|\right)^2$$

Thus $\|u + v\| \leq \|u\| + \|v\|$. This is the triangle inequality.

Fourier Theory

20.1 Introduction

Fourier series, Fourier transform, and certain special transforms related to Fourier transforms are explored in this chapter.

20.2 Fourier Series

A Fourier series is a representation of a periodic function in terms of trigonometric functions. Such representations are generally termed Fourier series. The series are named in honor of the French mathematician Jean Baptiste Joseph Fourier (1768–1830).

Examples of periodic functions each with period 2π are $\sin x$ and $\cos x$, where $x \in \mathbb{R}$. A linear combination of these elementary trigonometric functions is also periodic. A generalization of this concept is the expansion of a periodic function in terms of elementary trigonometric functions like $\sin(\cdot)$ and $\cos(\cdot)$. Fourier series are also useful in studying transform techniques. Fourier transform, short-time Fourier transform, and Wigner–Ville transforms are also studied in the chapter.

Generalized functions are a useful tool to study Fourier series and continuous transform techniques. In addition to generalized functions, the following topics are also discussed: conditions for the existence of the Fourier series, complex Fourier series, and trigonometric Fourier series.

20.2.1 Generalized Functions

A study of generalized functions is useful in understanding continuous transform techniques, like Fourier and wavelet transforms.

Definition 20.1. *The unit impulse function $\delta(t)$, $t \in \mathbb{R}$, is also called the delta function (δ-function), or Dirac's delta function. It is typically specified as:*

$$\delta(t) = \begin{cases} 0, & t \neq 0 \\ \infty, & t = 0 \end{cases} \tag{20.1a}$$

$$\int_{-\infty}^{\infty} \delta(t) \, dt = \int_{-\epsilon}^{\epsilon} \delta(t) \, dt = 1, \quad \epsilon > 0 \tag{20.1b}$$

□

This definition is not mathematically sound. This is because a function, which is zero everywhere except at a single point, must have the integral value equal to zero. The integration is assumed to be Riemannian. Therefore, it is alternately defined in terms of generalized functions.

Definition 20.2. $\delta(\cdot)$ *is a generalized (or symbolic) function, and $\phi(\cdot)$ is a test function, such that*

$$\int_{-\infty}^{\infty} \delta(t) \, \phi(t) \, dt = \phi(0) \tag{20.2}$$

□

Observe in the above definition, that we can only interpret about the *values of integrals* involving $\delta(t)$, and *not* about *its* value.

Observations 20.1. Let $t \in \mathbb{R}$.

1. $\delta(t) = \delta(-t)$.
2. $f(t) \delta(t) = f(0) \delta(t)$, where it is assumed that $f(t)$ is continuous at $t = 0$. If $f(t)$ is continuous at $t = t_0$, then $f(t)\delta(t - t_0) = f(t_0)\delta(t - t_0)$.
3. $\int_{-\infty}^{\infty} \delta(t - t_0) \, \phi(t) \, dt = \phi(t_0)$.
4. $\delta(at) = \delta(t) / |a|$, where $a \in \mathbb{R} \setminus \{0\}$.
5. Denote $*$ by the convolution operator. Then

$$f(t) * \delta(t) = \int_{-\infty}^{\infty} f(t - \tau) \delta(\tau) \, d\tau = f(t)$$

6. $\delta(t - \alpha) * \delta(t - \beta) = \delta(t - \alpha - \beta)$.
7. Denote the nth derivative of $\delta(t)$ and $\phi(t)$ with respect to t by $\delta^{(n)}(t)$ and $\phi^{(n)}(t)$ respectively. Then

$$\int_{-\infty}^{\infty} \delta^{(n)}(t) \, \phi(t) \, dt = (-1)^n \, \phi^{(n)}(0), \quad \forall \, n \in \mathbb{P}$$

8. Denote the first derivative of $f(x)$ with respect to x by $f'(x)$. Let $f(x) = 0$ have real roots x_n, where $1 \leq n \leq K$. Then

$$\delta(f(x)) = \sum_{n=1}^{K} \frac{\delta(x - x_n)}{|f'(x_n)|}$$

where it is assumed that $f'(x_n) \neq 0$ (that is, no repeated roots) for $1 \leq n \leq K$.

9. Integral representation of $\delta(t)$

$$\delta(t) = \frac{1}{2\pi} \int_{-\infty}^{\infty} e^{i\omega t} d\omega = \frac{1}{\pi} \int_{0}^{\infty} \cos(\omega t)\, d\omega \qquad (20.3)$$

where $i = \sqrt{-1}$.   □

20.2.2 Conditions for the Existence of Fourier Series

A periodic function is initially defined, and then the conditions for the existence of Fourier series are stated.

   Definition 20.3. *Let $f(t)$, $t \in \mathbb{R}$, be a real-valued function and $T_0 \in \mathbb{R}^+$. The function $f(\cdot)$ is periodic, if $f(t) = f(t+T_0)$, $\forall t \in \mathbb{R}$. The smallest such value of T_0 is called the period of the function $f(\cdot)$.*   □

   Examples 20.1. Elementary examples.

1. Some examples of periodic functions are $\sin(\omega_0 t)$, $\cos(\omega_0 t)$, and $e^{i\omega_0 t}$; where $\omega_0 = 2\pi/T_0$, $i = \sqrt{-1}$, and $t \in \mathbb{R}$.

2. Let $f(t)$, $t \in \mathbb{R}$ be a periodic function with period T_0. For any $a, b, c \in \mathbb{R}$

$$\int_{0}^{T_0} f(t)dt = \int_{a}^{T_0+a} f(t)dt$$

$$\int_{b}^{c} f(t)dt = \int_{T_0+b}^{T_0+c} f(t)dt$$

3. The sum, difference, product, or quotient (if defined properly) of two functions each of period T_0, is also a function of period T_0.   □

   A periodic function $f(t)$, $t \in \mathbb{R}$, of period $T_0 \in \mathbb{R}^+$ has a Fourier series representation if the so-called *Dirichlet conditions* are satisfied. These conditions are named after the mathematician Peter Gustav Lejeune Dirichlet (1805–1859). The Dirichlet conditions are sufficient but not necessary for the Fourier series representation (existence) of a periodic function.

   Dirichlet Conditions. Let the function $f(t)$ be defined over $t \in \mathbb{R}$.

1. The function $f(\cdot)$ is periodic with period T_0.

2. The function $f(\cdot)$ is well-defined and single-valued except possibly at a finite number of points in a single periodic interval $I = (a, a + T_0)$, where $a \in \mathbb{R}$.

3. Let $f'(t)$ be the first derivative of $f(t)$ with respect t. The functions $f(\cdot)$ and $f'(\cdot)$ are piecewise-continuous in the periodic interval I. This implies that the function $f(\cdot)$ is piecewise-smooth in the periodic interval I.
   Then the Fourier series expansion of the function $f(\cdot)$ converges to:

(a) $f(t)$ if the function is continuous at point t.

(b) $\{f(t_+) + f(t_-)\}/2$ if the function is discontinuous at point t. □

The proof of correctness of these conditions can be found in any standard text-book on harmonic analysis.

20.2.3 Complex Fourier Series

There are two equivalent types of Fourier series. These are the complex and trigono-metric forms of Fourier series representations. Each series representation can be transformed to the other. Complex Fourier series are discussed in this subsection.

Definition 20.4. *Let* $T_0 \in \mathbb{R}^+$ *be the period of a real-valued periodic function* $f(t), t \in \mathbb{R}$. *Also, let* $\omega_0 = 2\pi/T_0$, *then for any* $a \in \mathbb{R}$,

$$f(t) = \sum_{n \in \mathbb{Z}} c_n e^{in\omega_0 t} \tag{20.4a}$$

$$c_n = \frac{1}{T_0} \int_a^{a+T_0} f(t) e^{-in\omega_0 t} dt, \quad \forall\, n \in \mathbb{Z} \tag{20.4b}$$

In this series representation, it is assumed that Dirichlet conditions hold, and that $f(t)$ *is continuous at t. If* $f(t)$ *is discontinuous at t, then* $f(t)$ *in the above expan-sion should be replaced by* $\{f(t_+) + f(t_-)\}/2$. *The* c_n*'s are called coefficients of the complex Fourier series.* □

The above expansion is evident from the following relationship for any $m, n \in \mathbb{Z}$.

$$\frac{1}{T_0} \int_a^{a+T_0} e^{i\omega_0 t(m-n)} dt = \delta_{mn}$$

where

$$\delta_{mn} = \begin{cases} 1, & m = n \\ 0, & m \neq n \end{cases}$$

The function δ_{mn} is called Kronecker's delta function. It is named after the math-ematician Leopold Kronecker (1823–1891). The next set of observations follow im-mediately from the complex Fourier series representation of the periodic function $f(t), t \in \mathbb{R}$.

Observations 20.2. Some basic observations.

1. For any $a \in \mathbb{R}$, Parseval's relationship is

$$\frac{1}{T_0} \int_a^{a+T_0} |f(t)|^2 dt = \sum_{n \in \mathbb{Z}} |c_n|^2 \tag{20.5}$$

This relationship is named after the French mathematician Marc-Antoine Parse-val (1755–1836).

2. The coefficients of the complex Fourier series of the periodic function $f(\cdot)$, are related by $c_n = \bar{c}_{-n}, \forall\, n \in \mathbb{Z}$.

3. $f(t) = f(t + nT_0), \forall\, n \in \mathbb{Z}$.   ☐

An alternative to a complex Fourier series representation of a periodic function, is its trigonometric Fourier series representation.

20.2.4 Trigonometric Fourier Series

Let $T_0 \in \mathbb{R}^+$, and $\omega_0 = 2\pi/T_0$. For $t \in \mathbb{R}$, and any $a \in \mathbb{R}$, the sequence of functions

$$\{\cos n\omega_0 t \mid n \in \mathbb{N}\}, \quad \text{and} \quad \{\sin n\omega_0 t \mid n \in \mathbb{P}\}$$

form an orthogonal set of functions in the interval $[a, a + T_0]$. Observe that

$$\frac{2}{T_0} \int_0^{T_0} \cos m\omega_0 t \, \cos n\omega_0 t \, dt = \delta_{mn}, \quad \forall\, m, n \in \mathbb{P}$$

$$\frac{2}{T_0} \int_0^{T_0} \sin m\omega_0 t \, \sin n\omega_0 t \, dt = \delta_{mn}, \quad \forall\, m, n \in \mathbb{P}$$

$$\int_0^{T_0} \sin m\omega_0 t \, \cos n\omega_0 t \, dt = 0, \quad \forall\, m, n \in \mathbb{N}$$

Similarly

$$\int_0^{T_0} \cos m\omega_0 t \, dt = 0, \quad \forall\, m \in \mathbb{P}$$

$$\int_0^{T_0} \sin m\omega_0 t \, dt = 0, \quad \forall\, m \in \mathbb{N}$$

Definition 20.5. *If $f(t)$, $t \in \mathbb{R}$, is a periodic real-valued function with period $T_0 \in \mathbb{R}^+$, and $\omega_0 = 2\pi/T_0$. Then for any $a \in \mathbb{R}$*

$$f(t) = \frac{a_0}{2} + \sum_{n \in \mathbb{P}} (a_n \cos n\omega_0 t + b_n \sin n\omega_0 t) \tag{20.6a}$$

$$a_n = \frac{2}{T_0} \int_a^{a+T_0} f(t) \cos n\omega_0 t \, dt, \quad \forall\, n \in \mathbb{N} \tag{20.6b}$$

$$b_n = \frac{2}{T_0} \int_a^{a+T_0} f(t) \sin n\omega_0 t \, dt, \quad \forall\, n \in \mathbb{P} \tag{20.6c}$$

In this series representation, it is assumed that Dirichlet conditions hold, and that $f(t)$ is continuous at t. If $f(t)$ is discontinuous at t, then $f(t)$ in the above expansion should be replaced by $\{f(t_+) + f(t_-)\}/2$.   ☐

Some textbooks use the period $T_0 = 2\pi$, in the Fourier series representation. In this case, the above Fourier series representation and the corresponding coefficients can be suitably modified.

Observations 20.3. Let $t \in \mathbb{R}$.

1. For any $a \in \mathbb{R}$, Parseval's relationship is

$$\frac{1}{T_0} \int_a^{a+T_0} |f(t)|^2 \, dt = \frac{a_0^2}{4} + \frac{1}{2} \sum_{n \in \mathbb{P}} (a_n^2 + b_n^2) \qquad (20.7)$$

2. If $f(\cdot)$ is an even function, that is $f(t) = f(-t)$, $\forall\, t \in \mathbb{R}$, then $b_n = 0$ for all values of $n \in \mathbb{P}$. However, if $f(\cdot)$ is an odd function, that is $f(t) = -f(-t)$, $\forall\, t \in \mathbb{R}$, then $a_n = 0$ for all values of $n \in \mathbb{N}$.   □

The Fourier coefficients of the complex and trigonometric Fourier series are related as follows.

Observation 20.4. Note that

$$c_0 = \frac{1}{2}a_0, \; c_n = \frac{1}{2}(a_n - ib_n), \; c_{-n} = \frac{1}{2}(a_n + ib_n), \; \forall\, n \in \mathbb{P} \qquad (20.8a)$$

$$a_0 = 2c_0, \; a_n = (c_n + c_{-n}), \; b_n = i(c_n - c_{-n}), \qquad \forall\, n \in \mathbb{P} \qquad (20.8b)$$

□

20.2.5 Generalized Fourier Series

It is also possible to describe a generalized Fourier series. Let the field $\mathbb{F}$ be equal to either $\mathbb{R}$ or $\mathbb{C}$.

Definition 20.6. Let $\{\phi_n : [a,b] \to \mathbb{F} \mid n \in \mathbb{P}, \; (a,b) \subset \mathbb{R}\}$ be an orthonormal sequence of square integrable functions. That is, if

$$\delta_{mn} = \begin{cases} 1 & m = n \\ 0 & m \neq n \end{cases} \quad m, n \in \mathbb{P}$$

$$\int_a^b w(t)\, \phi_m(t)\, \overline{\phi_n}(t) \, dt = \delta_{mn}, \qquad m, n \in \mathbb{P}$$

where $w(\cdot)$ is the weight function, and δ_{mn} is the Kronecker delta function. Note that $\overline{\phi_n}(\cdot) = \phi_n(\cdot)$, if $\mathbb{F} = \mathbb{R}$. The generalized Fourier series of a function $f(t)$, $t \in (a,b) \subset \mathbb{R}$ is given by

$$f(t) = \sum_{n \in \mathbb{P}} c_n \phi_n(t), \quad \text{where} \quad c_n = \int_a^b w(t)\, f(t)\, \overline{\phi_n}(t)\, dt, \qquad n \in \mathbb{P}$$

☐

The corresponding Parseval identity is

$$\sum_{n \in \mathbb{P}} |c_n|^2 = \int_a^b |f(t)|^2 \, w(t) \, dt$$

20.3 Transform Techniques

A complement of the Fourier series technique is the Fourier transform of a function. A Fourier series representation is useful in studying periodic functions. In contrast, Fourier transform technique is used to study nonperiodic functions.

A transform is a mapping of a function from one space to another. Specially crafted transforms help us see patterns. A problem or a physical scenario can sometimes be addressed more easily in the transform domain than in the time domain. The purpose of transform analysis is to represent a function as a linear combination of some basis functions. This is in a sense a decomposition of a function into some "elementary" functions. These elementary functions are the building blocks of the transform. Transforms can be either continuous or discrete.

Some examples of continuous transforms are the Fourier, Laplace, Wigner–Ville, and wavelet transforms. All of these transforms are useful in studying functions in different domains. The different transform techniques also complement each other in their applications.

The discrete transform techniques are evidently related to their continuous counterpart. Furthermore, the discrete transforms are well suited for computer implementation. The discrete Fourier transform is discussed in a different chapter.

20.3.1 Fourier Transform

As mentioned earlier, Fourier series representation is used to study periodic functions. In direct contrast, Fourier transforms are used to study nonperiodic functions. An alternate viewpoint is to think that the Fourier series is used to analyze functions which are defined only over a finite interval, while the Fourier transform is used to examine functions defined over the entire real line $\mathbb{R}$. A Fourier transform converts a time-domain function into a function defined over the frequency domain.

One of the conditions for the existence of the Fourier transform of $f(t), t \in \mathbb{R}$ is that $\int_{-\infty}^{\infty} |f(t)| \, dt$ be convergent. If this integral exists, then the function $f(\cdot)$ is said to be *absolutely integrable* on $\mathbb{R}$.

Definition 20.7. *The Fourier transform of $f(t), t \in \mathbb{R}$ is*

$$F(\omega) \triangleq \Im[f(t)] = \int_{-\infty}^{\infty} f(t)e^{-i\omega t}dt \qquad (20.9)$$

where $i = \sqrt{-1}$, $\omega \in \mathbb{R}$, $f(\cdot)$ is piecewise-continuous $\forall\, t \in \mathbb{R}$, and $f(\cdot)$ is absolutely integrable on $\mathbb{R}$. The functions $f(\cdot)$ and $F(\cdot)$ are called a Fourier transform pair. This relationship is denoted by $f(t) \leftrightarrow F(\omega)$. $\square$

The transformed domain is often referred to as the frequency domain.

Observations 20.5. Let $f(t)$, $t \in \mathbb{R}$, be a piecewise-continuous function and absolutely integrable on $\mathbb{R}$. Also, let $f(t) \leftrightarrow F(\omega)$.

1. The function $f(\cdot)$ is absolutely integrable if $\int_{-\infty}^{\infty} |f(t)|\, dt < \infty$, that is $f(t) \in L^1(\mathbb{R})$.

2. The condition of absolute integrability of a function is sufficient but not necessary for the existence of a Fourier transform. For example, functions which are not absolutely integrable but have a Fourier transform are $\sin \omega_0 t$, and $\cos \omega_0 t$.

3. The function $f(\cdot)$ is piecewise-continuous if $f(\cdot)$ is continuous, except for a finite number of finite jumps in every finite subinterval of $\mathbb{R}$. Thus the function $f(\cdot)$ can possibly have an infinite number of discontinuities, but only a finite number in each finite subinterval.

4. It can be proved that:
    (a) $F(\omega)$ is properly defined (bounded) $\forall\, \omega \in \mathbb{R}$.
    (b) $F(\omega)$ is a continuous function defined on $\mathbb{R}$.
    (c) $F(\omega)$ tends to 0 as $\omega \to \pm\infty$.

5. The *inverse Fourier transform* of $F(\omega)$ is given by

$$f(t) = \Im^{-1}[F(\omega)](t) = \frac{1}{2\pi} \int_{-\infty}^{\infty} F(\omega)\, e^{i\omega t}d\omega \qquad (20.10a)$$

If $f(t)$ is discontinuous at a point t, and the discontinuity is finite, then the Fourier inverse transformation yields

$$f(t) = \frac{(f(t_+) + f(t_-))}{2} \qquad (20.10b)$$

$\square$

The constants 1 and $1/(2\pi)$ preceding the integration signs in the definition of the Fourier transform, and the expression for the inverse Fourier transform respectively, can be replaced by any two constants whose product is equal to $1/(2\pi)$. In the interest of symmetry some authors prefer to use the constant $1/\sqrt{2\pi}$ preceding the definition of the Fourier transform, and the expression for the inverse Fourier transform.

Derivation of Fourier Transform from Fourier Series

Let $f(t)$ be an absolutely integrable function. Further assume that $f(t)$ is a non-periodic signal of finite duration. That is, $f(t) = 0$ for $|t| > \tau$. Define $f_{T_0}(t)$, to be a periodic function formed by replicating $f(t)$ with period T_0. Notice that as $T_0 \to \infty$, $f_{T_0}(t) \to f(t)$. Also let $\omega_0 = 2\pi/T_0$.

$$f_{T_0}(t) = \sum_{n \in \mathbb{Z}} c_n e^{in\omega_0 t}, \quad \text{where} \quad c_n = \frac{1}{T_0} \int_{-T_0/2}^{T_0/2} f(t) e^{-in\omega_0 t} dt, \quad n \in \mathbb{Z}$$

As $T_0 \to \infty$, $c_n \to 0$, and ω_0 becomes small. Let $\omega_0 = \Delta\omega = 2\pi/T_0$. Then $c_n T_0 = F(n\Delta\omega)$.

$$\lim_{T_0 \to \infty} f_{T_0}(t) = \frac{1}{T_0} \sum_{n \in \mathbb{Z}} F(n\Delta\omega) e^{in\Delta\omega t}$$

$$= \frac{1}{2\pi} \sum_{n \in \mathbb{Z}} F(n\Delta\omega) e^{in\Delta\omega t} \Delta\omega$$

Therefore,

$$f(t) = \frac{1}{2\pi} \int_{-\infty}^{\infty} F(\omega) e^{i\omega t} d\omega$$

The above equation is a Fourier representation of a nonperiodic function $f(t)$.

Properties of the Fourier Transform

Let $a, t, \omega \in \mathbb{R}$. Also let $\alpha_1, \alpha_2 \in \mathbb{C}$, and $f(t) \leftrightarrow F(\omega)$, $f_1(t) \leftrightarrow F_1(\omega)$, and $f_2(t) \leftrightarrow F_2(\omega)$.

1. Linearity: $\alpha_1 f_1(t) + \alpha_2 f_2(t) \leftrightarrow \alpha_1 F_1(\omega) + \alpha_2 F_2(\omega)$

2. Time reversal: $f(-t) \leftrightarrow F(-\omega)$

3. Conjugate function: $\overline{f(t)} \leftrightarrow \overline{F(-\omega)}$

4. Symmetry or duality: $F(t) \leftrightarrow 2\pi f(-\omega)$

5. Time shift: $f(t - t_0) \leftrightarrow e^{-i\omega t_0} F(\omega)$

6. Frequency shift: $e^{i\omega_0 t} f(t) \leftrightarrow F(\omega - \omega_0)$

7. Time scaling:

$$f(at) \leftrightarrow \frac{1}{|a|} F\left(\frac{\omega}{a}\right), \quad \text{where} \quad a \neq 0$$

8. Convolution:

$$\int_{-\infty}^{\infty} f_1(\tau) f_2(t - \tau) d\tau \triangleq f_1(t) * f_2(t) \leftrightarrow F_1(\omega) F_2(\omega)$$

where $*$ is called the convolution operator.

9. Multiplication:

$$f_1(t) f_2(t) \leftrightarrow \frac{1}{2\pi} F_1(\omega) * F_2(\omega)$$

where $*$ is called the convolution operator.

10. Time differentiation:

$$\frac{d^n}{dt^n} f(t) \leftrightarrow (i\omega)^n F(\omega), \quad \forall\, n \in \mathbb{P}$$

11. Frequency differentiation:

$$(-it)^n f(t) \leftrightarrow \frac{d^n}{d\omega^n} F(\omega), \quad \forall\, n \in \mathbb{P}$$

12. Integration:

$$\int_{-\infty}^{t} f(\tau)\, d\tau \leftrightarrow \frac{F(\omega)}{i\omega} + \pi F(0)\,\delta(\omega)$$

13. Modulation identities: Let $\omega_0 \in \mathbb{R}$, then

$$f(t) \cos \omega_0 t \leftrightarrow \frac{1}{2} \{ F(\omega - \omega_0) + F(\omega + \omega_0) \}$$

$$f(t) \sin \omega_0 t \leftrightarrow \frac{1}{2i} \{ F(\omega - \omega_0) - F(\omega + \omega_0) \}$$

14. Parseval's relationships:

$$\int_{-\infty}^{\infty} |f(t)|^2\, dt = \frac{1}{2\pi} \int_{-\infty}^{\infty} |F(\omega)|^2\, d\omega$$

$$\int_{-\infty}^{\infty} f_1(t) f_2(t)\, dt = \frac{1}{2\pi} \int_{-\infty}^{\infty} F_1(-\omega) F_2(\omega)\, d\omega$$

$$\int_{-\infty}^{\infty} \overline{f_1(t)} f_2(t)\, dt = \frac{1}{2\pi} \int_{-\infty}^{\infty} \overline{F_1(\omega)} F_2(\omega)\, d\omega$$

$$\int_{-\infty}^{\infty} f_1(t) F_2(t)\, dt = \int_{-\infty}^{\infty} F_1(\omega) f_2(\omega)\, d\omega$$

15. Fourier transform of a series: Let $f(\cdot)$ be a periodic function with period $T_0 \in \mathbb{R}^+$. For the periodic function $f(\cdot)$, $\int_{-\infty}^{\infty} |f(t)\, dt| \to \infty$. However, assume that the Fourier transform of $f(\cdot)$ exists in the sense of a generalized function. Let $\omega_0 = 2\pi/T_0$, and $f(t) \leftrightarrow F(\omega)$. If

$$f(t) = \sum_{n \in \mathbb{Z}} c_n e^{in\omega_0 t}$$

then

$$F(\omega) = 2\pi \sum_{n \in \mathbb{Z}} c_n \delta(\omega - n\omega_0)$$

$\square$

Before the Fourier transform pairs are listed, certain useful functions are first defined. In all these functions $\alpha, t \in \mathbb{R}$.

Signum function $\mathrm{sgn}(\cdot)$:

$$\mathrm{sgn}(t) = \begin{cases} 1, & t > 0 \\ -1, & t < 0 \end{cases}$$

$\mathrm{sgn}(\cdot)$ is not defined at $t = 0$. It follows that

$$\frac{d}{dt}\mathrm{sgn}(t) = 2\delta(t)$$

Unit step function $u(\cdot)$:

$$u(t) = \begin{cases} 1, & t > 0 \\ 0, & t < 0 \end{cases}$$

$u(t)$ is not defined at $t = 0$. It follows that

$$u(t) = \frac{1}{2} + \frac{1}{2}\mathrm{sgn}(t)$$

Gate function $g_\alpha(\cdot)$, $\alpha > 0$:

$$g_\alpha(t) = \begin{cases} 1, & |t| < \alpha \\ 0, & |t| > \alpha \end{cases}$$

Sinc function $\mathrm{sinc}(\cdot)$:

$$\mathrm{sinc}(t) = \frac{\sin t}{t}$$

Some useful Fourier transform pairs are listed below.

1. $\delta(t) \leftrightarrow 1$
2. $\delta(t - t_0) \leftrightarrow e^{-i\omega t_0}$
3. Let $\delta_{T_0}(t) = \sum_{n \in \mathbb{Z}} \delta(t - nT_0)$ and $\delta_{\omega_0}(\omega) = \sum_{n \in \mathbb{Z}} \delta(\omega - n\omega_0)$, where $\omega_0 = 2\pi/T_0$, then $\delta_{T_0}(t) \leftrightarrow \omega_0 \delta_{\omega_0}(\omega)$.
4. $1 \leftrightarrow 2\pi\delta(\omega)$
5. $e^{i\omega_0 t} \leftrightarrow 2\pi\delta(\omega - \omega_0)$
6. $\sin\omega_0 t \leftrightarrow i\pi[\delta(\omega + \omega_0) - \delta(\omega - \omega_0)]$
7. $\cos\omega_0 t \leftrightarrow \pi[\delta(\omega + \omega_0) + \delta(\omega - \omega_0)]$
8. $\mathrm{sgn}(t) \leftrightarrow \frac{2}{i\omega}$
9. $u(t) \leftrightarrow \pi\delta(\omega) + \frac{1}{i\omega}$
10. Let $\alpha > 0$ then:

(a) $g_\alpha(t) \leftrightarrow 2\alpha \, sinc\,(\omega\alpha)$

(b) $\frac{\alpha}{\pi} sinc(\alpha t) \leftrightarrow g_\alpha(\omega)$

11. Let $\alpha > 0$ then:

$$\frac{1}{\sqrt{2\pi}\alpha} e^{-\frac{t^2}{2\alpha^2}} \leftrightarrow e^{-\frac{\alpha^2\omega^2}{2}}$$

12. Let $\alpha > 0$ then:

(a)

$$e^{-\alpha t} u(t) \leftrightarrow \frac{1}{(\alpha + i\omega)}$$

(b)

$$e^{-\alpha|t|} \leftrightarrow \frac{2\alpha}{(\alpha^2 + \omega^2)}$$

13. Let

$$g(t) = \begin{cases} \dfrac{t^{n-1}}{(n-1)!}, & t \geq 0 \\ 0, & \text{otherwise} \end{cases} \quad , \quad \forall n \in \mathbb{P}$$

then

$$g(t) \leftrightarrow \frac{1}{(i\omega)^n}$$

$\square$

Poisson's summation formulae are next derived.

Theorem 20.1. *Let $T_0, \tau \in \mathbb{R}^+$. Also let $\omega_0 = 2\pi/T_0$, $\Omega_0 = 2\pi/\tau$, $t \in \mathbb{R}$ and $f(t)$ be an arbitrary function such that $f(t) \leftrightarrow F(\omega)$. Define*

$$f_s(t) = \sum_{n \in \mathbb{Z}} f(t + nT_0), \quad t \in \mathbb{R} \tag{20.11a}$$

$$F_s(\omega) = \sum_{n \in \mathbb{Z}} F(\omega + n\Omega_0), \quad \omega \in \mathbb{R} \tag{20.11b}$$

Then

$$f_s(t) = \frac{1}{T_0} \sum_{n \in \mathbb{Z}} F(n\omega_0) e^{in\omega_0 t} \tag{20.11c}$$

$$F_s(\omega) = \tau \sum_{n \in \mathbb{Z}} f(n\tau) e^{-in\omega\tau} \tag{20.11d}$$

Proof. See the problem section. $\square$

Note that $f_s(t)$ and $F_s(\omega)$ are not a Fourier transform pair. The following formulae are immediate from the above theorem. These formulae are known as *Poisson's summation formulae* after the mathematician Siméon–Denis Poisson (1781–1840).

$$\sum_{n\in\mathbb{Z}} f(nT_0) = \frac{1}{T_0} \sum_{n\in\mathbb{Z}} F(n\omega_0) \tag{20.12a}$$

$$\sum_{n\in\mathbb{Z}} F(n\Omega_0) = \tau \sum_{n\in\mathbb{Z}} f(n\tau) \tag{20.12b}$$

Uncertainty Principle

Two uncertainty principles are enunciated. These uncertainty principles essentially assert that, resolution in the time domain cannot be traded for resolution in the ω (frequency) domain, and vice versa.

Definition 20.8. *Effective time duration and spectral width. Let $f(t) \leftrightarrow F(\omega)$, where $t, \omega \in \mathbb{R}$. Also let f_{max} be the largest value of $|f(t)|$ and F_{max} be the largest value of $|F(\omega)|$ in their respective domains. The effective time duration is Δ_T and effective spectral width is Δ_ω, where*

$$\Delta_T = \frac{1}{f_{max}} \int_{-\infty}^{\infty} |f(t)|\, dt$$

$$\Delta_\omega = \frac{1}{F_{max}} \int_{-\infty}^{\infty} |F(\omega)|\, d\omega$$

$\square$

Theorem 20.2. *Uncertainty principle of the first order. The effective time duration and spectral width product is*

$$\Delta_\omega \Delta_T \geq 2\pi \frac{f(0)}{f_{max}} \frac{F(0)}{F_{max}}$$

Proof. Observe that

$$\Delta_T f_{max} = \int_{-\infty}^{\infty} |f(t)|\, dt \geq \int_{-\infty}^{\infty} f(t)\, dt = F(0)$$

$$\Delta_\omega F_{max} = \int_{-\infty}^{\infty} |F(\omega)|\, d\omega \geq \int_{-\infty}^{\infty} F(\omega)\, d\omega = 2\pi f(0)$$

The result follows. $\square$

Example 20.2. Let $t \in \mathbb{R}$, and

$$f(t) = e^{-\alpha|t|}, \quad \alpha > 0$$

$$F(\omega) = \frac{2\alpha}{(\alpha^2 + \omega^2)}$$

Then $f(0) = f_{max} = 1$, and $F(0) = F_{max} = 2/\alpha$. Also Δ_T and Δ_ω are evaluated to be $2/\alpha$ and $\alpha\pi$ respectively. Then $\Delta_\omega \Delta_T = 2\pi$. $\square$

It is also possible to obtain results about the uncertainty principle of the second order. It asserts that $f(t)$ and $F(\omega)$ cannot both be small in magnitude.

Definition 20.9. *Let $f(t) \leftrightarrow F(\omega)$, where $t, \omega \in \mathbb{R}$. Let*

$$\sigma_T^2 = \frac{\int_{-\infty}^{\infty} t^2 \, |f(t)|^2 \, dt}{\int_{-\infty}^{\infty} |f(t)|^2 \, dt} \qquad (20.13a)$$

$$\sigma_\omega^2 = \frac{\int_{-\infty}^{\infty} \omega^2 \, |F(\omega)|^2 \, d\omega}{\int_{-\infty}^{\infty} |F(\omega)|^2 \, d\omega} \qquad (20.13b)$$

$\square$

Theorem 20.3. *If $f(t)$ is differentiable, and $t \, |f(t)|^2 \to 0$ as $t \to \pm\infty$. In other words $f(t)$ vanishes faster than $1/\sqrt{|t|}$ as $t \to \pm\infty$, then*

$$\sigma_\omega \sigma_T \geq \frac{1}{2} \qquad (20.14)$$

This is an equality if $f(t) = ae^{bt^2}$, where $a \in \mathbb{C}$, and b is a negative real number.
   Proof. See the problem section. $\square$

Orthonormal Sequences

The following observations are about orthonormality of a sequence, and its implications in the frequency domain.

Observations 20.6. Orthonormality in the frequency domain.

1. Let $\{\theta(t - n) \mid n \in \mathbb{Z}\}$ form an orthonormal set. If $\theta(t) \leftrightarrow \Theta(\omega)$, $\omega \in \mathbb{R}$, then

$$\sum_{n \in \mathbb{Z}} |\Theta(\omega + 2\pi n)|^2 = 1$$

2. Let the sequence of functions $\{a(t - n) \mid n \in \mathbb{Z}\}$, form a basis of space S. Also, let $a(t) \leftrightarrow A(\omega)$. Define

$$b(t) = \Im^{-1} \left[\frac{A(\omega)}{\sqrt{\sum_{n \in \mathbb{Z}} |A(\omega + 2\pi n)|^2}} \right]$$

Then $\{b(t - n) \mid n \in \mathbb{Z}\}$ is an orthonormal sequence which spans S. The sequence $\{a(t - n) \mid n \in \mathbb{Z}\}$ is said to be orthogonalized by the sequence $\{b(t - n) \mid n \in \mathbb{Z}\}$. This orthogonalization procedure is used occasionally in constructing wavelet bases. It was first proposed by Battle and Lemarié. $\square$

The first of the above observations is established in the problem section.

20.3.2 Short-Time Fourier Transform

An important problem in Fourier theory is the computation of $F(\omega)$ from $f(t)$. In practice $f(t)$ is not known for values of $|t| > t_0$. Therefore, $F(\omega)$ can only be estimated from this partial information. In order to determine $F(\omega)$, a more precise windowing technique is used. The corresponding Fourier transform is called the short-time Fourier transform or windowed Fourier transform. To compute this Fourier transform, $f(t)$ is multiplied by a window function $g(t - \tau)$ and then the Fourier transform is taken. The windowed Fourier transform is given by $F(\omega, \tau)$. Generally, the function $g(\cdot)$ has either a compact support, or is decaying rapidly.

Definition 20.10. *Let* $f(t) \leftrightarrow F(\omega)$, $t, \omega \in \mathbb{R}$, *and* $g(\cdot)$ *be a window function, such that* $g(\cdot) \in L^2(\mathbb{R})$. *The short-time Fourier transform* $F(\omega, \tau)$ *is given by*

$$F(\omega, \tau) = \int_{-\infty}^{\infty} f(t)g(t - \tau)e^{-i\omega t}dt, \quad \text{where} \quad \tau \in \mathbb{R} \tag{20.15}$$

□

The function $f(t)$ can be recovered as follows. The result is stated as a theorem.

Theorem 20.4. *Let* $\|g\|_2$ *be the* $L^2(\mathbb{R})$ *norm of the window function* $g(\cdot)$. *Then*

$$f(t) = \frac{1}{2\pi \|g\|_2^2} \int_{-\infty}^{\infty} \int_{-\infty}^{\infty} F(\omega, \tau)\overline{g(t - \tau)}e^{i\omega t}d\omega d\tau \tag{20.16a}$$

If the window is chosen such that $\|g\|_2 = 1$, *then*

$$f(t) = \frac{1}{2\pi} \int_{-\infty}^{\infty} \int_{-\infty}^{\infty} F(\omega, \tau)\overline{g(t - \tau)}e^{i\omega t}d\omega d\tau \tag{20.16b}$$

Proof. The inverse Fourier transform of $F(\omega, \tau)$ is

$$f(t)g(t - \tau) = \frac{1}{2\pi} \int_{-\infty}^{\infty} F(\omega, \tau)e^{i\omega t}d\omega$$

Multiply both sides of the above equation by $\overline{g(t - \tau)}$ and integrate over all values of $\tau \in \mathbb{R}$. This gives the stated result.   □

A Parseval-type relationship also holds for windowed Fourier transforms.

Theorem 20.5.

$$\int_{-\infty}^{\infty} |f(t)|^2 dt = \frac{1}{2\pi \|g\|_2^2} \int_{-\infty}^{\infty} \int_{-\infty}^{\infty} |F(\omega, \tau)|^2 d\omega d\tau \tag{20.17}$$

Proof. See the problem section.   □

Dennis Gabor initially used a Gaussian window of the form $g(t) = ae^{bt^2}$, where b is a negative real number. We have also observed that its Fourier transform is also Gaussian. Also recall that Gaussian windows achieve the lower bound obtained in the second-order uncertainty principle. A short-time Fourier transform with a Gaussian window is also called Gabor transform. Gabor won the Nobel prize in physics in the year 1971 for his work on holography.

20.3.3 Wigner–Ville Transform

The Wigner–Ville distribution is a second-order or bilinear transform that performs the mapping of time-domain functions into time-frequency space. It is an alternative to the short-time Fourier transform for nonstationary and transient signal (function) analysis. A nonstationary signal is a time varying signal in a statistical sense. This transform is named after E. P. Wigner (1902–1995) and J. Ville (1910–1989).

Definition 20.11. *The Wigner–Ville transform (distribution) of $f(t)$, $t \in \mathbb{R}$ is specified by*

$$\widetilde{W}_f(\tau, \omega) = \int_{-\infty}^{\infty} f\left(\tau + \frac{t}{2}\right) \overline{f\left(\tau - \frac{t}{2}\right)} e^{-i\omega t} dt; \quad \tau, \omega \in \mathbb{R} \qquad (20.18)$$

$\square$

Properties of Wigner–Ville Transform

Certain useful results about this transform are listed below. Let $f(t) \leftrightarrow F(\omega)$, where $t, \omega \in \mathbb{R}$. In these observations $\tau, t, t_1, t_2, \omega, \omega_1, \omega_2 \in \mathbb{R}$.

1. $\widetilde{W}_f(\tau, \omega) = \frac{1}{2\pi} \int_{-\infty}^{\infty} F\left(\omega + \frac{\xi}{2}\right) \overline{F\left(\omega - \frac{\xi}{2}\right)} e^{i\tau\xi} d\xi$

2. $f(t_1) \overline{f(t_2)} = \frac{1}{2\pi} \int_{-\infty}^{\infty} \widetilde{W}_f\left(\frac{t_1+t_2}{2}, \omega\right) e^{i\omega(t_1-t_2)} d\omega$

3. $f(t)\overline{f(0)} = \frac{1}{2\pi} \int_{-\infty}^{\infty} \widetilde{W}_f\left(\frac{t}{2}, \omega\right) e^{i\omega t} d\omega$

4. $F(\omega_1) \overline{F(\omega_2)} = \int_{-\infty}^{\infty} \widetilde{W}_f\left(\tau, \frac{\omega_1+\omega_2}{2}\right) e^{-i(\omega_1-\omega_2)\tau} d\tau$

5. $F(\omega) \overline{F(0)} = \int_{-\infty}^{\infty} \widetilde{W}_f\left(\tau, \frac{\omega}{2}\right) e^{-i\omega\tau} d\tau$

6. $|f(t)|^2 = \frac{1}{2\pi} \int_{-\infty}^{\infty} \widetilde{W}_f(t, \omega) d\omega$

7. $|F(\omega)|^2 = \int_{-\infty}^{\infty} \widetilde{W}_f(\tau, \omega) d\tau$

8. $\int_{-\infty}^{\infty} |f(t)|^2 dt = \frac{1}{2\pi} \int_{-\infty}^{\infty} |F(\omega)|^2 d\omega = \frac{1}{2\pi} \int_{-\infty}^{\infty} \int_{-\infty}^{\infty} \widetilde{W}_f(\tau, \omega) d\omega d\tau$ $\square$

Examples 20.3. In the following examples $t, \omega \in \mathbb{R}$.

1. If $f(t) = \delta(t - t_0)$, then $\widetilde{W}_f(\tau, \omega) = \delta(\tau - t_0)$.

2. If $F(\omega) = \delta(\omega - \omega_0)$, then $\widetilde{W}_f(\tau, \omega) = \delta(\omega - \omega_0)/(2\pi)$.

3. If $f(t) = \frac{1}{\sqrt{2\pi\alpha}} e^{-t^2/(2\alpha^2)}$, $\alpha \in \mathbb{R}^+$, then $\widetilde{W}_f(\tau, \omega) = \frac{1}{\sqrt{\pi\alpha}} e^{-\alpha^2\omega^2 - \tau^2/\alpha^2}$. □

Problems

1. A working definition of Dirac's delta function $\delta(\cdot)$ is provided in this problem. Prove that

$$\delta(x) = \lim_{\epsilon \to 0} \frac{\epsilon}{\pi(x^2 + \epsilon^2)}$$

Hint: Prove that

$$\int_{-\infty}^{\infty} \delta(x)\, dx = 1$$

2. Let $g(t)$ and $h(t)$ be periodic signals with period T_0. Also, let $\omega_0 = 2\pi/T_0$. Then for any $a \in \mathbb{R}$, the Fourier expansions of these functions are

$$g(t) = \sum_{n \in \mathbb{Z}} p_n e^{in\omega_0 t}, \quad p_n = \frac{1}{T_0} \int_a^{a+T_0} g(t) e^{-in\omega_0 t}\, dt, \qquad n \in \mathbb{Z}$$

$$h(t) = \sum_{n \in \mathbb{Z}} q_n e^{in\omega_0 t}, \quad q_n = \frac{1}{T_0} \int_a^{a+T_0} h(t) e^{-in\omega_0 t}\, dt, \qquad n \in \mathbb{Z}$$

Define $f(t) = g(t)h(t)$. Then $f(t)$ is a periodic function with period T_0. Let

$$f(t) = \sum_{n \in \mathbb{Z}} c_n e^{in\omega_0 t}, \quad c_n = \frac{1}{T_0} \int_a^{a+T_0} f(t) e^{-in\omega_0 t}\, dt, \qquad n \in \mathbb{Z}$$

(a) Show that

$$c_n = \sum_{m \in \mathbb{Z}} p_m q_{n-m}, \qquad n \in \mathbb{Z}$$

$$\frac{1}{T_0} \int_a^{a+T_0} g(t)h(t)\, dt = \sum_{n \in \mathbb{Z}} p_n q_{-n}$$

(b) Prove the above result, by substituting $g(t) = f(t)$ and $h(t) = \overline{f(t)}$ to obtain Parseval's relation:

$$\frac{1}{T_0} \int_a^{a+T_0} |f(t)|^2\, dt = \sum_{n \in \mathbb{Z}} |c_n|^2$$

3. Establish the following Fourier transform pairs.

   (a)
   $$\int_{-\infty}^{t} f(\tau)\, d\tau \leftrightarrow \frac{F(\omega)}{i\omega} + \pi F(0)\, \delta(\omega)$$

   (b) Let $\delta_{T_0}(t) = \sum_{n \in \mathbb{Z}} \delta(t - nT_0)$ and $\delta_{w_0}(\omega) = \sum_{n \in \mathbb{Z}} \delta(\omega - n\omega_0)$, where
   $\omega_0 = 2\pi/T_0$, then $\delta_{T_0}(t) \leftrightarrow \omega_0 \delta_{w_0}(\omega)$.

   Hints: See Hsu (1984).

   (a) $\int_{-\infty}^{t} f(\tau)\, d\tau = f(t) * u(t)$, where $*$ is the convolution operator, and $u(\cdot)$
   is the unit step function. Then

   $$\int_{-\infty}^{t} f(\tau)\, d\tau \leftrightarrow F(\omega) U(\omega)$$

   where
   $$U(\omega) = \pi\delta(\omega) + \frac{1}{i\omega}$$

   The result follows.

   (b) The Fourier series expansion of $\delta_{T_0}(t) = \frac{1}{T_0} \sum_{n \in \mathbb{Z}} e^{in\omega_0 t}$. Therefore,

   $$\delta_{T_0}(t) \leftrightarrow \frac{1}{T_0} \sum_{n \in \mathbb{Z}} 2\pi\delta(\omega - n\omega_0) = \omega_0 \delta_{w_0}(\omega)$$

4. Establish the following Fourier transform pairs. In all these functions $\alpha, t \in \mathbb{R}$.

   (a) Let $\alpha > 0$ then
   $$\frac{1}{\sqrt{2\pi}\alpha} e^{-\frac{t^2}{2\alpha^2}} \leftrightarrow e^{-\frac{\alpha^2 \omega^2}{2}}$$

   (b) Let $\alpha > 0$ then
   $$e^{-\alpha t} u(t) \leftrightarrow (\alpha + i\omega)^{-1}$$

   (c) Let $\alpha > 0$ then
   $$e^{-\alpha|t|} \leftrightarrow 2\alpha \left(\alpha^2 + \omega^2\right)^{-1}$$

   (d) Let $\alpha > 0$ then
   $$\frac{1}{(\alpha^2 + t^2)} \leftrightarrow \frac{\pi}{\alpha} e^{-\alpha|\omega|}$$

   (e) Let
   $$g(t) = \begin{cases} \dfrac{t^{n-1}}{(n-1)!}, & t \geq 0 \\ 0, & \text{otherwise} \end{cases} , \qquad \forall\, n \in \mathbb{P}$$

   then
   $$g(t) \leftrightarrow \frac{1}{(i\omega)^n}$$

(f) Let $f(t)$, $t \in \mathbb{R}$ be the probability density function of a continuously distributed random variable. A useful technique for computing the nth moment of the random variable is via the use of the Fourier transform. If

$$m_n(t) \triangleq \int_{-\infty}^{\infty} t^n f(t)dt$$

show that

$$m_n(t) = i^n \left.\frac{d^n}{d\omega^n} F(\omega)\right|_{\omega=0}, \quad \forall\, n \in \mathbb{N}$$

where $f(t) \leftrightarrow F(\omega)$.

5. Let T_0 and τ be positive real numbers. Also let $\omega_0 = 2\pi/T_0$, $\Omega_0 = 2\pi/\tau$, $t \in \mathbb{R}$ and $f(\cdot)$ be an arbitrary function such that $f(t) \leftrightarrow F(\omega)$. Define

$$f_s(t) = \sum_{n \in \mathbb{Z}} f(t + nT_0), \quad t \in \mathbb{R}$$

$$F_s(\omega) = \sum_{n \in \mathbb{Z}} F(\omega + n\Omega_0), \quad \omega \in \mathbb{R}$$

Note that $f_s(t)$ and $F_s(\omega)$ are not a Fourier transform pair. Establish Poisson's summation formulae.

(a) $f_s(t) = \frac{1}{T_0} \sum_{n \in \mathbb{Z}} F(n\omega_0) e^{in\omega_0 t}$
(b) $F_s(\omega) = \tau \sum_{n \in \mathbb{Z}} f(n\tau) e^{-in\omega\tau}$

Hint: See Hsu (1984).

(a) It is evident that

$$f_s(t) = f(t) * \delta_{T_0}(t), \quad \delta_{T_0}(t) = \sum_{n \in \mathbb{Z}} \delta(t - nT_0)$$

It is known that

$$\delta_{T_0}(t) \leftrightarrow \omega_0 \delta_{\omega_0}(\omega), \quad \delta_{\omega_0}(\omega) = \sum_{n \in \mathbb{Z}} \delta(\omega - n\omega_0)$$

Thus

$$\Im(f_s(t)) = F(\omega) \omega_0 \delta_{\omega_0}(\omega) = \omega_0 \sum_{n \in \mathbb{Z}} F(n\omega_0) \delta(\omega - n\omega_0)$$

Since $e^{in\omega_0 t} \leftrightarrow 2\pi\delta(\omega - n\omega_0)$, $\forall\, n \in \mathbb{Z}$, the result follows by taking the inverse Fourier transform of both sides.

(b) Observe that $F_s(\omega) = F(\omega) * \delta_{\Omega_0}(\omega)$, where

$$\delta_{\Omega_0}(\omega) = \sum_{n \in \mathbb{Z}} \delta(\omega - n\Omega_0)$$

Since $\delta_\tau(t) \leftrightarrow \Omega_0 \delta_{\Omega_0}(\omega)$, upon taking the Fourier inverse of $F_s(\omega)$ yields

$$\Im^{-1}\left(F_s\left(\omega\right)\right) = \frac{2\pi}{\Omega_0} f\left(t\right) \delta_\tau\left(t\right) = \tau \sum_{n \in \mathbb{Z}} f\left(n\tau\right) \delta\left(t - n\tau\right)$$

Since $\delta\left(t - n\tau\right) \leftrightarrow e^{-in\omega\tau}$, $\forall\, n \in \mathbb{Z}$, the result follows by taking the Fourier transform of both sides.

6. If $f(t)$ is differentiable, and $t\,|f(t)|^2 \to 0$ as $t \to \pm\infty$. In other words $f(t)$ vanishes faster than $1/\sqrt{|t|}$ as $t \to \pm\infty$, then

$$\sigma_\omega \sigma_T \geq \frac{1}{2}$$

This is an equality if $f(t) = ae^{bt^2}$, where $a \in \mathbb{C}$, and b is a negative real number. Hint: We have

$$\int_{-\infty}^{\infty} t\overline{f(t)}\frac{df(t)}{dt}\,dt = \frac{1}{2}\int_{-\infty}^{\infty} t\,d\,|f(t)|^2$$

$$= \frac{1}{2}\left[t\,|f(t)|^2 \Big|_{-\infty}^{\infty} - \int_{-\infty}^{\infty} |f(t)|^2\,dt \right]$$

$$= -\frac{1}{2}\int_{-\infty}^{\infty} |f(t)|^2\,dt$$

The last step is justified, as $t\,|f(t)|^2 \to 0$ for $t \to \pm\infty$, via the hypothesis of the theorem. Therefore,

$$\frac{1}{4}\left[\int_{-\infty}^{\infty} |f(t)|^2\,dt\right]^2 = \left|\int_{-\infty}^{\infty} t\overline{f(t)}\frac{df(t)}{dt}\,dt\right|^2$$

Using the Bunyakovsky–Cauchy–Schwartz inequality we obtain

$$\frac{1}{4}\left[\int_{-\infty}^{\infty} |f(t)|^2\,dt\right]^2 \leq \int_{-\infty}^{\infty} t^2\,|f(t)|^2\,dt \int_{-\infty}^{\infty}\left|\frac{df(t)}{dt}\right|^2\,dt$$

Since

$$\frac{df(t)}{dt} \leftrightarrow i\omega F(\omega)$$

$$\int_{-\infty}^{\infty} |f(t)|^2\,dt = \frac{1}{2\pi}\int_{-\infty}^{\infty} |F(\omega)|^2\,d\omega$$

we have

$$\frac{1}{4}\left\{\int_{-\infty}^{\infty} |f(t)|^2\,dt\right\}\left\{\frac{1}{2\pi}\int_{-\infty}^{\infty} |F(\omega)|^2\,d\omega\right\}$$

$$\leq \left\{\int_{-\infty}^{\infty} t^2\,|f(t)|^2\,dt\right\}\left\{\frac{1}{2\pi}\int_{-\infty}^{\infty} \omega^2\,|F(\omega)|^2\,dt\right\}$$

Using the definitions of σ_T and σ_ω we get $\sigma_\omega \sigma_T \geq 1/2$. Equality occurs if

$$\frac{df(t)}{dt} = 2bt f(t), \quad b < 0$$

which implies $f(t) = ae^{bt^2}$, where $a \in \mathbb{C}$ and b is a negative real number.

7. Let $\{\theta(t-n) \mid n \in \mathbb{Z}\}$ form an orthonormal set. If $\theta(t) \leftrightarrow \Theta(\omega)$, $\omega \in \mathbb{R}$, then

$$\sum_{n \in \mathbb{Z}} |\Theta(\omega + 2\pi n)|^2 = 1$$

Hint: For any $m \in \mathbb{Z}$

$$\delta_{m,0} = \int_{-\infty}^{\infty} \theta(t)\, \overline{\theta(t-m)}\, dt$$

$$= \frac{1}{2\pi} \int_{-\infty}^{\infty} |\Theta(\omega)|^2\, e^{i\omega m}\, d\omega = \frac{1}{2\pi} \sum_{n \in \mathbb{Z}} \int_{2\pi n}^{2\pi(n+1)} |\Theta(\omega)|^2\, e^{i\omega m}\, d\omega$$

$$= \frac{1}{2\pi} \sum_{n \in \mathbb{Z}} \int_{0}^{2\pi} |\Theta(\omega + 2\pi n)|^2\, e^{i\omega m}\, d\omega$$

$$= \frac{1}{2\pi} \int_{0}^{2\pi} e^{i\omega m} \sum_{n \in \mathbb{Z}} |\Theta(\omega + 2\pi n)|^2\, d\omega$$

As

$$\delta_{m,0} = \frac{1}{2\pi} \int_{0}^{2\pi} e^{i\omega m}\, d\omega$$

The result follows.

8. Establish the Parseval-type relationship for windowed Fourier transforms. It is

$$\int_{-\infty}^{\infty} |f(t)|^2\, dt = \frac{1}{2\pi \|g\|_2^2} \int_{-\infty}^{\infty} \int_{-\infty}^{\infty} |F(\omega, \tau)|^2\, d\omega d\tau$$

Hint: Let $g(t) \leftrightarrow G(\omega)$. The short-time Fourier transform of the function $f(t)$ is

$$F(\omega, \tau) = \int_{-\infty}^{\infty} f(t)g(t-\tau)e^{-i\omega t}\, dt$$

Observe that

$$e^{-i\omega_0 t}g(t-\tau) \leftrightarrow e^{-i(\omega+\omega_0)\tau}G(\omega+\omega_0)$$

Apply Parseval's relationship to the expression for $F(\omega, \tau)$. This results in

$$F(\omega, \tau) = \frac{e^{-i\omega\tau}}{2\pi} \int_{-\infty}^{\infty} F(\Omega)\, G(\omega - \Omega)\, e^{i\Omega\tau}\, d\Omega$$

$$= e^{-i\omega\tau} \mathfrak{F}^{-1}\left[F(\Omega)\, G(\omega - \Omega)\right](\tau)$$

Then

$$\frac{1}{2\pi \|g\|_2^2} \int_{-\infty}^{\infty} \int_{-\infty}^{\infty} |F(\omega, \tau)|^2 \, d\omega d\tau$$

$$= \frac{1}{2\pi \|g\|_2^2} \int_{-\infty}^{\infty} \int_{-\infty}^{\infty} |\mathfrak{S}^{-1}[F(\Omega) G(\omega - \Omega)](\tau)|^2 \, d\tau d\omega$$

Using Parseval's relationship again we get

$$\frac{1}{2\pi \|g\|_2^2} \int_{-\infty}^{\infty} \int_{-\infty}^{\infty} |F(\omega, \tau)|^2 \, d\omega d\tau$$

$$= \frac{1}{4\pi^2 \|g\|_2^2} \int_{-\infty}^{\infty} \int_{-\infty}^{\infty} |F(\Omega) G(\omega - \Omega)|^2 \, d\Omega d\omega$$

$$= \frac{1}{4\pi^2 \|g\|_2^2} \int_{-\infty}^{\infty} |F(\Omega)|^2 \int_{-\infty}^{\infty} |G(\omega - \Omega)|^2 \, d\omega d\Omega$$

$$= \frac{1}{2\pi} \int_{-\infty}^{\infty} |F(\Omega)|^2 \, d\Omega$$

$$= \int_{-\infty}^{\infty} |f(t)|^2 \, dt$$

9. Let $f(t) \leftrightarrow F(\omega)$, $t, \omega \in \mathbb{R}$. Prove the following result about the Wigner–Ville transform.

$$\widetilde{W}_f(\tau, \omega) = \frac{1}{2\pi} \int_{-\infty}^{\infty} F\left(\omega + \frac{\xi}{2}\right) \overline{F\left(\omega - \frac{\xi}{2}\right)} e^{i\tau\xi} d\xi, \qquad \tau, \omega \in \mathbb{R}$$

Hint:

$$\widetilde{W}_f(\tau, \omega)$$

$$= \int_{-\infty}^{\infty} f\left(\tau + \frac{t}{2}\right) \overline{f\left(\tau - \frac{t}{2}\right)} e^{-i\omega t} dt$$

$$= \frac{1}{(2\pi)^2} \int_{-\infty}^{\infty} \int_{-\infty}^{\infty} \int_{-\infty}^{\infty} F(\omega_1) \overline{F(\omega_2)} e^{i(\omega_1 - \omega_2)\tau + i(\omega_1 + \omega_2 - 2\omega)\frac{t}{2}} dt d\omega_1 d\omega_2$$

Note that

$$\frac{1}{2\pi} \int_{-\infty}^{\infty} e^{it\left(\frac{\omega_1 + \omega_2}{2} - \omega\right)} dt = \delta\left(\frac{\omega_1 + \omega_2}{2} - \omega\right)$$

Therefore,

$$\widetilde{W}_f(\tau, \omega)$$

$$= \frac{1}{2\pi} \int_{-\infty}^{\infty} \int_{-\infty}^{\infty} F(\omega_1) \overline{F(\omega_2)} e^{i(\omega_1 - \omega_2)\tau} \delta\left(\frac{\omega_1 + \omega_2}{2} - \omega\right) d\omega_1 d\omega_2$$

In the above equation, substitute $(\omega_1 - \omega_2) = \xi$ and $\left(\frac{\omega_1 + \omega_2}{2} - \omega\right) = y$. Thus

$$\widetilde{W}_f (\tau, \omega)$$

$$= \frac{1}{2\pi} \int_{-\infty}^{\infty} \int_{-\infty}^{\infty} F \left(\frac{2y + \xi + 2\omega}{2} \right) \overline{F \left(\frac{2y - \xi + 2\omega}{2} \right)} e^{i\tau\xi} \delta (y) \, dy d\xi$$

The result follows immediately.

CHAPTER 21

Probability Theory and Stochastic Processes

21.1 Introduction

A basic knowledge of probability theory and stochastic processes is necessary for proper and judicious application of wavelet transform theory. An overview of probabilistic tools and techniques to study nondeterministic events is provided in this chapter. Postulates (axioms) of probability theory are initially stated. The concept of the random variable is next introduced. Descriptions of average measures such as expectation of a random variable are also provided. Typical second-order measures, and the concept of independent random variables are also introduced. These ideas are also clarified via examples of discrete and continuous random variables. A brief introduction to stochastic processes is also provided.

21.2 Postulates of Probability Theory

Probability theory is developed on the basis of a set of postulates. These postulates were first promulgated by A. N. Kolmogorov (1903–1987) in the year 1933. In these postulates, an *experiment* is a mental or physical activity which produces a *measurable* outcome.

   Postulates of Probability Theory. *Probability is defined as the triple* $(S, \mathcal{F}, P)$, *where*:

(a) S *is the sample space. It is the set of all possible mutually exclusive outcomes of a specified experiment. Each such possible outcome* ω, *is called a sample point.*

(b) $\mathcal{F}$ *is a family of events.* $\mathcal{F} = \{A, B, C, \ldots\}$, *where each event is a set of sample points* $\{\omega \mid \omega \in S\}$. *Thus an event is a subset of* S. *All subsets of* S *are not necessarily events in the set* $\mathcal{F}$. *The collection of events in the set* $\mathcal{F}$ *observe the following rules.*

   (i) $S \in \mathcal{F}$.

(ii) *If $A \in \mathcal{F}$, then $A^c \in \mathcal{F}$.*

(iii) *If $A_i \in \mathcal{F}, \forall i \in \mathbb{P}$; then $\bigcup_{i \in \mathbb{P}} A_i \in \mathcal{F}$.*

Such collection of events is called an algebra.

(c) *P is a real-valued mapping (function) defined on $\mathcal{F}$, where $P(A)$ is the probability of the event A. It is also called the probability measure. The function $P(\cdot)$ also has to satisfy the following postulates.*

[*Postulate 1*] *For any event A, $P(A) \geq 0$.*

[*Postulate 2*] *$P(\mathcal{S}) = 1$.*

[*Postulate 3*] *If $A \cap B = \varnothing$, that is A and B are mutually exclusive events, then*

$$P(A \cup B) = P(A) + P(B) \tag{21.1a}$$

[*Postulate 3′*] *Let $A_1, A_2, \ldots$ be a sequence of events, such that $A_j \cap A_k = \varnothing, j \neq k$, where $j, k \in \mathbb{P}$, then*

$$P(A_1 \cup A_2 \cup \ldots) = P(A_1) + P(A_2) + \ldots \tag{21.1b}$$

□

Observe that the Postulate 3′ does not follow from Postulate 3. However, Postulate 3′ is superfluous if the sample space $\mathcal{S}$ is finite.

Observations 21.1. Let A and B be any events. Then

1. Let $\mathcal{F}$ be the family of events.
    (a) $\varnothing \in \mathcal{F}$, where $\varnothing$ is called the null event.
    (b) If $A, B \in \mathcal{F}$, then $A \cup B \in \mathcal{F}$, and $A \cap B \in \mathcal{F}$.
2. $P(\varnothing) = 0$.
3. $P(A^c) = (1 - P(A))$, where A^c is the complement of the event A.
4. $P(A) \leq 1$.
5. $P(A) \leq P(B)$, if $A \subseteq B$.
6. $P(A \cup B) = (P(A) + P(B) - P(A \cap B))$.   □

The following definitions are related to the concept of independence of two events. Independent events, as the name says, are events which do not affect the outcome of one another.

Definition 21.1. *Independence of events. Events A and B are independent of each other if and only if*

$$P(A \cap B) = P(A) P(B) \tag{21.2}$$

If the above relationship does not hold, then the events A and B are said to be dependent.   □

The three events $A, B,$ and C are independent of each other, if:

$$P(A \cap B) = P(A)P(B), \ P(B \cap C) = P(B)P(C),$$
$$P(C \cap A) = P(C)P(A), \ \text{and} \ P(A \cap B \cap C) = P(A)P(B)P(C)$$

21.3 Random Variables

In order to study occurrences of events further, random variables have to be studied. A random variable generally takes real values. A random variable, distribution function, probability mass function, and probability density function are defined. A real-valued random variable is either discrete or continuous.

Definitions 21.2. *Random variable and related functions.*

1. *A random variable is a function X which maps a sample point $\omega \in S$ into the real line. That is, $X(\omega) \in \mathbb{R}$. The random variable is often simply denoted as X.*

2. *The distribution function $F_X(\cdot)$ of the random variable X is defined for any $x \in \mathbb{R}$ as $F_X(x) = P(X \leq x)$. It is also sometimes referred to as the cumulative distribution function. The complementary cumulative distribution function $F_X^c(\cdot)$ of the random variable X, is specified by $F_X^c(x) = P(X > x) = (1 - F_X(x))$.*

3. *A random variable X is discrete, if its set of possible values is countable. If the random variable X takes on values $x_j, j = 1, 2, 3, \ldots,$ then the probabilities $P(X = x_j) \triangleq p_X(x_j), j = 1, 2, 3, \ldots,$ are called the probability mass function (or distribution) of the random variable X. The corresponding cumulative distribution function is said to be discrete.*

4. *A random variable X is continuous, if its image set $X(S)$ is a continuum of numbers. It is assumed that there exists a piecewise-continuous function $f_X(\cdot)$ that maps real numbers into real numbers such that*

$$P(a < X \leq b) = \int_a^b f_X(x)\,dx, \ \forall\, a < b \tag{21.3}$$

The function $f_X(\cdot)$ is called the probability density function. The corresponding cumulative distribution function is said to be continuous.   □

Observations 21.2. Some facts about the cumulative distribution function of a random variable.

1. The distribution function $F_X(\cdot)$ of the random variable X, is a monotonically nondecreasing function. That is, if $x < y$ then $F_X(x) \leq F_X(y)$. Also $0 \leq F_X(x) \leq 1$. Furthermore, $\lim_{x \to -\infty} F_X(x) = 0$, and $\lim_{x \to \infty} F_X(x) = 1$. In addition, for $h > 0$, $F_X(x) = \lim_{h \to 0} F_X(x+h) = F_X(x_+)$.

2. Let X be a discrete random variable, which takes on values $x_j, j = 1, 2, 3, \ldots$. The probabilities $P(X = x_j) = p_X(x_j), j = 1, 2, 3, \ldots$ satisfy

$$p_X(x_j) \geq 0, \quad \forall j \in \mathbb{P}; \quad \text{and} \quad \sum_{j \in \mathbb{P}} p_X(x_j) = 1 \qquad (21.4a)$$

$$F_X(x) = \sum_{x_j \leq x} p_X(x_j) \qquad (21.4b)$$

3. Let X be a continuous random variable, and its probability density function be $f_X(x)$, $x \in \mathbb{R}$. The probability density function satisfies the following relationships.

$$F_X(x) = \int_{-\infty}^{x} f_X(t)\, dt, \quad f_X(x) = \frac{d}{dx} F_X(x) \qquad (21.5a)$$

$$\int_{\mathbb{R}} f_X(x)\, dx = 1 \qquad (21.5b)$$

It is assumed that the derivative exists. It follows from the monotonicity of $F_X(\cdot)$, that $f_X(x) \geq 0$ for each $x \in \mathbb{R}$. $\qquad \square$

Jointly Distributed Random Variables

Jointly distributed random variables are initially defined for two random variables. This is then extended to N random variables.

Definitions 21.3. *Let X and Y be jointly distributed random variables which take real values.*

1. *Joint distributions.*
    (a) *The joint cumulative distribution function of the two random variables X and Y is $F_{X,Y}(\cdot, \cdot)$, where*

    $$F_{X,Y}(x, y) = P(X \leq x, Y \leq y) \qquad (21.6a)$$

    (b) *If X and Y are two discrete random variables, then the joint probability mass function of the two random variables X and Y is $p_{X,Y}(\cdot, \cdot)$, where*

    $$p_{X,Y}(x, y) = P(X = x, Y = y) \qquad (21.6b)$$

(c) *Let the two random variables X and Y be continuous. The random variables X and Y are jointly continuous if there exists a function $f_{X,Y}(\cdot,\cdot)$ such that*

$$P\left(X \in \widetilde{A}, Y \in \widetilde{B}\right) = \int_{\widetilde{B}}\int_{\widetilde{A}} f_{X,Y}(x,y)\,dx dy \qquad (21.6c)$$

where $\widetilde{A}$ and $\widetilde{B}$ are any subsets of real numbers. The function $f_{X,Y}(\cdot,\cdot)$ is called the joint probability density function.

2. *Marginal distributions.*

   (a) *As y tends to ∞, $F_{X,Y}(x,y)$ tends to $F_X(x)$. Similarly as x tends to ∞, $F_{X,Y}(x,y)$ tends to $F_Y(y)$. $F_X(\cdot)$ and $F_Y(\cdot)$ are called marginal cumulative distribution functions of X and Y respectively.*

   (b) *Let X and Y be both discrete random variables with joint probability mass function $p_{X,Y}(\cdot,\cdot)$. Then*

$$p_X(x) = \sum_y p_{X,Y}(x,y), \ \ and \ \ p_Y(y) = \sum_x p_{X,Y}(x,y) \qquad (21.7a)$$

   where $p_X(\cdot)$ and $p_Y(\cdot)$ are called the marginal mass functions of X and Y respectively.

   (c) *Let X and Y be both continuous random variables with joint probability density function $f_{X,Y}(\cdot,\cdot)$. Then*

$$f_X(x) = \int_{-\infty}^{\infty} f_{X,Y}(x,y)\,dy, \ \ and \ \ f_Y(y) = \int_{-\infty}^{\infty} f_{X,Y}(x,y)\,dx$$

$$(21.7b)$$

   where $f_X(\cdot)$ and $f_Y(\cdot)$ are called marginal probability density functions of X and Y respectively.

3. *Let $X_1, X_2, \ldots, X_N$ be $N \in \mathbb{P}\backslash\{1\}$ jointly distributed random variables. Then $F(\cdot,\cdot,\ldots,\cdot)$ is their joint cumulative distribution function, where*

$$F(x_1, x_2, \ldots, x_N) = P(X_1 \leq x_1, X_2 \leq x_2, \ldots, X_N \leq x_N) \qquad (21.8)$$

The joint probability mass function (for discrete random variables) and joint probability density function (for continuous random variables) for N random variables can be similarly defined. □

21.4 Average Measures

Expectation of a random variable, expectation of a function of a random variable, and common second-order expectations are defined and discussed in this section.

21.4.1 Expectation

The expectation of a discrete and continuous random variable is defined below.

Definition 21.4. *The expectation or mean or average value of a random variable X is denoted by $\mathcal{E}(X)$. It is*

$$\mathcal{E}(X) = \int_{-\infty}^{\infty} x dF_X(x) \tag{21.9a}$$

Specifically:

(a) *If X is a discrete random variable,*

$$\mathcal{E}(X) = \sum_{x:p_X(x)>0} x p_X(x) \tag{21.9b}$$

provided the summation exists.

(b) *If X is a continuous random variable,*

$$\mathcal{E}(X) = \int_{-\infty}^{\infty} x f_X(x)\, dx \tag{21.9c}$$

provided the integral exists.   □

Let $g(\cdot)$ be a function of a random variable X. The expectation of $g(X)$ is determined as follows.

(a) If X is a discrete random variable:

$$\mathcal{E}(g(X)) = \sum_{x:p_X(x)>0} g(x) p_X(x)$$

(b) If X is a continuous random variable:

$$\mathcal{E}(g(X)) = \int_{-\infty}^{\infty} g(x)\, dF_X(x)$$

Let $c_1, c_2, \ldots, c_N \in \mathbb{R}$, and $X_1, X_2, \ldots, X_N$ be N jointly distributed random variables, then

$$\mathcal{E}(\sum_{j=1}^{N} c_j X_j) = \sum_{j=1}^{N} c_j \mathcal{E}(X_j) \tag{21.10}$$

The mean of a random variable X is also called its first moment. Higher moments of the random variable are similarly defined.

Definition 21.5. *Let X be a random variable, and $r \in \mathbb{P}$. The rth moment of X is $\mu_r = \mathcal{E}(X^r)$. The parameter r is called the order of the moment.*   □

21.4.2 Second-Order Expectations

Some useful second-order expectations of a single random variable are variance, standard deviation, and squared coefficient of variation. Similarly, the common second-order expectations of two jointly distributed random variables are covariance, and correlation coefficient.

Definitions 21.6. *Common second-order expectations.*

1. *The variance* $Var(X)$ *of a random variable* X *is*

$$Var(X) = \mathcal{E}\left((X - \mathcal{E}(X))^2\right) \tag{21.11a}$$

   That is, $Var(X) = \mathcal{E}(X^2) - (\mathcal{E}(X))^2 = (\mu_2 - \mu_1^2).$

2. *The standard deviation* σ_X *of a random variable* X, *is* $\sigma_X = \sqrt{Var(X)}.$

3. *The squared coefficient of variation* C_X^2, *of a random variable* X *where* $\mathcal{E}(X) \neq 0$ *is*

$$C_X^2 = \frac{Var(X)}{\{\mathcal{E}(X)\}^2} \tag{21.11b}$$

4. *The covariance* $Cov(X,Y)$ *of two jointly distributed random variables* X *and* Y *is*

$$Cov(X,Y) = \mathcal{E}((X - \mathcal{E}(X))(Y - \mathcal{E}(Y))) \tag{21.11c}$$

   That is, $Cov(X,Y) = \mathcal{E}(XY) - \mathcal{E}(X)\mathcal{E}(Y).$

5. *If* $Cov(X,Y) = 0$, *then the random variables* X *and* Y *are said to be uncorrelated.*

6. *Let* σ_X *and* σ_Y *be the standard deviation of the jointly distributed random variables* X *and* Y *respectively, where* $\sigma_X \neq 0$ *and* $\sigma_Y \neq 0$. *The correlation coefficient* $Cor(X,Y)$ *of these random variables is*

$$Cor(X,Y) = \frac{Cov(X,Y)}{\sigma_X \sigma_Y} \tag{21.11d}$$

   If $Cor(X,Y) = 0$, *then the random variables* X *and* Y *are uncorrelated.*   □

The mean of a random variable X is also called its first moment. Higher moments of the random variable are similarly defined. It can be shown that $-1 \leq Cor(X,Y) \leq 1$.

21.5 Independent Random Variables

A precise definition of stochastic independence is as follows.

Definition 21.7. *Random variables X and Y are stochastically independent (or simply independent) random variables if for all values of x and y*

$$F_{X,Y}(x,y) = F_X(x) F_Y(y) \tag{21.12}$$

where $F_{X,Y}(\cdot,\cdot)$ is the joint cumulative distribution function of the random variables X and Y. Also $F_X(\cdot)$ and $F_Y(\cdot)$ are the marginal cumulative distribution functions of the random variables X and Y respectively. □

Observations 21.3. Let X and Y be independent random variables.

1. $\mathcal{E}(XY) = \mathcal{E}(X)\mathcal{E}(Y)$. Note that the reverse is not true. That is, $\mathcal{E}(XY) = \mathcal{E}(X)\mathcal{E}(Y)$ does not imply the independence of random variables X and Y.

2. $Var(X+Y) = Var(X) + Var(Y)$

3. $Cov(X,Y) = Cor(X,Y) = 0$

4. Given any N mutually independent random variables $X_1, X_2, \ldots X_N$, and $b_1, b_2, \ldots, b_N \in \mathbb{R}$

$$\mathcal{E}(\prod_{j=1}^{N} X_j) = \prod_{j=1}^{N} \mathcal{E}(X_j)$$

$$Var(\sum_{j=1}^{N} b_j X_j) = \sum_{j=1}^{N} b_j^2 Var(X_j)$$

□

21.6 Moment-Generating Function

The moment-generating function of a random variable is a convenient technique to determine its moments.

Definition 21.8. *Let X be a random variable, and its rth moment be μ_r, where $r \in \mathbb{P}$. The moment-generating function of X is given by $\mathcal{M}_X(t) = \mathcal{E}(e^{tX})$.*

(a) *If X is a discrete random variable, then $\mathcal{M}_X(t) = \sum_x e^{tx} p_X(x)$.*

(b) *If X is a continuous random variable, then $\mathcal{M}_X(t) = \int_{-\infty}^{\infty} e^{tx} f_X(x)\, dx$.*

It is assumed that $\mathcal{M}_X(t)$ exists for all $t \in (-h, h)$, for some $h > 0$. □

From these definitions it follows that

$$\mu_r = \left. \frac{d^r}{dt^r} \mathcal{M}_X(t) \right|_{t=0}, \qquad \forall\, r \in \mathbb{P}$$

21.7 Examples of Some Distributions

Some examples of discrete and continuous distributions are outlined in this section. The multivariate Gaussian distribution is also defined.

21.7.1 Discrete Distributions

Properties of discrete distributions, like the Bernoulli distribution, binomial distribution, and Poisson distribution are listed below.

Bernoulli distribution: X is a random variable with Bernoulli distribution. Its parameter is p, where $0 \leq p \leq 1$. The probability mass function of X is given by

$$p_X(x) = \begin{cases} q, & x = 0 \\ p, & x = 1 \end{cases} \tag{21.13}$$

where $q = (1 - p)$. Also $\mathcal{E}(X) = p$, and $Var(X) = pq$, and $\mathcal{M}_X(t) = (q + pe^t)$.

Binomial distribution: X is a random variable with binomial distribution. Its parameters are p and n, where $0 \leq p \leq 1$, and $n \in \mathbb{P}$. The probability mass function of X is given by

$$p_X(x) = \begin{cases} \binom{n}{x} p^x q^{n-x}, & x = 0, 1, 2, \ldots, n \\ 0, & \text{otherwise} \end{cases} \tag{21.14}$$

where $q = (1 - p)$. Also $\mathcal{E}(X) = np$, and $Var(X) = npq$, and $\mathcal{M}_X(t) = (q + pe^t)^n$. Note that $n = 1$, leads to a Bernoulli distribution.

Poisson distribution: Let X be a random variable with Poisson distribution. Its parameter is $\lambda \in \mathbb{R}^+$. The probability mass function of X is given by

$$p_X(x) = \begin{cases} e^{-\lambda} \dfrac{\lambda^x}{x!}, & \forall x \in \mathbb{N} \\ 0, & \text{otherwise} \end{cases} \tag{21.15}$$

Also $\mathcal{E}(X) = \lambda$, and $Var(X) = \lambda$, and $\mathcal{M}_X(t) = e^{\lambda(e^t - 1)}$.

21.7.2 Continuous Distributions

Properties of continuous distributions like the uniform distribution, exponential distribution, and normal distribution are listed below.

Uniform distribution: A random variable X has a uniform distribution, if the probability density function of X is given by

$$f_X(x) = \begin{cases} \dfrac{1}{(b-a)}, & x \in [a, b] \\ 0, & \text{otherwise} \end{cases} \qquad (21.16)$$

Its parameter space is $a, b \in \mathbb{R}$, where $a < b$. Also $\mathcal{E}(X) = (a+b)/2$, $Var(X) = (b-a)^2/12$. Further

$$F_X(x) = \begin{cases} 0, & x < a \\ \dfrac{(x-a)}{(b-a)}, & x \in [a, b] \\ 1, & x > b \end{cases}$$

$$\mathcal{M}_X(t) = \frac{(e^{bt} - e^{at})}{(b-a)t}$$

Exponential distribution: A random variable X has an exponential distribution, if the probability density function of X is given by

$$f_X(x) = \begin{cases} 0, & x \in (-\infty, 0) \\ \lambda e^{-\lambda x}, & x \in [0, \infty) \end{cases} \qquad (21.17)$$

Its parameter is $\lambda \in \mathbb{R}^+$. Also $\mathcal{E}(X) = 1/\lambda$, $Var(X) = 1/\lambda^2$. And

$$F_X(x) = \begin{cases} 0, & x \in (-\infty, 0) \\ (1 - e^{-\lambda x}), & x \in [0, \infty) \end{cases}$$

$$\mathcal{M}_X(t) = \frac{\lambda}{(\lambda - t)}, \quad t < \lambda$$

Normal distribution: A random variable X has a normal (or Gaussian) distribution, if the probability density function of X is given by

$$f_X(x) = \frac{1}{\sqrt{2\pi}\sigma} \exp\left\{-\frac{1}{2}\left(\frac{x-\mu}{\sigma}\right)^2\right\}, \quad x \in \mathbb{R} \qquad (21.18)$$

where $\mu \in \mathbb{R}$ and $\sigma \in \mathbb{R}^+$ are its parameters. Also $\mathcal{E}(X) = \mu$, and $Var(X) = \sigma^2$. Its moment-generating function is given by

$$\mathcal{M}_X(t) = \exp\left(\mu t + \frac{\sigma^2 t^2}{2}\right)$$

A normally distributed random variable X with mean μ and variance σ^2 is generally denoted by

$$X \sim \mathcal{N}(\mu, \sigma^2)$$

If a normal random variable has $\mu = 0$, and $\sigma = 1$, then it is called a *standard normal random variable*. Its probability density function $\phi(\cdot)$, and cumulative distribution function $\Phi(\cdot)$ are given by

$$\phi(x) = \frac{1}{\sqrt{2\pi}} e^{-\frac{x^2}{2}}, \qquad x \in \mathbb{R}$$

$$\Phi(x) = \frac{1}{\sqrt{2\pi}} \int_{-\infty}^{x} e^{-\frac{y^2}{2}} dy, \quad x \in \mathbb{R}$$

Also note that $\Phi(x) = (1 - \Phi(-x))$. The function $\Phi(\cdot)$ is generally evaluated numerically. The cumulative distribution function $\Phi(\cdot)$ can also be expressed in terms of the error function. The error function is defined as

$$\operatorname{erf}(z) = \frac{2}{\sqrt{\pi}} \int_0^z e^{-t^2} dt, \quad z \in \mathbb{C}$$

Therefore,

$$\Phi(x) = \frac{1}{2} \left\{ 1 + \operatorname{erf}\left(\frac{x}{\sqrt{2}}\right) \right\}, \quad x \in \mathbb{R}$$

Its moment-generating function is given by

$$\mathcal{M}_X(t) = \exp\left(\frac{t^2}{2}\right)$$

21.7.3 Multivariate Gaussian Distribution

Definition and some elementary properties of the multivariate Gaussian (or normal) distribution are given in this subsection.

Definition 21.9. *The random variables* $X_1, X_2, \ldots, X_m$ *are said to have a multivariate normal distribution, if their joint probability density function has the form*

$$f_X(x) = \frac{1}{(2\pi)^{m/2} (\det \Xi)^{1/2}} \exp\left\{ -\frac{1}{2} (x - \eta)^T \Xi^{-1} (x - \eta) \right\} \qquad (21.19a)$$

where

$$X = \begin{bmatrix} X_1 \ X_2 \ \cdots \ X_m \end{bmatrix}^T \qquad\qquad (21.19b)$$

$$x = \begin{bmatrix} x_1 \ x_2 \ \cdots \ x_m \end{bmatrix}^T \in \mathbb{R}^m \qquad (21.19c)$$

$$\eta = \begin{bmatrix} \eta_1 \ \eta_2 \ \cdots \ \eta_m \end{bmatrix}^T \in \mathbb{R}^m \qquad (21.19d)$$

The vector η *is constant, and the covariance matrix* $\Xi = [\xi_{ij}]$ *is positive definite. This distribution is denoted compactly as* $X \sim \mathcal{N}(\eta, \Xi)$. □

Definition 21.10. *The joint moment-generating function of the random variables* $X_1, X_2, \ldots, X_m$ *is*

$$\mathcal{M}_{X_1, X_2, \ldots, X_N}(t_1, t_2, \ldots, t_N) = \mathcal{E}\left(\exp\left\{ \sum_{j=1}^{N} t_j X_j \right\} \right) \qquad (21.20)$$

$\Box$

Observations 21.4. Some useful facts about multivariate Gaussian distribution.

1. $\mathcal{E}(X_i) = \eta_i, Var(X_i) = \xi_{ii}$ for $1 \le i \le m$.

2. $\xi_{ij} = Cov(X_i, X_j), 1 \le i, j \le m$.

3. $\xi_{ij} = \xi_{ji}$, for $1 \le i, j \le m$. That is, the covariance matrix Ξ is symmetric.

4. The covariance matrix Ξ is positive definite. Therefore, its diagonal elements are all positive.

5. Let $t = \begin{bmatrix} t_1 & t_2 & \cdots & t_m \end{bmatrix}^T$. The joint moment-generating function of the random variables $X_1, X_2, \ldots, X_m$ is

$$M_X(t) = \exp\left\{ \eta^T t + \frac{1}{2} t^T \Xi t \right\}$$

$\Box$

Observations 21.5.

1. Let X and Y be random vectors of the same size, where $X \sim \mathcal{N}(\eta, \Xi)$, and $Y \sim \mathcal{N}(\mu, \Psi)$. Also, let the elements of the vector X be uncorrelated with the elements of the vector Y. If $Z = (X + Y)$, then $Z \sim \mathcal{N}((\eta + \mu), (\Xi + \Psi))$.

2. Let X be a random vector of size $n \in \mathbb{P}$, where $X \sim \mathcal{N}(\eta, \Xi)$. Also, let A be a real-valued $r \times n$ matrix of rank $r \le n$; and c be a real-valued column matrix of size r. If $Y = AX + c$, then $Y \sim \mathcal{N}(\mu, \Psi)$, where

$$\mu = A\eta + c, \quad \text{and} \quad \Psi = A\Xi A^T$$

This result implies that under linear transformation, Gaussian distributions are preserved. $\Box$

21.8 Stochastic Processes

A sequence of random variables which are indexed by some parameter, say time, are called stochastic processes. Systems whose properties vary in a random manner can best be described in terms of stochastic processes. Terminology used in specifying stochastic processes is provided.

Definitions 21.11. *Terminology related to stochastic processes.*

1. *A stochastic or random process is a family of random variables. Let T be the index set of the stochastic process, and S be its sample space (or state space). Then $\{X(t, \omega), t \in T, \omega \in S\}$ is a stochastic process, where the variable t is typically time.*

   Note that a stochastic process is a function of two variables. For a specific value of time t, it is a random variable. For a specific value of random outcome $\omega \in S$, it is a function of time. This function of time is called a trajectory or sample path of the stochastic process.

   Usually the dependence of $X(\cdot, \cdot)$ on ω is dropped. Therefore, the stochastic process is generally denoted by $\{X(t), t \in T\}$.

2. *The stochastic process is a discrete-time stochastic process, if the set T is countable. The stochastic process is a continuous-time stochastic process, if the set T is an interval (either closed or open) on the real line.*

3. *An index set T is linear, if for any $t, h \in T$, then $(t + h) \in T$. Examples of linear index set are $\mathbb{Z}, \mathbb{N}, \mathbb{P}$ and $\mathbb{R}$.*

4. *The index set T, of a stochastic process is linear, and $t_i \in T$, for $0 \le i \le n$. Define a random vector $\mathcal{X}(t_0, t_1, t_2, \dots, t_n)$ as*

$$\mathcal{X}(t_0, t_1, t_2, \dots, t_n) = (X(t_0), X(t_1), \dots, X(t_n)) \qquad (21.21)$$

   A stochastic process is a stationary process, if for any $n \in \mathbb{N}$ and $\tau \in T$, and for all values of $t_0, t_1, t_2, \dots, t_n \in T$, the vectors

$$\mathcal{X}(t_0 + \tau, t_1 + \tau, t_2 + \tau, \dots, t_n + \tau) \quad and \quad \mathcal{X}(t_0, t_1, t_2, \dots, t_n)$$

   have identical distribution. In other words, the stochastic process is stationary if the distribution of the random vector $\mathcal{X}(t_0, t_1, t_2, \dots, t_n)$ is invariant with respect to translations in time for all values of its arguments.

5. *A stochastic process is second-order stationary if:*

   Its index set is linear, the first moment $\mathcal{E}(X(t))$ is independent of time t, and the second moment $\mathcal{E}(X(t)X(t + \tau))$ depends only on τ and not on t. This stationarity is also referred to as wide-sense stationarity.

6. *For a wide-sense stationary process, let:*

$$\mathcal{E}(X(t)) \triangleq \mu, \quad and \quad \sigma^2 \triangleq \mathcal{E}\left((X(t) - \mu)^2\right)$$

   (a) *The autocovariance $\gamma(\tau)$ of this process is*

$$\gamma(\tau) = \mathcal{E}((X(t + \tau) - \mu)(X(t) - \mu)) \qquad (21.22a)$$

   Observe that $\gamma(0) = \sigma^2$. The autocovariance $\gamma(\tau)$ measures the covariance between elements of the stochastic process separated by an interval of τ time units.

(b) *The autocorrelation function $\zeta\left(\cdot\right)$ of this process is*

$$\zeta\left(\tau\right) = \frac{\gamma\left(\tau\right)}{\gamma\left(0\right)} \tag{21.22b}$$

(c) *The Fourier transform of the autocovariance function of this stochastic process is called its spectral density function.*   □

Notice in the above definitions that all stationary processes are stationary in the second order, but the converse is not true in general. Furthermore, the concept of independence of random processes is a generalization of the concept of independence of random variables.

An example of a wide-sense stationary process is the autoregressive process of order one. This process is denoted by $AR\left(1\right)$. It is discussed in the chapter on lapped orthogonal transform.

Discrete -Time White Noise Process

The white noise process in discrete-time is a discrete signal whose samples have a zero mean and a finite variance. Further, these samples are stochastically uncorrelated with each other. It is also possible to describe the white noise process as a sequence of independent identically distributed random variables. The sequence is Gaussian white noise if the random variables have a Gaussian distribution with zero mean.

Problems

1. A point is selected at random inside a circle. Prove that the probability that the point is closer to the center of the circle than to its circumference is equal to 0.25.

2. A die is a cube with indentations on each of the six faces. One face has a single indentation. The second, third, fourth, fifth, and sixth face, each have $2, 3, 4, 5$, and 6 indentations respectively. That is, there are different number of indentations on each face. A die is generally used for gambling. Find the probability that the sum of the faces of two independently thrown dice totals 7. Find the expected value of the sum.

    Hint: Let the sum of the two faces be i, where $2 \leq i \leq 12$. Denote the probability of the sum of the two faces by $p\left(i\right)$. Then $p\left(7\right) = 6/36 = 1/6$, and $\sum_{i=2}^{12} ip\left(i\right) = 7$.

3. If X and Y are two jointly distributed random variables, then show that

$$|Cov(X,Y)| \leq \sigma_X \sigma_Y, \quad \text{and} \quad -1 \leq Cor(X,Y) \leq 1$$

4. Let X and Y be independent random variables with Gaussian distribution. Prove that the random variable $Z = (aX + bY)$ has a Gaussian distribution, where $a, b \in \mathbb{R}$.

5. Let $X_1, X_2, \ldots, X_n$ be a sequence of independent and continuously distributed random variables. If

$$U = \min\{X_1, X_2, \ldots, X_n\}, \quad \text{and} \quad V = \max\{X_1, X_2, \ldots, X_n\}$$

find the cumulative distribution and probability density functions of the random variables U and V.

Hint: See Mood, Graybill, and Boes (1974). Let the cumulative distribution and probability density functions of the random variable X_i, be $F_{X_i}(\cdot)$ and $f_{X_i}(\cdot)$ respectively, for $1 \leq i \leq n$.

Also, let the cumulative distribution and probability density functions of the random variable U, be $F_U(\cdot)$ and $f_U(\cdot)$ respectively. We have

$$1 - F_U(u) = P(U > u) = P(\min\{X_1, X_2, \ldots, X_n\} > u)$$
$$= P(X_1 > u, X_2 > u, \ldots, X_n > u)$$
$$= P(X_1 > u) P(X_2 > u) \ldots P(X_n > u)$$

The last step follows from the independence hypothesis of the sequence of the random variables $X_1, X_2, \ldots, X_n$. This leads to

$$1 - F_U(u) = \prod_{i=1}^{n} \{1 - F_{X_i}(u)\}, \quad u \in \mathbb{R}$$

Thus

$$F_U(u) = 1 - \prod_{i=1}^{n} \{1 - F_{X_i}(u)\}, \quad u \in \mathbb{R}$$

The corresponding probability density function is obtained by differentiating both sides of the above expression with respect to u. Further assume that the random variables X_i's are distributed as random variable X. Let the cumulative distribution and probability density functions of the random variable X, be $F(\cdot)$ and $f(\cdot)$ respectively. In this case

$$F_U(u) = 1 - \{1 - F(u)\}^n, \quad \text{and} \quad f_U(u) = n\{1 - F(u)\}^{n-1} f(u), \quad u \in \mathbb{R}$$

Similarly, let the cumulative distribution and probability density functions of the random variable V, be $F_V(\cdot)$ and $f_V(\cdot)$ respectively. Then

$$F_V(v) = P(V \le v) = P(\max\{X_1, X_2, \ldots, X_n\} \le v)$$
$$= P(X_1 \le v, X_2 \le v, \ldots, X_n \le v)$$
$$= P(X_1 \le v) P(X_2 \le v) \ldots P(X_n \le v)$$

The last step follows from the independence hypothesis of the sequence of random variables $X_1, X_2, \ldots, X_n$. This leads to

$$F_V(v) = \prod_{i=1}^{n} F_{X_i}(v), \quad v \in \mathbb{R}$$

The corresponding probability density function is obtained by differentiating both sides of the above expression with respect to v. Further assume that the random variables X_i's are distributed as random variable X. Let the cumulative distribution and probability density functions of the random variable X, be $F(\cdot)$ and $f(\cdot)$ respectively. In this case

$$F_V(v) = \{F(v)\}^n, \quad \text{and} \quad f_V(v) = n\{F(v)\}^{n-1} f(v), \quad v \in \mathbb{R}$$

6. X is a continuously distributed random variable with probability density function $f_X(x)$, $x \in \mathbb{R}$. Let $Y = |X|$, and $f_Y(\cdot)$, be its probability density function. Let the cumulative distribution function of the random variables X and Y be $F_X(\cdot)$ and $F_Y(\cdot)$ respectively. Prove that

$$F_Y(y) = F_X(y) - F_X(-y), \quad y \in \mathbb{R}_0^+$$
$$f_Y(y) = \begin{cases} f_X(y) + f_X(-y), & y > 0 \\ 0, & y < 0 \end{cases}$$
$$\mathcal{E}(Y) = \int_0^\infty y f_X(y)\, dy + \int_0^\infty y f_X(-y)\, dy$$

Hint: See Parzen (1960).

$$F_Y(y) = P(Y \le y) = P(|X| \le y) = P(-y \le X \le y)$$
$$= F_X(y) - F_X(-y)$$
$$= \int_{-y}^{y} f_X(x)\, dx$$

The result follows, by differentiating both sides with respect to y.

7. Show that the tail probability of the standard normal random variable is

$$P(X > x) \simeq \frac{\exp(-x^2/2)}{x\sqrt{2\pi}}, \quad \text{as } x \to \infty$$

Hint: See Grimmett and Stirzaker (2001). Let $\phi'(x)$ be the first derivative of $\phi(x)$ with respect to x. Use the relationship $\phi'(x) = -x\phi(x)$, and integration by parts to establish that

$$P(X > x) = \int_x^\infty \phi(t)\, dt$$

$$= \frac{\phi(x)}{x} - \int_x^\infty \frac{\phi(t)}{t^2}\, dt$$

Letting $x \to \infty$ leads to the stated result.

8. Let Y be a normally distributed random variable with mean 0 and variance σ^2. Also let $Z = |Y|$. Show that

$$F_Z^c(z) \simeq \frac{2\sigma \exp\left(-z^2 / (2\sigma^2)\right)}{\sqrt{2\pi z}}, \quad \text{as } z \to \infty$$

Hint: We have

$$F_Z(z) = P(Z \le z) = \int_{-z}^z f_Y(y)\, dy = 2 \int_0^z f_Y(y)\, dy$$
$$= 2(F_Y(z) - 0.5) = 2(1 - F_Y^c(z) - 0.5)$$
$$= 1 - 2F_Y^c(z)$$

This leads to

$$F_Z^c(z) = 2F_Y^c(z)$$

Let $X = Y/\sigma$. Then X has a standard normal distribution. Also

$$F_Y^c(z) = P(Y > z) = P(Y/\sigma > z/\sigma) = P(X > z/\sigma) = F_X^c(z/\sigma)$$

Therefore,

$$F_Z^c(z) = 2F_X^c(z/\sigma)$$

Use of the result in the last problem gives the stated result.

Bibliography

1. Aach, T., 2003. "Fourier, Block, and Lapped Transforms," in *Advances in Imaging and Electron Physics*, P. W. Hawkes, Ed., Vol. 128. San Diego: Academic Press, 2003, pp. 1-52.

2. Aboufadel, E., and Schlicker, S., 1999. *Discovering Wavelets*, John Wiley & Sons, Inc., New York, New York.

3. Abramowitz, M., and Stegun, I. A., 1965. *Handbook of Mathematical Functions*, Dover Publications, Inc., New York.

4. Akansu, A. N., and Haddad, R. A., 2001. *Multiresolution Signal Decomposition: Transforms, Subbands, and Wavelets*, Second Edition, Academic Press, New York, New York.

5. Alexandridis, A. K., E., and Zapranis, A. D., 2014. *Wavelet Neural Networks: With Applications in Financial Engineering, Chaos, and Classification*, John Wiley & Sons, Inc., New York, New York.

6. Apostol, T. M., 1976. *Introduction to Analytic Number Theory*, Springer-Verlag, Berlin, Germany.

7. Arora, S., and Barak, B., 2009. *Computational Complexity: A Modern Approach*, Cambridge University Press, Cambridge, Great Britain.

8. Atallah, M. J., and Blanton, M., Editors, 2010. *Algorithms and Theory of Computation Handbook: General Concepts and Techniques*, Second Edition, Chapman and Hall/CRC Press, New York, New York.

9. Atallah, M. J., and Blanton, M., Editors, 2010. *Algorithms and Theory of Computation Handbook: Special Topics and Techniques*, Second Edition, Chapman and Hall/CRC Press, New York, New York.

10. Ayres Jr., F., 1962. *Matrices*, Schaum's Outline Series, McGraw-Hill Book Company: New York.

11. Bachman, G., and Narici, L., 2000. *Functional Analysis*, Dover Publications, Inc., New York, New York.

12. Baldoni, M. W., Ciliberto, C., and Cattaneo, G. M. P., 2009. *Elementary Number Theory Cryptography and Codes*, Springer-Verlag, Berlin, Germany.

13. Bellman, R., 1995. *Introduction to Matrix Analysis*, Society of Industrial and Applied Mathematics, Philadelphia, Pennsylvania.

14. Blahut, R. E., 1985. *Fast Algorithms for Digital Signal Processing*, Addison-Wesley Publishing Company Inc., Menlo Park California.

15. Blatter, C., 1998. *Wavelets A Primer*, A. K. Peters, Ltd., Natick, Massachusetts.

16. Bhatnagar, N., 1995. "On Computation of Certain Discrete Fourier Transforms Using Binary Calculus," Signal Processing, Volume 43, Pages 93-101.

17. Bhatnagar, N., 2019. *Mathematical Principles of the Internet, Volume I: Engineering Fundamentals*, CRC Press: New York, New York.

18. Bhatnagar, N., 2019. *Mathematical Principles of the Internet, Volume II: Mathematical Concepts*, CRC Press: New York, New York.

19. Boggess, A., and Narcowich, F. J., 2001. *A First Course in Wavelets with Fourier Analysis*, Prentice Hall: Up Saddle River, New Jersey.

20. Boyer, K. G., 1995. "The Fast Wavelet Transform (FWT)," Master of Science Thesis, University of Colorado, Denver.

21. Bremaud, P., 2002. *Mathematical Principles of Signal Processing, Fourier and Wavelet Analysis*, Springer, New York.

22. Briggs, W. L., and Henson, V. E., 1995. *The DFT, An Owner's Manual for the Discrete Fourier Transform*, SIAM, Philadelphia.

23. Britanak, V., Yip, P. C., and Rao, K. R., 2007. *Discrete Cosine and Sine Transforms: General Properties, Fast Algorithms, and Integer Approximations,* Academic Press, Inc.: San Diego, California.

24. Bronshtein, I. N., and Semendyayev, K. A., 1985. *Handbook of Mathematics*, Van Nostrand Reinhold Company, New York, New York.

25. Burrus, S., Gopinath, R., and Guo, H., 1998. *Introduction to Wavelets and Wavelet Transforms, A Primer*, Prentice Hall: Up Saddle River, New Jersey.

26. Cameron, P. J., 1994. *Combinatorics: Topics, Techniques, Algorithms*, Cambridge University Press, Cambridge, Great Britain.

27. Chahal, J. S., 1988. *Topics in Number Theory*, Plenum Press, New York.

28. Chen, W., Editor, 2000. *Mathematics for Circuits and Filters*, CRC Press: New York.

29. Chui, C. K., 1997. *Wavelets a Mathematical Tool for Signal Analysis*, Society for Indus-
    trial and Applied Mathematics, Philadelphia, Pennsylvania.

30. Cohen, A., Daubechies, I., and Feauveau, J.-C., 1992. "Biorthogonal Bases of Compactly
    Supported Wavelets," Communications on Pure and Applied Mathematics, Volume 45,
    Pages 485-560.

31. Conway, J. B., 1978. *Functions of One Complex Variable*, Second Edition, Springer-
    Verlag, Berlin, Germany.

32. Cooley, J. W., and Tukey, J. W., April 1965. "An Algorithm for the Machine Calculation
    of Complex Fourier Series," Mathematics of Computation, Volume 19, Pages 297-301.

33. Cormen, T. H., Leiserson, C. E., Rivest, R. L., and Stein, C., 2009. *Introduction to Algo-
    rithms*, Third Edition, The MIT Press, Cambridge, Massachusetts.

34. Daubechies, I., 1988. "Orthonormal Bases of Compactly Supported Wavelets," Comm.
    Pure Appl. Math., Vol. 41, pp. 909-996.

35. Daubechies, I., 1992. *Ten Lectures on Wavelets*, Society for Industrial and Applied Math-
    ematics, Philadelphia.

36. Daubechies, I., 1993. "Orthonormal Bases of Compactly Supported Wavelets II. Varia-
    tions on a Theme," SIAM J. Math. Anal., Vol. 24, No. 2, pp. 499-519.

37. Daubechies, I., and Sweldens, W., 1998. "Factoring Wavelet Transforms into Lifting
    Steps," The Journal of Fourier Analysis and Applications Vol. 4, No. 3.

38. Debnath, L., and Bhatta, D., 2007. *Integral Transforms and Their Applications*, Second
    Edition, Chapman and Hall/CRC Press, New York, New York.

39. Debnath, L., and Shah, F. A., 2015. *Wavelet Transforms and Their Applications*, Second
    Edition, Birkhauser, Boston, Massachusetts.

40. Donoho, D. L., (1993). "Nonlinear Wavelet Methods for Recovery of Signals, Densities
    and Spectra from Indirect and Noisy Data," Proc. Symposia in Applied Mathematics (I.
    Daubechies, ed.), American Mathematical Society.

41. Donoho, D., and Johnstone, I., 1992. Ideal Spatial Adaptation Via Wavelet Shrinkage,
    Technical Report 409, Department of Statistics, Stanford University.

42. Durrett, R., 2005. *Probability Theory and Examples*, Third Edition, Thomas Learning -
    Brooks/Cole, Belmont, California.

43. Elliott, D. F., 1987. *Handbook of Digital Signal Processing*, Academic Press, Inc.: New
    York.

44. Feller, W., 1968. *An Introduction to Probability Theory and Its Applications, Vol. I*, Third
    Edition, John Wiley & Sons, Inc., New York, New York.

45. Feller, W., 1971. *An Introduction to Probability Theory and Its Applications, Vol. II*,
    Second Edition, John Wiley & Sons, Inc., New York, New York.

46. Fournier, A., Editor, 1995. "Wavelets and their Applications in Computer Graphics," SIG-GRAPH'95 Course Notes.

47. Garrity, T. A., 2002. *All the Mathematics You Missed*, Cambridge University Press, Cambridge, Great Britain.

48. Gnedenko, B. V., 1978. *The Theory of Probability*, Mir Publishers, Moscow.

49. Golub, G. H., and Loan, C. F. V., 1983. *Matrix Computations*, The John Hopkins University Press, Baltimore, Maryland.

50. Gomes, J., and Velho, L., 1999. "From Fourier Analysis to Wavelets," Course Notes - SIGGRAPH 99.

51. Goswami, J. C., and Chan, A. K., 1999. *Fundamentals of Wavelets, Theory, Algorithms, and Applications*, John Wiley & Sons, Inc., New York, New York.

52. Graham, R. L., Knuth, D. E., and Patashnik, O., 1994. *Concrete Mathematics: A Foundation for Computer Science*, Second Edition, Addison-Wesley Publishing Company, New York, New York.

53. Grimmett, G. R., and Stirzaker, D. R., 2001. *Probability and Random Processes,* Third Edition, Oxford University Press, Oxford, Great Britain.

54. Hall, S. R., 1993. "Filtering, Coding, and Compression with Malvar Wavelets," M. S. Thesis, Air Force Institute of Technology, Air University, USA.

55. Hamming, R. W., 1991. *The Art of Probability for Scientists and Engineers*, Addison-Wesley Publishing Company, New York, New York.

56. Hardy, G. H., and Wright, E. M. 1979. *An Introduction to the Theory of Numbers,* Fifth Edition, Oxford University Press, Oxford, Great Britain.

57. Hayes, M. H., 1999. *Digital Signal Processing*, Schaum's Outline Series, McGraw-Hill Book Company, New York, New York.

58. Hight, D. W., 1977. *A Concept of Limits,* Dover Publications, Inc., New York, New York.

59. Hoffman, K., 1975. *Analysis in Euclidean Space,* Dover Publications, Inc., New York, New York.

60. Hogben, L., Editor-in-Chief, 2007. *Handbook of Linear Algebra,* CRC Press: New York, New York.

61. Hong, D., Wang, J., and Gardner, R., 2005. *Real Analysis with an Introduction to Wavelets and Applications*, Elsevier Academic Press, New York, New York.

62. Horn, R. A., and Johnson, C. R., 1985. *Matrix Analysis,* Cambridge University Press, Cambridge, Great Britain.

63. Horowitz, E., and Sahni, S., 1978. *Fundamentals of Computer Algorithms*, Computer Science Press, Maryland.

64. Hsu, H. P., 1984. *Applied Fourier Analysis,* Harcourt Brace College Publishers, New York, New York.

65. Hsu, H. P., 1995. *Signals and Systems,* Schaum's Outline Series, McGraw-Hill Book Company, New York, New York.

66. Hua, L. K., 1982. *Introduction to Number Theory*, Springer-Verlag, Berlin, Germany.

67. Hubbard, B. B., 1996. *The World According to Wavelets. The Story of Mathematical Technique in the Making*, A. K. Peters, Ltd., Wellesley, Massachusetts.

68. Kahane, Jean-Pierre, and Lemarié-Rieusset, Pierre-Gilles, 1995. *Fourier Series and Wavelets*, Gordon and Breach Publishers, India.

69. Kantorovich, L. V., and Akilov, G. P., 1982. *Functional Analysis,* Second Edition, Pergamon Press, New York, New York.

70. Keinert, F., 2004. *Wavelets and Multiwavelets*, CRC Press: New York, New York.

71. Kolmogorov, A. N., and Fomin, S. V., 1970. *Introductory Real Analysis,* Dover Publications, Inc., New York, New York.

72. Koornwinder, T. H., Editor, 1993. *Wavelets: An elementary Treatment of Theory and Applications*, World Scientific, Singapore.

73. Korn, G. A., and Korn, T. M., 1968. *Mathematical Handbook for Scientists and Engineers*, Second Edition, McGraw-Hill Book Company, New York, New York.

74. Körner, T. W., 1988. *Fourier Analysis,* Cambridge University Press, Cambridge, Great Britain.

75. Lancaster, P., 1969. *Theory of Matrices*, Academic Press, New York, New York.

76. Leon-Garcia, A., 1994. *Probability and Random Processes for Electrical Engineering*, Second Edition, Addison-Wesley Publishing Company, New York, New York.

77. LeVeque, W. J., 1977. *Fundamentals of Number Theory*, Addison-Wesley Publishing Company, New York, New York.

78. Levinson, N., and Redheffer, R. M., 1970. *Complex Variables,* Holden-Day, San Francisco, California.

79. Linz, P., 2001. *Theoretical Numerical Analysis, An Introduction to Advanced Techniques*, Dover Publications, Inc. New York.

80. Lipschutz, S., 1965. *Probability*, Schaum's Outline Series, McGraw-Hill Book Company, New York.

81. Lipschutz, S., 1968. *Linear Algebra*, Schaum's Outline Series, McGraw-Hill Book Company, New York.

82. Lipschutz, S., 1998. *Set Theory and Related Topics*, Schaum's Outline Series, McGraw-Hill Book Company, New York, New York.

83. Louis, A. K., Maaβ, P., and Rieder, A., 1997. *Wavelets: Theory and Applications*, John Wiley and Sons, New York.

84. Mallat, S., 2009. *A Wavelet Tour of Signal Processing, The Sparse Way*, Third Edition, Academic Press, New York, New York.

85. Malvar, H. S., and Staelin, D. H., 1989. "The LOT: Transform Coding without Blocking Effects," IEEE Trans. Acoustics, Speech, Signal Process. Vol. 37, No. 4, pp. 553-559.

86. Malvar, H. S., 1990. "Lapped Transforms for Efficient Transform/Subband Coding," IEEE Trans. Acoustics, Speech, Signal Process. Vol. 38, No. 6, pp. 969-978.

87. Meyer, Y., 1993. *Wavelets Algorithms & Applications*, Society for Industrial and Applied Mathematics, Philadelphia.

88. Meyer, C., 2000. *Matrix Analysis and Applied Linear Algebra,* Society of Industrial and Applied Mathematics, Philadelphia, Pennsylvania.

89. Milne, R. D., 1980. *Applied Functional Analysis: An Introductory Treatment*, Pitman Advanced Publishing Program, London, Great Britain.

90. Mood, A. M., Graybill, F. A., and Boes, D. C., 1974. *Introduction to the Theory of Statistics*, Third Edition, McGraw-Hill Book Company, New York.

91. Moon, T. K., and Stirling, W. C., 2000. *Mathematical Methods and Algorithms for Signal Processing*, Prentice Hall: Up Saddle River, New Jersey.

92. Moore, R. E., 1985. *Computational Functional Analysis*, John Wiley & Sons, Inc., New York, New York.

93. Nickolas, P., 2017. *Wavelets: A Student Guide*, Cambridge University Press, Cambridge, U.K.

94. Nielsen, O. M., 1998. "Wavelets in Scientific Computing," Ph.D. Dissertation, Technical University of Denmark, Lyngby, Denmark.

95. Nievergelt, Y., 1999. *Wavelets Made Easy*, Birkhäuser, Boston, Massachusetts.

96. Niven, I., and Zuckerman, H. S., 1972. *An Introduction to the Theory of Numbers*, Third Edition, John Wiley & Sons, Inc., New York, New York.

97. Noble, B., 1969, *Applied Linear Algebra*, Prentice-Hall, Englewood Cliffs, New Jersey.

98. Nussbaumer, H. J., 1982. *Fast Fourier Transform and Convolution Algorithms*, Springer-Verlag, New York.

99. Ogden, R. T., 1997. *Essential Wavelets for Statistical Applications and Data Analysis*, Birkhauser, Boston, Massachusetts.

100. Oppenheim, A. V., and Schafer, R. W., 1975. *Digital Signal Processing*, Prentice-Hall, Inc.: Englewood Cliffs, New Jersey.

101. Oussar, Y., Rivals, I., Personnaz, L., and Dreyfus, G., 1998. "Training Wavelet Networks for Nonlinear Dynamic Input-Output Modeling," Neurocomputing, Elsevier, Vol. 20, Nos. 1-3, pp. 173-188.

102. Papoulis, A., 1962. *The Fourier Integral and Its Applications*, McGraw-Hill Book Company: New York.

103. Papoulis, A., 1965. *Probability, Random Variables, and Stochastic Processes*, McGraw-Hill Book Company, New York, New York.

104. Papoulis, A., 1977. *Signal Analysis*, McGraw-Hill Book Company: New York.

105. Parzen, E., 1960. *Modern Probability Theory and Its Applications,* John Wiley & Sons, Inc., New York, New York.

106. Pinkus, A., and Zafrany, S., 1997. *Fourier Series and Integral Transforms*, Cambridge University Press, Cambridge, U.K.

107. Poularikas, A. D., Editor-in-Chief, 2000. *The Handbook of Formulas and Tables for Signal Processing*, CRC Press: New York, New York.

108. Prasad, L., and Iyengar, S. S., 1997. *Wavelet Analysis with Applications to Image Processing*, CRC Press LLC, Boca Raton, Florida.

109. Rao, M. R., and Bopardikar, A. S, 1998. *Wavelet Transforms*, Addison-Wesley Longman, Inc., Menlo Park, California.

110. Resnikoff, H. L., and Wells, R. O., 1998. *Wavelet Analysis, The Scalable Structure of Information*, Springer, New York.

111. Rich, E., 2008. *Automata, Computability, and Computing: Theory and Applications*, Pearson Prentice-Hall, Upper Saddle River, New Jersey.

112. Rivlin, T. J., *Chebyshev Polynomials*, John Wiley & Sons Inc., New York.

113. Rosen, K. H., Editor-in-Chief, 2000. *Handbook of Discrete and Combinatorial Mathematics*, CRC Press: New York.

114. Ross, S. M., 1970. *Applied Probability Models with Optimization Applications,* Holden-Day, Inc., San Francisco, California.

115. Ruskai, M. B., Beylkin, G., Coifman, R., Daubechies, I., Mallat, S., Meyer, Y., and Raphael, L., 1992. *Wavelets and Their Applications*, Jones and Bartlett Publishers, Boston, Massachusetts.

116. Serpedin, E., Chen, T., and Rajan, D., Editors, 2012. *Mathematical Foundations for Signal Processing, Communications, and Networking,* CRC Press: New York, New York.

117. Shilov, G. E., 1996. *Elementary Real and Complex Analysis,* Dover Publications, Inc., New York, New York.

118. Sirovich, L., 1988. *Introduction to Applied Mathematics,* Springer-Verlag, Berlin, Germany.

119. Spiegel, M. R., 1959. *Vector Analysis*, Schaum's Outline Series, McGraw-Hill Book Company, New York, New York.

120. Spiegel, M. R., 1963. *Advanced Calculus*, Schaum's Outline Series, McGraw-Hill Book Company, New York, New York.

121. Spiegel, M. R., 1964. *Complex Variables*, Schaum's Outline Series, McGraw-Hill Book Company, New York, New York.

122. Spiegel, M. R., 1969. *Real Variables*, Schaum's Outline Series, McGraw-Hill Book Company, New York, New York.

123. Stark, H., and Yang, Y., 1998. *Vector Space Projections - A Numerical Approach to Signal and Image Processing, Neural Nets, and Optics,* John Wiley & Sons, Inc.: New York.

124. Stirzaker, D. R., 2003. *Elementary Probability,* Second Edition, Cambridge University Press, Cambridge, Great Britain.

125. Stollnitz, E. J., DeRose, T. D., and Salesin, D. H., 1996. *Wavelets for Computer Graphics, Theory and Applications*, Morgan Kaufmann Publishers, Inc., San Francisco, California.

126. Strang, G., and Nguyen, T. 1996. *Wavelets and Filter Banks*, Wellesley-Cambridge Press, Wellesley, Massachusetts.

127. Sveshnikov, A. A., 1968. *Problems in Probability Theory, Mathematical Statistics, and Theory of Random Functions*, Dover Publications, Inc., New York, New York.

128. Taswell, C., 2000. "The What, How, and Why of Wavelet Shrinkage Denoising," Computing in Science & Engineering, Vol. 2, Issue No. 3, pp. 12 – 19.

129. Tolstov, G. P., 1962. *Fourier Series,* Dover Publications, Inc., New York, New York.

130. Uytterhoeven, G. 1999. "Wavelets: Software and Applications," Ph. D. Thesis, Katholieke Universiteit Leuven, Belgium.

131. van Fleet, P. J., 2008. *Discrete Wavelet Transformations, An Elementary Approach with Applications*, John Wiley & Sons, Inc.: New York.

132. Veitch, D., 2005. "Wavelet Neural Networks, and Their Application in the Study of Dynamical Systems," M. Sc. Thesis, University of York, UK.

133. Vetterli, M, and Kovačević, J., 1995. *Wavelets and Subband Coding*, Prentice Hall, Up Saddle River, New Jersey.

134. Vetterli, M, Kovačević, J., and Goyal, V. K., 2014. *Foundations of Signal Processing*, Third Edition, Cambridge University Press, Cambridge, Great Britain.

135. Vidakovic, B., 1999. *Statistical Modeling by Wavelets*, John Wiley & Sons, Inc.: New York.

136. Villani, C., 2016. *Birth of a Theorem*: A Mathematical Adventure, Farrar, Straus, and Giroux, New York, New York.

137. Vretblad, A., 2003. *Fourier Analysis and Its Applications,* Springer-Verlag, Berlin, Germany.

138. Walker, J. S., 1999. *A Primer on Wavelets and their Scientific Applications*, Chapman & Hall / CRC Press LLC, Boca Raton, Florida.

139. Wickerhauser, M. V., 1994. *Adapted Wavelet Analysis from Theory to Software*, A. K. Peters, Ltd., Wellesley, Massachusetts.

140. Wilf, H. S., 1978. *Mathematics for the Physical Sciences,* Dover Publications, Inc., New York, New York.

141. Zhang, Q., and Benveniste, A., 1992. "Wavelet Networks," IEEE Trans. Neural Networks. Vol. 3, No. 6, pp. 889-898.

142. Zayed, A. I., 1996. *Handbook of Function and Generalized Function Transformations*, CRC Press: New York.

Index

Printed in the United States
by Baker & Taylor Publisher Services